The Editor

HASIA R. DINER is Director of the Goldstein-Goren Center for American Jewish History and Paul S. and Sylvia Steinberg Professor of American Jewish History at New York University. She is the author of *We Remember with Reverence and Love: American Jews and the Myth of Silence after the Holocaust* (2009); also *From Arrival to Incorporation: Migrants to the United States in a Global Age* (co-editor); *The Jews of the United States, 1654 to 2000; Hungering for America: Italian, Irish and Jewish Foodways in the Age of Migration; Her Works Praise Her: A History of Jewish Women in America from Colonial Times to the Present* (co-author); *Lower East Side Memories: Jewish Place in America; Erin's Daughters in America: Irish Women in the Nineteenth Century; In the Almost Promised Land: American Jews and Blacks, 1915–1935;* and *A Time for Gathering: The Second Migration, 1820–1880* (Volume 2 of *The Jewish People in America*, edited by Henry L. Feingold) and co-editor of *Remembering the Lower East Side: American Jewish Reflections.*

W. W. NORTON & COMPANY, INC.
Also Publishes

A NORTON CRITICAL EDITION

Jacob Riis

HOW THE OTHER HALF LIVES

AUTHORITATIVE TEXT

CONTEXTS

CRITICISM

Edited by

HASIA R. DINER
NEW YORK UNIVERSITY

*With photographs from the
Jacob A. Riis Collection
at the Museum of the City of New York*

W • W • NORTON & COMPANY • *New York* • *London*

W. W. Norton & Company has been independent since its founding in 1923, when William Warder Norton and Mary D. Herter Norton first published lectures delivered at the People's Institute, the adult education division of New York City's Cooper Union. The firm soon expanded its program beyond the Institute, publishing books by celebrated academics from America and abroad. By mid-century, the two major pillars of Norton's publishing program—trade books and college texts—were firmly established. In the 1950s, the Norton family transferred control of the company to its employees, and today—with a staff of four hundred and a comparable number of trade, college, and professional titles published each year—W. W. Norton & Company stands as the largest and oldest publishing house owned wholly by its employees.

The text of this book is composed in Fairfield Medium with the display set in Bernhard Modern.
Manufacturing by the Courier Companies—Westford division.
Book design by Antonina Krass.
Composition by Westchester Book Group.
Production manager: Eric Pier-Hocking.

Library of Congress Cataloging-in-Publication Data

Riis, Jacob A. (Jacob August), 1849–1914.
    How the other half lives : authoritative text, contexts, criticism / Jacob Riis ; edited by Hasia R. Diner.—1st ed.
        p.   cm.—(A Norton critical edition)
    Includes bibliographical references.
                    ISBN: 978-0-393-93026-9 (pbk.)
    1. Poor—New York (State)—New York.   2. Tenement houses—New York (State)—
New York.   3. Riis, Jacob A. (Jacob August), 1849–1914. How the other half lives.
I. Diner, Hasia R.   II. Title.
    HV4046.N6R58   2009
    305.5'69097471—dc22

                                                                                    2009015561

W. W. Norton & Company, Inc., 500 Fifth Avenue, New York, N.Y. 10110
www.wwnorton.com

W. W. Norton & Company Ltd., Castle House, 75/76 Wells Street, London W1T 3QT

1   2   3   4   5   6   7   8   9   0

Contents

Introduction

On November 15, 1890, the publishing house Charles Scribner's Sons, released *How the Other Half Lives*. Based on a magazine article of the same title that had appeared the previous year in *Scribner's Magazine*, the book, written by a reporter who had already achieved a relatively high-profile local reputation, Jacob Riis, became an instant best-seller. This sensationalistic, yet deeply moralistic, expose of the squalid living conditions of New York's urban poor, "the other half," caused an immediate stir among socially conscious members of the better-off "half" for whom the author penned his words and took the forty-three pictures that accompanied the text. Almost immediately upon its publication, Riis's book held a premier place among a string of other contemporary works that sought to drive home to Americans, particularly those with influence and power in government and business, the imperative of addressing the problems of the poor in America's cities, specifically in its ever-growing immigrant enclaves. No one would, Riis asserted, start working for a solution without first being exposed to the faces and facts of the urban crisis. This book catapulted Riis from local to national visibility as he told Americans of the comfortable classes that if they did not tackle these problems, the problems would come back to haunt them.

How the Other Half Lives also occupies a premier place on a selective list of American books that, on hindsight, unmistakably changed public opinion, began the process of altering public policy, and left an indelible mark on history. The only book among these transformative works that preceded *How the Other Half Lived*, Harriet Beecher Stowe's *Uncle Tom's Cabin* of 1852, played a role in awakening antislavery sentiment among Northerners as it depicted "life among the lowly" and the tragic human price levied by bondage. Two and a half decades after Riis challenged Americans to consider the effect of urban crowding and the greed of landlords who insouciantly gouged the poor in their quest for profits, Upton Sinclair launched his scathing attack on the exploitation of the immigrant poor, while highlighting the lax conditions in the meatpacking industry in *The Jungle* (1906), which propelled the federal government to involve itself in regulating the quality of what Americans ate. Three books of the 1960s, in addition, take their places on this distinguished shelf of books that transformed Americans' consciousness and changed the ways they lived: Rachel Carson's *The Silent Spring* (1962), Betty Friedan's *The Feminine Mystique* (1963) and Ralph Nader's *Unsafe at Any Speed* (1965). These writers and their works did no less than jump-start the environmentalist, feminist, and consumer movements, which went on to transform American law, politics, and social practice.

Each of these books inspired readers to demand action from those who could rectify the evils chronicled in their pages. Subsequent to their publication, other texts, including books, speeches, sermons, essays, exhibitions, and government reports, cited these volumes as conclusive evidence of the existence of a deep and profound problem that cried out for a solution. Later commentators would hail these books as the catalysts for broad public discussion and real political action. And, although all of these books had been preceded by other works that tackled the same problems, these particular texts captured public attention as none before, or after, had. All can be understood as having been the right book at, and for, the right time and as works that thoroughly galvanized the consciousness of their readers.

How the Other Half Lives appeared at a propitious moment. Looking backward, we see how it reflected much about the social gospel movement of the Gilded Age, which in heavily Protestant, evangelical tones, called on Americans to recognize that they had, or should feel as though they had, a connection to and responsibility for the increasing number of immigrants and other poor people who crowded into the industrial cities. Reformers of that era, whether writing with a Christian perspective or not, challenged the prevailing laissez-faire spirit, with its deep roots in America's national ideology that considered individualism as the only explanation for human success or failure. The long-standing American emphasis on very limited government had been strengthened in the 1860s and 1870s with the rise of social Darwinism, which claimed that in the natural order of things, those who could adapt would, while those who could not had to fall, plain and simple. Competition weeded out the weak, elevated the competent, and no amount of social tinkering could change natural processes.

Reform efforts of the post–Civil War era, like the social gospel movement, and Riis's book stood as rhetorical rebukes to William Graham Sumner's 1883 work, *What the Social Classes Owe Each Other,* in which the sociologist argued emphatically, nothing. Rather, Riis like the other socially conscious women and men of the late nineteenth century answered in the affirmative, declaring that, to the contrary, the classes owed much to each other.

The efforts of these individuals, like those of their counterparts in Great Britain, strove to convince the better-off that the problems of the city, its poverty, crime, disease, and political corruption, had left their mark on the upper classes as surely as they did on the dwellers of the slums and the tenements. Those with means had a role to play in rectifying these problems because the problems involved them as well.

Those who participated in this Gilded Age reform enterprise hoped to make the middle and upper classes aware of the breadth, depth, and anguish of poverty so they would voluntarily participate in projects to alleviate suffering. Such endeavors could be undertaken by church groups, clubs, other kinds of associations, and certainly by individuals, who could dip into their own pockets and give to the poor and to those in distress. They should, according to the reformist enterprise of the age, devote time to working with the poor and helping build bridges across the chasm that separated the social classes.

Riis drew much from that way of social thinking and reflected its thoughts about racial differences that had been inherited from the Enlightenment. Reformers asserted that changed and improved circumstances could alter, for the better, the basic character of the people who made up the various "inferior" groups at the bottom rungs of the social and economic ladders. Such a way of thinking about race ranked cultures and groups along a continuum from better to worst, but Riis and others confidently expected that altered conditions could erase the worst traits of the deprived.

Riis inherited much of his vision from the earlier, highly moralistic yet optimistic ethos of the mid-nineteenth century, which assumed the absence of fixed types and which believed that individuals and society could change by good works. People merely needed to be shown the way. Riis had little doubt that some styles of living should be seen as superior to others and that on such matters as home life, leisure-time activity, and gender expectations, one could comfortably talk about good and bad, better and worse, acceptable and not. People like himself, those who knew the best way, had a responsibility to point it out to those who did not.

While Riis reflected much of the social gospel's underlying ideology, he did part company with it on a number of matters, as borne out in the pages of How the Other Half Lives. Unlike many of those who had preceded him or indeed some of his contemporaries, he did not encounter the other half with a goal of converting them to his religious vision. At a time when missionaries honeycombed the immigrant neighborhoods and combined outreach services to the poor with a clear message that Catholics and Jews would be well served by embracing Protestantism, Riis, despite his own religiosity and his admiration for many of the programs undertaken by churches, did not devote his text to trying to further the evangelical cause. This put him well in line with the emerging progressive paradigm.

How the Other Half Lives also took on much of the substance of this new turn in reform activism, which understood social problems in decidedly pessimistic ways and which demanded that the state become an active force in changing the circumstances of the other half. While clinging to the belief that individuals might be able to effect changes once their sensibilities had been heightened, Riis believed the law had to lead the way. Progressivism did not trust the good will of individuals to solve the escalating crises that beset society, nor did it assume that much goodwill existed in the first place. A degree of compulsion had to be added.

Riis in How the Other Half Lives also embraced new ways of thinking about race. He, like contemporary scientists and ethnologists, comfortably spoke about "Jews," "Italians," and "Bohemians," lumping all under a single-group rubric, seeing essentially no variation. Consistent with much of late-nineteenth-century rhetoric, this book refered without hesitation to "the Negro" and "the Chinaman," reflecting a tendency to consider individuals as exemplars of entire populations and entire populations as the bearers of particular habits, tastes, and patterns of behavior. Riis predicted that some groups would move up and others would not as a result of basic racial traits. This assessment of the effect of race and the fixed nature of "the group" emerged in force in the 1890s. The formation of the Immigration Restriction League in 1893 showed how white, affluent, native-born Americans had come to view the growing number of immigrants from southern and eastern Europe as a fundamental threat to American life. The League can claim credit for having inspired a movement that culminated in the 1920s with the passage of the National Origins Act, comprehensive immigration legislation that fixed the number of immigrants who could enter the United States in any year and assigned quotas to immigrants on the basis of nationality. Although Riis never called for restriction or joined with the nativists, his assertions as to which groups would rise and which would not, which had admirable traits and which did not, fed into the xenophobes' triumph after the end of World War I.

In line with the spirit of the progressive era, conventionally dated by historians as beginning in 1890, the year of *How the Other Half Lives*, through the end of World War I, Riis placed a great deal of attention on the causative effect of physical spaces on character. The book, through words and photographs, first and foremost explored the world of the tenement and the tenement district. It fretted over the moral and health implications of fetid air, over the lack of greenery, over the absence of healthful places for children to play, and over the deleterious effect of crowding on those who lived in slums. It chided the cabal of landlords, crooked politicians, corrupt police officers, and saloon keepers who derived power and profit from the miserable circumstances of the men, women, and especially children forced to make their homes there. It drew a straight line from the filthy, overpopulated tenement apartments to the dangerous streets, to the grim asylums that warehoused the poor, and, ultimately, to the unmarked graves in Potter's Field, the final resting place, Riis believed, of those born of the slums.

Progressives as a group, like Riis, put much emphasis on the physical environment as a force in and of itself and went to great efforts to demonstrate graphically to the more comfortable classes the effect of degraded spaces on those who dwelled there. Conversely, progressives believed passionately in the ameliorative power of fresh air, the out-of-doors, trees, grass, and wide expanses of space for play. But, in lieu of shipping the poor to the countryside, something that had been tried at least for urban orphans by one of Riis's heroes, Charles Loring Brace, Riis and other urban progressives lobbied for the creation of parks and playgrounds in the slums, places that could counteract the dank and crowded apartments, the breeding places, as they saw it, of disease and criminality.

Normal and pure domestic life could not flourish in the slums, Riis and the progressives believed. These reformers put much emphasis on the family and had no doubt that an ideal family type, one resembling that of middle-class white America, existed as the standard against which to measure others and by which to assess the negative effects of the tenement environment.

The culture of the tenements and the streets around them destroyed families, as did that of the sweatshops, in which the poor labored, the saloons in which the men squandered their wages on drink, and the dives in which all sorts of temptations flourished. In the pages of *How the Other Half Lives* and in the flood of late-nineteenth- and early-twentieth-century articles, books, exhibitions, and investigative reports, which constituted the public works of the progressive era, all social evils worked together to crush families under their weight.

Riis did not blame the poor for their circumstances. Earlier commentators who wrote about poverty asserted that the poor had only themselves to blame for their poverty. Many of Riis's contemporaries continued to consider that the poor bore responsibility for their own fate. They had made bad choices and as such suffered the consequences of their own actions. Riis never engaged in this kind of blaming the victims. He also disagreed with those who considered poverty to be natural and inevitable. The poor, many Americans assumed, would always be there.

Riis believed poverty and the congested tenements and unsanitary streets could be eradicated. He pointed his finger directly at the landlords who charged excessive rents, which fostered crowded apartments and created an environment in which diseases could run rampant, wrecking the bodies of the other half. Riis also blamed employers who, in their quest for cutting costs, subjected workers to oppressive conditions and failed to pay a wage that would allow men to provide decent housing for their families. He lambasted corrupt politicians and policemen for ignoring the actions of saloonkeepers who, he contended, spread their poison throughout the tenement district, eating away at the poor. Riis and other progressives worried particularly about how such conditions affected the children of the slums.

In Riis's writing, as in so much of the reform discourse of the era, the poor emerge as victims, unable to lift themselves out of squalid circumstances. He stressed the pathos of their lives, the high rate of infant mortality, the debilitating diseases, and the lives lost to crime and drunkenness. He wrote about how the hopes of immigrants seeking a better life in America died in the tenement districts.

Yet, however sympathetically he portrayed the other half, Riis, like many progressives, had no doubt that some ways of living deserved condemnation and others, praise. Riis's moral vision pervaded nearly every page of *How the Other Half Lives,* every vignette, and he comfortably set himself up as the arbiter of the right way. No cultural relativist, Riis boldly asserted that the poor could no more be trusted to know what to do with their children, as landlords, saloonkeepers, politicians, or the police could be left to their own devices. He and the others of the progressive crusade had the obligation to speak for the poor and help the middle class participate in stemming the crisis.

Riis's book and the voluminous corpus of his subsequent writings and public addresses all reflected the progressives' abhorrence of disorder. *How the Other Half Lives* pulsated with images of crowded and chaotic streets, jumbled apartments into which light could not penetrate, filthy saloons swathed in darkness, fetid alleys used for sleeping and the commission of violent crimes, and, finally, the horrors of the unmarked grave.

Riis and the progressives relied on the written word to let the comfortable classes know about the conditions of the poor and to convince them that, despite their distance from the tenement districts, they too would suffer if society did not eliminate poverty, congestion, and disorder. They showed through the recently launched field of statistics that crime would spread as would disease. Unrest among the poor could be manipulated by political agitators and lead to the crumbling of society. The multitude of progressive-inflected works, of which *How the Other Half Lives* early on became a key text, provided graphic portraits of the tragic lives of the urban poor.

This age of the social exposé went in tandem with the efflorescence of literary realism. In both Europe and America, writers such as William Dean Howells, Stephen Crane, and Émile Zola began to shift literature away from sentimentality, with its emphasis on uplifting portraits of noble and genteel lives, to a harsh emphasis on the facts of life, regardless of the discomfort the reader might experience. Indeed, the imaginative literature and the reform writings together hoped to inspire unease because such unease would mean that the reader had learned the truth.

The style and structure of Riis's work owed much to the emergence of photography in the decades after the Civil War. Technological innovations such as flashlight powder proved crucial to Riis and other progressives who documented the brutal reality of poverty by going into the streets, apartments, and workshops to capture the faces of the poor and the spaces of their suffering. So too the development of new kinds of lenses and more adaptable cameras brought about the birth of photojournalism in the latter part of the nineteenth century. Photography made it possible for Riis to accomplish his goal of showing people something otherwise hidden to them. To present his story to a wide audience, he needed more than words. The photographs Riis and the others took functioned as crucial companions to the texts and not as just as interesting illustrations.

The ethos that infused Riis's book reflected some of the basic details of his life, a spectacular success story. This immigrant came to the United States with no contacts to help ease his way, no capital with which to invest in his future, no obvious assets to give him a quick start as he tried to make something of himself. Yet by the time he died in 1914 he had achieved national, even international, renown and could claim, among other notables, President Theodore Roosevelt as a friend. Indeed Roosevelt wrote a laudatory introduction to Riis's 1900 autobiography, *The Making of an American*. To reciprocate, in 1904 Riis wrote a book-length biographical tribute to Roosevelt, who was seeking to win reelection to the White House.

Riis's life began in 1849 in Ribe, Denmark, as the third child of Niels and Carolina Riis. His father taught school and edited the town newspaper, including in his work principles that would make his son famous, such as placing tremendous importance on education as a tool to uplift the poor. An avid reader, Jacob particularly enjoyed the writings of James Fenimore Cooper, celebrant of the American wilderness, and Charles Dickens, whose bleak portrayals of urban poverty, albeit told in sentimental terms, may have awakened the boy's social conscience.

But all that lay in the future. Jacob arrived in the United States in 1870 on the steamship *Iowa*. His training as a carpenter seemed to have prepared him for little in his new home, and he spent the years from his landing until 1873 moving around the northeastern part of the country, working odd jobs and observing and learning about America. Occasionally, he slept in shelters, lodging houses, and even a police station, all of which provided him with his first exposure to some of the conditions faced by the homeless, details of which eventually showed up in *How the Other Half Lives*.

In the fall of 1873 Riis made a momentous decision about his future direction. Evidently his command of English had become fairly good because he landed the position of city editor of a weekly magazine, *The Review*, published in Long Island. Although he lasted only two weeks in the job and never got paid for it, he transformed himself into a journalist, entering the field that would give him the platform from which to make a living, express himself, and ultimately influence public opinion and policy.

Over the course of the next several years he wrote for a variety of publications, including the *South Brooklyn News*, which he purchased within a few months of becoming one of its reporters. He stuck with the Brooklyn publication as publisher and writer and made enough money within a year to go back to Denmark, get married, and bring his bride back with him to Brooklyn, where he continued to work for the *News* as its editor.

In 1877, a year of great industrial strife in America, Riis expanded his horizons into areas that would eventually be reflected in *How the Other Half Lives*. He left the Brooklyn paper to give the advertising business a try. In that endeavor he began to make use of a fairly new piece of technology, the stereopticon, a projector with two lenses, known also as a *magic lantern*. Riis's fascination with the stereopticon as a way to market a product and his growing sense of the power of visual images to influence the public grew. Over the course of the 1880s he learned how to use flashlight powder, taught himself photography, and returned to journalism.

After a few months Riis jettisoned his career in advertising and went on the payroll of the *New York Tribune*, working the streets as a police reporter and covering life in the city as it revealed itself to him. For his first assignment, Riis ensconced himself in an office on Mulberry Street, directly across the street from police headquarters. Riis, who worked nights, sat in the thick of city life, covering not just the activities of the police but also the doings of the coroner's office, the fire department, and the health department. The experience provided the source of the dramatic stuff that would make *How the Other Half Lives* a vibrant and gritty text.

By the early 1880s Riis shifted to day work, which introduced him to another swathe of New York life: the deliberative bodies of state and municipal governments, the reform-oriented associations, and the social problems conferences that explored the many concerns that had accompanied the growth of the city via continued immigration. He met reformers bent on fixing the ills of the city. He attended lectures and sat in on meetings of commissions that took testimony from experts on matters of housing and health. In 1884 he covered the proceedings of the Tenement House Commission for the *Tribune*, following up on his 1881 report of the work of Dr. Roger Tracy, a sanitary inspector and statistician employed by the health department.

In the meantime Riis continued to experiment with and solidify his skills as a photographer. By 1888 he felt confident enough in this work that he began delivering an illustrated lecture, "The Other Half: How It Lives and Dies in New York," to a number of audiences, starting on January 25 with a presentation to the New York Society of Amateur Photographers. That year saw him take a number of other steps that would culminate in the 1890 publication of *How the Other Half Lives*. In March, he copyrighted the title "The Other Half: How It Lives and Dies in New York. With One Hundred Illustrations, Photographs from Real Life, of the Haunts of Poverty and Vice in the Great City." He also published "The Tenement House Question," an essay in two installments, in the *Christian Union*, thereby linking his name with the subject.

In December 1889 *Scribner's Magazine* published "How the Other Half Lives," chunks of which would appear in book form on November 15, 1890. The launch of Riis's most important work, and probably the most electrifying book of the progressive era, caused New Yorkers and many other Americans to sit up and take note.

Riis's fascination with the lower half and its social ills extended beyond the text of *How the Other Half Lives*. He published a string of books, all bearing a striking similarity to his first and most significant one. They included *The Children of the Poor* (1892), *Out of Mulberry Street* (1898), and *A Ten Years' War* (1900), the tenth anniversary of the publication of *How the Other Half Lives*. By this point Riis had become an important figure in both the city's and the nation's life. In 1895 he had struck up a friendship with Theodore Roosevelt, then a member of New York City's Board of Police Commissioners. Riis met Roosevelt when he guided him on tour of some of the city's worst immigrant slums and then went on to help him campaign for the governorship in 1898 and for the presidency in 1904.

All of Riis's books concentrated on the linked themes of the slums, the pathologies of the poor, and the evils of congestion. In *The Battle with the Slum* (1902) he recounted his efforts and those of others to expose the horrors of slum life to the public and, more important, to get government to act in response to that information. The next year saw the release of *Children of the Tenements* and *The Peril and Preservation of the Home*. Riis became in essence the spokesman for New York's tenement dwellers in as much as others recognized him as the expert, as the individual most able to explain how the poor lived and to expose their way of life. In 1904, for example, he led Booker T. Washington and the archbishop of Canterbury on tours of the immigrant east side.

Two years after his wife, Elisabeth, died in 1905, Riis married his secretary, Mary Phillips. Riis, then suffering from heart disease, and Mary moved to a farm in Barre, Massachusetts, where he died, on May 26, 1914.

His contemporaries recognized Riis as the authority on the plight of the urban poor. A century later, however, scholars and social critics in a very different era launched a critique of Riis, stripping away the conceit that any one person could speak for millions of immigrants, whose languages he did not know, whose cultures he could only guess at, and whose values he did not share. Modern critics noted the basically conservative underpinning of *How the Other Half Lives,* its fear of the crowd and its abhorrence of disorder, and depicted Riis as a voyeur who went out of his way to show the most decadent, the most macabre, the most prurient examples of urban life. They pointed out the prejudices that lay at the heart of the book and the highly subjective assumptions that blinded Riis from seeing the dense networks of social life that gave meaning to the poor and that provided them with much of what Riis assumed they lacked: family life, neighborliness, morality, bonds of support, and even the ability to assert control over their daily lives. Riis had no place in his vision, later critics noted, for the class-based actions of the urban masses to change their work lives through collective action, such as labor organizing.

Yet at the time of the book's publication and for many decades thereafter, Riis stood as a symbol of a particular aspect of American life, a liberal progressive strand of social conscience and consciousness. Historians and spokespeople for liberal causes have represented Riis, in both the popular and scholarly press, as an American success story, the immigrant who made it but who, in the process of achieving his own personal triumph, recognized that most would not. He stands out in the American liberal tradition as someone who witnessed horrible conditions, perceived the profound and very real social problems of others, spoke out about those problems, and chided the public to share in solving the escalating crisis. He took upon himself a cause of grave significance and prodded others, comfortable women and men like himself, to learn and to act. Riis came to stand for enlightened civic activism, as someone who believed, and wanted others to believe as well, that the two "halves" of society had an inextricable responsibility toward each other.   HASIA R. DINER

A Note on the Text

How the Other Half Lives was first published by Charles Scribner's Sons in 1890. This Norton Critical Edition is based on the 1901/02 Scribner's edition of the work.

The reproductions in this edition are from photographs in the Jacob A. Riis Collection at the Museum of the City of New York, which comprises the original complete compilation of Riis's pioneering works of photojournalism, including 415 original negatives, 326 glass lantern slides, and 191 vintage prints made by Riis in the 1880s and 1890s. After Riis's death in 1914, his collection remained undiscovered in the attic of the family's Long Island home until 1946. It was then that the photographer's son, Roger William Riis, donated Riis's photographic works to the Museum of the City of New York. Jacob A. Riis never considered himself a photographer and only took pictures he could not otherwise acquire. Today, his photographs are universally valued by social and photographic historians.

Illustrations

The Text of
HOW THE OTHER HALF LIVES

Preface

The belief that every man's experience ought to be worth something to the community from which he drew it, no matter what that experience may be, so long as it was gleaned along the line of some decent, honest work, made me begin this book. With the result before him, the reader can judge for himself now whether or not I was right. Right or wrong, the many and exacting duties of a newspaper man's life would hardly have allowed me to bring it to an end but for frequent friendly lifts given me by willing hands. To the President of the Board of Health, Mr. Charles G. Wilson, and to Chief Inspector Byrnes of the Police Force I am indebted for much kindness. The patient friendship of Dr. Roger S. Tracy, the Registrar of Vital Statistics, has done for me what I never could have done for myself; for I know nothing of tables, statistics and percentages, while there is nothing about them that he does not know. Most of all I owe in this, as in all things else, to the womanly sympathy and the loving companionship of my dear wife, ever my chief helper, my wisest counsellor, and my gentlest critic.

J. A. R.

"With gates of silver and bars of gold
Ye have fenced my sheep from their father's fold;
I have heard the dropping of their tears
In heaven these eighteen hundred years."

"O Lord and Master, not ours the guilt,
We build but as our fathers built;
Behold thine images, how they stand,
Sovereign and sole, through all our land."

Then Christ sought out an artisan,
A low-browed, stunted, haggard man,
And a motherless girl, whose fingers thin
Pushed from her faintly want and sin.

These set he in the midst of them,
And as they drew back their garment-hem,
For fear of defilement, "Lo, here," said he,
"The *images* ye have made of me!"

                          JAMES RUSSELL LOWELL[1]

---

1. "The Parable" (1848), by James Russell Lowell (1819–1891).

Introduction

Long ago it was said that "one half of the world does not know how the other half lives."[2] That was true then. It did not know because it did not care. The half that was on top cared little for the struggles, and less for the fate of those who were underneath, so long as it was able to hold them there and keep its own seat. There came a time when the discomfort and crowding below were so great, and the consequent upheavals so violent, that it was no longer an easy thing to do, and then the upper half fell to inquiring what was the matter. Information on the subject has been accumulating rapidly since, and the whole world has had its hands full answering for its old ignorance.

In New York, the youngest of the world's great cities, that time came later than elsewhere, because the crowding had not been so great. There were those who believed that it would never come; but their hopes were vain. Greed and reckless selfishness wrought like results here as in the cities of older lands. "When the great riot occurred in 1863,"[3] so reads the testimony of the Secretary of the Prison Association of New York before a legislative committee appointed to investigate causes of the increase of crime in the State twenty-five years ago, "every hiding-place and nursery of crime discovered itself by immediate and active participation in the operations of the mob. Those very places and domiciles, and all that are like them, are to-day nurseries of crime, and of the vices and disorderly courses which lead to crime. By far the largest part—eighty per cent. at least—of crimes against property and against the person are perpetrated by individuals who have either lost connection with home life, or never had any, or whose *homes had ceased to be sufficiently separate, decent, and desirable to afford what are regarded as ordinary wholesome influences of home and family. . . .* The younger criminals seem to come almost exclusively from the worst tenement[4] house districts, that is, when traced back to the very places where they had their homes in the city here." Of one thing New York made sure at that early stage of the inquiry: the boundary line of the Other Half lies through the tenements.

It is ten years and over, now, since that line divided New York's population evenly. To-day three-fourths of its people live in the tenements, and the nineteenth century drift of the population to the cities is sending ever-increasing multitudes to crowd them. The fifteen thousand tenant houses that were the despair of the sanitarian in the past generation have swelled into thirty-seven thousand, and more than twelve hundred thousand persons call them home. The one way out he saw—rapid transit to the suburbs—has brought no relief. We know now that there is no way out; that

2. Riis may very well have gotten this quotation from Benjamin Franklin's *Poor Richard's Almanck,* in which Franklin wrote, "It is a common saying that one half of the world does not know how the other half lives."
3. Riots that raged in New York City from July 13 to 16, 1863, sparked in large part by the announcement that the federal government would enforce military conscription. The participants came primarily from the ranks of poor Irish immigrants who lived in the city's most southern parts. They deeply resented the fact that those who paid a fee of $300 could avoid being drafted.
4. A residential building consisting of multiple units, dated back to the 1830s. Housing primarily the poor and the working class and immigrants in particular, tenements first attracted negative public attention in the years after the Civil War. New York State enacted the Tenement House Law in 1867, the first piece of legislation to attempt to improve tenement life.

the "system" that was the evil offspring of public neglect and private greed
has come to stay, a storm-centre forever of our civilization. Nothing is left
but to make the best of a bad bargain.

What the tenements are and how they grew to what they are, we shall
see hereafter. The story is dark enough, drawn from the plain public records, to send a chill to any heart. If it shall appear that the sufferings and
the sins of the "other half," and the evil they breed, are but as a just punishment upon the community that gave it no other choice, it will be
because that is the truth. The boundary line lies there because, while the
forces for good on one side vastly outweigh the bad—it were not well
otherwise—in the tenements all the influences make for evil; because they
are the hot-beds of the epidemics that carry death to rich and poor alike;
the nurseries of pauperism and crime that fill our jails and police courts;
that throw off a scum of forty thousand human wrecks to the island asylums and workhouses year by year; that turned out in the last eight years a
round half million beggars to prey upon our charities; that maintain a
standing army of ten thousand tramps with all that that implies; because,
above all, they touch the family life with deadly moral contagion. This is
their worst crime, inseparable from the system. That we have to own it the
child of our own wrong does not excuse it, even though it gives it claim
upon our utmost patience and tenderest charity.

What are you going to do about it? is the question of to-day. It was asked
once of our city in taunting defiance by a band of political cutthroats,[5] the
legitimate outgrowth of life on the tenement-house level. Law and order
found the answer then and prevailed. With our enormously swelling population held in this galling bondage, will that answer always be given? It will
depend on how fully the situation that prompted the challenge is grasped.
Forty per cent. of the distress among the poor, said a recent official report,
is due to drunkenness. But the first legislative committee ever appointed to
probe this sore went deeper down and uncovered its roots. The "conclusion
forced itself upon it that certain conditions and associations of human life
and habitation are the prolific parents of corresponding habits and morals,"
and it recommended "the prevention of drunkenness by providing for every
man a clean and comfortable home." Years after, a sanitary inquiry brought
to light the fact that "more than one-half of the tenements with two-thirds
of their population were held by owners who made the keeping of them
a business, *generally a speculation.* The owner was seeking a certain percentage on his outlay, and that percentage very rarely fell below fifteen per
cent., and frequently exceeded thirty. . . . The complaint was universal
among the tenants that they were entirely uncared for, and that the only
answer to their requests to have the place put in order by repairs and necessary improvements was that they must pay their rent or leave. The agent's
instructions were simple but emphatic: 'Collect the rent in advance, or, failing, eject the occupants.'" Upon such a stock grew this upas-tree. Small
wonder the fruit is bitter. The remedy that shall be an effective answer to
the coming appeal for justice must proceed from the public conscience.
Neither legislation nor charity can cover the ground. The greed of capital

---

5. The group of corrupt politicians linked to William M. "Boss" Tweed, who controlled the city government and the Democratic Party's Tammany Hall during the 1860s. By 1871 newspaper exposés
   and general public disgust drove Tweed and his followers out of political power.

that wrought the evil must itself undo it, as far as it can now be undone. Homes must be built for the working masses by those who employ their labor; but tenements must cease to be "good property" in the old, heartless sense. "Philanthropy and five per cent." is the penance exacted.

If this is true from a purely economic point of view, what then of the outlook from the Christian standpoint? Not long ago a great meeting was held in this city, of all denominations of religious faith, to discuss the question how to lay hold of these teeming masses in the tenements with Christian influences, to which they are now too often strangers. Might not the conference have found in the warning of one Brooklyn builder, who has invested his capital on this plan and made it pay more than a money interest, a hint worth heeding: "How shall the love of God be understood by those who have been nurtured in sight only of the greed of man?"

1. Genesis of the Tenement

The first tenement New York knew bore the mark of Cain from its birth, though a generation passed before the writing was deciphered. It was the "rear house," infamous ever after in our city's history. There had been tenant-houses before, but they were not built for the purpose. Nothing would probably have shocked their original owners more than the idea of their harboring a promiscuous crowd; for they were the decorous homes of the old Knicker-bockers, the proud aristocracy of Manhattan in the early days.

It was the stir and bustle of trade, together with the tremendous immigration that followed upon the war of 1812, that dislodged them. In thirty-five years the city of less than a hundred thousand came to harbor half a million souls, for whom homes had to be found. Within the memory of men not yet in their prime, Washington had moved from his house on Cherry Hill as too far out of town to be easily reached. Now the old residents followed his example; but they moved in a different direction and for a different reason. Their comfortable dwellings in the once fashionable streets along the East River front fell into the hands of real-estate agents and boarding-house keepers; and here, says the report to the Legislature of 1857, when the evils engendered had excited just alarm, "in its beginning, the tenant-house became a real blessing to that class of industrious poor whose small earnings limited their expenses, and whose employment in workshops, stores, or about the warehouses and thoroughfares, render a near residence of much importance." Not for long, however. As business increased, and the city grew with rapid strides, the necessities of the poor became the opportunity of their wealthier neighbors, and the stamp was set upon the old houses, suddenly become valuable, which the best thought and effort of a later age have vainly struggled to efface. Their "*large* rooms were partitioned into *several smaller ones*, without regard to light or ventilation, the rate of rent being lower in proportion to space or height from the street; and they soon became filled from cellar to garret with a class of tenantry living from hand to mouth, loose in morals, improvident in habits, degraded, and squalid as beggary itself." It was thus the dark bedroom, prolific of untold depravities, came into the world. It was destined to survive the old houses. In their new rôle, says the old report, eloquent in its indignant denunciation of "evils more destructive than wars," "they were not intended to last. Rents were fixed high enough to cover damage and abuse from this class, from whom nothing was expected, and the most was made of them while they lasted. Neatness, order, cleanliness, were never dreamed of in connection with the tenant-house system, as it spread its localities from year to year; while reckless slovenliness, discontent, privation, and ignorance were left to work out their invariable results, until the entire premises reached the level of tenant-house dilapidation, containing, but sheltering not, the miserable hordes that crowded beneath mouldering, water-rotted roofs or burrowed among the rats of clammy cellars." Yet so illogical is human greed that, at a later day, when called to account, "the proprietors frequently urged the filthy habits of the tenants as an excuse for the condition of their property, utterly losing sight of the fact that it was the tolerance of those habits which was the real evil, and that for this they themselves were alone responsible."

Still the pressure of the crowds did not abate, and in the old garden where the stolid Dutch burgher[1] grew his tulips or early cabbages a rear house was built, generally of wood, two stories high at first. Presently it was carried up another story, and another. Where two families had lived ten moved in. The front house followed suit, if the brick walls were strong enough. The question was not always asked, judging from complaints made by a contemporary witness, that the old buildings were "often carried up to a great height without regard to the strength of the foundation walls." It was rent the owner was after; nothing was said in the contract about either the safety or the comfort of the tenants. The garden gate no longer swung on its rusty hinges. The shell-paved walk had become an alley; what the rear house had left of the garden, a "court." Plenty such are yet to be found in the Fourth Ward,[2] with here and there one of the original rear tenements.

Worse was to follow. It was "soon perceived by estate owners and agents of property that a greater percentage of profits could be realized by the conversion of houses and blocks into barracks, and dividing their space into smaller proportions capable of containing human life within four walls. . . . Blocks were rented of real estate owners, or 'purchased on time,' or taken in charge at a percentage, and held for under-letting." With the appearance of the middle-man, wholly irresponsible, and utterly reckless and unrestrained, began the era of tenement building which turned out such blocks as Gotham Court,[3] where, in one cholera epidemic[4] that scarcely touched the clean wards, the tenants died at the rate of one hundred and ninety-five to the thousand of population; which forced the general mortality of the city up from 1 in 41.83 in 1815, to 1 in 27.33 in 1855, a year of unusual freedom from epidemic disease, and which wrung from the early organizers of the Health Department[5] this wail: "There are numerous examples of

1. Solid citizen. The word is of Dutch derivation and appropriate as such to a city that began as New Amsterdam.
2. On the banks of the East River. The ward, the smallest political unit in New York City, came to be identified by number in 1791. The Fourth Ward was one of the original city wards.
3. The Quaker philanthropist Silas Wood constructed a "model tenement" in 1851 on a block near Franklin Square. Made up of two rows of six buildings, each one rising five stories high, Gotham Court consisted of 144 apartments, each with a living room and a bedroom. (Riis describes the history of Gotham Court in Chapter 4)
4. Serious outbreaks of the dread disease swept through New York in 1832, 1849, 1854, and 1866. Middle-class New Yorkers tended to blame the immigrants as the carriers of the disease. In reality humans can contract the disease by ingesting infected water or food.
5. The Metropolitan Board of Health was created in 1866 as a result of the Metropolitan Health Act. It, along with the New York Quarantine Station, used cholera cultures for the first time in 1887 to prevent the disease from entering the city.

tenement-houses in which are lodged several hundred people that have a *pro rata* allotment of ground area scarcely equal to two square yards upon the city lot, courtyards and all included." The tenement-house population had swelled to half a million souls by that time, and on the East Side, in what is still the most densely populated district in all the world, China not excluded, it was packed at the rate of 290,000 to the square mile, a state of affairs wholly unexampled. The utmost cupidity of other lands and other days had never contrived to herd much more than half that number within the same space. The greatest crowding of Old London was at the rate of 175,816. Swine roamed the streets and gutters as their principal scavengers.[6] The death of a child in a tenement was registered at the Bureau of Vital Statistics as "plainly due to suffocation in the foul air of an unventilated apartment," and the Senators, who had come down from Albany to find out what was the matter with New York, reported that "there are annually cut off from the population by disease and death enough human beings to people a city, and enough human labor to sustain it." And yet experts had testified that, as compared with uptown, rents were from twenty-five to thirty per cent. higher in the worst slums of the lower wards, with such accommodations as were enjoyed, for instance, by a "family with boarders" in Cedar Street, who fed hogs in the cellar that contained eight or ten loads of manure; or "one room 12 × 12 with five families living in it, comprising twenty persons of both sexes and all ages, with only two beds, without partition, screen, chair, or table." The rate of rent has been successfully maintained to the present day, though the hog at least has been eliminated.

Tenement of 1863, for twelve families on each flat. D, dark. L, light. H, halls.

Lest anybody flatter himself with the notion that these were evils of a day that is happily past and may safely be forgotten, let me mention here three very recent instances of tenement-house life that came under my notice. One was the burning of a rear house in Mott Street, from appearances one of the original tenant-houses that made their owners rich. The fire made homeless ten families, who had paid an average of $5 a month for their mean little cubby-holes. The owner himself told me that it was *fully* insured for $800, though it brought him in $600 a year rent. He evidently considered himself especially entitled to be pitied for losing such valuable property. Another was the case of a hard-working family of man and wife, young people from the old country, who took poison together in a Crosby Street tenement because

---

6. Many tenement dwellers kept pigs. In 1867 the city passed an ordinance prohibiting swine from roaming in the inhabited and developed parts of the city.

Hell's Kitchen and Sebastopol

they were "tired." There was no other explanation, and none was needed when I stood in the room in which they had lived. It was in the attic with sloping ceiling and a single window so far out on the roof that it seemed not to belong to the place at all. With scarcely room enough to turn around in they had been compelled to pay five dollars and a half a month in advance. There were four such rooms in that attic, and together they brought in as much as many a handsome little cottage in a pleasant part of Brooklyn. The third instance was that of a colored family of husband, wife, and baby in a wretched rear rookery in West Third Street. Their rent was eight dollars and a half for a single room on the top-story, so small that I was unable to get a photograph of it even by placing the camera outside the open door. Three short steps across either way would have measured its full extent.

There was just one excuse for the early tenement-house builders, and their successors may plead it with nearly as good right for what it is worth. "Such," says an official report, "is the lack of houseroom in the city that any kind of tenement can be immediately crowded with lodgers, if there is space offered." Thousands were living in cellars. There were three hundred underground lodging-houses in the city when the Health Department was organized. Some fifteen years before that the old Baptist Church in Mulberry Street, just off Chatham Street, had been sold, and the rear half of the frame structure had been converted into tenements that with their swarming population became the scandal even of that reckless age. The wretched pile harbored no less than forty families, and the annual rate of deaths to the population was officially stated to be 75 in 1,000. These tenements were an extreme type of very many, for the big barracks had by this time spread east and west and far up the island into the sparsely settled wards. Whether or not the title was clear to the land upon which they were built was of less account than that the rents were collected. If there were damages to pay, the tenant had to foot them. Cases were "very frequent when property was in litigation, and two or three different parties were collecting rents." Of course under such circumstances "no repairs were ever made."

The climax had been reached. The situation was summed up by the Society for the Improvement of the Condition of the Poor[7] in these words: "Crazy old buildings, crowded rear tenements in filthy yards, dark, damp basements, leaking garrets, shops, outhouses, and stables converted into dwellings, though scarcely fit to shelter brutes, are habitations of thousands of our fellow-beings in this wealthy, Christian city." "The city," says its historian, Mrs. Martha Lamb,[8] commenting on the era of aqueduct building between 1835 and 1845, "was a general asylum for vagrants." Young vagabonds, the natural offspring of such "home" conditions, overran the streets. Juvenile crime increased fearfully year by year. The Children's Aid Society[9] and kindred philanthropic organizations were yet unborn, but in the city directory was to be found the address of the "American Society for the Promotion of Education in Africa."

---

7. Riis may be referring here to the Association for Improvement of the Condition of the Poor, founded in 1843. See page 30, n. 6.
8. Lamb (1826–1893) moved to New York in 1866 from Chicago. A writer of children's literature and newspaper articles, she also authored *The History of the City of New York: Its Origins, Rise, and Progress*, vol. 1 (New York, 1877–1880).
9. Founded in 1853 by Charles Loring Brace (1826–1890). The society emphasized self-help in its work with homeless boys, particularly the children of immigrants.

The Ashbarrel of Old

2. *The Awakening*

The dread of advancing cholera, with the guilty knowledge of the harvest field that awaited the plague in New York's slums, pricked the conscience of the community into action soon after the close of the war.[1] A citizens' movement resulted in the organization of a Board of Health and the adoption of the "Tenement-House Act" of 1867, the first step toward remedial legislation. A thorough canvass of the tenements had been begun already in the previous year; but the cholera first, and next a scourge of smallpox,[2] delayed the work, while emphasizing the need of it, so that it was 1869 before it got fairly under way and began to tell. The dark bedroom fell under the ban first. In that year the Board ordered the cutting of more than forty-six thousand windows in interior rooms, chiefly for ventilation—for little or no light was to be had from the dark hallways. Air-shafts were unknown. The saw had a job all that summer; by early fall nearly all the orders had been carried out. Not without opposition; obstacles were thrown in the way of the officials on the one side by the owners of the tenements, who saw in every order to repair or clean up only an item of added expense to diminish their income from the rent; on the other side by the tenants themselves, who had sunk, after a generation of unavailing protest, to the level of their surroundings, and were at last content to remain there. The tenements had bred their Nemesis, a proletariat ready and able to avenge the wrongs of their crowds. Already it taxed the city heavily for the support of its jails and charities. The basis of opposition, curiously enough, was the same at both extremes; owner and tenant alike considered official interference an infringement of personal rights, and a hardship. It took long years of weary labor to make good the claim of the sunlight to such corners of the dens as it could reach at all. Not until five years after did the department succeed at last in ousting the "cave-dwellers" and closing some five hundred and fifty cellars south of Houston Street, many of them below tide-water, that had been used as living apartments. In many instances the police had to drag the tenants out by force.

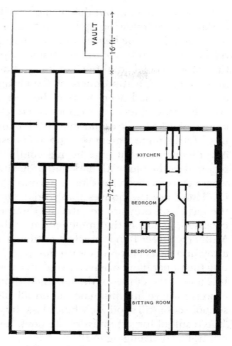

Tenement of the old style. Birth of the air-shaft.

1. I.e., the Civil War (1861–65).
2. This viral disease plagued New York since the colonial period, killing thousands annually. As of 1850 smallpox was the cause of about 25 of every 1,000 deaths in New York.

The work went on; but the need of it only grew with the effort. The Sanitarians[3] were following up an evil that grew faster than they went; like a fire, it could only be headed off, not chased, with success. Official reports, read in the churches in 1879, characterized the younger criminals as victims of low social conditions of life and unhealthy, overcrowded lodgings, brought up in "an atmosphere of actual darkness, moral and physical." This after the saw had been busy in the dark corners ten years! "If we could see the air breathed by these poor creatures in their tenements," said a well-known physician, "it would show itself to be fouler than the mud of the gutters." Little improvement was apparent despite all that had been done. "The new tenements, that have been recently built, have been usually as badly planned as the old, with dark and unhealthy rooms, often over wet cellars, where extreme overcrowding is permitted," was the verdict of one authority. These are the houses that to-day perpetuate the worst traditions of the past, and they are counted by thousands. The Five Points[4] had been cleansed, as far as the immediate neighborhood was concerned, but the Mulberry Street Bend[5] was fast outdoing it in foulness not a stone's throw away, and new centres of corruption were continually springing up and getting the upper hand whenever vigilance was relaxed for ever so short a time. It is one of the curses of the tenement-house system that the worst houses exercise a levelling influence upon all the rest, just as one bad boy in a school-room will spoil the whole class. It is one of the ways the evil that was "the result of forgetfulness of the poor," as the Council of Hygiene[6] mildly put it, has of avenging itself.

The determined effort to head it off by laying a strong hand upon the tenement builders that has been the chief business of the Health Board of recent years, dates from this period. The era of the air-shaft has not solved the problem of housing the poor, but it has made good use of limited opportunities. Over the new houses sanitary law exercises full control. But the old remain. They cannot be summarily torn down, though in extreme cases the authorities can order them cleared. The outrageous overcrowding, too, remains. It is characteristic of the tenements. Poverty, their badge and typical condition, invites—compels it. All efforts to abate it result only in temporary relief. As long as they exist it will exist with them. And the tenements will exist in New York forever.

To-day, what is a tenement? The law defines it as a house "occupied by three or more families, living independently and doing their cooking on the premises; or by more than two families on a floor, so living and cooking and having a common right in the halls, stairways, yards, etc." That is the legal meaning, and includes flats and apartment-houses, with which we have nothing to do. In its narrower sense the typical tenement was thus described when last arraigned before the bar of public justice: "It is gener-

3. It is not clear if Riis is referring here to a specific organization or to individuals of good will and civic concern.
4. A New York City neighborhood named for the intersection of five streets: Anthony Street (now Worth), Cross (now Park), Orange (Baxter), Mulberry, and Little Water (no longer in existence). A poor section since the 1820s that was inhabited by immigrants, particularly from Ireland, it included such areas as "Murderers' Alley" and "Den of Thieves." The city oversaw the demolition of most of the tenements there between 1887 and 1894.
5. A stretch of Mulberry Street in the Five Points neighborhood.
6. Established by a citizens group in 1864 to survey the unsanitary conditions endured by many poor New Yorkers. The council relied heavily on statistical data to make its case.

ally a brick building from four to six stories high on the street, frequently with a store on the first floor which, when used for the sale of liquor, has a side opening for the benefit of the inmates and to evade the Sunday law;[7] four families occupy each floor, and a set of rooms consists of one or two dark closets, used as bedrooms, with a living room twelve feet by ten. The staircase is too often a dark well in the centre of the house, and no direct through ventilation is possible, each family being separated from the other by partitions. Frequently the rear of the lot is occupied by another building of three stories high with two families on a floor." The picture is nearly as true to-day as ten years ago, and will be for a long time to come. The dim light admitted by the air-shaft shines upon greater crowds than ever. Tenements are still "good property," and the poverty of the poor man his destruction. A barrack down town where he *has to live* because he is poor brings in a third more rent than a decent flat house in Harlem. The statement once made a sensation that between seventy and eighty children had been found in one tenement. It no longer excites even passing attention, when the sanitary police report counting 101 adults and 91 children in a Crosby Street house, one of twins, built together. The children in the other, if I am not mistaken, numbered 89, a total of 180 for two tenements! Or when a midnight inspection in Mulberry Street unearths a hundred and fifty "lodgers" sleeping on filthy floors in two buildings. Spite of brownstone trimmings, plate-glass and mosaic vestibule floors, the water does not rise in summer to the second story, while the beer flows unchecked to the all-night picnics on the roof. The saloon with the side-door and the landlord divide the prosperity of the place between them, and the tenant, in sullen submission, foots the bills.

Where are the tenements of to-day? Say rather: where are they not? In fifty years they have crept up from the Fourth Ward slums and the Five Points the whole length of the island, and have polluted the Annexed District to the Westchester line.[8] Crowding all the lower wards, wherever business leaves a foot of ground unclaimed; strung along both rivers, like ball and chain tied to the foot of every street, and filling up Harlem with their restless, pent-up multitudes they hold within their clutch the wealth and business of New York, hold them at their mercy in the day of mob-rule and wrath. The bullet-proof shutters, the stacks of hand-grenades, and the Gatling guns of the Sub-Treasury[9] are tacit admissions of the fact and of the quality of the mercy expected. The tenements to-day are New York, harboring three-fourths of its population. When another generation shall have doubled the census of our city, and to that vast army of workers, held captive by poverty, the very name of home shall be as a bitter mockery, what will the harvest be?

3. *The Mixed Crowd*

When once I asked the agent of a notorious Fourth Ward alley how many people might be living in it I was told: One hundred and forty families, one

---

7. Laws prohibiting most commercial transactions, including the sale of alcohol, on Sunday.
8. Areas of what became the Bronx, annexed by New York City in 1874. This included Kingsbridge, Morrisania, and West Farms.
9. An agency for collecting federal taxes, founded in 1846, which had its headquarters on Wall Street from 1862 to 1925. "Gatling guns": Similar to machine guns.

hundred Irish,[1] thirty-eight Italian,[2] and two that spoke the German[3] tongue. Barring the agent herself, there was not a native-born individual in the court. The answer was characteristic of the cosmopolitan character of lower New York, very nearly so of the whole of it, wherever it runs to alleys and courts. One may find for the asking an Italian, a German, a French, African, Spanish, Bohemian, Russian, Scandinavian, Jewish, and Chinese colony.[4] Even the Arab, who peddles "holy earth" from the Battery as a direct importation from Jerusalem, has his exclusive preserves at the lower end of Washington Street. The one thing you shall vainly ask for in the chief city of America is a distinctively American community. There is none; certainly not among the tenements. Where have they gone to, the old inhabitants? I put the question to one who might fairly be presumed to be of the number, since I had found him sighing for the "good old days" when the legend "no Irish need apply" was familiar in the advertising columns of the newspapers. He looked at me with a puzzled air. "I don't know," he said. "I wish I did. Some went to California in '49, some to the war and never came back. The rest, I expect, have gone to heaven, or somewhere. I don't see them 'round here."

Whatever the merit of the good man's conjectures, his eyes did not deceive him. They are not here. In their place has come this queer conglomerate mass of heterogeneous elements, ever striving and working like whiskey and water in one glass, and with the like result: final union and a prevailing taint of whiskey. The once unwelcome Irishman has been followed in his turn by the Italian, the Russian Jew, and the Chinaman, and has himself taken a hand at opposition, quite as bitter and quite as ineffectual, against these later hordes. Wherever these have gone they have crowded him out, possessing the block, the street, the ward with their denser swarms. But the Irishman's revenge is complete. Victorious in defeat over his recent as over his more ancient foe, the one who opposed his coming no less than the one who drove him out, he dictates to both their politics, and, secure in possession of the offices, returns the native his greeting with interest, while collecting the rents of the Italian whose house he has bought with the profits of his saloon. As a landlord he is picturesquely autocratic. An amusing instance of his methods came under my notice while writing these lines. An inspector of the Health Department found an Italian

1. While an Irish presence had been seen in New York since the colonial period, the era of the greatest Irish immigration began in the mid-1840s with the potato famine, which ravaged Ireland. As of 1855 Irish immigrants constituted nearly a quarter of the city's population in sixteen of its twenty-two wards. Well into the early twentieth century more Irish-born women and men lived in New York than in any other American city. They arrived in New York extremely poor and endured generations of poverty. Protestant, native-born New Yorkers evinced a high degree of antipathy to the Irish based on their national origins and, of possibly greater significance, their Roman Catholic religion.
2. The greatest influx of Italian immigrants began in the 1890s, mostly from the nation's southern regions. Italian immigrant women and girls tended to work in the garment trades, many of them doing home work, while men labored in construction and manufacturing. They arrived quite poor and settled in several dense enclaves in Manhattan.
3. Like the Irish, German settlement in New York went back to the colonial period, but in the decades after the 1840s substantial waves of German immigrants made their homes there. The largest German neighborhood, known as *Kleindeutschland*, or "Little Germany," formed in the 1840s east of the Bowery and north of Division Street, up through Avenue D. This religiously and economically diverse group consisted of Lutherans, Catholics, Jews, Evangelicals, and antireligious socialists and ranged from solidly middle-class proprietors to working-class laborers.
4. In ticking off this list of immigrant groups, Riis reflected the vast diversity of backgrounds from which women and men who settled in New York hailed. According to the 1890 census, the foreign-born made up 42 percent of the population of Manhattan. Adding in their American-born children further demonstrates the degree to which the city took much of its character from the immigrants' presence. The same census enumerated more than three dozen places from which immigrants had come.

family paying a man with a Celtic name twenty-five dollars a month for three small rooms in a ramshackle rear tenement—more than twice what they were worth—and expressed his astonishment to the tenant, an ignorant Sicilian laborer. He replied that he had once asked the landlord to reduce the rent, but he would not do it.

"Well! What did he say?" asked the inspector.

" 'Damma, man!' he said; 'if you speaka thata way to me, I fira you and your things in the streeta.' " And the frightened Italian paid the rent.

In justice to the Irish landlord it must be said that like an apt pupil he was merely showing forth the result of the schooling he had received, reenacting, in his own way, the scheme of the tenements. It is only his frankness that shocks. The Irishman does not naturally take kindly to tenement life, though with characteristic versatility he adapts himself to its conditions at once. It does violence, nevertheless, to the best that is in him, and for that very reason of all who come within its sphere soonest corrupts him. The result is a sediment, the product of more than a generation in the city's slums, that, as distinguished from the larger body of his class, justly ranks at the foot of tenement dwellers, the so-called "low Irish."

It is not to be assumed, of course, that the whole body of the population living in the tenements, of which New Yorkers are in the habit of speaking vaguely as "the poor," or even the larger part of it, is to be classed as vicious or as poor in the sense of verging on beggary.

New York's wage-earners have no other place to live, more is the pity. They are truly poor for having no better homes; waxing poorer in purse as the exorbitant rents to which they are tied, as ever was serf to soil, keep rising. The wonder is that they are not all corrupted, and speedily, by their surroundings. If, on the contrary, there be a steady working up, if not out of the slough, the fact is a powerful argument for the optimist's belief that the world is, after all, growing better, not worse, and would go far toward disarming apprehension, were it not for the steadier growth of the sediment of the slums and its constant menace. Such an impulse toward better things there certainly is. The German rag-picker[5] of thirty years ago, quite as low in the scale as his Italian successor, is the thrifty tradesman or prosperous farmer of to-day.

The Italian scavenger of our time is fast graduating into exclusive control of the corner fruit-stands, while his black-eyed boy monopolizes the boot-blacking industry[6] in which a few years ago he was an intruder. The Irish hod-carrier[7] in the second generation has become a bricklayer, if not the Alderman of his ward, while the Chinese coolie is in almost exclusive possession of the laundry business.[8] The reason is obvious. The poorest immigrant comes here with the purpose and ambition to better himself and, given half a chance, might be reasonably expected to make the most of it. To the false plea that he prefers the squalid homes in which his kind are housed

---

5. One who made his or her living by scavenging rags and other kinds of refuse and then selling them. Others reworked these bits and pieces into sellable items.

6. I.e., shoe shining. "Corner fruit-stands": One of the first areas of Italian entrepreneurship, these establishments helped establish the Italian economic niche and provided produce for the public as a whole.

7. Unskilled work; specifically the transporting by hand of coal. The Irish in the immigrant generation performed much of this kind of labor.

8. One of the most ubiquitous commercial establishments in New York and elsewhere, operated by Chinese immigrants. "Coolie": A derisive term initially used to refer to Chinese and Indian laborers who engaged in low-level, unskilled work. The term was later used to refer to Chinese people in general.

there could be no better answer. The truth is, his half chance has too long been wanting, and for the bad result he has been unjustly blamed.

As emigration from east to west follows the latitude, so does the foreign influx in New York distribute itself along certain well-defined lines that waver and break only under the stronger pressure of a more gregarious race or the encroachments of inexorable business. A feeling of dependence upon mutual effort, natural to strangers in a strange land, unaquainted with its language and customs, sufficiently accounts for this.

The Irishman is the true cosmopolitan immigrant. All-pervading, he shares his lodging with perfect impartiality with the Italian, the Greek, and the "Dutchman,"[9] yielding only to sheer force of numbers, and objects equally to them all. A map of the city, colored to designate nationalities, would show more stripes than on the skin of a zebra, and more colors than any rainbow. The city on such a map would fall into two great halves, green for the Irish prevailing in the West Side tenement districts, and blue for the Germans on the East Side. But intermingled with these ground colors would be an odd variety of tints that would give the whole the appearance of an extraordinary crazy-quilt. From down in the Sixth Ward, upon the site of the old Collect Pond[1] that in the days of the fathers drained the hills which are no more, the red of the Italian would be seen forcing its way northward along the line of Mulberry Street to the quarter of the French purple on Bleecker Street and South Fifth Avenue, to lose itself and reappear, after a lapse of miles, in the "Little Italy" of Harlem, east of Second Avenue. Dashes of red, sharply defined, would be seen strung through the Annexed District, northward to the city line. On the West Side the red would be seen overrunning the old Africa of Thompson Street, pushing the black of the negro rapidly uptown, against querulous but unavailing protests, occupying his home, his church, his trade and all, with merciless impartiality. There is a church in Mulberry Street that has stood for two generations as a sort of mile-stone of these migrations. Built originally for the worship of staid New Yorkers of the "old stock," it was engulfed by the colored tide, when the draft-riots drove the negroes out of reach of Cherry Street and the Five Points. Within the past decade the advance wave of the Italian onset reached it, and to-day the arms of United Italy adorn its front. The negroes have made a stand at several points along Seventh and Eighth Avenues; but their main body, still pursued by the Italian foe, is on the march yet, and the black mark will be found overshadowing to-day many blocks on the East Side, with One Hundredth Street as the centre, where colonies of them have settled recently.

Hardly less aggressive than the Italian, the Russian and Polish Jew, having overrun the district between Rivington and Division Streets, east of the Bowery, to the point of suffocation, is filling the tenements of the old Seventh Ward[2] to the river front, and disputing with the Italian every foot of available space in the back alleys of Mulberry Street. The two races, differing hopelessly in much, have this in common: they carry their slums with them wherever they go, if allowed to do it. Little Italy already rivals its par-

---

9. I.e., a person of German background. The term came from a mispronunciation of the word for the German language, *Deutsch*.
1. A large pond in the middle of the Five Points neighborhood (see page 14, n. 4). It was filled in 1808; but by the 1820s the landfill began to sink, giving the neighborhood a malodorous quality. "Sixth Ward": Between Walker Street and Park Row.
2. An area outlined by Catherine Street, Division, Grand, South Street, and the East River.

ent, the "Bend," in foulness. Other nationalities that begin at the bottom make a fresh start when crowded up the ladder. Happily both are manageable, the one by rabbinical, the other by the civil law. Between the dull gray of the Jew, his favorite color, and the Italian red, would be seen squeezed in on the map a sharp streak of yellow, marking the narrow boundaries of Chinatown. Dovetailed in with the German population, the poor but thrifty Bohemian[3] might be picked out by the sombre hue of his life as of his philosophy, struggling against heavy odds in the big human bee-hives of the East Side. Colonies of his people extend northward, with long lapses of space, from below the Cooper Institute[4] more than three miles. The Bohemian is the only foreigner with any considerable representation in the city who counts no wealthy man of his race, none who has not to work hard for a living, or has got beyond the reach of the tenement.

Down near the Battery[5] the West Side emerald would be soiled by a dirty stain, spreading rapidly like a splash of ink on a sheet of blotting paper, headquarters of the Arab tribe, that in a single year has swelled from the original dozen to twelve hundred, intent, every mother's son, on trade and barter. Dots and dashes of color here and there would show where the Finnish sailors worship their djumala (God), the Greek pedlars the ancient name of their race, and the Swiss the goddess of thrift. And so on to the end of the long register, all toiling together in the galling fetters of the tenement. Were the question raised who makes the most of life thus mortgaged, who resists most stubbornly its levelling tendency—knows how to drag even the barracks upward a part of the way at least toward the ideal plane of the home—the palm must be unhesitatingly awarded the Teuton.[6] The Italian and the poor Jew rise only by compulsion. The Chinaman does not rise at all; here, as at home, he simply remains stationary. The Irishman's genius runs to public affairs rather than domestic life; wherever he is mustered in force the saloon is the gorgeous centre of political activity. The German struggles vainly to learn his trick; his Teutonic wit is too heavy, and the political ladder he raises from his saloon usually too short or too clumsy to reach the desired goal. The best part of his life is lived at home, and he makes himself a home independent of the surroundings, giving the lie to the saying, unhappily become a maxim of social truth, that pauperism and drunkenness naturally grow in the tenements. He makes the most of his tenement, and it should be added that whenever and as soon as he can save up money enough, he gets out and never crosses the threshold of one again.

4. The Down Town Back-alleys

Down below Chatham Square, in the old Fourth Ward, where the cradle of the tenement stood, we shall find New York's Other Half at home, receiving such as care to call and are not afraid. Not all of it, to be sure, there is not room for that; but a fairly representative gathering, representative of its earliest and worst traditions. There is nothing to be afraid of. In this metropo-

---

3. An immigrant from the section of the Austro-Hungarian Empire that became part of Czechoslovakia after World War I.
4. A tuition-free college created by Peter Cooper in 1859 to provide education for workers. Situated at Astor Place, it offered lectures and exhibitions as well as classes.
5. Occupying the southern tip of Manhattan, the area derived its name from the guns placed there by the Dutch to prevent a British invasion.
6. The reference here is to Germans.

At the cradle of the tenement. Doorway of an old-fashioned dwelling
on Cherry Hill.

lis, let it be understood, there is no public street where the stranger may not
go safely by day and by night, provided he knows how to mind his own business and is sober. His coming and going will excite little interest, unless he
is suspected of being a truant officer, in which case he will be impressed
with the truth of the observation that the American stock is dying out for
want of children. If he escapes this suspicion and the risk of trampling upon,
or being himself run down by the bewildering swarms of youngsters that are
everywhere or nowhere as the exigency and their quick scent of danger
direct, he will see no reason for dissenting from that observation. Glimpses
caught of the parents watching the youngsters play from windows or open
doorways will soon convince him that the native stock is in no way involved.

Leaving the Elevated Railroad where it dives under the Brooklyn Bridge[1]
at Franklin Square, scarce a dozen steps will take us where we wish to go.
With its rush and roar echoing yet in our ears, we have turned the corner
from prosperity to poverty. We stand upon the domain of the tenement. In
the shadow of the great stone abutments the old Knickerbocker[2] houses
linger like ghosts of a departed day. Down the winding slope of Cherry
Street—proud and fashionable Cherry Hill that was—their broad steps,
sloping roofs, and dormer windows are easily made out; all the more easily
for the contrast with the ugly barracks that elbow them right and left. These
never had other design than to shelter, at as little outlay as possible, the
greatest crowds out of which rent could be wrung. They were the bad after-

1. The steel suspension bridge that links Manhattan and Brooklyn went up in 1883. Its opening
played a key role in the development of housing in Brooklyn and helped, in the long run, siphon
many people out of some of Manhattan's most crowded neighborhoods, including those Riis wrote
about. "Elevated Railroad": The first elevated trains went up in New York at the end of the 1860s,
but they did not become widespread or particularly popular until the end of the 1870s.
2. I.e., the descendants of the old Dutch settlers of New Amsterdam.

Upstairs in Blindman's Alley

thought of a heedless day. The years have brought to the old houses unhonored age, a querulous second childhood that is out of tune with the time, their tenants, the neighbors, and cries out against them and against you in fretful protest in every step on their rotten floors or squeaky stairs. Good cause have they for their fretting. This one, with its shabby front and poorly patched roof, what glowing firesides, what happy children may it once have owned? Heavy feet, too often with unsteady step, for the pot-house is next door—where is it not next door in these slums?—have worn away the brown-stone steps since; the broken columns at the door have rotted away at the base. Of the handsome cornice barely a trace is left. Dirt and desolation reign in the wide hall-way, and danger lurks on the stairs. Rough pine boards fence off the roomy fire-places—where coal is bought by the pail at the rate of twelve dollars a ton these have no place. The arched gateway leads no longer to a shady bower on the banks of the rushing stream, inviting to day-dreams with its gentle repose, but to a dark and nameless alley, shut in by high brick walls, cheerless as the lives of those they shelter. The wolf knocks loudly at the gate in the troubled dreams that come to this alley, echoes of the day's cares. A horde of dirty children play about the dripping hydrant, the only thing in the alley that thinks enough of its chance to make the most of it: it is the best it can do. These are the children of the tenements, the growing generation of the slums; this their home. From the great highway overhead, along which throbs the life-tide of two great cities, one might drop a pebble into half a dozen such alleys.

One yawns just across the street; not very broadly, but it is not to blame. The builder of the old gateway had no thought of its ever becoming a public thoroughfare. Once inside it widens, but only to make room for a big box-like building with the worn and greasy look of the slum tenement that is stamped alike on the houses and their tenants down here, even on the homeless cur that romps with the children in yonder building lot, with an air of expectant interest plainly betraying the forlorn hope that at some stage of the game a meat-bone may show up in the role of "It." Vain hope, truly! Nothing more appetizing than a bare-legged ragamuffin appears. Meat-bones, not long since picked clean, are as scarce in Blind Man's Alley as elbow-room in any Fourth Ward back-yard. The shouts of the children come hushed over the house-tops, as if apologizing for the intrusion. Few glad noises make this old alley ring. Morning and evening it echoes with the gentle, groping tap of the blind man's staff as he feels his way to the street. Blind Man's Alley bears its name for a reason. Until little more than a year ago its dark burrows harbored a colony of blind beggars, tenants of a blind landlord, old Daniel Murphy, whom every child in the ward knows, if he never heard of the President of the United States.[3] "Old Dan" made a big fortune—he told me once four hundred thousand dollars—out of his alley and the surrounding tenements, only to grow blind himself in extreme old age, sharing in the end the chief hardship of the wretched beings whose lot he had stubbornly refused to better that he might increase his wealth. Even when the Board of Health at last compelled him to repair and clean up the worst of the old buildings, under threat of driving out the tenants and locking the doors behind them, the work was accomplished against the old man's angry protests. He appeared in person before the Board to argue his case, and his argument was characteristic.

"I have made my will," he said. "My monument stands waiting for me in Calvary. I stand on the very brink of the grave, blind and helpless, and now (here the pathos of the appeal was swept under in a burst of angry indignation) do you want me to build and get skinned, skinned? These people are not fit to live in a nice house. Let them go where they can, and let my house stand."

In spite of the genuine anguish of the appeal, it was downright amusing to find that his anger was provoked less by the anticipated waste of luxury on his tenants than by distrust of his own kind, the builder. He knew intuitively what to expect. The result showed that Mr. Murphy had gauged his tenants correctly. The cleaning up process apparently destroyed the home-feeling of the alley; many of the blind people moved away and did not return. Some remained, however, and the name has clung to the place.

---

3. Benjamin Harrison (1889–93).

Some idea of what is meant by a sanitary "cleaning up" in these slums may be gained from the account of a mishap I met with once, in taking a flash-light picture of a group of blind beggars in one of the tenements down here. With unpractised hands I managed to set fire to the house. When the blind-ing effect of the flash had passed away and I could see once more, I discov-ered that a lot of paper and rags that hung on the wall were ablaze. There were six of us, five blind men and women who knew nothing of their danger, and myself, in an attic room with a dozen crooked, rickety stairs between us and the street, and as many households as helpless as the one whose guest I was all about us. The thought: how were they ever to be got out? made my blood run cold as I saw the flames creeping up the wall, and my first impulse was to bolt for the street and shout for help. The next was to smother the fire myself, and I did, with a vast deal of trouble. Afterward, when I came down to the street I told a friendly policeman of my trouble. For some reason he thought it rather a good joke, and laughed immoderately at my concern lest even then sparks should be burrowing in the rotten wall that might yet break out in flame and destroy the house with all that were in it. He told me why, when he found time to draw breath. "Why, don't you know," he said, "that house is the Dirty Spoon? It caught fire six times last winter, but it wouldn't burn. The dirt was so thick on the walls, it smothered the fire!" Which, if true, shows that water and dirt, not usually held to be harmonious elements, work together for the good of those who insure houses.

Sunless and joyless though it be, Blind Man's Alley has that which its compeers of the slums vainly yearn for. It has a pay-day. Once a year sun-light shines into the lives of its forlorn crew, past and present. In June, when the Superintendent of Out-door[4] Poor distributes the twenty thousand dol-lars annually allowed the poor blind by the city, in half-hearted recognition of its failure to otherwise provide for them, Blind Man's Alley takes a day off and goes to "see" Mr. Blake. That night it is noisy with unwonted mer-riment. There is scraping of squeaky fiddles in the dark rooms, and cracked old voices sing long-forgotten songs. Even the blind landlord rejoices, for much of the money goes into his coffers.

From their perch up among the rafters Mrs. Gallagher's blind boarders might hear, did they listen, the tramp of the policeman always on duty in Gotham Court, half a stone's throw away. His beat, though it takes in but a small portion of a single block, is quite as lively as most larger patrol rounds. A double row of five-story tenements, back to back under a com-mon roof, extending back from the street two hundred and thirty-four feet, with barred openings in the dividing wall, so that the tenants may see but cannot get at each other from the stairs, makes the "court." Alleys—one wider by a couple of feet than the other, whence the distinction Single and Double Alley—skirt the barracks on either side. Such, briefly, is the tene-ment that has challenged public attention more than any other in the whole city and tested the power of sanitary law and rule for forty years. The name of the pile is not down in the City Directory,[5] but in the public records it holds an unenviable place. It was here the mortality rose during the last

4. Reference to the provision of charity outside of alms houses. Those who provided the relief distri-buted food, coal, clothing, and other necessities. By the 1870s public opposition in New York mounted against this kind of assistance, partly because of the increasing number of poor due to the Panic of 1873 and partly because of revelations about the collaboration between the providers of the relief and corrupt Tammany Hall politicians.
5. A predecessor to the telephone book, it listed names and addresses of city residents.

great cholera epidemic[6] to the unprecedented rate of 195 in 1,000 inhabitants. In its worst days a full thousand could not be packed into the court,
though the number did probably not fall far short of it. Even now, under
the management of men of conscience, and an agent, a King's Daughter,[7]
whose practical energy, kindliness and good sense have done much to
redeem its foul reputation, the swarms it shelters would make more than
one fair-sized country village. The mixed character of the population, by
this time about equally divided between the Celtic and the Italian stock,
accounts for the iron bars and the policeman. It was an eminently Irish
suggestion that the latter was to be credited to the presence of two German
families in the court, who "made trouble all the time." A Chinaman whom
I questioned as he hurried past the iron gate of the alley, put the matter in
a different light. "Lem Ilish velly bad," he said. Gotham Court has been the
entering wedge for the Italian hordes, which until recently had not attained
a foothold in the Fourth Ward, but are now trailing across Chatham Street
from their stronghold in "the Bend" in ever increasing numbers, seeking,
according to their wont, the lowest level.

It is curious to find that this notorious block, whose name was so long synonymous with all that was desperately bad, was originally built (in 1851) by
a benevolent Quaker for the express purpose of rescuing the poor people from
the dreadful rookeries they were then living in. How long it continued a model
tenement is not on record. It could not have been very long, for already in
1862, ten years after it was finished, a sanitary official counted 146 cases of
sickness in the court, including "all kinds of infectious disease," from small-
pox down, and reported that of 138 children born in it in less than three years
61 had died, mostly before they were one year old. Seven years later the
inspector of the district reported to the Board of Health that "nearly ten per
cent. of the population is sent to the public hospitals each year." When the
alley was finally taken in hand by the authorities, and, as a first step toward
its reclamation, the entire population was driven out by the police, experience
dictated, as one of the first improvements to be made, the putting in of a kind
of sewer-grating, so constructed, as the official report patiently puts it, "as to
prevent the ingress of persons disposed to make a hiding-place" of the sewer
and the cellars into which they opened. The fact was that the big vaulted sewers had long been a runway for thieves—the Swamp Angels—who through
them easily escaped when chased by the police, as well as a storehouse for
their plunder. The sewers are there to-day; in fact the two alleys are nothing
but the roofs of these enormous tunnels in which a man may walk upright the
full distance of the block and into Cherry Street sewer—if he likes the fun and
is not afraid of rats. Could their grimy walls speak, the big canals might tell
many a startling tale. But they are silent enough, and so are most of those
whose secrets they might betray. The flood-gates connecting with the Cherry
Street main are closed now, except when the water is drained off. Then there
were no gates, and it is on record that the sewers were chosen as a short cut
habitually by residents of the court whose business lay on the line of them,
near a manhole, perhaps, in Cherry Street, or at the river mouth of the big
pipe when it was clear at low tide. "Me Jimmy," said one wrinkled old dame,
who looked in while we were nosing about under Double Alley, "he used to

6. The epidemic of 1866 killed 1,137 New Yorkers.
7. A member of a group of church women who established a nursery school on Henry Street to provide poor working mothers with care for their children.

go to his work along down Cherry Street that way every morning and come back at night." The associations must have been congenial. Probably "Jimmy" himself fitted into the landscape.

Half-way back from the street in this latter alley is a tenement, facing the main building, on the west side of the way, that was not originally part of the court proper. It stands there a curious monument to a Quaker's revenge, a living illustration of the power of hate to perpetuate its bitter fruit beyond the grave. The lot upon which it is built was the property of John Wood, brother of Silas, the builder of Gotham Court. He sold the Cherry Street front to a man who built upon it a tenement with entrance only from the street. Mr. Wood afterward quarreled about the partition line with his neighbor, Alderman Mullins, who had put up a long tenement barrack on his lot after the style of the Court, and the Alderman knocked him down. Tradition records that the Quaker picked himself up with the quiet remark, "I will pay thee for that, friend Alderman," and went his way. His manner of paying was to put up the big building in the rear of 34 Cherry Street with an immense blank wall right in front of the windows of Alderman Mullins's tenements, shutting out effectually light and air from them. But as he had no access to the street from his building for many years it could not be let or used for anything, and remained vacant until it passed under the management of the Gotham Court property. Mullins's Court is there yet, and so is the Quaker's vengeful wall that has cursed the lives of thousands of innocent people since. At its farther end the alley between the two that begins inside the Cherry Street tenement, six or seven feet wide, narrows down to less than two feet. It is barely possible to squeeze through; but few care to do it, for the rift leads to the jail of the Oak Street police station, and therefore is not popular with the growing youth of the district.

There is crape on the door of the Alderman's court as we pass out, and upstairs in one of the tenements preparations are making for a wake. A man lies dead in the hospital who was cut to pieces in a "can racket"[8] in the alley on Sunday. The sway of the excise law is not extended to these back alleys. It would matter little if it were. There are secret byways, and some it is not held worth while to keep secret, along which the "growler"[9] wanders at all hours and all seasons unmolested. It climbed the stairs so long and so often that day that murder resulted. It is nothing unusual on Cherry Street, nothing to "make a fuss" about. Not a week before, two or three blocks up the street, the police felt called upon to interfere in one of these can rackets at two o'clock in the morning, to secure peace for the neighborhood. The interference took the form of a general fusillade, during which one of the disturbers fell off the roof and was killed. There was the usual wake and nothing more was heard of it. What, indeed, was there to say?

The "Rock of Ages" is the name over the door of a low saloon that blocks the entrance to another alley, if possible more forlorn and dreary than the rest, as we pass out of the Alderman's court. It sounds like a jeer from the days, happily past, when the "wickedest man in New York"[1] lived around the corner a little way and boasted of his title. One cannot take many steps in Cherry Street without encountering some relic of past or present prominence

8. A street fight fought out with tin cans.
9. A vessel for carrying beer from the saloon to one's home.
1. I.e., Thedore Allen, who owned several New York dives and was a minor player in city politics and a gambler, gave himself this name.

Gotham Court

in the ways of crime, scarce one that does not turn up specimen bricks of the coming thief. The Cherry Street tough is all-pervading. Ask Superintendent Murray, who, as captain of the Oak Street squad, in seven months secured convictions for theft, robbery, and murder aggregating no less than five hundred and thirty years of penal servitude, and he will tell you his opinion that the Fourth Ward, even in the last twenty years, has turned out more criminals than all the rest of the city together.

But though the "Swamp Angels" have gone to their reward, their successors carry on business at the old stand as successfully, if not as boldly. There goes one who was once a shining light in thiefdom. He has reformed since, they say. The policeman on the corner, who is addicted to a professional unbelief in reform of any kind, will tell you that while on the Island once he sailed away on a shutter, paddling along until he was picked up in Hell Gate[2] by a schooner's crew, whom he persuaded that he was a fanatic performing some sort of religious penance by his singular expedition. Over yonder, Tweed, [3] the arch-thief, worked in a brush-shop and earned an honest living before he took to politics. As we stroll from one narrow street to another the odd contrast between the low, old-looking houses in front and the towering tenements in the back yards grows even more striking, perhaps because we expect and are looking for it. Nobody who was not would suspect the presence of the rear houses, though they have been there long enough. Here is one seven stories high behind one with only three floors. Take a look into this Roosevelt Street alley; just about one step wide, with a five-story house on one side that gets its light and air—God help us for pitiful mockery!—from this slit between brick walls. There are no windows in the wall on the other side; it is perfectly blank. The fire-escapes of the long tenement fairly touch it; but the rays of the sun, rising, setting, or at high noon, never do. It never shone into the alley from the day the devil planned and man built it. There was once an English doctor who experimented with the sunlight in the soldiers' barracks, and found that on the side that was shut off altogether from the sun the mortality was one hundred per cent. greater than on the light side, where its rays had free access. But then soldiers are of some account, have a fixed value, if not a very high one. The people who live here have not. The horse that pulls the dirt-cart one of these laborers loads and unloads is of ever so much more account to the employer of his labor than he and all that belongs to him. Ask the owner; he will not attempt to deny it, if the horse is worth anything. The man too knows it. It is the one thought that occasionally troubles the owner of the horse in the enjoyment of his prosperity, built of and upon the successful assertion of the truth that all men are created equal.

With what a shock did the story of yonder Madison Street alley come home to New Yorkers one morning, eight or ten years ago, when a fire that broke

2. The dangerous strait connecting the East River and Long Island Sound. "The Island": I.e., Blackwell's Island, purchased in 1829 by the city of New York from the Blackwell family. This long strip of land in the East River housed many of the city's institutions, including prisons, the almshouse, the workhouse, asylums for the insane, and several hospitals.

3. William Magear "Boss" Tweed (1823–1878) may have been New York City's most notorious politician. [Sometimes the "M" is cited as standing for "Marcy"] Associated with Tammany Hall from the middle of the 1840s, he earned the moniker "Boss" in 1861 when he took over leadership of Tammany. He served in the New York State Senate starting in 1867. The senator—with his associates, known as "the Tweed Ring"—directed much state money to New York City for various municipal projects, enriching himself. Owing to public outcry at his corruption, he was arrested several times; stood trial several times; and spent time in prison, where he died in 1878.

out after the men had gone to their work swept up those narrow stairs and burned up women and children to the number of a full half score. There were fire-escapes, yes! but so placed that they could not be reached. The firemen had to look twice before they could find the opening that passes for a thoroughfare; a stout man would never venture in. Some wonderfully heroic rescues were made at that fire by people living in the adjoining tenements. Danger and trouble—of the imminent kind, not the every-day sort that excites neither interest not commiseration—run even this common clay into heroic moulds on occasion; occasions that help us to remember that the gap that separates the man with the patched coat from his wealthy neighbor is, after all, perhaps but a tenement. Yet, what a gap! and of whose making? Here, as we stroll along Madison Street, workmen are busy putting the finishing touches to the brown-stone[4] front of a tall new tenement. This one will probably be called an apartment house. They are carving satyrs' heads in the stone, with a crowd of gaping youngsters looking on in admiring wonder. Next door are two other tenements, likewise with brown-stone fronts, fair to look at. The youngest of the children in the group is not too young to remember how their army of tenants was turned out by the health officers because the houses had been condemned as unfit for human beings to live in. The owner was a wealthy builder who "stood high in the community." Is it only in our fancy that the sardonic leer on the stone faces seems to list that way? Or is it an introspective grin? We will not ask if the new house belongs to the same builder. He too may have reformed.

We have crossed the boundary of the Seventh Ward. Penitentiary Row, suggestive name for a block of Cherry Street tenements, is behind us. Within recent days it has become peopled wholly with Hebrews, the overflow from Jewtown adjoining, pedlars and tailors, all of them. It is odd to read this legend from other days over the door: "No pedlars allowed in this house." These thrifty people are not only crowding into the tenements of this once exclusive district—they are buying them. The Jew runs to real estate as soon as he can save up enough for a deposit to clinch the bargain. As fast as the old houses are torn down, towering structures go up in their place, and Hebrews are found to be the builders. Here is a whole alley nicknamed after the intruder, Jews' Alley. But abuse and ridicule are not weapons to fight the Israelite with. He pockets them quietly with the rent and bides his time. He knows from experience, both sweet and bitter, that all things come to those who wait, including the houses and lands of their persecutors.

Here comes a pleasure party, as gay as any on the avenue, though the carry-all is an ash-cart. The father is the driver and he has taken his brown-legged boy for a ride. How proud and happy they both look up there on their perch! The queer old building they have halted in front of is "The Ship," famous for fifty years as a ramshackle tenement filled with the oddest crowd. No one knows why it is called "The Ship," though there is a tradition that once the river came clear up here to Hamilton Street, and boats were moored along-side it. More likely it is because it is as bewildering inside as a crazy old ship, with its ups and downs of ladders parading as stairs, and its unexpected pitfalls. But Hamilton Street, like Water Street, is not what it was. The missions drove from the latter the worst of its dives. A sailors'

---

4. A red-brown stone, quarried in Passaic County, New Jersey, that came to be used in much New York City residential construction in the 1850s.

An Old Rear-Tenement in Roosevelt Street

mission[5] has lately made its appearance in Hamilton Street, but there are no dives there, nothing worse than the ubiquitous saloon and tough tenements.

Enough of them everywhere. Suppose we look into one. No.—— Cherry Street. Be a little careful, please! The hall is dark and you might stumble over the children pitching pennies back there. Not that it would hurt them; kicks and cuffs are their daily diet. They have little else. Here where the hall turns and dives into utter darkness is a step, and another, another. A flight of stairs. You can feel your way, if you cannot see it. Close? Yes! What would you have? All the fresh air that ever enters these stairs comes from the hall-door that is forever slamming, and from the windows of dark bedrooms that in turn receive from the stairs their sole supply of the elements God meant to be free, but man deals out with such niggardly hand. That was a woman filling her pail by the hydrant you just bumped against. The sinks are in the hallway, that all the tenants may have access—and all be poisoned alike by their summer stenches. Hear the pump squeak! It is the lullaby of tenement-house babes. In summer, when a thousand thirsty throats pant for a cooling drink in this block, it is worked in vain. But the saloon, whose open door you passed in

5. New York, because of its crucial role as a seaport had a constant floating population of sailors and seamen who spent time in the city. Various Christian groups set up missions to provide food for these transients, also offering a religious environment in an effort to combat the temptations of the city.

the hall, is always there. The smell of it has followed you up. Here is a door. Listen! That short hacking cough, that tiny, helpless wail—what do they mean? They mean that the soiled bow of white you saw on the door downstairs will have another story to tell—Oh! a sadly familiar story—before the day is at an end. The child is dying with measles. With half a chance it might have lived; but it had none. That dark bedroom killed it.

"It was took all of a suddint," says the mother, smoothing the throbbing little body with trembling hands. There is no unkindness in the rough voice of the man in the jumper, who sits by the window grimly smoking a clay pipe, with the little life ebbing out in his sight, bitter as his words sound: "Hush, Mary! If we cannot keep the baby, need we complain—such as we?"

Such as we! What if the words ring in your ears as we grope our way up the stairs and down from floor to floor, listening to the sounds behind the closed doors—some of quarrelling, some of coarse songs, more of profanity. They are true. When the summer heats come with their suffering they have meaning more terrible than words can tell. Come over here. Step carefully over this baby—it is a baby, spite of its rags and dirt—under these iron bridges called fire-escapes, but loaded down, despite the incessant watchfulness of the firemen, with broken household goods, with washtubs and barrels, over which no man could climb from a fire. This gap between dingy brick-walls is the yard. That strip of smoke-colored sky up there is the heaven of these people. Do you wonder the name does not attract them to the churches? That baby's parents live in the rear tenement here. She is at least as clean as the steps we are now climbing. There are plenty of houses with half a hundred such in. The tenement is much like the one in front we just left, only fouler, closer, darker—we will not say more cheerless. The word is a mockery. A hundred thousand people lived in rear tenements in New York last year. Here is a room neater than the rest. The woman, a stout matron with hard lines of care in her face, is at the wash-tub. "I try to keep the childer clean," she says, apologetically, but with a hopeless glance around. The spice of hot soap-suds is added to the air already tainted with the smell of boiling cabbage, of rags and uncleanliness all about. It makes an overpowering compound. It is Thursday, but patched linen is hung upon the pulley-line from the window. There is no Monday cleaning in the tenements. It is wash-day all the week round, for a change of clothing is scarce among the poor. They are poverty's honest badge, these perennial lines of rags hung out to dry, those that are not the washerwoman's professional shingle. The true line to be drawn between pauperism and honest poverty is the clothes-line. With it begins the effort to be clean that is the first and the best evidence of a desire to be honest.

What sort of an answer, think you, would come from these tenements to the question "Is life worth living?" were they heard at all in the discussion? It may be that this, cut from the last report but one of the Association for the Improvement of the Condition of the Poor,[6] a long name for a weary task, has a suggestion of it: "In the depth of winter the attention of the Association was called to a Protestant family living in a garret in a miserable tenement in Cherry Street. The family's condition was most deplorable. The man, his wife, and three small children shivering in one room through the roof of which the

6. Founded in 1843 by Robert M. Hartley, this association of volunteers reflected the emergence of scientific charity in the mid-nineteenth century. The association constructed bathhouses for the poor, built model tenements, and advocated for various kinds of municipal reforms, particularly in the area of sanitary matters. In 1891 it joined with the Charity Organization Society, the New York City Mission and Tract Society, and the Children's Aid Society to build and occupy the United Charities Building on East Twenty-second Street.

pitiless winds of winter whistled. The room was almost barren of furniture; the parents slept on the floor, the elder children in boxes, and the baby was swung in an old shawl attached to the rafters by cords by way of a hammock. The father, a seaman, had been obliged to give up that calling because he was in consumption, and was unable to provide either bread or fire for his little ones."

Perhaps this may be put down as an exceptional case, but one that came to my notice some months ago in a Seventh Ward tenement was typical enough to escape that reproach. There were nine in the family: husband, wife, an aged grandmother, and six children; honest, hardworking Germans, scrupulously neat, but poor. All nine lived in two rooms, one about ten feet square that served as parlor, bedroom, and eating-room, the other a small hall-room made into a kitchen. The rent was seven dollars and a half a month, more than a week's wages for the husband and father, who was the only bread-winner in the family. That day the mother had thrown herself out of the window, and was carried up from the street dead. She was "discouraged," said some of the other women from the tenement, who had come in to look after the children while a messenger carried the news to the father at the shop. They went stolidly about their task, although they were evidently not without feeling for the dead woman. No doubt she was wrong in not taking life philosophically, as did the four families a city missionary found housekeeping in the four corners of one room. They got along well enough together until one of the families took a boarder and made trouble. Philosophy, according to my optimistic friend, naturally inhabits the tenements. The people who live there come to look upon death in a different way from the rest of us—do not take it as hard. He has never found time to explain how the fact fits into his general theory that life is not unbearable in the tenements. Unhappily for the philosophy of the slums, it is too apt to be of the kind that readily recognizes the saloon, always handy, as the refuge from every trouble, and shapes its practice according to the discovery.

5. *The Italian in New York*

Certainly a picturesque, if not very tidy, element has been added to the population in the "assisted"[1] Italian immigrant who claims so large a share of public attention, partly because he keeps coming at such a tremendous rate, but chiefly because he elects to stay in New York, or near enough for it to serve as his base of operations, and here promptly reproduces conditions of destitution and disorder which, set in the frame-work of Mediterranean exuberance, are the delight of the artist, but in a matter-of-fact American community become its danger and reproach. The reproduction is made easier in New York because he finds the material ready to hand in the worst of the slum tenements; but even where it is not he soon reduces what he does find to his own level, if allowed to follow his natural bent. The Italian comes in at the bottom, and in the generation that came over the sea he stays there. In the slums he is welcomed as a tenant who "makes less trouble" than the contentious Irishman or the order-loving German, that is to say: is content to live in a pig-sty and submits to robbery at the hands of the rent-collector without murmur. Yet this very tractability makes of him in good hands, when

1. Many Italian men were able to come to the United States through the aid of a *padrone*, or labor agent, who paid the fare. The immigrant then worked off the fare. Many Americans considered this a form of slavery, and in 1885 Congress passed the Foran Act, or the Alien Contract Labor Act, to ban this practice. However, it persisted.

firmly and intelligently managed, a really desirable tenant. But it is not his good fortune often to fall in with other hospitality upon his coming than that which brought him here for its own profit, and has no idea of letting go its grip upon him as long as there is a cent to be made out of him.

Recent Congressional inquiries[2] have shown the nature of the "assistance" he receives from greedy steamship agents and "bankers," who persuade him by false promises to mortgage his home, his few belongings, and his wages for months to come for a ticket to the land where plenty of work is to be had at princely wages. The padrone—the "banker" is nothing else—having made his ten per cent. out of him en route, receives him at the landing and turns him to double account as a wage-earner and a rent-payer. In each of these roles he is made to yield a profit to his unscrupulous countryman, whom he trusts implicitly with the instinct of utter helplessness. The man is so ignorant that, as one of the sharpers who prey upon him put it once, it "would be downright sinful not to take him in." His ignorance and unconquerable suspicion of strangers dig the pit into which he falls. He not only knows no word of English, but he does not know enough to learn. Rarely only can he write his own language. Unlike the German, who begins learning English the day he lands as a matter of duty, or the Polish Jew, who takes it up as soon as he is able as an investment, the Italian learns slowly, if at all. Even his boy, born here, often speaks his native tongue indifferently. He is forced, therefore, to have constant recourse to the middle-man who makes him pay handsomely at every turn. He hires him out to the rail-road contractor, receiving a commission from the employer as well as from the laborer, and repeats the performance monthly, or as often as he can have him dismissed. In the city he contracts for his lodging, subletting to him space in the vilest tenements at extortionate rents, and sets an example that does not lack imitators. The "princely wages" have vanished with his coming, and in their place hardships and a dollar a day, beheft with the padrone's merciless mortgage, confront him. Bred to even worse fare, he takes both as a matter of course, and, applying the maxim that it is not what one makes but what he saves that makes him rich, manages to turn the very dirt of the streets into a hoard of gold, with which he either returns to his Southern home, or brings over his family to join in his work and in his fortunes the next season.

The discovery was made by earlier explorers that there is money in New York's ash-barrel, but it was left to the genius of the padrone to develop the full resources of the mine that has become the exclusive preserve of the Italian immigrant. Only a few years ago, when rag-picking was carried on in a desultory and irresponsible sort of way, the city hired gangs of men to trim the ash-scows[3] before they were sent out to sea. The trimming consisted in leveling out the dirt as it was dumped from the carts, so that the scow might be evenly loaded. The men were paid a dollar and a half a day, kept what they found that was worth having, and allowed the swarms of Italians who hung about the dumps to do the heavy work for them, letting them have their pick of the loads for their trouble. To-day Italians contract for the work, paying large sums to be permitted to do it. The city received not less than $80,000 last year for the sale of this privilege to the contractors, who in addition have to pay gangs of their countrymen for sorting out the bones, rags, tin cans and other waste that are found in the ashes and form the staples of their trade

2. I.e., the 1889 hearings held on the extensive evasions of the Foran Act.
3. Boats used to both store and transport waste material.

In the Home of an Italian Rag-picker, Jersey Street

and their sources of revenue. The effect has been vastly to increase the power of the padrone, or his ally, the contractor, by giving him exclusive control of the one industry in which the Italian was formerly an independent "dealer," and reducing him literally to the plane of the dump. Whenever the back of the sanitary police is turned, he will make his home in the filthy burrows where he works by day, sleeping and eating his meals under the dump, on the edge of slimy depths and amid surroundings full of unutterable horror. The city did not bargain to house, though it is content to board, him so long as he can make the ash-barrels yield the food to keep him alive, and a vigorous campaign is carried on at intervals against these unlicensed dump settlements; but the temptation of having to pay no rent is too strong, and they are driven from one dump only to find lodgement under another a few blocks farther up or down the river. The fiercest warfare is waged over the patronage of the dumps by rival factions represented by opposing contractors, and it has happened that the defeated party has endeavored to capture by strategy what he failed to carry by assault. It augurs unsuspected adaptability in the Italian to our system of self-government that these rivalries have more than once been suspected of being behind the sharpening of city ordinances, that were apparently made in good faith to prevent meddling with the refuse in the ash-barrels or in transit.

Did the Italian always adapt himself as readily to the operation of the civil law as to the manipulation of political "pull" on occasion, he would save himself a good deal of unnecessary trouble. Ordinarily he is easily enough governed by authority—always excepting Sunday, when he settles down to a game of cards and lets loose all his bad passions. Like the Chinese, the Italian is a born gambler. His soul is in the game from the moment the cards are on the table, and very frequently his knife is in it too before the game is ended. No Sunday has passed in New York since "the Bend" became a suburb of Naples without one or more of these murderous affrays coming to the notice of the police. As a rule that happens only when the man the game went against is either dead or so badly wounded as to require instant surgical help. As to the other, unless he be caught red-handed, the chances that the police will ever get him are slim indeed. The wounded man can seldom be persuaded to betray him. He wards off all inquiries with a wicked "I fix him myself," and there the matter rests until he either dies or recovers. If the latter, the community hears after a while of another Italian affray, a man stabbed in a quarrel, dead or dying, and the police know that "he" has been fixed, and the account squared.

With all his conspicuous faults, the swarthy Italian immigrant has his redeeming traits. He is as honest as he is hot-headed. There are no Italian burglars in the Rogues' Gallery;[4] the ex-brigand toils peacefully with pickaxe and shovel on American ground. His boy occasionally shows, as a pick-pocket, the results of his training with the toughs of the Sixth Ward slums. The only criminal business to which the father occasionally lends his hand, outside of

4. The collection of photographs of particularly notorious criminals maintained by the police department.

murder, is a bunco game,[5] of which his confiding countrymen, returning with
their hoard to their native land, are the victims. The women are faithful wives
and devoted mothers. Their vivid and picturesque costumes lend a tinge of
color to the otherwise dull monotony of the slums they inhabit. The Italian is
gay, lighthearted and, if his fur is not stroked the wrong way, inoffensive as a
child. His worst offence is that he keeps the stale-beer dives.[6] Where his headquarters is, in the Mulberry Street Bend, these vile dens flourish and gather
about them all the wrecks, the utterly wretched, the hopelessly lost, on the
lowest slope of depraved humanity. And out of their misery he makes a profit.

6. *The Bend*

Where Mulberry Street crooks like an elbow within hail of the old depravity of the Five Points, is "the Bend," foul core of New York's slums. Long
years ago the cows coming home from the pasture trod a path over this hill.
Echoes of thinkling bells linger there still, but they do not call up memories of green meadows and summer fields; they proclaim the homecoming
of the rag-picker's cart. In the memory of man the old cow-path has never
been other than a vast human pig-sty. There is but one "Bend" in the world,
and it is enough. The city authorities, moved by the angry protests of ten
years of sanitary reform effort, have decided that it is too much and must
come down. Another Paradise Park[1] will take its place and let in sunlight
and air to work such transformation as at the Five Points, around the corner of the next block. Never was change more urgently needed. Around "the
Bend" cluster the bulk of the tenements that are stamped as altogether bad,
even by the optimists of the Health Department. Incessant raids cannot
keep down the crowds that make them their home. In the scores of back
alleys, of stable lanes and hidden byways, of which the rent collector alone
can keep track, they share such shelter as the ramshackle structures afford
with every kind of abomination rifled from the dumps and ash barrels of the
city. Here, too, shunning the light, skulks the unclean beast of dishonest
idleness. "The Bend" is the home of the tramp as well as the rag-picker.

It is not much more than twenty years since a census of "the Bend" district returned only twenty-four of the six hundred and nine tenements as
in decent condition. Three-fourths of the population of the "Bloody Sixth"
Ward were then Irish. The army of tramps that grew up after the disband-
ment of the armies in the field, and has kept up its muster-roll, together
with the in-rush of the Italian tide, have ever since opposed a stubborn barrier to all efforts at permanent improvement. The more that has been done,
the less it has seemed to accomplish in the way of real relief, until it has at
last become clear that nothing short of entire demolition will ever prove of
radical benefit. Corruption could not have chosen ground for its stand with
better promise of success. The whole district is a maze of narrow, often
unsuspected passage-ways—necessarily, for there is scarce a lot that has
not two, three, or four tenements upon it, swarming with unwholesome
crowds. What a bird's-eye view of "the Bend" would be like is a matter of

5. A con game.
6. Saloons selling the cheapest form of beer.
1. Constructed over the site of the former Five Points, this park was one of the efforts of New York
   City to bring green spaces to city dwellers. In 1870 the city created the Department of Public Parks,
   and in 1881 private citizens formed the New York Park Association to stimulate the development
   of more such places.

The Mulberry Bend

bewildering conjecture. Its everyday appearance, as seen from the corner of Bayard Street on a sunny day, is one of the sights of New York.

Bayard Street is the high road to Jewtown across the Bowery, picketed from end to end with the outposts of Israel. Hebrew faces, Hebrew signs, and incessant chatter in the queer lingo[2] that passes for Hebrew on the East Side attend the curious wanderer to the very corner of Mulberry Street. But the moment he turns the corner the scene changes abruptly. Before him lies spread out what might better be the market-place in some town in Southern Italy than a street in New York—all but the houses; they are still the same old tenements of the unromantic type. But for once they do not make the foreground in a slum picture from the American metropolis. The interest centres not in them, but in the crowd they shelter only when the street is not preferable, and that with the Italian is only when it rains or he is sick. When the sun shines the entire population seeks the street, carrying on its household work, its bargaining, its lovemaking on street or sidewalk, or idling there when it has nothing better to do, with the reverse of the impulse that makes the Polish Jew coop himself up in his den with the thermometer at stewing heat. Along the curb women sit in rows, young and old alike with the odd head-covering, pad or turban, that is their badge of servitude—hers to bear the burden as long as she lives—haggling over baskets of frowsy weeds, some sort of salad probably, stale tomatoes, and oranges not above suspicion. Ash-barrels serve them as counters, and not infrequently does the arrival of the official cart en route for the dump cause a temporary suspension of trade until the barrels have been emptied and restored. Hucksters[3] and pedlars' carts make two rows of booths in the street itself, and along the houses is still another—a perpetual market doing a very lively trade in its own queer staples, found nowhere on American ground save in "the Bend." Two old hags, camping on the pavement, are dispensing stale bread, baked not in loaves, but in the shape of big wreaths like exaggerated crullers, out of bags of dirty bed-tick. There is no use disguising the fact: they look like and they probably are old mattresses mustered into service under the pressure of a rush of trade. Stale bread was the one article the health officers, after a raid on the market, once reported as "not unwholesome." It was only disgusting. Here is a brawny butcher, sleeves rolled up above the elbows and clay pipe in mouth, skinning a kid that hangs from his hook. They will tell you with a laugh at the Elizabeth Street police station that only a few days ago when a dead goat had been reported lying in Pell Street it was mysteriously missing by the time the offal-cart came to take it away. It turned out that an Italian had carried it off in his sack to a wake or feast of some sort in one of the back alleys.

On either side of the narrow entrance to Bandits' Roost, one of the most notorious of these, is a shop that is a fair sample of the sort of invention necessity is the mother of in "the Bend." It is not enough that trucks and ash-barrels have provided four distinct lines of shops that are not down on the insurance maps, to accommodate the crowds. Here have the very hallways been made into shops. Three feet wide by four deep, they have just room for one, the shop-keeper, who, himself within, does his business outside, his wares displayed on a board hung across what was once the hall door. Back of

---

2. I.e., Yiddish, spoken by nearly all of the eastern European Jewish immigrants who settled in New York.
3. Urban peddlers, an occupation of many immigrants in New York.

Bandits' Roost

the rear wall of this unique shop a hole has been punched from the hall into the alley and the tenants go that way. One of the shops is a "tobacco bureau," presided over by an unknown saint, done in yellow and red—there is not a shop, a stand, or an ash-barrel doing duty for a counter, that has not its patron saint—the other is a fish-stand full of slimy, odd-looking creatures, fish that never swam in American waters, or if they did, were never seen on an American fish-stand, and snails. Big, awkward sausages, anything but appetizing, hang in the grocer's doorway, knocking against the customer's head as if to remind him that they are there waiting to be bought. What they are I never had the courage to ask. Down the street comes a file of women carrying enormous bundles of fire-wood on their heads, loads of decaying vegetables from the market wagons in their aprons, and each a baby at the breast supported by a sort of sling that prevents it from tumbling down. The women do all the carrying, all the work one sees going on in "the Bend." The men sit or stand in the streets, on trucks, or in the open doors of the saloons smoking black clay pipes, talking and gesticulating as if forever on the point of

DEATH AND DEATH-RATES IN 1888 IN BAXTER AND MULBERRY
STREETS, BETWEEN PARK AND BAYARD STREETS.

	Population		
	Five Years old and over	Under five years	Total
Baxter Street	1,918	315	2,233
Mulberry Street	2,788	629	3,417
Total	4,706	944	5,650

	Deaths		
	Five years old and over	Under five years	Total
Baxter Street	26	46	72
Mulberry Street	44	86	130
Total	70	132	202

	Death-Rate		
	Five years old and over	Under five years	General
Baxter Street	13.56	146.02	32.24
Mulberry Street	15.78	136.70	38.05
Total	14.87	139.83	35.75

coming to blows. Near a particularly boisterous group, a really pretty girl with a string of amber beads twisted artlessly in the knot of her raven hair has been bargaining long and earnestly with an old granny, who presides over a wheelbarrow load of second-hand stockings and faded cotton yarn, industriously darning the biggest holes while she extols the virtues of her stock. One of the rude swains, with patched overalls tucked into his boots, to whom the girl's eyes have strayed more than once, steps up and gallantly offers to pick her out the handsomest pair, whereat she laughs and pushes him away with a gesture which he interprets as an invitation to stay; and he does, evidently to the satisfaction of the beldame, who forthwith raises her prices fifty per cent. without being detected by the girl.

Red bandannas and yellow kerchiefs are everywhere; so is the Italian tongue, infinitely sweeter than the harsh gutturals of the Russian Jew around the corner. So are the "ristorantes" of innumerable Pasquales; half of the people in "the Bend" are christened Pasquale, or get the name in some other way. When the police do not know the name of an escaped murderer, they guess at Pasquale and send the name out on alarm; in nine cases out of ten it fits. So are the "banks" that hang out their shingle as tempting bait on every hand. There are half a dozen in the single block, steamship agencies, employment offices, and savings-banks, all in one. So are the toddling youngsters, bow-legged half of them, and so are no end of mothers, present and prospective, some of them scarce yet in their teens. Those who are not in the street are hanging half way out of the windows, shouting at some one below. All "the Bend" must be, if not altogether, at least half out of doors when the sun shines.

In the street, where the city wields the broom, there is at least an effort at cleaning up. There has to be, or it would be swamped in filth overrunning from the courts and alleys where the rag-pickers live. It requires more than ordinary courage to explore these on a hot day. The undertaker has to do it then, the police always. Right here, in this tenement on the east side of the street, they found little Antonia Candia, victim of fiendish cruelty, "covered," says the account found in the records of the Society for the Prevention of Cruelty to Children,[4] "with sores, and her hair matted with dried blood." Abuse is the normal condition of "the Bend," murder its everyday crop, with the tenants not always the criminals. In this block between Bayard, Park, Mulberry, and Baxter Streets, "the Bend" proper, the late Tenement House Commission counted 155 deaths of children in a specimen year (1882). Their percentage of the total mortality in the block was 68.28, while for the whole city the proportion was only 46.20. The infant mortality in any city or place as compared with the whole number of deaths is justly considered a good barometer of its general sanitary condition. Here, in this tenement, No. 59½, next to Bandits' Roost, fourteen persons died that year, and eleven of them were children; in No. 61 eleven, and eight of them not yet five years old. According to the records in the Bureau of Vital Statistics only thirty-nine people lived in No. 59½ in the year 1888, nine of them little children. There were five baby funerals in that house the same year. Out of the alley itself, No. 59, nine dead were carried in 1888, five in baby coffins. Here is the record of the year for the whole block, as furnished by the Registrar of Vital Statistics, Dr. Roger S. Tracy [see table page 39].

The general death-rate for the whole city that year was 26.27.

These figures speak for themselves, when it is shown that in the model tenement across the way at Nos. 48 and 50, where the same class of people live in greater swarms (161, according to the record), but under good management, and in decent quarters, the hearse called that year only twice, once for a baby. The agent of the Christian people who built that tenement will tell you that Italians are good tenants, while the owner of the alley will oppose every order to put his property in repair with the claim that they are the worst of a bad lot. Both are right, from their different stand-points. It is the stand-point that makes the difference—and the tenant.

What if I were to tell you that this alley, and more tenement property in "the Bend," all of it notorious for years as the vilest and worst to be found anywhere, stood associated on the tax-books all through the long struggle to make its owners responsible, which has at last resulted in a qualified victory for the law, with the name of an honored family, one of the "oldest and best," rich in possessions and in influence, and high in the councils of the city's government? It would be but the plain truth. Nor would it be the only instance by very many that stand recorded on the Health Department's books of a kind that has come near to making the name of landlord as odious in New York as it has become in Ireland.

Bottle Alley is around the corner in Baxter Street; but it is a fair specimen of its kind, wherever found. Look into any of these houses, everywhere the same piles of rags, of malodorous bones and musty paper, all of which the sanitary police flatter themselves they have banished to the dumps and the

---

4. Founded in 1874 by Eldridge T. Gerry and John D. Wright, this association of volunteers advocated for children. It attempted to find and rescue abused children, and in 1881 the city gave it the power of law enforcement.

Bottle Alley

warehouses. Here is a "flat" of "parlor" and two pitch-dark coops called bedrooms. Truly, the bed is all there is room for. The family tea-kettle is on the stove, doing duty for the time being as a wash-boiler. By night it will have returned to its proper use again, a practical illustration of how poverty in "the Bend" makes both ends meet. One, two, three beds are there, if the old boxes and heaps of foul straw can be called by that name; a broken stove with crazy pipe from which the smoke leaks at every joint, a table of rough boards propped up on boxes, piles of rubbish in the corner. The closeness and smell are appalling. How many people sleep here? The woman with the red bandanna shakes her head sullenly, but the bare-legged girl with the bright face counts on her fingers—five, six!

"Six, sir!" Six grown people and five children.

"Only five," she says with a smile, swathing the little one on her lap in its cruel bandage. There is another in the cradle—actually a cradle. And how much the rent?

Nine and a half, and "please, sir! he won't put the paper on."

"He" is the landlord. The "paper" hangs in musty shreds on the wall.

Well do I recollect the visit of a health inspector to one of these tenements on a July day when the thermometer outside was climbing high in the nineties; but inside, in that awful room, with half a dozen persons washing, cooking, and sorting rags, lay the dying baby alongside the stove, where the doctor's thermometer ran up to 115°! Perishing for the want of a breath of fresh air in this city of untold charities! Did not the manager of the Fresh Air Fund[5] write to the pastor of an Italian Church only last year that "no one asked for Italian children," and hence he could not send any to the country?

Half a dozen blocks up Mulberry Street there is a rag-picker's settlement, a sort of overflow from "the Bend," that exists to-day in all its pristine nastiness. Something like forty families are packed into five old two-story and attic houses that were built to hold five, and out in the yards additional crowds are, or were until very recently, accommodated in sheds built of all sorts of old boards and used as drying racks for the Italian tenants' "stock." I found them empty when I visited the settlement while writing this. The last two tenants had just left. Their fate was characteristic. The "old man," who lived in the corner coop, with barely room to crouch beside the stove—there would not have been room for him to sleep had not age crooked his frame to fit his house—had been taken to the "crazy house," and the woman who was his neighbor and had lived in her shed for years had simply disappeared. The agent and the other tenants "guessed," doubtless correctly, that she might be found on the "island," but she was decrepit anyhow from rheumatism, and "not much good," and no one took the trouble to inquire for her. They had all they could do attending to their own business and raising the rent. No wonder; I found that for one front room and two "bedrooms" in the shameful old wrecks of buildings the tenant was paying $10 a month, for the back-room and one bedroom $9, and for the attic rooms, according to size, from $3.75 to $5.50.

There is a standing quarrel between the professional—I mean now the official—sanitarian and the unsalaried agitator for sanitary reform over the question of overcrowded tenements. The one puts the number a little vaguely at four or five hundred, while the other asserts that there are thirty-two thousand, the whole number of houses classed as tenements at the census of two years ago, taking no account of the better kind of flats. It depends on the angle from which one sees it which is right. At best the term overcrowding is a relative one, and the scale of official measurement conveniently sliding. Under the pressure of the Italian influx the standard of breathing space required for an adult by the health officers has been cut down from six to four hundred cubic feet. The "needs of the situation" is their plea, and no more perfect argument could be advanced for the reformer's position.

It is in "the Bend" the sanitary policeman locates the bulk of his four hundred, and the sanitary reformer gives up the task in despair. Of its vast homeless crowds the census takes no account. It is their instinct to shun the light, and they cannot be corralled in one place long enough to be counted. But

---

5. An association of volunteers, founded in 1877 by Willard Parsons, that provided summer vacations in the country for poor city children. Parsons gave control of the Fund to the *New York Tribune*.

Lodgers in a Crowded Bayard Street Tenement—"Five Cents a Spot"

the houses can, and the last count showed that in "the Bend" district between Broadway and the Bowery and Canal and Chatham Streets, in a total of four thousand three hundred and sixty-seven "apartments" only nine were for the moment vacant, while in the old "Africa," west of Broadway, that receives the overflow from Mulberry Street and is rapidly changing its character, the notice "standing room only" is up. Not a single vacant room was found there. Nearly a hundred and fifty "lodgers" were driven out of two adjoining Mulberry Street tenements, one of them aptly named "the House of Blazes," during that census. What squalor and degradation inhabit these dens the health officers know. Through the long summer days their carts patrol "the Bend," scattering disinfectants in streets and lanes, in sinks and cellars, and hidden hovels where the tramp burrows. From midnight till far into the small hours of the morning the policeman's thundering rap on closed doors is heard, with his stern command, *"Apri port'!"*[6] on his rounds gathering evidence of illegal overcrowding. The doors are opened unwillingly enough—but the order means business, and the tenant knows it even if he understands no word of English—upon such scenes as the one presented in the picture. It was photographed by flash-light on just such a visit. In a room not thirteen feet either way slept twelve men and women, two or three in bunks set in a sort of alcove, the rest on the floor. A kerosene lamp burned dimly in the fearful atmosphere, probably to guide other and later arrivals to their "beds," for it was only just past midnight. A baby's fretful wail came from an adjoining hall-room, where, in the semi-darkness, three recumbent figures could be made out. The "apartment" was one of three in two adjoining buildings we had found, within half an hour, similarly crowded. Most of the men were lodgers, who slept there for five cents a spot.

Another room on the top floor, that had been examined a few nights before, was comparatively empty. There were only four persons in it, two men, an old woman, and a young girl. The landlord opened the door with alacrity, and exhibited with a proud sweep of his hand the sacrifice he had made of his personal interests to satisfy the law. Our visit had been anticipated. The policeman's back was probably no sooner turned than the room was reopened for business.

7. A Raid on the Stale-beer Dives

Midnight roll-call was over in the Elizabeth Street police-station, but the reserves were held under orders. A raid was on foot, but whether on the Chinese fan-tan games,[1] on the opium joints of Mott and Pell Streets, or on dens of even worse character, was a matter of guess-work in the men's room. When the last patrolman had come in from his beat, all doubt was dispelled by the brief order "To the Bend!" The stale-beer dives were the object of the raid. The policemen buckled their belts tighter, and with expressive grunts of disgust took up their march toward Mulberry Street. Past the heathen temples[2] of Mott Street—there was some fun to be gotten out of a raid *there*—they trooped, into "the Bend," sending here and there a belated tramp scurrying in fright toward healthier quarters, and halted at

6. Open the door (Italian).
1. Gambling games of Chinese derivation played with buttons or beads and a bowl. Players bet on the number of objects left in the bowl.
2. Buddhist places of worship.

An All-Night Two-Cent Restaurant in "The Bend"

the mouth of one of the hidden alleys. Squads were told off and sent to make a simultaneous descent on all the known tramps' burrows in the block. Led by the sergeant, ours—I went along as a kind of war correspondent—groped its way in single file through the narrow rift between slimy walls to the tenements in the rear. Twice during our trip we stumbled over tramps, both women, asleep in the passage. They were quietly passed to the rear, receiving sundry prods and punches on the trip, and headed for the station in the grip of a policeman as a sort of advance guard of the coming army. After what seemed half a mile of groping in the dark we emerged finally into the alley proper, where light escaping through the cracks of closed shutters on both sides enabled us to make out the contour of three rickety frame tenements. Snatches of ribald songs and peals of coarse laughter reached us from now this, now that of the unseen burrows.

"School is in," said the sergeant drily as we stumbled down the worn steps of the next cellar-way. A kick of his boot-heel sent the door flying into the room.

A room perhaps a dozen feet square, with walls and ceiling that might once have been clean—assuredly the floor had not in the memory of man, if indeed there was other floor than hard-trodden mud—but were now covered with a brown crust that, touched with the end of a club, came off in shuddering showers of crawling bugs, revealing the blacker filth beneath. Grouped about a beer-keg that was propped on the wreck of a broken chair, a foul and ragged host of men and women, on boxes, benches, and stools. Tomato-cans filled at the keg were passed from hand to hand. In the centre of the group a sallow, wrinkled hag, evidently the ruler of the feast, dealt out the hideous stuff. A pile of copper coins rattled in her apron, the very pennies received with such showers of blessings upon the giver that afternoon; the faces of some of the women were familiar enough from the streets as those of beggars forever whining for a penny, "to keep a family from starving." Their whine and boisterous hilarity were alike hushed now. In sullen, cowed submission they sat, evidently knowing what to expect. At the first glimpse of the uniform in the open door some in the group, customers with a record probably, had turned their heads away to avoid the searching glance of the officer; while a few, less used to such scenes, stared defiantly.

A single stride took the sergeant into the middle of the room, and with a swinging blow of his club he knocked the faucet out of the keg and the half-filled can from the boss hag's hand. As the contents of both splashed upon the floor, half a dozen of the group made a sudden dash, and with shoulders humped above their heads to shield their skulls against the dreaded locust[3] broke for the door. They had not counted upon the policemen outside. There was a brief struggle, two or three heavy thumps, and the runaways were brought back to where their comrades crouched in dogged silence.

"Thirteen!" called the sergeant, completing his survey. "Take them out. 'Revolvers' all but one. Good for six months on the island, the whole lot." The exception was a young man not much if any over twenty, with a hard look of dissipation on his face. He seemed less unconcerned than the rest, but tried hard to make up for it by putting on the boldest air he could. "Come down early," commented the officer, shoving him along with his stick. "There is need of it. They don't last long at this. That stuff is brewed to kill at long range."

---

3. Policeman's billy club.

At the head of the cellar-steps we encountered a similar procession from farther back in the alley, where still another was forming to take up its march to the station. Out in the street was heard the tramp of the hosts already pursuing that well-trodden path, as with a fresh complement of men we entered the next stale-beer alley. There were four dives in one cellar here. The filth and the stench were utterly unbearable; even the sergeant turned his back and fled after scattering the crowd with his club and starting them toward the door. The very dog in the alley preferred the cold flags[4] for a berth to the stifling cellar. We found it lying outside. Seventy-five tramps, male and female, were arrested in the four small rooms. In one of them, where the air seemed thick enough to cut with a knife, we found a woman, a mother with a new-born babe on a heap of dirty straw. She was asleep and was left until an ambulance could be called to take her to the hospital.

Returning to the station with this batch, we found every window in the building thrown open to the cold October wind, and the men from the sergeant down smoking the strongest cigars that could be obtained by way of disinfecting the place. Two hundred and seventy-five tramps had been jammed into the cells to be arraigned next morning in the police court on the charge of vagrancy, with the certain prospect of six months "on the Island." Of the sentence at least they were sure. As to the length of the men's stay the experienced official at the desk was sceptical, it being then within a month of an important election. If tramps have nothing else to call their own they have votes, and votes that are for sale cheap for cash. About election time this gives them a "pull," at least by proxy. The sergeant observed, as if it were the most natural thing in the world, that he had more than once seen the same tramp sent to Blackwell's Island twice in twenty-four hours for six months at a time.

As a thief never owns to his calling, however devoid of moral scruples, preferring to style himself a speculator, so this real home-product of the slums, the stale-beer dive, is known about "the Bend" by the more dignified name of the two-cent restaurant. Usually, as in this instance, it is in some cellar giving on a back alley. Doctored, unlicensed beer is its chief ware. Sometimes a cup of "coffee" and a stale roll may be had for two cents. The men pay the score. To the women—unutterable horror of the suggestion—the place is free. The beer is collected from the kegs put on the sidewalk by the saloon-keeper to await the brewer's cart, and is touched up with drugs to put a froth on it. The privilege to sit all night on a chair, or sleep on a table, or in a barrel, goes with each round of drinks. Generally an Italian, sometimes a negro, occasionally a woman, "runs" the dive. Their customers, alike homeless and hopeless in their utter wretchedness, are the professional tramps, and these only. The meanest thief is infinitely above the stale-beer level. Once upon that plane there is no escape. To sink below it is impossible; no one ever rose from it. One night spent in a stale-beer dive is like the traditional putting on of the uniform of the caste, the discarded rags of an old tramp. That stile once crossed, the lane has no longer a turn; and contrary to the proverb, it is usually not long either.

---

4. I.e., flagstones.

With the gravitation of the Italian tramp landlord toward the old strong-hold of the African on the West Side, a share of the stale-beer traffic has left "the Bend"; but its headquarters will always remain there, the real home of trampdom, just as Fourteenth Street is its limit. No real tramp crosses that frontier after nightfall and in the daytime only to beg. Repulsive as the business is, its profits to the Italian dive-keeper are considerable; in fact, barring a slight outlay in the ingredients that serve to give "life" to the beer-dregs, it is all profit. The "banker" who curses the Italian colony does not despise taking a hand in it, and such a thing as a stale-beer trust on a Mulberry Street scale may yet be among the possibilities. One of these bankers, who was once known to the police as the keeper of one notorious stale-beer dive and the active backer of others, is to-day an extensive manufacturer of macaroni, the owner of several big tenements and other real estate; and the capital, it is said, has all come out of his old business. Very likely it is true.

On hot summer nights it is no rare experience when exploring the worst of the tenements in "the Bend" to find the hallways occupied by rows of "sitters," tramps whom laziness or hard luck has prevented from earning enough by their day's "labor" to pay the admission fee to a stale-beer dive, and who have their reasons for declining the hospitality of the police station lodging-rooms. Huddled together in loathsome files, they squat there over night, or until an inquisitive policeman breaks up the congregation with his club, which in Mulberry Street has always free swing. At that season the woman tramp predominates. The men, some of them at least, take to the railroad track and to camping out when the nights grow warm, returning in the fall to prey on the city and to recruit their ranks from the lazy, the shiftless, and the unfortunate. Like a foul loadstone, "the Bend" attracts and brings them back, no matter how far they have wandered. For next to idleness the tramp loves rum; next to rum stale beer, its equivalent of the gutter. And the first and last go best together.

As "sitters" they occasionally find a job in the saloons about Chatham and Pearl Streets on cold winter nights, when the hallway is not practicable, that enables them to pick up a charity drink now and then and a bite of an infrequent sandwich. The barkeeper permits them to sit about the stove and by shivering invite the sympathy of transient customers. The dodge works well, especially about Christmas and election time, and the sitters are able to keep comfortably filled up to the advantage of their host. But to look thoroughly miserable they must keep awake. A tramp placidly dozing at the fire would not be an object of sympathy. To make sure that they do keep awake, the wily bartender makes them sit constantly swinging one foot like the pendulum of a clock. When it stops the slothful "sitter" is roused with a kick and "fired out." It is said by those who profess to know that habit has come to the rescue of oversleepy tramps and that the old rounders can swing hand or foot in their sleep without betraying themselves. In some saloons "sitters" are let in at these seasons in fresh batches every hour.

On one of my visits to "the Bend" I came across a particularly ragged and disreputable tramp, who sat smoking his pipe on the rung of a ladder with such evident philosophic contentment in the busy labor of a score of rag-pickers all about him, that I bade him sit for a picture, offering him ten cents for the job. He accepted the offer with hardly a nod, and sat patiently watching me from his perch until I got ready for work. Then he took the

The Tramp

pipe out of his mouth and put it in his pocket, calmly declaring that it was not included in the contract, and that it was worth a quarter to have it go in the picture. The pipe, by the way, was of clay, and of the two-for-a-cent kind. But I had to give in. The man, scarce ten seconds employed at honest labor, even at sitting down, at which he was an undoubted expert, had gone on strike. He knew his rights and the value of "work," and was not to be cheated out of either.

Whence these tramps, and why the tramping? are questions oftener asked than answered. Ill-applied charity and idleness answer the first query. They are the whence, and to a large extent the why also. Once started on the career of a tramp, the man keeps to it because it is the laziest. Tramps and toughs profess the same doctrine, that the world owes them a living, but from stand-points that tend in different directions. The tough does not become a tramp, save in rare instances, when old and broken down. Even then usually he is otherwise disposed of. The devil has various ways of taking care of his own. Nor is the tramps' army recruited from any certain class. All occupations and most grades of society yield to it their contingent of idleness. Occasionally, from one cause or another, a recruit of a better stamp is forced into the ranks; but the first acceptance of alms puts a brand on the able-bodied man which his moral nature rarely holds out to efface. He seldom recovers his lost caste. The evolution is gradual, keeping step with the increasing shabbiness of his clothes and corresponding loss of self-respect, until he reaches the bottom in "the Bend."

Of the tough the tramp doctrine that the world owes him a living makes a thief; of the tramp a coward. Numbers only make him bold unless he has to do with defenceless women. In the city the policemen keep him straight enough. The women rob an occasional clothesline when no one is looking, or steal the pail and scrubbing-brush with which they are set to clean up in the station-house lodging-rooms after their night's sleep. At the police station the roads of the tramp and the tough again converge. In mid-winter, on the coldest nights, the sanitary police corral the tramps here and in their lodging-houses and vaccinate them, despite their struggles and many oaths that they have recently been "scraped." The station-house is the sieve that sifts out the chaff from the wheat, if there be any wheat there. A man goes from his first night's sleep on the hard slab of a police station lodging-room to a deck-hand's berth on an outgoing steamer, to the recruiting office, to any work that is honest, or he goes "to the devil or the dives, same thing," says my friend, the sergeant, who knows.

8. *The Cheap Lodging-houses*

When it comes to the question of numbers with this tramps' army, another factor of serious portent has to be taken into account: the cheap lodging-houses. In the caravanseries[1] that line Chatham Street and the Bowery, harboring nightly a population as large as that of many a thriving town, a home-made article of tramp and thief is turned out that is attracting the increasing attention of the police, and offers a field for the missionary's labors beside which most others seem of slight account. Within a year they have been stamped as nurseries of crime by the chief of the Secret Police,[2] the sort of crime that feeds especially on idleness and lies ready to the hand of fatal opportunity. In the same strain one of the justices on the police court bench sums up his long experience as a committing magistrate: "The ten-cent lodging-houses more than counterbalance the good done by the free reading-room, lectures, and all other agencies of reform. Such lodging-houses have caused more destitution, more beggary and crime than any other agency I know of." A very slight acquaintance with the subject is sufficient to convince the observer that neither authority overstates the fact. The two officials had reference, however, to two different grades of lodging-houses.

1. Middle Eastern inns, with central courtyards to provide accommodations for the caravans passing through.
2. Thomas F. Byrnes (1842–1910), who in 1883 won approval from the New York legislature to put all precinct detectives under his command. He became chief inspector in 1882. Byrnes ran the department in an autocratic manner. Riis refers here to an article Byrnes wrote for the *North American Review* in 1889 on lodging houses.

The cost of a night's lodging makes the difference. There is a wider gap between the "hotel"—they are all hotels—that charges a quarter and the one that furnishes a bed for a dime than between the bridal suite and the every-day hall bedroom of the ordinary hostelry.

The metropolis is to lots of people like a lighted candle to the moth. It attracts them in swarms that come year after year with the vague idea that they can get along here if anywhere; that something is bound to turn up among so many. Nearly all are young men, unsettled in life, many—most of them, perhaps—fresh from good homes, beyond a doubt with honest hopes of getting a start in the city and making a way for themselves. Few of them have much money to waste while looking around, and the cheapness of the lodging offered is an object. Fewer still know anything about the city and its pitfalls. They have come in search of crowds, of "life," and they gravitate naturally to the Bowery, the great democratic highway of the city, where the twenty-five-cent lodging-houses take them in. In the alleged reading-rooms of these great barracks, that often have accommodations, such as they are, for two, three, and even four hundred guests, they encounter three distinct classes of associates: the great mass adventurers like themselves, waiting there for something to turn up; a much smaller class of respectable clerks or mechanics, who, too poor or too lonely to have a home of their own, live this way from year to year; and lastly the thief in search of recruits for his trade. The sights the young stranger sees and the company he keeps in the Bowery are not of a kind to strengthen any moral principle he may have brought away from home, and by the time his money is gone, with no work yet in sight, and he goes down a step, a long step, to the fifteen-cent lodging-house, he is ready for the tempter whom he finds waiting for him there, reinforced by the contingent of ex-convicts returning from the prisons after having served out their sentences for robbery or theft. Then it is that the something he has been waiting for turns up. The police returns have the record of it. "In nine cases out of ten," says Inspector Byrnes, "he turns out a thief, or a burglar, if, indeed, he does not sooner or later become a murderer." As a matter of fact, some of the most atrocious of recent murders have been the result of schemes of robbery hatched in these houses, and so frequent and bold have become the depredations of the lodging-house thieves, that the authorities have been compelled to make a public demand for more effective laws that shall make them subject at all times to police regulation.

Inspector Byrnes observes that in the last two or three years at least four hundred young men have been arrested for petty crimes that originated in the lodging-houses, and that in many cases it was their first step in crime. He adds his testimony to the notorious fact that three-fourths of the young men called on to plead to generally petty offences in the courts are under twenty years of age, poorly clad, and without means. The bearing of the remark is obvious. One of the, to the police, well-known thieves who lived, when out of jail, at the Windsor, a well-known lodging-house in the Bowery, went to Johnstown after the flood[3] and was shot and killed there while robbing the dead.

An idea of just how this particular scheme of corruption works, with an extra touch of infamy thrown in, may be gathered from the story of David

---

3. On May 31, 1889, flooding in Johnstown, Pennsylvania, killed over two thousand people.

Smith, the "New York Fagin,"[4] who was convicted and sent to prison last year through the instrumentality of the Society for the Prevention of Cruelty to Children. Here is the account from the Society's last report:

"The boy, Edward Mulhearn, fourteen years old, had run away from his home in Jersey City, thinking he might find work and friends in New York. He may have been a trifle wild. He met Smith on the Bowery and recognized him as an acquaintance. When Smith offered him a supper and bed he was only too glad to accept. Smith led the boy to a vile lodging-house on the Bowery, where he introduced him to his 'pals' and swore he would make a man of him before he was a week older. Next day he took the unsuspecting Edward all over the Bowery and Grand Street, showed him the sights and drew his attention to the careless way the ladies carried their bags and purses and the easy thing it was to get them. He induced Edward to try his hand. Edward tried and won. He was richer by three dollars! It did seem easy. 'Of course it is,' said his companion. From that time Smith took the boy on a number of thieving raids, but he never seemed to become adept enough to be trusted out of range of the 'Fagin's' watchful eye. When he went out alone he generally returned empty-handed. This did not suit Smith. It was then he conceived the idea of turning this little inferior thief into a superior beggar. He took the boy into his room and burned his arms with a hot iron. The boy screamed and entreated in vain. The merciless wretch pressed the iron deep into the tender flesh, and afterward applied acid to the raw wound.

"Thus prepared, with his arm inflamed, swollen, and painful, Edward was sent out every day by this fiend, who never let him out of his sight and threatened to burn his arm off if he did not beg money enough. He was instructed to tell people the wound had been caused by acid falling upon his arm at the works. Edward was now too much under the man's influence to resist or disobey him. He begged hard and handed Smith the pennies faithfully. He received in return bad food and worse treatment."

The reckoning came when the wretch encountered the boy's father, in search of his child, in the Bowery, and fell under suspicion of knowing more than he pretended of the lad's whereabouts. He was found in his den with a half dozen of his chums revelling on the proceeds of the boy's begging for the day.

The twenty-five cent lodging-house keeps up the pretence of a bedroom, though the head-high partition enclosing a space just large enough to hold a cot and a chair and allow the man room to pull off his clothes is the shallowest of all pretences. The fifteen-cent bed stands boldly forth without screen in a room full of bunks with sheets as yellow and blankets as foul. At the ten-cent level the locker for the sleeper's clothes disappears. There is no longer need of it. The tramp limit is reached, and there is nothing to lock up save, on general principles, the lodger. Usually the ten- and seven-cent lodgings are different grades of the same abomination. Some sort of an apology for a bed, with mattress and blanket, represents the aristocratic purchase of the tramp who, by a lucky stroke of beggary, has exchanged the chance of an empty box or ash-barrel for shelter on the quality floor of one of these "hotels." A strip of canvas, strung between rough timbers, without

---

4. Fagin is a character in Charles Dickens's novel *Oliver Twist* who exploited street urchins, training them to steal for him.

Bunks in a Seven-Cent Lodging House, Pell Street

covering of any kind, does for the couch of the seven-cent lodger who prefers the questionable comfort of a red-hot stove close to his elbow to the revelry of the stale-beer dive. It is not the most secure perch in the world. Uneasy sleepers roll off at intervals, but they have not far to fall to the next tier of bunks, and the commotion that ensues is speedily quieted by the boss and his club. On cold winter nights, when every bunk had its tenant, I have stood in such a lodging-room more than once, and listening to the snoring of the sleepers like the regular strokes of an engine, and the slow creaking of the beams under their restless weight, imagined myself on shipboard and experienced the very real nausea of sea-sickness. The one thing that did not favor the deception was the air; its character could not be mistaken.

The proprietor of one of these seven-cent houses was known to me as a man of reputed wealth and respectability. He "ran" three such establishments and made, it was said, $8,000 a year clear profit on his investment. He lived in a handsome house quite near to the stylish precincts of Murray Hill, where the nature of his occupation was not suspected. A notice that was posted on the wall of the lodger's room suggested at least an effort to maintain his up-town standing in the slums. It read: "No swearing or loud talking after nine o'clock." Before nine no exceptions were taken to the natural vulgarity of the place; but that was the limit.

There are no licensed lodging-houses known to me which charge less than seven cents for even such a bed as this canvas strip, though there are unlicensed ones enough where one may sleep on the floor for five cents a spot, or squat in a sheltered hallway for three. The police station lodging-house, where the soft side of a plank is the regulation couch, is next in order. The manner in which this police bed is "made up" is interesting in its simplicity. The loose planks that make the platform are simply turned over, and the job is done, with an occasional coat of whitewash thrown in to sweeten things. I know of only one easier way, but, so far as I am informed, it has never been introduced in this country. It used to be practised, if report spoke truly, in certain old-country towns. The "bed" was represented by clothes-lines stretched across the room upon which the sleepers hung by the arm-pits for a penny a night. In the morning the boss woke them up by simply untying the line at one end and letting it go with its load; a labor-saving device certainly, and highly successful in attaining the desired end.

According to the police figures, 4,974,025 separate lodgings were furnished last year by these dormitories, between two and three hundred in number, and, adding the 147,634 lodgings furnished by the station-houses, the total of the homeless army was 5,121,659, an average of over fourteen thousand homeless men[5] for every night in the year! The health officers, professional optimists always in matters that trench upon their official jurisdiction, insist that the number is not quite so large as here given. But, apart from any slight discrepancy in the figures, the more important fact remains that last year's record of lodgers is an all round increase over the previous year's of over three hundred thousand, and that this has been the ratio of growth of the business during the last three years, the period of which Inspector Byrnes complains as turning out so many young criminals with the lodging-house stamp upon them. More than half of the lodging-houses are in the Bowery district, that is to say, the Fourth, Sixth, and Tenth Wards,[6] and they harbor nearly three-fourths of their crowds. The calculation that more than nine thousand homeless young men lodge nightly along Chatham Street and the Bowery, between the City Hall and the Cooper Union, is probably not far out of the way. The City Missionary finds them there far less frequently than the thief in need of helpers. Appropriately enough, nearly one-fifth of all the pawn-shops in the city and one-sixth of all the saloons are located here, while twenty-seven per cent. of all the arrests on the police books have been credited to the district for the last two years.

About election time, especially in Presidential elections, the lodging-houses come out strong on the side of the political boss who has the biggest

5. The total includes 69,111 *women* lodgers in police stations.
6. Encompassing Rivington, Bowery, Norfolk, and Division Streets, the Tenth Ward ward was home to much of the Jewish enclave, later known as the Lower East Side.

"barrel."[7] The victory in political contests, in the three wards I have mentioned of all others, is distinctly to the general with the strongest battalions, and the lodging-houses are his favorite recruiting ground. The colonization of voters is an evil of the first magnitude, none the less because both parties smirch their hands with it, and for that reason next to hopeless. Honors are easy, where the two "machines,"[8] intrenched in their strongholds, outbid each other across the Bowery in open rivalry as to who shall commit the most flagrant frauds at the polls. Semi-occasionally a champion offender is caught and punished, as was, not long ago, the proprietor of one of the biggest Bowery lodging-houses. But such scenes are largely spectacular, if not prompted by some hidden motive of revenge that survives from the contest. Beyond a doubt Inspector Byrnes speaks by the card[9] when he observes that "usually this work is done in the interest of some local political boss, who stands by the owner of the house, in case the latter gets into trouble." For standing by, read twisting the machinery of outraged justice so that its hand shall fall not too heavily upon the culprit, or miss him altogether. One of the houses that achieved profitable notoriety in this way in many successive elections, a notorious tramps' resort in Houston Street, was lately given up, and has most appropriately been turned into a bar-factory, thus still contributing, though in a changed form, to the success of "the cause." It must be admitted that the black tramp who herds in the West Side "hotels" is more discriminating in this matter of electioneering than his white brother. He at least exhibits some real loyalty in invariably selling his vote to the Republican bidder for a dollar, while he charges the Democratic boss a dollar and a half. In view of the well-known facts, there is a good deal of force in the remark made by a friend of ballot reform during the recent struggle over that hotly contested issue, that real ballot reform will do more to knock out cheap lodging-houses than all the regulations of police and health officers together.

The experiment made by a well-known stove manufacturer a winter or two ago in the way of charity might have thrown much desired light on the question of the number of tramps in the city, could it have been carried to a successful end. He opened a sort of breakfast shop for the idle and unemployed in the region of Washington Square, offering to all who had no money a cup of coffee and a roll for nothing. The first morning he had a dozen customers, the next about two hundred. The number kept growing until one morning, at the end of two weeks, found by actual count 2,014 shivering creatures in line waiting their turn for a seat at his tables. The shop was closed that day. It was one of the rare instances of too great a rush of custom wrecking a promising business, and the great problem remained unsolved.

9. Chinatown

Between the tabernacles of Jewry and the shrines of the Bend, Joss[1] has cheekily planted his pagan worship of idols, chief among which are the

---

7. The largesse, both in terms of services and material goods, that politicians gave those who voted correctly, that is, for them.
8. Political organizations that became particularly crucial in mid- to late-nineteenth-century America, when cities and political operatives had much in the way of jobs, contracts, and other benefits to bestow on loyal supporters. Although Tammany Hall may have been the country's best known and most well developed political machine, similar organizations existed in all cities.
9. Accurately, according to a script.
1. Chinese people. The word is derived from the Portuguese *deos*, meaning "gods," and is associated with Western perceptions of Chinese religious practices.

celestial worshippers' own gain and lusts. Whatever may be said about the Chinaman being a thousand years behind the age on his own shores, here he is distinctly abreast of it in his successful scheming to "make it pay." It is doubtful if there is anything he does not turn to a paying account, from his religion down, or up, as one prefers. At the risk of distressing some well-meaning, but, I fear, too trustful people, I state it in advance as my opinion, based on the steady observation of years, that all attempts to make an effective Christian of John Chinaman will remain abortive in this generation; of the next I have, if anything, less hope. Ages of senseless idolatry, a mere grub-worship, have left him without the essential qualities for appreciating the gentle teachings of a faith whose motive and unselfish spirit are alike beyond his grasp. He lacks the handle of a strong faith in something, anything, however wrong, to catch him by. There is nothing strong about him, except his passions when aroused. I am convinced that he adopts Christianity, when he adopts it at all, as he puts on American clothes, with what the politicians would call an ulterior motive, some sort of gain in the near prospect—washing, a Christian wife perhaps, anything he happens to rate for the moment above his cherished pig-tail. It may be that I judge him too harshly. Exceptions may be found. Indeed, for the credit of the race, I hope there are such. But I am bound to say my hope is not backed by lively faith.

Chinatown as a spectacle is disappointing. Next-door neighbor to the Bend, it has little of its outdoor stir and life, none of its gaily-colored rags or picturesque filth and poverty. Mott Street is clean to distraction: the laundry stamp is on it, though the houses are chiefly of the conventional tenement-house type, with nothing to rescue them from the everyday dismal dreariness of their kind save here and there a splash of dull red or yellow, a sign, hung endways and with streamers of red flannel tacked on, that announces in Chinese characters that Dr. Chay Yen Chong sells Chinese herb medicines, or that Won Lung & Co.—queer contradiction—take in washing, or deal out tea and groceries. There are some gimcracks in the second story fire-escape of one of the houses, signifying that Joss or a club has a habitation there. An American patent medicine concern has seized the opportunity to decorate the back-ground with its cabalistic trade-mark, that in this company looks as foreign as the rest. Doubtless the privilege was bought for cash. It will buy anything in Chinatown, Joss himself included, as indeed, why should it not? He was bought for cash across the sea and came here under the law that shuts out the live Chinaman,[2] but lets in his dead god on payment of the statutory duty on bric-à-brac. Red and yellow are the holiday colors of Chinatown as of the Bend, but they do not lend brightness in Mott Street as around the corner in Mulberry. Rather, they seem to descend to the level of the general dulness, and glower at you from doors and windows, from the telegraph pole that is the official organ of Chinatown and from the store signs, with blank, unmeaning stare, suggesting nothing, asking no questions, and answering none. Fifth Avenue is not duller on a rainy day than Mott Street to one in search of excitement. Whatever is on foot goes on behind closed doors. Stealth and secretiveness are as much part of the Chinaman

---

2. The Chinese Exclusion Act of 1882 effectively suspended Chinese immigration to the United States; it remained in force until the 1940s. Congress passed legislation barring only Chinese immigration and no other group was named as being so problematic as needing to be barred.

Smoking Opium in a Joint

in New York as the cat-like tread of his felt shoes. His business, as his domestic life, shuns the light, less because there is anything to conceal than because that is the way of the man. Perhaps the attitude of American civilization toward the stranger, whom it invited in, has taught him that way. At any rate, the very doorways of his offices and shops are fenced off by queer, forbidding partitions suggestive of a continual state of siege. The stranger who enters through the crooked approach is received with sudden silence, a sullen stare, and an angry "Vat you vant?" that breathes annoyance and distrust.

Trust not him who trusts no one, is as safe a rule in Chinatown as out of it. Were not Mott Street overawed in its isolation, it would not be safe to descend this open cellar-way, through which come the pungent odor of burning opium and the clink of copper coins on the table. As it is, though safe, it is not profitable to intrude. At the first foot-fall of leather soles on the steps the hum of talk ceases, and the group of celestials,[3] crouching over their game of fan tan, stop playing and watch the comer with ugly looks. Fan tan is their ruling passion. The average Chinaman, the police will tell you, would rather gamble than eat any day, and they have ample experience to back them. Only the fellow in the bunk smokes away, indifferent to all else but his pipe and his own enjoyment. It is a mistake to assume that Chinatown is honeycombed with opium "joints." There are a good many more outside of it than in it. The celestials do not monopolize the pipe. In Mott Street there is no need of them. Not a Chinese home or burrow there but has its bunk and its layout, where they can be enjoyed safe from police interference. The Chinaman smokes opium as Caucasians smoke tobacco, and apparently with little worse effect upon himself. But woe unto the white victim upon which his pitiless drug gets its grip!

The bloused pedlars who, with arms buried half to the elbow in their trousers' pockets, lounge behind their stock of watermelon seed and sugar-cane, cut in lengths to suit the purse of the buyer, disdain to offer the barbarian their wares. Chinatown, that does most things by contraries, rules it holiday style to carry its hands in its pockets, and its denizens follow the fashion, whether in blue blouse, in gray, or in brown, with shining and braided pig-tail dangling below the knees, or with hair cropped short above a coat collar of "Melican"[4] cut. All kinds of men are met, but no women— none at least with almond eyes. The reason is simple: there are none. A few, a very few, Chinese merchants have wives of their own color, but they are seldom or never seen in the street. The "wives" of Chinatown are of a different stock that comes closer home.

From the teeming tenements to the right and left of it come the white slaves of its dens of vice and their infernal drug, that have infused into the "Bloody Sixth" Ward a subtler poison than ever the stale-beer dives knew, or the "sudden death" of the Old Brewery.[5] There are houses, dozens of

---

3. I.e., Chinese immigrants. This common nineteenth-century expression refers to the image of the Chinese as Sons of the Emperor in Heaven and emphasizes their paganism and superstitiousness.

4. I.e., American. The term emphasizes the accented English spoken by the Chinese.

5. A 1792 building near the Collect Pond that operated as a brewery until 1837. It then became a tenement that developed a notorious reputation in New York for its dense overcrowding, the poverty of its residents, and the inhabitants' depravities and criminality. In 1852 the Ladies Home Missionary Society of the Methodist Episcopal Church bought it and had it razed.

"The Official Organ of Chinatown": Telephone Pole with Notices Stuck On

them, in Mott and Pell Streets, that are literally jammed, from the "joint" in the cellar to the attic, with these hapless victims of a passion which, once acquired, demands the sacrifice of every instinct of decency to its insatiate desire. There is a church in Mott Street,[6] at the entrance to Chinatown, that stands as a barrier between it and the tenements beyond. Its young men have waged unceasing war upon the monstrous wickedness for years, but with very little real result. I have in mind a house in Pell Street that has been raided no end of times by the police, and its population emptied upon Blackwell's Island, or into the reformatories, yet is to-day honeycombed with scores of the conventional households of the Chinese quarter: the men worshippers of Joss; the women, all white, girls hardly yet grown to womanhood, worshipping nothing save the pipe that has enslaved them

6. The Church of the Transfiguration at 29 Mott Street.

body and soul. Easily tempted from homes that have no claim upon the name, they rarely or never return. Mott Street gives up its victims only to the Charity Hospital or the Potter's Field.[7] Of the depth of their fall no one is more thoroughly aware than these girls themselves; no one less concerned about it. The calmness with which they discuss it, while insisting illogically upon the fiction of a marriage that deceives no one, is disheartening. Their misery is peculiarly fond of company, and an amount of visiting goes on in these households that makes it extremely difficult for the stranger to untangle them. I came across a company of them "hitting the pipe"[8] together, on a tour through their dens one night with the police captain of the precinct. The girls knew him, called him by name, offered him a pipe, and chatted with him about the incidents of their acquaintance, how many times he had "sent them up," and their chances of "lasting" much longer. There was no shade of regret in their voices, nothing but utter indifference and surrender.

One thing about them was conspicuous: their scrupulous neatness. It is the distinguishing mark of Chinatown, outwardly and physically. It is not altogether by chance the Chinaman has chosen the laundry as his distinctive field. He is by nature as clean as the cat, which he resembles in his traits of cruel cunning and savage fury when aroused. On this point of cleanliness he insists in his domestic circle, yielding in others with crafty submissiveness to the caprice of the girls, who "boss" him in a very independent manner, fretting vengefully under the yoke they loathe, but which they know right well they can never shake off, once they have put the pipe to their lips and given Mott Street a mortgage upon their souls for all time. To the priest, whom they call in when the poison racks the body, they pretend that they are yet their own masters; but he knows that it is an idle boast, least of all believed by themselves. As he walks with them the few short steps to the Potter's Field, he hears the sad story he has heard told over and over again, of father, mother, home and friends given up for the accursed pipe, and stands hopeless and helpless before the colossal evil for which he knows no remedy.

The frequent assertions of the authorities that at least no girls under age are wrecked on this Chinese shoal, are disproved by the observation of those who go frequently among these dens, though the smallest girl will invariably, and usually without being asked, insist that she is sixteen, and so of age to choose the company she keeps. Such assertions are not to be taken seriously. Even while I am writing, the morning returns from one of the precincts that pass through my hands report the arrest of a Chinaman for "inveigling little girls into his laundry," one of the hundred outposts of Chinatown that are scattered all over the city, as the outer threads of the spider's web that holds its prey fast. Reference to case No. 39,499 in this year's report of the Society for the Prevention of Cruelty to Children, will discover one of the much travelled roads to Chinatown. The girl whose story it tells was thirteen, and one of six children abandoned by a dissipated father. She had been discharged from an Eighth Avenue store, where she was employed as cash girl, and, being afraid to tell her mother, floated about

7. New York's burial site for the indigent. As of 1869 it was maintained on Hart Island in Long Island Sound. The dead have no headstones but were given numbers.
8. Smoking opium, an aspect of Chinese culture very much reviled by Americans.

until she landed in a Chinese laundry. The judge heeded her tearful prayer, and sent her home with her mother, but she was back again in a little while despite all promises of reform.

Her tyrant knows well that she will come, and patiently bides his time. When her struggles in the web have ceased at last, he rules no longer with gloved hand. A specimen of celestial logic from the home circle at this period came home to me with a personal application one evening when I attempted, with a policeman, to stop a Chinaman whom we found beating his white "wife" with a broom-handle in a Mott Street cellar. He was angry at our interference, and declared vehemently that she was "bad."

"S'ppose your wifee bad, you no lickee her?" he asked, as if there could be no appeal from such a common-sense proposition as that. My assurance that I did not, that such a thing could not occur to me, struck him dumb with amazement. He eyed me a while in stupid silence, poked the linen in his tub, stole another look, and made up his mind. A gleam of intelligence shone in his eye, and pity and contempt struggled in his voice. "Then, I guess, she lickee you," he said.

No small commotion was caused in Chinatown once upon the occasion of an expedition I undertook, accompanied by a couple of police detectives, to photograph Joss. Some conscienceless wag spread the report, after we were gone, that his picture was wanted for the Rogues' Gallery at Headquarters. The insult was too gross to be passed over without atonement of some sort. Two roast pigs made matters all right with his offended majesty of Mott Street, and with his attendant priests, who bear a very practical hand in the worship by serving as the divine stomach, as it were. They eat the good things set before their rice-paper master, unless, as once happened, some sacrilegious tramp sneaks in and gets ahead of them. The practical way in which these people combine worship with business is certainly admirable. I was told that the scrawl covering the wall on both sides of the shrine stood for the names of the pillars of the church or club—the Joss House is both—that they might have their reward in this world, no matter what happened to them in the next. There was another inscription overhead that needed no interpreter. In familiar English letters, copied bodily from the trade dollar, was the sentiment: "In God we trust." The priest pointed to it with undisguised pride and attempted an explanation, from which I gathered that the inscription was intended as a diplomatic courtesy, a delicate international compliment to the "Melican Joss," the almighty dollar.

Chinatown has enlisted the telegraph for the dissemination of public intelligence, but it has got hold of the contrivance by the wrong end. As the wires serve us in newspaper-making, so the Chinaman makes use of the pole for the same purpose. The telegraph pole, of which I spoke as the real official organ of Chinatown, stands not far from the Joss House in Mott Street, in full view from Chatham Square. In it centres the real life of the colony, its gambling news. Every day yellow and red notices are posted upon it by unseen hands, announcing that in such and such a cellar a fan tan game will be running that night, or warning the faithful that a raid is intended on this or that game through the machination of a rival interest. A constant stream of plotting and counterplotting makes up the round of Chinese social and political existence. I do not pretend to understand the exact political structure of the colony or its internal government. Even discarding as idle the stories of a secret cabal with power over life and death, and authority to enforce its decrees, there is evidence enough that the Chinese consider themselves subject to the laws of the land only when submission is unavoidable, and that they are governed by a code of their own, the very essence of which is rejection of all other authority except under compulsion. If now and then some horrible crime in the Chinese colony, a murder of such hideous ferocity as one I have a very vivid recollection of, where the murderer stabbed his victim (both Chinamen, of course) in the back with a meat-knife, plunging it in to the hilt no less than seventeen times, arouses the popular prejudice to a suspicion that it was "ordered," only the suspected themselves are to blame, for they appear to rise up as one man to shield the criminal. The difficulty of tracing the motive of the crime and the murderer is extreme, and it is the rarest of all results that the police get on the track of either. The obstacles in the way of hunting down an Italian murderer are as nothing to the opposition encountered in Chinatown. Nor is the failure of the pursuit wholly to be ascribed to the familiar fact that to Caucasian eyes "all Chinamen look alike," but rather to their acting "alike," in a body, to defeat discovery at any cost.

Withal the police give the Chinese the name of being the "quietest people down there," meaning in the notoriously turbulent Sixth Ward; and they are. The one thing they desire above all is to be let alone, a very natural wish perhaps, considering all the circumstances. If it were a laudable or even an allowable ambition that prompts it, they might be humored with advantage, probably, to both sides. But the facts show too plainly that it is not, and that in their very exclusiveness and reserve they are a constant and terrible menace to society, wholly regardless of their influence upon the industrial problems which their presence confuses. The severest official scrutiny, the harshest repressive measures are justifiable in Chinatown, orderly as it appears on the surface, even more than in the Bend, and the case is infinitely more urgent. To the peril that threatens there all the senses are alert, whereas the poison that proceeds from Mott Street puts mind and body to sleep, to work out its deadly purpose in the corruption of the soul.

This again may be set down as a harsh judgment. I may be accused of inciting persecution of an unoffending people. Far from it. Granted, that the Chinese are in no sense a desirable element of the population, that they serve no useful purpose here, whatever they may have done elsewhere in other days, yet to this it is a sufficient answer that they are here, and that, having let them in, we must make the best of it. This is a time for very plain speaking on this subject. Rather than banish the Chinaman, I would have

the door opened wider—for his wife; make it a condition of his coming or staying that he bring his wife with him. Then, at least, he might not be what he now is and remains, a homeless stranger among us. Upon this hinges the real Chinese question, in our city at all events, as I see it. To assert that the victims of his drug and his base passions would go to the bad anyhow, is begging the question. They might and they might not. The chance is the span between life and death. From any other form of dissipation than that for which Chinatown stands there is recovery; for the victims of any other vice, hope. For these there is neither hope nor recovery; nothing but death—moral, mental, and physical death.

10. Jewtown

The tenements grow taller, and the gaps in their ranks close up rapidly as we cross the Bowery and, leaving Chinatown and the Italians behind, invade the Hebrew quarter. Baxter Street, with its interminable rows of old clothes shops and its brigades of pullers-in—nicknamed "the Bay" in honor, perhaps, of the tars who lay to there after a cruise to stock up their togs, or maybe after the "schooners"[1] of beer plentifully bespoke in that latitude—Bayard Street, with its synagogues and its crowds, gave us a foretaste of it. No need of asking here where we are. The jargon[2] of the street, the signs of the sidewalk, the manner and dress of the people, their unmistakable physiognomy, betray their race at every step. Men with queer skull-caps, venerable beard, and the outlandish long-skirted kaftan of the Russian Jew, elbow the ugliest and the handsomest women in the land. The contrast is startling. The old women are hags; the young, houris. Wives and mothers at sixteen, at thirty they are old. So thoroughly has the chosen people crowded out the Gentiles in the Tenth Ward that, when the great Jewish holidays come around every year, the public schools in the district have practically to close up. Of their thousands of pupils scarce a handful come to school. Nor is there any suspicion that the rest are playing hookey. They stay honestly home to celebrate. There is no mistaking it: we are in Jewtown.

It is said that nowhere in the world are so many people crowded together on a square mile as here. The average five-story tenement adds a story or two to its stature in Ludlow Street and an extra building on the rear lot, and yet the sign "To Let" is the rarest of all there. Here is one seven stories high. The sanitary policeman whose beat this is will tell you that it contains thirty-six families, but the term has a widely different meaning here and on the avenues. In this house, where a case of small-pox was reported, there were fifty-eight babies and thirty-eight children that were over five years of age. In Essex Street two small rooms in a six-story tenement were made to hold a "family" of father and mother, twelve children and six boarders. The boarder plays as important a part in the domestic economy of Jewtown as the lodger in the Mulberry Street Bend. These are samples of the packing of the population that has run up the record here to the rate of three hundred and thirty thousand per square mile. The densest crowding of Old

---

1. Tankards or steins for beer drinking. "Pullers-in": Since the middle of the nineteenth century Jewish clothing merchants in the lower areas of New York, particularly around Chatham Square, set up their wares outside and used them to lure customers into their shops. "Tars": sailors.
2. Yiddish

A tramp's nest in Ludlow Street

London, I pointed out before, never got beyond a hundred and seventy-five thousand. Even the alley is crowded out. Through dark hallways and filthy cellars, crowded, as is every foot of the street, with dirty children, the settlements in the rear are reached. Thieves know how to find them when pursued by the police, and the tramps that sneak in on chilly nights to fight for the warm spot in the yard over some baker's oven. They are out of place in this hive of busy industry, and they know it. It has nothing in common with them or with their philosophy of life, that the world owes the idler a living. Life here means the hardest kind of work almost from the cradle. The world as a debtor has no credit in Jewtown. Its promise to pay wouldn't buy one of the old hats that are hawked about Hester Street, unless backed by security representing labor done at lowest market rates. But this army of workers must have bread. It is cheap and filling, and bakeries abound. Wherever they are in the tenements the tramp will skulk in, if he can. There is such a tramps' roost in the rear of a tenement near the lower end of Ludlow Street, that is never without its tenants in winter. By a judicious practice of flopping over on the stone pavement at intervals and thus warming one side at a time, and with an empty box to put the feet in, it is possible to keep reasonably comfortable there even on a rainy night. In summer the yard is the only one in the neighborhood that does not do duty as a public dormitory.

Thrift is the watchword of Jewtown, as of its people the world over. It is at once its strength and its fatal weakness, its cardinal virtue and its foul disgrace. Become an over-mastering passion with these people who come here in droves from Eastern Europe to escape persecution, from which freedom could be bought only with gold, it has enslaved them in bondage worse than that from which they fled. Money is their God. Life itself is of little value compared with even the leanest bank account. In no other spot does life wear so intensely bald and materialistic an aspect as in Ludlow Street. Over and over again I have met with instances of these Polish or Russian Jews deliberately starving themselves to the point of physical exhaustion, while working night and day at a tremendous pressure to save a little money. An avenging Nemesis pursues this headlong hunt for wealth; there is no worse paid class anywhere. I once put the question to one of their own people, who, being a pawnbroker, and an unusually intelligent and charitable one, certainly enjoyed the advantage of a practical view of the situation: "Whence the many wretchedly poor people in such a colony of workers, where poverty, from a misfortune, has become a reproach, dreaded as the plague?"

"Immigration," he said, "brings us a lot. In five years it has averaged twenty-five thousand a year, of which more than seventy per cent. have stayed in New York. Half of them require and receive aid from the Hebrew Charities[3] from the very start, lest they starve. That is one explanation. There is another class than the one that cannot get work: those who have had too much of it; who have worked and hoarded and lived, crowded together like pigs, on the scantiest fare and the worst to be got, bound to save whatever their earnings, until, worn out, they could work no longer. Then their hoards were soon exhausted. That is their story." And I knew that what he said was true.

Penury and poverty are wedded everywhere to dirt and disease, and Jewtown is no exception. It could not well be otherwise in such crowds, considering especially their low intellectual status. The managers of the Eastern Dispensary,[4] which is in the very heart of their district, told the whole story when they said: "The diseases these people suffer from are not due to intemperance or immorality, but to ignorance, want of suitable food, and the foul air in which they live and work." The homes of the Hebrew quarter are its workshops also. Reference will be made to the economic conditions under which they work in a succeeding chapter. Here we are concerned simply with the fact. You are made fully aware of it before you have travelled the length of a single block in any of these East Side streets, by the whir of a thousand sewing-machines, worked at high pressure from earliest dawn till mind and muscle give out together. Every member of the family, from the youngest to the oldest, bears a hand, shut in the qualmy rooms, where meals are cooked and clothing washed and dried besides, the live-long day. It is not unusual to find a dozen persons—men, women, and children—at work in a single small room. The fact accounts for the contrast that strikes with wonder the observer who comes across from the Bend. Over there the entire population seems possessed of an uncontrollable impulse to get out into the street; here all its energies appear to be bent upon keeping in and away from it. Not that the streets are deserted. The overflow from these tenements is enough to make a crowd anywhere. The children alone would do it. Not old enough to work and no room for play, that is their story. In the home the child's place is usurped by the lodger, who performs the service of the Irishman's pig[5]—pays the rent. In the street the army of hucksters crowd him out. Typhus[6] fever and small-pox are bred here, and help solve the question what to do with him. Filth diseases both, they sprout naturally among the hordes that bring the germs with them from across the sea, and whose first instinct is to hide their sick lest the authorities carry them off to the hospital to be slaughtered, as they firmly believe. The health officers

---

3. Founded in 1874, this organization brought together five Jewish-relief associations. It provided direct aid to the poor, particularly for newly arrived immigrants, as well as loans funds, employment services, training schools, and a range of other resources to assist Jews in need in New York.
4. Founded in 1832 to serve the area of heaviest Jewish residence, the Lower East Side.
5. Irish immigrants kept pigs not so much to slaughter and eat them themselves but to sell to others, providing an additional source of income.
6. A disease carried by louse-borne bacteria and one of New York City's major scourges. It afflicted those in the poorer areas more than those in the affluent areas.

are on constant and sharp look-out for hidden fever-nests. Considering that half of the ready-made clothes that are sold in the big stores, if not a good deal more than half, are made in these tenement rooms, this is not excessive caution. It has happened more than once that a child recovering from small-pox, and in the most contagious stage of the disease, has been found crawling among heaps of half-finished clothing that the next day would be offered for sale on the counter of a Broadway store; or that a typhus fever patient has been discovered in a room whence perhaps a hundred coats had been sent home that week, each one with the wearer's death-warrant, unseen and unsuspected, basted in the lining.

The health officers call the Tenth the typhus ward; in the office where deaths are registered it passes as the "suicide ward," for reasons not hard to understand; and among the police as the "crooked ward," on account of the number of "crooks," petty thieves and their allies, the "fences," receivers of stolen goods, who find the dense crowds congenial. The nearness of the Bowery, the great "thieves' highway," helps to keep up the supply of these, but Jewtown does not support its dives. Its troubles with the police are the characteristic crop of its intense business rivalries. Oppression, persecution, have not shorn the Jew of his native combativeness one whit. He is as ready to fight for his rights, or what he considers his rights, in a business transaction—synonymous generally with his advantage—as if he had not been robbed of them for eighteen hundred years. One strong impression survives with him from his days of bondage: the power of the law. On the slightest provocation he rushes off to invoke it for his protection. Doubt-less the sensation is novel to him, and therefore pleasing. The police at the Eldridge Street station are in a constant turmoil over these everlasting fights. Somebody is always denouncing somebody else, and getting his enemy or himself locked up; frequently both, for the prisoner, when brought in, has generally as plausible a story to tell as his accuser, and as hot a charge to make. The day closes on a wild conflict of rival interests. Another dawns with the prisoner in court, but no complainant. Over night the case has been settled on a business basis, and the police dismiss their prisoner in deep disgust.

These quarrels have sometimes a comic aspect. Thus, with the numerous dancing-schools that are scattered among the synagogues, often keeping them company in the same tenement. They are generally kept by some man who works in the daytime at tailoring, cigarmaking, or something else. The young people in Jewtown are inordinately fond of dancing, and after their day's hard work will flock to these "schools" for a night's recreation. But even to their fun they carry their business preferences, and it happens that a school adjourns in a body to make a general raid on the rival establishment across the street, without the ceremony of paying the admission fee. Then the dance breaks up in a general fight, in which, likely enough, someone is badly hurt. The police come in, as usual, and ring down the curtain.

Bitter as are his private feuds, it is not until his religious life is invaded that a real inside view is obtained of this Jew, whom the history of Christian civilization has taught nothing but fear and hatred. There are two or three missions in the district conducting a hopeless propagandism for the Messiah whom the Tenth Ward rejects, and they attract occasional crowds, who come to hear the Christian preacher as the Jews of old gathered to hear the apostles expound the new doctrine. The result is often strikingly similar.

"For once," said a certain well-known minister of an uptown church to me, after such an experience, "I felt justified in comparing myself to Paul preaching salvation to the Jews. They kept still until I spoke of Jesus Christ as the Son of God. Then they got up and fell to arguing among themselves and to threatening me, until it looked as if they meant to take me out in Hester Street and stone me." As at Jerusalem, the Chief Captain was happily at hand with his centurions, in the person of a sergeant and three policemen, and the preacher was rescued. So, in all matters pertaining to their religious life that tinges all their customs, they stand, these East Side Jews, where the new day that dawned on Calvary[7] left them standing, stubbornly refusing to see the light. A visit to a Jewish house of mourning is like bridging the gap of two thousand years. The inexpressibly sad and sorrowful wail for the dead, as it swells and rises in the hush of all sounds of life, comes back from the ages like a mournful echo of the voice of Rachel "weeping for her children and refusing to be comforted, because they are not."[8]

Attached to many of the synagogues, which among the poorest Jews frequently consist of a scantily furnished room in a rear tenement, with a few wooden stools or benches for the congregation, are Talmudic schools that absorb a share of the growing youth. The school-master is not rarely a man of some attainments who has been stranded there, his native instinct for money-making having been smothered in the process that has made of him a learned man. It was of such a school in Eldridge Street that the wicked Isaac Iacob, who killed his enemy, his wife, and himself in one day, was janitor. But the majority of the children seek the public schools, where they are received sometimes with some misgivings on the part of the teachers, who find it necessary to inculcate lessons of cleanliness in the worst cases by practical demonstration with wash-bowl and soap. "He took hold of the soap as if it were some animal," said one of these teachers to me after such an experiment upon a new pupil, "and wiped three fingers across his face. He called that washing." In the Allen Street public school the experienced principal has embodied among the elementary lessons, to keep constantly before the children the duty that clearly lies next to their hands, a characteristic exercise. The question is asked daily from the teacher's desk: "What must I do to be healthy?" and the whole school responds:

> "I must keep my skin clean,
> Wear clean clothes,
> Breathe pure air,
> And live in the sunlight."

It seems little less than biting sarcasm to hear them say it, for to not a few of them all these things are known only by name. In their everyday life there is nothing even to suggest any of them. Only the demand of religious custom has power to make their parents clean up at stated intervals, and the young naturally are no better. As scholars, the children of the most ignorant Polish Jew keep fairly abreast of their more favored playmates, until it comes to mental arithmetic, when they leave them behind with a bound. It is surprising to see how strong the instinct of dollars and cents is in them. They can count, and correctly, almost before they can talk.

7. A hill in Jerusalem associated with Jesus' crucifixion.
8. Jeremiah 31:15.

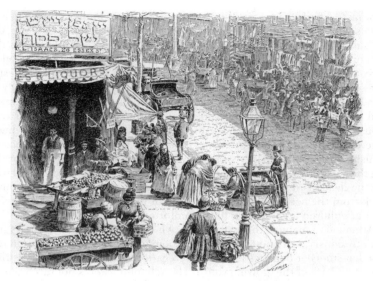

A market scene in the Jewish quarter

Within a few years the police captured on the East Side a band of firebugs[9] who made a business of setting fire to tenements for the insurance on their furniture. There has, unfortunately, been some evidence in the past year that another such conspiracy is on foot. The danger to which these fiends expose their fellow-tenants is appalling. A fire-panic at night in a tenement, by no means among the rare experiences in New York, with the surging, half-smothered crowds on stairs and fire-escapes, the frantic mothers and crying children, the wild struggle to save the little that is their all, is a horror that has few parallels in human experience.

I cannot think without a shudder of one such scene in a First Avenue tenement. It was in the middle of the night. The fire had swept up with sudden fury from a restaurant on the street floor, cutting off escape. Men and women threw themselves from the windows, or were carried down senseless by the firemen. Thirteen half-clad, apparently lifeless bodies were laid on the floor of an adjoining coal-office, and the ambulance surgeons worked over them with sleeves rolled up to the elbows. A half-grown girl with a baby in her arms walked about among the dead and dying with a stunned, vacant look, singing in a low, scared voice to the child. One of the doctors took her arm to lead her out, and patted the cheek of the baby soothingly. It was cold. The baby had been smothered with its father and mother; but the girl, her sister, did not know it. Her reason had fled.

Thursday night and Friday morning are bargain days in the "Pig-market." Then is the time to study the ways of this peculiar people to the

9. Businessmen who torched their own stores to collect the insurance money. Jews were frequently accused of this crime, and the image of the firebug became a stock element in anti-Jewish rhetoric of the nineteenth century.

The old clo'e's man—in the Jewish quarter

best advantage. A common pulse beats in the quarters of the Polish Jews and in the Mulberry Bend, though they have little else in common. Life over yonder in fine weather is a perpetual holiday, here a veritable tread-mill of industry. Friday brings out all the latent color and picturesque-ness of the Italians, as of these Semites. The crowds and the common poverty are the bonds of sympathy between them. The Pig-market is in Hester Street, extending either way from Ludlow Street, and up and down the side streets two or three blocks, as the state of trade demands. The name was given to it probably in derision, for pork is the one ware that is not on sale in the Pig-market. There is scarcely anything else that can be hawked from a wagon that is not to be found, and at ridiculously low prices. Bandannas and tin cups at two cents, peaches at a cent a quart, "damaged" eggs for a song, hats for a quarter, and spectacles, war-ranted to suit the eye, at the optician's who has opened shop on a Hes-ter Street door-step, for thirty-five cents; frowsy-looking chickens and half-plucked geese, hung by the neck and protesting with wildly strutting feet even in death against the outrage, are the great staple of the mar-ket. Half or a quarter of a chicken can be bought here by those who can-not afford a whole. It took more than ten years of persistent effort on the part of the sanitary authorities to drive the trade in live fowl from the streets to the fowl-market on Gouverneur Slip, where the killing is now done according to Jewish rite by priests detailed for the purpose by the chief rabbi.[1] Since then they have had a characteristic rumpus, that involved the entire Jewish community, over the fees for killing and the mode of collecting them. Here is a woman churning horse-radish on a machine she has chained and padlocked to a tree on the sidewalk, lest someone steal it. Beside her a butcher's stand with cuts at prices the avenues never dreamed of. Old coats are hawked for fifty cents, "as good as new," and "pants"—there are no trousers in Jewtown, only pants—at anything that can be got. There is a knot of half a dozen "pants" pedlars in the middle of the street, twice as many men of their own race finger-ing their wares and plucking at the seams with the anxious scrutiny of would-be buyers, though none of them has the least idea of investing in a pair. Yes, stop! This baker, fresh from his trough, bare-headed and with bare arms, has made an offer: for this pair thirty cents; a dollar and forty was the price asked. The pedlar shrugs his shoulders, and turns up his hands with a half pitying, wholly indignant air. What does the baker take him for? Such pants—. The baker has turned to go. With a jump like a panther's, the man with the pants has him by the sleeve. Will he give eighty cents? Sixty? Fifty? So help him, they are dirt cheap at that. Lose, will he, on the trade, lose all the profit of his day's peddling. The baker goes on unmoved. Forty then? What, not forty? Take them then for thirty, and wreck the life of a poor man. And the baker takes them and goes, well knowing that at least twenty cents of the thirty, two hundred per cent., were clear profit, if indeed the "pants" cost the pedlar anything.

The suspender pedlar is the mystery of the Pig-market, omnipresent and unfathomable. He is met at every step with his wares dangling over his shoulder, down his back, and in front. Millions of suspenders thus peram-bulate Jewtown all day on a sort of dress parade. Why suspenders, is the puzzle, and where do they all go to? The "pants" of Jewtown hang down with a common accord, as if they had never known the support of sus-penders. It appears to be as characteristic a trait of the race as the long beard and the Sabbath silk hat of ancient pedigree. I have asked again and again. No one has ever been able to tell me what becomes of the suspenders of Jewtown. Perhaps they are hung up as bric-à-brac in its homes, or laid away and saved up as the equivalent of cash. I cannot tell. I only know that more suspenders are hawked about the Pig-market every day than would supply the whole of New York for a year, were they all bought and turned to use.

The crowds that jostle each other at the wagons and about the sidewalk shops, where a gutter plank on two ash-barrels does duty for a counter! Pushing, struggling, babbling, and shouting in foreign tongues, a veritable Babel of confusion. An English word falls upon the ear almost with a sense of shock, as something unexpected and strange. In the midst of it all there is a sudden wild scattering, a hustling of things from the street into dark cellars, into back-yards and by-ways, a slamming and locking of doors hid-den under the improvised shelves and counters. The health officers' cart is

1. Rabbi Jacob Joseph of Vilna, brought to New York in 1887 to serve as the chief rabbi of the United States. He served in this post until 1902, but from the very start he had little power. Despite his lofty title, he actually worked for a group of Lower East Side congregations that had joined together under the equally pretentious title of the Association of the American Orthodox Congregations. He never could exert the authority that he believed he deserved.

coming down the street, preceded and followed by stalwart policemen, who shovel up with scant ceremony the eatables—musty bread, decayed fish and stale vegetables—indifferent to the curses that are showered on them from stoops and windows, and carry them off to the dump. In the wake of the wagon; as it makes its way to the East River after the raid, follow a line of despoiled hucksters shouting defiance from a safe distance. Their clamor dies away with the noise of the market. The endless panorama of the tenements, rows upon rows, between stony streets, stretches to the north, to the south, and to the west as far as the eye reaches.

11. The Sweaters[1] of Jewtown

Anything like an exhaustive discussion of the economical problem presented by the Tenth Ward[2] is beset by difficulties that increase in precise proportion to the efforts put forth to remove them. I have too vivid a recollection of weary days and nights spent in those stewing tenements, trying to get to the bottom of the vexatious question only to find myself in the end as far from the truth as at the beginning, asking with rising wrath Pilate's question, "What is truth?" to attempt to weary the reader by dragging him with me over that sterile and unprofitable ground. Nor are these pages the place for such a discussion. In it, let me confess it at once and have done with it, I should be like the blind leading the blind; between the real and apparent poverty, the hidden hoards and the unhesitating mendacity of these people, where they conceive their interests to be concerned in one way or another, the reader and I would fall together into the ditch of doubt and conjecture in which I have found company before.

The facts that lie on the surface indicate the causes as clearly as the nature of the trouble. In effect both have been already stated. A friend of mine who manufactures cloth once boasted to me that nowadays, on cheap clothing, New York "beats the world." "To what," I asked, "do you attribute it?" "To the cutter's long knife[3] and the Polish Jew," he said. Which of the two has cut deepest into the workman's wages is not a doubtful question. Practically the Jew has monopolized the business since the battle between East Broadway and Broadway ended in a complete victory for the East Side and cheap labor, and transferred to it the control of the trade in cheap clothing. Yet, not satisfied with having won the field, he strives as hotly with his own for the profit of half a cent as he fought with his Christian competitor for the dollar. If the victory is a barren one, the blame is his own. His price is not what he can get, but the lowest he can live for and underbid his neighbor. Just what that means we shall see. The manufacturer knows it, and is not slow to take advantage of his knowledge. He makes him hungry for work by keeping it from him as long as possible; then drives the closest bargain he can with the sweater.

Many harsh things have been said of the "sweater," that really apply to the system in which he is a necessary, logical link. It can at least be said of

1. Those who run the sweatshops, small apartment workshops where workers made garments.
2. Riis also refers to the Thirteenth Ward, which was also part of the Jewish quarter. It included the area between Division and Grand Streets, the East River, and Norfolk and Rivington Streets.
3. A knife that could cut through many layers of fabric, increasing the number of pieces that could be cut at one time.

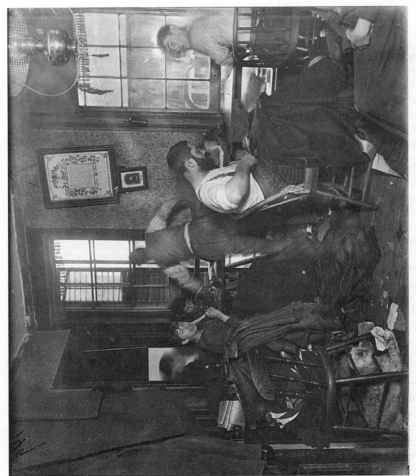

"Knee-pants" at Forty-Five Cents a Dozen—a Ludlow Street Sweater's Shop

him that he is no worse than the conditions that created him. The sweater is simply the middleman, the sub-contractor, a workman like his fellows, perhaps with the single distinction from the rest that he knows a little English; perhaps not even that, but with the accidental possession of two or three sewing-machines, or of credit enough to hire them, as his capital, who drums up work among the clothing-houses. Of workmen he can always get enough. Every ship-load from German ports brings them to his door in droves, clamoring for work. The sun sets upon the day of the arrival of many a Polish Jew, finding him at work in an East Side tenement, treading the machine and "learning the trade." Often there are two, sometimes three, sets of sweaters on one job. They work with the rest when they are not drumming up trade, driving their "hands" as they drive their machine, for all they are worth, and making a profit on their work, of course, though in most cases not nearly as extravagant a percentage, probably, as is often supposed. If it resolves itself into a margin of five or six cents, or even less, on a dozen pairs of boys' trousers, for instance, it is nevertheless enough to make the contractor with his thrifty instincts independent. The workman growls, not at the hard labor or poor pay, but over the pennies another is coining out of his sweat, and on the first opportunity turns sweater himself, and takes his revenge by driving an even closer bargain than his rival tyrant, thus reducing his profits.

The sweater knows well that the isolation of the workman in his helpless ignorance is his sure foundation, and he has done what he could—with merciless severity where he could—to smother every symptom of awakening intelligence in his slaves. In this effort to perpetuate his despotism he has had the effectual assistance of his own system and the sharp competition that keeps the men on starvation wages; of their constitutional greed, that will not permit the sacrifice of temporary advantage however slight, for permanent good, and above all, of the hungry hordes of immigrants to whom no argument appeals save the cry for bread. Within very recent times he has, however, been forced to partial surrender by the organization of the men to a considerable extent into trade unions, and by experiments in co-operation, under intelligent leadership, that presage the sweater's doom. But as long as the ignorant crowds continue to come and to herd in these tenements, his grip can never be shaken off. And the supply across the seas is apparently inexhaustible. Every fresh persecution of the Russian or Polish Jew on his native soil starts greater hordes hitherward to confound economical problems, and recruit the sweater's phalanx. The curse of bigotry and ignorance reaches half-way across the world, to sow its bitter seed in fertile soil in the East Side tenements. If the Jew himself was to blame for the resentment he aroused over there, he is amply punished. He gathers the first-fruits of the harvest here.

The bulk of the sweater's work is done in the tenements, which the law that regulates factory labor does not reach. To the factories themselves that are taking the place of the rear tenements in rapidly growing numbers, letting in bigger day-crowds than those the health officers banished, the tenement shops serve as a supplement through which the law is successfully evaded. Ten hours is the legal work-day in the factories, and nine o'clock the closing hour at the latest. Forty-five minutes at least must be allowed for dinner, and children under sixteen must not be employed unless they can read and write English; none at all under fourteen. The very fact that such a law should stand on the statute book, shows how desperate the plight of these people. But the tenement has defeated its benevolent purpose. In it the child works unchallenged from the day he is old enough to pull a thread. There is no such thing as a dinner hour; men and women eat while they work, and the "day" is lengthened at both ends far into the night. Factory hands take their work with them at the close of the lawful day to eke out their scanty earnings by working overtime at home. Little chance on this ground for the campaign of education that alone can bring the needed relief; small wonder that there are whole settlements on this East Side where English is practically an unknown tongue, though the people be both willing and anxious to learn. "When shall we find time to learn?" asked one of them of me once. I owe him the answer yet.

Take the Second Avenue Elevated Railroad at Chatham Square and ride up half a mile through the sweater's district. Every open window of the big tenements, that stand like a continuous brick wall on both sides of the way, gives you a glimpse of one of these shops as the train speeds by. Men and women bending over their machines, or ironing clothes at the window, half-naked. Proprieties do not count on the East Side; nothing counts that cannot be converted into hard cash. The road is like a big gangway through an endless work-room where vast multitudes are forever laboring. Morning, noon, or night, it makes no difference; the scene is always the same. At Rivington Street let us get off and continue our trip on foot. It is Sunday evening west of the Bowery. Here, under the rule of Mosaic law, the week of work is under full headway, its first day far spent. The hucksters' wagons are absent or stand idle at the curb; the saloons admit the thirsty crowds through the side-door labelled "Family Entrance"; a tin sign in a store-window announces that a "Sunday School" gathers in stray children of the new dispensation; but beyond these things there is little to suggest the Christian Sabbath. Men stagger along the sidewalk groaning under heavy burdens of unsewn garments, or enormous black bags stuffed full of finished coats and trousers. Let us follow one to his home and see how Sunday passes in a Ludlow Street tenement.

Up two flights of dark stairs, three, four, with new smells of cabbage, of onions, of frying fish, on every landing, whirring sewing machines behind closed doors betraying what goes on within, to the door that opens to admit the bundle and the man. A sweater, this, in a small way. Five men and a woman, two young girls, not fifteen, and a boy who says unasked that he is fifteen, and lies in saying it, are at the machines sewing knickerbockers, "knee-pants" in the Ludlow Street dialect. The floor is littered ankle-deep with half-sewn garments. In the alcove, on a couch of many dozens of "pants" ready for the finisher, a bare-legged baby with pinched face is asleep. A fence of piled-up clothing keeps him from rolling off on the floor. The faces, hands, and arms to the elbows of everyone in the room are black with the color of the cloth on which they are working. The boy and the woman alone look up at our entrance. The girls shoot sidelong glances, but at a warning look from the man with the bundle they tread their machines more energetically than ever. The men do not appear to be aware even of the presence of a stranger.

They are "learners," all of them, says the woman, who proves to be the wife of the boss, and have "come over" only a few weeks ago. She is disinclined to talk at first, but a few words in her own tongue from our guide set her fears, whatever they are, at rest, and she grows almost talkative. The learn-ers work for week's wages, she says. How much do they earn? She shrugs her shoulders with an expressive gesture. The workers themselves, asked in their own tongue, say indifferently, as though the question were of no inter-est: from two to five dollars. The children—there are four of them—are not old enough to work. The oldest is only six. They turn out one hundred and twenty dozen "knee-pants" a week, for which the manufacturer pays seventy cents a dozen. Five cents a dozen is the clear profit, but her own and her husband's work brings the family earnings up to twenty-five dollars a week, when they have work all the time. But often half the time is put in looking for it. They work no longer than to nine o'clock at night, from daybreak. There are ten machines in the room; six are hired at two dollars a month. For the two shabby, smoke-begrimed rooms, one somewhat larger than ordinary, they pay twenty dollars a month. She does not complain, though "times are not what they were, and it costs a good deal to live." Eight dollars a week for the family of six and two boarders. How do they do it? She laughs, as she goes over the bill of fare, at the silly question: Bread, fifteen cents a day, of milk two quarts a day at four cents a quart, one pound of meat for dinner at twelve cents, butter one pound a week at "eight cents a quarter of a pound." Coffee, potatoes, and pickles complete the list. At the least cal-culation, probably this sweater's family hoards up thirty dollars a month, and in a few years will own a tenement somewhere and profit by the example set by their landlord in rent-collecting. It is the way the savings of Jewtown are universally invested, and with the natural talent of its people for com-mercial speculation the investment is enormously profitable.

On the next floor, in a dimly lighted room with a big red-hot stove to keep the pressing irons ready for use, is a family of man, wife, three children, and a boarder. "Knee-pants" are made there too, of a still lower grade. Three cents and a half is all he clears, says the man, and lies probably out of at least two cents. The wife makes a dollar and a half finishing, the man about nine dollars at the machine. The boarder pays sixty-five cents a week. He is really only a lodger, getting his meals outside. The rent is two dollars and twenty-five cents a week, cost of living five dollars. Every floor has at least two, sometimes four, such shops. Here is one with a young family for which life is bright with promise. Husband and wife work together; just now the latter, a comely young woman, is eating her dinner of dry bread and green pickles. Pickles are favorite food in Jewtown. They are filling, and keep the children from crying with hunger. Those who have stomachs like ostriches thrive in spite of them and grow strong—plain proof that they are good to eat. The rest? "Well, they die," says our guide, dryly. No thought of untimely death comes to disturb this family with life all before it. In a few years the man will be a prosperous sweater. Already he employs an old man as ironer at three dollars a week, and a sweet-faced little Italian girl as finisher at a dollar and a half. She is twelve, she says, and can neither read nor write; will probably never learn. How should she? The family clears from ten to eleven dollars a week in brisk times, more than half of which goes into the bank.

A companion picture from across the hall. The man works on the machine for his sweater twelve hours a day, turning out three dozen "knee-pants," for which he receives forty-two cents a dozen. The finisher who works with him gets ten, and the ironer eight cents a dozen; buttonholes are extra, at eight to ten cents a hundred. This operator has four children at his home in Stanton Street, none old enough to work, and a sick wife. His rent is twelve dollars a month; his wages for a hard week's work less than eight dollars. Such as he, with their consuming desire for money thus smothered, recruit the ranks of the anarchists,[4] won over by the promise of a general "divide"; and an enlightened public sentiment turns up its nose at the vicious foreigner for whose perverted notions there is no room in this land of plenty.

Turning the corner into Hester Street, we stumble upon a nest of cloakmakers in their busy season. Six months of the year the cloak-maker is idle, or nearly so. Now is his harvest. Seventy-five cents a cloak, all complete, is the price in this shop. The cloak is of cheap plush, and might sell for eight or nine dollars over the store-counter. Seven dollars is the weekly wage of this man with wife and two children, and nine dollars and a half rent to pay per month. A boarder pays about a third of it. There was a time when he made ten dollars a week and thought himself rich. But wages have come down fearfully in the last two years. Think of it: "come down" to this. The other cloakmakers aver that they can make as much as twelve dollars a week, when they are employed, by taking their work home and sewing till midnight. One exhibits his account-book with a Ludlow Street sweater. It shows that he and his partner, working on first-class garments for a Broadway house in the four busiest weeks of the season, made together from $15.15 to $19.20 a week by striving from 6 A.M. to 11 P.M., that is to say, from $7.58 to $9.60 each. The sweater on this work probably made as much as fifty per cent. at least on their labor. Not far away is a factory in a rear yard where the factory inspector reports teams of tailors making men's coats at an average of twenty-seven cents a coat, all complete except buttons and buttonholes.

Turning back, we pass a towering double tenement in Ludlow Street, owned by a well-known Jewish liquor dealer and politician, a triple combination that bodes ill for his tenants. As a matter of fact, the cheapest "apartment," three rear rooms on the sixth floor, only one of which deserves the name, is rented for $13 a month. Here is a reminder of the Bend, a hallway turned into a shoemaker's shop. Two hallways side by side in adjoining tenements would be sinful waste in Jewtown, when one would do as well by knocking a hole in the wall. But this shoemaker knows a trick the Italian's ingenuity did not suggest. He has his "flat" as well as his shop there. A curtain hung back of his stool in the narrow passage half conceals his bed that fills it entirely from wall to wall. To get into it he has to crawl over the footboard, and he must come out the same way. Expedients more odd than this are born of the East Side crowding. In one of the houses we left, the coal-bin of a family on the fourth floor was on the roof of the adjoining tenement. A quarter of a ton of coal was being dumped there while we talked with the people.

We have reached Broome Street. The hum of industry in this six-story tenement on the corner leaves no doubt of the aspect Sunday wears within it. One flight up, we knock at the nearest door. The grocer, who keeps the store, lives on the "stoop," the first floor in East Side parlance. In this room a suspender-maker sleeps and works with his family of wife and four children. For a wonder there are no boarders. His wife and eighteen years old

4. Those who preached the fundamental nature of the class divide that existed between capital and labor. Anarchism as a political ideology attracted an appreciable number of adherents among the eastern European immigrant Jews. The same year that *How the Other Half Lives* appeared, Yiddish-speaking anarchists in New York began publication of the *Fraye Arbiter Shtime* (Free voice of labor).

daughter share in the work, but the girl's eyes are giving out from the strain. Three months in the year, when work is very brisk, the family makes by united efforts as high as fourteen and fifteen dollars a week. The other nine months it averages from three to four dollars. The oldest boy, a young man, earns four to six dollars in an Orchard Street factory, when he has work. The rent is ten dollars a month for the room and a miserable little coop of a bedroom where the old folks sleep. The girl makes her bed on the lounge in the front room; the big boys and the children sleep on the floor. Coal at ten cents a small pail, meat at twelve cents a pound, one and a half pound of butter a week at thirty-six cents, and a quarter of a pound of tea in the same space of time, are items of their house-keeping account as given by the daughter. Milk at four and five cents a quart, "according to quality." The sanitary authorities know what that means, know how miserably inadequate is the fine of fifty or a hundred dollars for the murder done in cold blood by the wretches who poison the babes of these tenements with the stuff that is half water, or swill. Their defence is that the demand is for "cheap milk." Scarcely a wonder that this suspender-maker will hardly be able to save up the *dot*[5] for his daughter, without which she stands no chance of marrying in Jewtown, even with her face that would be pretty had it a healthier tinge.

Up under the roof three men are making boys' jackets at twenty cents a piece, of which the sewer takes eight, the ironer three, the finisher five cents, and the buttonhole-maker two and a quarter, leaving a cent and three-quarters to pay for the drumming up, the fetching and bringing back of the goods. They bunk together in a room for which they pay eight dollars a month. All three are single here, that is: their wives are on the other side yet, waiting for them to earn enough to send for them. Their breakfast, eaten at the work-bench, consists of a couple of rolls at a cent a piece, and a draught of water, milk when business has been very good, a square meal at noon in a restaurant, and the morning meal over again at night. This square meal, that is the evidence of a very liberal disposition on the part of the consumer, is an affair of more than ordinary note; it may be justly called an institution. I know of a couple of restaurants at the lower end of Orchard Street that are favorite resorts for the Polish Jews, who remember the injunction that the ox that treadeth out the corn shall not be muzzled. Being neighbors, they are rivals of course, and cutting under. When I was last there one gave a dinner of soup, meat-stew, bread, pie, pickles, and a "schooner" of beer for thirteen cents; the other charged fifteen cents for a similar dinner, but with two schooners of beer and a cigar, or a cigarette, as the extra inducement. The two cents had won the day, however, and the thirteen-cent restaurant did such a thriving business that it was about to spread out into the adjoining store to accommodate the crowds of customers. At this rate the lodger of Jewtown can "live like a lord," as he says himself, for twenty-five cents a day, including the price of his bed, that ranges all the way from thirty to forty and fifty cents a week, and save money, no matter what his earnings. He does it, too, so long as work is to be had at any price, and by the standard he sets up Jewtown must abide.

It has thousands upon thousands of lodgers who help to pay its extortionate rents. At night there is scarce a room in all the district that has not one or more of them, some above half a score, sleeping on cots, or on the

5. Dowry.

floor. It is idle to speak of privacy in these "homes." The term carries no more meaning with it than would a lecture on social ethics to an audience of Hottentots. The picture is not overdrawn. In fact, in presenting the home life of these people I have been at some pains to avoid the extreme of privation, taking the cases just as they came to hand on the safer middle-ground of average earnings. Yet even the direst apparent poverty in Jewtown, unless dependent on absolute lack of work, would, were the truth known, in nine cases out of ten have a silver lining in the shape of a margin in the bank.

These are the economical conditions that enable my manufacturing friend to boast that New York can "beat the world"[6] on cheap clothing. In support of his claim he told me that a single Bowery firm last year sold fifteen thousand suits at $1.95 that averaged in cost $1.12½. With the material at fifteen cents a yard, he said, children's suits of assorted sizes can be sold at wholesale for seventy-five cents, and boys' cape over-coats at the same price. They are the same conditions that have perplexed the committee of benevolent Hebrews in charge of Baron de Hirsch's[7] munificent gift of ten thousand dollars a month for the relief of the Jewish poor in New York. To find proper channels through which to pour this money so that it shall effect its purpose without pauperizing, and without perpetuating the problem it is sought to solve, by attracting still greater swarms, is indeed no easy task. Colonization has not in the past been a success with these people. The great mass of them are too gregarious to take kindly to farming, and their strong commercial instinct hampers the experiment. To herd them in model tenements, though it relieve the physical suffering in a measure, would be to treat a symptom of the disease rather than strike at its root, even if land could be got cheap enough where they gather to build on a sufficiently large scale to make the plan a success. Trade schools for manual training could hardly be made to reach the adults, who in addition would have to be supported for months while learning. For the young this device has proved most excellent under the wise management of the United Hebrew Charities, an organization that gathers to its work the best thought and effort of many of our most public-spirited citizens. One, or all, of these plans may be tried, probably will. I state but the misgivings as to the result of some of the practical minds that have busied themselves with the problem. Its keynote evidently is the ignorance of the immigrants. They must be taught the language of the country they have chosen as their home, as the first and most necessary step. Whatever may follow, that is essential, absolutely vital. That done, it may well be that the case in its new aspect will not be nearly so hard to deal with.

Evening has worn into night as we take up our homeward journey through the streets, now no longer silent. The thousands of lighted windows in the tenements glow like dull red eyes in a huge stone wall. From every door multitudes of tired men and women pour forth for a half-hour's rest in the open air before sleep closes the eyes weary with incessant working. Crowds

---

6. By the 1890s, partly due to the influx into the United States of several million eastern European Jews, most of whom remained in New York, the city emerged as the world's chief producer of ready-made clothing.

7. A Jewish banker and renowned philanthropist, Baron Maurice de Hirsch provided material support for poor Jews around the world. He attempted to turn Jewish laborers into farmers by encouraging agricultural settlements. One year after Riis's book appeared, the colony of Woodbine, New Jersey, opened up as a model Jewish farming community. It, like most of de Hirsch's other projects in the United States, proved to be not very successful. Jewish immigrants preferred the city, in large measure because of the economic opportunities in the garment industry and other businesses.

of half-naked children tumble in the street and on the sidewalk, or doze fretfully on the stone steps. As we stop in front of a tenement to watch one of these groups, a dirty baby in a single brief garment—yet a sweet, human little baby despite its dirt and tatters—tumbles off the lowest step, rolls over once, clutches my leg with unconscious grip, and goes to sleep on the flagstones, its curly head pillowed on my boot.

12. The Bohemians—Tenement-house Cigarmaking

Evil as the part is which the tenement plays in Jewtown as the pretext for circumventing the law that was made to benefit and relieve the tenant, we have not far to go to find it in even a worse rôle. If the tenement is here continually dragged into the eye of public condemnation and scorn, it is because in one way or another it is found directly responsible for, or intimately associated with, three-fourths of the miseries of the poor. In the Bohemian quarter it is made the vehicle for enforcing upon a proud race a slavery as real as any that ever disgraced the South. Not content with simply robbing the tenant, the owner, in the dual capacity of landlord and employer, reduces him to virtual serfdom by making his becoming *his* tenant, on such terms as he sees fit to make, the condition of employment at wages likewise of his own making. It does not help the case that this landlord employer, almost always a Jew, is frequently of the thrifty Polish race just described.

Perhaps the Bohemian quarter is hardly the proper name to give to the colony, for though it has distinct boundaries it is scattered over a wide area on the East Side, in wedge-like streaks that relieve the monotony of the solid German population by their strong contrasts. The two races mingle no more on this side of the Atlantic than on the rugged slopes of the Bohemian mountains; the echoes of the thirty years' war[1] ring in New York, after two centuries and a half, with as fierce a hatred as the gigantic combat bred among the vanquished Czechs. A chief reason for this is doubtless the complete isolation of the Bohemian immigrant. Several causes operate to bring this about: his singularly harsh and unattractive language, which he can neither easily himself unlearn nor impart to others, his stubborn pride of race, and a popular prejudice which has forced upon him the unjust stigma of a disturber of the public peace and an enemy of organized labor. I greatly mistrust that the Bohemian on our shores is a much-abused man. To his traducer, who casts up anarchism against him, he replies that the last census (1880) shows his people to have the fewest criminals of all in proportion to numbers. In New York a Bohemian criminal is such a rarity that the case of two firebugs of several years ago is remembered with damaging distinctness. The accusation that he lives like the "rat" he is, cutting down wages by his underpaid labor, he throws back in the teeth of the trades unions with the counter-charge that they are the first cause of his attitude to the labor question.

A little way above Houston Street the first of his colonies is encountered, in Fifth Street and thereabouts. Then for a mile and a half scarce a Bohemian is to be found, until Thirty-eighth Street is reached. Fifty-fourth and Seventy-third Streets in their turn are the centres of populous Bohemian settlements. The location of the cigar factories, upon which he depends for a living, determines his choice of home, though there is less choice about it than with any

---

1. A series of wars fought extensively in central Europe from 1618 to 1648. One of the underlying causes of the war was conflict between Catholicism and Protestantism and the issue of which religion would dominate.

Bohemian Cigarmakers at Work in Their Tenement

other class in the community, save perhaps the colored people. Probably more than half of all the Bohemians in this city are cigarmakers, and it is the herding of these in great numbers in the so-called tenement factories, where the cheapest grade of work is done at the lowest wages, that constitutes at once their greatest hardship and the chief grudge of other workmen against them. The manufacturer who owns, say, from three or four to a dozen or more tenements contiguous to his shop, fills them up with these people, charging them outrageous rents, and demanding often even a preliminary deposit of five dollars "key money";[2] deals them out tobacco by the week, and devotes the rest of his energies to the paring down of wages to within a peg or two of the point where the tenant rebels in desperation. When he does rebel, he is given the alternative of submission, or eviction with entire loss of employment. His needs determine the issue. Usually he is not in a position to hesitate long. Unlike the Polish Jew, whose example of untiring industry he emulates, he has seldom much laid up against a rainy day. He is fond of a glass of beer, and likes to live as well as his means will permit. The shop triumphs, and fetters more galling than ever are forged for the tenant. In the opposite case, the newspapers have to record the throwing upon the street of a small army of people, with pitiful cases of destitution and family misery.

Men, women and children work together seven days in the week in these cheerless tenements to make a living for the family, from the break of day rill far into the night. Often the wife is the original cigarmaker from the old home, the husband having adopted her trade here as a matter of necessity, because, knowing no word of English, he could get so other work. As they state the cause of the bitter hostility of the trades unions, she was the primary bone of contention in the day of the early Bohemian immigration. The unions refused to admit the women, and, as the support of the family depended upon her to a large extent, such terms as were offered had to be accepted. The manufacturer has ever since industriously fanned the antagonism between the unions and his hands, for his own advantage. The victory rests with him, since the Court of Appeals decided that the law, passed a few years ago, to prohibit cigarmaking in tenements was unconstitutional, and thus put an end to the struggle. While it lasted, all sorts of frightful stories were told of the shocking conditions under which people lived and worked in these tenements, from a sanitary point of view especially, and a general impression survives to this day that they are particularly desperate. The Board of Health, after a careful canvass, did not find them so then. I am satisfied from personal inspection, at a much later day, guided in a number of instances by the union cigarmakers themselves to the tenements which they considered the worst, that the accounts were greatly exaggerated. Doubtless the people are poor, in many cases very poor; but they are not uncleanly, rather the reverse; they live much better than the clothing makers in the Tenth Ward, and in spite of their sallow look, that may be due to the all-pervading smell of tobacco, they do not appear to be less healthy than other in-door workers. I found on my tours of investigation several cases of consumption, of which one at least was said by the doctor to be due to the constant inhalation of tobacco fumes. But an examination of the death records in the Health Department does not support the claim that the Bohemian cigarmakers are peculiarly prone to that disease. On the contrary, the Bohemian percentage of deaths from consumption

---

2. Renters were required to pay a deposit before they could get the key to their apartments.

appears quite low. This, however, is a line of scientific inquiry which I leave
to others to pursue, along with the more involved problem whether the falling
off in the number of children, sometimes quite noticeable in the Bohemian
settlements, is, as has been suggested, dependent upon the character of the
parents' work. The sore grievances I found were the miserable wages and the
enormous rents exacted for the minimum of accommodation. And surely
these stand for enough of suffering.

Take a row of houses in East Tenth Street as an instance. They contained
thirty-five families of cigarmakers, with probably not half a dozen persons
in the whole lot of them, outside of the children, who could speak a word
of English, though many had been in the country half a lifetime. This room
with two windows giving on the street, and a rear attachment without windows, called a bedroom by courtesy, is rented at $12.25 a month. In the front
room man and wife work at the bench from six in the morning till nine
at night. They make a team, stripping the tobacco leaves together; then he
makes the filler, and she rolls the wrapper on and finishes the cigar. For
a thousand they receive $3.75, and can turn out together three thousand
cigars a week. The point has been reached where the rebellion comes in,
and the workers in these tenements are just now on a strike, demanding
$5.00 and $5.50 for their work. The manufacturer having refused, they are
expecting hourly to be served with notice to quit their homes, and the going
of a stranger among them excites their resentment, until his errand is
explained. While we are in the house, the ultimatum of the "boss" is received.
He will give $3.75 a thousand, not another cent. Our host is a man of seem-
ing intelligence, yet he has been nine years in New York and knows neither
English nor German. Three bright little children play about the floor.

His neighbor on the same floor has been here fifteen years, but shakes
his head when asked if he can speak English. He answers in a few broken
syllables when addressed in German. With $11.75 rent to pay for like accom-
modation, he has the advantage of his oldest boy's work besides his wife's
at the bench. Three properly make a team, and these three can turn out
four thousand cigars a week, at $3.75. This Bohemian has a large family;
there are four children, too small to work, to be cared for. A comparison
of the domestic bills of fare in Tenth and in Ludlow Streets results in the
discovery that this Bohemian's butcher's bill for the week, with meat at
twelve cents a pound as in Ludlow Street, is from two dollars and a half to
three dollars. The Polish Jew fed as big a family on one pound of meat a
day. The difference proves to be typical. Here is a suite of three rooms, two
dark, three flights up. The ceiling is partly down in one of the rooms. "It is
three months since we asked the landlord to fix it," says the oldest son, a
very intelligent lad who has learned English in the evening school. His
father has not had that advantage, and has sat at his bench, deaf and dumb
to the world about him except his own, for six years. He has improved his
time and become an expert at his trade. Father, mother and son together,
a full team, make from fifteen to sixteen dollars a week.

A man with venerable beard and keen eyes answers our questions through
an interpreter, in the next house. Very few brighter faces would be met in a
day's walk among American mechanics, yet he has in nine years learned no
syllable of English. German he probably does not want to learn. His story
supplies the explanation, as did the stories of the others. In all that time he
has been at work grubbing to earn bread. Wife and he by constant labor
make three thousand cigars a week, earning $11.25 when there is no lack

of material; when in winter they receive from the manufacturer tobacco for only two thousand, the rent of $10 for two rooms, practically one with a dark alcove, has nevertheless to be paid in full, and six mouths to be fed. He was a blacksmith in the old country, but cannot work at his trade here because he does not understand "Engliska." If he could, he says, with a bright look, he could do better work than he sees done here. It would seem happiness to him to knock off at 6 o'clock instead of working, as he now often has to do, till midnight. But how? He knows of no Bohemian blacksmith who can understand him; he should starve. Here, with his wife, he can make a living at least. "Aye," says she, turning, from listening, to her household duties, "it would be nice for sure to have father work at his trade." Then what a home she could make for them, and how happy they would be. Here is an unattainable ideal, indeed, of a workman in the most prosperous city in the world! There is genuine, if unspoken, pathos in the soft tap she gives her husband's hand as she goes about her work with a half-suppressed little sigh.

The very ash-barrels that stand in front of the big rows of tenements in Seventy-first and Seventy-third Streets advertise the business that is carried on within. They are filled to the brim with the stems of stripped tobacco leaves. The rank smell that waited for us on the corner of the block follows us into the hallways, penetrates every nook and cranny of the houses. As in the settlement farther down town, every room here has its work-bench with its stumpy knife and queer pouch of bed-tick, worn brown and greasy, fastened in front the whole length of the bench to receive the scraps of waste. This landlord-employer at all events gives three rooms for $12.50, if two be dark, one wholly and the other getting some light from the front room. The mother of the three bare-footed little children we met on the stairs was taken to the hospital the other day when she could no longer work. She will never come out alive. There is no waste in these tenements. Lives, like clothes, are worn through and out before put aside. Her place at the bench is taken already by another who divides with the head of the household his earnings of $15.50 a week. He has just come out successful of a strike that brought the pay of these tenements up to $4.50 per thousand cigars. Notice to quit had already been served on them, when the employer decided to give in, frightened by the prospective loss of rent. Asked how long he works, the man says: "from they can see till bed-time." Bed-time proves to be eleven o'clock. Seventeen hours a day, seven days in the week, at thirteen cents an hour for the two, six cents and a half for each! Good average earnings for a tenement-house cigarmaker in summer. In winter it is at least one-fourth less. In spite of it all, the rooms are cleanly kept. From the bedroom farthest back the woman brings out a pile of moist tobacco leaves to be stripped. They are kept there, under cover lest they dry and crack, from Friday to Friday, when an accounting is made and fresh supplies given out. The people sleep there too, but the smell, offensive to the unfamiliar nose, does not bother them. They are used to it.

In a house around the corner that is not a factory-tenement, lives now the cigarmaker I spoke of as suffering from consumption which the doctor said was due to the tobacco-fumes. Perhaps the lack of healthy exercise had as much to do with it. His case is interesting from its own stand-point. He too is one with a—for a Bohemian—large family. Six children sit at his table. By trade a shoemaker, for thirteen years he helped his wife make cigars in the manufacturer's tenement. She was a very good hand, and until his health gave out two years ago they were able to make from $17 to $25 a week, by lengthening the day at both ends. Now that he can work no more, and the family under the doctor's orders has moved away from the smell of tobacco, the burden of its support has fallen upon her alone, for none of the children is old enough to help. She has work in the shop at eight dollars a week, and this must go round; it is all there is. Happily, this being a tenement for revenue only, unmixed with cigars, the rent is cheaper: seven dollars for two bright rooms on the top floor. No housekeeping is attempted. A woman in Seventy-second Street supplies their meals, which the wife and mother fetches in a basket, her husband being too weak. Breakfast of coffee and hard-tack, or black bread, at twenty cents for the whole eight; a good many, the little woman says with a brave, patient smile, and there is seldom anything to spare, but—. The invalid is listening, and the sentence remains unfinished. What of dinner? One of the children brings it from the cook. Oh! it is a good dinner, meat, soup, greens and bread, all for thirty cents. It is the principal family meal. Does she come home for dinner? No; she cannot leave the shop, but gets a bite at her bench. The question: A bite of what? seems as merciless as the surgeon's knife, and she winces under it as one shrinks from physical pain. Bread, then. But at night they all have supper together—sausage and bread. For ten cents they can eat all they want. Can they not? she says, stroking the hair of the little boy at her knee; his eyes glisten hungrily at the thought, as he nods stoutly in support of his mother. Only, she adds, the week the rent is due, they have to shorten rations to pay the landlord.

But what of his being an Anarchist, this Bohemian—an infidel—I hear somebody say. Almost one might be persuaded by such facts as these—and they are everyday facts, not fancy—to retort: what more natural? With every hand raised against him in the old land and the new, in the land of his hoped-for freedom, what more logical than that his should be turned against society that seems to exist only for his oppression? But the charge is not half true. Naturally the Bohemian loves peace, as he loves music and song. As someone has said: He does not seek war, but when attacked knows better how to die than how to surrender. The Czech is the Irishman of Central Europe, with all his genius and his strong passions, with the same bitter traditions of landlord-robbery, perpetuated here where he thought to forget them; like him ever and on principle in the opposition, "again the government" wherever he goes. Among such a people, ground by poverty until their songs have died in curses upon their oppressors, hopelessly isolated and ignorant of our language and our laws, it would not be hard for bad men at any time to lead a few astray. And this is what has been done. Yet, even with the occasional noise made by the few, the criminal statistics already alluded to quite dispose of the charge that they incline to turbulence and riot. So it is with the infidel propaganda, the legacy perhaps of the fierce contention through hundreds of years between Catholics and Protestants on Bohemia's soil, of bad faith and savage persecutions in the name of the Christian's God that disgrace its history. The Bohemian clergyman, who spoke for his people at the Christian Conference held in Chickering Hall[3] two years ago, took even stronger ground. "They are Roman Catholics by birth, infidels by necessity, and Protestants by history and inclination," he said. Yet he added his testimony in the same breath to the fact that, though the Freethinkers[4] had started two schools

3. A concert hall that opened in 1875 and stood at Fifth Avenue and Eighteenth Street. Meetings as well as musical events took place there.
4. Religious skeptics.

in the immediate neighborhood of his church to counteract its influence, his flock had grown in a few years from a mere handful at the start to proportions far beyond his hopes, gathering in both Anarchists and Freethinkers, and making good church members of them.

Thus the whole matter resolves itself once more into a question of education, all the more urgent because these people are poor, miserably poor almost to a man. "There is not," said one of them, who knew thoroughly what he was speaking of, "there is not one of them all, who, if he were to sell all he was worth to-morrow, would have money enough to buy a house and lot in the country."

13. The Color Line in New York

The color line must be drawn through the tenements to give the picture its proper shading. The landlord does the drawing, does it with an absence of pretence, a frankness of despotism, that is nothing if not brutal. The Czar of all the Russias is not more absolute upon his own soil than the New York landlord in his dealings with colored tenants. Where he permits them to live, they go; where he shuts the door, stay out. By his grace they exist at all in certain localities; his ukase banishes them from others. He accepts the responsibility, when laid at his door, with unruffled complacency. It is business, he will tell you. And it is. He makes the prejudice in which he traffics pay him well, and that, as he thinks it quite superfluous to tell you, is what he is there for.

That his pencil does not make quite as black a mark as it did, that the hand that wields it does not bear down as hard as only a short half dozen years ago, is the hopeful sign of an awakening public conscience under the stress of which the line shows signs of wavering. But for this the landlord deserves no credit. It has come, is coming about despite him. The line may not be wholly effaced while the name of the negro, alone among the world's races, is spelled with a small n. Natural selection[1] will have more or less to do beyond a doubt in every age with dividing the races; only so, it may be, can they work out together their highest destiny. But with the despotism that deliberately assigns to the defenceless Black the lowest level for the purpose of robbing him there that has nothing to do. Of such slavery, different only in degree from the other kind that held him as a chattel, to be sold or bartered at the will of his master, this century, if signs fail not, will see the end in New York.

Ever since the war New York has been receiving the overflow of colored population from the Southern cities. In the last decade this migration has grown to such proportions that it is estimated that our Blacks have quite doubled in number since the Tenth Census.[2] Whether the exchange has been of advantage to the negro may well be questioned. Trades of which he had practical control in his Southern home are not open to him here. I know that it may be answered that there is no industrial proscription of color; that it is a matter of choice. Perhaps so. At all events he does not choose then. How many colored carpenters or masons has anyone seen at work in New

1. One of the forces of evolution as proposed by Charles Darwin. Natural selection referred to the process by which the traits that allow individuals to better adapt to their environment, find mates, and produce viable offspring tend to increase in a population, whereas traits that make it more difficult to adapt decrease.
2. According to the 1880 census (the "Tenth Census"), the number of African Americans in New York was 19,653; the 1890 census (the Eleventh Census) had the number at 23,601.

A Black-and-Tan Dive in "Africa"

York? In the South there are enough of them and, if the testimony of the most intelligent of their people is worth anything, plenty of them have come here. As a matter of fact the colored man takes in New York, without a struggle, the lower level of menial service for which his past traditions and natural love of ease perhaps as yet fit him best. Even the colored barber is rapidly getting to be a thing of the past. Along shore, at any unskilled labor, he works unmolested; but he does not appear to prefer the job. His sphere thus defined, he naturally takes his stand among the poor, and in the homes of the poor. Until very recent times—the years since a change was wrought can be counted on the fingers of one hand—he was practically restricted in the choice of a home to a narrow section on the West Side, that nevertheless had a social top and bottom to it—the top in the tenements on the line of Seventh Avenue as far north as Thirty-second Street, where he was allowed to occupy the houses of unsavory reputation which the police had cleared and for which decent white tenants could not be found; the bottom in the vile rookeries of Thompson Street and South Fifth Avenue, the old "Africa" that is now fast becoming a modern Italy. To-day there are black colonies in Yorkville and Morrisania.[3] The encroachment of business and the Italian below, and the swelling of the population above, have been the chief agents in working out his second emancipation, a very real one, for with his cutting loose from the old tenements there has come a distinct and gratifying improvement in the tenant, that argues louder than theories or speeches the influence of vile surroundings in debasing the man. The colored citizen whom this year's census man found in his Ninety-ninth Street "flat" is a very different individual from the "nigger" his predecessor counted in the black-and-tan slums of Thompson and Sullivan Streets. There is no more clean and orderly community in New York than the new settlement of colored people that is growing up on the East Side from Yorkville to Harlem.

Cleanliness is the characteristic of the negro in his new surroundings, as it was his virtue in the old. In this respect he is immensely the superior of the lowest of the whites, the Italians and the Polish Jews, below whom he has been classed in the past in the tenant scale. Nevertheless, he has always had to pay higher rents than even these for the poorest and most stinted rooms. The exceptions I have come across, in which the rents, though high, have seemed more nearly on a level with what was asked for the same number and size of rooms in the average tenement, were in the case of tumble-down rookeries in which no one else would live, and were always coupled with the condition that the landlord should "make no repairs." It can readily be seen that his profits were scarcely curtailed by his "humanity." The reason advanced for this systematic robbery is that white people will not live in the same house with colored tenants, or even in a house recently occupied by negroes, and that consequently its selling value is injured. The prejudice undoubtedly exists, but it is not lessened by the house agents, who have set up the maxim "once a colored house, always a colored house."

There is method in the maxim, as shown by an inquiry made last year by the *Real Estate Record*. It proved agents to be practically unanimous in the endorsement of the negro as a clean, orderly, and "profitable" tenant. Here is the testimony of one of the largest real estate firms in the city: "We would rather have negro tenants in our poorest class of tenements than the lower

---

3. A neighborhood in the Upper East Side and one in the southwestern part of the Bronx, respectively.

grades of foreign white people. We find the former cleaner than the latter, and they do not destroy the property so much. We also get higher prices. We have a tenement on Nineteenth Street, where we get $10 for two rooms which we could not get more than $7.50 for from white tenants previously. We have a four-story tenement on our books on Thirty-third Street, between Sixth and Seventh Avenues, with four rooms per floor—a parlor, two bedrooms, and a kitchen. We get $20 for the first floor, $24 for the second, $23 for the third and $20 for the fourth, in all $87 or $1,044 per annum. The size of the building is only 21 + 55." Another firm declared that in a specified instance they had saved fifteen to twenty per cent. on the gross rentals since they changed from white to colored tenants. Still another gave the following case of a front and rear tenement that had formerly been occupied by tenants of a "low European type," who had been turned out on account of filthy habits and poor pay. The negroes proved cleaner, better, and steadier tenants. Instead, however, of having their rents reduced in consequence, the comparison stood as follows:

Rents under White Tenants			Rents under Colored Tenants		
		Per Month			Per Month
Front	1st floor (store, etc.)	$21	Front	1st floor (store, etc.)	$21
	2d "	13		2d "	14
	3d "	13		3d "	14
	4th " (and rear)	21		4th "	14
Rear	2d "	12	Rear	2d "	12
	3d "	12		3d "	13
	4th " (see front)	–		4th "	13
Rear	1st "	8	Rear	1st "	10
house	2d "	10	house	2d "	12
	3d "	9		3d "	11
	4th "	8		4th "	10
	Total	$127		Total	$144

An increased rental of $17 per month, or $204 a year, and an advance of nearly thirteen and one-half per cent. on the gross rental "in favor" of the colored tenant. Profitable, surely!

I have quoted these cases at length in order to let in light on the quality of this landlord despotism that has purposely confused the public mind, and for its own selfish ends is propping up a waning prejudice. It will be cause for congratulation if indeed its time has come at last. Within a year, I am told by one of the most intelligent and best informed of our colored citizens, there has been evidence, simultaneous with the colored hegira from the low down-town tenements, of a movement toward less exorbitant rents. I cannot pass from this subject without adding a leaf from my own experience that deserves a place in this record, though, for the credit of humanity, I hope as an extreme case. It was last Christmas that I had occasion to visit the home of an old colored woman in Sixteenth Street, as the almoner of generous friends out of town who wished me to buy her a Christmas dinner. The old woman lived in a wretched shanty, occupying two mean, dilapidated rooms at the top of a sort of hen-ladder that went by the name of stairs. For these she paid ten dollars a month out of her hard-earned wages as a scrub-woman. I did not find her in and, being informed that she was "at the agent's," went around to hunt her up. The agent's wife appeared, to report that Ann was out. Being in a hurry it occurred to me that I might save time by making her employer the purveyor of my friend's bounty, and proposed to entrust the money, two dollars, to her to be expended for Old Ann's bene-fit. She fell in with the suggestion at once, and confided to me in the full-ness of her heart that she liked the plan, inasmuch as "I generally find her a Christmas dinner myself, and this money—she owes Mr.———(her hus-band, the agent) a lot of rent." Needless to state that there was a change of programme then and there, and that Ann was saved from the sort of Christ-mas cheer that woman's charity would have spread before her. When I had the old soul comfortably installed in her own den, with a chicken and "fixin's" and a bright fire in her stove, I asked her how much she owed of her rent. Her answer was that she did not really owe anything, her month not being quite up, but that the amount yet unpaid was—two dollars!

Poverty, abuse, and injustice alike the negro accepts with imperturbable cheerfulness. His philosophy is of the kind that has no room for repining. Whether he lives in an Eighth Ward barrack or in a tenement with a brown-stone front and pretensions to the title of "flat," he looks at the sunny side of life and enjoys it. He loves fine clothes and good living a good deal more than he does a bank account. The proverbial rainy day it would be rank ingratitude, from his point of view, to look for when the sun shines unclouded in a clear sky. His home surroundings, except when he is utterly depraved, reflect his blithesome temper. The poorest negro housekeeper's room in New York is bright with gaily-colored prints of his beloved "Abe Linkum," General Grant, President Garfield, Mrs. Cleveland, and other national celebrities, and cheery with flowers and singing birds. In the art of putting the best foot fore-most, of disguising his poverty by making a little go a long way, our negro has no equal. When a fair share of prosperity is his, he knows how to make life and home very pleasant to those about him. Pianos and parlor furniture abound in the uptown homes of colored tenants and give them a very pros-perous air. But even where the wolf howls at the door, he makes a bold and gorgeous front. The amount of "style" displayed on fine Sundays on Sixth and Seventh Avenues by colored holiday-makers would turn a pessimist black with wrath. The negro's great ambition is to rise in the social scale to which his color has made him a stranger and an outsider, and he is quite willing to accept the shadow for the substance where that is the best he can get. The claw-hammer coat[4] and white tie of a waiter in a first-class summer hotel, with the chance of taking his ease in six months of winter, are to him the next best thing to mingling with the white quality he serves, on equal terms. His festive gatherings, pre-eminently his cake-walks,[5] at which a sugared and frosted cake is the proud prize of the couple with the most aristocratic step and carriage, are comic mixtures of elaborate ceremonial and the joyous abandon of the natural man. With all his ludicrous incongruities, his sensu-ality and his lack of moral accountability, his superstition and other faults that are the effect of temperament and of centuries of slavery, he has his emi-nently good points. He is loyal to the backbone, proud of being an American

---

4. An elegant black coat with swallowtails in the back.
5. A dance popular among African Americans that had its origins in slavery days; it featured couples linked at the elbows.

and of his new-found citizenship.[6] He is at least as easily moulded for good as for evil. His churches are crowded to the doors on Sunday nights when the colored colony turns out to worship. His people own church property in this city upon which they have paid half a million dollars out of the depth of their poverty, with comparatively little assistance from their white brethren. He is both willing and anxious to learn, and his intellectual status is distinctly improving. If his emotions are not very deeply rooted, they are at least sincere while they last, and until the tempter gets the upper hand again.

Of all the temptations that beset him, the one that troubles him and the police most is his passion for gambling. The game of policy is a kind of unlawful penny lottery specially adapted to his means, but patronized extensively by poor white players as well. It is the meanest of swindles, but reaps for its backers rich fortunes wherever colored people congregate. Between the fortune-teller and the policy shop,[7] closely allied frauds always, the wages of many a hard day's work are wasted by the negro; but the loss causes him few regrets. Penniless, but with undaunted faith in his ultimate "luck," he looks forward to the time when he shall once more be able to take a hand at "beating policy."[8] When periodically the negro's lucky numbers, 4–11–44,[9] come out on the slips of the alleged daily drawings, that are supposed to be held in some far-off Western town, intense excitement reigns in Thompson Street and along the Avenue, where someone is always the winner. An immense impetus is given then to the bogus business that has no existence outside of the cigar stores and candy shops where it hides from the law, save in some cunning Bowery "broker's" back office, where the slips are printed and the "winnings" apportioned daily with due regard to the backer's interests.

It is a question whether "Africa" has been improved by the advent of the Italian, with the tramp from the Mulberry Street Bend in his train. The moral turpitude of Thompson Street has been notorious for years, and the mingling of the three elements does not seem to have wrought any change for the better. The border-land where the white and black races meet in common debauch, the aptly-named black-and-tan saloon,[1] has never been debatable ground from a moral stand-point. It has always been the worst of the desperately bad. Than this commingling of the utterly depraved of both sexes, white and black, on such ground, there can be no greater abomination. Usually it is some foul cellar dive, perhaps run by the political "leader" of the district, who is "in with" the police. In any event it gathers to itself all the law-breakers and all the human wrecks within reach. When a fight breaks out during the dance a dozen razors are handy in as many boot-legs, and there is always a job for the surgeon and the ambulance. The black "tough" is as handy with the razor in a fight as his peaceably inclined brother is with it in pursuit of his honest trade.[2] As the Chinaman hides his knife in his sleeve and the Italian his stiletto in the bosom, so the negro goes to the ball with a razor in his boot-leg, and on occasion does as much execution with

---

6. The Fourteenth Amendment to the Constitution, ratified in 1868, provided for the extension of the rights of citizenship to former slaves and indeed to all blacks, who had been denied such rights as a result of the *Dred Scott* decision articulated before the onset of the Civil War.
7. Places where gambling, particularly the numbers game, took place.
8. Hitting the lucky number.
9. Lucky numbers in policy gaming.
1. Low-class saloons where white and black customers mingled. These establishments tended to be viewed as highly disreputable by the police and offended middle-class New Yorkers.
2. Many African American men made a living as barbers.

it as both of the others together. More than three-fourths of the business the police have with the colored people in New York arises in the black-and-tan district, now no longer fairly representative of their color.

I have touched briefly upon such facts in the negro's life as may serve to throw light on the social condition of his people in New York. If, when the account is made up between the races, it shall be claimed that he falls short of the result to be expected from twenty-five years of freedom, it may be well to turn to the other side of the ledger and see how much of the blame is borne by the prejudice and greed that have kept him from rising under a burden of responsibility to which he could hardly be equal. And in this view he may be seen to have advanced much farther and faster than before suspected, and to promise, after all, with fair treatment, quite as well as the rest of us, his white-skinned fellow-citizens, had any right to expect.

14. The Common Herd

There is another line not always so readily drawn in the tenements, yet the real boundary line of the Other Half: the one that defines the "flat." The law does not draw it at all, accounting all flats tenements without distinction. The health officer draws it from observation, lumping all those which in his judgment have nothing, or not enough, to give them claim upon the name, with the common herd, and his way is, perhaps, on the whole, the surest and best. The outside of the building gives no valuable clew. Brass and brown-stone go well sometimes with dense crowds and dark and dingy rooms; but the first attempt to enter helps draw the line with tolerable distinctness. A locked door is a strong point in favor of the flat. It argues that the first step has been taken to secure privacy, the absence of which is the chief curse of the tenement. Behind a locked door the hoodlum is not at home, unless there be a jailor in place of a janitor to guard it. Not that the janitor and the door-bell are infallible. There may be a tenement behind a closed door; but never a "flat" without it. The hall that is a highway for all the world by night and by day is the tenement's proper badge. The Other Half ever receives with open doors.

With this introduction we shall not seek it long anywhere in the city. Below Houston Street the door-bell in our age is as extinct as the dodo. East of Second Avenue, and west of Ninth Avenue as far up as the Park, it is practically an unknown institution. The nearer the river and the great workshops the more numerous the tenements. The kind of work carried on in any locality to a large extent determines their character. Skilled and well-paid labor puts its stamp on a tenement even in spite of the open door, and usually soon supplies the missing bell. Gas-houses,[1] slaughterhouses and the docks, that attract the roughest crowds and support the vilest saloons, invariably form slum-centres. The city is full of such above the line of Fourteenth Street, that is erroneously supposed by some to fence off the good from the bad, separate the chaff from the wheat. There is nothing below that line that can outdo in wickedness Hell's Kitchen,[2] in the region of three-cent

1. The area between Twenty-seventh and Fourteenth Streets on the East Side, housed numerous facilities that stored gas tanks. The neighborhood came to be known as the Gashouse District, and leaking gas gave it its characteristically foul smell.
2. An area on the west side of Manhattan, between Thirtieth Street and Fifty-ninth along the Hudson River, that abounded with slaughterhouses, warehouses, factories, and lumberyards. It had a reputation in the late nineteenth century as one of New York's worst slums.

The open door

whiskey, or its counterpoise at the other end of Thirty-ninth Street, on the East River, the home of the infamous Rag Gang. Cherry Street is not "tougher" than Battle Row in East Sixty-third Street, or "the village" at Twenty-ninth Street and First Avenue, where stores of broken bricks, ammunition for the nightly conflicts with the police, are part of the regulation outfit of every tenement. The Mulberry Street Bend is scarce dirtier than Little Italy in Harlem.[3] Even across the Harlem River, Frog Hollow challenges the admiration of the earlier slums for the boldness and pernicious activity of its home gang. There are enough of these sore spots. We shall yet have occasion to look into the social conditions of some of them; were I to draw a picture of them here as they are, the subject, I fear, would outgrow alike the limits of this book and the reader's patience.

It is true that they tell only one side of the story; that there is another to tell. A story of thousands of devoted lives, laboring earnestly to make the most of their scant opportunities for good; of heroic men and women striving patiently against fearful odds and by their very courage coming off victors in the battle with the tenement; of womanhood pure and undefiled. That it should blossom in such an atmosphere is one of the unfathomable mysteries of life. And yet it is not an uncommon thing to find sweet and innocent girls, singularly untouched by the evil around them, true wives and faithful mothers, literally "like jewels in a swine's snout," in the worst of the infamous barracks. It is the experience of all who have intelligently observed this side of life in a great city, not to be explained—unless on the theory of my friend, the priest in the Mulberry Street Bend, that inherent purity revolts instinctively from the naked brutality of vice as seen in the slums—but to be thankfully accepted as the one gleam of hope in an otherwise hopeless desert.

But the relief is not great. In the dull content of life bred on the tenement-house dead level there is little to redeem it, or to claim apprehension for a society that has nothing better to offer its toilers; while the patient efforts of

3. East Harlem housed a sizable Italian population; 115th Street was at the heart of the community.

the lives finally attuned to it to render the situation tolerable, and the very success of these efforts, serve only to bring out in stronger contrast the general gloom of the picture by showing how much farther they might have gone with half a chance. Go into any of the "respectable" tenement neighborhoods—the fact that there are not more than two saloons on the corner, nor over three or four in the block will serve as a fair

Bird's-eye view of an East Side tenement block (from a drawing by Charles F. Wingate, Esq.)

guide—where live the great body of hard-working Irish and German immigrants and their descendants, who accept naturally the conditions of tenement life, because for them there is nothing else in New York; be with and among its people until you understand their ways, their aims, and the quality of their ambitions, and unless you can content yourself with the scriptural promise that the poor we shall have always with us, or with the menagerie view that, if fed, they have no cause of complaint, you shall come away agreeing with me that, humanly speaking, life there does not seem worth the living. Take at random one of these uptown tenement blocks, not of the worst nor yet of the most prosperous kind, within hail of what the newspapers would call a "fine residential section." These houses were built since the last cholera scare made people willing to listen to reason. The block is not like the one over on the East Side in which I actually lost my way once. There were thirty or forty rear houses in the heart of it, three or four on every lot, set at all sorts of angles, with odd, winding passages, or no passage at all, only "runways" for the thieves and toughs of the neighborhood. These yards are clear. There is air there, and it is about all there is. The view between brick walls outside is that of a stony street; inside, of rows of unpainted board fences, a bewildering maze of clothes-post and lines; under-foot, a desert of brown, hard-baked soil from which every blade of grass, every stray weed, every speck of green, has been trodden out, as must inevitably be every gentle thought and aspiration above the mere wants of the body in those whose moral natures such home surroundings are to nourish. In self-defence, you know, all life eventually accommodates itself to its environment, and human life is no exception. Within the house there is nothing to supply the want thus left unsatisfied. Tenement-houses have no æsthetic resources. If any are to be brought to bear on them, they must come from the outside. There is the common hall with doors opening softly on every landing as the strange step is heard on the stairs, the air-shaft that seems always so busy letting out foul stenches from below that it has no time to earn its name by bringing down fresh air, the squeaking pumps that hold no water, and the rent that is never less than one week's wages out of the four, quite as often half of the family earnings.

Why complete the sketch? It is drearily familiar already. Such as it is, it is the frame in which are set days, weeks, months, and years of unceasing toil, just able to fill the mouth and clothe the back. Such as it is, it is the world, and all of it, to which these weary workers return nightly to feed heart and brain after wearing out the body at the bench, or in the shop. To it come the

young with their restless yearnings, perhaps to pass on the threshold one of the daughters of sin, driven to the tenement by the police when they raided her den, sallying forth in silks and fine attire after her day of idleness. These in their coarse garments—girls with the love of youth for beautiful things, with this hard life before them—who shall save them from the tempter? Down in the street the saloon, always bright and gay, gathering to itself all the cheer of the block, beckons the boys. In many such blocks the census-taker found two thousand men, women, and children, and over, who called them home.

The picture is faithful enough to stand for its class wherever along both rivers the Irish brogue is heard. As already said, the Celt falls most readily victim to tenement influences since shanty-town and its original free-soilers have become things of the past. If he be thrifty and shrewd his progress thenceforward is along the plane of the tenement, on which he soon assumes to manage without improving things. The German has an advantage over his Celtic neighbor in his strong love for flowers, which not all the tenements on the East Side have power to smother. His garden goes with him wherever he goes. Not that it represents any high moral principle in the man; rather perhaps the capacity for it. He turns his saloon into a shrubbery as soon as his back-yard. But wherever he puts it in a tenement block its does the work of a dozen police clubs. In proportion as its spreads the neighborhood takes on a more orderly character. As the green dies out of the landscape and increases in political importance, the police find more to do. Where it disappears altogether from sight, lapsing into a mere sentiment, police-beats are shortened and the force patrols double at night. Neither the man nor the sentiment is wholly responsible for this. It is the tenement unadorned that is. The changing of Tompkins Square from a sand lot into a beautiful park put an end for good and all to the "Bread or Blood" riots of which it used to be the scene, and transformed a nest of dangerous agitators into a harmless, beer-craving band of Anarchists.[4] They have scarcely been heard of since. Opponents of the small parks system as a means of relieving the congested population of tenement districts, please take note.

With the first hot night in June police despatches, that record the killing of men and women by rolling off roofs and window-sills while asleep, announce that the time of greatest suffering among the poor is at hand. It is in hot weather, when life indoors is well-nigh unbearable with cooking, sleeping, and working, all crowded into the small rooms together, that the tenement expands, reckless of all restraint. Then a strange and picturesque life moves upon the flat roofs. In the day and early evening mothers air their

4. The area of Tompkins Square, between Seventh and Tenth Streets, and Avenues A and B, on the East Side, had been set aside in the 1830s as a place for military parades. It later became the site of numerous political rallies and gatherings. A rally in 1875, at the height of the economic depression, brought the police out to the square to confront the protesters. Other rallies took place in the tumultuous summer of 1877, when large numbers of the unemployed converged there, By the 1880s Tompkins Square had become a municipal park under the administration of the city.

babies there, the boys fly their kites from the house-tops, undismayed by police regulations, and the young men and girls court and pass the growler. In the stifling July nights, when the big barracks are like fiery furnaces, their very walls giving out absorbed heat, men and women lie in restless, sweltering rows, panting for air and sleep. Then every truck in the street, every crowded fire-escape, becomes a bedroom, infinitely preferable to any the house affords. A cooling shower on such a night is hailed as a heaven-sent blessing in a hundred thousand homes.

Life in the tenements in July and August spells death to an army of little ones whom the doctor's skill is powerless to save. When the white badge of mourning[5] flutters from every second door, sleepless mothers walk the streets in the gray of the early dawn, trying to stir a cooling breeze to fan the brow of the sick baby. There is no sadder sight than this patient devotion striving against fearfully hopeless odds. Fifty "summer doctors,"[6] especially trained to this work, are then sent into the tenements by the Board of Health, with free advice and medicine for the poor. Devoted women follow in their track with care and nursing for the sick. Fresh-air excursions run daily out of New York on land and water; but despite all efforts the grave-diggers in Calvary[7] work over-time, and little coffins are stacked mountain-high on the deck of the Charity Commissioners' boat when it makes its semi-weekly trips to the city cemetery.

Under the most favorable circumstance, an epidemic, which the well-to-do can afford to make light of as a thing to be got over or avoided by reasonable care, is excessively fatal among the children of the poor, by reason of the practical impossibility of isolating the patient in a tenement. The measles, ordinarily a harmless disease, furnishes a familiar example. Tread it ever so lightly on the avenues, in the tenements it kills right and left. Such an epidemic ravaged three crowded blocks in Elizabeth Street on the heels of the grippe[8] last winter, and, when it had spent its fury, the death-maps in the bureau of Vital Statistics looked as if a black hand had been laid across those blocks, overshadowing in part the contiguous tenements in Mott Street, and with the thumb covering a particularly packed settlement of half a dozen houses in Mulberry Street. The track of the epidemic through these teeming barracks was as clearly defined as the track of a tornado through a forest district. There were houses in which as many as eight little children had died in five months. The records showed that respiratory diseases, the common heritage of the grippe and the measles, had caused death in most cases, discovering the trouble to be, next to the inability to check the contagion in those crowds, in the poverty of the parents and the wretched home conditions that made proper care of the sick impossible. The fact was emphasized by the occurrence here and there of a few isolated deaths from diphtheria and scarlet fever. In the case of these diseases, considered more dangerous to the public health, the health officers exercised summary powers of removal to the hospital where proper treatment could be had, and the result was a low death-rate.

These were the tenements of the tall, modern type. A little more than a year ago, when a census was made of the tenements and compared with the mortality tables, no little surprise and congratulation was caused by the discovery

---

5. A sign posted on the door of an apartment in which someone had died.
6. Established in 1876, the Summer Corps enlisted doctors during the summer months, August in particular, to see to the medical needs of the poor.
7. A Catholic cemetery in Queens in which most of the interred came from poor immigrant communities, the Irish in particular.
8. Influenza

that as the buildings grew taller the death rate fell. The reason is plain, though the reverse had been expected by most people. The biggest tenements have been built in the last ten years of sanitary reform rule, and have been brought, in all but the crowding, under its laws. The old houses that from private dwellings were made into tenements, or were run up to house the biggest crowds in defiance of every moral and physical law, can be improved by no device short of demolition. They will ever remain the worst.

That ignorance plays its part, as well as poverty and bad hygienic surroundings, in the sacrifice of life is of course inevitable. They go usually hand in hand. A message came one day last spring summoning me to a Mott Street tenement in which lay a child dying from some unknown disease. With the "charity doctor" I found the patient on the top floor stretched upon two chairs in a dreadfully stifling room. She was gasping in the agony of peritonitis that had already written its death-sentence on her wan and pinched face. The whole family, father, mother, and four ragged children, sat around looking on with the stony resignation of helpless despair that had long since given up the fight against fate as useless. A glance around the wretched room left no doubt as to the cause of the child's condition. "Improper nourishment," said the doctor, which, translated to suit the place, meant starvation. The father's hands were crippled from lead poisoning. He had not been able to work for a year. A contagious disease of the eyes, too long neglected, had made the mother and one of the boys nearly blind. The children cried with hunger. They had not broken their fast that day, and it was then near noon. For months the family had subsisted on two dollars a week from the priest, and a few loaves and a piece of corned beef which the sisters sent them on Saturday. The doctor gave direction for the treatment of the child, knowing that it was possible only to alleviate its sufferings until death should end them, and left some money for food for the rest. An hour later, when I returned, I found them feeding the dying child with ginger ale, bought for two cents a bottle at the pedlar's cart down the street. A pitying neighbor had proposed it as the one thing she could think of as likely to make the child forget its misery. There was enough in the bottle to go round to the rest of the family. In fact, the wake had already begun; before night it was under way in dead earnest.

Every once in a while a case of downright starvation gets into the newspapers and makes a sensation. But this is the exception. Were the whole truth known, it would come home to the community with a shock that would rouse it to a more serious effort than the spasmodic undoing of its purse-strings. I am satisfied from my own observation that hundreds of men, women, and children are every day slowly starving to death in the tenements with my medical friend's complaint of "improper nourishment." Within a single week I have had this year three cases of insanity, provoked directly by poverty and want. One was that of a mother who in the middle of the night got up to murder her child, who was crying for food; another was the case of an Elizabeth Street truck-driver whom the newspapers never heard of. With a family to provide for, he had been unable to work for many months. There was neither food, nor a scrap of anything upon which money could be raised, left in the house; his mind gave way under the combined physical and mental suffering. In the third case I was just in time with the police to prevent the madman from murdering his whole family. He had the sharpened hatchet in his pocket when we seized him. He was an Irish laborer, and had been working in the sewers until the poisonous gases destroyed his health. Then he was laid off, and scarcely anything had been coming in all winter but the oldest child's earnings as cash-girl in a store, $2.50 a week. There were seven children to provide for, and the rent of the Mulberry Street attic in which the family lived was $10 a month. They had borrowed as long as anybody had a cent to lend. When at last the man got an odd job that would just buy the children bread, the week's wages only served to measure the depth of their misery. "It came in so on the tail-end of everything," said his wife in telling the story, with unconscious eloquence. The outlook worried him through sleepless nights until it destroyed his reason. In his madness he had only one conscious thought: that the town should not take the children. "Better that I take care of them myself," he repeated to himself as he ground the axe to an edge. Help came in abundance from many almost as poor as they when the desperate straits of the family became known through his arrest. The readiness of the poor to share what little they have with those who have even less is one of the few moral virtues of the tenements. Their enormous crowds touch elbow in a closeness of sympathy that is scarcely to be understood out of them, and has no parallel except among the unfortunate women whom the world scorns as outcasts. There is very little professed sentiment about it to draw a senti-mental tear from the eye of romantic philanthropy. The hard fact is that the instinct of self-preservation impels them to make common cause against the common misery.

No doubt intemperance bears a large share of the blame for it; judging from the stand-point of the policeman perhaps the greater share. Two such entries as I read in the police returns on successive days last March, of mothers in West Side tenements, who in their drunken sleep lay upon and killed their infants, go far to support such a position. And they are far from uncommon. But my experience has shown me another view of it, a view which the last report of the Society for Improving the Condition of the Poor seems more than half inclined to adopt in allotting to "intemperance the cause of distress, or distress the cause of intemperance," forty per cent. of the cases it is called upon to deal with. Even if it were all true, I should still load over upon the tenement the heaviest responsibility. A single factor, the scandalous scarcity of water in the hot summer when the thirst of the million tenants must be quenched, if not in that in something else, has in the past years more than all other causes encouraged drunkenness among the poor. But to my mind there is a closer connection between the wages of the tenements and the vices and improvidence of those who dwell in them than, with the guilt of the tenement upon out heads, we are willing to admit even to ourselves. Weak tea with a dry crust is not a diet to nurse moral strength. Yet how much better might the fare be expected to be in the family of this "widow with seven children, very energetic and prudent"—I quote again from the report of the Society for the Improvement of the Con-dition of the Poor—whose "eldest girl was employed as a learner in a tailor's shop at small wages, and one boy had a place as 'cash' in a store. There were two other little boys who sold papers and sometimes earned one dollar. The mother finishes pantaloons and can do three pairs in a day, thus earning thirty-nine cents. Here is a family of eight persons with rent to pay and an income of less than six dollars a week."

And yet she was better off in point of pay than this Sixth Street mother, who "had just brought home four pairs of pants to finish, at seven cents a pair. She was required to put the canvas in the bottom, basting and sewing three times around; to put the linings in the waistbands; to tack three pockets, three corners to each; to put on two stays and eight buttons, and make six buttonholes; to put the buckle on the back strap and sew on the ticket, all for seven cents." Better off than the "church-going mother of six children," and with a husband sick to death, who to support the family made shirts, averaging an income of one dollar and twenty cents a week, while her oldest girl, aged thirteen, was "employed downtown cutting out Hamburg edgings at one dollar and a half a week—two and a half cents per hour for ten hours of steady labor—making the total income of the family two dollars and seventy cents per week." Than the Harlem woman, who was "making a brave effort to support a sick husband and two children by taking in washing at thirty-five cents for the lot of fourteen large pieces, finding coal, soap, starch, and bluing herself, rather than depend on charity in any form." Specimen wages of the tenements these, seemingly inconsistent with the charge of improvidence.

But the connection on second thought is not obscure. There is nothing in the prospect of a sharp, unceasing battle for the bare necessaries of life to encourage looking ahead, everything to discourage the effort. Improvidence and wastefulness are natural results. The instalment plan secures to the tenant who lives from hand to mouth his few comforts; the evil day of reckoning is put off till a to-morrow that may never come. When it does come, with failure to pay and the loss of hard-earned dollars, it simply adds another hardship to a life measured from the cradle by such incidents. The children soon catch the spirit of this sort of thing. I remember once calling at the home of a poor washer-woman living in an East Side tenement, and finding the door locked. Some children in the hallway stopped their play and eyed me attentively while I knocked. The biggest girl volunteered the information that Mrs. Smith was out; but while I was thinking of how I was to get a message to her, the child put a question of her own: "Are you the spring man or the clock man?" When I assured her that I was neither one nor the other, but had brought work for her mother, Mrs. Smith, who had been hiding from the instalment collector, speedily appeared.

Perhaps of all the disheartening experiences of those who have devoted lives of unselfish thought and effort, and their number is not so small as often supposed, to the lifting of this great load, the indifference of those they would help is the most puzzling. They will not be helped. Dragged by main force out of their misery, they slip back again on the first opportunity, seemingly content only in the old rut. The explanation was supplied by two women of my acquaintance in an Elizabeth Street tenement, whom the city missionaries had taken from their wretched hovel and provided with work and a decent home somewhere in New Jersey. In three weeks they were back, saying that they preferred their dark rear room to the stumps out in the country. But to me the oldest, the mother, who had struggled along with her daughter making cloaks at half a dollar apiece, twelve long years since the daughter's husband was killed in a street accident and the city took the children, made the bitter confession: "We do get so kind o' downhearted living this way, that we have to be where something is going on, or we just can't stand it." And there was sadder pathos to me in her words than in the whole long story of their struggle with poverty; for unconsciously she voiced the sufferings of thousands misjudged by a happier world, deemed vicious because they are human and unfortunate.

In Poverty Gap, West Twenty-Fourth St. An English Coal-Heaver's Home

[*On the photograph, (p. 99), of the English coal-heaver's home.*] *Suspicions of murder, in the case of a woman who was found dead, covered with bruises, after a day's running fight with her husband, in which the beer-jug had been the bone of contention, brought me to this house, a ramshackle tenement on the tail-end of a lot over near the North River docks. The family in the picture lived above the rooms where the dead woman lay on a bed of straw, overrun by rats, and had been uninterested witnesses of the affray that was an every-day occurrence in the house. A patched and shaky stairway led up to their one bare and miserable room, in comparison with which a white-washed prison-cell seemed a real palace. A heap of old rags, in which the baby slept serenely, served as the common sleeping-bunk of father, mother, and children—two bright and pretty girls, singularly out of keeping in their clean, if coarse, dresses, with their surroundings. The father, a slow going, honest English coal-heaver, earned on the average five dollars a week, "when work was fairly brisk," at the docks. But there were long seasons when it was very "slack," he said, doubtfully. Yet the prospect did not seem to discourage them. The mother, a pleasant-faced woman, was cheerful, even light-hearted. Her smile seemed the most sadly hopeless of all in the utter wretchedness of the place, cheery though it was meant to be and really was. It seemed doomed to certain disappointment—the one thing there that was yet to know a greater depth of misery.*

It is a popular delusion, encouraged by all sorts of exaggerated stories when nothing more exciting demands public attention, that there are more evictions in the tenements of New York every year "than in all Ireland." I am not sure that it is doing much for the tenant to upset this fallacy. To my mind, to be put out of a tenement would be the height of good luck. The fact is, however, that evictions are not nearly as common in New York as supposed. The reason is that in the civil courts, the judges of which are elected in their districts, the tenant-voter has solid ground to stand upon at last. The law that takes his side to start with is usually twisted to the utmost to give him time and save him expense. In the busiest East Side court, that has been very appropriately dubbed the "Poor Man's Court,"[9] fully five thousand dispossess warrants are issued in a year, but probably not fifty evictions take place in the district. The landlord has only one vote, while there may be forty voters hiring his rooms in the house, all of which the judge takes into careful account as elements that have a direct bearing on the case. And so they have—on his case. There are sad cases, just as there are "rounders" who prefer to be moved at the landlord's expense and save the rent, but the former at least are unusual enough to attract more than their share of attention.

If his very poverty compels the tenant to live at a rate if not in a style that would beggar a Vanderbilt,[1] paying four prices for everything he needs, from his rent and coal down to the smallest item in his house keeping account, fashion, no less inexorable in the tenements than on the avenue, exacts of him that he must die in a style that is finally and utterly ruinous. The habit of expensive funerals—I know of no better classifica-

9. The Essex Market Court, at 69 Essex Street (the Third District Court).
1. Cornelius Vanderbilt (1794–1877), one America's wealthiest individuals, built his fortune in railroads. At his death, he left a fortune of $100 million.

tion for it than along with the
opium habit and similar grievous plagues of mankind—is a
distinctively Irish inheritance,
but it has taken root among all
classes of tenement dwellers,
curiously enough most firmly
among the Italians, who have
taken amazingly to the funeral
coach, perhaps because it furnishes the one opportunity
of their lives for a really grand
turn-out with a free ride
thrown in. It is not at all
uncommon to find the hoards
of a whole lifetime of hard
work and self-denial squan-

Dispossessed

dered on the empty show of a ludicrous funeral parade and a display of
flowers that ill comports with the humble life it is supposed to exalt. It is
easier to understand the wake as a sort of consolation cup for the survivors
for whom there is—as one of them, doubtless a heathenish pessimist, put
it to me once—"no such luck." The press and the pulpit have denounced
the wasteful practice that often entails bitter want upon the relatives of the
one buried with such pomp, but with little or no apparent result. Rather,
the undertaker's business prospers more than ever in the tenements since
the genius of politics has seen its way clear to make capital out of the dead
voter as well as of the living, by making him the means of a useful "show
of strength" and count of noses.

One free excursion awaits young and old whom bitter poverty has denied
the poor privilege of the choice of the home in death they were denied in

The trench in the Potter's Field

life, the ride up the Sound to the Potter's Field,[2] charitably styled the City Cemetery. But even there they do not escape their fate. In the common trench of the Poor Burying Ground they lie packed three stories deep, shoulder to shoulder, crowded in death as they were in life, to "save space"; for even on that desert island the ground is not for the exclusive possession of those who cannot afford to pay for it. There is an odd coincidence in this, that year by year the lives that are begun in the gutter, the little nameless waifs whom the police pick up and the city adopts as its wards, are balanced by the even more forlorn lives that are ended in the river. I do not know how or why it happens, or that it is more than a mere coincidence. But there it is. Year by year the balance is struck—a few more, a few less—substantially the same when the record is closed.

15. The Problem of the Children

The problem of the children becomes, in these swarms, to the last degree perplexing. Their very number makes one stand aghast. I have already given instances of the packing of the child population in East Side tenements. They might be continued indefinitely until the array would be enough to startle any community. For, be it remembered, these children with the training they receive—or do not receive—with the instincts they inherit and absorb in their growing up, are to be our future rulers, if our theory of government is worth anything. More than a working majority of our voters now register from the tenements. I counted the other day the little ones, up to ten years or so, in a Bayard Street tenement that for a yard has a triangular space in the centre with sides fourteen or fifteen feet long, just room enough for a row of ill-smelling closets at the base of the triangle and a hydrant at the apex. There was about as much light in this "yard" as in the average cellar. I gave up my self-imposed task in despair when I had counted one hundred and twenty-eight in forty families. Thirteen I had missed, or not found in. Applying the average for the forty to the whole fifty-three, the house contained one hundred and seventy children. It is not the only time I have had to give up such census work. I have in mind an alley—an inlet rather to a row of rear tenements—that is either two or four feet wide according as the wall of the crazy old building that gives on it bulges out or in. I tried to count the children that swarmed there, but could not. Sometimes I have doubted that anybody knows just how many there are about. Bodies of drowned children turn up in the rivers right along in summer whom no one seems to know anything about. When last spring some workmen, while moving a pile of lumber on a North River[1] pier, found under the last plank the body of a little lad crushed to death, no one had missed a boy, though his parents afterward turned up. The truant officer assuredly does not know, though he spends his life trying to find out, somewhat illogically perhaps since the department that employs him admits that thousands of poor children are crowded out of the schools year by year for want of room. There was a big tenement in the Sixth Ward, now happily appropriated by the beneficent spirit of business that blots out so many foul spots in New York—it figured not long ago in the official reports as "an out-

---

2. Place for the burial of the very poor and the unknown.
1. The segment of the Hudson River flowing between the Palisades and New York Bay.

and-out hogpen"—that had a record of one hundred and two arrests in four years among its four hundred and seventy-eight tenants, fifty-seven of them for drunken and disorderly conduct. I do not know how many children there were in it, but the inspector reported that he found only seven in the whole house who owned that they went to school. The rest gathered all the instruction they received running for beer for their elders. Some of them claimed the "flat" as their home as a mere matter of form. They slept in the streets at night. The official came upon a little party of four drinking beer out of the cover of a milk-can in the hallway. They were of the seven good boys and proved their claim to the title by offering him some.

The old question, what to do with the boy, assumes a new and serious phase in the tenements. Under the best conditions found there, it is not easily answered. In nine cases out of ten he would make an excellent mechanic, if trained early to work at a trade, for he is neither dull nor slow, but the short-sighted despotism of the trades unions has practically closed that avenue to him. Trade-schools, however excellent, cannot supply the opportunity thus denied him, and at the outset the boy stands condemned by his own to low and ill-paid drudgery, held down by the hand that of all should labor to raise him. Home, the greatest factor of all in the training of the young, means nothing to him but a pigeon-hole in a coop along with so many other human animals. Its influence is scarcely of the elevating kind, if it have any. The very games at which he takes a hand in the street become polluting in its atmosphere. With no steady hand to guide him, the boy takes naturally to idle ways. Caught in the street by the truant officer, or by agents of the Children's Societies, peddling, perhaps, or begging, to help out the family resources, he runs the risk of being sent to a reformatory, where contact with vicious boys older than himself soon develops the latent possibilities for evil that lie hidden in him. The city has no Truant Home in which to keep him, and all efforts of the children's friends to enforce school attendance are paralyzed by this want. The risk of the reformatory is too great. What is done in the end is to let him take chances— with the chances all against him. The result is the rough young savage, familiar from the street. Rough as he is, if any one doubt that this child of common clay have in him the instinct of beauty, of love for the ideal of which his life has no embodiment, let him put the matter to the test. Let him take into a tenement block a handful of flowers from the fields and watch the brightened faces, the sudden abandonment of play and fight that go ever hand in hand where there is no elbow-room, the wild entreaty for "posies," the eager love with which the little messengers of peace are shielded, once possessed; then let him change his mind. I have seen an armful of daisies keep the peace of a block better than a policeman and his club, seen instincts awaken under their gentle appeal, whose very existence the soil in which they grew made seem a mockery. I have not forgotten the deputation of ragamuffins from a Mulberry Street alley that knocked at my office door one morning on a mysterious expedition for flowers, not for themselves, but for "a lady," and having obtained what they wanted, trooped off to bestow them, a ragged and dirty little band, with a solemnity that was quite unusual. It was not until an old man called the next day to thank me for the flowers that I found out they had decked the bier of a pauper, in the dark rear room where she lay waiting in her pine-board coffin for the city's hearse. Yet, as I knew, that dismal alley with its bare brick walls, between which no sun ever rose or set, was the world of those children. It filled their young lives. Probably not one of them had ever been out of the sight of it. They were too dirty, too ragged, and too generally disreputable, too well hidden in their slum besides, to come into line with the Fresh Air summer boarders.

With such human instincts and cravings, forever unsatisfied, turned into a haunting curse; with appetite ground to keenest edge by a hunger that is never fed, the children of the poor grow up in joyless homes to lives of wearisome toil that claims them at an age when the play of their happier fellows has but just begun. Has a yard of turf been laid and a vine been coaxed to grow within their reach, they are banished and barred out from it as from a heaven that is not for such as they. I came upon a couple of youngsters in a Mulberry Street yard a while ago that were chalking on the fence their first lesson in "writin'." And this is what they wrote: "Keeb of te Grass." They had it by heart, for there was not, I verily believe, a green sod within a quarter of a mile. Home to them is an empty name. Pleasure? A gentleman once catechized a ragged class in a down-town public school on this point, and recorded the result: Out of forty-eight boys twenty had never seen the Brooklyn Bridge that was scarcely five minutes' walk away, three only had been in Central Park, fifteen had known the joy of a ride in a horse-car. The street, with its ash-barrels and its dirt, the river that runs foul with mud, are their domain. What training they receive is picked up there. And they are apt pupils. If the mud and the dirt are easily reflected in their lives, what wonder? Scarce half-grown, such lads as these confront the world with the challenge to give them their due, too long withheld, or ————. Our jails supply the answer to the alternative.

A little fellow who seemed clad in but a single rag was among the flotsam and jetsam stranded at Police Headquarters one day last summer. No one knew where he came from or where he belonged. The boy himself knew as little about it as anybody, and was the least anxious to have light shed on the subject after he had spent a night in the matron's nursery. The discovery that beds were provided for boys to sleep in there, and that he could have "a whole egg" and three slices of bread for breakfast put him on the best of terms with the world in general, and he decided that Headquarters was "a bully place." He sang "McGinty"[2] all through, with Tenth Avenue variations, for the police, and then settled down to the serious business of giving an account of himself. The examination went on after this fashion:

"Where do you go to church, my boy?"

"We don't have no clothes to go to church." And indeed his appearance, as he was, in the door of any New York church would have caused a sensation.

"Well, where do you go to school, then?"

"I don't go to school," with a snort of contempt.

"Where do you buy your bread?"

"We don't buy no bread; we buy beer," said the boy, and it was eventually the saloon that led the police as a landmark to his "home." It was worthy of the boy. As he had said, his only bed was a heap of dirty straw on the floor, his daily diet a crust in the morning, nothing else.

2. "Down Went McGinty," by Joseph Flynn, was a popular song of the 1880s. The chorus repeated: "Down went McGinty to the bottom of the sea, dressed in his best suit of clothes."

Into the rooms of the Children's Aid Society were led two little girls whose father had "busted up the house" and put them on the street after their mother died. Another, who was turned out by her step-mother "because she had five of her own and could not afford to keep her," could not remember ever having been in church or Sunday-school, and only knew the name of Jesus through hearing people swear by it. She had no idea what they meant. These were specimens of the overflow from the tenements of our home-heathen that are growing up in New York's streets to-day, while tender hearted men and women are busying themselves with the socks and the hereafter of well-fed little Hottentots[3] thousands of miles away. According to Canon Taylor, of York, one hundred and nine missionaries in the four fields of Persia, Palestine, Arabia, and Egypt spent one year and sixty thousand dollars in converting one little heathen girl. If there is nothing the matter with those missionaries, they might come to New York with a good deal better prospect of success.

By those who lay flattering unction to their souls in the knowledge that to-day New York has, at all events, no brood of the gutters of tender years that can be homeless long unheeded, let it be remembered well through what effort this judgment has been averted. In thirty-seven years the Children's Aid Society, that came into existence as an emphatic protest against the tenement corruption of the young, has sheltered quite three hundred thousand outcast, homeless, and orphaned children in its lodging-houses, and has found homes in the West for seventy thousand that had none. Doubtless, as a mere stroke of finance, the five millions and a half thus spent were a wiser investment than to have let them grow up thieves and thugs. In the last fifteen years of this tireless battle for the safety of the State the intervention of the Society for the Prevention of Cruelty to Children has been invoked for 138,891 little ones; it has thrown its protection around more than twenty-five thousand helpless children, and has convicted nearly sixteen thousand wretches of child-beating and abuse. Add to this the standing army of fifteen thousand dependent children in New York's asylums and institutions, and some idea is gained of the crop that is garnered day by day in the tenements, of the enormous force employed to check their inroads on our social life, and of the cause for apprehension that would exist did their efforts flag for ever so brief a time.

Nothing is now better understood than that the rescue of the children is the key to the problem of city poverty, as presented for our solution to-day; that a character may be formed where to reform it would be a hopeless task. The concurrent testimony of all who have to undertake it at a later stage: that the young are naturally neither vicious nor hardened, simply weak and undeveloped, except by the bad influences of the street, makes this duty all the more urgent as well as hopeful. Helping hands are held out on every side. To private charity the municipality leaves the entire care of its proletariat of tender years, lulling its conscience to sleep with liberal appropriations of money to foot the bills. Indeed, it is held by those whose opinions are entitled to weight that it is far too liberal a paymaster for its own best interests and those of its wards. It deals with the evil in the seed to a limited extent in gathering in the outcast babies from the streets. To the ripe fruit

---

3. An African tribe that called itself the Khoikhoi. The term *Hottentots* referred in the nineteenth century to the lowest level of civilization possible.

the gates of its prisons, its reformatories, and its workhouses are opened wide the year round. What the showing would be at this end of the line were it not for the barriers wise charity has thrown across the broad highway to ruin—is building day by day—may be measured by such results as those quoted above in the span of a single life.

16. Waifs of the City's Slums

First among these barriers is the Foundling Asylum.[1] It stands at the very outset of the waste of life that goes on in a population of nearly two millions of people; powerless to prevent it, though it gather in the outcasts by night and by day. In a score of years an army of twenty-five thousand of these forlorn little waifs have cried out from the streets of New York in arraignment of a Christian civilization under the blessings of which the instinct of motherhood even was smothered by poverty and want. Only the poor abandon their children. The stories of richly-dressed foundlings that are dished up in the newspapers at intervals are pure fiction. Not one instance of even a well-dressed infant having been picked up in the streets is on record. They came in rags, a newspaper often the only wrap, semi-occasionally one in a clean slip with some evidence of loving care; a little slip of paper pinned on, perhaps, with some message as this I once read, in a woman's trembling hand: "Take care of Johnny, for God's sake. I cannot." But even that is the rarest of all happenings.

The city divides with the Sisters of Charity[2] the task of gathering them in. The real foundlings, the children of the gutter that are picked up by the police, are the city's wards. In midwinter, when the poor shiver in their homes, and in the dog-days when the fierce heat and foul air of the tenements smother their babies by thousands, they are found, something three and four in a night, in hallways, in areas and on the doorsteps of the rich, with whose comfort in luxurious homes the wretched mother somehow connects her own misery. Perhaps, as the drowning man clutches at a straw, she hopes that these happier hearts may have love to spare even for her little one. In this she is mistaken. Unauthorized babies especially are not popular in the abodes of the wealthy. It never happens outside of the story-books that a baby so deserted finds home and friends at once. Its career, though rather more official, is less romantic, and generally brief. After a night spent at Police Headquarters it travels up to the Infants' Hospital on Randall's Island[3] in the morning, fitted out with a cumber and a bottle, that seldom see much wear before they are laid aside for a fresh recruit. Few outcast babies survive their desertion long. Murder is the true name of the mother's crime in eight cases out of ten. Of 508 babies received at the Randall's Island Hospital last year 333 died, 65.55 percent. But of the 508 only 170 were picked up in the streets, and among these the mortality was much greater, probably nearer ninety per cent., if the truth were told. The rest

---

1. Founded in 1869 by the American Sisters of Charity (see next note), the New York Foundling Hospital took care of illegitimate infants.
2. Established in 1809 by Elizabeth Bayley Seton, this was the first religious order founded in the United States. The order built the Roman Catholic Orphan Asylum in New York in 1817, establishing its long-standing interest in the care of poor children.
3. Located at the confluence point of the East and Harlem Rivers. The city purchased the island in 1830 and established on it a cemetery for the indigent, an almshouse, a reformatory, and the Idiot's and Children's Hospital.

were born in the hospitals. The high mortality among the foundlings is not to be marvelled at. The wonder is, rather, that any survive. The stormier the night, the more certain is the police nursery to echo with the feeble cries of abandoned babes. Often they came half dead from exposure. One live baby came in a little pine coffin which a policeman found an inhuman wretch trying to bury in an up-town lot. But many do not live to be officially registered as a charge upon the county. Seventy-two dead babies were picked up in the streets last year. Some of them were doubtless put out by very poor parents to save funeral expenses. In hard times the number of dead and live foundlings always increases very noticeably. But whether travelling by way of the Morgue or the Infants' Hospital, the little army of waifs meets, reunited soon, in the trench in the Potter's Field where, if no medical student is in need of a subject, they are laid in squads of a dozen.

Most of the foundlings come from the East Side, where they are left by young mothers without wedding-ring or other name than their own to bestow upon the baby, returning from the island hospital to face an unpitying world with the evidence of their shame. Not infrequently they wear the bed-tick regimentals of the Public Charities, and thus their origin is easily enough traced. Oftener no ray of light penetrates the gloom, and no effort is made to probe the mystery of sin and sorrow. This also is the policy pursued in the great Foundling Asylum of the Sisters of Charity in Sixty-eighth Street, known all over the world as Sister Irene's Asylum. Years ago the crib that now stands just inside the street door, under the great main portal, was placed outside at night; but it filled up too rapidly. The babies took to coming in little squads instead of in single file, and in self-defence the sisters were forced to take the cradle in. Now the mother must bring her child inside and put it in the crib where she is seen by the sister on guard. No effort is made to question her, or discover the child's antecedents, but she is asked to stay and nurse her own and another baby. If she refuses, she is allowed to depart unhindered. If willing, she enters at once into the great family of the good Sister who in twenty-one years has gathered as many thousand homeless babies into her fold. One was brought in when I was last in the asylum, in the middle of July, that received in its crib the number 20715. The death-rate is of course lowered a good deal where exposure of the child is prevented. Among the eleven hundred infants in the asylum it was something over nineteen per cent. last year; but among those actually received in the twelvemonth nearer twice that figure. Even the nineteen per cent., remarkably low for a Foundling Asylum, was equal to the startling death-rate of Gotham Court in the cholera scourge.

Four hundred and sixty mothers, who could not or would not keep their own babies, did voluntary penance for their sin in the asylum last year by nursing a strange waif besides their own until both should be strong enough to take their chances in life's battle. An even large number than the eleven hundred were "pay babies," put out to be nursed by "mothers" outside the asylum. The money thus earned pays the rent of hundreds of poor families. It is no trifle, quite half of the quarter of a million dollars contributed annually by the city for the support of the asylum. The procession of these nurse-mothers, when they come to the asylum on the first Wednesday of each month to receive their pay and have the babies inspected by the sisters, is one of the sights of the city. The nurses, who are under strict supervision, grow to love their little charges and part from them with tears when, at the age of four or five, they are sent to Western homes to be adopted. The sisters carefully encourage the home-feeling in the child as their strongest ally in seeking its mental and moral elevation, and the toddlers depart happy to join their "papas and mammas" in the far-away, unknown home.

An infinitely more fiendish, if to surface appearances less deliberate, plan of child-murder than desertion has flourished in New York for years under the title of baby-farming.[4] The name, put into plain English, means starving babies to death. The law has fought this most heinous of crimes by compelling the registry of all baby-farms. As well might it require all persons intending murder to register their purpose with time and place of the deed under the penalty of exemplary fines. Murderers do not hang out a shingle. "Baby-farms," said once Mr. Elbridge T. Gerry,[5] the President of the Society charged with the execution of the law that was passed through his efforts, "are concerns by means of which persons, usually of disreputable character, eke out a living by taking two, or three, or four babies to board. They are the charges of outcasts, or illegitimate children. They feed them on sour milk, and give them paregoric to keep them quiet, until they die, when they get some young medical man without experience to sign a certificate to the Board of Health that the child died of inanition, and so the matter ends. The baby is dead, and there is no one to complain." A handful of baby-farms have been registered and licensed by the Board of Health with the approval of the Society for the Prevention of Cruelty to Children in the last five years, but none of this kind. The devil keeps the only complete register to be found anywhere. Their trace is found oftenest by the coroner or the police; sometimes they may be discovered hiding in the advertising columns of certain newspapers, under the guise of the scarcely less heartless traffic in helpless children that is dignified with the pretence of adoption—for cash. An idea of how this scheme works was obtained through the disclosures in a celebrated divorce case, a year or two ago. The society has among its records a very recent case of a baby a week old (Baby "Blue Eyes") that was offered for sale—adoption, the dealer called it—in a newspaper. The agent bought it after some haggling for a dollar, and arrested the woman slave trader; but the law was powerless to punish her for her crime. Twelve unfortunate women awaiting dishonored motherhood were found in her house.

One gets a glimpse of the frightful depths to which human nature, perverted by avarice bred of ignorance and rasping poverty, can descend, in the mere suggestion of systematic insurance *for profit* of children's lives. A woman was put on trial in this city last year for incredible cruelty in her treatment of a step-child. The evidence aroused a strong suspicion that a pitifully small amount of insurance on the child's life was one of the motives for the woman's savagery. A little investigation brought out the fact that three companies that were in the business of insuring children's lives, for sums varying from $17 up, had insured not less than a million such policies! The premiums ranged from five to twenty-five cents a week. What untold horrors this business may conceal was suggested by a formal agreement entered into by some of the companies, "for the purpose

4. Taking in an infant and breast-feeding it, for pay; the term took on pejorative connotations.
5. Founder and president of New York's Association for Preventing Cruelty to Children.

Prayer Time in the Nursery, Five Points House of Industry

of preventing speculation in the insurance of children's lives." By the terms of this compact, "no higher premium than ten cents could be accepted on children under six years old." Barbarism forsooth! Did ever heathen cruelty invent a more fiendish plot than the one written down between the lines of this legal paper?

It is with a sense of glad relief that one turns from this misery to the brighter page of the helping hands stretched forth on every side to save the young and the helpless. New York is, I firmly believe, the most charitable city in the world. Nowhere is there so eager a readiness to help, when it is known that help is worthily wanted; nowhere are such armies of devoted workers, nowhere such abundance of means ready to the hand of those who know the need and how rightly to supply it. Its poverty, its slums, and its suffering are the result of unprecedented growth with the consequent disorder and crowding, and the common penalty of metropolitan greatness. If the structure shows signs of being top-heavy, evidences are not wanting—they are multiplying day by day—that patient toilers are at work among the underpinnings. The Day Nurseries, the numberless Kindergartens and charitable schools in the poor quarters, the Fresh Air Funds, the thousand and one charities that in one way or another reach the homes and the lives of the poor with sweetening touch, are proof that if much is yet to be done, if the need only grows with the effort, hearts and hands will be found to do it in ever-increasing measure. Black as the cloud is it has a silver lining, bright with promise. New York is to-day a hundredfold cleaner, better, purer, city than it was even ten years ago.

Two powerful agents that were among the pioneers in this work of moral and physical regeneration stand in Paradise Park to-day as milestones on the rocky, uphill road. The handful of noble women, who braved the foul depravity of Old Brewery to rescue its child victims, rolled away the first and heaviest bowlder, which legislatures and city councils had tackled in vain. The Five Points Mission and the Five Points House of Industry[6] have accomplished what no machinery of government availed to do. Sixty thousand children have been rescued by them from the streets and had their little feet set in the better way. Their work still goes on, increasing and gathering in the waifs, instructing and feeding them, and helping their parents with advice and more substantial aid. Their charity knows not creed or nationality. The House of Industry is an enormous nursery-school with an average of more than four hundred day scholars and constant boarders— "outsiders" and "insiders." Its influence is felt for many blocks around in that crowded part of the city. It is one of the most touching sights in the world to see a score of babies, rescued from homes of brutality and desolation, where no other blessing than a drunken curse was ever heard, saying their prayers in the nursery at bedtime. Too often their white night-gowns hide tortured little bodies and limbs cruelly bruised by inhuman hands. In the shelter of this fold they are safe, and a happier little group one may seek long and far in vain.

---

6. Located at 155 Worth Street, it functioned as a workhouse for the poor. The mission, founded in 1848 by women of the Ladies Home Missionary Society, grew out of the Methodist Episcopal Church. It opened its first mission in a former saloon and by 1852 took over the space once occupied by the Old Brewery.

17. The Street Arab[1]

Not all the barriers erected by society against its nether life, not the labor of unnumbered societies for the rescue and relief of its outcast waifs, can dam the stream of homelessness that issues from a source where the very name of home is a mockery. The Street Arab is as much of an institution in New York as Newspaper Row,[2] to which he gravitates naturally, following his Bohemian instinct. Crowded out of the tenements to shift for himself, and quite ready to do it, he meets there the host of adventurous runaways from every State in the Union and from across the sea, whom New York attracts with a queer fascination, as it attracts the older emigrants from all parts of the world. A census of the population in the Newsboys' Lodging-house on any night will show such an odd mixture of small humanity as could hardly be got together in any other spot. It is a mistake to think that they are helpless little creatures, to be pitied and cried over because they are alone in the world. The unmerciful "guying"[3] the good man would receive, who went to them with such a programme, would soon convince him that that sort of pity was wasted, and would very likely give him the idea that they were a set of hardened little scoundrels, quite beyond the reach of missionary effort.

But that would only be his second mistake. The Street Arab has all the faults and all the virtues of the lawless life he leads. Vagabond that he is, acknowledging no authority and owing no allegiance to anybody or anything, with his grimy fist raised against society whenever it tries to coerce him, he is as bright and sharp as the weasel, which, among all the predatory beasts, he most resembles. His sturdy independence, love of freedom and absolute self-reliance, together with his rude sense of justice that enables him to govern his little community, not always in accordance with municipal law or city ordinances, but often a good deal closer to the saving line of "doing to others as one would be done by"—these are strong handles by which those who know how can catch the boy and make him useful. Successful bankers, clergymen, and lawyers all over the country, statesmen in some instances of national repute, bear evidence in their lives to the potency of such missionary efforts. There is scarcely a learned profession, or branch of honorable business, that has not in the last twenty years borrowed some of its brightest light from the poverty and gloom of New York's streets.

Anyone, whom business or curiosity has taken through Park Row or across Printing House Square in the midnight hour, when the air is filled with the roar of great presses spinning with printers' ink on endless rolls of white paper the history of the world in the twenty-four hours that have just passed away, has seen little groups of these boys hanging about the newspaper offices; in winter, when snow is on the streets, fighting for warm spots around the grated vent-holes that let out the heat and steam from the underground press-rooms with their noise and clatter, and in summer playing craps and 7–11[4] on the

1. A street urchin or slum child who spends most of his or her time in the streets.
2. Since the 1840s a section of Park Row, between Frankfort and Beekman Street, housed the offices of some of New York's most important newspapers, including the *New York Times*, the *Globe and Commercial Advertiser*, and the *Recorder*. In addition, paper manufacturers, advertising agencies, printers and photographers all maintained a presence in this area.
3. Teasing.
4. Street game with dice.

Street Arabs, Mulberry Street, Retreat in Church Corner

curb for their hard-earned pennies, with all the absorbing concern of hard-ened gamblers. This is their beat. Here the agent of the Society for the Pre-vention of Cruelty to Children finds those he thinks too young for "business," but does not always capture them. Like rabbits in their burrows, the little ragamuffins sleep with at least one eye open, and every sense alert to the approach of danger: of their enemy, the policeman, whose chief busi-ness in life is to move them on, and of the agent bent on robbing them of their cherished freedom. At the first warning shout they scatter and are off. To pursue them would be like chasing the fleet-footed mountain goat in his rocky fastnesses. There is not an open door, a hidden turn or runway which they do not know, with lots of secret passages and short cuts no one else ever found. To steal a march on them is the only way. There is a coal chute from the sidewalk to the boiler-room in the sub-cellar of the Post Office which the Society's officer found the boys had made into a sort of tobog-gan slide to a snug berth in wintry weather. They used to slyly raise the cover in the street, slide down in single file, and snuggle up to the warm boiler out of harm's way, as they thought. It proved a trap, however. The agent slid down himself one cold night—there was no other way of getting there—and, landing right in the midst of the sleeping colony, had it at his mercy. After repeated raids upon their headquarters, the boys forsook it last summer, and were next found herding under the shore-end of one of the East River banana docks, where they had fitted up a regular club-room that was shared by thirty or forty homeless boys and about a million rats.

Newspaper Row is merely their headquarters. They are to be found all over the city, these Street Arabs, where the neighborhood offers a chance of pick-ing up a living in the daytime and of "turning in" at night with a promise of security from surprise. In warm weather a truck in the street, a convenient out-house, or a dug-out in a hay-barge at the wharf make good bunks. Two were found making their nest once in the end of a big iron pipe up by the Harlem Bridge, and an old boiler at the East River served as an elegant flat for another couple, who kept house there with a thief the police had long sought, little suspecting that he was hiding under their very noses for months together. When the Children's Aid Society first opened its lodging-houses, and with some difficulty persuaded the boys that their charity was no "pious dodge" to trap them into a treasonable "Sunday-school racket," its managers overhead a laughable discussion among the boys in their unwontedly com-fortable beds—perhaps the first some of them had ever slept in—as to the relative merits of the different styles of their everyday berths. Preferences were divided between the steam-grating and a sand-box; but the weight of the evidence was decided to be in favor of the sand-box, because, as its advocate put it, "you could curl all up in it." The new "find" was voted a good way ahead of any previous experience, however. "My eyes, ain't it nice!" said one of the lads, tucked in under his blanket up to the chin, and the roomful of boys echoed the sentiment. The compact silently made that night between the Street Arabs and their hosts has never been broken. They have been fast friends ever since.

Whence this army of homeless boys? is a question often asked. The answer is supplied by the procession of mothers that go out and in at Police Headquarters the year round, inquiring for missing boys, often not until they have been gone for weeks and months, and then sometimes rather as a matter of decent form than from any real interest in the lad's fate. The stereotyped promise of the clerks who fail to find his name on the books among the arrests, that he "will come back when he gets hungry," does not always come true. More likely he went away because he was hungry. Some are orphans, actually or in effect, thrown upon the world when their parents were "sent up" to the island or to Sing Sing,[5] and somehow overlooked by the "Society," which thenceforth became the enemy to be shunned until growth and dirt and the hardships of the street, that make old early, offer some hope of successfully floating the lie that they are "sixteen." A drunken father explains the matter in other cases, as in that of John and Willie, aged ten and eight, picked up by the police. They "didn't live nowhere," never went to school, could neither read nor write. Their twelve-year-old sister kept house for the father, who turned the boys out to beg, or steal, or starve. Grinding poverty and hard work beyond the years of the lad; blows and curses for breakfast, dinner, and supper; all these are recruiting agents for the homeless army. Sickness in the house, too many mouths to feed:

"We wuz six," said an urchin of twelve or thirteen I came across in the Newsboys' Lodging-house, "and we ain't got no father. Some on us had to go." And so he went, to make a living by blacking boots. The going is easy enough. There is very little to hold the boy who has never known anything but a home in a tenement. Very soon the wild life in the streets holds him fast, and thenceforward by his own effort there is no escape. Left alone to himself, he soon enough finds a place in the police books, and there would be no other answer to the second question: "what becomes of the boy?" than that given by the criminal courts every day in the week.

But he is not left alone. Society in our day has no such suicidal intention. Right here, at the parting of the ways, it has thrown up the strongest of all its defences for itself and for the boy. What the Society for the Prevention of Cruelty to Children is to the baby-waif, the Children's Aid Society is to the homeless boy at this real turning-point in his career. The good it has done cannot easily be over-estimated. Its lodging-houses, its schools and its homes block every avenue of escape with their offer of shelter upon terms which the boy soon accepts, as on the whole cheap and fair. In the great Duane Street lodging-house for newsboys, they are succinctly stated in a "notice" over the door that reads thus: "Boys who swear and chew tobacco cannot sleep here." There is another unwritten condition, viz.: that the boy shall be really without a home; but upon this the managers wisely do not insist too obstinately, accepting without too close inquiry his account of himself where that seems advisable, well knowing that many a home that sends forth such lads far less deserves the name than the one they are able to give them.

With these simple preliminaries the outcast boy may enter. Rags do not count; to ignorance the door is only opened wider. Dirt does not survive long, once within the walls of the lodging-house. It is the settled belief of the men who conduct them that soap and water are as powerful moral agents in their particular field as preaching, and they have experience to back them. The boy may come and go as he pleases so long as he behaves himself. No restraint of any sort is put on his independence. He is as free as any other guest at a hotel, and, like him, he is expected to pay for what

---

5. The State of New York prison, established in 1825 in Ossining, up the Hudson River from the city.

"Didn't Live Nowhere"

he gets. How wisely the men planned who laid the foundation of this great rescue work and yet carry it on, is shown by no single feature of it better than by this. No pauper was ever bred within these houses. Nothing would have been easier with such material, or more fatal. But charity of the kind that pauperizes is furthest from their scheme. Self-help is its very key-note, and it strikes a response in the boy's sturdiest trait that raises him at once to a level with the effort made in his behalf. Recognized as an independent trader, capable of and bound to take care of himself, he is in a position to ask trust if trade has gone against him and he cannot pay cash for his "grub" and his bed, and to get it without question. He can even have the loan of the small capital required to start him in business with a boot-black's kit, or an armful of papers, if he is known or vouched for; but every cent is charged to him as carefully as though the transaction involved as many hundreds of dollars, and he is expected to pay back the money as soon as he has made enough to keep him going without it. He very rarely betrays the trust reposed in him. Quite on the contrary, around this sound core of self-help, thus encouraged, habits of thrift and ambitious industry are seen to grow up in a majority of instances. The boy is "growing" a character, and he goes out to the man's work in life with that which for him is better than if he had found a fortune.

Six cents for his bed, six for his breakfast of bread and coffee, and six for his supper of pork and beans, as much as he can eat, are the rates of the boys' "hotel" for those who bunk together in the great dormitories that sometimes hold more than a hundred berths, two tiers high, made of iron, clean and neat. For the "upper ten," the young financiers who early take the lead among their fellows, hire them to work for wages and add a share of their profits to their own, and for the lads who are learning a trade and getting paid by the week, there are ten-cent beds with a locker and with curtains hung about. Night schools and Sunday night meetings are held in the building and are always well attended, in winter especially, when the lodging-houses are crowded. In summer the tow-path and the country attract their share of the bigger boys. The "Sunday-school racket" has ceased to have terror for them. They follow the proceedings with the liveliest interest, quick to detect cant of any sort, should any stray in. No one has any just conception of what congregational singing is until he has witnessed a roomful of these boys roll up their sleeves and start in on "He is the lily of the valley." The swinging trapeze in the gymnasium on the top floor is scarcely more popular with the boys than this tremendously vocal worship. The Street Arab puts his whole little soul into what interests him for the moment, whether it be pulverizing a rival who has done a mean trick to a smaller boy, or attending at the "gospel shop" on Sundays. This characteristic made necessary some extra supervision when recently the lads in the Duane Street Lodging-house "chipped in" and bought a set of boxing gloves. The trapeze suffered a temporary eclipse until this new toy had been tested to the extent of several miniature black eyes upon which soap had no effect, and sundry little scores had been settled that evened things up, as it were, for a fresh start.

I tried one night, not with the best of success I confess, to photograph the boys in their wash-room, while they were cleaning up for supper. They were quite turbulent, to the disgust of one of their number who assumed, unasked, the office of general manager of the show, and expressed his mortification to me in very polite language. "If they would only behave, sir!" he complained, "you could make a good picture."

"Yes," I said, "but it isn't in them, I suppose."

"No, b'gosh!" said he, lapsing suddenly from grace under the provocation, "them kids ain't got no sense, no-how!"

The Society maintains five of these boys' lodging-houses, and one for girls, in the city. The Duane Street Lodging-house alone has sheltered since its foundation in 1855 nearly a quarter of a million different boys, at a total expense of a good deal less than half a million dollars. Of this amount, up to the beginning of the present year, the boys and the earnings of the house had contributed no less than $172,776.38. In all of the lodging-houses together, 12,153 boys and girls were sheltered and taught last year. The boys saved up no inconsiderable amount of money in the savings banks provided for them in the houses, a simple system of lock boxes that are emptied

Street Arabs at Night, Mulberry Street

for their benefit once a month. Besides these, the Society has established and operates in the tenement districts twenty-one industrial schools, co-ordinate with the public schools in authority, for the children of the poor who cannot find room in the city's school-houses, or are too ragged to go there; two free reading-rooms, a dress-making and typewriting school and a laundry for the instruction of girls; a sick-children's mission in the city and two on the sea-shore, where poor mothers may take their babies; a cottage by the sea for crippled girls, and a brush factory for crippled boys in Forty-fourth Street. The Italian school in Leonard Street, alone, had an average attendance of over six hundred pupils last year. The daily average attendance at all of them was 4,105, while 11,331 children were registered and taught. When the fact that there were among these 1,132 children of drunken parents, and 416 that had been found begging in the street, is contrasted with the showing of $1,337.21 deposited in the school savings banks by 1,745 pupils, something like an adequate idea is gained of the scope of the Society's work in the city.

A large share of it, in a sense the largest, certainly that productive of the happiest results, lies outside of the city, however. From the lodging-houses and the schools are drawn the battalions of young emigrants that go every year to homes in the Far West, to grow up self-supporting men and women safe from the temptations and the vice of the city. Their number runs far up in the thousands. The Society never loses sight of them. The records show that the great mass, with this start given them, become useful citizens, an honor to the communities in which their lot is cast. Not a few achieve place and prominence in their new surroundings. Rarely bad reports come of them. Occasionally one comes back, lured by homesickness even for the slums; but the briefest stay generally cures the disease for good. I helped once to see a party off for Michigan, the last sent out by that great friend of the homeless children, Mrs. Astor,[6] before she died. In the party was a boy who had been an "Insider" at the Five Points House of Industry, and brought along as his only baggage a padlocked and iron-bound box that contained all his wealth, two little white mice of the friendliest disposition. They were going with him out to live on the fat of the land in the fertile West, where they would never be wanting for a crust. Alas! for the best-laid plans of mice and men. The Western diet did not agree with either. I saw their owner some months later in the old home at the Five Points. He had come back, walking part of the way, and was now pleading to be sent out once more. He had at last had enough of the city. His face fell when I asked him about the mice. It was a sad story, indeed. "They had so much corn to eat," he said, "and they couldn't stand it. They burned all up inside, and then they busted."

Mrs. Astor set an example during her noble and useful life in gathering every year a company of homeless boys from the streets and sending them to good homes, with decent clothes on their backs—she had sent out no less than thirteen hundred when she died, and left funds to carry on her work— that has been followed by many who, like her, had the means and the heart for such a labor of love. Most of the lodging-houses and school-buildings

---

6. Charlotte Augusta Astor (1825–1887), wife of John Jacob Astor III. Unlike her husband, who had little interest in philanthropic work, Charlotte, a religious woman, gave much and sat on the boards of the Children's Aid Society and the Women's Hospital of New York.

Getting Ready for Supper in the Newsboys' Lodging House

of the society were built by some one rich man or woman who paid all the bills, and often objected to have even the name of the giver made known to the world. It is one of the pleasant experiences of life that give one hope and courage in the midst of all this misery to find names, that stand to the unthinking mass only for money-getting and grasping, associated with such unheralded benefactions that carry their blessings down to generations yet unborn. It is not so long since I found the carriage of a woman, whose name is synonymous with millions, standing in front of the boys' lodging-house in Thirty-fifth Street. Its owner was at that moment busy with a surgeon making a census of the crippled lads in the brush-shop, the most miserable of all the Society's charges, as a preliminary to fitting them out with artificial limbs.

Farther uptown than any reared by the Children's Aid Society, in Sixty-seventh Street, stands a lodging-house intended for boys of a somewhat larger growth than most of those whom the Society shelters. Unlike the others, too, it was built by the actual labor of the young men it was designed to benefit. In the day when more of the boys from our streets shall find their way to it and to the New York Trade Schools,[7] of which it is a kind of home annex, we shall be in a fair way of solving in the most natural of all ways the question what to do with this boy, in spite of the ignorant opposition of the men whose tyrannical policy is now to blame for the showing that, out of twenty-three millions of dollars paid annually to mechanics in the building trades in this city, less than six millions go to the workman born in New York, while his boy roams the streets with every chance of growing up a vagabond and next to none of becoming an honest artisan. Colonel Auchmuty is a practical philanthropist to whom the growing youth of New York will one day owe a debt of gratitude not easily paid. The progress of the system of trade schools established by him, at which a young man may acquire the theory as well as the practice of a trade in a few months at a merely nominal outlay, has not been nearly as rapid as was to be desired, though the fact that other cities are copying the model, with their master mechanics as the prime movers in the enterprise, testifies to its excellence. But it has at last taken a real start, and with union men and even the officers of unions[8] now sending their sons to the trade schools to be taught, one may perhaps be permitted to hope that an era of better sense is dawning that shall witness a rescue work upon lines which, when the leaven has fairly had time to work, will put an end to the existence of the New York Street Arab, of the native breed at least.

18. The Reign of Rum[1]

Where God builds a church the devil builds next door—a saloon, is an old saying that has lost its point in New York. Either the Devil was on the ground first, or he has been doing a good deal more in the way of building. I tried

---

7. Architect Richard Tylden Auchmuty (1831–1893) founded this school, which specialized in teaching mechanical and building trades.
8. As a result of the depression of the 1870s, the unions for the building trades put in place a series of measures that restricted employment in the field to union members. They instituted hefty initiation fees and rules of apprenticeship, which highly restricted who could get work.
1. Denotes alcohol in general. In 1884 the Republican Party adopted the slogan, "Rum, Romanism, and Rebellion," as a way to tar the Democrats and their candidate Grover Cleveland with the image of being the party of the Catholics and of those who opposed curtailing the sale and consumption of alcohol.

A Downtown "Morgue"

once to find out how the account stood, and counted to 111 Protestant churches, chapels, and places of worship of every kind below Fourteenth Street, 4,065 saloons. The worst half of the tenement population lives down there, and it has to this day the worst half of the saloons. Uptown the account stands a little better, but there are easily ten saloons to every church to-day. I am afraid, too, that the congregations are larger by a good deal; certainly the attendance is steadier and the contributions more liberal the week round, Sunday included. Turn and twist it as we may, over against every bulwark for decency and morality which society erects, the saloon projects its colossal shadow, omen of evil wherever it falls into the lives of the poor.

Nowhere is its mark so broad or so black. To their misery it sticketh closer than a brother, persuading them that within its doors only is refuge, relief. It has the best of the argument, too, for it is true, worse pity, that in many a tenement-house block the saloon is the one bright and cheery and humanly decent spot to be found. It is a sorry admission to make, that to bring the rest of the neighborhood up to the level of the saloon would be one way of squelching it; but it is so. Wherever the tenements thicken, it multiplies. Upon the direst poverty of their crowds it grows fat and prosperous, levying upon it a tax heavier than all the rest of its grievous burdens combined. It is not yet two years since the Excise Board made the rule that no three corners of any street-crossing, not already so occupied, should thenceforward be licensed for rum-selling. And the tardy prohibition was intended for the tenement districts. Nowhere else is there need of it. One may walk many miles through the homes of the poor searching vainly for an open reading-room, a cheerful coffee-house, a decent club that is not a cloak for the traffic in rum. The dramshop[2] yawns at every step, the poor man's club, his forum and his haven of rest when weary and disgusted with the crowding, the quarrelling, and the wretchedness at home. With the poison dealt out there he takes his politics, in quality not far apart. As the source, so the stream. The rumshop turns the political crank in New York. The natural yield is rum politics. Of what that means, successive Boards of Aldermen, composed in a measure, if not of a majority, of dive-keepers, have given New York a taste. The disgrace of the infamous "Boodle Board"[3] will be remembered until some corruption even fouler crops out and throws it into the shade.

What relation the saloon bears to the crowds, let me illustrate by a comparison. Below Fourteenth Street were, when the Health Department took its first accurate census of the tenements a year and a half ago, 13,220 of the 32,390 buildings classed as such in the whole city. Of the eleven hundred thousand tenants, not quite half a million, embracing a host of more than sixty-three thousand children under five years of age, lived below that line. Below it, also, were 234 of the cheap lodging-houses accounted for by the police last year, with a total of four millions and a half of lodgers for the twelvemonth, 59 of the city's 110 pawnshops, and 4,065 of its 7,884 saloons. The four most densely peopled precincts, the fourth, Sixth, Tenth, and Eleventh, supported together in round numbers twelve hundred

---

2. Any institution that sold alcoholic beverages.
3. The word *boodle* referred to money received and distributed by corrupt politicians. The term here links boodle with the Tweed Ring.

saloons, and their returns showed twenty-seven per cent. of the whole number of arrests for the year. The Eleventh Precinct, that has the greatest and the poorest crowds of all—it is the Tenth Ward—and harbored one-third of the army of homeless lodgers and fourteen per cent. of all the prisoners of the year, kept 485 saloons going in 1889. It is not on record that one of them all failed for want of support. A number of them, on the contrary, had brought their owners wealth and prominence. From their bars these eminent citizens stepped proudly into the councils of the city and the State. The very floor of one of the bar-rooms, in a neighborhood that lately resounded with the cry for bread of starving workmen, is paved with silver dollars!

East Side poverty is not alone in thus rewarding the tyrants that sweeten its cup of bitterness with their treacherous poison. The Fourth Ward points with pride to the honorable record of the conductors of its "Tub of Blood," and a dozen bar-rooms with less startling titles; the West Side to the wealth and "social" standing of the owners of such resorts as the "Witches' Broth" and the "Plug Hat" in the region of Hell's Kitchen three-cent whiskey, names ominous of the concoctions brewed there and of their fatally generous measure. Another ward, that boasts some of the best residences and the bluest blood on Manhattan Island, honors with political leadership in the ruling party the proprietor of one of the most disreputable black-and-tan dives and dancing-hells to be found anywhere. Criminals and policemen alike do him homage. The list might be strung out to make texts for sermons with a stronger home flavor than many that are preached in our pulpits on Sunday. But I have not set out to write the political history of New York. Besides, the list would not be complete. Secret dives are skulking in the slums and out of them, that are not labelled respectable by a Board of Excise and support no "family entrance." Their business, like that of the stale-beer dives, is done through a side-door the week through. No one knows the number of unlicensed saloons in the city. Those who have made the matter a study estimate it at a thousand, more or less. The police make occasional schedules of a few and report them to headquarters. Perhaps there is a farce in the police court, and there the matter ends. Rum and "influence" are synonymous terms. The interests of the one rarely suffer for the want of attention from the other.

With the exception of these free lances that treat the law openly with contempt, the saloons all hang out a sign announcing in fat type that no beer or liquor is sold to children. In the down-town "morgues" that make the lowest degradation of tramp-humanity pan out a paying interest, as in the "reputable resorts" uptown where Inspector Byrnes's men spot their worthier quarry elbowing citizens whom the idea of associating with a burglar would give a shock they would not get over for a week, this sign is seen conspicuously displayed. Though apparently it means submission to a beneficent law, in reality the sign is a heartless, cruel joke. I doubt if one child in a thousand, who brings his growler to be filled at the average New York bar, is sent away empty-handed, if able to pay for what he wants. I once followed a little boy, who shivered in bare feet on a cold November night so that he seemed in danger of smashing his pitcher on the icy pavement, into a Mulberry Street saloon where just such a sign hung on the wall, and forbade the barkeeper to serve the boy. The man was as astonished at my interference as if I had told him to shut up his shop and go home, which in fact

I might have done with as good a right, for it was after 1 A.M., the legal closing hour. He was mighty indignant too, and told me roughly to go away and
mind my business, while he filled the pitcher. The law prohibiting the selling of beer to minors is about as much respected in the tenement-house
districts as the ordinance against swearing. Newspaper readers will recall
the story, told little more than a year ago, of a boy who after carrying beer
a whole day for a shopful of men over on the East Side, where his father
worked, crept into the cellar to sleep off the effects of his own share in the
rioting. It was Saturday evening. Sunday his parents sought him high and
low; but it was not until Monday morning, when the shop was opened, that
he was found, killed and half-eaten by the rats that overran the place.

All the evil the saloon does in breeding poverty and in corrupting politics; all the suffering it brings into the lives of its thousands of innocent
victims, the wives and children of drunkards it sends forth to curse the
community; its fostering of crime and its shielding of criminals—it is all
as nothing to this, its worst offence. In its affinity for the thief there is at
least this compensation that, as it makes, it also unmakes him. It starts
him on his career only to trip him up and betray him into the hands of the
law, when the rum he exchanged for his honesty has stolen his brains as
well. For the corruption of the child there is no restitution. None is possible. It saps the very vitals of society; undermines its strongest defences,
and delivers them over to the enemy. Fostered and filled by the saloon, the
"growler" looms up in the New York street boy's life, baffling the most persistent efforts to reclaim him. There is no escape from it; no hope for the
boy, once its blighting grip is upon him. Thenceforward the logic of the
slums, that the world which gave him poverty and ignorance for his portion "owes him a living," is his creed, and the career of the "tough" lies
open before him, a beaten track to be blindly followed to a bad end in the
wake of the growler.

19. The Harvest of Tares[1]

The "growler" stood at the cradle of the tough. It bosses him through his
boyhood apprenticeship in the "gang," and leaves him, for a time only, at
the door of the jail that receives him to finish his training and turn him
loose upon the world a thief, to collect by stealth or by force the living his
philosophy tells him that it owes him, and will not voluntarily surrender
without an equivalent in the work which he hates. From the moment he,
almost a baby, for the first time carries the growler for beer, he is never out
of its reach, and the two soon form a partnership that lasts through life. It
has at least the merit, such as it is, of being loyal. The saloon is the only
thing that takes kindly to the lad. Honest play is interdicted in the streets.
The policeman arrests the ball-tossers, and there is no room in the back-
yard. In one of these, between two enormous tenements that swarmed with
children, I read this ominous notice: "*All boys caught in this yard will be delt
with accorden to law.*"

Along the water-fronts, in the holes of the dock-rats, and on the avenues,
the young tough finds plenty of kindred spirits. Every corner has its gang, not
always on the best of terms with the rivals in the next block, but all with a

---

1. A particularly noxious weed.

common programme: defiance of law and order, and with a common ambition: to get "pinched," *i.e.*, arrested, so as to pose as heroes before their fellows. A successful raid on the grocer's till is a good mark, "doing up" a policeman cause for promotion. The gang is an institution in New York. The police deny its existence while nursing the bruises received in nightly battles with it that tax their utmost resources. The newspapers chronicle its doings daily, with a sensational minuteness of detail that does its share toward keeping up its evil traditions and inflaming the ambition of its members to be as bad as the worst. The gang is the ripe fruit of tenement-house growth. It was born there, endowed with a heritage of instinctive hostility to restraint by a generation that sacrificed home to freedom, or left its country for its country's good. The tenement received and nursed the seed. The intensity of the American temper stood sponsor to the murderer in what would have been the common "bruiser" of a more phlegmatic clime. New York's tough represents the essence of reaction against the old and the new oppression, nursed in the rank soil of its slums. Its gangs are made up of the American-born sons of English, Irish, and German parents. They reflect exactly the conditions of the tenements from which they sprang. Murder is as congenial to Cherry Street or to Battle Row, as quiet and order to Murray Hill. The "assimilation" of Europe's oppressed hordes, upon which our Fourth of July orators are fond of dwelling, is perfect. The product is our own.

Such is the genesis of New York's gangs. Their history is not so easily written. It would embrace the largest share of our city's criminal history for two generations back, every page of it dyed red with blood. The guillotine Paris set up a century ago to avenge its wrongs was not more relentless, or

Typical Toughs (From the Rogues' Gallery)

less discriminating, than this Nemesis of New York. The difference is of intent. Murder with that was the serious purpose; with ours it is the careless incident, the wanton brutality of the moment. Bravado and robbery are the real purposes of the gangs; the former prompts the attack upon the policeman, the latter that upon the citizen. Within a single week last spring, the newspapers recorded six murderous assaults on unoffending people, committed by young highwaymen in the public streets. How many more were suppressed by the police, who always do their utmost to hush up such outrages "in the interests of justice," I shall not say. There has been no lack of such occurrences since, as the records of the criminal courts show. In fact, the past summer has seen, after a period of comparative quiescence of the gangs, a reawakening to renewed turbulence of the East Side tribes, and over and over again the reserve forces of a precinct have been called out to club them into submission. It is a peculiarity of the gangs that they usually break out in spots, as it were. When the West Side is in a state of eruption, the East Side gangs "lie low," and when the toughs along the North River are nursing broken heads at home, or their revenge in Sing Sing, fresh trouble breaks out in the tenements east of Third Avenue. This result is brought about by the very efforts made by the police to put down the gangs. In spite of local feuds, there is between them a species of ruffianly Freemasonry[2] that readily admits to full fellowship a hunted rival in the face of the common enemy. The gangs belt the city like a huge chain from the Battery to Harlem—the collective name of the "chain gang" has been given to their scattered groups in the belief that a much closer connection exists between them than commonly supposed— and the ruffian for whom the East Side has become too hot, has only to step across town and change his name, a matter usually much easier for him than to change his shirt, to find a sanctuary in which to plot fresh outrages. The more notorious he is, the warmer the welcome, and if he has "done" his man he is by common consent accorded the leadership in his new field.

From all this it might be inferred that the New York tough is a very fierce individual, of indomitable courage and naturally as blood-thirsty as a tiger. On the contrary he is an arrant coward. His instincts of ferocity are those of the wolf rather than the tiger. It is only when he hunts with the pack that he is dangerous. Then his inordinate vanity makes him forget all fear or caution in the desire to distinguish himself before his fellows, a result of his swallowing all the flash literature and penny-dreadfuls[3] he can beg, borrow, or steal—and there is never any lack of them—and of the strongly dramatic element in his nature that is nursed by such a diet into rank and morbid growth. He is a queer bundle of contradictions at all times. Drunk and foul-mouthed, ready to cut the throat of a defenceless stranger at the toss of a cent, fresh from beating his decent mother black and blue to get money for rum, he will resent as an intolerable insult the imputation that he is "no gentleman." Fighting his battles with the coward's weapons, the brass-knuckles and the deadly sand-bag, or with brick-bats from the

2. A fraternal order dating back to the mid-seventeenth century. Its members take vows of secrecy about its rituals and activities.
3. The middle of the nineteenth century saw a vast explosion in popular literature, from inexpensive books to newspapers and magazines, much of which was highly sensationalistic.

housetops, he is still in all seriousness a lover of fair play, and as likely as not, when his gang has downed a policeman in a battle that has cost a dozen broken heads, to be found next saving a drowning child or woman at the peril of his own life. It depends on the angle at which he is seen, whether he is a cowardly ruffian, or a possible hero with different training and under different social conditions. Ready wit he has at all times, and there is less meanness in his make-up than in that of the bully of the London slums; but an intense love of show and applause, that carries him to any length of bravado, which his twin-brother across the sea entirely lacks. I have a very vivid recollection of seeing one of his tribe, a robber and murderer before he was nineteen, go to the gallows unmoved, all fear of the rope overcome, as it seemed, by the secret, exultant pride of being the centre of a first-class show, shortly to be followed by that acme of tenement-life bliss, a big funeral. He had his reward. His name is to this day a talisman among West Side ruffians, and is proudly borne by the gang of which, up till the night when he "knocked out his man," he was an obscure though aspiring member.

The crime that made McGloin[4] famous was the cowardly murder of an unarmed saloonkeeper who came upon the gang while it was sacking his bar-room at the dead of night. McGloin might easily have fled, but disdained to "run for a Dutchman."[5] His act was a fair measure of the standard of heroism set up by his class in its conflicts with society. The finish is worthy of the start. The first long step in crime taken by the half-grown boy, fired with ambition to earn a standing in his gang, is usually to rob a "lush," i.e., a drunken man who has strayed his way, likely enough is lying asleep in a hallway. He has served an apprenticeship on copper-bottom wash-boilers and like articles found lying around loose, and capable of being converted into cash enough to give the growler a trip or two; but his first venture at robbery moves him up into full fellowship at once. He is no longer a "kid," though his years may be few, but a tough with the rest. He may even in time—he is reasonably certain of it—get his name in the papers as a murderous scoundrel, and have his cup of glory filled to the brim. I came once upon a gang of such young rascals passing the growler after a successful raid of some sort, down at the West Thirty-seventh Street dock, and, having my camera along, offered to "take" them.[6] They were not old and wary enough to be shy of the photographer, whose acquaintance they usually first make in handcuffs and the grip of a policeman; or their vanity overcame their caution. It is entirely in keeping with the tough's character that he should love of all things to pose before a photographer and the ambition is usually the stronger the more repulsive the tough. These were of that sort, and accepted the offer with great readiness, dragging into their group a disreputable-looking sheep that roamed about with them (the slaughter-houses were close at hand) as one of the band. The homeliest ruffian of the lot, who insisted on being taken with the growler to his "mug," took the opportunity to pour what was left in it down his throat and this

4. Mike McGloin (1862–1883) led the Whyo gang that operated in Hell's Kitchen. Police detective Thomas F. Byrnes headed the investigation that led to McGloin's arrest. McGloin went to the gallows on March 7, 1883.
5. Hide or run away in cowardice.
6. I.e., take their photograph.

caused a brief unpleasantness, but otherwise the performance was a success. While I was getting the camera ready, I threw out a vague suggestion of cigarette-pictures, and it took root at once. Nothing would do then but that I must take the boldest spirits of the company "in character." One of them tumbled over against a shed, as if asleep, while two of the others bent over him, searching his pockets with a deftness that was highly suggestive. This, they explained for my benefit, was to show how they "did the trick." The rest of the band were so impressed with the importance of this exhibition that they insisted on crowding into the picture by climbing upon the shed, sitting on the roof with their feet dangling over the edge, and disposing themselves in every imaginable manner within view, as they thought. Lest any reader be led into the error of supposing them to have been harmless young fellows enjoying themselves in peace, let me say that within half an hour after our meeting, when I called at the police station three blocks away, I found there two of my friends of the "Montgomery Guards" under arrest for robbing a Jewish pedlar who had passed that way after I left them, and trying to saw his head off, as they put it, "just for fun. The sheeny cum along an' the saw was there, an' we socked it to him." The prisoners were described to me by the police as Dennis, "the Bum," and "Mud" Foley.

It is not always that their little diversions end as harmlessly as did this, even from the standpoint of the Jew, who was pretty badly hurt. Not far from the preserves of the Montgomery Guards, in Poverty Gap, directly opposite the scene of the murder to which I have referred in a note explaining the picture of the Cunningham family (p. 100), a young lad, who was the only support of his aged parents, was beaten to death within a few months by the "Alley Gang," for the same offence that drew down the displeasure of its neighbors upon the pedlar: that of being at work trying to earn an honest living. I found a part of the gang asleep the next morning, before young Healey's death was known, in a heap of straw on the floor of an unoccupied room in the same row of rear tenements in which the murdered boy's home was. One of the tenants, who secretly directed me to their lair, assuring me that no worse scoundrels went unhung, ten minutes later gave the gang, to its face, an official character for sobriety and inoffensiveness that very nearly startled me into an unguarded rebuke of his duplicity. I caught his eye in time and held my peace. The man was simply trying to protect his own home, while giving such aid as he safely could toward bringing the murderous ruffians to justice. The incident shows to what extent a neighborhood may be terrorized by a determined gang of these reckless toughs.

In Poverty Gap there were still a few decent people left. When it comes to Hell's Kitchen, or to its compeers at the other end of Thirty-ninth Street over by the East River, and further down First Avenue in "the Village," the Rag Gang and its allies have no need of fearing treachery in their periodical battles with the police. The entire neighborhood takes a hand on these occasions, the women in the front rank, partly from sheer love of the "fun," but chiefly because husbands, brothers, and sweethearts are in the fight to a man and need their help. Chimney-tops form the staple of ammunition then, and stacks of loose brick and paving-stones, carefully hoarded in upper rooms as a prudent provision against emergencies. Regular patrol posts are established by the police on the housetops in times of trouble in these localities, but even then they do not escape whole-skinned, if, indeed, with their lives; neither does the gang. The policeman knows of but one cure for the tough, the club, and he lays it on without stint whenever and wherever he has the chance, knowing right well that, if caught at a disadvantage, he will get his outlay back with interest. Words are worse than wasted in the gang-districts. It is a blow at sight, and the tough thus accosted never stops to ask questions. Unless he is "wanted" for some signal outrage, the policeman rarely bothers with arresting him. He can point out half a dozen at sight against whom indictments are pending by the basketful, but whom no jail ever held many hours. They only serve to make him more reckless, for he knows that the political backing that has saved him in the past can do it again. It is a commodity that is only exchangeable "for value received," and it is not hard to imagine what sort of value is in demand. The saloon, in ninety-nine cases out of a hundred, stands behind the bargain.

For these reasons, as well as because he knows from frequent experience his own way to be the best, the policeman lets the gangs alone except when they come within reach of his long night-stick. They have their "club-rooms" where they meet, generally in a tenement, sometimes under a pier or a dump, to carouse, play cards, and plan their raids; their "fences," who dispose of the stolen property. When the necessity presents itself for a descent upon the gang after some particularly flagrant outrage, the police have a task on hand that is not of the easiest. The gangs, like foxes, have more than one hole to their dens. In some localities, where the interior of a block is filled with rear tenements, often set at all sorts of odd angles, surprise alone is practicable. Pursuit through the winding ways and passages is impossible. The young thieves know them all by heart. They have their run-ways over roofs and fences which no one else could find. Their lair is generally selected with special reference to its possibilities of escape. Once pitched upon, its occupation by the gang, with its earmark of nightly symposiums, "can-rackets" in the slang of the street, is the signal for a rapid deterioration of the tenement, if that is possible. Relief is only to be had by ousting the intruders. An instance came under my notice in which valuable property had been well-nigh ruined by being made the thoroughfare of thieves by night and by day. They had chosen it because of a passage that led through the block by way of several connecting halls and yards. The place came soon to be known as "Murderers Alley." Complaint was made to the Board of Health, as a last resort, of the condition of the property. The practical inspector who was sent to report upon it suggested to the owner that he build a brick-wall in a place where it would shut off communication between the streets, and he took the advice. Within the brief space of a few months the house changed character entirely, and became as decent as it had been before the convenient runway was discovered.

This was in the Sixth Ward, where the infamous Whyo Gang until a few years ago absorbed the worst depravity of the Bend and what is left of the Five Points. The gang was finally broken up when its leader was hanged for murder after a life of uninterrupted and unavenged crimes, the recital of which made his father confessor turn pale, listening in the shadow of the scaffold, though many years of labor as chaplain of the Tombs[7] had hardened him to such rehearsals. The great Whyo had been a "power in the ward," handy at carrying elections for the party or faction that happened to stand in need of his services and was willing to pay for them in money or in kind. Other gangs have sprung up since with as high ambition and a fair prospect of outdoing their predecessor. The conditions that bred it still exist, practically unchanged. Inspector Byrnes is authority for the statement that throughout the city the young tough has more "ability" and "nerve" than the thief whose example he successfully emulates. He begins earlier, too. Speaking of the increase of the native element among criminal prisoners exhibited in the census returns of the last thirty years, the Rev. Fred. H. Wines[8] says, "their youth is a very striking fact." Had he confined his observations to the police courts of New York, he might have emphasized that remark and found an explanation of the discovery that "the ratio of prisoners in cities is two and one-quarter times as great as in the country at large," a computation that takes no account of the reformatories for juvenile delinquents, or the exhibit would have been still more striking. Of the 82,200 persons arrested by the police in 1889, 10,505 were under twenty years old. The last report of the Society for the Prevention of Cruelty to Children enumerates, as "a few typical cases," eighteen "professional cracksmen,"[9] between nine and fifteen years old, who had been caught with burglars' tools, or in the act of robbery. Four of them, hardly yet in long trousers, had "held up" a wayfarer in the public street and robbed him of $73. One, aged sixteen, "was the leader of a noted gang of young robbers in Forty-ninth Street. He committed murder, for which he is now serving a term of nineteen years in State's Prison." Four of the eighteen were girls and quite as bad as the worst. In a few years they would have been living with the toughs of their choice without the ceremony of a marriage, egging them on by their pride in their lawless achievements, and fighting side by side with them in their encounters with the "cops."

The exploits of the Paradise Park Gang in the way of highway robbery showed last summer that the embers of the scattered Whyo Gang, upon the wreck of which it grew, were smouldering still. The hanging of Driscoll[1] broke up the Whyos because they were a comparatively small band, and, with the incomparable master-spirit gone, were unable to resist the angry rush of public indignation that followed the crowning outrage. This is the history of the passing away of famous gangs from time to time. The passing is more apparent than real, however. Some other daring leader gathers the scattered elements about him soon, and the war on society is resumed. A bare enumeration of the names of the best-known gangs would occupy pages of this book. The Rock Gang, the Rag Gang, the Stable Gang, and the Short Tail Gang down about the "Hook"[2] have all achieved bad eminence, along with scores of others that have not paraded so frequently in the newspapers. By day they loaf in the corner-groggeries on their beat, at

7. The Manhattan House of Detention for Men, which stood at 100 Centre Street.
8. Minister from Springfield, Illinois, who investigated the causes of crime.
9. Safecrackers.
1. Danny Driscoll, a captain of the Whyo gang, was hanged in the Tombs because he accidentally shot and killed a woman bystander.
2. This lower Manhattan neighborhood, located south of Delancy, north of Montgomery Street, and along the East River, housed many poor, immigrant families.

A Growler Gang in Session

night they plunder the stores along the avenues, or lie in wait at the river for unsteady feet straying their way. The man who is sober and minds his own business they seldom molest, unless he be a stranger inquiring his way, or a policeman and the gang twenty against the one. The tipsy wayfarer is their chosen victim, and they seldom have to look for him long. One has not far to go to the river from any point in New York. The man who does not know where he is going is sure to reach it sooner or later. Should he foolishly resist or make an outcry—dead men tell no tales. "Floaters"[3] come ashore every now and then with pockets turned inside out, not always evidence of a postmortem inspection by dock-rats. Police patrol the rivers as well as the shore on constant look-out for these, but

3. Bodies dumped in the water.

seldom catch up with them. If overtaken after a race during which shots are often exchanged from the boats, the thieves have an easy way of escaping and at the same time destroying the evidence against them; they simply upset the boat. They swim, one and all, like real rats; the lost plunder can be recovered at leisure the next day by diving or grappling. The loss of the boat counts for little. Another is stolen, and the gang is ready for business again.

The fiction of a social "club," which most of the gangs keep up, helps them to a pretext for blackmailing the politicians and the storekeepers in their bailiwick at the annual seasons of their picnic, or ball. The "thieves' ball" is as well known and recognized an institution on the East Side as the Charity Ball in a different social stratum, although it does not go by that name, in print at least. Indeed, the last thing a New York tough will admit is that he is a thief. He dignifies his calling with the pretence of gambling. He does not steal: he "wins" your money or your watch, and on the police returns he is a "speculator." If, when he passes around the hat for "voluntary" contributions, any storekeeper should have the temerity to refuse to chip in, he may look for a visit from the gang on the first dark night, and account himself lucky if his place escapes being altogether wrecked. The Hell's Kitchen Gang and the Rag Gang have both distinguished themselves within recent times by blowing up objectionable stores with stolen gunpowder. But if no such episode mar the celebration, the excursion comes off and is the occasion for a series of drunken fights that as likely as not end in murder. No season has passed within my memory that has not seen the police reserves called out to receive some howling pandemonium returning from a picnic grove on the Hudson or on the Sound. At least one peaceful community up the river, that had borne with this nuisance until patience had ceased to be a virtue, received a boat-load of such picnickers in a style befitting the occasion and the cargo. The outraged citizens planted a howitzer on the dock, and bade the party land at their peril. With the loaded gun pointed dead at them, the furious toughs gave up and the peace was not broken on the Hudson that day, at least not ashore. It is good cause for congratulation that the worst of all forms of recreation popular among the city's toughs, the moonlight picnic, has been effectually discouraged. Its opportunities for disgraceful revelry and immorality were unrivalled anywhere.

In spite of influence and protection, the tough reaches eventually the end of his rope. Occasionally—not too often—there is a noose on it. If not, the world that owes him a living, according to his creed, will insist on his earning it on the safe side of a prison wall. A few, a very few, have been clubbed into an approach to righteousness from the police standpoint. The condemned tough goes up to serve his "bit" or couple of "stretches," followed by the applause of his gang. In the prison he meets older thieves than himself, and sits at their feet listening with respectful admiration to their accounts of the great doings that sent them before. He returns with the brand of the jail upon him, to encounter the hero-worship of his old associates as an offset to the cold shoulder given him by all the rest of the world. Even if he is willing to work, disgusted with the restraint and hard labor of prison life, and in a majority of cases that thought is probably uppermost in his mind, no one will have him around. If, with the assistance of Inspec-

Hunting River Thieves

tor Byrnes, who is a philanthropist in his own practical way, he secures a job, he is discharged on the slightest provocation, and for the most trifling fault. Very soon he sinks back into his old surroundings, to rise no more until he is lost to view in the queer, mysterious way in which thieves and fallen women disappear. No one can tell how. In the ranks of criminals he never rises above that of the "laborer," the small thief or burglar, or general crook, who blindly does the work planned for him by others, and runs the biggest risk for the poorest pay. It cannot be said that the "growler" brought him luck, or its friendship fortune. And yet, if his misdeeds have helped to make manifest that all effort to reclaim his kind must begin with the conditions of life against which his very existence is a protest, even the tough has not lived in vain. This measure of credit at least should be accorded him, that, with or without his good-will, he has been a factor in urging on the battle against the slums that bred him. It is a fight in which eternal vigilance is truly the price of liberty and the preservation of society.

20. The Working Girls of New York

Of the harvest of tares, sown in iniquity and reaped in wrath, the police returns tell the story. The pen that wrote the "Song of the Shirt"[1] is needed to tell of the sad and toil-worn lives of New York's workingwomen. The cry echoes by night and by day through its tenements:

> Oh, God! that bread should be so dear,
> And flesh and blood so cheap!

Six months have not passed since at a great public meeting in this city, the Working Women's Society reported: "It is a known fact that men's wages cannot fall below a limit upon which they can exist, but woman's wages have no limit, since the paths of shame are always open to her. It is simply impossible for any woman to live without assistance on the low salary a saleswoman earns, without depriving herself of real necessities. . . . It is inevitable that they must in many instances resort to evil." It was only a few brief weeks before that verdict was uttered, that the community was shocked by the story of a gentle and refined woman who, left in direst poverty to earn her own living alone among strangers, threw herself from her attic window, preferring death to dishonor. "I would have done any honest work, even to scrubbing," she wrote, drenched and starving, after a vain search for work in a driving storm. She had tramped the streets for weeks on her weary errand, and the only living wages that were offered her were the wages of sin. The ink was not dry upon her letter before a woman in an East Side tenement wrote down her reason for self-murder: "Weakness, sleeplessness, and yet obliged to work. My strength fails me. Sing at my coffin: 'Where does the soul find a home and rest?'" Her story may be found as one of two typical "cases of despair" in one little church community, in the *City Mission Society's*[2] *Monthly* for last February. It is a story that has many parallels in the experience of every missionary, every police reporter and every family doctor whose practice is among the poor.

It is estimated that at least one hundred and fifty thousand women and girls earn their own living in New York; but there is reason to believe that this estimate falls far short of the truth when sufficient account is taken of the large number who are not wholly dependent upon their own labor, while contributing by it to the family's earnings. These alone constitute a large class of the women wage-earners, and it is characteristic of the situation that the very fact that some need not starve on their wages condemns the rest to that fate. The pay they are willing to accept all have to take. What the "everlasting law of supply and demand," that serves as such a convenient gag for public indignation, has to do with it, one learns from observation all along the road of inquiry into these real woman's wrongs.

---

1. An 1843 poem by English poet Thomas Hood. It gained immediate attention for its attack on worker exploitation, particularly that of working women.
2. Founded in 1812 to serve both religious and physical needs of the poor, the society lead to two important spin-off institutions: the Fresh Air Fund and the Association for Improvement of the Conditions of the Poor.

To take the case of the saleswomen for illustration: The investigation of the Working Women's Society[3] disclosed the fact that wages averaging from $2 to $4.50 a week were reduced by excessive fines, "the employers placing a value upon time lost that is not given to services rendered." A little girl, who received two dollars a week, made cash-sales amounting to $167 in a single day, while the receipts of a fifteen-dollar male clerk in the same department footed up only $125; yet for some trivial mistake the girl was fined sixty cents out of her two dollars. The practice prevailed in some stores of dividing the fines between the superintendent and the time-keeper at the end of the year. In one instance they amounted to $3,000, and "the superintendent was heard to charge the time-keeper with not being strict enough in his duties." One of the causes for fine in a certain large store was sitting down. The law requiring seats for saleswomen, generally ignored, was obeyed faithfully in this establishment. The seats were there, but the girls were fined when found using them.

Cash-girls receiving $1.75 a week for work that at certain seasons lengthened their day to sixteen hours were sometimes required to pay for their aprons. A common cause for discharge from stores in which, on account of the oppressive heat and lack of ventilation, "girls fainted day after day and came out looking like corpses," was too long service. No other fault was found with the discharged saleswomen than that they had been long enough in the employ of the firm to justly expect an increase of salary. The reason was even given with brutal frankness, in some instances.

These facts give a slight idea of the hardships and the poor pay of a business that notoriously absorbs child-labor. The girls are sent to the store before they have fairly entered their teens, because the money they can earn there is needed for the support of the family. If the boys will not work, if the street tempts them from home, among the girls at least there must be no drones. To keep their places they are told to lie about their age and to say that they are over fourteen. The precaution is usually superfluous. The Women's Investigating Committee[4] found the majority of the children employed in the stores to be under age, but heard only in a single instance of the truant officers calling. In that case they came once a year and sent the youngest children home; but in a month's time they were all back in their places, and were not again disturbed. When it comes to the factories, where hard bodily labor is added to long hours, stifling rooms, and starvation wages, matters are even worse. The Legislature has passed laws to prevent the employment of children,[5] as it has forbidden saloon-keepers to sell them beer, and it has provided means of enforcing its mandate, so efficient, that the very number of factories in New York is *guessed* at as in the neighborhood of twelve thousand. Up till this summer, a single inspector was charged with the duty of keeping the run of them all, and of seeing to it that the law was respected by the owners.

Sixty cents is put as the average day's earnings of the 150,000, but into this computation enters the stylish "cashier's" two dollars a day, as well

3. Founded in 1888, the society dedicated itself to protecting working women.
4. Founded to investigate illegal labor practices, particularly the employment of underage children.
5. In 1886 the New York State Legislature passed the Factory Act, which barred factories from employing children under the age of twelve. In 1889 the law raised the bar to age fourteen. It also imposed a variety of other limitations on child labor. The state, however, employed only two inspectors to monitor the forty-three thousand factories covered by the legislation.

as the thirty cents of the poor little girl who pulls threads in an East Side factory, and, if anything, the average is probably too high. Such as it is, however, it represents board, rent, clothing, and "pleasure" to this army of workers. Here is the case of a woman employed in the manufacturing department of a Broadway house. It stands for a hundred like her own. She averages three dollars a week. Pays $1.50 for her room; for breakfast she has a cup of coffee; lunch she cannot afford. One meal a day is her allowance. This woman is young, she is pretty. She has "the world before her." Is it anything less than a miracle if she is guilty of nothing worse than the "early and improvident marriage," against which moralists exclaim as one of the prolific causes of the distress of the poor? Almost any door might seem to offer welcome escape from such slavery as this. "I feel so much healthier since I got three square meals a day," said a lodger in one of the Girls' Homes.[6] Two young sewing-girls came in seeking domestic service, so that they might get enough to eat. They had been only half-fed for some time, and starvation had driven them to the one door at which the pride of the American-born girl will not permit her to knock, though poverty be the price of her independence.

The tenement and the competition of public institutions and farmers' wives and daughters, have done the tyrant shirt to death, but they have not bettered the lot of the needle-women. The sweater of the East Side has appropriated the flannel shirt. He turns them out to-day at forty-five cents a dozen, paying his Jewish workers from twenty to thirty-five cents. One of these testified before the State Board of Arbitration, during the shirtmakers' strike,[7] that she worked eleven hours in the shop and four at home, and had never in the best of times made over six dollars a week. Another stated that she worked from 4 o'clock in the morning to 11 at night. These girls had to find their own thread and pay for their own machines out of their wages. The white shirt has gone to the public and private institutions that shelter large numbers of young girls, and to the country. There are not half as many shirtmakers in New York to-day as only a few years ago, and some of the largest firms have closed their city shops. The same is true of the manufacturers of underwear. One large Broadway firm has nearly all its work done by farmers' girls in Maine, who think themselves well off if they can earn two or three dollars a week to pay for a Sunday silk, or the wedding outfit, little dreaming of the part they are playing in starving their city sisters. Literally, they sew "with double thread, a shroud as well as a shirt." Their pin-money[8] sets the rate of wages for thousands of poor sewing-girls in New York. The average earnings of the worker on underwear to-day do not exceed the three dollars which her competitor among the Eastern hills is willing to accept as the price of her play. The shirtmaker's pay is better only because the very finest custom work is all there is left for her to do.

6. Created by various charitable groups to provide living space and meals to homeless girls.
7. In 1890 unionized and non-unionized shirtmakers went on strike for a ten-hour day and weekly wages. "State Board of Arbitration": founded in 1887, the New York State Board of Arbitration and Mediation attempted to reconcile disputes between workers and employers. It functioned through the state's Department of Labor.
8. A small amount of money put aside for incidentals. Many, including leaders of the labor movement, claimed that women did not work out of necessity. Riis may have been engaging in wordplay here because he is describing the experiences of women in the garment industry, who did in fact work with pins.

Calico wrappers at a dollar and a half a dozen—the very expert sewers able to make from eight to ten, the common run five or six—neckties at from 25 to 75 cents a dozen, with a dozen as a good day's work, are specimens of women's wages. And yet people persist in wondering at the poor quality of work done in the tenements! Italian cheap labor has come of late also to possess this poor field, with the sweater in its train. There is scarce a branch of woman's work outside of the home in which wages, long since at low-water mark, have not fallen to the point of actual starvation. A case was brought to my notice recently by a woman doctor, whose heart as well as her life-work is with the poor, of a widow with two little children she found at work in an East Side attic, making paper-bags. Her father, she told the doctor, had made good wages at it; but she received only five cents for six hundred of the little three-cornered bags, and her fingers had to be very swift and handle the paste-brush very deftly to bring her earnings up to twenty-five and thirty cents a day. She paid four dollars a month for her room. The rest went to buy food for herself and the children. The physician's purse, rather than her skill, had healing for their complaint.

I have aimed to set down a few dry facts merely. They carry their own comment. Back of the shop with its weary, grinding toil—the home in the tenement, of which it was said in a report of the State Labor Bureau: "Decency and womanly reserve cannot be maintained there—what wonder so many fall away from virtue?" Of the outlook, what? Last Christmas Eve my business took me to an obscure street among the West Side tenements. An old woman had just fallen on the doorstep, stricken with paralysis. The doctor said she would never again move her right hand or foot. The whole side was dead. By her bedside, in their cheerless room, sat the patient's aged sister, a hopeless cripple, in dumb despair. Forty years ago the sisters had come, five in number then, with their mother, from the North of Ireland to make their home and earn a living among strangers. They were lace embroiderers and found work easily at good wages. All the rest had died as the years went by. The two remained and, firmly resolved to lead an honest life, worked on though wages fell and fell as age and toil stiffened their once nimble fingers and dimmed their sight. Then one of them dropped out, her hands palsied and her courage gone. Still the other toiled on, resting neither by night nor by day, that the sister might not want. Now that she too had been stricken, as she was going to the store for the work that was to keep them through the holidays, the battle was over at last. There was before them starvation, or the poor-house. And the proud spirits of the sisters, helpless now, quailed at the outlook.

These were old, with life behind them. For them nothing was left but to sit in the shadow and wait. But of the thousands, who are travelling the road they trod to the end, with the hot blood of youth in their veins, with the love of life and of the beautiful world to which not even sixty cents a day can shut their eyes—who is to blame if their feet find the paths of shame that are "always open to them"? The very paths that have effaced the saving "limit," and to which it is declared to be "inevitable that they must in many instances resort." Let the moralist answer. Let the wise economist apply his rule of supply and demand, and let the answer be heard in this city of a thousand charities where justice goes begging.

To the everlasting credit of New York's working girl let it be said that, rough though her road be, all but hopeless her battle with life, only in the

Sewing and Starving in an Elizabeth Street Attic

rarest instances does she go astray. As a class she is brave, virtuous, and true. New York's army of profligate women is not, as in some foreign cities, recruited from her ranks. She is as plucky as she is proud. That "American girls never whimper" became a proverb long ago, and she accepts her lot uncomplainingly, doing the best she can and holding her cherished independence cheap at the cost of a meal, or of half her daily ration, if need be. The home in the tenement and the traditions of her childhood have neither trained her to luxury nor predisposed her in favor of domestic labor in preference to the shop. So, to the world she presents a cheerful, uncomplaining front that sometimes deceives it. Her courage will not be without its reward. Slowly, as the conviction is thrust upon society that woman's work must enter more and more into its planning, a better day is dawning. The organization of working girls' clubs, unions, and societies with a community of interests, despite the obstacles to such a movement, bears testimony to it, as to the devotion of the unselfish women who have made their poorer sister's cause their own, and will yet wring from an unfair world the justice too long denied her.

21. Pauperism in the Tenements

The reader who has followed with me the fate of the Other Half thus far, may not experience much of a shock at being told that in eight years 135,595 families in New York were registered as asking or receiving charity. Perhaps, however, the intelligence will rouse him that for five years past one person in every ten who died in this city was buried in the Potter's Field. These facts tell a terrible story. The first means that in a population of a million and a half, very nearly, if not quite, half a million persons were driven, or chose, to beg for food, or to accept it in charity at some period of the eight years, if not during the whole of it. There is no mistake about these figures. They are drawn from the records of the Charity Organization Society,[1] and represent the time during which it has been in existence. It is not even pretended that the record is complete. To be well within the limits, the Society's statisticians allow only three and a half to the family, instead of the four and a half that are accepted as the standard of calculations which deal with New York's population as a whole. They estimate upon the basis of their every-day experience that, allowing for those who have died, moved away, or become for the time being at least self-supporting, eighty-five per cent. of the registry are still within, or lingering upon, the borders of dependence. Precisely how the case stands with this great horde of the indigent is shown by a classification of 5,169 cases that were investigated by the Society in one year. This was the way it turned out: 327 worthy of continuous relief, or 6.4 per cent.; 1,269 worthy of temporary relief, or 24.4 per cent.; 2,698 in need of work, rather than relief, or 52.2 per cent.; 875 unworthy of relief, or 17 per cent.

That is, nearly six and a half per cent. of all were utterly helpless—orphans, cripples, or the very aged; nearly one-fourth needed just a lift to start them on the road to independence, or to permanent pauperism,

---

1. Founded by Josephine Shaw Lowell in 1882, the society evaluated applicants for charity, investigating their worthiness and need. An exemplar of scientific charity, its members went into the apartments of applicants to establish a bond and to research the home's conditions.

according to the wisdom with which the lever was applied. More than half were destitute because they had no work and were unable to find any, and one-sixth were frauds, professional beggars, training their children to follow in their footsteps—a veritable "tribe of Ishmael,"[2] tightening its grip on society as the years pass, until society shall summon up pluck to say with Paul,[3] "if any man will not work neither shall he eat," and stick to it. It is worthy of note that almost precisely the same results followed a similar investigation in Boston. There were a few more helpless cases of the sort true charity accounts it a gain to care for, but the proportion of a given lot that was crippled for want of work, or unworthy, was exactly the same as in this city. The bankrupt in hope, in courage, in purse, and in purpose, are not peculiar to New York. They are found the world over, but we have our full share. If further proof were wanted, it is found in the prevalence of pauper burials. The Potter's Field stands ever for utter, hopeless surrender. The last the poor will let go, however miserable their lot in life, is the hope of a decent burial. But for the five years ending with 1888 the average of burials in the Potter's Field has been 10.03 per cent. of all. In 1889 it was 9.64. In that year the proportion to the total mortality of those who died in hospitals, institutions, and in the Almshouse was as 1 in 5.

The 135,595 families inhabited no fewer than 31,000 different tenements. I say tenements advisedly, though the society calls them buildings, because at least ninety-nine per cent. were found in the big barracks, the rest in shanties scattered here and there, and now and then a fraud or an exceptional case of distress in a dwelling-house of better class. Here, undoubtedly, allowance must be made for the constant moving about of those who live on charity, which enables one active beggar to blacklist a dozen houses in the year. Still the great mass of the tenements are shown to be harboring almsseekers. They might almost as safely harbor the small-pox. That scourge is not more contagious than the alms-seeker's complaint. There are houses that have been corrupted through and through by this pestilence, until their very atmosphere breathes beggary. More than a hundred and twenty pauper families have been reported from time to time as living in one such tenement.

The truth is that pauperism grows in the tenements as naturally as weeds in a garden lot. A moral distemper, like crime, it finds there its most fertile soil. All the surroundings of tenement-house life favor its growth, and where once it has taken root it is harder to dislodge than the most virulent of physical diseases. The thief is infinitely easier to deal with than the pauper, because the very fact of his being a thief presupposes some bottom to the man. Granted that it is bad, there is still something, a possible handle by which to catch him. To the pauper there is none. He is as hopeless as his own poverty. I speak of the *pauper*, not of the honestly poor. There is a sharp line between the two; but athwart it stands the tenement, all the time blurring and blotting it out. "It all comes down to character in the end," was the verdict of a philanthropist whose life has been spent wrestling with this weary problem. And so it comes down to the tenement, the destroyer of individuality and character everywhere. "In nine years," said a wise and

2. A reference to the narrative in Genesis 21 of Abraham casting out his concubine Hagar along with their son, Ishamael.
3. Saint Paul.

charitable physician, sadly, to me, "I have known of but a single case of permanent improvement in a poor tenement family." I have known of some whose experience, extending over an even longer stretch, was little better.

The beggar follows the "tough's" rule of life that the world owes him a living, but his scheme of collecting it stops short of violence. He has not the pluck to rob even a drunken man. His highest flights take in at most an unguarded clothes-line, or a little child sent to buy bread or beer with the pennies he clutches tightly as he skips along. Even then he prefers to attain his end by stratagem rather than by force, though occasionally, when the coast is clear, he rises to the height of the bully. The ways he finds of "collecting" under the cloak of undeserved poverty are numberless, and often reflect credit on the man's ingenuity, if not on the man himself. I remember the shock with which my first experience with his kind—her kind,

A Flat in the Pauper Barracks, West Thirty-Eighth Street, with All Its Furniture

rather, in this case: the beggar was a woman—came home to me. On my way to and from the office I had been giving charity regularly, as I fondly believed, to an old woman who sat in Chatham Square with a baby done up in a bundle of rages, moaning piteously in sunshine and rain, "Please, help the poor." It was the baby I pitied and thought I was doing my little to help, until one night I was just in time to rescue it from rolling out of her lap, and found the bundle I had been wasting my pennies upon just rags and nothing more, and the old hag dead drunk. Since then I have encountered bogus babies, borrowed babies, and drugged babies in the streets, and fought shy of them all. Most of them, I am glad to say, have been banished from the street since; but they are still occasionally to be found. It was only last winter that the officers of the Society for the Prevention of Cruelty to Children arrested an Italian woman who was begging along Madison Avenue with a poor little wreck of a girl, whose rags and pinched face were calculated to tug hard at the purse-strings of a miser. Over five dollars in nickles and pennies were taken from the woman's pockets, and when her story of poverty and hunger was investigated at the family's home in a Baxter Street tenement, bank-books turned up that showed the Masonis to be regular pauper capitalists, able to draw their check for three thousand dollars, had they been so disposed. The woman was fined $250, a worse punishment undoubtedly than to have sent her to prison for the rest of her natural life. Her class has, unhappily, representatives in New York that have not yet been brought to grief.

Nothing short of making street begging a crime has availed to clear our city of this pest to an appreciable extent. By how much of an effort this result has been accomplished may be gleaned from the fact that the Charity Organization Society alone, in five years, caused the taking up of 2,594 street beggars, and the arrest and conviction of 1,474 persistent offenders. Last year it dealt with 612 perambulating mendicants. The police report only 19 arrests for begging during the year 1889, but the real facts of the case are found under the heading "vagrancy." In all, 2,633 persons were charged with this offence, 947 of them women. A goodly proportion of these latter came from the low groggeries[4] of the Tenth Ward, where a peculiar variety of the female tramp-beggar is at home, the "scrub." The scrub is one degree perhaps above the average pauper in this, that she is willing to work at least one day in the week, generally the Jewish Sabbath.[5] The orthodox Jew can do no work of any sort from Friday evening till sunset on Saturday, and this interim the scrub fills out in Ludlow Street. The pittance she receives for this vicarious sacrifice of herself upon the altar of the ancient faith buys her rum for at least two days of the week at one of the neighborhood "morgues."[6] She lives through the other four by begging. There are distilleries in Jewtown, or just across its borders, that depend almost wholly on her custom. Recently, when one in Hester Street was raided because the neighbors had complained of the boisterous hilarity of the hags over their beer, thirty-two aged "scrubs" were marched off to the station-house.

---

4. Saloons.
5. Known as a *shabbes goy*, the scrub described here earned money by doing work for an Orthodox Jewish family, who, according to Jewish law, could not labor on the Sabbath.
6. Saloons.

It is curious to find preconceived notions quite upset in a review of the nationalities that go to make up this squad of street beggars. The Irish head the list with fifteen per cent., and the native American is only a little way behind with twelve per cent., while the Italian, who in his own country turns beggary into a fine art, has less than two per cent. Eight per cent. were Germans. The relative prevalence of the races in our population does not account for this showing. Various causes operate, no doubt, to produce it. Chief among them is, I think, the tenement itself. It has no power to corrupt the Italian, who comes here in almost every instance to work—no beggar would ever emigrate from anywhere unless forced to do so. He is distinctly on its lowest level from the start. With the Irishman the case is different. The tenement, especially its lowest type, appears to possess a peculiar affinity for the worse nature of the Celt, to whose best and strongest instincts it does violence, and soonest and most thoroughly corrupts him. The "native" twelve per cent. represent the result of this process, the hereditary beggar of the second or third generation in the slums.

The blind beggar alone is winked at in New York's streets, because the authorities do not know what else to do with him. There is no provision for him anywhere after he is old enough to strike out for himself. The annual pittance of thirty or forty dollars which he receives from the city serves to keep his landlord in good humor; for the rest his misfortune and his thin disguise of selling pencils on the street corners must provide. Until the city affords him some systematic way of earning his living by work (as Philadelphia has done, for instance) to banish him from the street would be tantamount to sentencing him to death by starvation. So he possesses it in peace, that is, if he is blind in good earnest, and begs without "encumbrance."[7] Professional mendicancy does not hesitate to make use of the greatest of human afflictions as a pretence for enlisting the sympathy upon which it thrives. Many New Yorkers will remember the French schoolmaster who was "blinded by a shell at the siege of Paris," but miraculously recovered his sight when arrested and deprived of his children by the officers of Mr. Gerry's society. When last heard of he kept a "museum" in Hartford, and acted the overseer with financial success. His sign with its pitiful tale, that was a familiar sight in our streets for years and earned for him the capital upon which he started his business, might have found a place among the curiosities exhibited there, had it not been kept in a different sort of museum here as a memento of his rascality. There was another of his tribe, a woman, who begged for years with a deformed child in her arms, which she was found to have hired at an almshouse in Genoa for fifteen francs a month. It was a good investment, for she proved to be possessed of a comfortable fortune. Some time before that, the Society for the Prevention of Cruelty to Children, that found her out, had broken up the dreadful padrone system, a real slave trade in Italian children who were bought of poor parents across the sea and made to beg their way on foot through France to the port whence they were shipped to this city, to be beaten and starved here by their cruel masters and sent out to beg, often after merciless mutilation to make them "take" better with a pitying public.

7. Children.

Coffee at one cent

But, after all, the tenement offers a better chance of fraud on impulsive but thoughtless charity, than all the wretchedness of the street, and with fewer risks. To the tender-hearted and unwary it is, in itself, the strongest plea for help. When such a cry goes up as was heard recently from a Mott Street den, where the family of a "sick" husband, a despairing mother, and half a dozen children in rags and dirt were destitute of the "first necessities of life," it is not to be wondered at that a stream of gold comes pouring in to relieve. It happens too often, as in that case, that a little critical inquiry or reference to the "black list" of the Charity Organization Society, justly dreaded only by the frauds, discovers the "sickness" to stand for laziness, and the destitution to be the family's stock in trade; and the community receives a shock that for once is downright wholesome, if it imposes a check on an undiscriminating charity that is worse than none at all.

The case referred to furnished an apt illustration of how thoroughly corrupting paupersim is in such a setting. The tenement woke up early to the gold mine that was being worked under its roof, and before the day was three hours old the stream of callers who responded to the newspaper appeal found the alley blocked by a couple of "toughs," who exacted toll of a silver quarter from each tearful sympathizer with the misery in the attic.

A volume might be written about the tricks of the professional beggar, and the uses to which he turns the tenement in his trade. The Boston "widow" whose husband turned up alive and well after she had buried him seventeen times with tears and lamentation, and made the public pay for the weekly funerals, is not without representatives in New York. The "gentleman tramp" is a familiar type from our streets, and the "once respectable Methodist" who patronized all the revivals in town with his profitable story of repentance, only to fall from grace into the saloon door nearest the church after the service was over, merely transferred the scene of his operations from the tenement to the church as the proper setting for his specialty. There is enough of real suffering in the homes of the poor to make one wish that there were some effective way of enforcing Paul's plan of starving the drones into the paths of self-support: no work, nothing to eat.

The message came from one of the Health Department's summer doctors, last July, to The King's Daughters' Tenement-house Committee, that a family with a sick child was absolutely famishing in an uptown tenement. The address was not given. The doctor had forgotten to write it down, and before he could be found and a visitor sent to the house the baby was dead, and the mother had gone mad. The nurse found the father, who was an honest laborer long out of work, packing the little corpse in an orange-box partly filled with straw, that he might take it to the Morgue for pauper burial. There was absolutely not a crust to eat in the house, and the other children were crying for food. The great immediate need in that case, as in more than half of all according to the record, was work and living wages. Alms do not meet the emergency at all. They frequently aggravate it, degrading and pauperizing where true help should aim at raising the sufferer to self-respect and self-dependence. The experience of the Charity Organization Society in raising, in eight years, 4,500 families out of the rut of pauperism into proud, if modest, independence, without alms, but by a system of "friendly visitation," and the work of the Society for Improving the Condition of the Poor and kindred organizations along the same line, shows what can be done by well-directed effort. It is estimated that New York spends in public and private charity every year a round $8,000,000. A small part of this sum intelligently invested in a great labor bureau, that would bring the seeker of work and the one with work to give together under auspices offering some degree of mutual security, would certainly repay the amount of the investment in the saving of much capital now worse than wasted, and would be prolific of the best results. The ultimate and greatest need, however, the real remedy, is to remove the cause—the tenement that was built for "a class of whom nothing was expected," and which has come fully up to the expectation. Tenement-house reform holds the key to the problem of pauperism in the city. We can never get rid of either the tenement or the pauper. The two will always exist together in New York. But by reforming the one, we can do more toward exterminating the other than can be done by all other means together that have yet been invented, or ever will be.

22. The Wrecks and the Waste

Pauperdom is to blame for the unjust yoking of poverty with punishment, "charities" with "correction," in our municipal ministering to the needs of the Nether Half. The shadow of the workhouse points like a scornful finger toward its neighbor, the almshouse, when the sun sets behind the teeming city across the East River, as if, could its stones speak, it would say before night drops its black curtain between them: "You and I are brothers. I am not more bankrupt in moral purpose than you. A common parent begat us. Twin breasts, the tenement and the saloon, nourished us. Vice and unthrift go hand in hand. Pauper, behold thy brother!" And the almshouse owns the bitter relationship in silence.

Over on the islands that lie strung along the river and far up the Sound[1] the Nether Half hides its deformity, except on show-days, when distinguished visitors have to be entertained and the sore is uncovered by the authorities with due municipal pride in the exhibit. I shall spare the reader

1. Long Island Sound; Randall's Island and Blackwell's Island are along the East River.

the sight. The aim of these pages has been to lay bare its source. But a brief glance at our proscribed population is needed to give background and tone to the picture. The review begins with the Charity Hospital with its thousand helpless human wrecks; takes in the penitentiary, where the "tough" from Battle Row and Poverty Gap is made to earn behind stone walls the living the world owes him; a thoughtless, jolly convict-band with opportunity at last "to think" behind the iron bars, but little desire to improve it; governed like unruly boys, which in fact most of them are. Three of them were taken from the dinner-table while I was there one day, for sticking pins into each other, and were set with their faces to the wall in sight of six hundred of their comrades for punishment. Pleading incessantly for tobacco, when the keeper's back is turned, as the next best thing to the whiskey they cannot get, though they can plainly make out the saloon-signs across the stream where they robbed or "slugged" their way to prison. Every once in a while the longing gets the best of some prisoner from the penitentiary or the workhouse, and he risks his life in the swift currents to reach the goal that tantalizes him with the promise of "just one more drunk." The chances are at least even of his being run down by some passing steamer and drowned, even if he is not overtaken by the armed guards who patrol the shore in boats, or his strength does not give out.

This workhouse come next, with the broken-down hordes from the dives, the lodging-houses, and the tramps' nests, the "hell-box"[2] rather than the repair-shop of the city. In 1889 the registry at the workhouse footed up 22,477, of whom some had been there as many as twenty times before. It is the popular summer resort of the slums, but business is brisk at this stand the year round. Not a few of its patrons drift back periodically without the formality of a commitment, to take their chances on the island when there is no escape from the alternative of work in the city. Work, but not too much work, is the motto of the establishment. The "workhouse step" is an institution that must be observed on the island, in order to draw any comparison between it and the snail's pace that shall do justice to the snail. Nature and man's art have made these islands beautiful; but weeds grow luxuriantly in their gardens, and spiders spin their cobwebs unmolested in the borders of sweet-smelling box. The work which two score of hired men could do well is too much for these thousands.

Rows of old women, some smoking stumpy, black clay-pipes, others knitting or idling, all grumbling, sit or stand under the trees that hedge in the almshouse, or limp about in the sunshine, leaning on crutches or bean-pole staffs. They are a "growler-gang" of another sort than may be seen in session on the rocks of the opposite shore at that very moment. They grumble and growl from sunrise to sunset, at the weather, the breakfast, the dinner, the supper; at pork and beans as at corned beef and cabbage; at their Thanksgiving dinner as at the half rations of the sick ward; at the past that had no joy, at the present whose comfort they deny, and at the future without promise. The crusty old men in the next building are not a circumstance to them. The warden, who was in charge of the almshouse for many years, had become so snappish and profane by constant association with a thousand cross old women that I approached him with some misgivings, to

---

2. In a printing house, the receptacle for old or broken type. The metal would be recast at a foundry. "Workhouse": An institution on Blackwell's Island.

request his permission to "take" a group of a hundred or so who were within shot of my camera. He misunderstood me.

"Take them?" he yelled. "Take the thousand of them and be welcome. They will never be still, by ———, till they are sent up on Hart's Island in a box, and I'll be blamed if I don't think they will growl then at the style of the funeral."

And he threw his arms around me in an outburst of enthusiasm over the wondrous good luck that had sent a friend indeed to his door. I felt it to be a painful duty to undeceive him. When I told him that I simply wanted the old women's picture, he turned away in speechless disgust, and to his dying day, I have no doubt, remembered my call as the day of the champion fool's visit to the island.

When it is known that many of these old people have been sent to the almshouse to die by their heartless children, for whom they had worked faithfully as long as they were able, their growling and discontent is not hard to understand. Bitter poverty threw them all "on the county," often on the wrong county at that. Very many of them are old-country poor, sent, there is reason to believe, to America by the authorities to get rid of the obligation to support them. "The almshouse," wrote a good missionary, "affords a sad illustration of St. Paul's description of the 'last days.' The class from which comes our poorhouse population is to a large extent 'without natural affection.'" I was reminded by his words of what my friend, the doctor, had said to me a little while before: "Many a mother has told me at her child's death-bed, 'I cannot afford to lose it. It costs too much to bury it.' And when the little one did die there was no time for the mother's grief. The question crowded on at once, 'where shall the money come from?' Natural feelings and affections are smothered in the tenements." The doctor's experience furnished a sadly appropriate text for the priest's sermon.

Pitiful as these are, sights and sounds infinitely more saddening await us beyond the gate that shuts this world of woe off from whence the light of hope and reason have gone out together. The shuffling of many feet on the macadamized roads heralds the approach of a host of women, hundreds upon hundreds—beyond the turn in the road they still keep coming, marching with the faltering step, the unseeing look and the incessant, senseless chatter that betrays the darkened mind. The lunatic women of the Blackwell's Island Asylum are taking their afternoon walk. Beyond, on the wide lawn, moves another still stranger procession, a file of women in the asylum dress of dull gray, hitched to a queer little wagon that, with its gaudy adornments, suggests a cross between a baby-carriage and a circus-chariot. One crazy woman is strapped in the seat; forty tug at the rope to which they are securely bound. This is the "chain-gang," so called once in scoffing ignorance of the humane purpose the contrivance serves. These are the patients afflicted with suicidal mania, who cannot be trusted at large for a moment with the river in sight, yet must have their daily walk as a necessary part of their treatment. So this wagon was invented by a clever doctor to afford them at once exercise and amusement. A merry-go-round in the grounds suggests a variation of this scheme. Ghastly suggestion of mirth, with that stricken host advancing on its aimless journey! As we stop to see it pass, the plaintive strains of a familiar song float through a barred window in the gray stone building. The voice is sweet, but inexpressibly sad: "Oh, how my heart grows weary, far from—" The song breaks off suddenly in a low, troubled laugh. She has forgotten, forgotten—. A woman in the ranks, whose head has been turned toward the window, throws up her hands with a scream. The rest stir uneasily. The nurse is by her side in an instant with words half soothing, half stern. A messenger comes in haste from the asylum to ask us not to stop. Strangers may not linger where the patients pass. It is apt to excite them. As we go in with him the human file is passing yet, quiet restored. The troubled voice of the unseen singer still gropes vainly among the lost memories of the past for the missing key: "Oh! how my heart grows weary, far from—"

"Who is she, doctor?"

"Hopeless case. She will never see home again."

An average of seventeen hundred women this asylum harbors; the asylum for men up on Ward's Island even more. Altogether 1,419 patients were admitted to the city asylums for the insane in 1889, and at the end of the year 4,913 remained in them. There is a constant ominous increase in this class of helpless unfortunates that are thrown on the city's charity. Quite two hundred are added year by year, and the asylums were long since so overcrowded that a great "farm" had to be established on Long Island to receive the surplus. The strain of our hurried, over-worked life has something to do with this. Poverty has more. For these are all of the poor. It is the harvest of sixty and a hundred-fold, the "fearful rolling up and rolling down from generation to generation, through all the ages, of the weakness, vice, and moral darkness of the past." The curse of the island haunts all that come once within its reach. "No man or woman," says Dr. Louis L. Seaman, who speaks from many years' experience in a position that gave him full opportunity to observe the facts, "who is 'sent up' to these colonies ever returns to the city scot-free. There is a lien, visible or hidden, upon his or her present or future, which too often proves stronger than the best purposes and fairest opportunities of social rehabilitation. The under world holds in rigorous bondage every unfortunate or miscreant who has once 'served time.' There is often tragic interest in the struggles of the ensnared wretches to break away from the meshes spun about them. But the maelstrom has no bowels of mercy; and the would-be fugitives are flung back again and again into the devouring whirlpool of crime and poverty, until the end is reached on the dissecting-table, or in the Potter's Field. What can the moralist or scientist do by way of resuscitation? Very little at best. The flotsam and jetsam are mere shreds and fragments of wasted lives. Such a ministry must begin at the sources—is necessarily prophylactic, nutritive, educational. On these islands there are no flexible twigs, only gnarled, blasted, blighted trunks, insensible to moral or social influences."

Sad words, but true. The commonest keeper soon learns to pick out almost at sight the "cases" that will leave the penitentiary, the work-house, the almshouse, only to return again and again, each time more hopeless, to spend their wasted lives in the bondage of the island.

The alcoholic cells in Bellevue Hospital,[3] are a way-station for a goodly share of them on their journeys back and forth across the East River. Last

3. Established in 1736, the hospital was long associated with the poor and the victims of epidemics. However, it had developed a range of services and ancillary programs that provided much-needed medical service to New Yorkers. By the time Riis wrote *How the Other Half Lives*, Bellevue had opened a medical college; a school to train nurses; and special wards for alcoholics, the insane, emergency care, and special surgery.

year they held altogether 3,694 prisoners, considerably more than one-fourth of the whole number of 13,813 patients that went in through the hospital gates. The daily average of "cases" in this, the hospital of the poor, is over six hundred. The average daily census of all the prisons, hospitals, workhouses, and asylums in the charge of the Department of Charities and Correction last year was about 14,000, and about one employee was required for every ten of this army to keep its machinery running smoothly. The total number admitted in 1889 to all the jails and institutions in the city and on the islands was 138,332. To the almshouse alone 38,600 were admitted; 9,765 were there to start the new year with, and 553 were born with the dark shadow of the poorhouse overhanging their lives, making a total of 48,918. In the care of all their wards the commissioners expanded $2,343,372. The appropriation for the police force in 1889 was $4,409,550.94, and for the criminal courts and their machinery $403,190. Thus the first cost of maintaining our standing army of paupers, criminals, and sick poor, by direct taxation, was last year $7,156,112.94.

23. The Man with the Knife

A man stood at the corner of Fifth Avenue and Fourteenth Street the other day, looking gloomily at the carriages that rolled by, carrying the wealth and fashion of the avenues to and from the big stores down town. He was poor, and hungry, and ragged. This thought was in his mind: "They behind their well-fed teams have no thought for the morrow; they know hunger only by name, and ride down to spend in an hour's shopping what would keep me and my little ones from want a whole year." There rose up before him the picture of those little ones crying for bread around the cold and cheerless hearth—then he sprang into the throng and slashed about him with a knife, blindly seeking to kill, to revenge.

The man was arrested, of course, and locked up. To-day he is probably in a mad-house, forgotten. And the carriages roll by to and from the big stores with their gay throng of shoppers. The world forgets easily, too easily, what it does not like to remember.

Nevertheless the man and his knife had a mission. They spoke in their ignorant, impatient way the warning one of the most conservative, dispassionate of public bodies had sounded only a little while before: "Our only fear is that reform may come in a burst of public indignation destructive to property and to good morals." They represented one solution of the problem of ignorant poverty *versus* ignorant wealth that has come down to us unsolved, the danger-cry of which we have lately heard in the shout that never should have been raised on American soil—the shout of "the masses against the classes"—the solution of violence.

There is another solution, that of justice. The choice is between the two. Which shall it be?

"Well!" say some well-meaning people; "we don't see the need of putting it in that way. We have been down among the tenements, looked them over. There are a good many people there; they are not comfortable, perhaps. What would you have? They are poor. And their houses are not such hovels as we have seen and read of in the slums of the Old World. They are decent in comparison. Why, some of them have brown-stone fronts. You will own at least that they make a decent show."

Yes! that is true. The worst tenements in New York do not, as a rule, *look bad*. Neither Hell's Kitchen, nor Murderers' Row bears its true character stamped on the front. They are not quite old enough, perhaps. The same is true of their tenants. The New York tough may be ready to kill where his London brother would do little more than scowl; yet, as a general thing he is less repulsively brutal in looks. Here again the reason may be the same: the breed is not so old. A few generations more in the slums, and all that will be changed. To get at the pregnant facts of tenement-house life one must look beneath the surface. Many an apple has a fair skin and a rotten core. There is a much better argument for the tenements in the assurance of the Registrar of Vital Statistics that the death-rate of these houses has of late been brought below the general death-rate of the city, and that it is lowest in the biggest houses. This means two things: one, that the almost exclusive attention given to the tenements by the sanitary authorities in twenty years has borne some fruit, and that the newer tenements are better than the old—there is some hope in that; the other, that the whole strain of tenement-house dwellers has been bred down to the conditions under which it exists, that the struggle with corruption has begotten the power to resist it. This is a familiar law of nature, necessary to its first and strongest impulse of self-preservation. To a certain extent, we are all creatures of the conditions that surround us, physically and morally. But is the knowledge reassuring? In the light of what we have seen, does not the question arise: what sort of creature, then, this of the tenement? I tried to draw his likeness from observation in telling the story of the "tough." Has it nothing to suggest the man with the knife?

I will go further. I am not willing even to admit it to be an unqualified advantage that our New York tenements have less of the slum look than those of older cities. It helps to delay the recognition of their true character on the part of the well-meaning, but uninstructed, who are always in the majority.

The "dangerous classes" of New York long ago compelled recognition. They are dangerous less because of their own crimes than because of the criminal ignorance of those who are not of their kind. The danger to society comes not from the poverty of the tenements, but from the ill-spent wealth that reared them, that it might earn a usurious interest from a class from which "nothing else was expected." That was the broad foundation laid down, and the edifice built upon it corresponds to the groundwork. That this is well understood on the "unsafe" side of the line that separates the rich from the poor, much better than by those who have all the advantages of discriminating education, is good cause for disquietude. In it a keen foresight may again dimly discern the shadow of the man with the knife.

Two years ago a great meeting was held at Chickering Hall—I have spoken of it before—a meeting that discussed for days and nights the question how to banish this spectre; how to lay hold with good influences of this enormous mass of more than a million people, who were drifting away faster and faster from the safe moorings of the old faith. Clergymen and laymen from all the Protestant denominations took part in the discussion; nor was a good word forgotten for the brethren of the other great Christian fold who labor among the poor. Much was said that was good and true, and ways were found of reaching the spiritual needs of the tenement population that promise success. But at no time throughout the conference was the real key-note of the situation so boldly struck as has been done by a few far-seeing business men, who had listened to the cry of that Christian builder: "How shall the love of God be understood by those who have been nurtured in sight only of the greed of man?" Their practical programme of "Philanthropy and five per cent."[1] has set examples in tenement building that show, though they are yet few and scattered, what may in time be accomplished even with such poor opportunities as New York offers to-day of undoing the old wrong. This is the gospel of justice, the solution that must be sought as the one alternative to the man with the knife.

"Are you not looking too much to the material condition of these people," said a good minister to me after a lecture in a Harlem church last winter, "and forgetting the inner man?" I told him, "No! for you cannot expect to find an inner man to appeal to in the worst tenement-house surroundings. You must first put the man where he can respect himself. To reverse the argument of the apple: you cannot expect to find a sound core in a rotten fruit."

24. What Has Been Done

In twenty years what has been done in New York to solve the tenement-house problem?

The law has done what it could. That was not always a great deal, seldom more than barely sufficient for the moment. An aroused municipal conscience endowed the Health Department with almost autocratic powers in dealing with this subject, but the desire to educate rather than force the community into a better way dictated their exercise with a slow conservatism that did not always seem wise to the impatient reformer. New York has its St. Antoine, and it has often sadly missed a Napoleon III,[1] to clean up and make light in the dark corners. The obstacles, too, have been many and great. Nevertheless the authorities have not been idle, though it is a grave question whether all the improvements made under the sanitary regulations of recent years deserve the name. Tenements quite as bad as the worst are too numerous yet; but one tremendous factor for evil in the lives of the poor has been taken by the throat, and something has unquestionably been done, where that was possible, to lift those lives out of the rut where they were equally beyond the reach of hope and of ambition. It is no longer lawful to construct barracks to cover the whole of a lot. Air and sunlight have a legal claim, and the day of rear tenements is past. Two years ago a hundred thousand people burrowed in these inhuman dens; but some have been torn down since. Their number will decrease steadily until they shall have become a bad tradition of a heedless past. The dark, unventilated bedroom is going with them, and the open sewer. The day is at hand when the greatest of all evils that now curse life in the tenements—the dearth of water in the hot summer days—will also have been remedied, and a long step taken toward the moral and physical redemption of their tenants.

1. A slogan used by reformers who tried to talk builders and landlords into giving 5 percent of their profits to the construction of model tenements.
1. Louis Napoleon (1808–1873), nephew of Napoleon Bonaparte, ruled as emperor of France from 1852 to 1870. Under his rule a massive project was undertaken by Baron Haussmann to clear many Paris slums to make way for a set of grand boulevards. "St. Antoine": Saint Anthony of Padua.

Public sentiment has done something also, but very far from enough. As a rule, it has slumbered peacefully until some flagrant outrage on decency and the health of the community aroused it to noisy but ephemeral indignation, or until a dreaded epidemic knocked at our door. It is this unsteadiness of purpose that has been to a large extent responsible for the apparent lagging of the authorities in cases not involving immediate danger to the general health. The law needs a much stronger and readier backing of a thoroughly enlightened public sentiment to make it as effective as it might be made. It is to be remembered that the health officers, in dealing with this subject of dangerous houses, are constantly trenching upon what each landlord considers his private rights, for which he is ready and bound to fight to the last. Nothing short of the strongest pressure will avail to convince him that these individual rights are to be surrendered for the clear benefit of the whole. It is easy enough to convince a man that he ought not to harbor the thief who steals people's property; but to make him see that he has no right to slowly kill his neighbors, or his tenants, by making a death-trap of his house, seems to be the hardest of all tasks. It is apparently the slowness of the process that obscures his mental sight. The man who

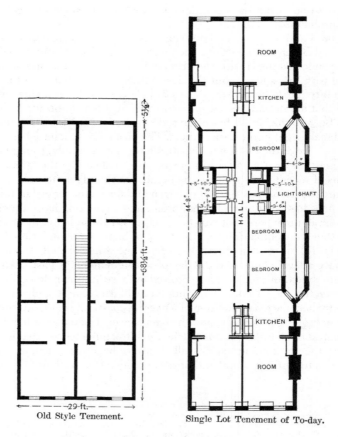

Old Style Tenement.   Single Lot Tenement of To-day.

Evolution of the tenement in twenty years

will fight an order to repair the plumbing in his house through every court he can reach, would suffer tortures rather than shed the blood of a fellow-man by actual violence. Clearly, it is a matter of education on the part of the landlord no less than the tenant.

In spite of this, the landlord has done his share; chiefly perhaps by yielding—not always gracefully—when it was no longer of any use to fight. There have been exceptions, however: men and women who have mended and built with an eye to the real welfare of their tenants as well as to their own pockets. Let it be well understood that the two are inseparable, if any good is to come of it. The business of housing the poor, if it is to amount to anything, must be business, as it was business with our fathers to put them where they are. As charity, pastime, or fad, it will miserably fail, always and everywhere. This is an inexorable rule, now thoroughly well understood in England and continental Europe, and by all who have given the matter serious thought here. Call it poetic justice, or divine justice, or anything else, it is a hard fact, not to be gotten over. Upon any other plan than the assumption that the workman has a just claim to a decent home, and the right to demand it, any scheme for his relief fails. It must be a fair exchange of the man's money for what he can afford to buy at a reasonable price. Any charity scheme merely turns him into a pauper, however it may be disguised, and drowns him hopelessly in the mire out of which it proposed to pull him. And this principle must pervade the whole plan. Expert management of model tenements succeeds where amateur management, with the best intentions, gives up the task, discouraged, as a flat failure. Some of the best-conceived enterprises, backed by abundant capital and good-will, have been wrecked on this rock. Sentiment, having prompted the effort, forgot to stand aside and let business make it.

Business, in a wider sense, has done more than all other agencies together to wipe out the worst tenements. It has been New York's real Napoleon III, from whose decree there was no appeal. In ten years I have seen plague-spots disappear before its onward march, with which health officers, police, and sanitary science had struggled vainly since such struggling began as a serious business. And the process goes on still. Unfortunately, the crowding in some of the most densely packed quarters down-town has made the property there so valuable, that relief from this source is less confidently to be expected, at all events in the near future. Still, their time may come also. It comes so quickly sometimes as to fairly take one's breath away. More than once I have returned, after a few brief weeks, to some specimen rookery in which I was interested, to find it gone and an army of workmen delving twenty feet underground to lay the foundation of a mighty warehouse. That was the case with the "Big Flat" in Mott Street. I had not had occasion to visit it for several months last winter, and when I went there, entirely unprepared for a change, I could not find it. It had always been conspicuous enough in the landscape before, and I marvelled much at my own stupidity until, by examining the number of the house, I found out that I had gone right. It was the "flat" that had disappeared. In its place towered a six-story carriage factory with business going on on every floor, as if it had been there for years and years.

This same "Big Flat" furnished a good illustration of why some well-meant efforts in tenement building have failed. Like Gotham Court, it was originally built as a model tenement, but speedily came to rival the Court in foulness. It became a regular hot-bed of thieves and peace-breakers, and made no end of trouble for the police. The immediate reason, outside of the lack of proper supervision, was that it had open access to two streets in a neighborhood where thieves and "toughs" abounded. These took advantage of an arrangement that had been supposed by the builders to be a real advantage as a means of ventilation, and their occupancy drove honest folk away. Murderers' Alley, of which I have spoken elsewhere, and the sanitary inspector's experiment with building a brick wall athwart it to shut off travel through the block, is a parallel case.

The causes that operate to obstruct efforts to better the lot of the tenement population are, in our day, largely found among the tenants themselves. This is true particularly of the poorest. They are shiftless, destructive, and stupid; in a word, they are what the tenements have made them. It is a dreary old truth that those who would fight for the poor must fight the poor to do it. It must be confessed that there is little enough in their past experience to inspire confidence in the sincerity of the effort to help them. I recall the discomfiture of a certain well-known philanthropist, since deceased, whose heart beat responsive to other suffering than that of human kind. He was a large owner of tenement property, and once undertook to fit out his houses with stationary tubs, sanitary plumbing, wood-closets, and all the latest improvements. He introduced his rough tenants to all this magnificence without taking the precaution of providing a competent housekeeper, to see that the new acquaintances got on together. He felt that his tenants ought to be grateful for the interest he took in them. They were. They found the boards in the wood-closets fine kindling wood, while the pipes and faucets were as good as cash at the junk shop. In three months the owner had to remove what was left of his improvements. The pipes were cut and the houses running full of water, the stationary tubs were put to all sorts of uses except washing, and of the wood-closets not a trace was left. The philanthropist was ever after a firm believer in the total depravity of tenement-house people. Others have been led to like reasoning by as plausible arguments, without discovering that the shiftlessness and ignorance that offended them were the consistent crop of the tenement they were trying to reform, and had to be included in the effort. The owners of a block of model tenements uptown had got their tenants comfortably settled, and were indulging in high hopes of their redemption under proper management, when a contractor ran up a row of "skin" tenements, shaky but fair to look at, with brown-stone trimmings and gewgaws.[2] The result was to tempt a lot of the well-housed tenants away. It was a very astonishing instance of perversity to the planners of the benevolent scheme; but, after all, there was nothing strange in it. It is all a matter of education, as I said about the landlord.

That the education comes slowly need excite no surprise. The forces on the other side are ever active. The faculty of the tenement for appropriating to itself every foul thing that comes within its reach, and piling up and intensifying its corruption until out of all proportion to the beginning, is something marvellous. Drop a case of scarlet fever, of measles, or of diphtheria into one of these barracks, and, unless it is caught at the very start

2. Bric-a-brac, ornamentation. "Skin tenements": Tenements with elaborate facades that were, however, poorly built.

and stamped out, the contagion of the one case will sweep block after block, and half people a graveyard. Let the police break up a vile dive, goaded by the angry protests of the neighborhood—forthwith the outcasts set in circulation by the raid betake themselves to the tenements, where in their hired rooms, safe from interference, they set up as many independent centres of contagion, infinitely more destructive, each and every one, than was the known dive before. I am not willing to affirm that this is the police reason for letting so many of the dives alone; but it might well be. They are perfectly familiar with the process, and quite powerless to prevent it.

This faculty, as inherent in the problem itself—the prodigious increase of the tenement-house population that goes on without cessation, and its consequent greater crowding—is the chief obstacle to its solution. In 1869 there were 14,872 tenements in New York, with a population of 468,492 persons. In 1879 the number of the tenements was estimated at 21,000, and their tenants had passed the half-million mark. At the end of the year 1888, when a regular census was made for the first time since 1869, the showing was: 32,390 tenements, with a population of 1,093,701 souls. To-day we have 37,316 tenements, including 2,630 rear houses, and their population is over 1,250,000. A large share of this added population, especially of that which came to us from abroad, crowds in below Fourteenth Street, where the population is already packed beyond reason, and confounds all attempts to make matters better there. At the same time new slums are constantly growing up uptown, and have to be kept down with a firm hand. This drift of the population to the great cities has to be taken into account as a steady factor. It will probably increase rather than decrease for many years to come. At the beginning of the century the percentage of our population that lived in cities was as one in twenty-five. In 1880 it was one in four and one-half, and in 1890 the census will in all probability show it to be one in four. Against such tendencies, in the absence of suburban outlets for the crowding masses, all remedial measures must prove more or less ineffective. The "confident belief" expressed by the Board of Health in 1874, that rapid transit[3] would solve the problem, is now known to have been a vain hope.

Workingmen, in New York at all events, will live near their work, no matter at what sacrifice of comfort—one might almost say at whatever cost, and the city will never be less crowded than it is. To distribute the crowds as evenly as possible is the effort of the authorities, where nothing better can be done. In the first six months of the present year 1,068 persons were turned out of not quite two hundred tenements below Houston Street by the sanitary police on their midnight inspections, and this covered only a very small part of that field. The uptown tenements were practically left to take care of themselves in this respect.

The quick change of economic conditions in the city that often outpaces all plans of relief, rendering useless to-day what met the demands of the situation well enough yesterday, is another cause of perplexity. A common obstacle also—I am inclined to think quite as common as in Ireland,[4] though

---

3. By 1879 four elevated lines had opened up.
4. One of Ireland's most chronic economic problems, and one that exacerbated its dire poverty, involved the fact that many of its landlords lived in England, leaving the management of their estates to superintendents and showing no real concern for their tenants. Economists blamed absenteeism for much of the disrepair of the countryside and the relatively primitive nature of Irish farming.

we hear less of it in the newspapers—is the absentee landlord. The home article, who fights for his rights, as he chooses to consider them, is bad enough; but the absentee landlord is responsible for no end of trouble. He was one of the first obstructions the sanitary reformers stumbled over, when the Health Department took hold. It reported in 1869 that many of the tenants were entirely uncared for, and that the only answer to their requests to have the houses put in order was an invitation to pay their rent or get out. "Inquiry often disclosed the fact that the owner of the property was a wealthy gentleman or lady, either living in an aristocratic part of the city, or in a neighboring city, or, as was occasionally found to be the case, in Europe. The property is usually managed entirely by an agent, whose instructions are simple but emphatic: Collect the rent in advance, or, failing, eject the occupants." The Committee having the matter in charge proposed to compel owners of tenements with ten families or more to put a housekeeper in the house, who should be held responsible to the Health Department. Unluckily the powers of the Board gave out at that point, and the proposition was not acted upon then. Could it have been, much trouble would have been spared the Health Board, and untold suffering the tenants in many houses. The tribe of absentee landlords is by no means extinct in New York. Not a few who fled from across the sea to avoid being crushed by his heel there have groaned under it here, scarcely profiting by the exchange. Sometimes—it can hardly be said in extenuation—the heel that crunches is applied in saddening ignorance. I recall the angry indignation of one of these absentee landlords, a worthy man who, living far away in the country, had inherited city property, when he saw the condition of his slum tenements. The man was shocked beyond expression, all the more because he did not know whom to blame except himself for the state of things that had aroused his wrath, and yet, conscious of the integrity of his intentions, felt that he should not justly be held responsible.

The experience of this landlord points directly to the remedy which the law failed to supply to the early reformers. It has since been fully demonstrated that a competent agent on the premises, a man of the best and the highest stamp, who knows how to instruct and guide with a firm hand, is a prerequisite to the success of any reform tenement scheme. This is a plain business proposition, that has been proved entirely sound in some notable instances of tenement building, of which more hereafter. Even among the poorer tenements, those are always the best in which the owner himself lives. It is a hopeful sign in any case. The difficulty of procuring such assistance without having to pay a ruinous price, is one of the obstructions that have vexed in this city efforts to solve the problem of housing the poor properly, because it presupposes that the effort must be made on a larger scale than has often been attempted.

The readiness with which the tenants respond to intelligent efforts in their behalf, when made under fair conditions, is as surprising as it is gratifying, and fully proves the claim that tenants are only satisfied in filthy and unwholesome surroundings because nothing better is offered. The moral effect is as great as the improvement of their physical health. It is clearly discernible in the better class of tenement dwellers to-day. The change in the character of the colored population in the few years since it began to move out of the wicked rookeries[5] of the old "Africa" to the decent tenements

5. Slums, nineteenth-century slang.

in Yorkville, furnishes a notable illustration, and a still better one is found in the contrast between the model tenement in the Mulberry Street Bend and the barracks across the way, of which I spoke in the chapter devoted to the Italian. The Italian himself is the strongest argument of all. With his fatal contentment in the filthiest surroundings, he gives undoubted evidence of having in him the instinct of cleanliness that, properly cultivated, would work his rescue in a very little while. It is a queer contradiction, but the fact is patent to anyone who has observed the man in his home-life. And he is not alone in this. I came across an instance, this past summer, of how a refined, benevolent personality works like a leaven in even the roughest tenement-house crowd. This was no model tenement; far from it. It was a towering barrack in the Tenth Ward, sheltering more than twenty families. All the light and air that entered its interior came through an air-shaft two feet square, upon which two bedrooms and the hall gave in every story. In three years I had known of two domestic tragedies, prompted by poverty and justifiable disgust with life, occurring in the house, and had come to look upon it as a typically bad tenement, quite beyond the pale of possible improvement. What was my surprise, when chance led me to it once more after a while, to find the character of the occupants entirely changed. Some of the old ones were there still, but they did not seem to be the same people. I discovered the secret to be the new housekeeper, a tidy, mild-mannered, but exceedingly strict little body, who had a natural faculty of drawing her depraved surroundings within the beneficent sphere of her strong sympathy, and withal of exacting respect for her orders. The worst elements had been banished from the house in short order under her management, and for the rest a new era of self-respect had dawned. They were, as a body, as vastly superior to the general run of their class as they had before seemed below it. And this had been effected in the short space of a single year.

My observations on this point are more than confirmed by those of nearly all the practical tenement reformers I have known, who have patiently held to the course they had laid down. One of these,[6] whose experience exceeds that of all of the rest together, and whose influence for good has been very great, said to me recently: "I hold that not ten per cent. of the people now living in tenements would refuse to avail themselves of the best improved conditions offered, and come fully up to the use of them, properly instructed; but they cannot get them. They are up to them now, fully, if the chances were only offered. They don't have to come up. It is all a gigantic mistake on the part of the public, of which these poor people are the victims. I have built homes for more than five hundred families in fourteen years, and I have been getting daily more faith in human nature from my work among the poor tenants, though approaching that nature on a plane and under conditions that could scarcely promise better for disappointment." It is true that my friend has built his houses in Brooklyn; but human nature does not differ greatly on the two shores of the East River. For those who think it does, it may be well to remember that only five years ago the Tenement-house Commission summed up the situation in this city in the declaration that, "the condition of the tenants is in advance of the houses which they occupy," quite the severest arraignment of the tenement that had yet been uttered.

6. Alfred Tredway White, president of the Brooklyn Bureau of Charities, who developed several model tenement complexes in Brooklyn in 1878 and 1890.

The many philanthropic efforts that have been made in the last few years to render less intolerable the lot of the tenants in the homes where many of them must continue to live, have undoubtedly had their effect in creating a disposition to accept better things, that will make plainer sailing for future builders of model tenements. In many ways, as in the "College Settlement" of courageous girls, the Neighborhood Guilds,[7] through the efforts of The King's Daughters, and numerous other schemes of practical mission work, the poor and the well-to-do have been brought closer together, in an every-day companionship that cannot but be productive of the best results, to the one who gives no less than to the one who receives. And thus, as a good lady wrote to me once, though the problem stands yet unsolved, more perplexing than ever; though the bright spots in the dreary picture be too often bright only by comparison, and many of the expedients hit upon for relief sad makeshifts, we can dimly discern behind it all that good is somehow working out of even this slough of despond the while it is deepening and widening in our sight, and in His own good season, if we labor on with courage and patience, will bear fruit sixty and a hundred fold.

25. How the Case Stands

What, then, are the bald facts with which we have to deal in New York?

I. That we have a tremendous, ever swelling crowd of wage-earners which it is our business to house decently.

II. That it is not housed decently.

III. That it must be so housed *here* for the present, and for a long time to come, all schemes of suburban relief being as yet utopian, impracticable.

IV. That it pays high enough rents to entitle it to be so housed, as a right.

V. That nothing but our own slothfulness is in the way of so housing it, since "the condition of the tenants is in advance of the condition of the houses which they occupy" (Report of Tenement-house Commission[1]).

VI. That the security of the one no less than of the other half demands, on sanitary, moral, and economic grounds, that it be decently housed.

VII. That it will pay to do it. As an investment, I mean, and in hard cash. This I shall immediately proceed to prove.

VIII. That the tenement has come to stay, and must itself be the solution of the problem with which it confronts us.

7. Riis is unlikely to be referring to the College Settlement that opened in 1899 but rather to settlement houses in general, which had begun to crop up in the years surrounding the writing of *How the Other Half Lives*. The oldest of these, University Settlement, opened its doors at 146 Forsyth Street in 1886, then called the Lily Pleasure Club, as an effort by divinity students to bring recreational and other programs to poor boys in the slum neighborhood. It took the name of the Neighborhood Guild in 1887 and became the University Settlement in 1891. In Chicago, Jane Addams and Ellen Gates Starr opened Hull House in 1889.

1. The city had been attempting to upgrade tenements since 1867 when it passed the first Tenement House Law, which defined the tenement and imposed some obligations on landlords, such as providing fire ladders and privies and making provisions for light and air to penetrate interior rooms. The Tenement House Law of 1879 attempted to enforce the earlier law and led to the development of "dumbbell tenements," buildings that looked like a dumbbell if seen from above, owing to the indentation between the front and back rooms to crate air shafts.

This is the fact from which we cannot get away, however we may deplore it. Doubtless the best would be to get rid of it altogether; but as we cannot, all argument on that score may at this time be dismissed as idle. The practical question is what to do with the tenement. I watched a Mott Street landlord, the owner of a row of barracks that have made no end of trouble for the health authorities for twenty years, solve that question for himself the other day. His way was to give the wretched pile a coat of paint, and put a gorgeous tin cornice on with the years 1890 in letters a yard long. From where I stood watching the operation, I looked down upon the same dirty crowds camping on the roof, foremost among them an Italian mother with two stark-naked children who had apparently never made the acquaintance of a wash-tub. That was a landlord's way, and will not get us out of the mire.

The "flat" is another way that does not solve the problem. Rather, it extends it. The flat is not a model, though it is a modern, tenement. It gets rid of some of the nuisances of the low tenement, and of the worst of them, the over-crowding—if it gets rid of them at all—at a cost that takes it at once out of the catalogue of "homes for the poor," while imposing some of the evils from which they suffer upon those who ought to escape from them.

There are three effective ways of dealing with the tenements in New York:

   I. By law.

   II. By remodelling and making the most out of the old houses.

   III. By building new, model tenements.

Private enterprise—conscience, to put it in the category of duties, where it belongs—must do the lion's share under these last two heads. Of what the law has effected I have spoken already. The drastic measures adopted in Paris, in Glasgow, and in London[2] are not practicable here on anything like as large a scale. Still it can, under strong pressure of public opinion, rid us of the worst plague-spots. The Mulberry Street Bend will go the way of the Five Points when all the red tape that binds the hands of municipal effort has been unwound. Prizes were offered in public competition, some years ago, for the best plans of modern tenement-houses. It may be that we shall see the day when the building of model tenements will be encouraged by subsidies in the way of a rebate of taxes. Meanwhile the arrest and summary punishment of landlords, or their agents, who persistently violate law and decency, will have a salutary effect. If a few of the wealthy absentee landlords, who are the worst offenders, could be got within the jurisdiction of the city, and by arrest be compelled to employ proper overseers, it would be a proud day for New York. To remedy the overcrowding, with which the night inspections of the sanitary police cannot keep step, tenements may eventually have to be licensed, as now the lodging-houses, to hold so many tenants, and no more; or the State may have to bring down the rents that cause the crowding, by assuming the right to regulate them as it regulates

2. These three cities undertook massive urban renewal projects, which involved slum clearance. Glasgow, for example, embarked on its projects in 1875. The issues of housing and poverty in the industrial city extended far beyond the specific situation of New York, and reformers participated in a transatlantic discussion about the best ways to deal with matters of congestion, disease, unsanitary conditions, and crime.

the fares on the elevated roads. I throw out the suggestion, knowing quite well that it is open to attack. It emanated originally from one of the brightest minds that have had to struggle officially with this tenement-house question in the last ten years. In any event, to succeed, reform by law must aim at making it unprofitable to own a bad tenement. At best, it is apt to travel at a snail's pace, while the enemy it pursues is putting the best foot foremost.

In this matter of profit the law ought to have its strongest ally in the landlord himself, though the reverse is the case. This condition of things I believe to rest on a monstrous error. It cannot be that tenement property that is worth preserving at all can continue to yield larger returns, if allowed to run down, than if properly cared for and kept in good repair. The point must be reached, and soon, where the cost of repairs, necessary with a house full of the lowest, most ignorant tenants, must overbalance the saving of the first few years of neglect; for this class is everywhere the most destructive, as well as the poorest paying. I have the experience of owners, who have found this out to their cost, to back me up in the assertion, even if it were not the statement of a plain business fact that proves itself. I do not include tenement property that is deliberately allowed to fall into decay because at some future time the ground will be valuable for business or other purposes. There is unfortunately enough of that kind in New York, often leasehold property owned by wealthy estates or soulless corporations that oppose all their great influence to the efforts of the law in behalf of their tenants.

There is abundant evidence, on the other hand, that it can be made to pay to improve and make the most of the worst tenement property, even in the most wretched locality. The example set by Miss Ellen Collins[3] in her Water Street houses will always stand as a decisive answer to all doubts on this point. It is quite ten years since she bought three old tenements at the corner of Water and Roosevelt Streets, then as now one of the lowest localities in the city. Since then she has leased three more adjoining her purchase, and so much of Water Street has at all events been purified. Her first effort was to let in the light in the hallways, and with the darkness disappeared, as if by magic, the heaps of refuse that used to be piled up beside the sinks. A few of the most refractory tenants disappeared with them, but a very considerable proportion stayed, conforming readily to the new rules, and are there yet. It should here be stated that Miss Collins's tenants are distinctly of the poorest. Her purpose was to experiment with this class, and her experiment has been more than satisfactory. Her plan was, as she puts it herself, fair play between tenant and landlord. To this end the rents were put as low as consistent with the idea of a business investment that must return a reasonable interest to be successful. The houses were thoroughly refitted with proper plumbing. A competent janitor was put in charge to see that the rules were observed by the tenants, when Miss Collins herself was not there. Of late years she has had to give very little time to personal superintendence, and the care-taker told me only the other day that very little

3. A member of the New York Mission Society and the Society for Improving the Condition of the Poor, Collins (1828–1912) purchased four rookeries on Water Street and tried to transform them into model tenements. She rented the apartments to tenants who had to agree to follow a strict code of behavior to live there. She limited herself to a profit margin of 6 percent.

was needed. The houses seemed to run themselves in the groove once laid down. Once the reputed haunt of thieves, they have become the most orderly in the neighborhood. Clothes are left hanging on the lines all night with impunity, and the pretty flower-beds in the yard where the children not only from the six houses, but of the whole block, play, skip, and swing, are undisturbed. The tenants, by the way, provide the flowers themselves in the spring, and take all the more pride in them because they are their own. The six houses contain forty-five families, and there "has never been any need of putting up a bill." As to the income from the property, Miss Collins said to me last August: "I have had six and even six and three-quarters per cent. on the capital invested; on the whole, you may safely say five and a half per cent. This I regard as entirely satisfactory." It should be added that she has persistently refused to let the corner-store, now occupied by a butcher, as a saloon; or her income from it might have been considerably increased.

Miss Collins's experience is of value chiefly as showing what can be accomplished with the worst possible material, by the sort of personal interest in the poor that alone will meet their real needs. All the charity in the world, scattered with the most lavish hand, will not take its place. "Fair play" between landlord and tenant is the key, too long mislaid, that unlocks the door to success everywhere as it did for Miss Collins. She has not lacked imitators whose experience has been akin to her own. The case of Gotham Court has been already cited. On the other hand, instances are not wanting of landlords who have undertaken the task, but have tired of it or sold their property before it had been fully redeemed, with the result that it relapsed into its former bad condition faster than it had improved, and the tenants with it. I am inclined to think that such houses are liable to fall even below the average level. Backsliding in brick and mortar does not greatly differ from similar performances in flesh and blood.

Backed by a strong and steady sentiment, such as these pioneers have evinced, that would make it the personal business of wealthy owners with time to spare to look after their tenants, the law would be able in a very short time to work a salutary transformation in the worst quarters, to the lasting advantage, I am well persuaded, of the landlord no less than the tenant. Unfortunately, it is in this quality of personal effort that the sentiment of interest in the poor, upon which we have to depend, is too often lacking. People who are willing to give money feel that that ought to be enough. It is not. The money thus given is too apt to be wasted along with the sentiment that prompted the gift.

Even when it comes to the third of the ways I spoke of as effective in dealing with the tenement-house problem, the building of model structures, the personal interest in the matter must form a large share of the capital invested, if it is to yield full returns. Where that is the case, there is even less doubt about its paying, with ordinary business management, than in the case of reclaiming an old building, which is, like putting life into a defunct newspaper, pretty apt to be up-hill work. Model tenement building has not been attempted in New York on anything like as large a scale as in many other great cities, and it is perhaps owing to this, in a measure, that a belief prevails that it cannot succeed here. This is a wrong notion entirely. The various undertakings of that sort that have been made here under intelligent management have, as far as I know, all been successful.

From the managers of the two best-known experiments in model tenement building in the city, the Improved Dwellings Association and the
Tenement-house Building Company,[4] I have letters dated last August,
declaring their enterprises eminently successful. There is no reason why
their experience should not be conclusive. That the Philadelphia plan is not
practicable in New York is not a good reason why our own plan, which is precisely the reverse of our neighbor's, should not be. In fact it is an argument
for its success. The very reason why we cannot house our working masses
in cottages, as has been done in Philadelphia—viz., that they must live on
Manhattan Island, where the land is too costly for small houses—is the best
guarantee of the success of the model tenement house, properly located and
managed. The drift in tenement building, as in everything else, is toward
concentration, and helps smooth the way. Four families on the floor,
twenty in the house, is the rule of to-day. As the crowds increase, the need
of guiding this drift into safe channels becomes more urgent. The larger the
scale upon which the model tenement is planned, the more certain the
promise of success. The utmost ingenuity cannot build a house for sixteen
or twenty families on a lot 25×100 feet in the middle of a block like it, that
shall give them the amount of air and sunlight to be had by the erection of
a dozen or twenty houses on a common plan around a central yard. This was
the view of the committee that awarded the prizes for the best plan for
the conventional tenement, ten years ago. It coupled its verdict with the
emphatic declaration that, in its view, it was "impossible to secure the
requirements of physical and moral health within these narrow and arbitrary
limits." Houses have been built since on better plans than any the committee saw, but its judgment stands unimpaired. A point, too, that is not to be
overlooked, is the reduced cost of expert superintendence—the first condition of successful management—in the larger buildings.

The Improved Dwellings Association put up its block of thirteen houses in
East Seventy-second Street nine years ago. Their cost, estimated at about
$240,000 with the land, was increased to $285,000 by troubles with the contractor engaged to build them. Thus the Association's task did not begin
under the happiest auspices. Unexpected expenses came to deplete its treasury. The neighborhood was new and not crowded at the start. No expense
was spared, and the benefit of all the best and most recent experience in tenement building was given to the tenants. The families were provided with from
two to four rooms, all "outer" rooms, of course, at rents ranging from $14 per
month for the four on the ground floor, to $6.25 for two rooms on the top
floor. Coal lifts, ash-chutes, common laundries in the basement, and free
baths, are features of these buildings that were then new enough to be looked
upon with suspicion by the doubting Thomases who predicted disaster.
There are rooms in the block for 218 families, and when I looked in recently
all but nine of the apartments were let. One of the nine was rented while I
was in the building. The superintendent told me that he had little trouble
with disorderly tenants, though the buildings shelter all sorts of people. Mr.
W. Bayard Cutting, the President of the Association, writes to me:

---

4. In 1887 this company built the city's second improved tenement block, spanning 338 to 344
Cherry Street. "Improved Dwellings Association": Founded in 1879, this organization, headed by
W. Bayard Cutting, built the first planned, reform-inspired tenement in New York, on First Avenue,
between Seventy-first and Seventy-second Street. Cutting (1850–1912): financier, real estate
developer, and philanthropist.

"By the terms of subscription to the stock before incorporation, dividends were limited to five per cent. on the stock of the Improved Dwellings Association. These dividends have been paid (two per cent. each six months) ever since the expiration of the first six months of the buildings operation. All surplus has been expended upon the buildings. New and expensive roofs have been put on for the comfort of such tenants as might choose to use them. The buildings have been completely painted inside and out in a manner not contemplated at the outset. An expensive set of fire-escapes has been put on at the command of the Fire Department, and a considerable number of other improvements made. *I regard the experiment as eminently successful and satisfactory,* particularly when it is considered that the buildings were the first erected in this city upon anything like a large scale, where it was proposed to meet the architectural difficulties that present themselves in the tenement-house problem. I have no doubt that the experiment could be tried to-day with the improved knowledge which has come with time, and a much larger return be shown upon the investment. The results referred to have been attained in spite of the provision which prevents the selling of liquor upon the Association's premises. You are aware, of course, how much larger rent can be obtained for a liquor saloon than for an ordinary store. An investment at five per cent. net upon real estate security worth more than the principal sum, ought to be considered desirable."

The Tenement-house Building Company made its "experiment" in a much more difficult neighborhood, Cherry Street, some six years later. Its houses shelter many Russian Jews, and the difficulty of keeping them in order is correspondingly increased, particularly as there are no ash-chutes in the houses. It has been necessary even to shut the children out of the yards upon which the kitchen windows give, lest they be struck by something thrown out by the tenants, and killed. It is the Cherry Street style, not easily got rid of. Nevertheless, the houses are well kept. Of the one hundred and six "apartments," only four were vacant in August. Professor Edwin R. A. Seligman,[5] the secretary of the company, writes to me: "The tenements are now a decided success." In the three years since they were built, they have returned an interest of from five to five and a half per cent. on the capital invested. The original intention of making the tenants profit-shares on a plan of rent insurance, under which all earnings above four per cent. would be put to the credit of the tenants, has not yet been carried out.

A scheme of dividends to tenants on a somewhat similar plan has been carried out by a Brooklyn builder, Mr. A. T. White,[6] who has devoted a life of beneficent activity to tenement building, and whose experience, though it has been altogether across the East River, I regard as justly applying to New York as well. He so regards it himself. Discussing the cost of building, he says: "There is not the slightest reason to doubt that the financial result of a similar undertaking in any tenement-house district of New York City would be equally good. . . . High cost of land is no detriment, provided the

5. Seligman (1861–1939), economics professor at Columbia University, also participated in numerous progress reforms in the city.
6. Alfred Treadway White (1846–1920), housing reformer whose first project involved the Tower and Home Building, which opened in Brooklyn in 1877. Inspired by similar housing projects in London, he offered model tenements for respectable but poor people and limited his own profit to 5 percent.

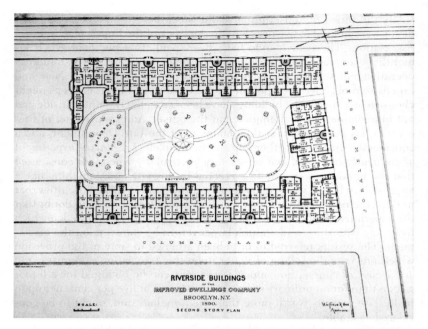

General plan of the Riverside Buildings (A. T. White's) in Brooklyn

value is made by the pressure of people seeking residence there. Rents in New York City bear a higher ratio to Brooklyn rents than would the cost of land and building in the one city to that in the other." The assertion that Brooklyn furnishes a better class of tenants than the tenement districts in New York would not be worth discussing seriously, even if Mr. White did not meet it himself with the statement that the proportion of day-laborers and sewing-women in his houses is greater than in any of the London model tenements, showing that they reach the humblest classes.

Mr. White has built homes for five hundred poor families since he began his work, and has made it pay well enough to allow good tenants a share in the profits, averaging nearly one month's rent out of the twelve, as a premium upon promptness and order. The plan of his last tenements, reproduced on p. 165; may be justly regarded as the *beau ideal* of the model tenement for a great city like New York. It embodies all the good features of Sir Sydney Waterlow's[7] London plan, with improvements suggested by the builder's own experience. Its chief merit is that it gathers three hundred real homes, not simply three hundred families, under one roof. Three tenants, it will be seen, use each entrance hall. Of the rest of the three hundred they may never know, rarely see, one. Each has his private front-door. The common hall, with all that it stands for, has disappeared. The fire-proof stairs are outside the house, a perfect fire-escape. Each tenant has his own scullery and ash-flue. There are no air-shafts, for they are not needed. Every room, under the admirable arrangement of the plan, looks out either upon the street or the yard, that is nothing less than a great park with a

7. British philanthropist (1822–1906), who in the 1860s served as chair of the Improved Industrial Dwellings Company.

PLAN OF APARTMENTS.

Floor plan of one division in the "RIVERSIDE," showing six
apartments, four of four rooms and two of three rooms.

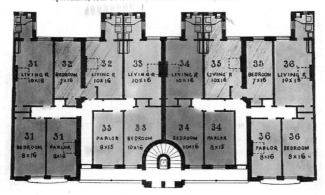

Floor plan of one division in the Riverside Buildings, showing six "apartments"

play-ground set apart for the children, where they may dig in the sand to
their heart's content. Weekly concerts are given in the park by a brass band.
The drying of clothes is done on the roof, where racks are fitted up for the
purpose. The outside stairways end in turrets that give the buildings a very
smart appearance. Mr. White never has any trouble with his tenants,
though he gathers in the poorest; nor do his tenements have anything of
the "institution character" that occasionally attaches to ventures of this
sort, to their damage. They are like a big village of contented people, who
live in peace with one another because they have elbow-room even under
one big roof.

Enough has been said to show that model tenements can be built successfully and made to pay in New York, if the owner will be content with
the five or six per cent. he does not even dream of when investing his funds
in "governments" at three or four. It is true that in the latter case he has
only to cut off his coupons and cash them. But the extra trouble of looking
after his tenement property, that is the condition of his highest and lasting
success, is the penalty exacted for the sins of our fathers that "shall be visited upon the children, unto the third and fourth generation." We shall
indeed be well off, if it stop there. I fear there is too much reason to believe
that our own iniquities must be added to transmit the curse still further.
And yet, such is the leavening influence of a good deed in that dreary desert
of sin and suffering, that the erection of a single good tenement has the
power to change, gradually but surely, the character of a whole bad block.
It sets up a standard to which the neighborhood must rise, if it cannot succeed in dragging it down to its own low level.

And so this task, too, has come to an end. Whatsoever a man soweth, that
shall he also reap. I have aimed to tell the truth as I saw it. If this book shall
have borne ever so feeble a hand in garnering a harvest of justice, it has
served its purpose. While I was writing these lines I went down to the sea,
where thousands from the city were enjoying their summer rest. The ocean

slumbered under a cloudless sky. Gentle waves washed lazily over the white sand, where children fled before them with screams of laughter. Standing there and watching their play, I was told that during the fierce storms of winter it happened that this sea, now so calm, rose in rage and beat down, broke over the bluff, sweeping all before it. No barrier built by human hands had power to stay it then. The sea of a mighty population, held in galling fetters, heaves uneasily in the tenements. Once already our city, to which have come the duties and responsibilities of metropolitan greatness before it was able to fairly measure its task, has felt the swell of its resistless flood. If it rise once more, no human power may avail to check it. The gap between the classes in which it surges, unseen, unsuspected by the thoughtless, is widening day by day. No tardy enactment of law, no political expedient, can close it. Against all other dangers our system of government may offer defence and shelter; against this not. I know of but one bridge that will carry us over safe, a bridge founded upon justice and built of human hearts. I believe that the danger of such conditions as are fast growing up around us is greater for the very freedom which they mock. The words of the poet, with whose lines I prefaced this book, are truer to-day, have far deeper meaning to us, than when they were penned forty years ago:

> —Think ye that building shall endure
> Which shelters the noble and crushes the poor?[8]

8. From "The Parable," by James Russell Lowell.

CONTEXTS

Lower Manhattan, Late 1800s

1 BATTERY
2 THOMPSON ST.
3 MULBERRY ST.
4 POST OFFICE
5 FERRY WHARF
6 COLLECT POND
7 FIVE POINTS
8 WASHINGTON SQUARE
9 CHATHAM SQUARE
10 PEARL ST.
11 VESEY ST.
12 TRINITY CHURCH
13 CUSTOM HOUSE
14 WALL ST. FERRY TO BROOKLYN
15 TOMBS PRISON.
16 MOTT ST.
17 NEWSBOY'S LODGING HOUSE
18 OLD BOWERY THEATRE
19 SPRUCE ST.
20 BAXTER ST.
21 TRIBUNE
22 CITY HALL
23 NASSAU ST.
24 ANN ST.
25 BROADWAY
26 CHATHAM ST.
27 CORNER OF BROADWAY
   AND CHAMBERS ST.
28 NEW YORK HOSPITAL
29 PARK PLACE

BROOKLYN

NEW
JERSEY

168

The Five Points in the 1800s

★ The Five Points Intersection.
1 The Tombs Prison, erected 1838.
2 The Bowery Theatre.

About Riis—In His Own Words

JACOB A. RIIS
From The Making of an American[†]

Introduction by Theodore Roosevelt

It is difficult for me to write of Jacob Riis only from the public standpoint. He was one of my truest and closest friends. I have ever prized the fact that once, in speaking of me, he said, "Since I met him he has been my brother." I have not only admired and respected him beyond measure, but I have loved him dearly, and I mourn him as if he were one of my own family.

But this has little to do with what I wish to say. Jacob Riis was one of those men who by his writings contributed most to raising the standard of unselfishness, of disinterestedness, of sane and kindly good citizenship, in this country. But in addition to this he was one of the few great writers for clean and decent living and for upright conduct who was also a great doer. He never wrote sentences which he did not in good faith try to act whenever he could find the opportunity for action. He was emphatically a "doer of the word," and not either a mere hearer or a mere preacher. Moreover, he was one of those good men whose goodness was free from the least taint of priggishness or self-righteousness. He had a white soul; but he had the keenest sympathy for his brethren who stumbled and fell. He had the most flaming intensity of passion for righteousness, but he also had kindliness and a most humorously human way of looking at life and a sense of companionship with his fellows. He did not come to this country until he was almost a young man; but if I were asked to name a fellow-man who came nearest to being the ideal American citizen, I should name Jacob Riis.

—From The Outlook, June 6, 1914.

Chapter XI. *The Bend Is Laid by the Heels*

If there be any to whom the travail through which we have just come seems like a mighty tempest in a teapot, let him quit thinking so. It was not a small matter. To be sure, the wrong could have been undone in a day by the authorities, had they been so minded. That it was not undone was largely, and illogically, because no one had a word to say in its defence. When there are two sides to a thing, it is not difficult to get at the right of it in an argument, and to carry public opinion for the right. But when there is absolutely nothing to be said against a proposed reform, it seems to be human

---

[†] New York: Macmillan, 1947. All footnotes are Riis's.

nature—American human nature, at all events—to expect it to carry itself
through with the general good wishes but no particular lift from any one.
It is a very charming expression of our faith in the power of the right to
make its way, only it is all wrong: it will not make its way in the generation
that sits by to see it move. It has got to be moved along, like everything else
in this world, by men. That is how we take title to the name. That is what
is the matter with half our dead-letter laws. The other half were just still-
born. It is so, at this moment, with the children's playgrounds in New York.
Probably all thinking people subscribe to-day to the statement that it is the
business of the municipality to give its children a chance to play, just as
much as to give them schools to go to. Everybody applauds it. The authorities do not question it; but still they do not provide playgrounds. Private
charity has to keep a beggarly half-dozen going where there ought to be
forty or fifty, as a matter of right, not of charity. Call it official conservatism,
inertia, treachery, call it by soft names or hard; in the end it comes to this,
I suppose, that it is the whetstone upon which our purpose is sharpened,
and in that sense we have apparently got to be thankful for it. So a man may
pummel his adversary and accept him as a means of grace at the same time.
If there were no snags, there would be no wits to clear them away, or strong
arms to wield the axe. It was the same story with the Mulberry Bend. Until
the tramp lodging-houses were closed, until the Bend was gone, it seemed
as if progress were flat down impossible. As I said, decency had to begin
there, or not at all.

Before I tackle the Bend, perhaps I had better explain how I came to take
up photographing as a—no, not exactly as a pastime. It was never that with
me. I had use for it, and beyond that I never went. I am downright sorry to
confess here that I am no good at all as a photographer, for I would like
to be. The thing is a constant marvel to me, and an unending delight. To
watch the picture come out upon the plate that was blank before, and that
saw with me for perhaps the merest fraction of a second, maybe months
before, the thing it has never forgotten, is a new miracle every time. If I
were a clergyman I would practice photography and preach about it. But I
am jealous of the miracle. I do not want it explained to me in terms of HO_2
or such like formulas, learned, but so hopelessly unsatisfying. I do not want
my butterfly stuck on a pin and put in a glass case. I want to see the sunlight on its wings as it flits from flower to flower, and I don't care a rap what
its Latin name may be. Anyway, it is not its name. The sun and the flower
and the butterfly know that. The man who sticks a pin in it does not, and
never will, for he knows not its language. Only the poet does among men.
So, you see, I am disqualified from being a photographer. Also, I am clumsy,
and impatient of details. The axe was ever more to my liking than the
graving-tool. I have lived to see the day of the axe and enjoy it, and now I
rejoice in the coming of the men and women who know; the Jane
Addamses, who to heart add knowledge and training, and with gentle hands
bind up wounds which, alas! too often I struck. It is as it should be. I only
wish they would see it and leave me out for my sins.

But there! I started out to tell about how I came to be a photographer,
and here I am, off on the subject of philanthropy and social settlements.
To be precise, then, I began taking pictures by proxy. It was upon my midnight trips with the sanitary police that the wish kept cropping up in me
that there were some way of putting before the people what I saw there.

A drawing might have done it, but I cannot draw, never could. There are certain sketches of mine now on record that always arouse the boisterous hilarity of the family. They were made for the instruction of our first baby in wolf-lore, and I know they were highly appreciated by him at the time. Maybe the fashion in wolves has changed since. But, anyway, a drawing would not have been evidence of the kind I wanted. We used to go in the small hours of the morning into the worst tenements to count noses and see if the law against overcrowding was violated, and the sights I saw there gripped my heart until I felt that I must tell of them, or burst, or turn anarchist, or something. "A man may be a man even in a palace" in modern New York as in ancient Rome, but not in a slum tenement. So it seemed to me, and in anger I looked around for something to strike off his fetters with. But there was nothing.

I wrote, but it seemed to make no impression. One morning, scanning my newspaper at the breakfast table, I put it down with an outcry that startled my wife, sitting opposite. There it was, the thing I had been looking for all those years. A four-line despatch from somewhere in Germany, if I remember right, had it all. A way had been discovered, it ran, to take pictures by flashlight. The darkest corner might be photographed that way. I went to the office full of the idea, and lost no time in looking up Dr. John T. Nagle, at the time in charge of the Bureau of Vital Statistics in the Health Department, to tell him of it. Dr. Nagle was an amateur photographer of merit and a good fellow besides, who entered into my plans with great readiness. The news had already excited much interest among New York photographers, professional and otherwise, and no time was lost in communicating with the other side. Within a fortnight a raiding party composed of Dr. Henry G. Piffard and Richard Hoe Lawrence, two distinguished amateurs, Dr. Nagle and myself, and sometimes a policeman or two, invaded the East Side by night, bent on letting in the light where it was so much needed.

At least that was my purpose. To the photographers it was a voyage of discovery of the greatest interest; but the interest centred in the camera and the flashlight. The police went along from curiosity; sometimes for protection. For that they were hardly needed. It is not too much to say that our party carried terror wherever it went. The flashlight of those days was contained in cartridges fired from a revolver. The spectacle of half a dozen strange men invading a house in the midnight hour armed with big pistols which they shot off recklessly was hardly reassuring, however sugary our speech, and it was not to be wondered at if the tenants bolted through windows and down fire-escapes wherever we went. But as no one was murdered, things calmed down after a while, though months after I found the recollection of our visits hanging over a Stanton Street block like a nightmare. We got some good pictures; but very soon the slum and the awkward hours palled upon the amateurs. I found myself alone just when I needed help most. I had made out by the flashlight possibilities my companions little dreamed of.

I hired a professional photographer next whom I found in dire straits. He was even less willing to get up at 2 A.M. than my friends who had a good excuse. He had none, for I paid him well. He repaid me by trying to sell my photographs behind my back. I had to replevin the negatives to get them away from him. He was a pious man, I take it, for when I tried to

have him photograph the waifs in the baby nursery at the Five Points
House of Industry, as they were saying their "Now I lay me down to sleep,"
and the plate came out blank the second time, he owned up that it was his
doing: it went against his principles to take a picture of any one at prayers.
So I had to get another man with some trouble and expense. But on the
whole I think the experience was worth what it cost. The spectacle of a
man prevented by religious scruples from photographing children at
prayers, while plotting at the same time to rob his employer, has been a
kind of chart to me that has piloted me through more than one quagmire
of queer human nature. Nothing could stump me after that. The man was
just as sincere in the matter of his scruple as he was rascally in his business dealings with me.

There was at last but one way out of it; namely, for me to get a camera
myself. This I did, and with a dozen plates took myself up the Sound to the
Potter's Field on its desert island to make my first observations. There at
least I should be alone, with no one to bother me. And I wanted a picture
of the open trench. I got it, too. When I say that with the sunlight of a January day on the white snow I exposed that extra-quick instantaneous plate
first for six seconds, then for twelve, to make sure I got the picture,[1] and
then put the plate-holder back among the rest so that I did not know which
was which, amateur photographers will understand the situation. I had to
develop the whole twelve to get one picture. That was so dark, almost black,
from over-exposure as to be almost hopeless. But where there is life there
is hope, if you can apply that maxim to the Potter's Field, where there are
none but dead men. The very blackness of my picture proved later on, when
I came to use it with a magic lantern, the taking feature of it. It added a
gloom to the show more realistic than any the utmost art of professional
skill might have attained.

So I became a photographer, after a fashion, and thereafter took the
pictures myself. I substituted a frying-pan for the revolver, and flashed the
light on that. It seemed more homelike. But, as I said, I am clumsy. Twice
I set fire to the house with the apparatus, and once to myself. I blew the
light into my own eyes on that occasion, and only my spectacles saved me
from being blinded for life. For more than an hour after I could see nothing and was led about by my companion, helpless. Photographing Joss in
Chinatown nearly caused a riot there. It seems that it was against *their*
religious principles. Peace was made only upon express assurance being
given the guardians of Joss that his picture would be hung in the "gallery
at Police Headquarters." They took it as a compliment. The "gallery at
Headquarters is the rogues' gallery, not generally much desired. Those
Chinese are a queer lot, but when I remembered my Christian friend of
the nursery I did not find it in me to blame them Once, when I was taking pictures about Hell's Kitchen, I was confronted by a wild-looking man
with a club, who required me to subscribe to a general condemnation of
reporters as "hardly fit to be flayed alive," before he would let me go; the
which I did with a right good will, though with somewhat of a mental

1. Men are ever prone to doubt what they cannot understand. With all the accumulated information
   on the subject, even to this day, when it comes to taking a snap-shot, at the last moment I weaken
   and take it under protest, refusing to believe that it can be. A little more faith would make a much
   better photographer of me.

reservation in favor of my rivals in Mulberry Street, who just then stood in need of special correction.

What with one thing and another, and in spite of all obstacles, I got my pictures, and put some of them to practical use at once. I recall a midnight expedition to the Mulberry Bend with the sanitary police that had turned up a couple of characteristic cases of overcrowding. In one instance two rooms that should at most have held four or five sleepers were found to contain fifteen, a week-old baby among them. Most of them were lodgers and slept there for "five cents a spot." There was no pretence of beds. When the report was submitted to the Health Board the next day, it did not make much of an impression—these things rarely do, put in mere words—until my negatives, still dripping from the dark-room, came to reënforce them. From them there was no appeal. It was not the only instance of the kind by a good many. Neither the landlord's protests nor the tenant's plea "went" in face of the camera's evidence, and I was satisfied.

I had at last an ally in the fight with the Bend. It was needed, worse even than in the campaign against the police lodging-houses, for in that we were a company; in the Bend I was alone. From the day—I think it was in the winter of 1886—when it was officially doomed to go by act of legislature until it did go, nine years later, I cannot remember that a cat stirred to urge it on. Whether it was that it had been bad so long that people thought it could not be otherwise, or because the Five Points had taken all the reform the Sixth Ward had coming to it, or because, by a sort of tacit consent, the whole matter was left to me as the recognized Mulberry Bend crank—whichever it was, this last was the practical turn it took. I was left to fight it out by myself. Which being so, I laid in a stock of dry plates and buckled to.

The Bend was a much jollier adversary than the police lodging-houses. It kicked back. It did not have to be dragged into the discussion at intervals, but crowded in unbidden. In the twenty years of my acquaintance with it as a reporter I do not believe there was a week in which it was not heard from in the police reports, generally in connection with a crime of violence, a murder or a stabbing affray. It was usually on Sunday, when the Italians who lived there were idle and quarrelled over their cards. Every fight was the signal for at least two more, sometimes a dozen, for they clung to their traditions and met all efforts of the police to get at the facts with their stubborn "fix him myself." And when the detectives had given up in dismay and the man who was cut had got out of the hospital, pretty soon there was news of another fight, and the feud had been sent on one step. By far the most cheering testimony that our Italian is becoming one of us came to me a year or two ago in the evidence that on two occasions Mulberry Street had refused to hide a murderer even in his own village.[2] That was conclusive. It was not so in those days. So, between the vendetta, the mafia, the ordinary neighborhood feuds, and the Bend itself, always picturesque if outrageously dirty, it was not hard to keep it in the foreground. My scrap-book from the year 1883 to 1896 is one running comment on the Bend and upon the official indolence that delayed its demolition nearly a decade after it

---

2. The Italians here live usually grouped by "villages," that is, those from the same community with the same patron saint keep close together. The saint's name-day is their local holiday. If the police want to find an Italian scamp, they find out first from what village he hails, then it is a simple matter, usually, to find where he is located in the city.

had been decreed. But it all availed nothing to hurry up things, until, in a swaggering moment, after four years of that sort of thing, one of the City Hall officials condescended to inform me of the real cause of the delay. It was simply that "no one down there had been taking any interest in the thing."

I could not have laid it out for him to suit my case better than he did. It was in the silly season, and the newspapers fell greedily upon the sensation I made. The Bend, moreover, smelled rather worse than usual that August. They made "the people's cause" their own, and shouted treason until the commission charged with condemning the Bend actually did meet and greased its wheels. But at the next turn they were down in a rut again, and the team had to be prodded some more. It had taken two years to get a map of the proposed park filed under the law that authorized the laying out of it. The commission consumed nearly six years in condemning the forty-one lots of property, and charged the city $45,498.60 for it. The Bend itself cost a million, and an assessment of half a million was laid upon surrounding property for the supposed benefit of making it over from a pig-sty into a park. Those property-owners knew better. They hired a lawyer who in less than six weeks persuaded the Legislature that it was an injury, not a benefit. The town had to foot the whole bill. But at last it owned the Bend.

Instead of destroying it neck and crop, it settled down complacently to collect the rents; that is to say, such rents as it could collect. A good many of the tenants refused to pay, and lived rent free for a year. It was a rare chance for the reporter, and I did not miss it. The city as landlord in the Bend was fair game. The old houses came down at last, and for a twelvemonth, while a reform government sat at the City Hall, the three-acre lot lay, a veritable slough of despond filled with unutterable nastiness, festering in the sight of men. No amount of prodding seemed able to get it out of that, and all the while money given for the relief of the people was going to waste at the rate of a million dollars a year. The Small Parks Act of 1887 appropriated that amount, and it was to be had for the asking. But no one who had the authority asked, and as the appropriation was not cumulative, each passing year saw the loss of just so much to the cause of decency that was waiting without. Eight millions had been thrown away when they finally came to ask a million and a half to pay for the Mulberry Bend park, and then they had to get a special law and a special appropriation because the amount was more than "a million in one year." This in spite of the fact that we were then in the Christmas holidays with one year just closing and the other opening, each with its unclaimed appropriation. I suggested that to the powers that were, but they threw up their hands: that would have been irregular and quite without precedent. Oh, for irregularity enough to throttle precedent finally and for good! It has made more mischief in the world, I verily believe, than all the other lawbreakers together. At the very outset it had wrecked my hopes of getting the first school playground in New York planted in the Bend by simply joining park and school together. There was a public school in the block that went with the rest. The Small Parks Law expressly provided for the construction of "such and so many" buildings for the comfort, health, and "instruction" of the people, as might be necessary. But a school in a park! The thing had never been heard of. It would lead to conflict between two departments! And to this day there is no playground in the Mulberry Bend, though the school is right opposite.

It was, nevertheless, that sort of thing that lent the inspiration which in the end made the old Bend go. It was when, in the midst of the discussion, they showed me a check for three cents, hung up and framed in the Comptroller's office as a kind of red-tape joss for the clerks to kow-tow to, I suppose. They were part of the system it glorified. The three cents had miscarried in the purchase of a school site, and, when the error was found, were checked out with all the fuss and flourish of a transaction in millions and at a cost, I was told, of fifty dollars' worth of time and trouble. Therefore it was hung up to be forever admired as the ripe fruit of an infallible system. No doubt it will be there when another Tweed has cleaned out the city's treasury to the last cent. However, it suggested a way out to me. Two could play at that game. There is a familiar principle of sanitary law, expressed in more than one ordinance, that no citizen has a right to maintain a nuisance on his premises because he is lazy or it suits his convenience in other ways. The city is merely the aggregate of citizens in a corporation, and must be subject to the same rules. I drew up a complaint in proper official phrase, charging that the state of Mulberry Bend was "detrimental to health and dangerous to life," and formally arraigned the municipality before the Health Board for maintaining a nuisance upon its premises.

I have still a copy of that complaint, and, as the parting shot to the worst slum that ever was, and, let us hope, ever will be, I quote it here in part:—

"The Bend is a mass of wreck, a dumping-ground for all manner of filth from the surrounding tenements. The Street-cleaning Department has no jurisdiction over it, and the Park Department, in charge of which it is, exercises none.

"The numerous old cellars are a source of danger to the children that swarm over the block. Water stagnating in the holes will shortly add the peril of epidemic disease. Such a condition as that now prevailing in this block, with its dense surrounding population, would not be tolerated by your department for a single day if on private property. It has lasted here many months.

"The property is owned by the city, having been taken for the purposes of a park and left in this condition after the demolition of the old buildings. The undersigned respectfully represents that the city, in the proposed Mulberry Bend park, is at present maintaining a nuisance, and that it is the duty of your honorable Board to see to it that it is forthwith abolished, to which end he prays that you will proceed at once with the enforcement of the rules of your department prohibiting the maintaining of nuisances within the city's limits."

If my complaint caused a smile in official quarters, it was short-lived, except in the Sanitary Bureau, where I fancy it lurked. For the Bend was under its windows. One whiff of it was enough to determine the kind of report the health inspectors would have to make when forced to act. That night, before they got around, some boys playing with a truck in the lots ran it down into one of the cellar holes spoken of and were crushed under it, and so put a point upon the matter that took the laughter out of it for good. They went ahead with the park then.

When they had laid the sod, and I came and walked on it in defiance of the sign to "keep off the grass," I was whacked by a policeman for doing it, as I told in the "Ten Years' War."[3] But that was all right. We had the park. And I had been "moved on" before when I sat and shivered in reeking hallways in that very spot, alone and forlorn in the long ago; so that I did not mind. The children who were dancing there in the sunlight were to have a better time, please God! We had given them their lost chance. Looking at them in their delight now, it is not hard to understand what happened: the place that had been redolent of crime and murder became the most orderly in the city. When the last house was torn down in the Bend, I counted seventeen murders in the block all the details of which I remembered. No doubt I had forgotten several times that number. In the four years after that, during which I remained in Mulberry Street, I was called only once to record a deed of violence in the neighborhood, and that was when a stranger came in and killed himself. Nor had the Bend simply sloughed off its wickedness, for it to lodge and take root in some other place. That would have been something; but it was not that. The Bend had become decent and orderly because the sunlight was let in, and shone upon children who had at last the right to play, even if the sign "keep off the grass" was still there. That was what the Mulberry Bend park meant. It was the story it had to tell. And as for the sign, we shall see the last of that yet. The park has notice served upon it that its time is up.

So the Bend went, and mighty glad am I that I had a hand in making it go. The newspapers puzzled over the fact that I was not invited to the formal opening. I was Secretary of the Small Parks Committee at the time, and presumably even officially entitled to be bidden to the show; though, come to think of it, our committee was a citizens' affair and not on the pay-rolls! The Tammany Mayor who came in the year after said that we had as much authority as "a committee of bootblacks" about the City Hall, no more. So that it seems as if there is a something that governs those things which survives the accidents of politics, and which mere citizens are not supposed to understand or meddle with. Anyway, it was best so. Colonel Waring, splendid fellow that he was, when he grew tired of the much talk, made a little speech of ten words that was not on the programme, and after that the politicians went home, leaving the park to the children. There it was in the right hands. What mattered the rest, then?

And now let me go back from the slum to my Brooklyn home for just a look. I did every night, or I do not think I could have stood it. I never lived in New York since I had a home, except for the briefest spell of a couple of months once when my family were away, and that nearly stifled me. I have to be where there are trees and birds and green hills, and where the sky is blue above. So we built our nest in Brooklyn, on the outskirts of the great park, while the fledglings grew, and the nest was full when the last of our little pile had gone to make it snug. Rent was getting higher all the time, and the deeper I burrowed in the slum, the more my thoughts turned, by a son of defensive instinct, to the country. My wife laughed, and said I should have thought of that while we yet had some money to buy or build with, but I borrowed no trouble on that score. I was never a good business man, as I have said before, and yet—no! I will take that back. It is going back on the record. I trusted my accounts with the Great Pay-

---

3. Now, "The Battle with the Slum."

I saw, too, that I had put my hand to a task that was too great for me, yet which I might not give over, once I had taken it up. Every day the slum showed me that more clearly. The hunger for the beautiful that gnawed at its heart was a constant revelation. Those little ones at home were wiser than I. At most I had made out its stomach. This was like cutting windows for souls that were being shrunk and dwarfed in their mean setting. Shut them up once the sunlight had poured in—never! I could only drive ahead, then, until a way opened. Somewhere beyond it was sure to do that.

And it did. Among the boxes from somewhere out in Jersey came one with the letters I. H. N. on. I paid little attention to it then, but when more came so marked, I noticed that they were not all from one place, and made inquiries as to what the letters meant. So I was led to the King's Daughters' headquarters, where I learned that they stood for "In His Name." I liked the sentiment; I took to it at once. And I liked the silver cross upon which it was inscribed. I sometimes wish I had lived—no! I do not. That's dreaming. I have lived in the best of all times, when you do not have to dream things good, but can help make them so. All the same, when I put on the old crusader's cross which King Christian sent me a year ago from Denmark, and think of the valiant knights who wore it, I feel glad and proud that, however far behind, I may ride in their train.

So I put on the silver cross, and in the Broadway Tabernacle spoke to the members of the order, asking them to make this work theirs. They and it at once. A committee was formed, and in the summer of 1890 it opened an office in the basement of the Mariners' Temple, down in the Fourth Ward. The Health Department's summer doctors were enlisted, and the work took a practical turn from the start. There were fifty of the doctors, whose duty it was to canvass the thirty thousand tenements during the hot season and prescribe for the sick poor. They had two months to do it in, and with the utmost effort, if they were to cover their ground, could only get around once to each family In a great many cases that was as good as nothing. They might as well have stayed away, for what was wanted was advice, instruction, a friendly lift out of a hopeless rut, more than medicine. We hired a nurse, and where they pointed there she went, following their track and bringing the things the doctor could not give. It worked well. At the end of the year, when we would have shut up shop, we found ourselves with three hundred families on our hands, to leave whom would have been rank treachery. So we took a couple of rooms in a tenement, amd held on. And from this small beginning has grown the King's Daughters' settlement, which to-day occupies two houses at 48 and 50 Henry Street, doing exactly the same kind of work as when they began in the next block. The flowers were and are the open sesame to every home. They were laughed at by some at the start; but that was because they did not know. They are not needed now to open doors; the little cross is known for a friend wherever it goes.

We sometimes hear it said, and it is true, that the poor are more charitable among themselves than the outside world is to them. It is because they know the want; and it only goes to prove that human nature is at bottom good, not bad. In real straits it comes out strongest. So, if you can only make the others see, will they do. The trouble is, they do not know, and some of us seem to have cotton in our ears: we are a little hard of hearing. Yet, whenever we put it to the test, up-town rang true. I remember the widow with three or four little ones who had to be wheeled if she were to be able to get about as the doctor insisted. There was no nursery within reach. And I remember the procession of baby-carriages that answered our appeal. It strung clear across the street into Chatham Square. Whatever we needed we got. We saw the great heart of our city, and it was good to see.

Personally I had little to do with it, except to form the link with the official end of it, the summer doctors, etc., and to make trouble occasionally. As, for instance, when I surreptitiously supplied an old couple we had charge of with plug tobacco. The ladies took it ill, but, then, they had never smoked. I had, and I know what it is to do without tobacco, for the doctor cut my supply off a long while ago. Those two were old, very old, and they wanted their pipe, and they got it. I suppose it was irregular, but I might as well say it here that I would do the same thing again, without doubt. I feel it in my bones. So little have I profited. But, good land! a pipe is not a deadly sin. For the rest, I was mighty glad to see things managed with system. It was a new experience to me. On the *Tribune* I had a kind of license to appeal now and again for some poor family I had come across, and sometimes a good deal of money came in. It was hateful to find that it did not always do the good it ought to. I bring to mind the aged bookkeeper and his wife whom I found in a Greene Street attic in a state of horrid want. He had seen much better days, and it was altogether a very pitiful case. My appeal brought in over $300, which, in my delight, I brought him in a lump. The next morning, when going home at three o'clock, whom should I see in a vile Chatham Street dive, gloriously drunk, and in the clutches of a gang of Sixth Ward cutthroats, but my protégé, the bookkeeper, squandering money right and left. I caught sight of him through the open door, and in hot indignation went in and yanked him out, giving him a good talking to. The gang followed, and began hostilities at once. But for the providential coming of two policemen, we should probably have both fared ill. I had the old man locked up in the Oak Street Station. For a wonder, he had most of the money yet, and thereafter I spent it for him.

On another occasion we were deliberately victimized—the reporters in Mulberry Street, I mean—by a man with a pitiful story of hardship, which we took as truth and printed. When I got around there the next morning to see about it, I found that some neighborhood roughs had established a toll-gate in the alley charging the pitying visitors who came in shoals a quarter for admission to the show in the garret. The man was a fraud. That was right around the corner from a place where, years before, I used to drop a nickel in a beggar woman's hand night after night as I went past, because she had a baby cradled on her wheezy little hand-organ, until one night the baby rolled into the gutter, and I saw that it was a rag baby, and that the woman was drunk. It was on such evidence as this, both as to them and myself, that I early pinned my faith to organized charity as just orderly charity, and I have found good reasons since to confirm me in the choice. If any doubt had lingered in my mind, my experience in helping distribute the relief fund to the tornado sufferers at Woodhaven a dozen years ago would have dispelled it. It does seem as if the chance of getting something for nothing is, on the whole, the greatest temptation one can hold out to frail human nature, whether in the slum, in Wall Street, or out where the daisies grow.

Everything takes money. Our work takes a good deal. It happened more than once, when the bills came in, that there was nothing to pay them with.

Now these were times to put to the test my faith, as recorded above. My associates in the Board will bear me out that it was justified. It is true that the strain was heavy once or twice. I recall one afternoon, as do they, when we sat with bills amounting to $150 before us and not a cent in the bank, so the treasurer reported. Even as she did, the mail-carrier brought two letters, both from the same town, as it happened—Morristown, N.J. Each of them contained a check for $75, one from a happy mother "in gratitude and joy," the other from "one stricken by a great sorrow" that had darkened her life. Together they made the sum needed. We sat and looked at each other dumbly. To me it was not strange: that was my mother's faith. But I do not think we, any of us, doubted after that; and we had what we needed, as we needed it.

Chapter XII. I Become an Author and Resume My Interrupted Career as a Lecturer

For more than a year I had knocked at the doors of the various magazine editors with my pictures, proposing to tell them how the other half lived, but no one wanted to know. One of the Harpers, indeed, took to the idea, but the editor to whom he sent me treated me very cavalierly. Hearing that I had taken the pictures myself, he proposed to buy them at regular photographer's rates and "find a man who could write" to tell the story. We did not part with mutual expressions of esteem. I gave up writing for a time then, and tried the church doors. That which was bottled up within me was, perhaps, getting a trifle too hot for pen and ink. In the church one might, at all events, tell the truth unhindered. So I thought; but there were cautious souls there, too, who held the doors against Mulberry Street and the police reporter. It was fair, of course, that they should know who I was, but I thought it sufficient introduction that I was a deacon in my own church out on Long Island. They did not, it seemed. My stock of patience, never very large, was showing signs of giving out, and I retorted hotly that then, if they wanted to know, I was a reporter, and perhaps Mulberry Street had as much sanctity in it as a church that would not listen to its wrongs. They only shut the doors a little tighter at that. It did not mend matters that about that time I tried a little truth-telling in my own fold and came to grief. It did not prove to be any more popular on Long Island than in New York. I resigned the diaconate and was thinking of hiring a hall—a theatre could be had on Sunday—wherein to preach my lay sermon, when I came across Dr. Schauffler, the manager of the City Mission Society, and Dr. Josiah Strong, the author of "Our Country." They happened to be together, and saw at once the bearing of my pictures. Remembering my early experience with the magic lantern, I had had slides made from my negatives, and on February 28, 1888, I told their story in the Broadway Tabernacle. Thereafter things mended somewhat. Plymouth Church and Dr. Parkhurst's opened their doors to me and the others fell slowly into line.

I had my say and felt better. I found a note from Dr. Schauffler among my papers the other day that was written on the morning after that first speech. He was pleased with it and with the collection of $143.50 for the mission cause. I remember it made me smile a little grimly. The fifty cents would have come handy for lunch that day. It just happened that I did not have any. It happened quite often. I was, as I said, ever a bad manager.

I mention it here because of two letters that came while I have been writing this, and which I may as well answer now. One asks me to lift the mortgage from the writer's home. I get a good many of that kind. The writers seem to think I have much money and might want to help them. I should like nothing better. To go around, if one were rich, and pay off mortgages on little homes, so that the owners when they had got the interest together by pinching and scraping should find it all gone and paid up without knowing how, seems to me must be the very finest fun in all the world. But I shall never be able to do it, for I haven't any other money than what I earn with my pen and by lecturing, and never had. So their appeals only make me poorer by a two-cent stamp for an answer to tell them that, and make them no richer. The other letter asks why I and other young men who have had to battle with the world did not go to the Young Men's Christian Association, or to the missionaries, for help. I do not know about the others, but I did not want anybody to help me. There were plenty that were worse off and needed help more. The only time I tried was when Pater Breton, the good French priest in Buffalo, tried to get me across to France to fight for his country, and happily did not succeed. As to battling with the world, that is good for a young man, much better than to hang on to somebody for support. A little starvation once in a while even is not out of the way. We eat too much anyhow, and when you have fought your way through a tight place, you are the better for it. I am afraid that is not always the case when you have been shoved through.

And then again, as I have just told, when I did go to the ministers with a fair proposition, they did not exactly jump at it. No, it was better the way it was.

The thing I had sought vainly so long came in the end by another road than I planned. One of the editors of *Scribner's Magazine* saw my pictures and heard their story in his church, and came to talk the matter over with me. As a result of that talk I wrote an article that appeared in the Christmas *Scribner's* 1889, under the title "How the Other Half Lives," and made an instant impression. That was the beginning of better days.

Before I let the old depart I must set down an incident of my reporter's experience that crowds in with a good hearty laugh, though it was not the slum that sent me to the Church of the Holy Communion over on Sixth Avenue. And though the door was shut in my face, it was not by the rector, or with malice prepense. A despatch from the Tenderloin police station had it that the wife of the Rev. Dr. Henry Mottet was locked up there, out of her mind. We had no means of knowing that Dr. Mottet was at that time a confirmed bachelor. So I went over to condole with him, and incidentally to ask what was the matter with his wife, any way. The servant who came to the door did not know whether the doctor was in; she would go and see. But even as she said it the wind blew the door shut behind her. It had a snap-lock.

"Oh!" she said, "I am shut out. If the doctor isn't in the house, I can't get in."

We rang, but no one came. There was only one way: to try the windows. The poor girl could not be left in the street. So we went around the rectory and found one unlatched. She gave me a leg up, and I raised the sash and crawled in.

Halfway in the room, with one leg over the sill, I became dimly conscious of a shape there. Tall and expectant, it stood between the door-curtains.

"Well, sir! and who are you?" it spoke sternly.

I climbed over the sill and put the question myself: "And who are you, sir?"

"I am Dr. Mottet, and live in this house." He had been it after all and had come down to hear what the ringing was about "And now may I ask, sir—?"

"Certainly, you may. I am a reporter from Police Head quarters, come up to tell you that your wife is locked up in the Thirtieth Street police station."

The doctor looked fixedly at me for a full minute. Then he slowly telescoped his tall frame into an armchair, and sank down, a look of comic despair settling upon his face.

"O Lord!" he sighed heavily. "A strange man climbs through my parlor window to tell me, a bachelor, that my wife is locked up in the police station. What will happen next?"

And then we laughed together and made friends. The woman was just an ordinary lunatic.

I was late home from the office one evening the week my Christmas article was printed. My wife was waiting for me at the door, looking down the street. I saw that she had something on her mind, but the children were all right, she said, nothing was amiss. Supper over, she drew a chair to the fire and brought out a letter.

"I read it," she nodded. It was our way. The commonest business letter is to me a human document when she has read it. Besides, she knows so much more than I. Her heart can find a way where my head bucks blindly against stone walls.

The letter was from Jeanette Gilder, of the *Critic*, asking if I had thought of making my article into a book. If so, she knew a publisher. My chance had come. I was at last to have my say.

I should have thought I would have shouted and carried on. I didn't. We sat looking into the fire together, she and I. Neither of us spoke. Then we went up to the children. They slept sweetly in their cribs. I saw a tear in her eye as she bent over the baby's cradle, and caught her to me, questioning.

"Shall we lose you now?" she whispered, and hid her head on my shoulder. I do not know what jealous thought of authors being wedded to their work had come into her mind; or, rather, I do. I felt it, and in my heart, while I held her close, I registered a vow which I have kept. It was the last tears she shed for me. Our daughter pouts at her father now and then; says I am "fierce." But She comes with her sewing to sit where I write, and when she comes the sun shines.

Necessarily, for a while, my new work held me very close. "How the Other Half Lives" was written at night while the house slept, for I had my office work to attend to in the day. Then it was my habit to light the lamps in all the rooms of the lower story and roam through them with my pipe, for I do most of my writing on my feet. I began the book with the new year. In November it was published, and on the day it came out I joined the staff of the *Evening Sun*. I merely moved up one flight of stairs. Mulberry Street was not done with me yet, nor I with it.

I had had a falling out with the manager of the Associated Press Bureau,— the *Tribune* had retired from the copartnership some years before,—and during one brief summer ran an opposition shop of my own. I sold police news to all the papers, and they fell away from the Bureau with such hearty unanimity that the manager came around and offered to farm out the department to me entirely if I would join forces. But independence was ever sweet to me, and in this instance it proved profitable even. I made at least three times as much money as before, but I did it at such cost of energy and effort that I soon found it could not last, even with the phenomenal streak of good luck I had struck. It seemed as if I had only to reach out to turn up news. I hear people saying once in a while that there is no such thing as luck. They are wrong. There is; I know it. It runs in streaks, like accidents and fires. The thing is to get in the way of it and keep there till it comes along, then hitch on, and away you go. It is the old story of the early bird. I got up at five o'clock, three hours before any of my competitors, and sometimes they came down to the office to find my news hawked about the street in extras of their own papers.

One way or another, a fight there was always on hand. That seemed foreordained. If it was not "the opposition" it was the police. When Mulberry Street took a rest the publisher's "reader" began it, and the proof-reader. This last is an enemy of human kind anyhow. Not only that he makes you say things you never dreamed of, but his being so cocksure that he knows better every time, is a direct challenge to a fight. The "reader" is tarred with the same stick. He is the one who passes on the manuscript, and he has an ingrown hatred of opinion. If a man has that, he is his enemy before he ever sets eye on him. He passed on my manuscript with a blue pencil that laid waste whole pages, once a whole chapter, with a stroke. It was like sacking a conquered city. But he did not die in his sins. I joined battle at the first sight of that blue pencil. The publishers said their reader was a very capable man. So he was, and a fine fellow to boot; had forgotten more than I ever knew, except as to the other half, of which he did not know anything. I suggested to the firm that if they did not think so, they had better let him write a book to suit, or else print mine as I wrote it. It was fair, and they took my view of it. So did he. The blue pencil went out of commission.

How deadly tired I was in those days I do not think I myself knew until I went to Boston one evening to help discuss sweating at the Institute of Technology. I had an hour to spare, and went around into Beacon Street to call upon a friend. I walked mechanically up the stoop and rang the bell. My friend was not in, said the servant who came to the door. Who should she say called? I stood and looked at her like a fool: I had forgotten my name. I was not asleep; I was rummaging in an agony of dread and excitement through every corner and crevice of my brain for my own name, but I did not find it. As slowly as I could, to gain time, I reached for my card-case and fumbled for a card, hoping to remember. But no ray came. Until I actually read my name on my card it was as utterly gone as if I had never heard it. If the people of Boston got anything out of my speech that day they did better than I. All the time I spoke something kept saying over within me: "You are a nice fellow to make a speech at the Institute of Technology; you don't even know your own name."

After that I was haunted by a feeling that I would lose myself altogether, and got into the habit of leaving private directions in the office where I would probably be found, should question arise. It arose at last in a Brooklyn church where I was making a speech with my magic-lantern pictures. While I spoke a feeling kept growing upon me that I ought to be down in the audience looking at the pictures. It all seemed a long way off and in no way related to me. Before I knew it, or any one had time to notice, I had gone down and taken a front seat. I sat there for as much as five minutes perhaps, while the man with the lantern fidgeted and the audience wondered, I suppose, what was coming next. Then it was the pictures that did not change which fretted me; with a cold chill I knew I had been lost, and went back and finished the speech. No one was any the wiser, apparently. But I was glad when, the following week, I wrote the last page in my book. That night, my wife insists, I deliberately turned a somerset on the parlor carpet while the big children cheered and the baby looked on, wide-eyed, from her high chair.

I preserve among my cherished treasures two letters of that period from James Russell Lowell. In one of them he gives me permission to use the verses with which I prefaced the book. They were the text from which I preached my sermon. He writes that he is "glad they have so much life left in them after forty years." But those verses will never die. They tell in a few lines all I tried to tell on three hundred pages. The other letter was written when he had read the book. * * *

For myself I have never been able to satisfactorily explain the great run "How the Other Half Lives" had. It is a curiously popular book even to-day. Perhaps it was that I had had it in me so long that it burst out at last with a rush that caught on. The title had a deal to do with it. Mr. Howells asked me once where I got it. I did not get it. It came of itself. Like Topsy, it growed. It had run in my mind ever since I thought of the things I tried to describe. Then there was the piece of real good luck that Booth's "In Darkest England" was published just then. People naturally asked, "how about New York?" That winter Ward McAllister wrote his book about society as he had found it, and the circuit was made. Ministers preached about the contrast. "How the Other Half Lives" ran from edition to edition. There was speedily a demand for more "copy," and I wrote "The Children of the Poor," following the same track. Critics said there were more "bones" in it, but it was never popular like the "Other Half."

By "bones" I suppose they meant facts to tie to. They were scarce enough at that stage of the inquiry. I have in my desk a table giving the ages at which children get their teeth that bears witness to that. I had been struggling with the problem of child-labor in some East Side factories, and was not making any headway. The children had certificates, one and all, declaring them to be "fourteen," and therefore fit to be employed. It was perfectly evident that they were not ten in scores of cases, but the employer shrugged his shoulders and pointed to the certificate. The father, usually a tailor, would not listen at all, but went right on ironing. There was no birth registry to fall back on; that end of it was neglected. There seemed to be no way of proving the fact, yet the fact was there and must be proven. My own children were teething at the time, and it gave me an idea. I got Dr. Tracy to write out that table for me, showing at what age the dog-teeth should appear, when the molars, etc. Armed with that I went into the factories and pried open the little workers' mouths. The girls objected: their teeth were quite generally bad; but I saw enough to enable me to speak positively. Even allowing for the backwardness of the slum, it was clear that a child that had not yet grown its dog-teeth was not "fourteen," for they should have been cut at twelve at the latest. Three years later the Reinhardt Committee reported to the Legislature that the net result of the Factory Law was a mass of perjury and child-labor, and day began to dawn for the little ones, too.

Rough ways and rough work? Yes, but you must use the tools that come to hand, and be glad for them, if you want to get things done. Bludgeons were needed just then, and, after all, you can get a good deal of fun out of one when it is needed. I know I did. By that time the whole battle with the slum had evolved itself out of the effort to clean one pig-sty, and, as for my own share in it, to settle for one dead dog. It was raging all along the line with demands for tenement-house reform and the destruction of the old rookeries; for parks for the people who were penned up in the slum; for playgrounds for their children; for decent teaching and decent schools. There were too many dark spots in New York where we had neither. So dense was the ignorance of the ruling powers of the needs and real condition of the public schools, which, on parade days, they spoke of sententiously as the "corner-stone of our liberties," while the people cheered the sentiment, that it was related how a Tammany Mayor had appointed to the office of school trustee in the Third Ward a man who had been dead a whole year, and how, when the world marvelled, it had been laughed off at the City Hall with the comment that what did it matter: there were no schools in the ward; it was the wholesale grocery district. I do not know how true it was, but there was no reason why it might not be. It was exactly on a par with the rest of it. I do not mean to say that there were no good schools in New York. There were some as good as anywhere; for there were high-souled teachers who redeemed even the slough we were in from utter despair. But they were there in spite of it and they were far from being the rule. Let us hope for the day when that shall have been reversed as a statement of fact. No one will hail it more gladly than I. There is an easy way of putting it to the test; we did it once before. Broach a measure of school reform and see what the question is that will be asked by the teachers. If it is, "How is it going to benefit the children?" hoist the flag; the day of deliverance is at hand. In the battle I refer to that question was not asked once. The teachers stood shoulder to shoulder for *their* rights, let the children fare as they might.

However, that is an old grievance. We had it out over it once, and I have no mind to rip it up again unless it is needed. My own father was a teacher; perhaps that is one reason why I revere the calling so that I would keep its skirts clear of politics at any hazard. Another is that I most heartily subscribe to the statement that the public school is the corner-stone of our liberties, and to the sentiment that would keep the flag flying over it always. Only I want as much respect for the flag: a clean school under an unsoiled flag! So we shall pull through; not otherwise. The thing requires no argument.

My own effort in that fight was mainly for decent schoolhouses, for playgrounds, and for a truant school to keep the boys out of jail. If I was not competent to argue over the curriculum with a professor of pedagogy, I could tell, at least, if a schoolroom was so jammed that to let me pass into the next room the children in the front seat had to rise and stand; or if there was light enough for them to see their slates or the blackboard. Nor did it take the wisdom of a Solomon to decide that a dark basement room, thirty by fifty feet, full of rats, was not a proper place for a thousand children to call their only "playground." Play, in the kindergarten scheme, is the "normal occupation of the child through which he first begins to perceive moral relations." Nice kind of morals burrowed there for him! There was, in the whole of Manhattan, but a single outdoor playground attached to a public school, and that was an old burial-ground in First Street that had been wrested from the dead with immense toil. When I had fed fat my grudge upon these things, I could still go where the public school children came, and learn, by a little judicious pumping, how my friend, the professor, had stored their minds. That is, if they did not come to me. Many hundreds of them did, when under Roosevelt we needed two thousand new policemen, and it was from some of them we learned that among the thirteen States which formed the Union were "England, Ireland, Wales, Belfast, and Cork"; that Abraham Lincoln was "murdered by Ballington Booth," and that the Fire Department was in charge of the city government when the Mayor was away. Don't I wish it were, and that they would turn the hose on a while! What a lot of trouble it would save us in November.

As for a truant school, the lack of one was the worst outrage of all, for it compelled the sending of boys, who had done no worse harm than to play hooky on a sunny spring day, to a jail with iron bars in the windows. For the boy who did this wicked thing—let me be plain about it and say that if he had not; if he had patiently preferred some of the schools I knew to a day of freedom out in the sunshine. I should have thought him a miserable little lunkhead quite beyond hope. As for those who locked him up, almost nothing I can think of would be bad enough for them. The whole effort of society should be, and is getting to be more and more, thank goodness and common sense, to keep the boy out of jail. To run to it with him the moment the sap begins to boil up in him and he does any one of the thousand things we have all done or wanted to do if we dared, why, it is sinful folly. I am not saying that there are not boys who ought to be in jail, though to my mind it is the poorest use you can put them to; but to put truants there, to learn all the tricks the jail has to teach, with them in the frame of mind in which it receives them,—for boys are not fools, whatever those who are set over them may be, and they know when they are ill-used,—I know of nothing so wickedly wasteful. That was our way; is still in fact, to a large extent, though the principle has been disavowed as both foul and foolish. But in those days the defenders of the system—Heaven save the mark!—fought for it yet, and it was give and take right along, every day and all day.

Before this, in time to bear a strong hand in it all, there had come into the field a new force that was destined to give both energy and direction to our scattered efforts for reform. Up till then we had been a band of guerillas, the incentive proceeding usually from Dr. Felix Adler, Mrs. Josephine Shaw Lowell, or some one of their stamp; and the rest of us joining in to push *that* cart up the hill, then taking time to breathe until another came along that needed a lift. The social settlements, starting as neighborhood guilds to reassert the lost brotherhood, became almost from the first the fulcrum, as it were, whence the lever for reform was applied, because the whole idea of that reform was to better the lot of those whom the prosperous uptown knew vaguely only as "the poor." If parks were wanted, if schools needed bettering, there were at the College Settlement, the University Settlement, the Nurses' Settlement, and at a score of other such places, young enthusiasts to collect the facts and to urge them, with the prestige of their non-political organization to back them. The Hull House out in Chicago set the pace, and it was kept up bravely at this end of the line. For one, I attached myself as a kind of volunteer "auxiliary" to the College Settlement—that was what the girls there called me—and to any one that would have me, and so in a few years' time slid easily into the day when my ruder methods were quite out of date and ready to be shelved.

How it came about that, almost before I knew it, my tongue was enlisted in the fight as well as my pen I do not know myself. It could not be because I had a "silver-tongue," for I read in the local newspaper one day when I had been lecturing in the western part of the state that "a voluble German with a voice like a squeaky cellar-door" had been in town. It seems that I had fallen into another newspaper row, all unsuspecting, and was in the opposition editor's camp. But, truly, I lay no claim to eloquence. So it must have been the facts, again. There is nothing like them. Whatever it was, it made me smile sometimes in the middle of a speech to think of the prophecies when I was a schoolboy that "my tongue would be my undoing," for here it was helping right wrongs instead. In fact, that was what it had tried to do in the old days when the teachers were tyrannical. It entered the lists here when Will Craig, a clerk in the Health Department, with whom I had struck up a friendship, helped me turn my photographs into magic-lantern slides by paying the bills, and grew from that, until now my winters are spent on the lecture platform altogether. I always liked the work. It tires less than office routine, and you feel the touch with your fellows more than when you sit and write your message. Also, if you wish to learn about a thing, the best way is always to go and try to teach some one else that thing. I never make a speech on a subject I am familiar with but that I come away knowing more about it than I did at the start, though no one else may have said a word.

Then there is the chairman. You never can tell what sort of surprise is in store for you. In a Massachusetts town last winter I was hailed on the stage by one of his tribe, a gaunt, funereal sort of man, who wanted to know what he should say about me.

"Oh," said I, in a spirit of levity, "say anything you like. Say I am the most distinguished citizen in the country. They generally do."

Whereupon my funereal friend marched upon the stage and calmly announced to the audience that he did not know this man Riis, whom he was charged with introducing, never heard of him.

"He tells me," he went on with never a wink, "that he is the most distinguished citizen in the country. You can judge for yourselves when you have heard him."

I thought at first it was some bad kind of joke; but no! He was not that kind of man. I do not suppose he had smiled since he was born. Maybe he was an undertaker. Assuredly, he ought to be. But he had bowels after all. Instead of going off the stage and leaving me blue with rage, he stayed to exhort the audience in a fifteen minutes' speech to vote right, or something of that sort. The single remark, when at last he turned his back, that it was a relief to have him "extinguished," made us men and brothers, that audience and me. I think of him with almost as much pleasure as I do of that city editor chap out in Illinois who came blowing upon the platform at the last minute and handed me a typewritten speech with the question if that would do. I read it over. It began with the statement that it was the general impression that all newspapermen were liars, and went on by easy stages to point out that there were exceptions, myself for instance. The rest was a lot of praise to which I had no claim. I said so, and that I wished he would leave it out.

"Oh, well," he said, with a happy smile, "don't you see it gives you your cue. Then you can turn around and say that anyway I am a liar."

With tongue or pen, the argument shaped itself finally into the fundamental one for the rescue of the home imperilled by the slum. There all roads met. Good citizenship hung upon that issue. Say what you will, a man cannot live like a pig and vote like a man. The dullest of us saw it. The tenement had given to New York the name of "the homeless city." But with that gone which made life worth living, what were liberty worth? With no home to cherish, how long before love of country would be an empty sound? Life, liberty, pursuit of happiness? Wind! says the slum, and the slum is right if we let it be. We cannot get rid of the tenements that shelter two million souls in New York to-day, but we set about making them at least as nearly fit to harbor human souls as might be. That will take a long time yet. But a beginning was made. With reform looming upon the heels of the Lexow disclosures came the Gilder Tenement-House Commission in the autumn of 1894.

Greater work was never done for New York than by that faithful body of men. The measure of it is not to be found in what was actually accomplished, though the volume of that was great, but in what it made possible. Upon the foundations they laid down we may build for all time and be the better for it. Light and air acquired a legal claim, and where the sun shines into the slum, the slum is doomed. The worst tenements were destroyed; parks were opened, schools built, playgrounds made. The children's rights were won back for them. The slum denied them even the chance to live, for it was shown that the worst rear tenements murdered the babies at the rate of one in five. The Commission made it clear that the legislation that was needed was "the kind that would root out every old ramshackle disease-breeding tenement in the city." That was the way to begin it. As to the rest of them, it laid the foundation deeper yet, for it made us see that life in them "conduces to the corruption of the young." That told it all. It meant that a mortgage was put on the civic life of the morrow, which was not to be borne. We were forewarned.

The corruption of the young! We move with rapid strides in our time. That which was a threat scoffed at by many, has become a present and dreadful peril in half a dozen brief years. We took a short cut to make it that when we tried to drain the pool of police blackmail of which the Lexow disclosures had shown us the hideous depths. We drained it into the tenements, and for the police infamy got a real-estate blackmail that is worse. The chairman of the Committee of Fifteen tells us that of more than a hundred tenements, full of growing children, which his committee has canvassed, not one had escaped the contamination that piles up the landlord's profits. Twelve dollars for an honest flat, thirty for the other kind and no questions asked! I find in my scrap-book this warning, sounded by me in the Christmas holidays, 1893, when the country was ringing with Dr. Parkhurst's name:—

"I would not, whatever else might happen, by any hasty or ill-advised system of wholesale raids crowd these women into the tenements and flats of our city. That is what will surely happen, is happening now. It is a danger infinitely greater than any flowing from their presence where they are, and as they are. Each centre of moral contagion by this scattering process becomes ten or twenty, planted where they will do the most possible harm. Think of the children brought in daily, hourly contact with this vice! Think of the thousands of young women looking vainly for work this hard winter! Be there ever so little money for woman's honest work, there is always enough to buy her virtue. Have tenement houses moral resources that can be trusted to keep her safe from this temptation?

"This is a wicked villany that must not be permitted, come whatever else may. We hear of danger to 'our young men,' from present conditions. What sort of young men must they be who would risk the sacrifice of their poorer sisters for their own 'safety'? And it is being risked wherever houses of this kind are being shut up and the women turned into the streets, there to shift for themselves. The jail does not keep them. Christian families will not receive them. They cannot be killed. No door opens to them: yet they have to go somewhere. And they go where they think they can hide from the police and still ply the trade that gives them the only living society is willing they shall have, though it says it is not."

And they did go there. Dr. Parkhurst was not to blame. He was fighting Tammany that dealt the cards and took all the tricks, and for that fight New York owes him a debt it hardly yet knows of. Besides, though those raids hastened the process, it was already well under way. The police extortion of itself would have finished it in time. A blackmailer in the long run always kills the goose that lays his golden egg. His greed gets the better of his sense. The interview I quoted was not a plea for legalizing wrong. That will get us no farther. It was rather a summons to our people to cease skulking behind lying phrases and look the matter squarely in the face. With a tenement-house law, passed this winter, which sends the woman to jail and fines the landlord and his house $1000, we shall be in the way shortly of doing so. Until we do that justice first, I do not see how we can. Poverty's back is burdened enough without our loading upon it the sins we are afraid to face. Meanwhile we shall be getting up courage to talk plainly about it, which is half the battle. Think of the shock it would have given our grandmothers to hear of a meeting of women in a public hall "to protest against protected vice." On a Sunday, too. Come to think of it, I do not know but that wholesome, plain speech on this subject is nearer the whole than half the battle. I rather guess it is.

Riis's Contemporaries Observe the "Other Half"

CHARLES LORING BRACE

From The Dangerous Classes of New York, and Twenty Years' Work among Them[†]

Chapter 1. Christ in Charity and Reform.

THE CONDITION OF NEGLECTED CHILDREN BEFORE CHRISTIANITY.

The central figure in the world's charity is Christ.

An eloquent rationalistic writer—Mr. Lecky—speaking of the Christian efforts in early ages in behalf of exposed children and against infanticide, says:

"Whatever mistakes may have been made, the entire movement I have traced displays an anxiety not only for the life, but for the moral well-being, of the castaways of society, such as the most humane nations of antiquity had never reached. This minute and scrupulous care for human life and human virtue in the humblest forms, in the slave, the gladiator, the savage, or the infant, was indeed wholly foreign to the genius of Paganism. It was produced by the Christian doctrine of the inestimable value of each immortal soul.

"It is the distinguishing and transcendent characteristic of every society into which the spirit of Christianity has passed."

Christ has indeed given a new value to the poorest and most despised human being.

When one thinks what was the fate before He lived, throughout the civilized world, of for instance one large and pitiable class of human beings—unfortunate children, destitute orphans, foundlings, the deformed and sickly, and female children of the poor; how almost universal, even under the highest pagan civilization—the Greek and Roman—infanticide was; how Plato and Aristotle both approved of it; how even more common was the dreadful exposure of children who were physically imperfect or for any cause disagreeable to their parents, so that crowds of these little unfortunates were to be seen exposed around a column near the Velabrum at Rome—some being taken to be raised as slaves, others as prostitutes, others carried off by beggars and maimed for exhibition, or captured by witches to

† Third Edition. New York: Wynkoop & Hallenbeck, 1880.

be murdered, and their bodies used in their magical preparations; when one remembers for how many centuries, even after the nominal introduction of Christianity, the sale of free children was permitted by law, and then recalls how utterly the spirit of the Founder of Christianity has exterminated these barbarous practices from the civilized world; what vast and ingenious charities exist in every Christian country for this unfortunate class; what time and wealth and thought are bestowed to heal the diseases, purify the morals, raise the character, and make happy the life of foundlings, outcast girls and boys and orphans, we can easily understand that the source of the charities of civilized nations has been especially in Christ; and knowing how vital the moral care of unfortunate children is to civilization itself, the most skeptical among us may still put Him at the head of even modern social reform.

EXPOSURE OF CHILDREN.

The "exposure of children" is spoken of casually and with indifference by numerous Latin authors. The comedians include the custom in their pictures of the daily Roman life, usually without even a passing condemnation. Thus, in Terence's play (Heauton: Act iii., sc. v.), the very character who uttered the apothegm which has become a proverb of humanity for all ages—"I am a man, and nothing belonging to man is alien to me"— is represented, on the eve of his departure on a long journey, as urging his wife to destroy the infant soon to be born, if it should prove to be a girl, rather than expose it. She, however, exposes it, and it was taken, as was usual, and brought up as a prostitute. This play turns in its plot, as is true of many popular comedies, on this exposition of the abandoned child.

It is frequently commented on by Roman dramatists, and subsequently by the early Christian preachers, that, owing to this terrible custom, brothers might marry sisters, or fathers share in the ruin of their unknown daughters in houses of crime.

Seneca, who certainly always writes with propriety and aims to be governed by reason, in his treatise on Anger (De Irâ: i., 15), comments thus calmly on the practice: "Portentos fœtus extinguimus; liberos quoque si debiles, monstrosique editi sunt, mergimus. Non ira, sed *ratio* est, a sanis, inutilia secernere." (Monstrous offspring we destroy; children too, if weak and unnaturally formed from birth, we drown. It is not anger, but reason, thus to separate the useless from the sound.)

In another work (Controversi, lib. v., 33), he denounces the horrible practice, common in Rome, of maiming these unfortunate children and then offering them to the gaze of the compassionate. He describes the miserable little creatures with shortened limbs, broken joints, and curved backs, exhibited by the villainous beggars who had gathered them at the *Lactaria*, and then deformed them: "Volo nosse," "I should like to know," says the moralist, with a burst of human indignation, "illam calamitatum humanarum officinam—illud infantum spoliarium!"—"that workshop of human misfortunes—those shambles of infants!"

On the day that Germanicus died, says Suetonius (in Calig., n. 5), "Subversæ Deûm aræ, partus conjugum expositi," parents exposed their newborn babes.

The early Christian preachers and writers were unceasing in their denunciations of the practice.

Quintilian (Decl. 306, vol vi., p. 236) draws a most moving picture of the fate of these unhappy children left in the Forum: "Rarum est ut expositi vivant! Vos ponite ante oculos puerum statim neglectum * * * inter feras et volucres."

"It is rare that the exposed survive!" he says.

Tertullian, in an eloquent passage (Apol., c. 9), asks: "Quot vultis ex his circumstantibus et in christianum sanguinem hiantibus * * * apud conscientias pulsem, qui natos sibi liberos enecent?"

"How many, do you suppose, of those standing about and panting for the blood of Christians, if I should put it to them before their very conscience, would deny that they killed their own children?"

Lactantius, who was the tutor of the son of Constantine, in a book dedicated to Constantine, protests: "It is impossible to grant that one has the right to strangle one's new-born children"; and speaks of exposition as exposing one's own blood—"ad servitutem vel ad lupanar"—"for slavery or the brothel." "It is a crime as execrable to expose a child as to kill him."

So fearfully did the numbers increase, under the Roman Empire, of these unfortunate children, that the spark of charity, which is never utterly extinguished in the human breast, began to kindle. Pliny the Younger is said to have appropriated a sum equivalent to $52,000 (see Epist., v., 7), to found an asylum for fathers unable to support their children.

THE FIRST CHILDREN'S ASYLUM.

Probably the first society or asylum in history for poor children was the foundation established by the Emperor Trajan (about A.D. 110) for destitute and abandoned children. The property thus established in perpetuity, with real estate and money at interest (at five per cent.), was equivalent in value to $920,000, and supported some five thousand children of both sexes. Singularly enough, there seems to have been only one illegitimate child to one hundred and fifty legitimate in these institutions.

The Antonines, as might be expected, did not neglect this charity; but both Antoninus Pius and Marcus Aurelius founded associations for destitute girls. Alexander Severus established one also for poor children. These form the only organized efforts made for this object, during many centuries, by the most civilized and refined state of antiquity.

The number, however, of these wretched creatures increased beyond all cure from scattered exceptional efforts like these. Everywhere the poor got rid of their children by exposure, or sold them as slaves. The rich, if indifferent to their offspring, or unwilling to take the trouble of rearing them, sent them out to the public square, where pimps, beggars, witches, and slave-dealers gleaned their horrible harvest. At length, under the influence of Christianity, legislation began to take cognizance of the practice.

The Emperor Constantine, the Emperor Valentian, Valens, and Gratian, sixty years later, continued this humane legislation.

They ordered, under strict penalties, that every one should nourish his own children, and forbade exposition; declaring also that no one had the right to reclaim the children he had abandoned; the motive to this law being the desire to make it for the interest of those "taking up" exposed children to keep them, even if necessary, as slaves, against any outside claims.

Unfortunately, at that period, slavery was held a less evil than the ordinary fate to which the poor left their children.

The punishment of death was also decreed against infanticide.

It is an interesting fact that a portion, and probably the whole, of our ancestral tribes looked with the greatest horror on abortion and infanticide. The laws of the Visigoths punished these offenses with death or blindness. Their influence, of course, should always be considered, as well as that of Christianity, in estimating the modern position of woman and the outcast child, as compared with their status under Greek and Roman civilization.

At a later period (412 A.D.) the imperial legislation again endeavored to prevent the reclaiming of exposed children from compassionate persons who had taken them. "Were they right to say that those children belonged to them when they had despised them even to the point of abandoning them to death?"

It was provided also, that in future no one should "take from the ground" exposed children except in the presence of witnesses, and that the archbishop should put his signature on the document of guardianship which was prepared. (Cod. Theod., lib. 5, tit. 7, De Expositis.)

Hitherto, exposed children had generally been taken and reared as slaves; but in A.D. 529, Justinian decreed that not only the father lost all legitimate authority over the child if he exposed it, but also that the child itself preserved its liberty.

This law applied only to the Eastern Empire; in the Western the slavery of exposed children continued for centuries. (Lecky: Hist. of Europ. Morals, vol. ii., p. 32.) The Christian churches throughout the early centuries took especial care of orphans, in parish orphan nurseries, or *orphanotrophiœ*.

The first asylums for deserted and foundling children which are recorded in the Christian era are one in Trêves in the sixth century, one at Angiers in the seventh, and a more famous one in Milan, A.D. 787.

Societies for the protection of children were also formed in Milan in the middle of the twelfth century.

At the end of that century a monk of Montpelier, Brother Guy, formed what may be called the first "Children's Aid Society," for the protection, shelter, and education of destitute children, a fraternity which subsequently spread over Europe.

One great cause of the final extreme corruption and extinction of ancient pagan society was the existence of large classes of unfortunate beings, whom no social moral movement of renovation ever reached—the slaves, the gladiators, the barbarian strangers, and the outcast children.

To all these deep strata of misery and crime Christianity gradually penetrated, and brought life and light, and finally an almost entire metamorphosis. As criminal and unfortunate classes, they have—with the exception only of the children—ceased to exist under modern civilization. We have no longer at the basis of modern society the dangers of a multitude of ignorant slaves, or of disaffected barbarous foreigners, or of a profession of gladiators—brutal, brutalizing; but we do still have masses of unfortunate youth, whose condition, though immensely improved and lightened by the influences of Christianity, is still one of the most threatening and painful phenomena of modern society in nearly all civilized countries.

Still, unlike the experience of Paganism under the Roman Empire and before it, rays of light, of intelligence, and of moral and spiritual influence penetrate to the depths of these masses. The spirit of Christ is slowly and irresistibly permeating even this lowest class of miserable, unfortunate, or criminal beings; inspiring those who perseveringly labor for them, drawing from wealth its dole and from intelligence its service of love, educating the fortunate in the habit of duty to the unfortunate, giving a dignity to the most degraded, and offering hope to the despairing.

Christ leads the Reform of the world, as well as its Charity.

Those who have much to do with alms-giving and plans of human improvement soon see how superficial and comparatively useless all assistance or organization is, which does not touch habits of life and the inner forces which form character. The poor helped each year become poorer in force and independence. Education is a better preventive of pauperism than charity. The best police and the most complete form of government are nothing if the individual morality be not there. But Christianity is the highest education of character. Give the poor that, and only seldom will either alms or punishment be necessary.

When one comes to know the peculiar overpowering temptations which beset the class of unfortunate children and similar classes; the inducements to sharpness, deception, roguery, lying, fraud, coarseness, vice in many forms, besides toward open offenses against the law; the few restraining influences in social opinion, good example, or inherited self-control; the forces without and the organization within impelling to crime, and then sees how immensely powerful the belief in and love for a supernatural and noble character and Friend is upon such wild natures; how it inspires to nobleness, restrains low passions, changes bad habits, and transforms base hearts; how the thoughts of this supernatural Friend can accompany a child of the street, and make his daily hard life an offering of loving service; how the unseen sympathy can dry the orphan's tears, and throw a light of cheerfulness around the wan, pale face of the little vagrant, and bring down something of the splendor of heaven to the dark cellars and dreary dens of a great city: whoever has had this experience—not once, but many times—will begin to understand that Christ must lead Reform as well as Charity, and that without Him the worst diseases of modern society can never be cured.

Chapter II. The Proletaires of New York.

New York is a much younger city than its European rivals; and with perhaps one-third the population of London, yet it presents varieties of life among the "masses" quite as picturesque, and elements of population even more dangerous. The throng of different nationalities in the American city gives a peculiarly variegated air to the life beneath the surface, and the enormous over-crowding in portions of the poor quarters intensifies the evils, peculiar to large towns, to a degree seen only in a few districts in such cities as London and Liverpool.

The *mass* of poverty and wretchedness is, of course, far greater in the English capital. There are classes with inherited pauperism and crime more deeply stamped in them, in London or Glasgow, than we ever behold in New York; but certain small districts can be found in our metropolis with the unhappy fame of containing more human beings packed to the square yard, and stained with more acts of blood and riot, within a given period, than is true of any other equal space of earth in the civilized world.

There are houses, well known to sanitary boards and the police, where Fever has taken a perennial lease, and will obey no legal summons to quit; where Cholera—if a single germ-seed of it float anywhere in American atmosphere—at once ripens a black harvest; where Murder has stained every floor of its gloomy stories, and Vice skulks or riots from one year's end to the other. Such houses are never reformed. The only hope for them is in the march of street improvements, which will utterly sweep them away.

It is often urged that the breaking-up of these "dens" and "fever-nests" only scatters the pestilence and moral disease, but does not put an end to them.

The objection is more apparent than real. The abolishing of one of these centres of crime and poverty is somewhat like withdrawing the virus from one diseased limb and diffusing it through an otherwise healthy body. It seems to lose its intensity. The diffusion weakens. Above all, it is less likely to become hereditary.

One of the remarkable and hopeful things about New York, to a close observer of its "dangerous classes," is, as I shall show in a future chapter, that they do not tend to become fixed and inherited, as in European cities.

But, though the crime and pauperism of New York are not so deeply stamped in the blood of the population, they are even more dangerous. The intensity of the American temperament is felt in every fibre of these children of poverty and vice. Their crimes have the unrestrained and sanguinary character of a race accustomed to overcome all obstacles. They rifle a bank, where English thieves pick a pocket; they murder, where European *proletaires* cudgel or fight with fists; in a riot, they begin what seems about to be the sacking of a city, where English rioters would merely batter policemen, or smash lamps. The "dangerous classes" of New York are mainly American-born, but the children of Irish and German immigrants. They are as ignorant as London flash-men or costermongers. They are far more brutal than the peasantry from whom they descend, and they are much banded together, in associations, such as "Dead Rabbit," "Plug-ugly," and various target companies. They are our *enfants perdus*, grown up to young manhood. The murder of an unoffending old man, like Mr. Rogers, is nothing to them. They are ready for any offense or crime, however degraded or bloody. New York has never experienced the full effect of the nurture of these youthful ruffians as she will one day. They showed their hand only slightly in the riots during the war. At present, they are like the athletes and gladiators of the Roman demagogues. They are the "roughs" who sustain the ward politicians, and frighten honest voters. They can "repeat" to an unlimited extent, and serve their employers. They live on *"panem et circenses,"* or City-Hall places and pot-houses, where they have full credit.

We shall speak more particularly of the causes of crime in future chapters, but we may say in brief, that the young ruffians of New York are the products of accident, ignorance, and vice. Among a million people, such as compose the population of this city and its suburbs, there will always be a great number of misfortunes; fathers die, and leave their children unprovided for; parents drink, and abuse their little ones, and they float away on the currents of the street; step-mothers or step-fathers drive out, by neglect and ill-treatment, their sons from home. Thousands are the children of poor foreigners, who have permitted them to grow up without school, education, or religion. All the neglect and bad education and evil example of a poor class tend to form others, who, as they mature, swell the ranks of ruffians and criminals. So, at length, a great multitude of ignorant, untrained, passionate, irreligious boys and young men are formed, who become the "dangerous class" of our city. They form the "Nineteenth-street Gangs," the young burglars and murderers, the garroters and rioters, the thieves and flash-men, the "repeaters" and ruffians, so well known to all who know this metropolis.

THE DANGERS.

It has been common, since the recent terrible Communistic outbreak in Paris, to assume that France alone is exposed to such horrors; but, in the judgment of one who has been familiar with our "dangerous classes" for twenty years, there are just the same explosive social elements beneath the surface of New York as of Paris.

There are thousands on thousands in New York who have no assignable home, and "flit" attic to attic, and cellar to cellar; there are other thousands more or less connected with criminal enterprises; and still other tens of thousands, poor, hard-pressed, and depending for daily bread on the day's earnings, swarming in tenement-houses, who behold the gilded rewards of toil all about them, but are never permitted to touch them.

All these great masses of destitute, miserable, and criminal persons believe that for ages the rich have had all the good things of life, while to them have been left the evil things. Capital to them is the tyrant.

Let but Law lift its hand from them for a season, or let the civilizing influences of American life fail to reach them, and, if the opportunity offered, we should see an explosion from this class which might leave this city in ashes and blood.

To those incredulous of this, we would recall the scenes in our streets during the riots in 1863; when, for a short period, the guardians of good order—the local militia—had been withdrawn for national purposes, and when the ignorant masses were excited by dread of the draft.

Who will ever forget the marvelous rapidity with which the better streets were filled with a ruffianly and desperate multitude, such as in ordinary times we seldom see—creatures who seemed to have crept from their burrows and dens to join in the plunder of the city—how quickly certain houses were marked out for sacking and ruin, and what wild and brutal crimes were committed on the unoffending negroes? It will be recalled, too, how much *women* figured in these horrible scenes, as they did in the Communistic outbreak in Paris. It was evident to all careful observers then, that had another day of license been given the crowd, the attack would have been directed at the apparent wealth of the city—the banks, jewelers' shops, and rich private houses.

No one doubted then, or during the Orange riot of 1871, the existence of "dangerous classes" in New York. And yet the separate members of these riotous and ruffianly masses are simply neglected and street-wandering children who have come to early manhood.

The true preventive of social catastrophes like these, are just such Christian reformatory and educational movements as we are about to describe.

Of the number of the distinctively homeless and vagrant youth in New York, it is difficult to speak with precision. We should be inclined to estimate it, after long observation, as fluctuating each year between 20,000 and 30,000.[1] But to these, as they mature, must be added, in the composition of the dangerous classes, all those who are professionally criminal, and who have homes and lodging-places. And again to these, portions of that vast and ignorant[2] multitude, who, in prosperous times, just keep their heads above water, who are pressed down by poverty or misfortune, and who look with envy and greed at the signs of wealth and luxury all around them, while they themselves have nothing but hardship, penury, and unceasing drudgery.

Chapter III. The Causes of Crime.

The great practical division of causes of crime may be made into preventible and non-preventible. Among the preventible, or those which can be in good part removed, may be placed ignorance, intemperance, over-crowding of population, want of work, idleness, vagrancy, the weakness of the marriage-tie, and bad legislation.

Among those which cannot be entirely removed are inheritance, the effects of emigration, orphanage, accident or misfortune, the strength of the sexual and other passions, and a natural weakness of moral or mental powers.

IGNORANCE.

There needs hardly a word to be said in this country on the intimate connection between ignorance and crime.

The precise statistical relation between them in the State of New York would seem to be this: about thirty-one per cent. of the adult criminals cannot read or write, while of the adult population at large about six (6.08) per cent. are illiterate; or nearly one-third of the crime is committed by six-hundredths of the population. In the city prisons for 1870, out of 49,423 criminals, 18,442 could not write and could barely read, or more than thirty-three per cent.

In the Reformatories of the country, according to the statement of Dr. Bittinger before the National Congress on prison-discipline at Cincinnati, out of the average number of the inmates for 1868, of 7,963 twenty-seven per cent. were wholly illiterate.

Very great criminality is, of course, possible with high education; but in the immense majority of cases a very small degree of mental training or intellectual tastes is a preventive of idleness and consequent crime and of extreme poverty. The difference between knowing how to read and not knowing will often be the line between utter poverty and a capacity for various occupations.

---

1. The homeless children who come each year under the charitable efforts afterwards to be described amount to some 12,000.
2. It should be remembered that there are in this city over 60,000 persons above ten years of age who cannot write their names.

Among the inmates of the city prisons a large percentage are without a trade, and no doubt this idle condition is largely due to their ignorance and is one of the great stimulants to their criminal course. Who can say how much the knowledge of Geography alone may stimulate a child or a youth to emigrate, and thus leave his immediate temptations and escape pressing poverty?

ORPHANAGE.

Out of 452 criminal children received into the House of Refuge in New York during 1870, only 187 had both parents living, so that nearly sixty per cent. had lost one or both of their parents, or were otherwise separated from them.

According to Dr. Bittinger,[3] of the 7,963 inmates of the reformatories in the United States in 1870, fifty-five per cent. were orphans or half orphans.

The following figures strikingly show the extent to which orphanage and inheritance influence the moral condition of children.

Mettrai, the celebrated French reformatory, has received since its foundation 3,580 youthful inmates. Of these, there are 707 whose parents are convicts; 308 whose parents live in concubinage; 534 "natural" children; 221 foundlings; 504 children of a second marriage; and 1,542 without either father or mother.[4]

An intelligent French writer, M. de Marsangy,[5] in writing of the causes of juvenile crime in France, says that "a fifth of those who have been the objects of judicial pursuit are composed of orphans; the half have no father, a quarter no mother, and as for those who have a family, nearly all are dragged by it into evil."

EMIGRATION.

There is no question that the breaking of the ties with one's country has a bad moral effect, especially on a laboring class. The Emigrant is released from the social inspection and judgment to which he has been subjected at home, and the tie of church and priesthood is weakened. If a Roman Catholic, he is often a worse Catholic, without being a better Protestant. If a Protestant, he often becomes indifferent. Moral ties are loosened with the religious. The intervening process which occurs here, between his abandoning the old state of things and fitting himself to the new, is not favorable to morals or character.

The consequence is, that an immense proportion of our ignorant and criminal class are foreign-born; and of the dangerous classes here, a very large part, though native-born, are of foreign parentage. Thus, out of the whole number of foreigners in New York State, in 1860, 16.69 per cent. could not read or write; while of the native-born only 1.83 per cent. were illiterate.

Of the 49,423 prisoners in our city prisons, in prison for one year before January, 1870, 32,225 were of foreign birth, and, no doubt, a large proportion of the remainder of foreign parentage. Of the foreign-born, 21,887 were from Ireland; and yet at home the Irish are one of the most law-abiding and virtuous of populations—the proportion of criminals being smaller than in England or Scotland.

3. Transactions of the National Congress, p. 279.
4. Une visite à Mettray. Paris, 1868.
5. Moralisation de l'enfance coupable, p. 13.

In the Eastern Penitentiary of Pennsylvania, according to Dr. Bittinger, from one-fourth to one-third of the inmates are foreigners; in Auburn, from a third to a half; in Clinton, one-half; in Sing Sing, between one-half and six-sevenths. In the Albany Penitentiary, the aggregate number of prisoners during the last twenty years was 18,390, of whom 10,770 were foreign-born.[6]

It is another marked instance of the demoralizing influence of emigration, that so large a proportion of the female criminal class should be Irish-born, though the Irish female laboring class are well known to be at home one of the most virtuous in the world.

A hopeful fact, however, begins to appear in regard to this matter; the worst effects of emigration in this country seem over. The machinery for protecting and forwarding the newly-arrived immigrants, so that they may escape the dangers and temptations of the city, has been much improved. Very few, comparatively, now remain in our sea-ports to swell the current of poverty and crime. The majority find their way at once to the country districts. The quality, too, of the immigration has improved. More well-to-do farmers and peasantry, with small savings, arrive than formerly, and the preponderance, as to nationality, is inclining to the Germans. It comparatively seldom happens now that paupers or persons absolutely without means, land in New York.

As one of the great causes of crime, Emigration will undoubtedly have a much feebler influence in the future in New York than it has had in the past.

WANT OF A TRADE.

It is remarkable how often, in questioning the youthful convicts in our prisons as to the causes of their downfall, they will reply that "if they had had a trade, they would not have been there." They disliked drudgery, they found places in offices and shops crowded; they would have enjoyed the companionship and the inventiveness of a trade, but they could not obtain one, and therefore they were led into stealing or gambling, as a quick mode of earning a living.

There is no doubt that a lad with a trade feels a peculiar independence of the world, and is much less likely to take up dishonest means of living than one depending on manual labor, or chance means of living.

There is nearly always a demand for his work; the lad feels himself a member of a craft and supported by the consciousness of this membership; the means of the "Unions" often sustain him when out of employment; his associates are more honest and respectable than those of boys depending on chance-labor, and so he is preserved from falling into crime.

Of course, if such a lad would walk forth to the nearest country village, he would find plenty of healthy and remunerative employment in the ground, as gardener or farmer. And to a country-lad, the farm offers a better chance than a trade. But many city boys and young men will not consent to leave the excitements of the city, so that the want of a mechanical occupation does expose them to many temptations.

The persons most responsible for this state of things are the members of such "Unions" as refuse to employ boys, or to encourage the training of apprentices. It is well-known that in many trades of New York, hardly any young laborers or apprentices are being trained. The result of this selfish

6. Transact. of Nat. Cong., p. 282.

policy will be to reduce the amount of skilled labor in this city, and thus compel the importation of foreign labor, and to increase juvenile crime and the burdens on the poor.

Another cause of this increasing separation from trades among the young is, no doubt, the increasing aversion of American children, whether poor or rich, to learn anything thoroughly; the boys of the street, like those of our merchants, preferring to make fortunes by lucky and sudden "turns," rather than by patient and steady industry.

Our hope in this matter is in the steady demand for juvenile labor in the country districts, and the substantial rewards which await industry there.

J. O. S. HUNTINGTON

Tenement-house Morality[†]

Some time ago a lad came back to me, after making his confession, and asked, in a troubled tone: "Father, must I confess what that man says at the shop?" That, it seems to me, is a fair example of the effect not only of the shops where tenement-house people work, but of the streets where they walk and the buildings in which they live. Here was a boy with strong impulses toward goodness, trying and struggling to do right and to keep himself pure, hating the blasphemy and obscenity which he heard from those around him, and yet compelled for so many hours each day to breathe an atmosphere foul with moral corruption that he had come to feel that the sin about him was somehow his own, and that he needed cleansing from others' guilt as if he were himself defiled. That this is the case in many shops where children work, is clear from their own pathetic acknowledgment. "How can we be good," they cry, "when we have to hear such talk all day?" Or, as the older ones say, in yet sadder tones: "When I first went to the factory I thought I couldn't stand it; then I got used to it; now I say the same things myself." Would that the evil stopped short at *words!*

But it is not of shops that I have to speak now, but of a more sacred place, of that which must over be the source from which the life of society flows forth—of the homes of our working people. And I solemnly aver that the tenement-house system surrounds the poor in their very families with just such corrupting influences as those found in the factories and shops; yes, and with yet more deadly moral contagion. How can it be otherwise? Take one block in a tenement-house district.[1] It will measure 700 by 200 feet. On all four sides are rows of tenements four or five stories high. Behind one-third of the houses in these rows are rear houses, with smaller rooms, darker and dirtier passages, backed often by another rear-house, a brewery, a stable, or a factory. Altogether there are 1,736 rooms. In these rooms live 2,076 souls, divided into 460 families; thus, on the average, each family of five persons occupies three rooms. The population of some parts of New York is 290,000 to the square mile: the most densely populated part of London has 170,000.

---

† From *Forum* 3.5 (1887).

1. I give the average of five such blocks which I have had thoroughly visited. The two young men whom I employed, though they have lived all their lives in the very district, came back horrified at the condition of things.

Of course in many cases the family is larger (some of the very poorest people take lodgers), and in a number of cases we have found fourteen or fifteen grown persons occupying two rooms, or even one. And then many of these "rooms" are hardly more than closets, and dark closets at that. Almost all the bedrooms measure only seven feet by nine, and have but one door and one window. The door leads into the apartment that serves as kitchen, parlor, sitting-room, laundry, and workshop, and the window opens on a dark stair-way, up which the moisture from the cellar and the sewer-gas from the drains are continually rising. One-fifth of these rooms, too, are in basements below the level of the street, and nearly half of even the outer rooms open into courts only twenty feet wide, in which there are usually several wooden priv-ies for the use of the fifteen or twenty families in the front and rear houses.

I know that these statistics will give but a faint conception of the density of the population to any except those who have gone in and out of the houses day and night for months, if not years; but most people, by a little effort of the imagination, can form some sort of an idea how impossible it is for dwellers in tenement blocks to get out of the sight and sound of their neighbors, whose names are often unknown, but whose voices and footsteps are as familiar as those of their own room-mates. At all seasons of the year the inhabitants of a tenement-house must meet one another in the entries (sometimes less than three feet wide), on the stairs, at the sink (there is but one on each floor); must see into one another's rooms as each person goes in and out; must use the roof, the doorway, the yard, in common. But when the summer heats are on, and men and women crowd together on the top of the house waiting for a breeze to come; when men will sit all night on a seat in the park to escape the closeness of a room where a fire has been burning all day (not for cooking, but to heat the irons for the laundry or the tailor's shop); when every window must stand open to let in what little air there is; then it may be seen that privacy in a tenement-house is not much more possible than in an Eastern caravansary or in the steerage of an emi-grant vessel. At such a time every loud word spoken reaches the ears of scores of people. From one room come the harsh tones of a husband and wife in the heat of a "family quarrel," oaths and imprecations ringing out on the fetid air; from another window come the shouts and frantic laughter of men and women (God pity them!) trying to drown their misery in liquor from the gin-mill on the corner; while from the roof of a neighboring house come the words of a ribald song flung out shamelessly to all within hearing, whether they choose or not. And, as if this were not debasing enough, in many of these blocks every other house has, on the ground floor, a saloon or rum-shop, from which the smell of alcohol issues at all times; where the monotonous click of balls on the pool table sounds till after midnight, when it gives place to the howls of drunken men turned out on the street; and past the door of which, often open into the entry, every person, every child, in the house must pass to and from his room.

And who are the people that crowd these tenements? Perhaps it will be thought that the very badness of the condition of such places shows that the people are all "filthy and debased creatures,"[2] and that, therefore, very little

---

2. This is the expression which was used to describe the inhabitants of tenement-houses before a committee of the New York Legislature last winter, by one of the opponents of two bills, which have since become laws, to amend the old statutes on tenement-houses, and to provide for the laying out of small parks in crowded districts.

can be done or need be done for them. Men will be inclined to dismiss the whole matter with a shrug of the shoulders and an impatient sigh. "It is all very dreadful, no doubt, but there will always be base, corrupt people; they naturally herd together, they create their own misery; if you root them out of one locality they will simply transfer themselves and their brutality and vice to some other." No doubt there are such people in tenement-houses, but that they represent the great body of the tenement-house population I entirely deny. Side by side with these poor outcasts of humanity are hard-working men and women who are leading lives of heroic purity and nobility. They are fighting, at fearful odds, to keep themselves and their children from the filth and pollution all about them. It is in their name that I plead; and not for their sake only, but for that great middle class of those who are not determinedly vicious, and yet are not striving with such desperate resolution as these others after goodness and truth—those who would gladly do right, but lack the courage to rise above the mass of simple low-living and coarseness around them. Surely the case of these people is pitiful enough. They are pressed together under conditions which make it well-nigh impossible for them to help themselves or one another. The bad almost inevitably drag down the good; and the good have not the chance to lift up the bad. Remember that the tenement population of most of our cities is a heterogeneous mixture of all the races and nationalities of the globe. There is no place in such a conglomeration for the public spirit and popular sentiment that so often exercise a restraining and elevating influence. There is no standard of morality. Human nature is left to do pretty nearly what it likes, and the lower passions are not slow to assert themselves.

This is all the more the case that so many of these people are emigrants. They have come from the villages of England, Germany, Russia, where they were under the constraint of a certain conventional morality, backed up by a strong and vigilant, even if a despotic, government that made it often easier to do right than to do wrong. Here they are jumbled together in utter disorder, Prussians, Bohemians, Swiss, Scotch, Chinese, Italians, Turks, Jews, and Christians, black and white; a restless, soothing mass of human beings, unable to talk together, unable to think together, able only, under some overmastering passion, to act together. In a city like New York may be found representatives of almost "every epoch of history and every locality of the world." One scholar says that in New York, he has heard eighty-four languages and distinct dialects spoken. The signs alone in the crowded parts of the city show the cosmopolitan character of the population.[3] Is it not evident that in such a chaotic state of things, with the reins of government held very loosely,[4] every one, man, woman, boy, and girl, must actually live in an atmosphere of defilement night and day; not merely going into it, as in the case of work in a shop, and then coming back into pure and elevating surroundings, but breathing in the polluted air with every breath? Why, the very tones of the voices that I have heard from my room

---

3. The following are a few signs copied down in the course of a short walk on the east side of New York: "G. Gelb, Junk Dealer. Highest Price paid," etc.—"Hier wird der höchiste Preis bezahlt für Alle Sorten Kupfer, Bloi, Zink, Eisen, Flaschen, Lumpen, Strick, u s. w."—"שותעם בשרלם ר צחק ורנוואלר בשר בשרי משתעת"—"Reverend L. Levy, Gesetzliche Eho Kontrakto Vollzogen."—"Janacek & Kysela Bankovní a Preplavni Obehod. Wechsel und Passage Gesehäft."—"Fotograficka Dilna."—"M. Bonedik Uhersky Pryphen Slovansky Hostinee."—"Cesky Pekarna,"—"Aechte Böhmische Schwarzbrod Bäckerei."
4. A crowd of men and women, on East Twelfth Street, lately boasted, "No policeman dare show his face down here."

in a tenement-house brought with them a sense of moral contamination. Even bodily cleanliness is almost impossible. Bath-rooms are unknown in tenement-houses, and the public baths, open only a few months of the year, often afford but fresh opportunities for vice. In most families what little washing is done must be done in the presence of others, and often all the water used must be carried up three or four flights of narrow winding stairs.

Of course sickness and death have their own horrors and their own depraving influences. What little privacy may be possible for the well is often denied to the sick, who, to get any air at all, must lie in the room used by the whole family for almost every purpose. Many of the diseases are infectious, but isolation is impossible, and therefore almost every child suffers from scarlet fever, measles, chicken-pox, and diphtheria, and often bears the results through life. And death, from its frequency, and the coarseness that surrounds it, loses, if not all its terrors, at least its dignity, and is regarded as one of the many disagreeable accidents of life, hardly worthy even of idle curiosity. The corpse lies for two days in the room where the family eats, works, and often sleeps.[5]

But this by no means exhausts the abominations of the system of tenement-house life. As I have said, it is only by an effort quite beyond the powers of many people that grown men and women can resist the lowering influences about them. What, then, must be the lot of the children? They must not only hear all that older people hear, and see all that they see, at an age when every such sight and sound leaves its impression, but they are practically forced into acquaintanceship with the other dwellers in the tenement which their elders can avoid. Many mothers do try to keep their children in their own rooms, but as the children grow up this is increasingly difficult, and at length impossible. Once beyond the mother's supervision, the child inevitably becomes one of a group of children representing, perhaps, almost all the nationalities and religions of which the population consists. This group of children finds its playground in the dirty street in front of the block, or in the dirty yard, half filled with privies, behind. Here and there is a yard where turf has been laid, and a few flowers coaxed to grow; but there, of course, is no room for children. When it rains the children play in the cellars, sailing their boats on the water that often stands there, or wading ankle-deep in it. Wherever they play they are without any real oversight. The fathers are at their work, or in the saloon; the mothers are working wearily at the sewing-machine or the wash-tub, too driven to stop and watch their children, even if they can see them from the window. Think of what possibilities of moral contagion lie in such associations, amid such surroundings. Think how horribly ruinous the presence of one older bad child can be. As a fact, I could not here relate what I know to be the effects of such companionship; I could not even describe the games at which they play.

But suppose that a child passes with some degree of safety through the period of mere unconscious and, even in tenement-houses, light-hearted childhood;[6] suppose the child has not been afflicted by many of the

5. As to physical suffering, take two points: The water the patient drinks must often be drawn at three o'clock in the morning, and kept standing all day; and the thermometer has been found to register 115° in the shade over the head of a sick child.

6. How prematurely this period passes, Dr. Daniels has lately borne witness from her wide experience. "One is struck with the extraordinarily early maturity of these little ones. I have sick babies of six months to two years brought to me daily, by boys and girls of eight to nine years, who answer my questions as well as the mother could."

disorders—granulated eyelids, scrofula, rickets, heart disease—so shockingly prevalent among these children, what then awaits these boys and girls? As life begins to open, and the desire for a little of the brightness and happiness of the world makes itself felt, what is the scene that confronts them? A wilderness of ignorance, poverty, and crime; a moral desert, beautiless, joyless, utterly unsatisfying to all the best and noblest instincts of their hearts. Do you realize that in a tenement-house district there is absolutely not one lovely thing on which the eyes can rest? Even the sky is often robbed of its fairness by the clouds of smoke and dust. The glories of sunrise and sunset are unknown. The sun crawls up from among the chimney-pots, and goes down behind brick walls and tin roofs. The streets are always filthy, the houses ugly, the shop-windows cheaply gaudy, or neglected and covered with dust; the blocks are wearily monotonous, the schoolrooms are bare and uninteresting, the factories are filled with fluff, and dirt, and noise; the air is charged with foul odors from close courts, open drains, or the neighboring oil and varnish works; the river is foul with mud and ooze and the refuse of a great city; the district ends in heaps of rubbish and empty lots, waiting for a rise in the market. And the rooms are often worst of all. There is many a "home" where a boy or girl over fourteen years old would not think of passing an evening unless compelled to do so. Think of coming back after a hard day's work in a shop to find the only sitting-room half filled with wash-tubs, the baby crying, children squabbling on the floor, or perhaps tumbling about on the bed; the walls hung with the soiled clothes and dresses of the family; the whole place reeking with the smell of fat and garlic from the hot stove; the table "set" with coarse, broken china, strewn on a dirty board; a kerosene lamp, without a shade, smoking in the middle; a loaf of bread, in the brown paper in which it was wrapped at the bakery; and a coffee-pot of black, bitter coffee. That is the scene which welcomes many a girl or boy, just beginning to realize how differently other people live. Is it strange that they gulp down their sugarless coffee, and at the first chance slip out into the street beneath, glad, perhaps, if they escape without a harsh scolding or a blow? And what has the world outside their homes to offer them? An avenue lighted by electricity, with plenty of young people with whom to "carry on," without any interruption from father or mother; the bright, warm saloon, with every chance of pleasant companionship and obsequious attendance; or the gay theater or dance hall, where all the troubles of life can be forgotten for a few hours in excitement or sin.[7] Is it strange that as we go about from house to house, every few weeks some mother tells us, with an affectation of indifference, but with a quiver in her voice, "Rosie isn't at home now; she's boarding. We don't just know where she is. She was a bad girl; she wouldn't work. Father licked her, and then she went away." Or, "Charlie done something wrong at the shop; he took some money from the boss, and we ain't seen him since." Is it strange that a young woman, attractive, intelligent, who has gone astray and found the misery of that, and now is trying to do right, and support a father and mother and little brother,

---

7. Of course something is being accomplished for a small portion of the young people in tenement districts by the various chapels, mission-rooms, guild and reading-rooms, schools and libraries, just as in other ways a good deal is being done for the bodies and souls of the poor; but these are, for the most part, only palliatives of the misery; and an increasing number of the hardest workers in the cause of philanthropy are beginning to question whether all our charitable agencies and institutions, by making the lives of tenement-house people just not intolerable, may not be actually increasing the evils that they are organized to redress.

should have said to me the other day: "There's nothing in the world that makes me happy; the only thing I can do is to keep working. I work at tailoring all day. Noontimes I work as soon as I've eaten my lunch. I bring my work home and sew until I fall asleep. That's the way I keep from going mad with my wretchedness."

I am quite aware that much of what I have written will seem overstated. It seems so to me, and yet I know that it is not. Every single fact has been verified, and can be verified in thousands of cases. And this is not more than half the truth. If any one is disposed to be skeptical, I can only ask him to make investigation on his own account. But let him be thorough. Let him not merely walk through the streets some breezy Monday morning; let him spend days and nights here; let him live, as we have done, in a tenement block; let him visit the people at all hours; let him, above all, spend a public holiday here; let him see the carnival of sin of a Fourth of July or a New Year's night. I do not say that he will even then understand the conditions of tenement-house existence; but I know that his incredulity will give place to a sad, bewildered realization of the horrors of a state of things where manhood is brutalized, womanhood dishonored, childhood poisoned at its very source.

That is the present witness of those who have looked unflinchingly at the facts. Two clergymen, one of them the rector of one of the largest of our city churches, the other now a missionary bishop, formerly a hard-working priest among the city poor,[8] have recently given public utterance to the statement that in many tenement-houses morality is practically impossible.

One question remains: Can anything be done to set things right? I can almost hear some one saying, "Oh, well, it is all very bad, no doubt; but it always has been, and I suppose it always must be." There is an answer to that. This is not a matter for sentiment, or pious condolence, but for justice. Thirty years ago Christian communities in many parts of this country were content that thousands of human beings should live in a condition of life where the marriage relation was unknown, and children grew up in utter ignorance and vice. But at last the conscience of the American people awoke to the wrong inflicted, and in its highest legislative assembly assured to the negro slaves of the South the rights of men.[9] And have not the tenement-house people of our own race, our own blood, capable, many of them, of education and refinement quite equal to our own—have not they and their children a right to live pure and good lives? And if this is their right, then the enjoyment of it must be theirs sooner or later. If there is a God in heaven, and if righteousness and judgment are the habitation of his throne, it cannot be his will that one of these little ones should perish. Shall we work with him that his will be done, that even the weakest and poorest shall find the way open before him to purity and peace; or shall we longer withhold the poor from their desire, and turn away the stranger from his right, and plunder the heritage of the needy, and so be called to answer to the God of the poor in the day when he shall arise to shake terribly the

8. The Rev. Dr. Rainsford, Rector of St. George's Church, New York city, and the Rt. Rev. W. D. Walker, S. T. D., Bishop of Northern Dakota, formerly in charge of Calvary Chapel, New York city.
9. It may be answered that the freedmen of the southern States are not as well off now as they were under servitude. Why this is so may be inferred from the saying common among southern planters to-day, "What fools we were to fight for slavery, when we can get so much more out of our niggers by setting them to compete with one another in the labor market."

earth? Already many hearts, among working people at any rate, are rising up to echo the call of a great English thinker:

> "Charitable persons suppose that the worst fault of the rich is to refuse the people meat; and the people cry for their meat, kept back by fraud, to the Lord of Multitudes. Alas! it is not meat of which the refusal is cruelest, or to which the claim is validest. The life is more than the meat. The rich not only refuse food to the poor; they refuse wisdom; they refuse salvation. Ye sheep without shepherd, it is not the pasture that has been shut from you, but the Presence. Meat: perhaps your right to that may be pleadable; but other rights have to be pleaded first. Claim the crumbs from the table, if you will; but claim them as children, not as dogs. Claim your right to be fed; but claim more loudly your right to be holy, perfect, pure."[1]

Let us acknowledge that claim, and strive for the destruction of the tenement-house system, for the bringing in, even in the midst of the darkness of our great cities, of the kingdom of light, liberty, and love.

WILLIAM T. ELSING

From The Poor in Great Cities†

Life in New York Tenement-Houses as Seen by a City Missionary

THE EAST SIDE—TENEMENT LIFE—CONTRASTS IN THE TENEMENTS—DIRT
AND CLEANLINESS—CLASSES OF HOMES IN THE TENEMENTS—RENTS—CHANGES
IN THE TENEMENT POPULATION—STATISTICS OF A TYPICAL
BLOCK—NATIONALITIES—INFLUENCES OF THE PUBLIC SCHOOLS—
THE FRESH-AIR EXCURSIONS—THE COLLEGE SETTLEMENTS—STORIES
OF THE POOR—THE CHARITY ORGANIZATIONS—THE CHURCH—SUGGESTIONS
TOWARD IMPROVING "DARKEST NEW YORK."

For nearly nine years I have spent much of my time in the homes of the working people, on the East Side, in the lower part of New York City. I have been with the people in their days of joy and hours of sorrow. I have been present at their marriage, baptismal, and funeral services. I have visited the sick and dying in cold, dark cellars in midwinter, and sat by the bedside of sufferers in midsummer in the low attic room, where the heat was so intense and the perspiration flowed so abundantly that it reminded me of a Turkish bath. I have been a frequent guest in the homes of the humble. I have become the confidant of many in days of trouble and anxiety.

I shall in this paper tell simply what I have heard, seen, and know. I shall endeavor to avoid giving a one-sided statement. I have noticed that nearly all those who work among the poor of our great cities fall into the natural habit of drawing too dark a picture of the real state of things. The outside world has always been more inclined to listen to weird, startling, and thrilling statements than to the more ordinary and commonplace facts. If

1. John Ruskin. "Unto This Last." *Ad Valorem.*
† New York: Charles Scribner's Sons, 1895.

I were to crowd into the space of one short chapter all the remarkable things which I have heard and seen during the past nine years, I might give an absolutely truthful account and produce a sensation, and yet, after all, I should give a most misleading idea of the actual condition of the homes and the people with whom I have been so intimately associated. We must not crowd all the sad and gloomy experiences of a lifetime into a history which can be read in an hour.

What I have said applies especially to the homes of the people in the tenement-houses. An ordinary tenement-house contains five stories and a basement, four families usually occupying a floor. The halls in nearly all the houses are more or less dark, even during the brightest part of the day. When groping my way in the passages I usually imitate the steam craft in a thick fog and give a danger-signal when I hear someone else approaching; but even when all is silent I proceed with caution, for once I have stumbled against a baby who was quietly sitting in the dark hall or on the stairs. In the old-style halls there is no way of getting light and air, except from the skylight in the roof, or from the glass transoms in the doors of the apartments. In the newer houses a scanty supply of air comes directly from the air-shafts at the side of the hall. The new houses are not much better lighted than the old ones. The air-shafts are too narrow to convey much light to the lower floors. In the older houses the sink is frequently found in the hall, where the four tenants living on the same floor get their water. These sinks in the dark halls are a source of great inconvenience. A person is liable to stumble against them, and they are frequently filthy and a menace to health. In the new tenements the sink is never placed in the hall. In addition to the owner and agent, in connection with every large tenement-house, there is a housekeeper. The housekeepers are usually strong and thrifty housewives who take care of the halls and stairs, light the gas, sweep the sidewalks, and show the rooms to new applicants, and frequently receive the rent until the agent or landlord calls for it. Sometimes the housekeeper deals directly with the landlord, who comes once or twice a month to look at his property and collect the rent. The housekeeper is frequently a widow, who gets free rent in exchange for her work, and by means of sewing or washing is able to provide food and clothing for her children. It pays the landlord to have one tenant rent free in order to have a clean house. If the house is small the housekeeper usually receives her rent at a reduced rate in exchange for her services. There is never any difficulty in getting a good housekeeper. The landlord or agent sees to it that the housekeeper does her duty and the housekeeper watches the tenants. If they soil the stairs and halls, she reminds them of the fact in no uncertain way. If a careless tenant gives unnecessary labor to the housekeeper that tenant will soon be compelled to seek other quarters. The result is that the stairs and halls in all the large tenement-houses are remarkably clean. I have visited a great number of them, and can confidently say that I have never seen the halls of a large tenement-house in as neglected and dirty a condition as the corridors of the New York Post-Office. But the moment you enter the rooms of the occupants you often step from cleanliness into filth. The influence of the housekeeper and the sight of the clean halls and stairs is to some the first lesson in cleanliness, and is not without its beneficial effects. There is a slow but constant improvement in this direction, and every year strangers from many lands are getting gradually acquainted with the use, value, and virtue of clean water.

The housekeeper is frequently wanting in the older and smaller houses, which were formerly occupied by one family, but now serve as homes for three or four. Every tenant is here expected to perform a portion of the housekeeper's duty without remuneration. These houses are sometimes extremely dirty, and the death-rate is higher than in the larger and better kept tenements.

Let us leave the hall and enter some of the homes in the larger houses. To many persons, living in a tenement-house is synonymous with living in the slums, yet nothing is further from the truth. It would be an easy matter for me to take a stranger into a dozen or more homes so poor, dirty, and wretched that he would not forget the sight for days, and he would be thoroughly convinced that a home cannot exist in a tenement-house; but I could take that same person to an equal number of homes in the same section of the city, and sometimes in the same house, which would turn him into a joyful optimist, and forever satisfy him that the state of things is not by any means as bad as it might be. To the casual observer the tenement-houses in many portions of New York present a remarkable degree of uniformity. The great brick buildings with their net-work of iron fire-escapes in front, their numerous clothes-lines running from every window in the rear, the well-worn stairs, the dark halls, the numerous odors, pleasant and otherwise, coming from a score of different kitchens presided over by housewives of various nationalities—these are all similar; but from the moment you enter the rooms you will find every variety of homes, many of them poor, neglected, wretched, and dirty; others clean, thrifty, and attractive; indeed, as great a variety as exists in the interior of homes in an ordinary town. There are homes where the floor is bare and dirty, the furniture broken and scanty, the table greasy, the bedlinen yellow, the air foul and heavy, the children pale, frowsy, and sticky, so that you squirm when the baby wants to kiss you; but there is also another and brighter side. There are at the same time thousands of cheerful, happy homes in the tenement-houses. The floor is frequently as clean and white as soap, water, and German muscle is able to make it. The tablecloth and bedlinen, although of coarse material, are snowy white. The stove has the brightness of a mirror, the cheap lace-curtains are the perfection of cleanliness, and the simple furniture shines with a recent polishing. There is nothing offensive about the well-washed faces of the children. A few favorite flowers are growing on the window-sill. The room contains a book-shelf with a few popular volumes. A bird-cage hangs from the ceiling; the little songster seems to feel that his music is appreciated in this tenement-kitchen, and pours forth more rich and tender notes than are ever heard in the silent chambers of the wealthy. In such homes the oft-recurring motto, "God Bless Our Home," is not an idle mockery.

A large number of tenement-houses in the lower portion of New York are only a little below the common up-town flat. It is often difficult to tell where the flat leaves off and the tenement begins. You get about as little air and sunshine in the one as in the other. The main difference lies in the number of rooms and the location. If some down-town tenement-houses stood up-town they would be called flats. The word *tenement* is becoming unpopular down-town, and many landlords have dubbed their great caravansaries by the more aristocratic name of "flat," and the term "rooms" has been changed to "apartments."

There are three distinct classes of homes in the tenement-houses; the cheapest and humblest of these is the attic home, which usually consists of one or two rooms, and is found only down-town. These are generally occupied by old persons. Occasionally three or four attic rooms are connected and rented to a family, but as small single rooms are sought after by lonely old people, the landlord often rents them separately. An old lady who has to earn her bread with the needle finds the attic at once the cheapest and best place for her needs. The rent of one or two unfurnished attic rooms ranges from $3 to $5 per month.

A large number of very poor people live in three rooms—a kitchen and two dark bedrooms. Where the family is large the kitchen lounge is opened and converted into a double bed at night. The rent for three rooms is generally from $8 to $12 per month.

The vast majority of respectable working people live in four rooms—a kitchen, two dark bedrooms, and a parlor. These parlors are generally provided with a bed-lounge, and are used as sleeping-rooms at night. The best room is always carpeted and often provided with upholstered chairs. The walls are generally decorated with family photographs and inexpensive pictures, and in some of them I have found a piano. These parlors compare very favorably with the best room in the house of the average farmer. The rent for four rooms is from $12 to $16 per month.

The rent is an ever-present and unceasing source of anxiety to a great many poor people. The family is sometimes obliged to go half clothed and live on the cheapest and coarsest food in order to provide the rent money. The monthly rent is a veritable sword of Damocles. To a poor woman who dreads the coming of the landlord, the most enticing and attractive description of heaven which I have been able to give is a place where they pay no rent. The landlords are of necessity compelled to be peremptory and sometimes arbitrary in their demands. If a landlord were even a little too lenient his tenement property would certainly prove a losing investment. The apparently unreasonable harshness of many landlords is often justifiable, and the only means of securing them against loss. Generally where a good tenant is unable to pay the rent on account of sickness or lack of work the landlord is willing to extend the time a few weeks. I frequently find families who are two or three months in arrears. In the majority of cases where dispossess papers are served, the landlord does not know his tenant sufficiently well to trust him, or the tenant is unworthy of trust. Very few of those who are evicted are compelled to take to the street. In most cases sufficient money is collected from friends, neighbors, and charitable people to procure another place of shelter. Occasionally, however, all the worldly possessions of an unfortunate tenant are placed on the street. It is a pathetic sight to see a small heap of poor household stuff standing on the sidewalk guarded by the children, while the distressed mother is frantically rushing from one charitable organization to another in search of help.

A poor German woman came to me on one occasion and informed me that her furniture was standing on the sidewalk, and she knew not what would become of her. She had with her a beautiful little girl. The child cried continually, but the mother's distress was too great for tears. She begged me in God's name to help her. I gave her but little encouragement, and dismissed her with a few kind words. She left without heaping abuse on me or cursing the church for its neglect of the poor. A little later I went to the place where she informed me her furniture was and found all her earthly goods on the sidewalk. I inquired of some of her former neighbors about her character, and on being convinced that she was a worthy woman, rented two small rooms in a rear tenement. I found some young street-corner loafers, told them about the woman, and asked them to lend a hand in getting the furniture moved. There is no man so bad that he will not do a good turn for another if you approach him properly. These young roughs went to work with a will, and when the poor woman returned from her last fruitless attempt to collect enough for a new home she found everything arranged. She was thankful and happy. I did not see her until two months later. Then she appeared in as great distress as before, and showed me a new dispossess paper. She informed me that she had failed to find work, everything had been against her, but she hoped to get on her feet if I would once more help her. I told her it was impossible for me to do anything more for her; so she thanked me for my former kindness and departed. That afternoon I heard of a lady in Orange, N. J., who wanted a house-servant and a little girl as waitress. I immediately thought of the German woman and promised if possible to send her out to Orange as soon as arrangements could be made. I was soon in the little rooms of the widow and her daughter and expected to be the bearer of joyful tidings. When I finished she looked sadly at the few scanty pieces of furniture and said:

"If I go to the country what shall I do with the stuff?"

"My good woman," I said, "the stuff is not worth fifty cents; give it to the boys to make a bonfire, and do what I tell you."

"But I have not money enough to leave the city."

I provided the fare, the boys had a glorious time around their fire, and that night, instead of sleeping in her comfortless room, the poor woman was on Orange Mountain. It would have been a losing investment for any landlord to give an extension of time to that woman, and yet she was a thoroughly worthy person, as the sequel proved; her old misery and trouble were at an end. She found a good home and gave perfect satisfaction.

Many other experiences like this, and my constant association with the conditions of tenement-house life, have, of course, led me to certain conclusions as to the best remedies, which I shall reserve for specific mention in the latter part of this paper.

The population of the tenement-houses in lower New York is continually changing. There is a constant graduation of the better element. As soon as the circumstances of the people improve they want better homes. A foreigner who took up his abode in a tenement-house fifteen or twenty years ago may be perfectly contented with his surroundings, but when his children grow up and earn good wages they are not satisfied with a tenement-house, and give the old people no peace until a new home is found. Sometimes a man who has led a bad life reforms and immediately seeks a better home for his wife and children. I know several men who were at one time low and degraded drunkards, who would have been satisfied with a pig-sty, who had torn the clothes from their children's backs, the blankets from their beds, and taken them to the pawnshop to get money for drink; but through the good influences that were thrown around them, the wise counsel of friends, and the saving power of the gospel they became changed men. Their circumstances began to improve, the children were provided with clothes, one piece of furniture after another was brought into the empty rooms, until the place began to look like a home again. These men were charmed with the new life. Home became so dear a place that they are willing to travel an hour each morning and evening in order to make it still more attractive. They began to see the disadvantages of life in a tenement and found a new home on Long Island or in New Jersey.

This constant sifting of the best elements makes religious and philanthropic work in lower New York exceedingly difficult and apparently unfruitful, but none the less encouraging and necessary. The fact that the people leave the tenements in search of better homes is the best proof that a good work is being accomplished. A few months ago we celebrated the tenth anniversary of the dedication of one of our city mission churches. There were six hundred present, and out of this number there were only twenty-four who were at the dedication ten years before. While the better class is being constantly sifted out of the tenements, a steady stream of new-comers flows in to take their places.

Successive waves of population follow each other in rapid succession. It is often impossible to tell what the character of the population will be in the next ten years. In 1830 the agents of the New York City Mission visited 34,542 families. Among this number there were only 264 who desired foreign tracts, showing that the population was then almost exclusively American or English-speaking. * * *

In 1892 I made a careful canvass of a typical block and found 300 families composed of 1,424 individuals. The nationalities of the families were as follows: 244 German, 16 Irish, 11 American, 13 Hungarian, 6 Polish, 4 Russian, 2 Bohemian, 1 English, 1 Dutch, and 2 Chinese. Among the 244 German families there were 192 Jews, 38 Protestants, and 14 Roman Catholics. The German Jews are the most highly respected, and on this account many call themselves German who are in reality Russian or Polish Jews. These 300 heads of families are engaged in 72 different trades, occupations, and professions. There are 73 tailors, 17 cigarmakers, 17 storekeepers, 12 pedlars, 11 painters, 9 butchers, and 9 shoemakers in the block. The remaining 65 trades and professions are represented by 148 different persons. Thirty of the heads of families are Roman Catholics, 47 Protestants, and 221 Jews, and 2 have no religion. The Jews do not as a rule mingle to any great extent with the Christians. When they come in large numbers into a street, the Christians gradually withdraw, and the neighborhood finally becomes a Jewish quarter. There are streets in New York where it is a rare thing to find a Christian family.

During the transition period, when a locality is neither Christian nor Jewish, an interesting state of things prevails—a Jewish family, a Roman Catholic family, a pious Protestant family, and a heathen family, as far as religion is concerned, frequently live on the same floor. Suffering appeals to our common humanity. In trouble and sickness these neighbors render each other assistance and often become warm friends. I have seen a Jewish woman watching anxiously by the bedside of a dying Christian. A Roman Catholic or Jewish woman will often stand as godmother at the baptism of a Protestant child. A pretty, black-eyed Jewess occasionally captures the heart of a young Roman Catholic or Protestant, and they have come to me to perform the marriage service. Persons of various nations and religious beliefs are sometimes present at a tenement-house funeral. Bigotry and national prejudice are gradually broken down and the much-abused tenement becomes a means of promoting the brotherhood of man and the union of Christendom. You may hear daily from the lips of devout Roman Catholics and Jews such words as these: "We belong to a different religion, but we have the same God and hope to go to the same heaven." Such confessions are not often heard in small towns and country districts, but they are frequent in the tenement-houses.

The Jews, who in all ages have been noted for their exclusiveness, are affected by this contact with Christians in the tenement-house. In De Witt Memorial Church, with which I am connected, an audience of three or four hundred Jews assembles every week to hear Christian instruction. From the stand-point of social science such a gathering every week for two or three years past is significant. The Jew in every land has preserved his identity. Persecution has isolated him; when he has been most hated he has flourished, when he has been despised he has prospered. Like the symbolic burning bush, the fires of persecution have not destroyed him. It remains to be seen whether he will preserve his identity in this country, where, as a citizen, he enjoys equal rights, and where the doors of the public school and the Christian church stand open to Jew and Gentile alike.

Whatever may be the nationality of the parents the children are always thorough Americans. The blond-haired, blue-eyed German children; the black-haired, dark-eyed Italians; the little Jews, both dark and blonde, from many lands, are all equally proud of being Americans. A patriotic Irishman gave a beautiful edition of "Picturesque Ireland" to one of the boys in my Sunday-school. The lad looked disappointed. His father asked him why he was not pleased with the present. He answered: "I want a history of the United States." We have a circulating library, patronized almost exclusively by foreigners. The librarian informs me that four boys out of every five call for United States histories.

The most powerful influence at work among the tenement-house population is the public school. Every public school is a great moral lighthouse, and stands for obedience, cleanliness, morality, and patriotism, as well as mental training. When the little children begin to attend the schools their hands and faces are inspected, and if they are not up to the standard, they are sent home for a washing. A boy who is especially dirty is sometimes sent down-stairs with the cleanest boy in school, and told to wash himself until he looks as well as his companion. Such lessons are not soon forgotten, and the result is the public-school children in lower New York present a very respectable appearance. The fresh-air excursions, with many other benefits, promote cleanliness. The heads of the children must be examined before they can enjoy a trip into the country. There is no more beautiful and beneficent charity than this fresh-air work. In two or three weeks the pale-faced children return to the crowded city with renewed health and with larger and better views of life. I know boys who became so enraptured with green fields, running brooks, waving grain, and life on the farm that they have fully resolved to leave the city when they become men. One little fellow was so anxious to become a farmer that he ran away because his parents would not permit him to leave home.

The fresh-air work usually closes in October, but the young ladies connected with the "College Settlement" have added a new feature, which will commend itself to everyone who is acquainted with the condition of life around us. Every Saturday afternoon during the winter two of the ladies take a small party of children to their summer home. Saturday evening is spent in playing various games, or enjoying a candy-pull, and having a general good time. On Sunday the children attend the country church, and Sunday evening, seated before a blazing open fire, a good book is read, or the ladies in charge give some practical talk to the children. On Monday the little party returns to the city and the house is locked until the following Saturday. Such a visit to the country will be indelibly impressed upon these children. You cannot do people very much good at long range. Hand-picked fruit is the best.

In the summer of 1891 I took my first party of boys from my mission church to Northfield, Mass., and attended Mr. Moody's students' conference. We pitched our tents in the forest, cooked our own food, and sang college songs around our camp-fire at night. In ten days I became thoroughly acquainted with the boys, and was able to help them in many ways. I believe if every minister, priest, rabbi, and Sunday-school superintendent would select eight or ten young men and spend two weeks with them under canvas by the side of a mountain-lake or trout-stream, more good might be done in permanently influencing their lives than by many weeks of eloquent preaching.

To keep the boys off the streets, and to train them to habits of cleanliness, obedience, and manliness, military companies have been formed in several of our down-town Sunday-schools. It is astonishing how well a number of wild boys will go through military tactics after a few months' drilling. The hope of our great cities lies in the children of the poor. If we can influence them to become upright, honorable men and women, we shall not only save them, but produce the most powerful lever for lifting up those of the same class who are sinking. I know scores of children and young people who are far better than their parents. Some of the noblest young men I have ever known have worthless, drunken parents. Some of the most beautiful flowers grow in mud-ponds, and some of the truest and best young women in our city come from homes devoid of good influences; but in all such cases uplifting outside help has moulded their characters.

While the people in tenement-houses are compelled to sleep in rooms where the sunlight never enters, and suffer many discomforts from overcrowding, especially in summer, there are certain compensations which must not be overlooked. The poor in large cities who have steady work are, as a rule, better fed and clothed than the same class in rural districts. Fresh vegetables, raised in hot-houses, or sent from Southern markets, are sold throughout the winter at reasonable prices, and in the early spring strawberries and various other fruits are for sale on the streets in the tenement district long before they reach the country towns and villages. In the poorest quarter of the city you find the so-called "delicatessen" shops, where the choicest groceries, preserves, and canned meats are sold. The clothing, too, worn by the young people is stylish and sometimes expensive; anyone who walks through these districts will be astonished at the number of well-dressed young people. A young woman who earns from $6 to $8 a week will often be dressed in silk or satin, made according to the fashion. The teeth, fingernails, and shoes are often the only signs of her poverty. When visiting a stylish young woman's plain mother, I have sometimes seen all the finery in which the daughter appeared at church on Sunday hanging on the wall of a bare, comfortless bedroom not much larger than a good-sized closet.

The tenement-house people are not all thriftless, as the records of the down-town savings-banks clearly prove. Seven hundred out of every thousand depositors in one of the banks on the Bowery live in tenement-houses, and if it were not for tenement-house depositors several of our down-town savings-banks would be compelled to give up business. An abundance of cruel and bitter poverty, however, can always be found. The "submerged tenth" is ever present.

A widow, for instance, with three or four young children who is obliged to earn her bread by sewing, is in a most pitiable and terrible position. Hundreds of such weary mothers continue their work far into the night, with smarting eyes, aching backs, and breaking hearts. There is nothing which makes a man who has any feeling for the suffering of his fellows so dissatisfied with our present social system as the sight of such a poor woman sewing shirts and overalls for twenty-nine cents a dozen. There are good people in all our large cities who live just above the starving-point. The average earnings of the unskilled laborers with whom I am acquainted is not over $10 per week. When a man is obliged to spend one-fourth of this for rent, and feed and clothe his family on the remainder, it is impossible to lay by anything for a rainy day. When the father is out of work for a considerable time, or when sickness or death enter the home, distress, hunger, and an urgent landlord stare him in the face.

It is easy for those who have never felt it to overlook the constant strain of poverty and the irritation which it causes in families which in circumstances of ordinary comfort would be contented. In such cases particularly can great good be accomplished by a visit from some clear-sighted and sympathetic person.

Not very long ago I was invited to act as referee between a husband and wife. There were three little children and a grandmother in the family. The man worked in a cigar-box factory; business was slack and he was employed only half time. His average weekly earnings were $5. They had a debt of $11 at a grocery-store and another of $35 at an undertaker's shop. I knew the family; both husband and wife were honest, sober, and industrious people. The wife wanted to break up housekeeping; the husband was opposed to this plan, and they had agreed to abide by my decision. I examined each one separately. I began with the husband and said:

"When a physician prescribes a remedy he must first know the disease. I want you, therefore, to tell me plainly why your wife wants to break up the home. There may be good reasons why her plan should be adopted. If you two cannot possibly agree, and are fighting like cats and dogs, then I may be in favor of breaking up. Tell me just how the matter stands."

He informed me that he and his wife had always lived in perfect peace. They never had any trouble except poverty. The wife had become completely discouraged, and the only way she saw out of the difficulty was to put the children into an orphan asylum and go out as a house-servant until she could earn enough to clear off the debt, after which she hoped to get her home together again. The wife and grandmother gave me the same account. The perpetual strain of poverty was the only reason for breaking up the home. For the sake of the three little children I decided that the home must not be broken up and promised to see that the debt at the grocery-store was wiped out and the family clothing was taken out of the pawn-shop. The grandmother was so pleased with the decision that she determined to become a servant and begged me to find a place for her.

In our large cities there is too much isolation between the rich and the poor. The charitable societies are often the only link between them. If the mother of every well-to-do home in our large cities would regularly visit, once a month, a needy family, a vast amount of good would be accomplished among the worthy poor, and distress would be unknown. Human nature is too selfish for such a happy state of things ever to be realized, but it is possible to bring the givers and receivers of charity closer together than they are. If some of the wealthier ladies who now give a few dollars each year to the charitable societies would seek through these societies to come into direct personal contact with the recipients of their charity, they would experience a deeper happiness and fully realize the blessedness of giving. Business men are too much occupied to make a monthly visit to the tenement-houses, but if their wives and daughters would undertake this work a new day would dawn for many a poor, heartbroken mother who is now hopeless and longing for death to end her misery. We are frequently asked, "Is it safe for a lady to visit these great tenement-houses?" We answer unhesitatingly, perfectly safe. The young ladies connected with the City Mission go unmolested into the darkest portions of New York. The first visit to a tenement-house might be made in the company of a city missionary, after which the most timid could go alone.

Nothing is easier than to make paupers out of the poor. Great discretion must be exercised, but the Charity Organization Society, the Society for Improving the Condition of the Poor, the City Mission, the Children's Aid Society, and other equally worthy institutions are ever ready to give direction to individuals who desire to do personal work. A few persons have through the City Mission come into personal contact with the poor, and the results are most gratifying.

While in a small town the distress of the poor is easily made known through friends and neighbors or the clergyman, in our large cities the most deserving are often overlooked and suffer most intensely; and it is these cases which are reached by personal visitation. The worthy poor are generally the silent poor. Their sufferings must be extreme before they make their wants known. There are many poor, upright, God-fearing old people who struggle against fearful odds to keep body and soul together, and yet they drift daily toward the almshouse on Blackwell's Island, the last and most dreaded halting-place on the way to Potter's Field. I have nothing to say against the administration of the almshouse or the treatment of its inmates, but I do not wonder that old men and women who have led a good moral life would rather die than be stranded on the island and take up their abode among the broken wrecks of humanity which fill that institution.

It is very unwise to give aid without a thorough investigation. Some time since a Polish Jew asked me the way to a certain street. I directed him, and he said: "Dear sir, I am in great distress; my furniture is standing on the sidewalk in Essex Street, and my children are watching the stuff, while I am trying to collect a little money to get another place." He drew from his pocket a few coppers, and asked me to add my gift. I said: "I do not know you, and I am acquainted with a great many poor people whom I would like to help, but I have not the means; how, then, can you expect any help from me?" Two streams burst from his eyes. The big tears rained down his beard and coat. "It is hard," he said, and bowed his head, buried his face in a red handkerchief, wiped off the tears, and passed on. I crossed the street. The tears of that sad man touched me. I turned, ran after him, and said: "Where is the stuff?" "In Essex Street." "What have you?" "A table, bureau, bed, and looking-glass," he replied. "Have you nothing small that I can take with me and loan you money on?" He pointed to his well-worn greasy coat, and said: "I have this." "Show me the stuff," I said. We walked together, and I endeavored to carry on a conversation with the stranger in German, for he was ignorant of English, but suddenly he seemed to have lost all knowledge of the German tongue in which he had before addressed me, and was perfectly dumb. When we reached Ridge Street he finally spoke, and asked me to wait for him a moment while he went to see a friend. I said: "Look here, I want you to take me to the stuff immediately." He looked amazed and said: "What have I to do with you?" "A good deal," I replied; "you either take me to the stuff or I take you to the police station." "Do you think I am a liar?" I said: "You must take me to the stuff or you are a liar." "Come," he said, "I will take you to the stuff." It was wonderful to see how that old man, who had moved so slowly before, walked through the crowded streets. I had all I could do to keep up with him. We soon reached Essex Street. It was Friday afternoon and Essex Street was in all its glory—old clothes, decayed meat, pungent fish, and stale fruit abounded. The Ghetto in Rome and the Jewish quarters in London and Amsterdam are nothing compared with Essex Street. At one place it was almost impossible to get through the crowd, and I left the sidewalk and took the street. In a moment my new acquaintance disappeared, and I have not seen him since. I have no doubt this man and many others like him are making a good deal of money by playing on the sympathies of poor people.

I have made it a rule never to give a homeless man money, but when his breath does not smell of whiskey I give him my card containing the name and address of a lodging-house. The card must be used the same day it is given. As some of those who ask for a lodging never use the cards, my bill is always less than the number of cards given out. One night a man told me he was tired of his bad life and he wanted to become a better man. I spoke a few encouraging words to him and was about to dismiss him, when he told me he was sick and needed just five cents to get a dose of salts. I took him at his word and immediately sent for the drug and made him take it on the spot. It is needless to say that he never troubled me again.

There remain many cases where charity is of no avail. Where poverty is caused by crime, no relief can come except by breaking up the home. Not long since I was called to take charge of the funeral of a little child. I groped my way up the creaking, filthy stairs of a small, old-fashioned rear tenement. I knocked, but heard no response; I pushed the door open, but found no one in the room, yet this was the place—"Rear, top floor, left door." I made no mistake. I entered the room and found a dead baby wrapped in an old towel lying on a table. I learned from the neighbors that the father and mother had been out collecting money to bury the child and both had become beastly drunk. I returned to the dead child, read the burial service, and thanked God that the little one was out of its misery. A little later a man came and took the body to Potter's Field. The parents had buried (it would be more accurate to say starved to death) six children before they were two years old. Very little can be done for such people. Cumulative sentences ought to be imposed upon them each time they are arrested for drunkenness, so that prison-bars may prevent them from bringing the little sufferers into the world.

A great deal is done by the various charitable societies for the relief of distress, but as far as my observation goes the most effective charitable work is done by the poor themselves. Thousands of dollars are given away in the tenement districts every year by the inhabitants of the tenements, of which no charitable society makes a record. I have never related a peculiarly distressing case of poverty to a poor person but there was a ready response, and out of their own poverty the poor have ministered to those who were in need of relief. The children of our City Mission school, who come from the tenement-houses, contribute every Thanksgiving-Day from $80 to $100 for the poor in our immediate neighborhood. A club of fifty small boys and girls saved their pennies one year and bought thirty-five Thanksgiving dinners for the poor, consisting of chickens, potatoes, beans, turnips, and cabbages. The original plan was to have a head of cabbage go with each chicken, but the money gave out; this did not in any way disconcert the children, for they quickly solved the difficulty by cutting a cabbage into four parts, and putting a quarter into each bag. The children worked from 7.30 to 11 P.M. distributing the provisions. The members of this club visit the hospitals, sing to the patients, and furnish them with reading matter. In ten months they distributed as many as 27,901 booklets and illustrated papers. One summer the children noticed that the flies troubled the sick people and there were no fans in some of the hospitals. They saved their pennies, which in most cases would have gone to the candy-store, and bought a lot of palm-leaf fans at a wholesale house. They bound the fans with variously colored ribbons and decorated them with scripture texts appropriate to the sick, and on Sunday afternoon presented them to the delighted patients. The poor give that which costs them something, and their joy is correspondingly greater. That the most spontaneous and beautiful charity flourishes in the tenement-houses will undoubtedly be a surprise to many, but it is a fact well known to all who have any large acquaintance with the poor in our great cities.

It is equally true that there is more virtue in tenement localities than is commonly supposed. Darkness and sin have much in common. The dark halls and crowded homes are not favorable to virtue, but nevertheless virtue is the rule and vice the exception. The people who live in tenement-houses are not fastidious about rules of etiquette and propriety. Young women sometimes allow young men to address them and caress them in a manner which would offend well-bred people, and yet these girls would indignantly resent any liberties which they consider dishonoring. Young people occasionally desire to be married secretly, and timidly ask if it is not possible for me to date back the wedding certificate three or four months; such cases, however, are not common. There are many hasty marriages where the consent of the parents has not been obtained; these sometimes end in a speedy separation. Young girls occasionally come to me accompanied by young men half drunk and ask me to perform the marriage ceremony. There are self-styled clergymen who put up conspicuous signs advertising the fact that they make a business of uniting young people in marriage. These hungry sharks are ever ready to give their services for one or two dollars, thus plunging thoughtless young people into misery. I have succeeded in breaking up matches which I knew would have brought certain ruin to the parties concerned. I always refuse to marry a young couple when I am not permitted to consult the parents before performing the ceremony. If a law were passed making it obligatory on young people to get a license from the civil courts before a clergyman could perform the marriage, some unfortunate marriages would be prevented. A few hours of sober reflection would bring both parties to their senses.

The young people in our cities are extravagant. Very few of them save anything. Many of them put all they earn on their backs, and sometimes have not enough to pay the wedding fee, and all the furniture for the new home has been bought on the instalment plan. When the young husband is sober and industrious the married life generally moves on smoothly. It frequently happens, however, that from the day of her marriage a girl begins to fade like a flower. In three or four years a bright young girl will degenerate into a careworn, ill-tempered, slovenly middle-aged woman, surrounded by two or three pale, ragged, ungoverned children. She spent her girlhood in a store or shop, and was never initiated into the art of housekeeping. Her husband finds the saloon a far more comfortable place than his home. When industrial training shall have been introduced into every public school and the girls get a thorough training in housekeeping we may look for improvement in the home life of the poor in our cities. The cooking classes in connection with the girls' clubs, the Young Women's Christian Association, and those opened in some of the City Mission churches are doing excellent service in training young women to assume the responsibilities of home-makers.

The influence of the church on the tenement population is not as great as it probably will be in the near future. The strongest churches have followed their constituents and moved up-town; those which remained have languished, and in some cases have been compelled to close for want of active support. A new era has dawned. All religious denominations are interested in the churchless masses. New churches and chapels are being erected down-town, and there is a strong feeling in every quarter that the old stations must be maintained. The wisest men fully recognize the fact that if the churches among the tenement population are to do efficient work they must be well manned, richly endowed, and run at high pressure all through the year. Wherever church work has been pursued on these lines the results have been most gratifying. The workingmen, although not hostile, are generally extremely indifferent to religion. They are concerned about food, clothing, and a place of shelter for the present, and trouble themselves but little about the future. The fact that the church is beginning to take an active interest in the temporal welfare of the working people is already producing beneficial results.

The daily press exerts as great an influence over the parents as the public school does over the children. The workingmen in the tenement-houses constantly read the newspapers, and they read almost nothing else. What we need is not more learned lectureship foundations on the evidences of

Christianity, but endowments to secure a large number of short, concise, popular prize essays on moral and religious subjects, especially adapted in language and style to the working people. If these prize essays were published in the Sunday papers they would be read by tens of thousands of workingmen, and be a most powerful means of doing good.

There are a great many things which might be done to improve the conditions of the poor, but most of the schemes proposed are altogether impracticable. If we could make the poor sober and industrious, and the rich unselfish and generous, poverty would soon disappear; unfortunately we can do neither. We must take the world as we find it, and employ the best means to reach the desired end. I have seen a great deal of wretchedness and poverty in lower New York, and for some of these evils I can offer no remedy; but if the following suggestions could be carried out I believe something would be done toward improving "darkest New York:"

First.—There is nothing the inhabitants of the tenement-houses need so much as more room, sunshine, and fresh air. At present the sun never shines in the bedrooms of three-quarters of the people of New York City. In some parts of our city the population is nearly twice as dense as in the most crowded part of London. Nowhere on the wide earth are human beings so crowded as in the tenement districts. The suffering in July and August is often intense. The bedrooms become unbearable, and the roofs, fire-escapes, and empty wagons are used as sleeping-places. Thousands of little children do not see green grass during the entire summer; they are virtually prisoners in their own homes. The only true remedy can come in a complete system of cheap rapid transit. If the happy day ever comes when a poor man can be carried to the green fields of Long Island, New Jersey, or Westchester County for five cents, then a wonderful change will take place. It is commonly supposed that the poor enjoy herding together like dumb brutes on a cattle train, but nothing is further from the truth. The only reason why so many people put up with the numerous inconveniences of a tenement-house is simply that stern necessity compels them to live in this way. At the present time, with all the inconveniences of travel, many persons are leaving tenement-houses and seeking better homes in Brooklyn, Jersey City, and upper New York. If the North and East Rivers were spanned with railroad bridges, so that in twenty minutes a workingman might be ten miles distant from the factory or store, there would be a great exodus from the tenement-houses, and many places now used as homes would be turned into shops and warehouses.

Second.—A great blessing will be conferred on the crowded multitudes of the East Side when the long-promised and eagerly-desired small parks are opened. There are stone, coal, and lumber yards on the river-front on the East Side which would make attractive breathing spots for the children of the poor. If the Park Commissioners would bestir themselves, and with all possible haste provide the children of the poor with small parks and play-grounds they would confer an inestimable blessing upon the city.

Third.—Great improvements have been made in the construction and sanitary arrangements of tenement-houses, but still more must be done in the same direction. There are scores of horrible, pestilential rat-holes which are utterly unfit for human habitation. All such places ought to be condemned, and the Board of Health must be backed up by public sentiment in its endeavor to root out these plague-spots. Our city lots are not of the proper size to erect the large rectangular European tenements with a court in the centre, from which light and air can be conveyed into every room. A few such model tenements, however, have been built by associations of philanthropists and private individuals. More of these model tenements are needed. They will bring down the exorbitantly high rents which are now exacted from the poorest people. The model tenement will confer a great boon upon large families. It is often exceedingly difficult for a man who has seven or eight children to get rooms in the better class houses. The first question asked is, "How many children have you?" I know families who have been compelled to pay a high rent for poor accommodations on account of the large number of children. A poor woman searched all day for rooms; wherever she saw a place that suited her the old question, "How many children have you?" was asked, and she was obliged to look elsewhere. One morning she sent all her children to Greenwood Cemetery, put on a black dress, and began the search of rooms. When she had found a suitable place the landlord asked, "How many children have you?" "Six," answered the woman, sadly; "but they are all in Greenwood." The landlord was satisfied that the children would do his place no harm. The woman paid a month's rent and took possession. There was a scene at night, but during the month the woman proved to be such a good tenant that she was allowed to remain permanently.

Fourth.—The saloon is the poor man's club, and flourishes most vigorously in the poorest sections of the city. Instead of denouncing the saloon on account of the numerous evils it afflicts on the poor, something better must be supplied to take its place. "Home is the sacred refuge of our life," but notwithstanding all that poets have sung and moralists have spoken, many workingmen are perfectly convinced that two dark bedrooms and a kitchen is not an attractive place in which to spend a pleasant evening with a friend. The saloon is the only substitute. When Orpheus passed by the cave of the siren he took his lyre and made such wondrous melody that sailors, enraptured by the music, spurned the seductive strains that were wafted from the dangerous cave. The fable has its application—give the workingmen something they will like as well as the saloon and you will strike at the root of the evil. There are excellent places, like Cooper Union and the Young Men's Institute; but these institutions cannot expect to draw those who live one or two miles away in another part of the city. If the workingmen were fully alive to the advantages afforded them they would undoubtedly be willing to walk a long distance, but the majority of them have no ambition to improve themselves. They spend their evenings in the saloons because they are always within easy reach and form agreeable meeting-places. It is absurd to denounce the saloon in unqualified terms. The multitudes who patronize them are not all absolute fools. Many simply seek to satisfy the craving after fellowship which the Creator has implanted in their natures. The saloons are well-lighted, conveniently located social clubs, provided in some cases with a pleasant reading-room, and always with obliging proprietors. Wise men are beginning to see that a substitute must be supplied to take the place of the saloon which shall retain all its good features and simply discard its evil elements. The churches of various denominations are taking a deep interest in providing attractive, well-lighted reading and club-rooms for the workingmen in our large cities. A great and beneficent work might be done by the Board of Education if free reading rooms and libraries were opened in connection with every public school in the crowded portions of the city.

Fifth.—Good old John Wesley said, "Cleanliness is next to godliness;" but bathing in tenement-houses is exceedingly difficult and sometimes impossible. On pleasant days, when vast numbers of young men prefer the street-corner to the saloon, I have often stopped among a group of young fellows and said: "Boys, suppose a first-class swimming-bath were opened somewhere in this neighborhood, where you could for five or ten cents dive from a spring-board and plunge into a tank 50 feet wide and 100 feet long, full of warm, clean water, would you patronize such a place?" and the spontaneous and united answer always is: "You bet your life we would." I am fully convinced that if a first-class natatorium, with reading-rooms, library, and restaurant attached, was opened in some crowded district, the result would surpass all expectation. The baths have been remarkably successful in London. In one of these institutions over two hundred thousand baths were taken in a single year, and the receipts were more than $3,000 over the expenditures. Every humanitarian effort which is successful across the ocean does not succeed here, but from the sights which I witness every summer, when hundreds of young men plunge from the docks, lumber-yards, and shipping, at the risk of being arrested and having their clothes stolen, I am convinced that a swimming-bath would at once become immensely popular. The old Romans were wise in this respect. One of their great baths in our modern cities would be an effective means of aiding all forms of good work.

At the Christian conference held in Chickering Hall, in 1888, I endeavored to impress upon the audience the need of public baths. The good work begun at that time by the City Mission has been completed by the Society for Improving the Condition of the Poor. The first bath was opened in August, 1891, and the results are most satisfactory. Sixteen thousand baths were taken during the first one hundred and fifteen days. One day in the latter part of August, 1891, there were six hundred and sixty-nine bathers.[1]

Sixth.—There has been great need of a universal loan association. The poor, as well as the rich, are frequently compelled to borrow money. Unfortunately the poor, until lately, have not been able to get it at a reasonable interest. There is no bank in the city that will loan a poor man money and take his old clothes, his wife's wedding-ring, or some little household treasure as security. Yet the poor man is forced to borrow. He has been out of work a few weeks. The landlord will come to-morrow. The children are hungry and call loudly for bread. In the dark bedroom lies a child with a burning fever. A physician has been to see the child. He is a kind-hearted man, he knows the hardships of the poor and does not expect his fee to-day; but of course the father cannot be expected to pay for the prescription he has just written. How shall the man get bread for those hungry children and medicine for this one who is sick? They have one last resort left—the household idols must be sacrificed. All the valuables are brought together. These little rings and lockets, and the silver cup which a proud uncle presented to the first baby boy; the father's overcoat and Sunday suit, with the mother's best dress, are all needed to make up the $10 for the landlord, and

---

1. Nearly one hundred thousand baths are now taken every year.

to get food and medicine for the children. The pawnbroker is ready to devour everything which has any value. The pawn-tickets are carefully put away, and the parents confidently hope that they will soon be able to redeem the things they have "put away." They redeem them at three per cent. a month, or else they finally lose them, not having received more than one-fifth of the actual value of the articles. I sent a boy to an East Side pawn-shop with a gold watch, the original cost of which was $150; its actual present value was certainly not less than $40. The boy received $5, and this was as much as he could get. I redeemed the watch the next day, much to the disgust of the pawnbroker. What has proved a great blessing to many people in distress, was the opening of the offices of the Provident Loan Society, in the United Charities Building on Fourth Avenue and Twenty-second Street.[2] I fear that heretofore, no charitable society has undertaken this work, from the mistaken idea many people have that such an institution would foster thriftless habits among the poor. Such persons forget that it is not a question of pawn-shops or no pawn-shops, but whether we shall have one large, reputable loan association, where the poor man's clothing and jewelry shall be as good as the rich man's real estate at a banking-house, or a vast number of little pawn-shops—those whirlpools in which the valuables of many poor families are swallowed. Thieves who want to get rid of stolen property, and thriftless drunkards who go to the pawnbroker to dispose permanently of their property at the highest prices, will continue to visit the pawn-shop; but persons who need a temporary loan to help them through a period of enforced idleness or sickness will be greatly benefited by a wisely managed loan association.

Seventh.—There is great need of trained nurses for the sick. Hundreds of mothers who are obliged to care for their homes during the day, are sitting at night by the bedside of sick children. If the sickness is of a temporary nature these periods of broken rest and double duty are passed without disaster. It frequently happens, however, that two or three children are sick at the same time. The mother is compelled to work night and day until nature gives way and she breaks down under the strain. Sickness brings increased expenses, therefore it is impossible for the husband to stay at home to take care of his family. If he does not work there will be no money next week for food, rent, and medicine. When the physician tells him that the end is near for wife or child, then he gives up his work. I have visited homes where I found the mother and all the children sick, and if it had not been for the occasional visit of a neighbor there would have been no one to give a cup of water to the sick or dying. Into such homes the trained nurse comes like a ministering angel. She lights a fire in the cold stove, bathes the sick, provides clean bedding, dresses the little children, puts in order the rooms, and when the place looks like home again, she takes from her basket some beef-tea, a little jelly, or some other tempting morsel for the sick. The mother, who has been lying hopeless in the dark bedroom, begins to revive, and watches with deep interest the ministering stranger, and with wet eyes says: "God bless you and reward you for what you have done this day." The nurse not only aids the sick, but is able by her counsel to help the mother when she has recovered. The friendly talks on housekeeping and the

2. Other loan associations have been opened since this paper was written.

care of the children are often of the greatest value. The nurse also forms the connecting link between the hospitals and the invalids hidden away in the tenement-houses, many of whom would have been left to rot and finally to die on their filthy beds if the nurses had not found them and sent them to the hospital. The nurse does not stop to ask what the nationality or creed of the sufferers is. The only recommendation required to receive her services is sickness and distress. The nurses of the City Mission are doing a noble work, but their number is too small and they must be constantly restrained lest they break down from overwork. Here is a work which can be done at once. Anyone who desires to relieve the suffering poor in the most direct and effective way can do it through a trained nurse. It would be a source of the purest happiness to many a man and woman, when they go to rest in their beautiful and luxurious homes, to know that $600, the saving, perhaps, of some needless luxury, is keeping a faithful nurse at work the entire year, moistening the fevered lips of the sick, or soothing the last hours of the dying. The Great Teacher of men consigned Dives to hell, not because of erroneous theological opinions, but because he neglected the beggar, who lay at his gate full of sores. Dives is among us to-day. He is clothed in the finest robes and fares sumptuously every day. Lazarus is also here. He lies in the cheerless bedroom of a tenement-house, hungry, sick, and full of sores. The two have been brought together for a purpose. The only salvation for our modern Dives lies in Lazarus.

Eighth.—There is need of greater co-operation among all good men. When we see anyone endeavoring to cast out social demons among us, let us not forbid him because he does not accept our creed or follow our party. Prejudice, narrow-mindedness, and bigotry have too long stood in the way of social reform. Wise men must recognize that whatever is good is of God. It makes no difference from what source it comes. When all good men shall work together on the broadest lines of social reform, great and beneficent changes will be brought about, and New York will continue to be a great, happy, and prosperous city.

THOMAS BYRNES

Nurseries of Crime[†]

The lodging-houses of New York constitute an evil of large and growing proportions. This fact is palpable to any one who has to deal with the criminal classes here, or who is familiar with the methods of life in the least respectable parts of the city through missionary work or in any other way. Of lodging-houses in other cities I have no personal knowledge; but it is fair to presume that the same evil exists in all large cities to a greater or less extent. In the following pages I speak only of New York, and the facts mentioned have all come within the range of my personal experience.

---

† From *The North American Review* 149. 394 (1889).

It is undeniable that the lodging-houses of the city have a powerful tendency to produce, foster, and increase crime. Instead of being places where respectable people reduced in circumstances or temporarily short of money can secure a clean bed for a small amount of money, they have come to be very largely frequented by thieves and other criminals of the lowest class, who lodge in these resorts regularly and here consort together and lay their plans for crimes of one sort or another. But this is not the worst feature of the matter. Take the case of a young man who runs away from his home in the country, or for any reason finds himself stranded in the great city. In searching for a cheap place to lodge in, he naturally drifts into one of these lodging-houses, and it is almost inevitable that association with the people who make these places their headquarters will corrupt him. In nine cases out of ten—I am quite confident that this proportion is not too large—he turns out a thief or a burglar, if, indeed, he does not sooner or later become a murderer. Hundreds of instances of this kind occur every year.

The lodging-house in New York is a modern institution. It was started by a man named Howe, who came here from Boston, about twelve years ago. He opened his first lodging-house in Chatham Street (now Park Row), near Tryon Row. It was a success, and he soon extended the business. When he died, seven years ago, he left a large fortune as the result of his shrewd management of this new enterprise. The number of lodging-houses has increased rapidly since Howe made his first venture, and there are now three hundred and forty-five such places in the city. There is one class in which fifteen, twenty, or twenty-five cents are charged for a night's lodging, while in another and lower class the prices are only five and ten cents. According to the "Report of the Police Department of the City of New York for the Year Ending December 31, 1888," the "enormous number of 4,649,660 cheap lodgings were furnished during the year" in these resorts. The following table, taken from the report, shows the distribution of lodging-houses among the various precincts:

	Lodging-houses and dormitories.				Lodging-houses and dormitories.		
PRECINCTS.	NUMBER.	NUMBER OF ROOMS.	LODGERS, 1888.	PRECINCTS.	NUMBER.	NUMBER OF ROOMS.	LODGERS, 1888.
First	9	325	77,925	Thirteenth	6	22	66,560
Second	21	346	73,045	Fourteenth	5	138	142,350
Fourth	39	2,307	597,870	Fifteenth	14	636	256,585
Fifth	3	24	45,150	Eighteenth	3	43	173,375
Sixth	44	2,086	913,050	Twentieth	1	90	. . . .
Seventh	13	294	127,155	Twenty-first . . .	9	159	63,837
Eighth	11	112	182,500	Twenty-fifth . . .	1	241	36,794
Ninth	3	279	77,600	Twenty-ninth. . .	13	549	104,287
Tenth	12	1,374	438,365				
Eleventh	58	1,293	1,243,200	Total	267	10,439	4,649,660
Twelfth	2	121	30,012				

These figures are obtained by inquiry among the keepers of the known lodging-houses, and, while they do not wholly agree with what I learn from other sources, they are, no doubt, fairly accurate.

There is no law that governs or applies to these places of which I am speaking, except certain sections of the Sanitary Code of the Board of Health, which give the Health Department the right to exercise supervision over them in the matter of cleanliness. In connection with this phase of the subject it will be of interest to quote further from the report of the Police Department for last year.

"Attention has repeatedly been called to that portion of the city covered by the Fourth, Sixth, Tenth and Eleventh Precincts. From the table of arrests it will be seen that in 1888 there were 23,146 persons arrested in this comparatively small district, or 27.24 per cent. of the entire number of arrests—an increase over the year 1887. Eighteen per cent. of the pawn-shops are located there; more than 16 per cent. of the liquor and beer saloons of the city are flourishing there; more than 57 per cent. of the cheap lodging-houses ply a busy trade, and they furnish nearly 70 per cent. of the lodgings indicated above.

"Again it is urged that there should be some legal regulation by which the cheap lodging-houses could be placed under police supervision. Though it is admitted that many of the patrons of these places are persons in distressed circumstances, yet, where so many are herded together daily and nightly, it is reasonable to suppose there are many disposed to crime. If tenement life tends to immorality and vice certainly the fifty-eight lodging-houses in the Eleventh Precinct, furnishing 1,213,200 lodgings in one year, must have the same or a worse tendency. Reflection upon the figures contained in the above table will lead to the conclusion that we have a large population of impecunious people (all males) which ought to be regarded with some concern.

"It is shown above that an average of 13,152 persons without homes and the influence of family lodged nightly in the station-houses[1] and in these poorly-provided dormitories—an army of idlers, willing or forced. It is respectfully submitted that social reformers would here find a field for speculation, it not for considerable activity."

The cheapest class of lodging-houses are generally the resort of drunkards and people of the lowest type, though all of them are infested with thieves, idlers, and loafers of every description. Hence it is no exaggeration to assert that they are very hot-beds of crime. More than one murder has been committed in these houses. One well-remembered crime of this sort was that of Quimbo Appo, who stabbed and killed a young man named John Kelly in a lodging-house in Chatham Street. Kelly was the son of respectable parents, but had fallen into dissolute habits, and was accustomed to spend his nights in these resorts. One night Quimbo got into an altercation with him; blows followed, and the result was that Kelly received fatal wounds. Another man was killed in the Phœnix lodging-house in the Bowery. He applied for a lodging, which for some reason was refused; he quarrelled with the clerk, and the clerk killed him, being subsequently acquitted

---

1. During 1888 there were 150,812 lodgings furnished at the station-houses of the city, making the total number of lodgings 4,800,472.

on the ground of justifiable homicide. It was at this same Phœnix house that I and my men not long ago arrested the notorious Greenwall and Miller on the charge of murdering Mr. Lyman S. Weeks in Brooklyn. There is little doubt in my mind that this murder, a most dastardly crime (Mr. Weeks being shot down in his own house by a burglar who had invaded it), was hatched in this or some other house of like character. In the very same place three men were arrested recently for a burglary committed in a residence in Mount Vernon. At the lodging-house No. 262 Bowery we secured a gang of thieves who had been engaged in a series of robberies at Kingston, N. Y., and they were sent up there for punishment. Among other cases of criminals who made their abode in houses of this sort may be mentioned the following, all the acts being of recent occurrence: Charles Hoffman, convicted of highway robbery and sent to the State-prison; James McGann, burglary, sent to the State-prison; Hugh O'Neill, burglary, sent to the State-prison; Jacob Meyer, burglary, sent to the State-prison. There are hundreds of other instances of the same kind.

A case somewhat out of the ordinary run was that of Henry Bishoff, who was convicted of forgery on the complaint of a well-known business man. Bishoff had only been in this country for a year, and for some months he had been out of employment. During this time he lived at the Victoria Hotel lodging-house, at No. 9 Bowery. There he was inoculated with criminal ideas, and he made it a practice to follow letter-carriers while making deliveries. When letters were deposited in small boxes in front of stores and lofts, and a good opportunity presented itself, Bishoff would abstract them by means of long keys and a piece of steel wire. In this way he got a letter out of the box of a leading clothing firm. It was from a Philadelphia house, and contained a check or draft for a large sum. He forged the indorsement of the New York firm, and obtained the money. Subsequently he was arrested by this bureau,[2] and sentenced to a long term in prison.

Within the last three years crime has increased very rapidly, so far as the lodging-houses of the city are concerned. A large number of young fellows hailing from these places have been arrested for stealing blankets from horses whose drivers have been compelled to leave them for a minute or two, or for picking up anything else of trifling value that they could lay hands on. These are beginners in crime, as a rule, and they undoubtedly associate with older and more experienced men, who tell them how and where to dispose of their booty for a small sum of money. It is in this way that young men get their initiation in crime. I personally have arrested a considerable number of men in lodging-houses for carrying burglars' tools. Hundreds of criminals must be made every year through the associations they form in these breeding-places of lawlessness.

Lying on my desk as I write are two tin-types of the cheapest sort, evidently taken in the Bowery. They represent two young "toughs," each holding a pistol at the head of the other. They were taken from the pockets of the young fellows, who were brought into my office the other day on charges of robbery. These photographs interested me, and I asked the boys how they came to be taken in that style. "Oh," they answered, "we held a pistol up to the head of a man one night and got his money, and we just

2. The Detective Bureau of the New York Police Department.

thought we would like to see how we looked." They seemed rather proud of their achievement. I mention this as an illustration of the sort of young criminals the lodging-houses of New York turn out.

During the last two or three years at least four hundred young men have been arrested for petty crimes that originated here. In many of these cases it was the first stop in crime that was being taken. Observation in the courts convinces me that three-fourths of the young men called on to plead to various offences are under twenty years of age; they are poorly clad and without means. Their crimes are petty ones as a rule, and they seem to have no realizing sense of the enormity of their deeds. It is the customary thing, when such people are arraigned in the Court of General Sessions, for the judges to assign counsel to defend them, since these criminals have no money to hire professional advice.

Some twelve or thirteen thousand persons sleep almost nightly in the lodging-houses of the city, some of which have as many as three hundred beds. Among the houses of the lowest order are the Kingston in East Broadway, some of those already mentioned, and those at the following numbers: 15, 23, 34, and 68 Bowery, 18 Pell Street, 9 Doyers Street, 197 Worth Street, 33, 35, and 62 Mulberry Street, 44 East Houston Street, 176, 184, and 194 Park Row, and 9 Mulberry Street. One of the very lowest of all is that at No. 18 Pell Street. The charge there is five cents a night, and the lodgers sleep on strips of canvas suspended by ropes, something after the fashion of hammocks. Suppose that a young man, who finds himself in the city without a home or friends or money, gets into a place of this kind; it will take not more than ten days at the furthest to familiarize him with crime and criminals, and the chances of his leading an honest life afterwards are not one in a hundred—hardly one in a thousand. There are a few Italian lodging-houses in the city; they are very low and dirty, and give the police the greatest trouble of all.

It has frequently been stated to me by thieves that large numbers of foreigners who are criminals have their passage paid to this country by the authorities or by somebody else. When they land here they have no money, or very little, and they immediately flock to the lodging-houses, where they can live for almost nothing, where they meet people congenial to them, and are soon put in the way of engaging again in their criminal pursuits. I remember the case of a boy named Fritz who came here from Antwerp not long ago, and secured employment with one Jacob Thoman. Thoman noticed that the boy acted in a queer, nervous way, and questioned him, whereupon the boy confessed that in Prussia, his native country, he had had a quarrel with another boy, and in a moment of passion had dashed his brains out. The boy was arrested by detectives from this office, and the matter was brought to the attention of the German consul. But the consul had no official advices regarding the matter, no charge was pressed against the boy, and he was discharged. He then went to live in one of the low lodging-houses, where, I suppose, he was instructed in crime. At all events, in a short time he was detected in the act of committing a burglary in the place of business of his former employer. Only recently I arrested a man who was engaged in robbing private houses in the upper part of the city. He told me that he had been sent here on account of being caught in thieving operations "on the other side." He had no money when he arrived except a few shillings, and almost the first place he got into was one of the cheap lodging-houses. He soon became acquainted with the inmates, who were mostly thieves, and in a little while they took him out over the city and set him to stealing. I have not the least doubt that there are numerous cases like this.

But the evils that have been already mentioned are not the only ones that are produced by the lodging-house system. It is notorious that these houses are used every year for the "colonization" of voters. A large number of men register regularly from these places, and they have not the slightest hesitation about swearing in their votes in case they are challenged. Now and then somebody comes to grief through this practice, but it still flourishes. Not long ago the proprietor of the Windsor, at No. 41 Bowery, was sent to prison for "colonizing" voters. But usually this work is done in the interest of some local political "boss," who stands by the owner of the house in case the latter gets into trouble. This alone is certainly an evil of large dimensions.

I might cite many other cases that have come under my personal observation, where crimes have been the direct offspring of life in lodging-houses. Take the case of "Mike" Drohan, a notorious thief, who lived at the Windsor, to which reference has just been made. Drohan went to Johnstown after the recent horrible disaster, and was shot and killed while engaged in the fiendish work of robbing the dead bodies of victims of the flood. Assuredly there was a case where a criminal got something like his just deserts. Again, these lodging-houses become the dwelling-places of many of the convicts who are released from prison. These men have little money, and very naturally they gravitate to these places, where they are likely to find people they know. These houses they use as their rendezvous, and there they soon arrange to meet their companions and to plot various crimes. Lodging-houses thus play an important part in causing ex-convicts to resume their former vocation.

It may be asked whether these resorts do not serve any useful purpose. Undoubtedly there are frequently worthy people who are glad of an opportunity to get a night's lodging for a trifle; but these are a small minority of the *habitués* of such houses. In the course of my professional duty here I have found among the patrons of these places a sprinkling of professional men who have held good positions in society—lawyers, doctors, civil-engineers, and even authors. In the usual course they have become drunkards, and have gone down the ladder step by step until they have been abandoned by their friends, and have become drunken sots in the lowest lodging-houses, presenting no difference in their personal appearance from the commonest patrons of such places. It would require a conversation with these people to show that they were educated, and had sunk from a lofty position through a lack of will-power. I remember one who was brought here on suspicion, who belonged to a family that had held an exalted position in society. He was the black sheep of the family, and had at length got so low as to consort with the class of people that are to be found in the cheapest lodging-houses. There seemed to be no possibility of reclaiming him, and I suppose he will spend his days there.

Such is the evil—a menace to good order and the well-being of society of rapidly enlarging proportions. And the remedy? That I conceive to lie outside of my province as a police official. But I am convinced that a remedy ought to be applied—a drastic, searching remedy—and applied without delay. This is not a case for a palliative; as Emerson would say, it is a "case for a gun"—for the knife, the blister, the amputating instruments. I will venture to offer one or two suggestions only, which philanthropists who endeavor to solve the problem may care to take into account. There should be stringent laws enacted by the Legislature for the regulation of lodging-houses in this city. The records and books of these houses should be open at all times to the inspection of the proper authorities. It should be made a misdemeanor for the proprietor of such a house to mutilate or destroy his books, and he should be compelled to keep an accurate record of all his lodgers. This would be important in the matter of preventing fraudulent registration, etc. No person who is not of good character should be permitted to own or maintain a lodging-house, and bonds should be required of and licenses issued to those who desire to carry on this business. In my judgment, based on many years' experience, the lodging-house business should be under the immediate supervision of the police, since they are the officials who practically enforce the laws, and because they have better opportunities than any others for ascertaining the character of persons and places.

MARCUS T. REYNOLDS

From The Housing of the Poor†

I. The Unsanitary Tenement—Origin, Growth and Present Condition of the Tenement-House System.

New York city offers the best example for the study of the origin, growth and evil effects of the tenement-house system in the New World. Not only was it here that overcrowding first made itself apparent, but the evil has grown here more rapidly than elsewhere. Constantly receiving additions from foreign ports, and recruiting its numbers from the country, it is to-day the most densely settled city of the world, while it is not rash to predict that long before another century its population will surpass that of London. The restricted limits of the city will cause it to be always the most crowded town of the continent, and therefore a more careful study of this problem will be required here than in other cities, more favorably situated. If the evils of the tenement are more striking in New York than elsewhere, it has the honor of being far in advance of any other city in respect of sanitary regulations, and has, indeed, become a standard for other cities throughout the country and in many of the European capitals.

The first effort to reform the tenement-house system in New York city was made in the winter of 1856–7, when a special committee was appointed by the legislature to examine and report upon the tenant-houses of the city. In its report this committee stated that, in its opinion, the causes of the tenant-house evil were over-population and destitution. Increasing traffic and manufacture had driven to the less thickly settled quarters of the city

† Publications of the American Economic Association 8.2/3 (1893).

the wealthier citizens, whose spacious dwellings were then used as boarding-houses, or let in suites of apartments to the industrious poor who were employed in workshops, stores and warehouses in the vicinity. Rents were, at first, moderate, and the accommodations offered were suitable to the needs of their occupants; but a further pressure of population caused an increase of rent, and, at the same time, a decrease in the value obtained by it, as large suites of apartments were subdivided into small ones, large and light rooms partitioned into small and dark ones. The greater percentage of profit to be realized on such houses after their conversion into barracks, led to large purchases of property to be employed in the construction of others.

For more than five years no radical improvement was made in the tenant-houses, and meanwhile their evils continued to increase, until the public became thoroughly aroused as the system extended from ward to ward, the density of population increased, and it became evident that crime, debauchery and disease were becoming the habits of a large part of the population.

*   *   *

III. Importance of Reform—Causes of Over-crowding—
Evils of Over-crowded Tenements.

Too much attention has been paid to the personal and merely bodily discomforts of the occupants of our unsanitary tenements, while the far-reaching and more deadly evils, which have their origin here, are lost sight of in the lengthy descriptions of the want and suffering of the unfortunate poor.

Descriptions of specific cases have, therefore, been omitted here purposely, as they have been fully dwelt on by those who have made it their life work to labor among the poor, and who have sketched the horrors of tenement life in the strongest and darkest colors. A score of such books and reports of various charitable organizations are given in the bibliography. It would seem to be more profitable, therefore, to examine into the evils which are inseparably connected with the tenement-house system, which affect the wealth, morality and the very being of the nation—evils from whose pernicious influence no one, no matter what his position, is entirely safe, and which it is the interest of all to lessen in every way possible.

The overcrowding which is at the root of all these evils is due to many causes. Prominent among them are the fascination which a large town exercises over the dwellers in the country; the opportunities offered the poor and lazy to dwell at the expense of the rich, and the greater demand for labor. Indeed, as Lord Salisbury says, "the evil is directly caused by prosperity; as competition for work becomes closer the suffering of the poor from bad housing becomes more severe." But whatever the causes of the overcrowded tenement may be, the evils which accompany it are many and terrible. I have made an attempt to tabulate them, but the task is a most difficult one, so inseparably connnected in cause and effect are many of them. The more important of the resulting evils will now be briefly considered.

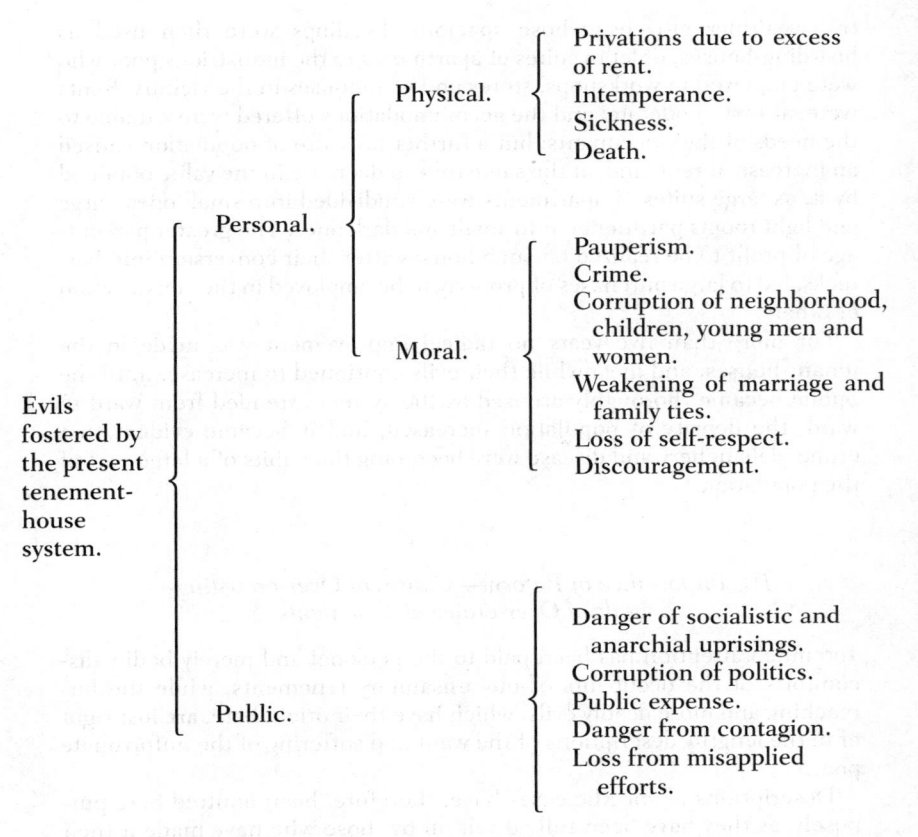

Evils fostered by the present tenement-house system.

Personal.

Physical.
- Privations due to excess of rent.
- Intemperance.
- Sickness.
- Death.

Moral.
- Pauperism.
- Crime.
- Corruption of neighborhood, children, young men and women.
- Weakening of marriage and family ties.
- Loss of self-respect.
- Discouragement.

Public.
- Danger of socialistic and anarchial uprisings.
- Corruption of politics.
- Public expense.
- Danger from contagion.
- Loss from misapplied efforts.

Privations Due to the Excess of Rent.—The exorbitant rent charged the very poor is the immediate source of much suffering, and too often of crime.

Over-crowding is made possible by the fact that the demand far exceeds the supply. A workman can live outside the city, but he is seldom willing to prolong the labor of the day by the hour or more which must be spent in reaching his place of employment in the morning and in returning to his home at night.

Many persons, who have been tenement lodgers, but who have in some way acquired a little capital, know how profitable this investment is and build tenements themselves. Their capital is small and the buildings are erected at the smallest expense. They know, also, that every room which is situated near the centres of employment is eagerly competed for, and that they are sure of tenants, no matter how wretched the rooms may be. Repairs and improvements are, therefore, seldom if ever made.

A few examples will show how excessive the rent is in many instances. In Bedford street, Philadelphia, a rookery worth $500 brought $80 a month. In New York the owner of a building destroyed by fire stated himself that it was fully insured for $800, though it brought him in $600 a year rent. Forty per cent. was declared by witnesses before a senate committee to be a fair average interest on tenement property. Instances were given of rates of interest being one hundred per cent. and over. The following are a few typical examples of the rents of tenements in New York: One room and dark alcove,

$10 per month; one room and dark alcove (a little larger), $12.25; one room and two dark alcoves, $12.50; one parlor, two bed-rooms and kitchen, $22.

Rents will continue to be excessive until there are offered the working classes enough cheap and healthy homes to supply the demand. Then no longer will they be forced to content themselves with whatever wretched places are offered, and to pay exorbitant prices.

Admitting that the rents charged are excessive, let us see what evils result therefrom. To do this it is necessary only to examine the ways in which the rent is met. The usual means is by taking boarders or lodgers; for these no larger accommodations are taken, and the new-comers share the room or rooms, none too large for the original family.

Many instances have been discovered where a family occupying a single room has taken, as boarders, not one other family but several. The debasing effect upon any family life which might otherwise exist is too obvious to need discussion.

It is a frequent practice to let the rooms by day to the men and women who busy themselves with making "tenement-made" clothing. The only limit to the number of persons thus accommodated is the seating capacity of the room. The demands of ventilation are disregarded, and the air, which was fetid in the morning from the nightly exhalations of its occupants, becomes saturated with germs from the unclean and often diseased bodies of the "sweaters" who breathe it again and again. This is continued day after day, until the room and all its contents reek with the accretions of filth accumulated during an indefinite period. The clothing made in these places is afterward exposed for sale in all parts of the city, and, when worn, meets us at every corner. In an atmosphere such as this, family ties and human life cannot exist. Still another way of making others pay the rent is the letting of the room by night for immoral purposes.

The excess of rent is also met by a proportional decrease in the purchase of fuel, food, clothing and other necessaries, and even then the family can often afford but a single room, whose evil influences are studied in a later portion of this article.

Intemperance.—It is a self-evident fact that unpleasant surroundings and intemperance are as closely allied as the sequence of cause and effect can bind them. A silent acknowledgment is the comfort with which a saloon in the slums is fitted up, the proprietor knowing well what bait will prove most attractive to his customers.

It is quite true that in many a tenement block the saloon is the one bright, cheerful place to be found, and it would be strange if the workman, returning tired from his day's labor, did not prefer the warm and comfortable saloon to the cold and cheerless place, which he calls his home. Writers on temperance, in both Europe and America, have reached the conclusion that the re-housing of the poor would be a substantial aid to their cause.

A legislative committee in New York, appointed to investigate the question, recommended "the prevention of drunkenness by providing every man a clean and comfortable home." The futility of all attempts to benefit labor before this remedy has been applied is affirmed by a writer in the *Fortnightly Review,* who thus disposes of the question: "It is useless to increase wages and to lessen the hours of labor, so long as the workman is compelled to live in the pesthouses we have described; nay, it is worse than useless, as extra wages and leisure operate as incentives to drunkenness."

Too great emphasis cannot be given to the fact that the saloon is merely the expression of the unconscious desire, prevalent in most men, for the comfort to body and mind offered by a warm, comfortably furnished and well lighted room. It is not the liquor which gives the saloon its chief attraction, but the companionship found there. As long as this is only offered in drinking places, just so long will the saloons be well patronized. As soon as the home means something more to the working man than a place in which he eats and sleeps, just so soon will the saloon lose its chief attraction for him.

Sickness and Mortality.—Of all the evils which are due to the tenement-house system, the one that concerns the public most directly is the danger, which at all times threatens the community, from the presence in the tenement district of contagious and infectious diseases.

That thousands of dwellings in all of our cities are in a more or less unsanitary condition, while their occupants lead lives conducive to the birth of disease, is too well known to need more than the mention.

The working people, who spend the night in such dirty and disease-breeding places, disperse in the morning, and by the nature of their occupations, find their way to all portions of the city, and are thrown in contact with all classes of society. It is not too much to say that there is not a home which is not entered daily by at least one person, who has his home in a dwelling occupied exclusively by the working classes.

Much of the clothing offered for sale by the best dry-good stores and tailors has passed through the hands of like persons, while no small portion has been made in their dwellings. Clothes sent out to be washed are usually carried to the homes of the working people.

Though we might prevent the actual entrance into our homes of persons carrying about with them the germs of disease, it is quite impossible to prevent contact in the street, or elsewhere, with such persons.

I do not wish to be understood as stating that all dwellings of the working classes are in a more or less unsanitary condition, or that all dirty and unhealthy dwellings are of necessity dangerous to the health of the community. The number of dwellings in an unsanitary condition is, however, very large, as the reports of various boards of health will testify, and even in buildings which are for the most part clean and in good condition, there usually exist one or more rooms, the tenants of which persist in keeping them in a filthy condition. While these places may not all produce contagious or infectious germs, there is a great probability that many of them do, while all are well fitted to harbor any disease which may present itself. In times of epidemics, if the disease obtains a foot-hold in the tenement-house district, it is almost impossible to overpower it, until it has burnt itself out. In Gotham Court, New York city, the mortality in the last great cholera epidemic reached the height of 195 in 1,000 inhabitants. Here it was that a sanitary inspector counted 146 cases of sickness, including all kinds of infectious diseases, from small-pox down. Of 138 children born in three years only 61 lived. In the old Baptist church not far away, the rear half of which had been divided into tenements, the annual death rate was 75 in 1,000. In the Bend the mortality in 1882 was 68.28; that of Mulberry street, in 1888 was 38.05.

The hand of disease and death falls most heavily on the children. The death rate for them reached in Baxter street 146.02; in Mulberry street 136.70.

Possibly the full importance of these figures can be appreciated only by comparing them with the mortality of various cities at nearly the same time:

Death rate in New York,   1889 . . . . 25.19
"   "   Boston,   " 24.42
"   "   Brooklyn,   " 22.5
"   "   Philadelphia, " 19.7
"   "   London,   " 17.4

The sanitary police of New York city took, in 1888, a census of the tenement-house population, to which the registrar of vital statistics draws attention in a preliminary report on the death rates of the city. Some unexpected conclusions are reached. With a total tenement-house population of 1,117,257 and 29,172 deaths, we have a death rate for the year of 26.11 per 1,000 living, as against a general death rate for the city of 26.33. The death rate of the tenement-house population is thus seen to be lower than that of the remaining population of the city.

The death rate of persons five years of age and over decreases with increase in number of tenants, while the death rate of children under five years increases, until there are more than eighty tenants to a house after which it decreases. The probable reason for the progressive decrease of death rate is that the tenants of the larger houses live under better sanitary conditions than those of the smaller, with the exception of density of population. These better sanitary conditions are largely owing to the greater facility of inspection and superintendence in the larger houses. As regards special diseases, it was found that while diarrhœal diseases and diphtheria show a greater death rate in the larger houses, phthisis and pneumonia show comparatively little difference, that little being in favor of the larger houses. It may be noted, as a possible partial explanation of the lesser death rate of the poorer classes, that they pass much of their lives out of doors, and when in-doors live in rooms without carpets or papered walls to catch and propagate micro-organisms, with bare floors that are washed frequently.

A comparison of the vital statistics of 1888 with those of 1869 shows that this disproportion has not always existed:

YEAR.	GENERAL DEATH-RATE.	TENEMENT DEATH-RATE.
1869.	28.13	28.35
1888.	26.33	22.71

The report of the board of health for 1891 shows the same remarkable fact presented in 1888, that the death rate is the highest in the houses which contain the fewest occupants. This report finds that the highest death rates for the thickly populated districts are in districts largely inhabited by Italians, and the lowest in the poor Jewish district. As regards particular diseases, the death rates from bronchitis, diarrhœal diseases, diphtheria and croup, measles, pneumonia and scarlet fever increase, while Brights' disease, heart diseases, influenza, malarial fevers, phthisis and typhoid fever decrease as the number of tenants increases. The report gives as a probable reason for the progressively decreasing death rate, more frequent removal to hospitals from the larger houses, adducing the above figures of special diseases to show decreasing death rate in such diseases as would be more likely to be removed to the hospitals.

The public dispensaries of New York alone annually provide medical aid for 1,500,000 persons, nearly all of whom are inhabitants of tenement districts. Healthy homes save twenty days of idleness yearly through sickness for every inhabitant, according to the estimate of an officer of the London board of health.

The public loss in money is enormous; the poor alone understand the full meaning of the individual loss of wages and money. But the greater evil is the danger to the community from disease. This may, perhaps, be the means, where all others have failed, of doing away with the most crying evils of the tenement, for it is self-interest which enforces the dictates of humanity.

Pauperism.—Pauperism may be considered as one of the contagious diseases common to the tenement-house system. Many instances might be cited of houses which at one time were occupied by hardworking persons, but which, by the contagious presence of one person, too lazy or too vicious to work, had become filled almost exclusively with paupers. More than a hundred and twenty paupers have been reported as living in a single tenement.

In a time of temporary embarrassment many persons, hitherto wage-earners, seek relief by appealing to the charity of others; then, finding it an easy matter to obtain a sufficient amount for support, all desire for earning wages is lost, and henceforth they become paupers.

Others in the same tenement, seeing how easy it is to obtain in a few hours without labor more money than they can earn by a day's hard work, soon follow their example.

This is not to be wondered at. The poor are not particularly endowed with moral courage, and are as anxious as the rest of the world to obtain the greatest returns for the least expenditure of labor.

There is no accurate estimate of the number of paupers in the United States. Mr. Charles D. Kellogg, secretary of the New York Charity Organization Society, has estimated that 3,000,000 were wholly or partially supported by alms during a single year, while the *State's Charities Record* reports 500,000 paupers in New York state as almsmen of the state.

Perhaps the figures which carry the greatest meaning are the number of pauper burials, which represent only the poorest of the poor. For the five years ending 1888 over 10 per cent of all the burials in New York city were in the potter's field, and this despite the fact that the poor have in most cases elaborate funerals, while many are provided by the numerous aid societies.

Professor Richard T. Ely, in an article investigating the causes of pauperism in the United States, reached the conclusion that "the most general statement possible is that the causes of poverty are heredity and environment, producing weak physical, mental and moral constitutions."

The influences of tenement life were also recognized by Dugdale, who, in his sociological study, "The Jukes," says: "The logical induction seems to be that environment is the ultimate controlling factor in determining careers, placing heredity itself as an organized result of invariable environments."[1]

---

1. "Pauperism in the United States," *North American Review*, April, 1891.

Tenement-house reform has long been recognized as the key to the problem of pauperism in the city. We can never get rid of the tenement-house system or of pauperism, but by the reform of the former we shall accomplish more towards exterminating the latter than by any other means that has yet been suggested.

Crime.—The legislative committee appointed in 1885 to investigate the causes of the increase of crime in New York state reached the conclusion that it was largely due to the evil influences of the tenement upon the young. The following extract, from the testimony of Dr. Elisha Harris, corresponding secretary of the Prison Association of New York, before that committee, clearly shows the connection between crime and the tenement:

> "The younger criminals seem to come almost exclusively from the worst tenement-house districts. When the great riot occurred in 1863 every hiding-place and nursery of crime discovered itself by immediate and active participation in the operations of the mob. Those very places and domiciles, and all that are like them, are to-day nurseries of crime, and of the vices and disorderly courses which lead to crime. By far the largest part—eighty per cent. at least—of the crimes against property and against the person are perpetrated by individuals who have either lost connection with home life, or never had any, or whose homes had ceased to be sufficiently separate, decent and desirable to afford what are regarded as ordinary wholesome influences of home and family."

In the *North American Review* of September, 1889, Superintendent Byrnes calls attention to the reformation of the tenement-house system as the most efficient method of reducing the number of our criminals. In this article, entitled "Nurseries of Crime," he emphatically states that the direct causes of many an honest man's fall are the absence of all home life and the consequent corrupting acquaintance of the young with the criminal classes.

The best proof of the intimate connection between crime and the loss of home influences is the fact that in many towns where a wide-reaching reform of the tenement-house system has taken place, the number of crimes committed during a given period has greatly fallen off. Glasgow is a striking example of this. Here the number of crimes fell from 10,899 in 1867 to 7,869 in 1873. This decrease is undoubtedly due to the extensive reforms effected in that city, by the appropriation and rebuilding of large districts.

In connection with this subject, it is well to point out the evils which the present system of cheap lodging-houses is responsible for. In such places congregate the stranger to the city, the honest-man-out-of-work, and the criminal.

The criminal and the easy method of obtaining a living at the expense of others, which he personifies, are thus brought to the notice of the other two classes. These persons, from the nature of their circumstances, are in danger of losing what moral courage they may possess, by the undermining influence of the absence of all home ties, of a desire for excitement and of actual want. From these classes the ranks of the criminals are constantly recruited, and many of them can look back upon the cheap lodging-house as the place where first the temptation was presented that caused their subsequent downfall.

Evil Influences.—One of the curses of the tenement system is the level-ing influence which the worst houses exercise upon all the others. Over-crowding results in the inevitable association of honest people with criminals. The effect of this association is especially bad for the young of both sexes. The boys' ideal hero is the clever thief or the successful burglar; the girls admire and envy the woman of evil life, who obtains such pleas-ures and comforts as they are capable of appreciating, at such an easy cost. The marriage tie also is weakened. As the conditions of life become too hard, the man is tempted to desert his family, either alone or with another companion.

If, as Cardinal Manning says, domestic life creates a people, it is perti-nent to ask ourselves, what sort of people the domestic life of our tene-ments will produce us. We may indeed inquire if there is any domestic life possible in our tenements as constituted to-day. The home life of a family, in which both parents drink and are mutually unfaithful, whose sons belong perhaps to the "gangs" of our streets, and whose girls seek a liveli-hood upon the pavement, can not be productive of good. A family which lets the room by day to the "sweaters," by night for immoral purposes, can hardly be of a kind to produce a very high grade of citizenship. Nor can the domestic life found in a "room 12×12, with five families living in it, com-prising twenty persons of both sexes and all ages, with only two beds, with-out partition, screen, chair or table," have a beneficial effect upon the characters of the younger members.

Habitual contact with uncleanliness lowers self-respect. Bishop Potter has said: "The connection between dirt and degradation is more intimate than most people are willing to recognize. No one, who has known any other condition, can be subjected to conditions of life in which cleanliness is practically impossible, whether of body or raiment, without a steady and sure deterioration of the whole moral tone."

Not the least evil of the overcrowded tenement is the depression of body and mind which they create, and which is an almost insuperable obstacle to the action of any elevating or refining agencies.

Public Dangers.—While the public is indirectly affected by the misfor-tunes of its component parts, it is also directly affected in more than one way by the over-crowded tenement. One danger, which grows more and more apparent every year, is the danger of a social revolution. What man-ner of men and women must these millions of paupers be, if they can see without resentment the complacent exhibition of opulence and ease, which is forever flaunted in their faces, within a few hundred yards of the noisome courts and alleys. The cry of distress is as yet almost inarticulate, but it will not always remain so. It would be strange, indeed, if the striking contrast between the luxury of the rich and the misery of the poor, jostling one another upon every street corner, did not provoke bitter remonstrance, and even active revolt, on the part of the less fortunate members of our body politic.

The wide circulation of such a book as "Progress and Poverty," and the acceptance which the suggestions it contains have found among the work-ing classes, are full of significance and warning.

The wanton display of riches and the unhappiness of the poor were little greater in France in 1789 than they are in America a century later, and while there is little present danger that similar results will follow, it is well to keep in mind that saying of Danton: "If you suffer the poor to grow up as animals, they may chance to become beasts and rend you."

The public seems able to bear with equanimity the story of the misfortunes of the poor; it only shudders when the danger from contagion is hinted at; but it might arouse itself if a revolution were threatened, for "when property becomes alarmed, the outcry which it makes is deafening."

The influence on politics is powerful for evil. Indifference to the conditions of the tenement house will always show itself in the corruption of public affairs. An instance of this is furnished by New York under the rule of Tweed, himself of tenement origin, when the administration of public affairs was notoriously corrupt, and the tenements in their worst condition. With the improvement of one went the reform of the other.

It is needless to point out the great public expense from the sickness and death, crime and pauperism, engendered in the tenement. The yearly loss from wasted efforts due to the same must not be lost sight of.

* * *

EDWARD W. TOWNSEND

From A Daughter of the Tenements[†]

Chapter VI. Eleanor's Glimpse of Tenement Hades.

Carminella was a marvel to Eleanor Hazelhurst, and she had heard there were beautiful faces, and sometimes beautiful forms, to be seen among the young women or older girls in the slums. But here was this child in years, although nearly a woman in stature, who not only had a face so beautiful that it startled, and an erect, slight figure carried with grace, but who was gentle in manner and speech. She expressed this surprise to an associate in her work once. "Oh," replied the more experienced woman, "you have our prize product, our daughter of the tenements, as we call her. All her life nearly she has been associated with teachers in our schools, or similar ones, and we boast of her, and point her out to our patrons as an example of what we could make of children here if we had them under our influence long enough. But they are usually taken from us at six or eight years of age to help their fathers and mothers sewing at home for sweaters. Before children are Carminella's age they are usually employed in a factory with certificates that they are fourteen, and long before that our efforts to save them have been nullified by their home and shop surroundings. Her mother is a monomaniac, and her mania, happily, is the care and education of that girl. I wonder what her life is to be?"

After this, Eleanor made an equal and a companion of Carminella in their school hours. Carminella planned, advised, and helped in the school work, and "Miss Helen" talked with her in their moments together as she would to an equal; gave her books to read which filled the child's mind with wonder and exaltation, and brightened her life until her candle-lit room in the dingy,

[†] New York: Lovell, Coryell & Company, 1895.

crowded tenement was peopled with the world's greatest, real and ideal; moving in scenes which Carminella could not but think must be wholly ideal, so completely they satisfied her stirred and broadening imagination. While Eleanor was giving Carminella glimpses of what to the child of the tenements was almost a dream-life, Carminella in turn showed the woman to whom until now every refinement of luxury had been accepted as a matter of course, realities which were to her as new and startling phases of life as anything she had revealed or suggested to Carminella had been to the child.

Eleanor had assumed and performed her task as a teacher in the charity school for some months before she saw the inside of the homes from which her pupils came. One six-year-old Jewish child, a pinched and withered little girl, had been in her school several weeks. Eleanor had observed and wondered that under the influences of fresh air and sunlight, of freedom from care and toil, of friendly treatment, of the laughter and frolic of the games she constantly provided for the children, the worn look of an aged toiler had slipped from the child's face, and been replaced by a look of baby joy and happiness. But for several days this child had been absent from the school. Instead of making inquiries through an inspector employed for that purpose, Eleanor decided to go and see for herself what the home lives were which produced the startling effects she saw in her pupils and sought to efface. In leaving her schoolroom one evening, the next day being a school holiday, she arranged with Carminella to meet her there in the morning, when Carminella should guide her to the home of the absent little Jewess. It was Eleanor's custom to drive as far down Broadway as Leonard Street, and leave her carriage at the side of the big white marble insurance building, to which place the carriage would return for her in the evening. On this morning, as there were to be no classes, she ordered the coachman to wait for her, and she walked as usual across the few blocks from Broadway where her quietly appointed equipage would be passed by endless throngs of people unremarked, into that other world where her liveried coachman and footman would have been assaulted on sight.

Carminella was waiting for her at the school, and they set out at once for the home of Lena, the absent one.

"It is in our block," said Carminella, "but it is on the Baxter Street side. It is a back tenement almost in a line with ours."

Perhaps with an unconscious intention to delay the revelation which she felt her companion did not foresee, and partly with a child's delight in showing off what to her were the attractions of her own side of the block, its brightness and gayety, Carminella led Eleanor up Park Street and turned into Mulberry Bend toward Bayard Street. That stretch of the Bend is one of the two places in New York City so affected by the adjacent conditions of living that the police there openly permit during certain hours of the day violations of the law concerning street obstructions. From seven until ten in the morning market stalls and booths are allowed to obstruct the sidewalk. The space in the houses, even to the ground floors and the cellars, is so urgently demanded as living and work room that without this street market the swarming inhabitants would have no place to conduct their daily household trade.

Eleanor and Carminella moved slowly along the Bend, for the obstructions were too numerous and the crowds too dense to permit of more than a slow working forward. It was a bright, early spring day, and it seemed to

Eleanor as if every man, woman, and child must have left the old rookeries on either side of the street to enjoy the sun and the gay companionship of the market-place. The gossip of the women, the strange cries of the vendors, the shouts of the children were all animated, light-hearted; the dress, even the rags of the poorest, were bright-colored, and the marvellous things they sold lent attractiveness to the scene; the glinting bronze of the open kegs of humble herrings, the scarlet of ropes of peppers, the green of barrels of olives; the gleaming white and purple of onions; the silver shining fresh fish heaped high in wagon-loads; the cords of high-stacked monster loaves of bread in every shade of brown; the almost startling degree and variety of color in the open booths where women's shawls, children's stockings, and men's neckerchiefs were displayed and offered for sale by women who laughed as they bantered their neighbors—rubber-booted men from the fish-market docks counting out eels from barrels, or a gardener from Long Island with bushels of dull-tinted winter vegetables, or a fruit vendor with a load of his red and gold and purple commodities, gathered from across oceans and continents.

Many of the women and some of the men stopped their barter and banter to good-naturedly hail Carminella as she passed, and ask her in their own language if the Signorina with her was the teacher from the mission, and would she not like to replenish her wardrobe or her cupboard from their wares. Before they had walked ten yards Eleanor was conscious that she was the object of polite attention. Once a fish vendor left his wagon to light his pipe with a coal from the brazier on which some dish was cooking in front of an area-way bread-stall. As he stood, big, square-shouldered, and seemingly immovable, holding with his fingers a live coal to his pipe, he was so engrossed with his occupation, and perhaps with the pretty eyes of the bread vendor, that he did not hear the first shout for him to clear the way for Carminella and the lady. Then forty people, men, women, and children, shouted at him, and some of the objurgations must have been very emphatic, for he jumped, startled, to the curb, and there, as they passed he stood smiling apologetically, lifting his soft woollen cap from his curling black hair and bowing with an accompanying backward sweep of one rubber-booted leg.

In the course of human events, as they are directed and advanced by municipal energy, Mulberry Bend is to be converted into a park. For the sunlight and air so introduced into that neighborhood we shall all feel appropriately proud of our share in the achievement, yet I cannot but regret that even with all the deliberation our rulers may exercise in this matter, the transformation of the Bend into the park will have taken place before any American painter shall have found time from working up his "Naples sketches" and elaborating his "scenes from Cairo streets" into ambitious canvases, to step over into the Bend and preserve its distinctive color and action for those of us who care. He might even conceal his indiscretion by labelling his picture "Street Scene in an Italian Town," and sell it, i' faith!

As they turned down Bayard Street, and then into Baxter, Eleanor shivered as one who steps from sunlight into the silent, solemn shade of a vault. Every condition of life which could affect mind or body was reversed. The people, from the youngest to the oldest, were speechless and grave and hopeless-looking. Men staggered past, their bodies bent almost double under what seemed impossible loads of clothing they were carrying to and from the sweaters' and the workshop-homes; women carrying similar bundles on their heads, or perhaps a bundle of wood from some builder's waste, hurried along, not speaking to those they passed; none of the children seen was much more than a baby in years, and they were silent too, and had no games: they were in the street because while the sweaters' work went on there was no room for them in their homes. In the dress of none was any bright color seen, and the only sounds were the occasional cry of a hurt child, the snarling of the low-browed men who solicited trade for the clothing stores, quarrelling for the possession of a chance victim; and always, as the grinding ocean surf mutters an accompaniment to all other shore sounds—always, always, always!—was heard the whirring monotone of the sewing-machine.

Carminella, who was looking for a number, stopped before the entrance to a low, dark, tunnel-like passageway, by the side of an equally low, dark and forbidding drinking-saloon.

"It is the back tenement of this number," said Carminella, and as she saw a slight, instinctive shrinking in her companion she took her hand. They walked through the long entrance, which was damp with the chill dampness which even midsummer heat never wholly dispels. They came out into a small, narrow court roughly paved with stone and bricks and so overshadowed by tall buildings it was only a little less dark than the passageway. An Italian had just brought into the court an enormous sack of waste paper, which his wife and three children were aiding him to assort.

"There are few of my people on this side of the block," said Carminella, as if she were sorry they had happened upon this group. "These have just come from Italy," she added, with a quick noting of their clothes, "and they will be on our side of the block as soon as some one dies there and makes room." Eleanor was looking at what seemed to be a low bank of refuse lying against the south wall of the court.

"Cannot we make some one at least take that away?" she said to Carminella. The child spoke to the man in Italian. The man grinned, and made a reply. Then Carminella said, "It is snow, Miss Helen. It must stay till it is melted. It takes a long time to warm these courts, and then to cool them." Carminella asked the woman if she knew in what rooms Lena's family lived: no, she did not know, she had only been there three weeks, and knew the name of no one in the tenement. Carminella stepped toward the open stairway, but Eleanor did not follow at once. She looked affrighted, and as Carminella returned to her, she heard her whisper: "God in heaven! Can nothing be done for such as these?" And then in a tenser whisper, "Inasmuch as ye have done it unto one of the least of these—" Carminella interrupted her by laying a hand softly on her arm. "Wait," the child whispered, "wait till you have seen the others. My people can smile. Did you not see these smile? The others never smile. They cannot."

This was the first actual glimpse Eleanor had ever caught of the picture which society, ever weaving pleasing harmonies in bright colors in the light, weaves in the dark on the reverse side of the social tapestry: but as yet merely the edge of the fabric had been turned for her inspection. Gathering herself with a start she followed Carminella into the entrance and up the stairway of the rear tenement. The effluvia from the reeking wooden stairs, the odor of cooking cabbage which came in clouds of steam from some of the open doors, the sense of what she had seen, the dawning suspicion of what she was to see, overcame her for a moment at the first landing. She clutched Carminella in the dark and gasped as though she were stifled. "It is silly, but I cannot go on now. How much further?"

They found their way at last and by a process of rejection, going one flight further when every tenant on a floor had professed ignorance of Lena.

At the rear of the fourth landing an open door led into a small room with two windows looking on a narrow court, little more than a passageway, facing some wooden sheds used to stable pedlers' horses. In this room, as in nearly every one they had passed, people were at work making clothing. Here there were four men, a woman, a girl of probably sixteen years of age, a boy younger than she, and two younger girls. The youngest of the girls was seated on the floor with disordered heaps of clothing all about her, pulling threads from finished garments the other workers tossed to her. Three men were running sewing-machines; the others were doing hand-sewing, or pressing, and the arms of all were black to the elbow from the dye of the coarse, cheap stuff they worked on. As Eleanor and her companion stopped at the open door all of the toilers looked up for one hasty glance, but without an instant's pause in their labor, all but the youngest child. It was Lena. She gave a little cry of recognition, and laid down her work as if to rise, but a scowl from one of the men, her father, caused her to continue her endless task. Lena could speak a little English, the two hundred words or so, of English, such as it is, which is the common language of all the children of the tenements, whatever may be the native tongue of their parents. Carminella knew this language and also knew a few words of the Hebrew jargon which was Lena's vernacular, and which she mixed with her street vocabulary. As Carminella stepped into the one little unoccupied space just inside the door, Eleanor leaned against the door frame, glad of that partial rest, for she was faint. Both the windows were closed, and on a little coal stove against the sides of which were propped a number of pressing irons, was a steaming kettle of cabbage. The men at work each wore above his trousers only a widely-gaping, sleeveless, cotton undershirt; the woman and the children, including the sixteen-year-old girl, were clothed above the waist in much the same fashion as the men. After the first short, suspicious scrutiny, none in the room except Lena showed any consciousness of the presence of the visitors. She, continuing her work with one hand, made an effort with the other to catch together at the throat the one garment over her shoulders, and she looked up at Carminella as if aware of the object of the visit, and ready to reply when she should be questioned. And when Carminella did question her, Lena explained in language which was nearly as incomprehensible to Eleanor as it was to Lena's work-fellows, although they considered it English. She had been kept from school by her father and mother to do the work an eight-year-old sister had been doing until she was taken sick. When she was well Lena would return to school.

Lena did not explain that her father wanted her to stay in school until she could speak and read, and write English so that she could communicate with the Christians who gave out work, and thus, perhaps, avert the calamity of idleness when the family could get no work from its own people.

Carminella translated what Lena said for Eleanor, who, when she heard of the sick eight-year-old, tried to peer into a dark inner room adjoining. "Ask her if her sister is in there or at the hospital, and what she is sick with," she said to Carminella. Lena explained again: her sister was sick of a fever; she did not know what fever. A woman in the tenement, whose husband was a rag-picker, had said she would tell him to stop where the doctors were and tell them of the sickness.

Lena's story was interrupted by a startled cry from Eleanor, who had seen in a corner of the room a stricken, fevered child's face rise slowly, staring at her with irrational eyes across a wall of unfinished work, built above a pile of finished clothing which made the child's sick-bed.

"It is the sick one," said Lena.

"Has she no bed?" exclaimed Eleanor. "Not even a cot in the other room?"

"No, the boarders"—Lena indicated the three men working by her father's side—"sleep in that room." The family, seven, all slept in the room in which they were working.

"Has the child no care, no nursing, no delicacies?" Eleanor asked.

Carminella could not make all of this understood by Lena. She said at last, however, that her, Lena's school-dress, had been pawned that morning, and with the money her father bought a quarter of a chicken in Hester Street, and it was now cooking in the pot with the cabbage. The others would have no chicken, they would have cabbage and black bread for dinner.

"Is it all you want to know?" whispered Carminella to Eleanor.

"No," said Eleanor, with tightly drawn lips, "I want to know all I can. I thought I knew something of this life; I know nothing. Ask her—ask her why, because her sister could not work, she could not go to school."

The sewing-machines clicked and whirred, the needles of the hand-sewers flashed in and out with the steady regularity of machinery, and all the toilers bent steadily, sombrely over their tasks as Lena, not neglecting her own work, however, again explained.

It was pitiful that she could explain, not so little, but so much as she did. This child—who in another condition of society would be treated as only emerging from babyhood, as just maturing at best into a mental capacity to be safely vexed with the mysteries of A, B, and C, with the sums of one and one, and two and two—told with a surprisingly flexible use of her frugal vocabulary (yet a vocabulary born of the necessity of understanding such matters, if nothing else, and God knows how seldom the understanding of anything else comes into their lives!), explained, I say, this six-year-old sweaters' slave, as her bare, thin, dye-blackened arms moved with sharp activity which never ceased from daylight until far into the night, when nature dragged them, listless, to her side and her head sank in restless sleep on a pillow of her own work, while her elders yet toiled on—that, when they all worked, the family earned six dollars a week! Not every week: sometimes more, much more than that. But sometimes, also, the cutters who prepared their work for them in the big shops were out on strike, and they earned nothing; sometimes trade was dull, and they earned less than six dollars a week: sometimes, too, when ships brought to the city many loads of their people who had escaped from the other country, wages went down, as now, when for finishing "pants" they were paid but five cents a pair; for "knee-pants" forty-two cents a dozen; for covering wooden buttons, the children's task when other work was light, four cents a gross. In good times and bad their wages came to six dollars a week at the end of the year, so she could not go to school when the fever took away one of the family from the work.

When her sister was well she would be back in school, and then she would only have to work from daylight until school-time, and after school hours until dark.

"But it will be better than this, something must make it better than this," interrupted Eleanor, with a sobbing break in her voice.

When Lena was made to understand the question she spoke to her father and translated his reply, given sombrely as he worked, "Nothing would ever be better. The wages always went down. The rent never did."

"Is there nothing to hope for then?" exclaimed Eleanor. Carminella tried, but tried in vain, to render this question to the little interpreter. Lena shook her head. She could not understand. The word hope was as foreign to her vocabulary as the thing it meant was to their lives.

Eleanor felt herself growing faint again, the air of the hot, close room was lifeless: the odors from the perspiring, unclean bodies of the workers, the coarse fumes from the boiling cabbage, the steam arising from the dampened shoddy under the hot iron of the presser, the indescribable scent from the fever-scorched, uncared-for patient, and the utter misery of it all made her weak and dizzy. She had just made a faint motion for Carminella to come away with her, when a health officer, of whose approach her ringing ears had taken no note, stood by her side at the door. He recognized her as a charity worker in the district in which his paid services were employed, and raised his hat respectfully as he said: "A case, supposed to be fever, has been reported from this apartment. Have you been investigating it?"

"I only learned of it by accident," Eleanor replied.

He noted her weak voice and swooning look, and promptly strode over the strewn confusion of garments to the windows and threw both of them open. The instant he entered the room the boy, probably ten years of age, and a girl a year his senior, cried, parrot-like, "Fourteen!"

"They are telling their age; they think he is a truant officer," Carminella whispered in explanation to Eleanor. "That is what they are all taught to say, so they will not be sent to school. It is the same in the shops, when the factory inspector comes."

Eleanor was not listening. She was eagerly watching the health officer, who had gone to the sick child, and was closely examining her. Then he went over to the door and said to Eleanor: "Do not be alarmed at what I say, but my duties require me to exercise some authority over your immediate movements. I happen to know who you are, and that Dr. Bailey is your family physician. I was in his office as a student. You have been exposed here to typhus fever. You must go home at once and send for Dr. Bailey."

He stopped as if in conjecture. Eleanor looked as if she had not understood a word he had spoken.

"How will you reach your home?" he asked, and added, "you would expose others in a street car."

"My carriage is just at Broadway," she answered.

Again he paused, as if determining a plan, and then said rapidly: "I will go and bring your carriage as far as Centre Street. You will reach there no sooner than I do. You will drive then to your stables, not to your house. I will telephone to Dr. Bailey, who will meet you there."

He started to go, but turned to the workers and asked sharply, "Any one speak English here?"

"Me," Lena replied. No one else even looked up.

"None of this clothing must be taken out, and none of you must leave the room until I return. You understand?"

"Yes," said Lena.

Eleanor reached the carriage, nervous and distressed. The health officer mistook the cause of her agitation and began to reassure her as to the remoteness, in her case at least, of the danger from contagion.

"No, no, you do not understand," she cried impetuously. "I do not fear or care for myself, but I have exposed this child, Carminella, here. It is I who am to blame if anything happens to her. She must come with me."

The officer forbade this. Carminella was near her own home, where he could take immediate precautions for her. He would go with her himself to her home. For her to go with Miss Hazelhurst would be only an additional possible danger to whoever attended them.

"Promise me then that Carminella shall have every attention from you Dr. Bailey will give me. There must be no question of expense," urged Eleanor.

"I promise you," he said.

Before the health officer had completed these promised arrangements for Carminella's safety, Lena's father had secured the aid of a tenant from another floor, who was soon staggering toward a clothing factory, bent beneath the mound of garments which had made the typhus-fever patient's bed; each garment to be offered for sale over some counter the next day; a bargain, verily, for a death-warrant would be included free with every garment!

WILLIAM DEAN HOWELLS

From Impressions and Experiences†

The Jewish East Side, 1881–1924

I do not know whether the Hebrew quarter, when I began to make my calls there, seemed any worse than the American quarter or not. But I noticed presently a curious subjective effect in myself, which I offer for the reader's speculation.

There is something in a very little experience of such places that blunts the perception, so that they do not seem so dreadful as they are; and I should feel as if I were exaggerating if I recorded my first impression of their loathsomeness. I soon came to look upon the conditions as normal, not for me, indeed, or for the kind of people I mostly consort with, but for the inmates of the dens and lairs about me. Perhaps this was partly their fault; they were uncomplaining, if not patient, in circumstances where I believe a single week's sojourn, with no more hope of a better lot than they could have, would make anarchists of the best people in the city. Perhaps the poor people themselves are not so thoroughly persuaded that there is anything very unjust in their fate, as the compassionate think. They at least do not know the better fortune of others, and they have the habit of pas-

† New York: Harper's, 1896.

sively enduring their own. I found them usually cheerful in the Hebrew quarter, and they had so much courage as enabled them to keep themselves noticeably clean in an environment where I am afraid their betters would scarcely have had heart to wash their faces and comb their hair. There was even a decent tidiness in their dress, which I did not find very ragged, though it often seemed unseasonable and insufficient. But here again, as in many other phases of life, I was struck by men's heroic superiority to their fate, if their fate is hard; and I felt anew that if prosperous and comfortable people were as good in proportion to their fortune as these people were they would be as the angels of light, which I am afraid they now but faintly resemble.

One of the places we visited was a court somewhat like that we had already seen in the American quarter, but rather smaller and with more the effect of a pit, since the walls around it were so much higher. There was the same row of closets at one side and the hydrant next them, but here the hydrant was bound up in rags to keep it from freezing, apparently, and the wretched place was by no means so foul under foot. To be sure, there was no stable to contribute its filth, but we learned that a suitable stench was not wanting from a bakery in one of the basements, which a man in good clothes and a large watch-chain told us rose from it in suffocating fumes at a certain hour, when the baker was doing some unimaginable thing to the bread. This man seemed to be the employer of labor in one of the rooms above, and he said that when the smell began they could hardly breathe. He caught promptly at the notion of the Board of Health, and I dare say that the baker will be duly abated. None of the other people complained, but that was perhaps because they had only their Yiddish to complain in, and knew that it would be wasted on us. They seemed neither curious nor suspicious concerning us; they let us go everywhere, as if they had no thought of hindering us. One of the tenements we entered had just been vacated; but there was a little girl of ten there, with some much smaller children, amusing them in the empty space. Through a public-spirited boy, who had taken charge of us from the beginning and had a justly humorous sense of the situation, we learned that this little maid was not the sister but the servant of the others, for even in these low levels society makes its distinctions. I dare say that the servant was not suffered to eat with the others when they had anything to eat, and that when they had nothing her inferiority was somehow brought home to her. She may have been made to wait and famish after the others had hungered some time. She was a cheerful and friendly creature and her small brood were kept tidy like herself.

The basement under this vacant tenement we found inhabited, and though it was a most preposterous place for people to live, it was not as dirty as one would think. To be sure, it was not very light and all the dirt may not have been visible. One of the smiling women who were there made their excuses, "Poor people; cannot keep very nice," and laughed as if she had said a good thing. There was nothing in the room but a table and a few chairs and a stove, without fire, but they were all contentedly there together in the dark, which hardly let them see one another's faces. My companion struck a match and held it to the cavernous mouth of an inner cellar half as large as the room we were in, where it winked and paled so soon that I had only a glimpse of the bed, with the rounded heap of bedding on it; but out of this hole, as if she had been a rat, scared from it by the light, a young girl came, rubbing her eyes and vaguely smiling, and vanished upstairs somewhere.

I found no shape or size of tenement but this. There was always the one room, where the inmates lived by day, and the one den, where they slept by night, apparently all in the same bed, though probably the children were strewn about the floor. If the tenement were high up the living-room had more light and air than if it were low down; but the sleeping-hole never had any light or air of its own. My calls were made on one of the mild days which fell before last Christmas, and so I suppose I saw these places at their best; but what they must be when the summer is seven times heated without, as it often is in New York, or when the arctic cold has pierced these hapless abodes and the inmates huddle together for their animal heat, the reader must imagine for himself. The Irish-Americans had flaming stoves, even on that soft day, but in the Hebrew tenements I found no fire. They were doubtless the better for this, and it is one of the comical anomalies of the whole affair that they are singularly healthy. The death rate among them is one of the lowest in the city, though whether for their final advantage it might not better be the highest, is one of the things one must not ask one's self. In their presence I should not dare to ask it, even in my deepest thought. They are then so like other human beings and really so little different from the best, except in their environment, that I had to get away from this before I could regard them as wild beasts.

I suppose there are and have been worse conditions of life, but if I stopped short of savage life I found it hard to imagine them. I did not exaggerate to myself the squalor that I saw, and I do not exaggerate it to the reader. As I have said, I was so far from sentimentalizing it that I almost immediately reconciled myself to it, as far as its victims were concerned. Still, it was squalor of a kind which, it seemed to me, it could not be possible to outrival anywhere in the life one commonly calls civilized. It is true that the Indians who formerly inhabited this island were no more comfortably lodged in their wigwams of bark and skins than these poor New Yorkers in their tenements. But the wild men pay no rent, and if they are crowded together upon terms that equally forbid decency and comfort in their shelter, they have the freedom of the forest and the prairie about them; they have the illimitable sky and the whole light of day and the four winds to breathe when they issue into the open air. The New York tenement dwellers, even when they leave their lairs, are still pent in their high-walled streets, and inhale a thousand stenches of their own and others' making. The street, except in snow and rain, is always better than their horrible houses, and it is doubtless because they pass so much of their time in the street that the death rate is so low among them. Perhaps their domiciles can be best likened for darkness and discomfort to the dugouts or sod huts of the settlers on the great plains. But these are only temporary shelters, while the tenement dwellers have no hope of better housing; they have neither the prospect of a happier fortune through their own energy as the settlers have, nor any chance from the humane efforts and teachings of missionaries, like the savages. With the tenement dwellers it is from generation to generation, if not for the individual, then for the class, since no one expects that there will not always be tenement dwellers in New York as long as our present economical conditions endure.

When I first set out on my calls I provided myself with some small silver, which I thought I might fitly give, at least to the children, and in some of the first places I did this. But presently I began to fancy an unseemliness in it, as if it were an indignity added to the hardship of their lot, and to feel that unless I gave all my worldly wealth to them I was in a manner mocking their misery. I could not give everything, for then I should have had to come upon charity myself, and so I mostly kept my little coins in my pocket; but when we mounted into the court again from that cellar apartment and found an old, old woman there, wrinkled and yellow, with twinkling eyes and a tooth-less smile, waiting to see us, as if she were as curious in her way as we were in ours, I was tempted. She said in her Yiddish, which the humorous boy interpreted, that she was eighty years old, and she looked a hundred, while she babbled unintelligibly but very cheerfully on. I gave her a piece of twenty-five cents and she burst into a blessing, that I should not have thought could be bought for money. We did not stay to hear it out, but the boy did, and he followed to report it to me, with a gleeful interest in its beneficent exaggera-tions. If it is fulfilled I shall live to be a man of many and prosperous years, and I shall die possessed of wealth that will endow a great many colleges and found a score of libraries. I do not know whether the boy envied me or not, but I wish I could have left that benediction to him, for I took a great liking to him, his shrewd smile, his gay eyes, his promise of a Hebrew nose, and his whole wise little visage. He said that he went to school and studied reading, writing, geography and everything. All the children we spoke to said that they went to school, and they were quick and intelligent. They could mostly speak English, while most of their elders knew only Yiddish.

The sound of this was around us on the street we issued into, and which seemed from end to end a vast bazaar, where there was a great deal of sell-ing, whether there was much buying or not. The place is humorously called the pig-market by the Christians, because everything in the world but pork is to be found there. To me its activity was a sorrowfully amusing satire upon the business ideal of our plutocratic civilization. These people were desperately poor, yet they preyed upon one another in the commerce, as if they could be enriched by selling dear or buying cheap. So far as I could see they would only impoverish each other more and more, but they traf-ficked as eagerly as if there were wealth in every bargain. The sidewalks and the roadways were thronged with peddlers and purchasers, and everywhere I saw splendid types of that old Hebrew world which had the sense if not the knowledge of God when all the rest of us lay sunk in heathen darkness. There were women with oval faces and olive tints, and clear, dark eyes, relu-cent as evening pools, and men with long beards of jetty black or silvery white, and the noble profiles of their race. I said to myself that it was among such throngs that Christ walked, it was from such people that he chose his Disciples and his friends; but I looked in vain for him in Hester Street. Probably he was at that moment in Fifth Avenue.

After all, I was loath to come away. I should have liked to stay and live awhile with such as they, if the terms of their life had been possible, for there were phases of it that were very attractive. That constant meeting and that neighborly intimacy were superficially at least of a very pleasant effect, and though the whole place seemed abandoned to mere trade, it may have been a necessity of the case, for I am told that many of these Hebrews have another ideal, and think and vote in the hope that the land of their refuge shall yet some day keep its word to the world, so that men shall be equally free in it to the pursuit of happiness. I suppose they are mostly fugitives from the Russian persecution, and that from the cradle their days must have been full of fear and care, and from the time they could toil that they must have toiled at whatever their hands found to do. Yet they had not the look of a degraded people; they were quiet and orderly, and I saw none of the drunkenness or the truculence of an Irish or low American neighborhood among them. There were no policemen in sight, and the quiet behavior that struck me so much seemed not to have been enforced. Very likely they may have moods different from that I saw, but I only tell of what I saw, and I am by no means ready yet to preach poverty as a saving grace. Though they seemed so patient and even cheerful in some cases, I do not think it is well for human beings to live whole families together in one room with a kennel out of it, where modesty may survive, but decency is impossible. Neither do I think they can be the better men and women for being insufficiently clothed and fed, though so many of us appear none the better for being housed in palaces and clad in purple and fine linen and faring sumptuously every day.

I have tried to report simply and honestly what I saw of the life of our poorest people that day. One might say it was not so bad as it is painted, but I think it is quite as bad as it appeared; and I could not see that in itself or in its conditions it held the promise or the hope of anything better. If it is tolerable, it must endure; if it is intolerable, still it must endure. Here and there one will release himself from it, and doubtless numbers are always doing this, as in the days of slavery there were always fugitives; but for the great mass the captivity remains. Upon the present terms of leaving the poor to be housed by private landlords, whose interest it is to get the greatest return of money for the money invested, the very poorest must always be housed as they are now. Nothing but public control in some form or other can secure them a shelter fit for human beings.

When I come home from these walks of mine, I have a vision of the wretched quarters through which I have passed, as blotches of disease upon the civic body, as loathsome sores, destined to eat deeper and deeper into it; and I am haunted by this sense of them, until I plunge deep into the Park, and wash my consciousness clean of it all for a while. But when I am actually in these leprous spots, I become hardened, for the moment, to the deeply underlying fact of human discomfort. I feel their picturesqueness, with a callous indifference to that ruin, or that defect, which must so largely constitute the charm of the picturesque. A street of tenement-houses is always more picturesque than a street of brownstone residences, which the same thoroughfare usually is before it slopes to either river. The fronts of the edifices are decorated with the iron balconies and ladders of the fire-escapes, and have in the perspective a false air of gayety, which is travestied in their rear by the lines thickly woven from the windows to the tall poles set between the backs of the houses, and fluttering with drying clothes as with banners.

The sidewalks swarm with children, and the air rings with their clamor, as they fly back and forth at play; on the thresholds, the mothers sit nursing their babes, and the old women gossip together; young girls lean from the casements, alow and aloft, or flirt from the doorways with the hucksters who leave their carts in the street, while they come forward with some bargain in fruit or vegetables, and then resume their leisurely progress and their jarring cries. The place has all the attraction of close neighborhood, which the poor love, and which affords them for nothing the spectacle of the human drama, with themselves for actors. In a picture it would be most pleasingly effective, for then you could be in it, and yet have the distance on it which it needs. But to be in it, and not have the distance, is to inhale the stenches of the neglected street, and to catch that yet fouler and dreadfuller poverty-smell which breathes from the open doorways. It is to see the children quarrelling in their games, and beating each other in the face, and rolling each other in the gutter, like the little savage outlaws they are. It is to see the work-worn look of the mothers, the squalor of the babes, the haggish ugliness of the old women, the slovenly frowziness of the young girls. All this makes you hasten your pace down to the river, where the tall buildings break and dwindle into stables and shanties of wood, and finally end in the piers, commanding the whole stretch of the mighty waterway with its shipping, and the wooded heights of its western bank.

I am supposing you to have walked down a street of tenement houses to the North River, as the New Yorkers call the Hudson; and I wish I could give some notion of the beauty and majesty of the stream, some sense of the mean and ignoble effect of the city's invasion of the hither shore. The ugliness is, indeed, only worse in degree, but not in kind, than that of all city water-fronts. Instead of pleasant homes, with green lawns and orchards sloping to the brink, huge factories and foundries, lumber yards, breweries, slaughter-houses, and warehouses, abruptly interspersed with stables and hovels and drinking-saloons, disfigure the shore, and in the nearest avenue the freight trains come and go on lines of railroads, in all the middle portion of New York. South of it, in the business section, the poverty section, the river region is a mere chaos of industrial and commercial strife and pauper wretchedness. North of it there are gardened drive-ways following the shore; and even at many points between, when you finally reach the river, there is a kind of peace, or at least a truce to the frantic activities of business. To be sure, the heavy trucks grind up and down the long piers, but on either side the docks are full of leisurely canal-boats, and if you could come with me in the late afternoon, you would see the smoke curling upward from their cabin roofs, as from the chimneys of so many rustic cottages, and smell the evening meal cooking within, while the canal-wives lounged at the gangway hatches for a breath of the sunset air, and the boatmen smoked on the gunwales or indolently plied the long sweeps of their pumps. All the hurry and turmoil of the city is lost among these people, whose clumsy craft recall the grassy inland levels remote from the metropolis, and the slow movement of life in the quiet country ways. Some of the mothers from the tenement-houses stroll down on the piers with their babies in their arms, and watch their men-kind, of all ages, fishing along the sides of the dock, or casting their lines far out into the current at the end. They do not seem to catch many fish, and never large ones, but they silently enjoy the sport, which they probably find leisure for in the general want of work in these hard times; if they swear a little at their luck, now and then, it is, perhaps, no more than their luck deserves. Some do not even fish, but sit with their legs dangling over the water, and watch the swift tugs, or the lagging sloops that pass, with now and then a larger sail, or a towering passenger steamboat. Far down the stream they can see the forests of masts, fringing either shore, and following the point of the island round and up into the great channel called the East River. These vessels seem as multitudinous as the houses that spread everywhere from them over the shore farther than the eye can reach. They bring the commerce of the world to this mighty city, which, with all its riches, is the parent of such misery, and with all its traffic abounds in idle men who cannot find work. The ships look happy and free, in the stream, but they are of the overworked world, too, as well as the houses; and let them spread their wings ever so widely, they still bear with them the sorrows of the poor.

The other evening I walked over to the East River through one of the tenement streets, and I reached the waterside just as the soft night was beginning to fall in all its autumnal beauty. The afterglow died from the river, while I hung upon a parapet over a gulf ravined out of the bank for a street, and experienced that artistic delight which cultivated people are often proud of feeling, in the aspect of the long prison island which breaks the expanse of the channel. I knew the buildings on it were prisons, and that the men and women in them, bad before, could only come out of them worse than before, and doomed to a life of outlawry and of crime. I was aware that they were each an image of that loveless and hopeless perdition which men once imagined that God had prepared for the souls of the damned, but I could not see the barred windows of those hells in the waning light. I could only see the trees along their walks; their dim lawns and gardens, and the castellated forms of the prisons; and the æsthetic sense, which is careful to keep itself pure from pity, was tickled with an agreeable impression of something old and fair. The dusk thickened, and the vast steamboats which ply between the city and the New England ports on Long Island Sound, and daily convey whole populations of passengers between New York and Boston, began to sweep by silently, swiftly, luminous masses on the black water. Their lights aloft at bow and stern, floated with them like lambent planets; the lights of lesser craft dipped by, and came and went in the distance; the lamps of the nearer and farther shores twinkled into sight, and a peace that ignored all the misery of it, fell upon the scene.

From First Report of the Tenement House Department of the City of New York, 1902–03[†]

General Instructions No. 1.

UNIFORMS.

To all Inspectors:—

Inspectors are directed while on duty to wear the departmental uniform, badge, hat and hat band.

Inspectors are required to furnish their own uniforms and hats, and to keep them in good condition and repair. The department will furnish badges, uniform buttons and departmental hat-bands, which will be loaned to the inspector, who will be held personally and financially responsible for them.

Inspectors on appointment will order their uniform and hat from the contractor to whom the latest contract for the departmental uniform has been awarded.

ROBERT W. DE FOREST,
Commissioner.

CHARLES B. BALL,
        Chief Inspector.
Issued May 21, 1902.
Reissued September 14, 1903.

No. 4.

VACCINATION.

All employees on reporting for duty at appointment are required to make a written statement on Form 1008 (the "S" card) of the date on which they were last vaccinated, as nearly as ascertainable, the name of the vaccinator, if known, and whether such vaccination "took."

In view of their special danger from exposure to small-pox, inspectors are required to be vaccinated in an effective manner at least once a year.

Issued July 12, 1902.
Reissued September 14, 1903.

No. 5.

ENTRY TO BUILDING REFUSED.

Inspectors are directed that if admission to a building is refused an inspector in the course of his duty, he should at once show to the proper person the text of Section 1344E of the Greater New York Charter, which gives to the officers of the Tenement House Department full right and power to enter and examine all premises.

If admission is still refused, the inspector should then telephone the office, whereupon a police officer will be sent to accompany the inspector to the building, who will explain to the proper person that the inspector has a lawful right to enter the premises.

† *The Journal of Political Economy* 13.2 (1905).

If the admission is still refused, then the inspector and the police officer should apply to the nearest police magistrate and obtain a summons for the person refusing admission.

It should be distinctly understood, however, that application for a summons should not be made except as prescribed in Rule 36 of the departmental regulations.

For the information of inspectors the following statement is made as to the legal rights of the department:

Sections 47 and 124 of the Penal Code provide that any person who wilfully resists, delays or obstructs any executive officer in the performance of his duty is guilty of a misdemeanor.

Section 1264 of the Greater New York Charter makes the same provision with regard to resisting an officer of the Department of Health, and by Section 1344-H of the Charter this provision is made applicable to the inspectors of the Tenement House Department. Section 1344-E gives full power to the Tenement House Department.

Issued August 4, 1902.

Reissued September 14, 1903.

No. 10.

REPORTING FIRES.

Employees are requested to call to the attention of their immediate superiors, by submitting clippings from newspapers, or by otherwise reporting on Form 1008 (the "S" card), all fires in tenement houses, which attract attention either by reason of loss of life or by rescue of tenants. The purpose of making this report is to enable the department to investigate the circumstances attending such fires.

Issued, August 25, 1902.

Reissued, September 14, 1903.

No. 11.

OBSTRUCTED FIRE ESCAPES.

Inspectors are directed, whenever making an inspection of a building which involves entering an individual apartment, to note whether the fire escapes connected with such apartment are obstructed, giving especial attention to the fire escape openings.

If found obstructed, the inspectors will kindly, but firmly, advise the tenants that they are endangering their lives in placing these obstructions upon the fire escapes, and in case of fire that they may suffer seriously because of this practice; that it is contrary to law, and that these encumbrances must be removed, and kept removed.

Issued, August 25, 1902.

Reissued, September 14, 1903.

No. 12.

PROSTITUTION.

Inspectors are directed to report on Form 1008 (the "S" card), any circumstances which lead them to believe that prostitution is being carried on in any of the tenement houses which they inspect, and which are occupied, in whole or in part, by families.

Inspectors should understand that they are not directed to hunt out cases of prostitution, but only to report suspicious circumstances as observed in their regular work, so that further special investigation may be made, if necessary.

No inspector will be called upon as a witness, or for any further testimony in regard to such reports.

Issued, September 11, 1902.

Reissued, September 14, 1903.

No. 14.

UNSAFE OR DANGEROUS BUILDINGS.

Inspectors are directed to report on Form 1008 (the "S" card), all unsafe or dangerous buildings which they may discover in the course of their work. The report should state the defects which lead the inspector to the conclusion that the building is unsafe. Where it appears that the circumstances are exceptional, and that the building is in a condition where it is liable to fall at any moment, such information should be immediately telephoned to the office.

Issued, September 25, 1902.

Reissued, September 14, 1903.

No. 18.

ADDITIONAL OR UNNECESSARY FIRE ESCAPES NOT TO
BE ORDERED REMOVED.

Inspectors are directed that where there are sufficient fire escapes on a tenement house, and there are also additional fire escapes which are unnecessary, and the latter are located in air shafts or are in violation of the law in other respects, the department will not issue an order to remove such additional or unnecessary fire escapes.

Issued October 28, 1902.

Reissued September 14, 1903.

No. 19.

KEEPING OF ANIMALS ON TENEMENT HOUSE PREMISES
AND NUISANCES ARISING THEREFROM.

Inspectors are directed not to report as violations the keeping on tenement house premises of animals other than those specified in Section 110 of the Tenement House Act.

Where, however, nuisances exist because of the keeping of cats, dogs, chickens, pigeons or any other animal, a report of the existence of such nuisance should be made on the violation form, so that such accumulation of filth may be ordered to be removed.

Inspectors should understand that it is not the part of the functions of the department to require the removal of fleas or other vermin from tenement houses or from particular apartments.

Issued October 28, 1902.

Reissued September 14, 1903.

No. 20.

COMMON SEWER CONNECTIONS FOR TWO OR MORE HOUSES.

Inspectors are directed that where two or more adjacent houses are found to have a common connection to the public sewer, if this connection is defective, a report to this effect should be made on the violation form for each house.

Issued October 28, 1902.

Reissued September 14, 1903.

No. 26.

CELLAR AND BASEMENT LIVING ROOMS.

Inspectors are directed that whenever, in making an inspection, they observe cellar or basement rooms occupied for living purposes, to report this fact on Form 1008 (the "S" card).

Issued November 3, 1902.

Reissued September 14, 1903.

No. 28.

INTERPRETATION OF THE WORD "DISINFECTION" IN RELATION TO ACCUMULATIONS OF RUBBISH.

Inspectors are directed that where there is an accumulation of rubbish or other offensive material in the cellar or other parts of a tenement house, and the department has issued Orders 401, 402 or 404, requiring the disinfection of the site of such accumulation, that the cleansing of such site with a soda solution is sufficient disinfection. Inspectors must not report such orders as being complied with until this has been done.

Issued November 5, 1902.

Reissued September 14, 1903.

No. 29.

ACCUMULATIONS OF FILTH IN HOUSES DAMAGED BY FIRE AND UNOCCUPIED.

Inspectors are directed that where a tenement house has been damaged by fire, and there is an accumulation of filth or other offensive material therein, and the building is unoccupied, or is occupied by less than three (3) families, they should report this fact on Form 1008 (the "S" card), and should not report a violation.

Issued November 5, 1902.

Reissued September 14, 1903.

No. 31.

REMOVAL OF SCHOOL-SINKS, ETC.—DISINFECTION OF SITE TO BE SUPERVISED.

Inspectors are directed that where the department has issued an order to remove a school-sink, privy vault or latrine, and to provide water-closets, that before the violation is dismissed the removal of the iron trough and the demolition of the masonry vault must be viewed, and the disinfection of the site supervised by an inspector of this department.

The procedure in such cases should be as follows:

1. The removal of the iron trough.

2. A layer of quicklime should be sprinkled over it in the bottom of the pit, and this quicklime should be moistened.

3. The masonry should be demolished and tumbled into the pit, or should be entirely removed.

4. A second layer of quicklime should be laid over the tumbled in masonry and over the sides of the pit.

5. The excavation should then be filled in with fresh earth.

Issued November 7, 1902.

Reissued September 14, 1903.

No. 35.

PAN WATER-CLOSETS.

Inspectors are directed, in rendering a report in regard to a particular pan water-closet in a tenement house, to state whether there are other pan water-closets in the building, their number, location and condition.

Issued November 12, 1902.

Reissued September 14, 1903.

No. 36.

SMOKE FROM NEIGHBORING CHIMNEYS AND ODORS
FROM NEIGHBORING PLUMBING PIPES ENTERING WINDOWS
OF ADJOINING TENEMENTS.

Inspectors are directed, in cases where smoke from neighboring chimneys enters the windows of adjoining houses, or where foul odors from neighboring plumbing pipes enter similar windows, that no violation should be reported, but that a statement of the conditions should be made on Form 1008 (the "S" card).

Issued November 12, 1902.

Reissued September 14, 1903.

No. 42.

CASES OF CONTAGIOUS DISEASE TO BE REPORTED AS DISCOVERED.

Inspectors are directed that where they discover a case of contagious disease (other than tuberculosis) in a tenement house, and there is no sign posted by the Department of Health, that they should, upon leaving such building, immediately telephone this fact to the office, stating the street, the number of the house, the exact location of the particular apartment, the nature of the disease, the name of the tenant, and, if ascertainable, the age of the patient.

A written report confirming this information on Form 1008 (the "S" card), should be handed in on the following morning.

Cases of tuberculosis may be reported simply on a Form 1008 (the "S" card) without telephoning.

Issued, December 10, 1902.
Reissued, September 14, 1903.

No. 43.

VIOLATIONS FOR STABLES ON THE SAME LOT WITH TENEMENT HOUSES.

Inspectors are directed, when reporting the existence of a stable on the same premises with a tenement house, not to report a violation unless the stable is in an insanitary condition, and sufficiently so to be deemed a nuisance. In every case they must give the following information:

1. Whether the stable is in an in insanitary condition, and sufficiently so to be deemed a nuisance.
2. The number of horses actually kept on the premises.
3. The number of horses that the building can accommodate.

Issued, December 10, 1902.
Reissued, September 14, 1903.

No. 46.

FURNISHED ROOM HOUSES.

What is known ordinarily as a "furnished room house" will not, for the present at least, be deemed in the department a tenement house for the purpose of the Tenement House Act. A building of this type may be defined for departmental purposes as: "One occupied by single men or women, or by married couples living generally in one room to each domicile, having no independent washtubs or sinks, and having possibly a small stove for heating the room, upon which occasional meals are prepared."

In reporting in regard to such a house, a detailed statement as to the occupancy and arrangement should always be made, and where the inspector is of opinion that the house is a "furnished room house" no violation should be reported. Where, however, the inspector is in doubt, a violation should be reported, and the statement on a separate piece of paper that he is in doubt as to the classification of the building should be appended thereto.

Issued, January 9, 1903.
Reissued, September 14, 1903.

No. 49.

WATERPROOFING OF FLOORS IN CONNECTION WITH THE REMOVAL OF PAN AND SIMILAR WATER-CLOSETS.

Inspectors are directed, whenever reporting the existence of a pan, plunger, offset or long hopper water-closet, which should be replaced by a closet of modern type, that they must in every case state:

1st. Whether the compartment in which the fixture is located is lighted and ventilated by a window to the outer air. If such window does not open on the street, but on a yard, shaft or court, the dimensions of such space must be stated, and if a court or shaft, whether it is open or closed at the top.

2d. The size of the water-closet compartment.

3d. Whether there are other fixtures in the same compartment with the water-closet, and what such fixtures are.

4th. Where there are other fixtures, whether it is practicable to provide a waterproof slab under the new water-closet, extending across the entire end of the room, and if not, why not.

Issued January 22, 1903.
Reissued September 14, 1903.

No. 50.

INSUFFICIENT ROOF EGRESS.

Inspectors are directed that, wherever there is insufficient egress from the roof of a tenement house, because of the fact that egress to the adjoining building is shut off by means of a fence of any kind, that a violation should be reported, so that the fence in question may be removed, or a proper gate or door provided in such fence, such gate or door to be so fastened as to easily open from the inside by hook or otherwise, but without a lock.

Where there are fences on each side of a tenement house, and egress exists to one of the adjoining buildings, or can be provided, the inspector should understand that this is sufficient, and that it is not necessary to provide egress to both adjoining buildings.

Issued January 22, 1903.
Reissued September 14, 1903.

No. 56.

HOUSES UNFIT FOR HUMAN HABITATION.

Inspectors are directed at all times to call the attention of the department to all buildings (whether tenement houses or not) which they find, in their judgment, to be unfit for human habitation, stating their reasons therefor. Such report should be made on Form 1008 (the "S" card), and should state whether the building is a tenement house, and the number of families occupying it at the time of report.

Inspectors are cautioned to be conservative in their judgment as to whether a house is unfit for human habitation.

Issued February 13, 1903.
Reissued September 14, 1903.

No. 64.

BASEMENT AND CELLAR LIVING ROOMS.

Inspectors are directed, in making out the card report in relation to rooms in basements or cellars occupied for living purposes (the "B" card), to observe especially the following points:

1st. In each case a diagram of the particular rooms must be made.

2d. All windows, whether in exterior walls or in interior partitions, must be indicated on the diagram, and the size given, with the further statement as to whether they are fixed or made to open. A statement must be made as to what such windows open upon, whether the street, yard, court or shaft. If on a yard, court or shaft, the size must be given and the statement made whether it is an inner or outer court or shaft, and whether open or closed at the top.

Where such rooms are found to be technically in violation of Section 97 of the Tenement House Act in one or two particulars, such as the height of the ceiling above the curb or street, or where the height of the rooms is slightly less than that prescribed, it is not the intention of the department to prevent the use of such rooms for living purposes, provided they conform in all other respects to the provisions of the Tenement House Act, and are sufficiently light, are well drained and dry, and are fit for human habitation.

When an inspector reports that a room is not sufficiently light, he must state why, and what proportion of the room is so dark that he is not able to read, also the nature of the weather and the time of day when the report is made.

When an inspector reports that a room is not well drained and dry, he must state why, and must report in detail what conditions of dampness exist in the floors and walls, and the relation between the bottom of the adjoining yards, courts and shafts and the floors of the living room in question.

Where an inspector reports that a room is not fit for human habitation, it means that the room is actually in this condition, without reference to the technical violations which exist, and the inspector must state the facts which lead to this conclusion.

Where such rooms can readily be made to have sufficient light, to be well drained and dry, and to be fit for human habitation, the inspector should recommend the means by which this can be accomplished.

Issued April 7, 1903.

Reissued September 14, 1903.

No. 66.

INSPECTORS TO ACQUIRE PLUMBING KNOWLEDGE.

Inspectors are directed that they must, as rapidly as possible, familiarize themselves with the general principles of plumbing.

On and after June 1, 1903, the competency of the inspectors for this work will be a subject of inquiry.

Inspectors are advised to read current plumbing periodicals, such as "Domestic Engineering," as well as such books as the following:

"Sanitary Fittings and Plumbing," by G. Lister Sutcliffe; publishers, D. Van Nostrand Company.

"Drainage and Plumbing," by N. R. Maguire.

"House Drainage and Sanitary Plumbing," by W. P. Gerhard.

"Recent Practice in the Sanitary Drainage of Buildings," by W. P. Gerhard.

"Sanitary Engineering of Buildings," by W. P. Gerhard.

"Plumber and Sanitary Houses," by Hellyer.

"Practical Hygiene," by Harrington.

Most of the books referred to, as well as others on sanitary science, can be consulted at the library of the American Society of Civil Engineers, No. 220 West Fifty-seventh street, on all week days up to 10 P. M. Any of the inspectors will be welcome to make use of the privilege of this institution.

Issued April 17, 1903.

Reissued September 14, 1903.

No. 68.

SINKS ON STAIR LANDINGS.

Inspectors are directed that where a sink is provided on the stair landing half-way between two stories, or in a similar convenient location, that it is deemed a compliance with the provision of the Tenement House Act which requires that there be running water in one place on each floor.

Issued April 23, 1903.
Reissued September 14, 1903.

No. 74.

FIRE ESCAPE CERTIFICATE EXAMINATIONS.

Inspectors are directed in reporting results of examination of fire-escapes, where a fire-escape certificate has been applied for (Form 59), or an "F" card has been requested, that they should report on Form 59 or on 1006 the variations found, but should not report such variations on Form 137 (the violation form).

In making subsequent examinations, they should report only such variations as occur on the revised 1036, and which have not been remedied at the time of such subsequent inspection.

Issued April 30, 1903.
Reissued September 14, 1903.

No. 75.

GARBAGE AND ASH CANS.

Inspectors are directed, in reporting in relation to garbage and ash cans, to state in every case the following:

1st. Whether there are separate cans for garbage and ashes.
2d. The number of each.
3d. The material and approximate size.
4th. Their condition.
5th. Why they are not sufficient.
Issued May 2, 1903.
Reissued September 14, 1903.

No. 76.

ATTEMPTS AT BRIBERY.

Inspectors are directed to promptly report on Form 1008 (the "S" card) every attempt made by any one to influence their actions, directly or indirectly, either by bribe or otherwise, with full particulars, and all circumstances attending such attempt, including name, time and place.

Issued May 6, 1903, June 23, 1903.
Reissued September 14, 1903.

No. 78.

REMOVAL OF LONG HOPPER WATER-CLOSETS.

Inspectors are directed that, for the present, violations will not be reported for the removal of long hopper water-closets in tenement houses, except enameled iron pipe-wash long hopper fixtures when found to be defective, or in a badly corroded condition. Where other types of long hopper water-closets are found to be in a filthy condition, the fact should be so reported, so that an order to clean them may be issued.

Issued May 11, 1903.

Reissued September 14, 1903.

No. 81.

DEMOLISHED HOUSES.

Inspectors are directed to note all tenement houses that are demolished in their district, and to promptly report such fact on Form 1008 (the "S" card), describing the house by street and number. A house is not considered demolished until it is torn down to the ground or thereabouts.

Issued May 14, 1903.

Reissued September 14, 1903.

No. 82.

EMPLOYMENT AGENCIES IN TENEMENT HOUSES.

Inspectors are directed to report on Form 1008 (the "S" card) all apparent employment agencies that they may discover in tenement houses in the course of their work; whether such agencies are reputable or disreputable, genuine or bogus.

The inspector should give the location of the house, and state as follows:

Apparent employment agency in apartment (third floor, rear, north) (giving the name of the tenant, if possible).

No further information is desired; the report should be signed and dated by the inspector.

Issued May 19, 1903.

Reissued September 14, 1903.

No. 83.

CASES OF APPARENT POVERTY.

Inspectors are directed to report on Form 1008 (the "S" card) all cases of apparent poverty which they may discover in tenement houses in the course of their work. These reports should include the following information:

1. Location of the building.
2. Location of the particular apartment in which the persons reside.
3. The name of the person, and whether the person is Jewish or non-Jewish.

If the circumstances are exceptional, and the case seems an extreme one, this report should be made over the telephone and confirmed next morning by a card report.

Issued June 1, 1903.

Reissued September 14, 1903.

No. 84.

CASES OF APPARENT TUBERCULOSIS.

Inspectors are directed to report on Form 1008 (the "S" card) all cases of apparent tuberculosis that they may discover in tenement houses in the course of their work; such reports should include the following information:

1. Location of the house.
2. Location of the particular apartment in which the person resides.
3. The name and age of the patient, if possible.

The purpose of this inquiry is to enable the department to refer such cases to the Department of Health.

Issued June 1, 1903.

Reissued September 14, 1903.

No. 87.

ACCUMULATIONS OF HAY, STRAW, ETC., IN FRUIT CELLARS.

Inspectors are directed that where they find slight accumulations of hay, straw and similar material in fruit cellars, used in connection with the storage of fruit, that no violation for the storage of material of this kind should be reported, unless the quantity stored is plainly in excess of the amount required for the carrying on of a business of this nature or is clearly and without question an excessive amount, and objectionable from the fire point of view or from the sanitary point of view.

Issued June 9, 1903.

Reissued September 14, 1903.

No. 89.

INSUFFICIENT WATER-CLOSET ACCOMMODATIONS.

Inspectors are directed, in investigating complaints in relation to insufficient water-closet accommodations to note carefully whether there are sufficient water-closet accommodations for the living apartments of the house, and in addition to note whether there are sufficient independent water-closet accommodations for the use of such stores as may be located in the building.

In regard to the sufficiency of accommodations for families, Section 100 of the Tenement House Act will govern; in regard to the insufficiency of accommodations for the use of stores in the building, inspectors will not report violations unless there has been a complaint made, or unless there are clearly serious sanitary abuses resulting from the lack of such accommodations.

In reporting insufficient water-closet accommodations for stores, inspectors must always give the following information:

1. The number of persons using each fixture.
2. Whether there are separate fixtures for the different sexes.
3. What sanitary abuses exist.
4. Whether the fixture is accessible from each store, or from the public parts of the building.
Issued June 19, 1903.
Reissued September 14, 1903.

No. 93.

REPORTS AS TO OCCUPANCY AND ARRANGEMENT OF BUILDINGS.

Inspectors are directed that when they are requested to report how a building is occupied or arranged, they must state in detail both the occupancy and arrangement on each floor. They should note especially what arrangements for living purposes in the nature of fixtures exist, especially wash-tubs, stoves, water-closets and sinks, also the presence of cooking utensils.

Such reports must be arranged in accordance with the sample accompanying this letter. Each report should state at the beginning:

"I respectfully report inspection of above premises (date) The building is occupied and arranged as follows:"

A blank line should be left after this introductory statement. There should then follow the headings running across the card:

Story. Use. Apts. Occupancy. Fixtures.

as shown in the sample, which should be filled out for each story of the building. These columns should be totaled at the bottom, and the report should end with the statement from the inspector as to whether the building is a tenement house or not.

Issued, July 1, 1903.
Reissued, September 21, 1903.

I respectfully report inspection of above premises on . . . . Building is occupied and arranged as follows:

Story.	Use.	Apartments.	Occupancy.	Fixtures.
Cellar	Storage	0		
First	2 stores	2	2 families	Sink in each apartment, 1 water-closet in hall.
Second . . .	Living	4	4 families	Sink in each apartment, 2 water closets in hall.
Third	Living	4	4 families	Sink in each apartment, 2 water closets in hall.
Fourth . . .	Living	4	4 families	Sink in each apartment, 2 water-closets in hall.
Fifth	Living	4	4 families	Sink in each apartment, 2 water-closets in hall.

Total, 18 families—a tenement house.

John Smith,
Inspector.

No. 94.

INSANITARY CONDITIONS TO BE REPORTED.

Inspectors are directed when investigating a complaint in relation to a specific matter, that they should note at the same time all general insanitary conditions at the premises, and report such violations as may be found, giving especial attention to accumulations of filth and rubbish, as well as notable defects in the plumbing.

Issued, July 2, 1903.

Reissued, September 14, 1903.

No. 96.

INSANITARY BAKERIES IN TENEMENT HOUSES.

Inspectors are directed, when in the course of their work they discover a bakery in a tenement house, the light or ventilation of which is inadequate, or where there are foul odors, fumes or noxious gases from such bakery which constitute a nuisance, or the bakery is in an insanitary condition, that a report of these facts should be made on Form 1008 (the "S" card), so that the attention of the State Factory inspector may be called to these conditions. No violation should be reported.

Issued, July 6, 1903.

Reissued, September 14, 1903.

No. 97.

OIL-SOAKED WOODWORK, OR OTHER DANGEROUS FIRE CONDITIONS.

Inspectors are directed, when in the course of their work they discover oil-soaked woodwork in cellars, or other parts of tenement houses, or other conditions which render a building dangerous in case of fire, to report this fact on Form 1008 (the "S" card), so that the matter may be referred to the Fire Department. No violation should be reported.

Issued, July 6, 1903.

Reissued, September 14, 1903.

No. 98.

COMPLAINTS IN REGARD TO QUALITY OF WATER IN TENEMENT HOUSES.

Inspectors are directed, when investigating complaints in relation to the quality of the water supply, that they must first determine whether there is a roof tank.

If there is no roof tank, no further investigation is necessary.

If there is a roof tank, the first thing to determine is whether the sides and bottom of the tank are clean. This can seldom be determined if the tank is full at the time of inspection; the inspector should arrange with the janitor to have the water drawn off at an appointed time, so that he may reinspect, to determine the conditions and report a violation if the tank is found unclean.

Issued August 4, 1903.

Reissued September 14, 1903.

No. 101.

UNUSUAL AND STRIKING CONDITIONS TO BE REPORTED.

Inspectors are directed whenever in the course of their work they encounter unusual and striking conditions, to make a brief report, in popular form, of the facts observed, on Form 1008 (the "S" card).

The purpose of this requirement is to enable the department to have a series of illustrative cases explaining its work.

Issued August 10, 1903.

Reissued September 14, 1903.

No. 104.

PAN CLOSETS.

Inspectors are directed whenever reporting in relation to a pan water-closet found to be in an unsanitary condition, that they must in every case state the following facts:

1st. Whether the condition of the closet is such as to constitute a nuisance.

2d. The condition of the receivers, whether they are corroded and foul, and contain incrustations of fecal matter.

3d. Similar statements should also be made in regard to the condition of the exposed portions of the fixture.

4th. The type of flushing apparatus for the closet, viz.: whether valve or from a tank.

Issued August 13, 1903.

Reissued September 14, 1903.

No. 109.

DOORS FROM PAINT, OIL, DRUG AND LIQUOR STORES.

Inspectors are directed, in reporting violations of section 42 of the Tenement House Act, in relation to doors leading from stores in tenement houses where paint, oil, liquors or drugs are kept or sold, that in every case the inspector must state the material of the partition in which the doors or other openings exist, viz.: Whether brick wall, lath and plaster or sheathing.

In fireproofing doors leading from such stores the department requires that the doors shall be of metal or be covered with metal on both sides and edges; the jambs and trim need be covered with metal on the store side only.

Issued August 26, 1903.

Reissued September 14, 1903.

No. 112.

FIREPROOF FURRING STRIPS IN BAKERY CEILINGS.

Inspectors are directed that the department will not at present accept as "fireproof furring strips" strips of any material except plaster board, metal or terra cotta.

It should be distinctly understood that "fireproof wood" furring strips are not permitted.

Issued August 29, 1903.
Reissued September 14, 1903.

No. 114.

LEAKY ROOFS.

Inspectors are directed that before reporting a violation in reference to a leak in a roof, they must have satisfactory evidence that the defect exists. A stained ceiling or wall in a particular apartment is not deemed sufficient evidence, unless it is damp or wet at the time of the inspection. In every case where there are such stains the inspector should ascertain, before reporting a violation, whether the roof has been repaired or whether the leak still exists. A water-stained ceiling is not insanitary.

Inspectors should not recommend for dismissal violations for leaky roofs until the roof has been tested by at least one rain storm after it has been repaired.

If they report the violation "not complied with" for this reason solely, they should make a full explanation on such report.

Issued September 14, 1903.

No. 115.

VIOLATIONS RELATING SOLELY TO ACCUMULATIONS OF FILTH AND RUBBISH.

Inspectors are directed that where the sole violation found as a result of inspection is an accumulation of filth or rubbish, that they need not report such violation on Form 137, but in every case report the fact on Form 1008 (the "S" card).

It should be clearly understood that this direction relates only to cases where the sole violation is of this nature. If there are violations of any other nature found, then all violations must be reported on Form 137.

Issued September 14, 1903.

No. 124.

SKYLIGHT VENTILATION IN OLD BUILDINGS.

Inspectors are directed to note for their information the following points in connection with the provisions of the Tenement House Law in relation to ventilation of skylights in now existing tenement houses.

1. Houses that have Halls with Windows to the Outer Air—In this class of building all the law requires is either ridge ventilators or louvres. The louvres may be fixed or movable, at the option of the owner.

2. Houses that have Halls with no Windows to the Outer Air:

   a. Where the Halls Are Steam Heated—In such houses the law requires that there shall be ridge ventilators and louvres. The louvres may be fixed or movable, at the option of the owner.

   b. Where the Halls are not Steam Heated—The requirements of the law in relation to this class of houses divides itself into two classes:

      1. Houses Over Four Stories or Containing Over Four Families—In such houses the law requires ridge ventilators and fixed louvres.

2. Houses that are not Over Four Stories and do not Contain Over Four Families—In such houses the law requires ridge ventilators and louvres, but the louvres may be fixed or movable, at the option of the owner.

Accompanying this letter will be found a diagramatic explanation of the above provisions of law.

Issued September 21, 1903.

No. 125.

WIRE OR STEEL CABLE FIRE ESCAPES.

Inspectors are directed that the department has approved solely for use in tenement houses which are less than four stories in height, and which also do not contain accommodations for more than four families in all, certain wire or steel cable fire escapes, as provided for in Section 12 of the Tenement House Act. A building three stories and basement in height is deemed for the purpose of this section a building less than four stories in height.

The fire escapes approved are as follows:

The Harris fire escape, a sample of which is on file in the office of the department.

Inspectors should be careful to note the following points:

1. Each apartment above the ground floor must be provided with not less than one such fire escape.

2. Such fire escape must be of sufficient length to reach the ground.

3. It must be constantly maintained ready for use both as respects its location and condition.

4. The rungs must be not less than fifteen inches long and not more than twelve inches apart.

5. Such fire escapes must comply in every respect with the provisions of Section 12 of the Tenement House Act relating thereto.

A Straight Vertical Ladder—The details of the specifications for the construction of this fire escape are set forth in the printed circular accompanying this letter.

Inspectors are advised that it is not necessary to obtain special permission from the department to install either of the above fire escapes in tenement houses less than four stories in height, and which are not arranged to accommodate more than four families. Inspectors are cautioned against giving any contrary impression to the public or against expressing a personal opinion as to the relative merits of different kinds of fire escapes.

Issued September 21, 1903.

No. 126.

WIDTH OF NEW STAIRS ON EXISTING FIRE ESCAPE BALCONIES.

Inspectors are directed that where an order is issued by the department to equip existing fire escape balconies with stairways, and the present balconies are not of sufficient width to permit stairs twenty inches wide, and also to leave a passageway of fourteen inches between the stairs and the wall of the house, or the outer rail of the balcony, as the case may be, that the department will, in such cases, permit the construction of stairs sixteen inches wide in the clear instead of twenty inches wide, thus leaving a clear passageway of thirteen inches.

This information is solely for the use of the inspectors. If new stairs are this width, the violation must not be dismissed unless a modification to this effect has been granted by the Executive Division.

Issued September 21, 1903.

No. 127.

CLEANING OF WALLS, CEILINGS, WOODWORK AND WATER-CLOSETS IN INDIVIDUAL APARTMENTS.

Inspectors are directed that it is not the policy of the department, at the present time, to issue violations requiring owners of tenement houses to clean the walls, ceilings, woodwork and water-closet floors in individual apartments which are solely within the control of the tenants. Such orders should be limited entirely to the public parts of the building, for which the owner is responsible.

When an inspector finds accumulations of filth or filthy water-closets in individual apartments that are tenanted, and the conditions require prompt remedy, he should report such facts upon Form 1008 (the "S" card), but should not report a violation.

When an apartment or store is vacant, it is to be considered as a public part of the building, and, if conditions warrant, a violation should be reported, as under such circumstances it is appropriate to send a notice to the owner. A statement to the effect that the apartment or store is vacant should be included in the report of violation.

Issued September 21, 1903.

No. 136.

HINGING OF SCUTTLES.

Inspectors are directed to report that a scuttle requires hinging if it is not easily practicable for the ordinary female tenants of the house in question to lift the scuttle in case of fire.

Issued September 21, 1903.

No. 137.

INADEQUATE WATER SUPPLY.

Inspectors are directed, in making examinations in reference to complaint of inadequate water supply, and reporting violations in relation thereto, to state in every case the following:

1. The day of the week (Monday, Tuesday, etc.) on which the inspection was made, and the time (11.10 A. M.).

2. At what specific floors and apartments in the building the water supply is inadequate.

3. Whether inadequate to flush water-closets or simply inadequate for sinks, tubs or baths.

4. Whether there are pumps or similar appliances for the sinks, tubs or water-closets, as the case may be, and whether such pumps are in use. (In

this connection it should be understood that the department does not permit the use of hand pumps as the sole means of flushing water-closets.)

5. Whether there is a roof tank on the building.

6. Whether there is a power pump in the cellar to force water to the roof tank.

7. Whether the supply in the upper story, or in the particular apartment in question, does not flow when a faucet in one of the lower stories is open; if so, the size of the rising lines must be given.

8. The adequacy of the water supply in the upper story in adjoining houses on each side of the building in question, and whether such adjoining houses have roof tanks.

9. What is necessary to make the water supply adequate.

Before dismissing a violation for inadequate water supply, the inspector must make a definite report on the following points:

1. What has actually been done at the building to remedy the conditions originally found defective. Thus:

(A roof tank has been provided; a power pump has been placed in the cellar; the defect was in the water main in that district, which has been remedied by the Water Department in the following manner:)

2. The inspector must state that he has made inquiry of the tenants in the upper story; and also in the apartment where the supply had been inadequate, and that the tenants report such supply now to be adequate.

3. The inspector must test the water-closets and the flow at the sink foucets throughout the upper story and throughout the apartments where the supply had previously been inadequate, and if not found adequate he must not dismiss the violation.

4. His report must include a statement as to the day of the week and the time at which such inspection prior to dismissal is made.

Issued September 21, 1903.

No. 140.

REPLACEMENT OF WATER-CLOSETS, TUBS AND OTHER FIXTURES IN BASEMENT AND CELLAR ROOMS.

Inspectors are directed, in reporting in relation to water-closets, wash tubs, sinks or other fixtures in basement or cellars where the replacement of the fixture is involved, to append to the violation in every case a note as to whether such fixture is used in connection with basement or cellar living rooms, and if so, whether the rooms are lawful or unlawful; if unlawful, stating why. It will not be necessary to make out a "B" card, but there should be a definite statement in the report as above indicated.

The reason for requiring such report is that the department does not desire to order owners to replace such defective water-closets or wash tubs if the apartments in question are unlawful and these fixtures will ultimately have to be removed.

Issued September 21, 1903.

No. 141.

UNLAWFUL BASEMENT OR CELLAR ROOMS.

Inspectors are directed that wherever the department has issued an order to discontinue the use of basement or cellar rooms for living purposes, before such violations can be dismissed not only must the tenants vacate, but all wash tubs, baths, etc., which may have existed, must be removed and the openings sealed.

Issued September 21, 1903.

No. 142.

ACCESS TO APARTMENTS NOT OBTAINED—TENANTS ABSENT.

Inspectors are directed, in making an inspection on a complaint, "U" card or "CU" card, where they are unable to obtain access to certain apartments because of the absence of the tenants, that they should in every case make a second visit to the apartment in question, if possible arranging beforehand with the janitor for a definite hour at which access can be obtained.

If access cannot be obtained upon the second visit, the report should be turned in, stating the day and hour of both visits, but without the information in relation to this particular apartment, and an abstract should be made on a separate "S" card, calling attention to this fact, so that this matter may be placed in the hands of a special inspector and be taken up at some subsequent date.

In this connection, where inspectors find pan or other objectionable types of water-closet throughout a building, but are unable to state positively that there are pan-closets in certain apartments because they could not obtain access to such apartments after two visits, they should assume that the type of closets in the particular apartment in question is the same as the type of closets throughout the building, and report a violation accordingly. A statement to this effect, however, should be appended in the form of a note to the violation.

Issued September 21, 1903.

No. 143.

DISUSED PLUMBING FIXTURES.

Inspectors are directed that where disused plumbing fixtures are found care should be taken to note whether such fixtures are located in a store or apartment which is temporarily vacant.

If the disused fixture is a school-sink, privy vault or latrine, it should be so reported, so that it may be ordered removed. If the disused fixtures are wash trays located in unlawful basement or cellar living rooms, a report to this effect should be made.

In every case care should be taken to note whether the fixtures are necessary and are likely to be used again. In every case there must be a definite statement that the seal of the trap has evaporated before a violation is reported.

Issued September 21, 1903.

FRANCIS R. COPE JR.

Tenement House Reform: Its Practical Results in the "Battle Row" District, New York[†]

The present paper does not attempt to deal with the whole housing problem. It is simply a small contribution to a certain phase of that problem—the question of the erection and management of "model" tenement houses by private corporations—based largely on practical observation.

In order to accomplish the best results the writer thought it expedient to limit his studies in this case to a certain section of New York city where both bad tenements and good tenements existed side by side, and then to compare the leading features of both and show the influence which the latter were having upon the former. Accordingly he sought an interview with the president of the company which recently erected the new buildings on the borders of the "Battle Row" district, Dr. E. R. L. Gould, who was kind enough to place at his disposal much of his own vast store of knowledge on tenement-house reform, and especially his experience as the head of the City and Suburban Homes Company. Besides this valuable interview with Dr. Gould, I made a personal inspection of the model tenements on E. Sixty-fourth street, gathered much valuable information from their matron, Miss Geary, and then endeavored to get some idea of the character of the old-style tenements and the population of the neighboring district.

Whatever value, therefore, this paper may have will be due largely to personal observation of things as they actually exist in a certain corner of the largest city in the United States, rather than to any general knowledge of the subject. And I trust enough actual facts have been revealed to show that the tenement-house-reform problem is full of hope, and that it has already been, and therefore can be in the future, at least partially solved on the principles and methods of Dr. Gould's semi-philanthropic company.

I. Origin and Importance of the Housing Problem.

The marvelous growth of cities in the United States has already become a commonplace fact. The once startling announcement that during the last hundred years the number of persons living in cities of over 5,000 inhabitants had increased from about 3 per cent. in 1790 to over 29 per cent. in 1890 no longer causes any unusual comment. And yet this steady movement of population from the rural districts goes on at an ever-increasing rate. One has but to travel through the mountainous farming districts of New England or the Middle States to observe the restlessness of the country people. Everywhere the young farmers of pluck and energy are seeking a new outlet for their abilities. The farming districts of the East are altogether too slow for them, and they either turn to the cities or else go west to where there is "more doing." And what is the result? A steady decrease in the numbers and character of our rural population, and a steady rise in the population of our larger towns and cities.

† *The American Journal of Sociology* 7.3 (1901).

Nor is this steady increase in urban life confined to the United States. On the contrary, it is one of the great movements of the times, and one that is going on in European countries, and especially in England, just as in our own land. But it is to the United States that I wish mainly to confine my remarks in the present paper, not alone because this is a field which is naturally the most interesting, but because it offers exceptional opportunities for a study of the housing problem.

Add now to this growth in city population, caused by the constant influx of persons from the country, the tremendous increase from foreign immigration, and we see at once the chief cause of the overcrowding of the working classes. Such, then, is the *origin* of the tenement-house problem.

The *importance* of the housing conditions in our large cities and its far-reaching effect on the morals and physical capacity of our citizens should be self-evident. And yet it is in but very recent years that the subject has received any serious attention in America. New Yorkers march up and down Fifth avenue, ride in and out every day from their cosy, comfortable homes in the suburbs to the fashionable shopping and business quarters of the city, and perhaps never dream that but a few blocks away, down in the lower portion of Manhattan Island and up along the East and West Side, there is massed together a vast body of human beings who have no place to live in but a dark, crowded, filthy, and half-ventilated tenement house. If these good people of New York, these wealthy men and women who can afford to live in comfortable homes, would only visit the slums of their own city and see with their own eyes how many of their fellow-citizens are forced to live in dwellings unfit for any human habitation, they would no longer stand idly by, but would be up in arms in support of a reform movement which would sweep away forever these death-breeding, crime-breeding hovels!

This may sound like mere sensation, but it is a very mild statement of the actual conditions which prevail today in some of the largest and wealthiest cities of the United States. And besides, it takes strong language to arouse the American citizen. The whole history of the tenement-house problem in New York, from 1834 to the present time, is but the history of sporadic and widely separated movements in favor of reform. Thus, for instance, the Gilder Commission of 1894, while it did much good by arousing public sentiment on this subject for the time being, failed to accomplish any sweeping reform simply because public interest soon flagged again.

But if now anyone still doubts that the proper housing of the poor in our large cities is one of the most vitally important social problems of the present day, let him do what the writer did a few weeks ago—take even a casual walk through part of what is known as the "Ghetto" district in New York. Let him pass along Rutgers street to Division and up Division to Suffolk and Rivington and Ludlow streets. I venture to predict that he will no longer question my assertion. It was in this quarter of the city that I saw the streets filled with a mob of Hebrews—men, women, and children. The sidewalks were jammed with ragged men and boys selling bread and other necessaries; the streets were filled with a swarm of children who have no possible place to play except among the heaps of refuse and filth that line the gutters. Many of the individuals were scarcely clothed at all, even on cold winter days; others carried around them but a bundle of rags. One sees a few cheerful, smiling faces, but many more tired and haggard ones, and all begrimed with dirt. The odor, too, that fills these streets is something one cannot soon forget; and when, on one or two occasions, I ventured inside a tenement house, the absence of any proper ventilation made the stench arising from the filthy halls and living-rooms almost unendurable. Does anyone still doubt the facts? Then let him remember that in this district of the tenth ward there was, according to the careful estimate of the Gilder Commission of 1894, an average density of population of 700 persons per acre![1]

It is not within the limits of the present paper to give any detailed account of the tenement-house problem in New York. Nevertheless it may be interesting in this connection to record that this same Gilder Commission, in one wing of its investigations, found a population of 255,033 persons, out of which only 306 had access to bath-rooms in the houses in which they lived.

Here is a population larger than that of Providence, R. I.; Newark, N. J.; Minneapolis or St. Paul; Omaha, Indianapolis, or Kansas City; and only a shade smaller than Washington, D. C., or New Orleans; with only 306 persons able to take a bath in the houses in which they lived.[2]

Again, in the same department of investigation 15,726 families, numbering 67,897 persons, or an average of 4⅓ persons to the family, were found living in tenements of an average size of 284.4 square feet of floor area. To obtain an idea of the contraction of these quarters we have but to measure an ordinary-sized room, say 12×24 feet, and we find it to contain 288 square feet in floor space. And, besides the small size of the apartments, it must be remembered that these were in old, filth-soaked buildings without any decent ventilation or plumbing facilities.

It is no wonder that under such conditions the death-rate among children under five years of age runs up to 254.4 per thousand, while under the most favorable conditions it is only 30 per thousand. This is a "slaughter of the innocents," compared with which the butchery of Herod, over which centuries of Christendom have shuddered, sinks into insignificance. Under the same conditions, too, the general death-rate rises from an average of 21.03 for the entire city to 61.97 per thousand. The horror of this is intensified by the fact that adequate experiments in many of the largest cities of the world have proved that this murder may be prevented by properly built houses, with plenty of light and air, and generous bathing facilities—in all of which New York is criminally behind the age, so far as concerns her city wage-earning population.

What can we expect in the way of character and morals from persons brought up under such conditions as these? What kind of citizens will the children make when they have been reared under the influences of such an environment? What kind of fathers and mothers will they make to the children of the next generation? What kind of a purification of politics can we hope for in the future from men who have been brought up in an atmosphere

1. *Report of the New York Tenement-House Committee of 1894,* Table 1, pp. 266, 267. According to the police census of 1895, two blocks in this district contained an average of 1,526 and 1,774 persons respectively per acre.
2. *Review of Reviews,* Vol. XVI, p. 695.

of crime and drunkenness, who have been taught to cheat and believe in the righteousness of the principle that "to the victors belong the spoils"? It is this thought of the hopelessness of ever trying to educate to a high standard of morality the boys and girls who are brought up in the atmosphere of the average New York tenement of today, that impresses upon us the importance of this housing problem. It is the certain knowledge of the life of sickness and misery, of crime and impurity, to which the thousands and thousands of poor little children in the New York slums are doomed, which has led to the recent movements in that city for a radical reform of the living conditions of the poor. And it is this sad knowledge of similar conditions in Boston and Chicago, and other large cities, that should rouse all citizens to the importance and influence of the home life on character and morals.

Listen to what Governor Roosevelt said in his address at the Tenement House Exhibition in New York in 1900:

> I have come from Albany to be here this evening because it seems to me, literally, that on the whole no movement is so vital to the well-being of our people as that into a part of which you are looking now. If we succeed in upbuilding the material and, therefore, moral side of what is the foundation of the real life of the Greater New York, we shall have taken a longer stride than is possible in any other way toward a solution of the great civic problems with which we are confronted.
>
> Go and look through the charts downstairs, which show the centers of disease and poverty, and remember that it is there that the greatest number of votes are cast. We hear complaints of corruption in the city government of New York, but how can we expect the stream to rise so very far when the source is polluted? We have got to strive for the elementary physical benefit of the people first.
>
> Every wretched tenement that a city allows to exist revenges itself on the city by being a hotbed of disease and pauperism. It tends steadily to lower the tone of our city life and of our social life. The present movement for better tenement houses is an effort to cut at the roots of the diseases which eat at the body social and the body politic.[3]

Even that far-sighted social reformer, Arnold Toynbee, speaking of the dwellings of the working people in 1882, said:

> The importance of the home it is impossible to exaggerate. What is liberty without it? What is education in schools without it? The greatness of no nation can be secure that is not based upon a pure home life. But is a pure life possible under present conditions for the bulk of the laboring class? I answer, No. I do not deny that artisans have good dwellings in many towns; but I assert that the dwellings of the great mass of people are a danger to our civilization. . . . . People have no idea of the universality of the evil.[4]

So much for the moral and ethical aspects of the question. It remains for us to consider the importance of the housing problem in its economic and physical effects.

3. *Charities*, February 11, 1900, pp. 6, 7.
4. Quoted by BALDWIN, *The Housing Problem*, p. 3. See also DR. E. R. L. GOULD's article, "The Housing Problem in Great Cities," *Municipal Affairs*, March, 1899, p. 110.

In the first place, bad housing means a bad distribution of wealth, and this again means high rents for poor accommodations and a heavy tax upon the income of the working class. Now, careful investigations have shown it to be a notorious fact that there is no better-paying property than cheap unsanitary tenement houses. Thus witnesses before investigating committees in New York have cited instances of rents of 100 per cent. and more upon the value of the property. The Boston tenement house census of 1891 showed that the average return to owners of 646 tenements found to be in bad sanitary condition was 12½ per cent. upon the assessed valuation. Seventeen unsanitary houses in Ward 6, at the North End, yielded 15 per cent. In London also it has been ascertained that in some districts 42 per cent. of the *poor* population pay from one-fifth to one-fourth of their earnings in rent; 46 per cent. from one-fourth to one-half; while only 12 per cent. pay less than one-fifth.[5] Yet economists tell us that 20 per cent. of the wages of the head of the family should be the maximum outlay for rents in the city.

The cause of this increase in rents is obviously in the constantly increasing demand for housing accommodations. In other words, it is due to the overcrowding and congestion of the population in our large cities. And this in turn is traceable to three different causes, viz.: (1) natural increase, especially among the poor classes; (2) immigration; (3) encroachments of business upon the poorer residence sections.

Regarding the high birth-rate among the lower classes little need be said, for it is a well-known fact that the natural rate of increase is much higher among the low strata of society than among the high. And this in itself would be sufficient to produce overcrowding and high rents.

As to immigration, it is impossible to obtain any reliable data, for the simple reason that we have no means of telling what proportion of the immigrants to the United States remain in the cities in which they land. However, it is interesting to note the figures furnished by the United States commission at Ellis Island, N. Y., and quoted by the Tenement House Committee of 1894:[6]

	Total to United States	Total Arriving at New York	Total Destined to New York
Year ending June 30, 1891	560,319	405,664	169,841
Year ending June 30, 1892	579,663	445,987	234,311
Year ending June 30, 1893	439,730	343,422	153,223
Year ending June 30, 1894	285,631	219,046	91,109

It will be seen that 45.85 per cent. of all the immigrants landed at New York city were destined at least to the *state* of New York. But in any case the percentage of foreign-born citizens in the United States must be very great, the New York committee[7] placing the foreign-born whites of the city of New York as comprising 42 8/10 per cent. (not counting the nearly 26,000 of African descent born in America) of the total population.[8]

5. *Cf.* Baldwin, *The Housing Problem*, p. 4.
6. *Report of the New York Tenement-House Committee of 1894*, p. 9.
7. *Report of the New York Tenement-House Committee of 1894*, p. 10.
8. Taken from United States census of 1890.

The third cause of overcrowding—the encroachment of business upon the poorer residence sections—is well illustrated by what is now taking place in the North and West Ends of Boston. Thus, as Professor Baldwin says, "the high rents of tenement-house property, which severely handicap the working class, are seen to be the natural result of increasing demand and diminishing supply."

But there are other important economic aspects of the housing question which should be mentioned, viz.: (1) low productive efficiency of the working classes as the direct results of disease and bad housing; (2) drunkenness; (3) crime.

First, let us consider the low productive efficiency of many laboring men due to disease brought on by bad housing. Good health certainly means good earning power, other things being equal, and as most workingmen lead a hand-to-mouth existence, any loss of earning power is naturally a serious matter. Indeed, few people seem to realize the loss of productive energy through sickness brought on by bad living environment. Sir James Paget, the distinguished English physician, estimates that the loss inflicted upon English wage-earners amounts to over fifteen millions of dollars annually. Yet this is a purely preventable loss, he adds. Some years ago, also, the London health authorities instituted inquiries in certain congested neighborhoods to estimate the value of labor lost in a year, not by sickness, but from sheer exhaustion caused by bad living conditions. The result of this inquiry was the knowledge that, upon the lowest estimate, every workman lost, on an average, about twenty days each year from this cause. Dr. E. R. L. Gould, of New York, bears testimony on this point when he says that

> The economic value of sanitary reform has never been fully appreciated. The loss to any nation by allowing unsanitary conditions to prevail is simply tremendous. It is likewise twofold. There is, in the first place, a great waste of productive power which might otherwise have been utilized; and, secondly, there is the expense of maintenance of hospitals and pauper institutions, a large number of the inmates of which are recruited through sickness caused by unhealthy living environment.

Again, bad housing is undoubtedly one of the principal causes of drunkenness and crime. How can we expect any reform in the matter of intemperance so long as the cheerless, unhealthy home of many a laboring man compels him to seek the relaxation and companionship which are always centered about the saloon? Instead of making the home the most attractive spot on earth, we have, in hundreds of thousands of cases in our large cities, permitted it to become a veritable pest hole of disease and crime. I say "we" have permitted this state of affairs to exist, because it is an absolute fact that the "upper half," the rich and well-to-do, are in many cases directly responsible for the misery of the poor. It has been clearly demonstrated, I think, that it lies in our power, if not wholly to remove the unhealthy and cheerless surroundings of the city poor, at least in large measure to improve those surroundings and make them more cheerful. But for the present let me leave this discussion of remedies and their actual effects, and simply mention a few facts regarding the intimate connection between drunkenness and bad housing. Of course, it is dangerous to go too far in our search for cause and effect in conjunction with circumstances, yet, as Dr. Gould has remarked, "the sequel to the massing of saloons in low neighborhoods where the worst housing conditions exist is more than a coincidence."[9] Take, for example, the undisputed fact that the most crowded districts of New York are also the districts where liquor saloons are most numerous and most profitable. Thus in one place there are 148 saloons all located within a space 514 yards long by 375 yards wide! It is the same, or perhaps even worse, in many European cities. In Edinburgh, too, in St. Giles' ward there are 127 drinking places to 234 shops where food is sold. And we have a fair index to patronage in the fact that the rental of the latter amounts to only 80 per cent. of the rental of the former. This ward contains one-eleventh of the total population of the city, and it furnishes just about one-third of its crime. In spite of the fact that 17½; per cent. of its area is made up of parks, the death-rate is 40 per cent. higher than for the whole city. Then, again, Glasgow's famous district No. 14 contains upward of 43 public schoolhouses to 104 premises for food, and the rental of the former exceeds the latter. "This district consumes more life than it produces," not to speak of the fact that it entails enormous burdens upon public and private charity.[1]

In the light of these few simple facts, can anyone longer deny the vital importance of the housing problem in our great cities? Can one longer deny the fact that the main hope for a solution of the political, civic, and labor troubles, which are bound to be the great problems of the twentieth century, rests upon providing a pure, healthy home life, where character and morals are most firmly molded? Once surround the masses with wholesome, uplifting conditions, where virtue will become easy and crime difficult, and more than half the fight which is being waged for a pure city government and an honest ballot will have been won. That such a reform in the living conditions of the working classes is not only *possible*, but that it has actually been tried and found *profitable* in the largest and perhaps the most corrupt city in America, it is the object of the present paper to show.

II. The Reform Movement and Its Practical Results in the "Battle Row" District, New York.

In the first place, what is the so-called "Battle Row" district, and where is it located?

In answer to the above question it may be said that, roughly speaking, all that small district in New York city which lies between First avenue on the west and the East River on the east, and between Fifty-ninth street on the south and Sixty-fourth street on the north, was known in local terminology as the "Battle Row." The name was derived from the fact that in former years the population of the district was composed almost exclusively of Irish, who, being suddenly invaded by an army of Bohemian immigrants, put up a determined and sometimes bloody defense against the newcomers. For years, while this fight was going on, the district acquired a decidedly unsavory reputation. Many crimes were committed within its borders, and an open street fight between an invader and one of the old inhabitants

9. GOULD, "The Housing Problem in Great Cities," *Municipal Affairs*, March, 1899, p. 110.
1. *Cf.* GOULD, *op. cit.*, p. 110.

was not by any means an uncommon occurrence. Gradually, however, the Irish gave way, until today they are outnumbered by both Germans and natives. But the bad reputation which this neighborhood acquired and its significant name still remain.

Such, then, was and is still the character of the district visited by the writer early in December, 1900; and it is to this district that I shall now confine my remarks.

What, now, did I see on my recent visit? Mostly large tenement houses from five to six stories high; also some smaller ones of two and three stories; and here and there, near the river, even a few old *wooden,* but very dingy and delapidated dwelling-houses. The streets in the district, from Fifty-ninth to Sixty-fourth street, are not particularly narrow and only moderately dirty. Indeed, compared with the "Ghetto" down-town the whole neighborhood might almost be called a little heaven. This, however, makes it none the less interesting, because, as we shall presently see, the man who recently erected the famous model tenement houses on the borders of the "Battle Row" district purposely chose for his experiment a part of the city representing the middle rather than the lowest strata of the working classes. But let us examine more closely the character of the average tenement house in the "Battle Row."

And, first of all, what do we find the typical old-style tenement, which comprises perhaps three-fourths of all the dwelling-houses of the district, to be like? I visited upward of fifteen of these, and all appeared to be much alike. They were not as bad as some of the down-town houses, but they were bad enough. All had long, dark hallways, and in all the only light and ventilation to which the rooms not immediately bordering on the street had access was that which came from a long, dark air-shaft. ⁎ ⁎ ⁎ Such shafts I found to be thoroughly representative of the kind used in the old-style tenement of the "Battle Row;" and it should be added that their average length and height for a five-story building was about 40 and 50 feet respectively, and the average width was not more than 2 feet 5 inches. When we remember that all the bedrooms in those houses which I visited were backrooms, and that their only contact with fresh air of any kind was through one small window opening onto one of these air-shafts, we get some idea of the misery and suffering which their inmates must be forced to endure. And when we remember, too, that most of the inhabitants live in suites of three rooms each, with two persons to a room, measuring on an average not more than 11×7 feet, we get a still more vivid picture of life in an old-style tenement in the "Battle Row."[2]

Such is the plan and arrangement of the old-style building; but how about the habits and cleanliness of the tenants? In many cases this is disgusting and almost beyond description. For instance, in two of the apartments visited the halls were literally deep in filth, while the bottom of the air-shafts, which were supposed to supply the bedrooms with fresh air, were in an even worse condition. I stepped inside the living-rooms, and in each case I found three adults and four children occupying a floor space 14×8 feet! All windows and doors were tightly closed; it was family washing day; and, as a result, the air was filled with steam, and close and foul beyond

---

2. In most of these "shafts" the sunlight never penetrates, even at midday, below the fifth story.

comprehension, while the temperature must have been little short of the nineties! Those were cases worse than the average, I must admit, but still the average was bad enough.

So this is where many thousands of human beings are reared every year! How can we wonder that they are filthy and dirty, and that disease carries off a very large number? None of the houses mentioned had any bathing arrangements, and in all cases the closets were down in the yard and generally in a very unsanitary condition. As for the poor little children, they had no playground whatever except the street or the close, unhealthy atmosphere of their own living-rooms.

Now let us pass on to a new type of tenement house, which has but recently appeared in the "Battle Row" district—an *old* building remodeled. Here we naturally find a more hopeful state of affairs. The halls are cleaner, lighter, and more airy, having a large window at the back end opening on a small court, besides several smaller windows opening on the air-shafts. The rooms, too, are larger and have access to more air and light. As for the "shafts," these are wider, and, instead of being closed overhead by a skylight, as in the old style, are directly open to the fresh air. In general, the whole building and its inmates have a much more cheerful, hopeful aspect. The children are cleaner and better kept, and the closets are at least usable. ⁎ ⁎ ⁎ There are a number of such buildings scattered along Sixty-third street, between First and Second avenues.

Lastly we come to still a third type of tenement house in the "Battle Row" district—the "new model." It is on these splendid buildings of the City and Suburban Homes Company, constructed by the most skilful architects on the most improved plans, that I wish especially to dwell. My desire is simply to show that in most parts of the city of New York, and, indeed, in any of our large American cities, it is perfectly possible to buy up the ground on which old, unsanitary buildings now stand, and to build in their stead a model tenement of the best modern sanitary type *which will yield a profitable return to the investors*. We have seen the great importance of the housing problem; we have shown that many of the worst features of that problem exist, or did exist a few years ago, in the "Battle Row" district in New York. Now let us observe how the City and Suburban Homes Company has met that problem in the "Battle Row," and how, as a result, it is slowly but surely working a reform, not alone on the character and morals of its own tenants, but on the neighboring inhabitants of the whole district.

The City and Suburban Homes Company was organized in 1896, with Dr. E. R. L. Gould as president and a board of directors composed of many of the most prominent New York businessmen. The broad underlying principle on which the company is founded is the recognition that the housing problem can be solved only by economic methods.[3] Philanthropy alone, according to Dr. Gould's ideas, is powerless to do much, because the field is altogether too vast. Then, too, there is the ever-present danger that movements in which philanthropy forms a part may become sporadic. Time and again movements of this kind have been restricted to very limited areas, and as a result have realized but half their promise. In order to avoid this

3. *Cf.* DR. GOULD, "The Housing Problem, etc.," *Municipal Affairs*, March, 1899, p. 122.

danger the company determined to choose as its leader a man who, from his previous study of the question, was not only a philanthropist, but a man of sound business principles. And yet the housing problem is a sociological one, as well as a business and economic one. Accordingly, the new company adopted a middle policy, or a policy of "investment philanthropy," as Dr. Gould calls it—that is, a philanthropy made seductive by co-ordination with a reasonable commercial dividend. It does not stand for "charity" in the common acceptation of that term; on the other hand, getting the largest possible economic outcome has been equally ignored.

> Realizing that in the future an investment which has New York improved real estate as security is likely to command notice, dividends are limited to 5 per cent. cumulative. Ordinary rents may yield more [and, indeed, they have, as we shall see presently], but whatever surplus accumulates will be invested for the extension of operations. The understanding which the company has with the public and with its stockholders is that participation in economic profits is limited to a fair commercial rate.[4]

The first distinguishing feature of the company, then, is its semi-philanthropic nature.

The second distinguishing characteristic of the company is "popularity"—using the word "popular" in its generic signification. It desires to place within reach of all, other things being equal, a sound security; "particularly ought the savings of the masses to be utilized more than they are at present for their direct benefit."[5] Hence its shares are limited to $10 each, in order that they may attract a large number of people of moderate means.

The third important principle of the Suburban Homes Company is the differentiation of its efforts in order to meet the needs of various classes of wage-earners. For the better classes of working people it provides attractive suburban cottages at remarkably reasonable rates, the tenants being encouraged to purchase on the instalment plan. For the poorer classes it provides model tenements in the city at moderate rents.

So much for the history and objects of one of the most interesting of private business enterprises engaged in ameliorating the housing conditions of the city's poor.

The first buildings erected by the company are situated on the West Side of New York, on Sixty-eighth and Sixty-ninth streets, between Amsterdam and West End avenues. They are known as the Alfred Corning Clark buildings, were built by the well-known architect, Mr. Ernest Flagg, on the best sanitary principles, and contain 373 apartments of two, three, and four rooms each. These houses were opened for occupancy in the spring of 1898, but, as the present paper deals with another section of New York city, I shall pass by any further description of the Clark buildings and confine my remarks to the company's other tenements on the East Side.

The second set of tenement-house buildings owned by the Suburban Homes Company is situated on First avenue between Sixty-fourth and Sixty-fifth streets, just on the borders of the "Battle Row" district, and were

4. *Ibid.*, p. 123.
5. GOULD, *loc. cit.*

opened to the public in April, 1900. These buildings were designed by Mr. James E. Ware, and are supposed to represent a slight improvement on the Clark houses. They contain 148 apartments of two, three, and four rooms, and six stores on the ground floor—the apartments renting at an average rate of about 93 cents a room per week.

The contrast, as one emerges from the old-style tenement on the south side of Sixty-fourth street and enters the new model buildings on the north side of the same street, is something wonderful. Instead of dark, dingy, foul-smelling halls, everything is sweet and clean. The tenants, while perhaps of a trifle higher class than those living farther down in "Battle Row," are noticeable, not for their wealth, but for their cheerful, happy faces and for the evident pride with which they keep their little homes—now "homes" in very truth—neat and cosy. Indeed, every apartment is a complete home in itself. Every room has quiet, light, and air, with thorough ventilation. Staircases and stair walls are entirely fireproof; walls of the first story and the dividing walls between each group of apartments are also fireproof. Halls and stairways are well lighted and steam-heated, and every apartment is furnished with a gas-range and steam radiators. The building is divided into houses with four separate entrances from the street, and every such division has two stairways and two dumb waiters. Showers and tub-baths are provided free on the first floor and in the basement, besides which there are free laundries, also in the basement. Special facilities are given for drying on the roofs, while each floor is provided with a dust-shoot, allowing convenient disposal of ashes without carrying them downstairs.

Each apartment also has certain conveniences reserved exclusively for its own occupants, such as plaster closets instead of wardrobes, separate water-closets constructed on the best modern hygienic principles, etc.

Throughout, the latest sanitary construction of houses has been followed, so that Dr. Gould's new tenement buildings really possess most of the advantages of the modern flat, though, of course, on a somewhat reduced scale.

Regarding the character and nationality of the tenants in these model houses, much interest has been expressed by those interested in the housing problem. According to the reports of reliable investigators, and even of Dr. Gould himself, many of the lodging and tenement houses provided by European municipalities have failed entirely to attract the low class of tenants for which they were primarily intended. But here we come to an important difference between the purpose underlying Dr. Gould's venture and that of the majority of similar enterprises, both public and private. The former has always contended that the best way to reform the tenement houses of our large cities as well as their tenants is not to cater at first to the *lowest* classes. On the contrary, it is best to begin with the *upper* strata of what Jacob Riis has called the "other half" of society. Providing for the best and most prosperous of these leaves just so much more room for those underneath. Beginning at the top relieves the pressure and prompts an upward movement all along the line. Accordingly, Dr. Gould and his company have purposely catered to the mechanics and better class of wage-earners. The result of this policy has been to gather together in the East Side buildings the better class of Germans, Bohemians, English, Swedish, Irish, Americans, Scotch, and Cubans. The following table, showing the

occupations of those tenants who had moved in by April 30, 1900, may be
of interest:[6]

Annuitant - - - - - -	1	Independent - - - - -	1
Bakers - - - - - -	2	Iron-worker - - - - -	1
Barber - - - - - - -	1	Laborer - - - - - -	1
Bartender - - - - - -	1	Laundry hands - - - -	3
Bookkeeper - - - - - -	1	Literary workers - - - -	4
Bottler - - - - - - -	1	Machinist - - - - -	1
Brass-worker - - - - -	1	Medical instrument maker - -	1
Butlers - - - - - -	2	Milliners - - - - - -	3
Caretakers - - - - - -	2	Neckwear embroiderer - - -	1
Carpenters - - - - - -	4	Nurses - - - - - - -	2
Chiropodist - - - - - -	1	Painters - - - - - - -	5
Cigarmakers - - - - -	3	Pipe caulker - - - - -	1
Cigar packer - - - - - -	1	Plasterer - - - - - -	1
Clerks - - - - - - -	3	Printers - - - - - - -	4
Coachmen - - - - - -	3	Salesmen - - - - - -	5
Conductors - - - - - -	2	School-teacher - - - -	1
Delicatessen storekeeper - -	1	Scrub-woman - - - - -	1
Detective - - - - - -	1	Store matron - - - - -	1
Dressmaker - - - - -	1	Suspender-maker - - - -	1
Drivers - - - - - -	3	Tape-measure maker - - -	1
Dry-goods business - - - -	1	Tea business - - - - -	1
Elevator man - - - - -	1	Traveler - - - - - -	1
Engineers - - - - - -	4	Upholsterer - - - - -	1
Factory hands - - - - -	3	Waiters - - - - - - -	3
Fish-market man - - - -	1	Watchmen - - - - - -	2
Furniture duster - - - -	1	Widows supported by children	5
Gardener - - - - - -	1		
Griddleman - - - - -	1	Total - - - - - - -	102
Gripmen - - - - - -	2		

During the same period the Alfred Corning Clark buildings seemed to
have contained a distinctly lower class of tenants (357 in all on April 30,
1900). And of these Dr. Gould estimated that 31 per cent. were men earning but $1.50 to $1.75 per day, while 21½ per cent. were either widows or
unmarried women—showing that three-fourths of the total number of
inhabitants were earning no more than the poorest unskilled laborer. They
therefore belonged to a class of society least able to afford better homes,
and yet they eagerly availed themselves of the opportunities offered by the
City and Suburban Homes Company. In this connection it is also interesting to note that Dr. Gould informed the writer that in the new buildings of the company now being erected on E. Sixty-fourth street, the

6. By October 1, 1900, when the buildings were practically filled for the first time, the total number
of tenants had risen to over 200. Of these, 4½ per cent. came from below Fourteenth street, 74
per cent. from between Fourteenth and Seventieth streets, 11 per cent. from above Seventieth
street on Manhattan Island, 3 per cent. from the Bronx, 3½ per cent. from Brooklyn, and 4 per
cent. from outside New York city. The record of tenancy also appears to have been satisfactory, 42
per cent. of all the tenants having been residents for more than one year, and 34 per cent. between
six months and a year.

number of four-room apartments would be very much reduced. It appears that in the present houses the three- and two-room apartments filled up almost immediately, while the four-room ones were not all occupied for six weeks after the opening of the buildings, doubtless because of the increased cost of rental. The company has become convinced, says the president, that, while it does not desire to cater to the lowest classes, its four-room apartments are too costly to attract the desired character of tenants.[7]

As to the cost of land used for purposes of "expropriation," Dr. Gould expressed the opinion that it would hardly be safe for any private enterprise to pay more than $12,000 for the regular 25 × 100 feet New York lot. Seven thousand dollars, he said, had been paid by the Suburban Homes Company for its land on E. Sixty-fourth street. If the doctor is right in his advice, it is evident that it will be almost impossible for a private corporation to purchase sufficient land for building purposes in the lower portions of Manhattan Island. And yet it would seem that this is the very portion of the whole city which is most in need of radical relief for its congested population. Perhaps here is the chance for the municipality to step in, as has been done with success in many English cities.

Another word should be said regarding the health of the occupants of the Gould buildings. In the East Side tenements the matron, Miss Geary, informed the writer that during the nine months of occupancy since April, 1900, there had been only two or three isolated cases of contagious diseases, and these were so well provided for, and could be so easily cut off from their neighbors, that the board of health had thought it unnecessary to remove them. In the West Side tenements the fourth annual report of the company states that the health of the tenants has been excellent, there being only two cases of contagious diseases during the past year. The vital statistics of the same buildings record thirty-six births during the year—thirteen boys and twenty-three girls. During the same period there were eleven deaths—six adults, two children, and three infants.

Dr. Gould alo called my attention to the necessity of providing competent domestic management, if the model tenement was to be run with success. He laid special emphasis on the desirability of having *women* rent collectors. Women are able to use more tact in this unpleasant task than men, and at the same time are more competent to offer helpful advice and suggestions to the tenants. In this respect the City and Suburban Homes Company has been particularly fortunate in securing as a matron and rent collector for its East Side buildings Miss Blanche Geary, who was trained in London in the methods of Miss Octavia Hill and her associates. Out of a total of $10,782.20 due from rents to date, President Gould told me that Miss Geary had failed to collect but $22.50. In the West Side buildings, where the rent collecting is also in charge of a woman, the showing is hardly less favorable, there being to date only $143.25 bad debts out of a total of $26,189.73.

---

7. Since the above was written, I learn that the new buildings on E. Sixty-fourth street are to contain 190 apartments, 10 of four rooms with private bath, 130 of three rooms, and 50 of two rooms. Plans for still another large building on the same street adjoining those now in construction are also contemplated, providing for about 290 apartments, chiefly of two rooms and three rooms each.

As for discipline, only a very few general regulations are laid down for the government of the tenants—only sixteen in all. All occupants of the Gould buildings, however, are expected to obey these simple rules, and if, after several warnings delivered at the suggestion of the superintendent, they persist in violating them, they are expelled from the premises. Such severe measures have seldom been found necessary, however, only 22 out of more than 373 families in the West Side tenements having been expelled.

Below is a table showing length of tenancy in the various houses of the Clark buildings:

SIXTY-EIGHTH STREET.

House Number.	Two Years and Over.	Eighteen Months to Two Years.	One Year to Eighteen Months.	Total Number of Apartments in Buildings.	Percentage of Tenants Living in Building One Year or Over.
217	4	5	4	35	37
219	14	7	2	41	56
225	9	6	1	41	39
227	8	6	4	41	44
233	8	13	4	41	61
	43	37	15		

SIXTY-NINTH STREET.

House Number.	Two Years and Over.	Eighteen Months to Two Years.	One Year to Eighteen Months.	Total Number of Apartments in Buildings.	Percentage of Tenants Living in Building One Year or Over.
214	20	2	8	45	67
216	13	8	6	42	64
218	8	7	6	42	50
220	15	9	3	45	60
	56	26	23		

Changes of tenancy seem to occur with the greatest frequency during the spring and early summer months, a fair proportion of the heads of families being waiters, coachmen, and personal attendants who are employed chiefly at country homes or seaside resorts during the summer.

III. Results of Gould's Reforms.

I. FINANCIAL SUCCESS.

The financial success of the City and Suburban Homes Company, especially of its large tenement houses in New York city, is beyond question.

The company's balance sheet made up on April 30, 1898, at which date the first fiscal year of its operations ended, showed receipts amounting to $1,174,595.61. Of this, $1,098,245.84 represents the capital accounts of the three estates belonging to the company, and $76,349.77 the balance in bank. One hundred and fifty thousand dollars of the receipts came from a temporary bank loan. On March 1, 1898, 5 per cent. interest was paid to shareholders upon instalments on account of subscriptions to the capital stock. This sum, as well as the company's general expenses for salaries, rent, printing and stationery, advertising, postage, etc.; for legal expenses, and for taxes on both real property and capital stock, were equitably apportioned among the three different estates and were included in the figures showing the capital expenditures on the various estates up to April 30, 1900. Furthermore, when the allotment of shares was made in January, 1897, 5,000 shares of the par value of $10 each were reserved for the benefit of those persons who might desire them, but who had neither underwritten nor subscribed at the public subscription. The object was to extend the area of interest in the company's operations as widely as possible. Without even announcing the fact that any shares remained unallotted, private applications made from time to time have taken all of these, with the exception of 193 shares which still remain unallotted.

The company's balance sheets for the years ending April, 1899 and 1900, as they show well its growth and prosperity, are given below:

	APRIL 30, 1899.	APRIL 30, 1900.	INCREASE.
Total assets	$1,491,504.22	$1,739,925.52	$248,421.30
Total liabilities ..	1,491,504.22	1,739,925,52	248,421.30
Profit and loss	13,785.22	20,883.98	7,098.65

In 1899 a dividend of 2 per cent. was paid and charged to profit and loss account on December 1, 1898, out of the net earnings of the company up to October 31, 1898 (= $20,000).

In 1900 a dividend of 1¾ per cent. on the capital stock, amounting to $17,500, was paid on December 4, 1899, out of net earnings for the six months ending October 31, 1899, and charged to profit and loss account. Later a further dividend of 1¾ per cent. was declared and ordered paid on May 9, 1900, thus making a total of 3½ per cent. in dividends paid during the fiscal year ending April, 1900.[8] The net income for the year on the Clark buildings was $19,266.58, representing 6.10 per cent per annum on the amount of capital stock invested in that estate. The following items may also be of interest:

Average weekly vacancies of stores - - - - - - - - - - - - - - None
Average weekly vacancies of apartments - - - - - - - - - - - - - 17
Aggregate loss from vacancies during year- - - - - - - - - - - $2,541.25
Percentage of loss from vacancies during year - - - - - - - - - - 4.56
Aggregate loss from irrevocable arrears - - - - - - - - - - - - 94.30
Percentage of loss from irrevocable arrears - - - - - - - - - - - 0.71

8. The dividend the previous year was 3 per cent. That during the following year ending April 30, 1901, according to the fifth annual report just received, was 4 per cent.

II. EFFECT ON THE TENANTS INHABITING THE "MODEL" BUILDINGS.

Both Dr. Gould and Miss Geary boldly assert that the effect of the healthy, cheerful environment of the new tenement house on E. Sixty-fourth street has been most marked.

In the first place, this was seen in their improved sanitary standards. Thus when a new tenant arrived and ventured to put in practice any of his old habits of uncleanness or carelessness, he was invariably frowned down by the old residents who had learned better. In other words, the new surroundings had developed an unwritten, but a far higher and more effective sanitary standard among the tenants than any which they had known before.

In the second place, the wholesome effect of the new surroundings on the tenants was seen in the development of a more *united family life*. And anyone who has studied the causes of immorality knows how much of it is due to this very absence of a high standard of domestic union. Whereas under the old system of herding many individuals of different sexes into the same room moral purity and decency had become almost impossible, now under the new and better mode of life a large measure of this danger was removed.

In the third place, a marked improvement in the health of the tenants was noticeable. The dangers of disease and sickness are, of course, much lessened under a proper sanitary environment (see p. 286).

III. EFFECT ON THE "BATTLE ROW" DISTRICT.

The most noticeable improvement in the "Battle Row" district which is clearly traceable to the stimulating effect of Dr. Gould's model tenements is the building of better houses by outside parties. This is the natural and almost inevitable result of competition. Just as soon as good housing is found to pay better than bad housing, because of the higher standard stimulated by the former among the tenants, then we may logically hope for a rapid improvement. Thus the remodeled houses on Sixty-third street, between First and Second avenues, as well as several entirely new tenements, notably those on Sixty-second street just west of First avenue, have all come into existence since Dr. Gould's buildings were opened.

Another noticeable improvement in the "Battle Row" region, undoubtedly due to the contact of neighbors with the new model tenements and their occupants, is in the better sanitary conditions which prevail generally. For example, Miss Geary told me that many of the neighboring halls and courts had recently been cleaned and repaired. There was also less rubbish on the fire escapes, and fewer clothes were seen hanging in the air-shafts to block up what little fresh air does actually penetrate those deep "wells"! These are little matters, to be sure, but they all show an evident rise in the sanitary standards of "Battle Row."

IV. Conclusions.

In the foregoing paper I have not attempted to go into even a brief account of the many proposed methods of tenement-house reform. I have simply

confined my remarks to showing, first the importance of the housing problem because of its vital effect on the character and health of our citizens,
and secondly the remedies which have been applied to this evil in a certain
district in New York city. The question of municipal *versus* private ownership of "model" tenement houses I have scarcely touched upon, except
in so far as the undoubted success of the City and Suburban Homes Company as a private enterprise bears upon this phase of the problem. Neither
have I attempted to show the importance of proper sanitary and building
laws or of the right of expropriation of property by the city government in
dealing with the proper housing of the poor. The value and necessity of
such laws have been taken for granted, as any adequate discussion of them
would take me beyond the limits of the present paper. My conclusions,
therefore, are valuable only in so far as they are based on an observation of
the actual effect which the Gould model tenements have already had, both
upon their own inhabitants and upon those of the immediate neighborhood.

However, I trust enough has already been written to show:

1. That a private company with moderate capital, with semi-philanthropic
motives, and run on sound business principles, can *profitably* undertake the
improved housing of the poor.

2. That such a company, when once firmly established, has a tremendous influence for good, not alone by raising the moral and physical standard of its own tenants, but, by sheer force of business competition,
compelling a higher standard of living in the whole neighborhood.

But if it be answered that the field of my observations has been too
limited to justify such sweeping conclusions, I would merely point to
similar results which have been achieved in Europe and America under
similar conditions. Take, for example, the careful investigations carried
on by Dr. Gould, both in this country and abroad, in which he shows that
of all the large companies throughout Europe and the United States
which have been formed for improving the housing conditions of the
poor, 86 per cent. earned clear profits, 6 per cent. earned a savings-bank
rate of interest, while only 6 per cent. were actually unsuccessful. Such
figures are not by any means conclusive in themselves, but, coupled with
the actual results which have been achieved by the City and Suburban
Homes Company in New York, go far to justify us in adding a third conclusion:

3. That, while the housing problem is one of the most important social
problems of the present day, we have every reason to hope and believe that
at least a partial reform may be worked out on the lines indicated in the
present paper.

LILLIAN W. BETTS

From The Leaven in a Great City[†]

Chapter III. The Homes under One Roof

The importance of environment is at last admitted as a factor in character-building. That light and air are indispensable to cleanliness, and physical cleanliness to health, and health to morals, is the gospel that the evils of the tenements have forced the philanthropists to declare until the thinking public is convinced of its truth.

There are tenement houses that have reputations as positive as individuals. Thoughtful, intelligent wives of workingmen would not, could not be persuaded to move into them because of their reputations. Often the evils of these tenements are justly attributed to the housekeepers. Housekeepers of tenements are women who pay the whole or a part of their rent by overseeing the house; attending to the cleaning, collecting the rents, letting the rooms, adjusting differences between tenants—"a go-between" between the agent or the owner and the tenants. The owner or agent employing these women upholds their decisions when differences between the tenants and housekeepers arise. This clothes them with great authority, and often enables them to do great injustice. They are feared usually. Families will endure restrictions of liberties, every deprivation of their rights, because protest would mean eviction or discomforts that would compel them to move.

Under some agents and owners these housekeepers have absolute control of the property. They frequently make and enforce rules that utterly ignore the rights of tenants. This rule is often as absolute as though they were the owners of the house. Strange as it may seem, this class of housekeepers usually make the property under their control pay; they usually keep up the character of the houses under their control because they have standards and compel those about them to live up to them.

On an East Side street a few blocks from the East River are four 27-foot front houses of the English-basement type. The plan of these houses indicates that they were designed as residences for people of ample means. The halls are broad, the stairways wide, ascending in recesses on the first floor that leaves the entrance halls clear from front to rear doorways. The yards of these four houses, wide and deep, are paved with broad flagging stones, such as are used on the sidewalks. The fences are kept in good order and well painted. Not a child living in these four houses dares to play in those yards. The housekeeper—one woman has charge of the four houses—would order them out. If the children did not leave at once, complaint would be made to the mothers; and if they did not uphold the housekeeper and insist that the children play in the street, the mothers who failed would have to move. Every mother-tenant knows this well. A mother of three children who had lived in these houses all her married life, when asked why the children could not play in the yard,

† New York: Dodd, Mead & Company, 1903.

where she could watch them, replied: "Why, if the children played in the yard they would make a lot of work for the housekeeper. She would not stand it." This mother's tone indicated that she thought the housekeeper was right. The youngest of the three children in another family living in these houses was ill all winter. When convalescent, the doctor ordered him to be kept out of doors as much as possible. The mother had all the work to do for five in family, and had to devise some means of keeping the child out that would not interfere with her work. She arranged the fire-escape outside of the window, putting pillows and toys out there. The little fellow climbed over the rail and struck a stone beneath, breaking his arms.

"Why did you not put him in the yard, where you could watch him, and where he could run about?"

"Oh! the housekeeper would be so angry; I wouldn't dare."

"Must you keep the children out of the yard?"

"Yes; they would make an awful lot of work for the housekeeper."

Investigation proved that the owner of this property supported the house-keeper in depriving even the babies of the use of these yards. A mother could not roll a baby carriage around the yards, because her older children, if she had any, would be sure to go into the yards to see her. The rents for four rooms, two absolutely dark, ventilated through the dark and unventi-lated halls by a window eighteen inches square, were $22, $20 and $18 per month, respectively, for each floor. The streets in front are overcrowded, dirty; when the trucks were in the streets, two were always standing in front of these houses. Push-carts now replace the trucks.

The people stay in these houses year after year. A bill never appears on them. The arbitrary restriction as to the use of the yard is not counted against the property, because it is so clean, kept in such good repair, and the character of the people scrutinized before they are accepted as tenants. It is generally understood that the renting of furnished rooms is not approved. The housekeeper finds a tenant who rents rooms objectionable. In a neighborhood where every house shows year after year a loss of char-acter, people poorer and more ignorant becoming tenants, these four houses retain the appearance of comfort and respectability. Among the ten-ants there is but little intimacy; they appear to have little in common. The women are never heard in the halls, nor do they loiter about the doorways. The men are all skilled workmen, earning good wages—clerks on small salaries, or in city departments, all natives of New York. The wives were all wage-earners before they were married. They dress well; most of them are fairly good housekeepers. All buy their children's clothes ready made; two make their own dresses. For their children they are ambitious, and expect to keep them in school until they are sixteen. This the children defeat. The boys get places during the summer vacations in their fourteenth year, refus-ing to go back to school. The girls are contented until fourteen, and then they grow restless, becoming wage-earners; all that they earn is spent for their clothes. The wages of the father may no more than meet the expenses of the family, but this is not considered. Clothes are the essentials. A man having a salary of $1,400, living in one of these houses, had to go in debt the first week of a serious illness of his wife. He did not have a dollar in advance to meet emergencies. He was a proud, indulgent, tender husband and father.

This type of house and this class of tenants are disappearing from the East Side. The remnant of this class who remain are held by political affiliations or family ties. The men enjoy the sense of power that comes from this connection, and realize fully that to leave the district would mean a loss of social prestige, or, if minor politicians, a loosening of their hold on the people to whom they represent political power. Many of this class remain in the section because they hold positions in the city departments in return for active service in the interest of the political machines.

Not far away from these tenements is another in which are sixteen families. The rents in this house range from $5 to $9.50 per month for two to three rooms. The house is dirty, neglected; violations of the sanitary laws are evident from the front door to the roof, on which tenants occupying the front rooms must dry their clothes. The water is in the dark halls; in winter, for days at a time, the pipes, both water and drain, are frozen and burst; yet the tenants stay year after year. One woman, the mother of four children, was born, married, her four children were born, and her husband, mother and father died in this house. She has never moved, except across the hall, up and downstairs, as she has been able to pay more or has been forced to reduce her rent. The women in this house know almost nothing of housekeeping. The men are employed only about half the time. The number of children in the house averages three to each family. It is a New England hamlet under one roof in this particular. If there is sickness in any family, it is the concern of every tenant; if a man is out of work, it is a community misfortune, and to be shared. A new hat for man or woman is the cause of rejoicing, for it is the badge of respectability for any in the house who may need it in an emergency. The whole household, for such it seems to be, are poor, very poor; thriftless, unambitious; the men somewhat given to drink to excess; yet the spirit of neighborliness shames criticism. A woman in this house ill four months was nursed by her neighbors night and day. Her house and children were cared for, food provided when necessary. Comment on their loyalty and devotion was met with the response: "God knows how soon she may be doing it for one of us." Yet when that woman, whom most of them had known all her life, gave evidence of pregnancy a few months after her husband's death, not a woman crossed her doorsill until the birth of twin babies within the period of time redeemed her character. Whether from remorse or love, ample return for this cruelty has been made many times.

In the two-room apartments in this house there is one closet, with shelves about six inches wide. This is in the one room that serves as living-room, kitchen, dining-room—a room less than eight feet wide. The bedroom is perfectly dark, ventilated by a square window into perfectly dark, unventilated halls. A full-sized bed leaves the width of the door between it and the wall. The three-room apartments have outside windows—five to the three rooms. There is a closet in the kitchen and one in the large room. People talk of poverty, but few people know what it is. A woman who had moved into the three-room apartment had hung all the clothing for five in family in the one bedroom on four nails. In reply to a protest, she said patiently and quietly: "There are no hooks in the closet in the front room, and I hadn't a penny to buy any." Ten cents provided that closet with hooks. A comment was made on the keeping of the washtub under the kitchen table. "Why do you not have the tub carried to the cellar?" An expression of self-pity passed over the woman's face as she explained that the tub would have to be carried down three flights of stairs, out on the street, around the corner, down the cellar stairs, and then to her coal cellar at the extreme end of the cellar.

The house stands on a corner, the entrance from the street at the extreme end of the west wall. The cellar door was formerly close to the entrance door, but the landlord built in the back end of the cellar an oven when a baker hired the store on the first floor. A cellar door was then opened at the farthest part of the front, or south wall, one hundred and twenty-five feet from the entrance door of the house. Is it surprising that coal is bought by the pail by all the tenants? That tubs are kept anywhere in their rooms where there is space?

Shiftlessness, thriftless uncleanliness marks even the sidewalk about this house. The dirt inside or out troubles nobody. Children will spill half the contents of the garbage pail they are carrying to the cans in the tiny yard, in halls and on the stairway. It is kicked out of the way without comment. Dogs or cats, and ofttimes both, are members of the families who live under this roof. The unsanitary conditions of the closets in the yard arouse pity for the tenants on the first floor; but no tenant thinks of complaining to either the housekeeper or the authorities. It would be useless, and would get them into trouble. The present owner is willing to kalsomine the bedrooms and halls each spring, but the tenants object because it makes a lot of work.

In August, two years ago, the writer was going up the first flight of stairs in this house, when a baby voice was heard pleading: "Pease tum fas'er; oh, pease tum fas'er; I 'ant to do p'ay; I 'ant to doe on steet; pease tum fas'er." On the third floor a tiny boy stood in front of the sink talking to the faucet, from which a tiny stream was flowing into a little tin pail. An infant's voice from one of the rooms told the story. The mother needed water and could not leave the baby. Perhaps this was the tiny nurse of mother and baby, big enough to call a neighbor to do what he could not do.

When it is remembered that this stream of water from the faucet represented the water supply for four families, the difficulties of cleanliness under those conditions may be slightly appreciated. In spite of the dirt, the darkness, the unsanitary conditions of this house, the thriftlessness and ignorance of the tenants, there is a spirit of neighborliness in it that puts the critical to blush. Without a doubt the housekeeper, who is a shrewd woman, fosters this spirit of neighborliness. She smiles as she says: "They gets so used to each other they hates to be separated." Neither house nor tenants seem to go below the level established twelve years ago.

There is a housekeeper who does mission work of which the world takes no note. She is the woman who in the true sense is an altruist. By her force of character, her hatred of inefficiency, her love of order, she compels the women who become tenants who do not know how to keep house to learn how.

The writer knows intimately such a housekeeper. She had charge of a four-story tenement on the lower East Side. The house was of the type known as "double decker." There were four apartments on each floor; the front consisting of a kitchen, living-room and two bedrooms; the back, of one room and two bedrooms. Small windows near the ceiling in kitchen and bedrooms opened on a narrow space between this and the next house, which was an old-fashioned residence. A similar opening in that house enabled the neighbors to look into each other's rooms. Water and refuse were thrown into this space between the two houses, and sometimes into the rooms of neighbors unintentionally. There was war, bitter war, because of this; for the large tenement was occupied by a part of the remnant having social standards left on the lower East Side.

There was water in all the kitchens of the large tenement. The halls were absolutely dark, but were free from the nuisances of hallways having sinks. Stairs and halls were covered with light oilcloth, the stairs having brass treads on the edge. Everything was kept as clean as soap, water and muscular strength could keep it.

The first visit was made to this house long before Colonel Waring had shown what clean streets would do in the tenement-house districts. On the street curb in front of the door stood three ash barrels filled within three inches of the top, carefully covered with newspapers tucked in around the edge of the contents. This indicates the standards of this housekeeper. She hated dirt and disorder. She could not be happy where it was. She forced by tact, coercion, persuasion, any and every means, her way to the heart and home of every ignorant housekeeper who came under that roof. She taught cooking by sending cake, bread, soup she had made to the tenants, and arousing the desire in them to learn how to make that particular dish. She instituted an exchange of skill among the tenants. The woman who could make a dress and not a hat exchanged skill with the one who had been a milliner. The woman who made bread and failed with cake exchanged skill with the cakemaker. They even took turns in going to the theatre, the neighbor staying home and taking care of the children.

The property was more valuable every year; no bill appeared at the door. It stood apart from its neighbors for years. This housekeeper was compelled to give up her responsibility and left the house, as she wisely said: "No one would manage it in my way. I could not get on in peace." Six months after every tenant had moved but the liquor dealer; and even his barroom had sunk to a lower level. A building in which many homes might be maintained is now merely a place of shelter. People move in and out; no relations are established; there is nothing to hold the tenant here above any other house. The owner has sold the property, hating its present character.

Again, tenants will be the victims of vindictive housekeepers, who for any and no reason will begin a system of petty persecutions to compel a tenant to move. Then there is the gossiping housekeeper, who keeps the tenants at war. It is no secret that the method of rent collecting of some housekeepers holds tenants year after year. They will take the rent in the smallest sums, daily or weekly. By the end of the month they will usually have the full amount collected. The houses where this system prevails are the most objectionable. The tenants for this leniency endure positive evils. The important thing is a place of shelter for the family. Work is uncertain, or long periods of idleness has made the payment of rent impossible for a period. The housekeeper understands and becomes responsible for keeping the tenant until the rent is paid. In return the tenants endure neglect of duty on the part of the housekeeper. Silence is their expression of gratitude. No repairs are made, for none are demanded. The house sinks lower and lower; anybody can move in on the payment of part of a month's rent. The vacant rooms are dirty—give visible evidence of the presence of vermin;

but the family evicted with only half a month's rent in hand cannot afford to be critical. This is the house that makes the slum.

Two housekeepers of tenements were discussing owners and tenants before the writer. One was rigid, keeping the house astonishingly clean, with rooms rarely vacant; the other, always in trouble with the tenants, always having some one to evict, threw the blame for her troubles on the tenants. The first one listened, finally saying slowly: "No, you are the one. You get cross and abuse the children. You make pets of some children and some mothers, and the others see it and get mad. Then there is a fight. To keep a house you must treat everybody the same. You must make good rules; you must do your part and make every tenant do her part. I've had two of the tenants you put out of your house five years. They are good tenants; watch yourself."

There are landlords who care for nothing but the income from their property. Any kind of tenant who will pay rent is acceptable. Any housekeeper who collects the specified amount may hold control without question. The housekeeper may have standards, but these are swept aside by the exactions of the landlord. The rents in such houses are usually high, because there is such a percentage of loss in rents. This house also contributes to the creation of the slum.

The careless and apparently malicious destruction of property by tenants is not appreciated by those who touch this question of tenement houses superficially. No means has yet been found to make the tenement-house population understand that the abuse of property is a factor in their rent problem. Within a year the writer was walking with a group of women, two of whom were housekeepers in tenement houses. This question of tenants was being discussed freely by the women who were tenants as well as the housekeepers. It was interesting to find that all agreed that one family could change the character of a tenement house for the worst, but one family could not improve its character. The reason was that the family above the tenement came only to reduce their rent during a hard time, while the family with evil tendencies stayed until they were put out, to go into a cheaper tenement and lower that. They agreed that where housekeeper and tenant got on well together both hated a change. The two things that dragged down the character of a tenement was beer-drinking and destructive children—children allowed to "run wild." These women insisted that there never would be quarrels in tenement houses were it not for these two causes. A woman who drank beer would invite her new neighbors to drink. They would treat in return, and the house would show it at once. The women who drink beer in this fashion grow careless of their persons and their homes; they get rid of their children, who soon learn to enjoy the freedom from control. The children destroy the property first in play, through carelessness, and later grow malicious.

If a housekeeper is sharp and shrewd, these women tenants claimed that she could at any time get rid of an objectionable tenant; but the housekeepers held that if the owner did not care for anything but rents, the housekeeper was often compelled to let in and keep in objectionable tenants. They admitted, one and all, that houses fairly indicated the character of the people who would live in them, and that rents regulated the class of tenants to a very great degree. They admitted that at times one could find tenants who had lived for many years in one house where conditions had changed for the worst. But it was unusual. People now selected houses where those of their own faith, and, if foreign, those of their own nationality, at least predominated. That this tendency was seen more and more every year. This group of women were among the remnant of Christians left on the lower East Side. All had been born there of Irish parentage. They lived in the houses bordering on the edge of the East River—old houses on the plan of the first tenements erected in New York, or in houses designed for one family and now holding four to eight. Two of them lived in houses built in a row erected eighty-three years ago. They were two-story, dormer windows and basement frame houses, built without an area, the door to the basements opening like a cellar door on the street. These basements were occupied by a family each. Fourteen of these houses are still standing. The people in this section live a life entirely their own. They have been crowded out, the more prosperous, by the Hebrews, while the remnant find themselves hemmed in by them.

These people live in the confines of a Roman Catholic parish that twenty years ago contained nearly eleven thousand souls of that faith. Three years ago the priest in charge estimated his parish at less than four thousand, and that four thousand remained because they were too poor to get away, he declared.

The Hebrews, as tenants will, on the same block show many social grades, many degrees of poverty and prosperity, many stages of development in American civilization. There is a sense of feeling of brotherhood that other people lack. The houses will range from the most uncleanly, ill-kept, to the new tenement with ornate entrance and modern improvements. The most modern will, on entering, be found with walls marked and broken when the wood-work is new. No one seems troubled by this destruction. The housekeeper does not struggle, for it is expected and charged for in the rent. Plumbing is of the simplest, for it is expected to present the largest percentage of loss in the administration of the property. One of the most elaborate of the new tenements erected on the lower East Side was visited three months after it was occupied. Every hallway from top to bottom of the house had broken plaster and was marked by pencil and crayon. The plumber was then a daily visitor. This house a year afterward bore on the interior evidences that years of hard usage might have brought. The housekeeper collected rents and attended to the garbage. She was utterly indifferent to the appearance of the house, which, intended for prosperous families, was a nest of sweat-shops, where even children of six and seven were employed. The rents had been collected; that was the owner's only requirement.

The West Side is congested, because manufacture and storehouses are displacing the houses. Rents are high, and the houses for the most part old residences occupied by several families. The people, generally, are Americans. They are deeply attached to this old section, because it is their birthplace; and for many of them an even deeper attachment prevails, for this section was the birthplace of parents. The houses often are found to have life-long friends, often relatives, as tenants. The tenants keep the halls and stairways clean in turn, and the houses generally are well kept up. Here one tenant is allowed a rebate on rent for renting rooms, collecting the rent, caring for the sidewalk and stoop, the garbage and ash-cans. The majority of the people in this section are Protestants. The Protestant churches are well maintained. The Trinity Corporation supports kindergartens, cooking and sewing schools. The Judson Memorial is a very attractive gymnasium, that brings children from as far west as the North River. The Methodist Church holds many who in no other section could find the same equality and freedom. The vocabulary of the people through this section shows the effect of the newer activities in the modern churches; the effect of the enlarging interests of the children in art and nature through the public school education.

While the people are living on small incomes, often on uncertain incomes, life is lived at a much higher level than on the East Side. Children are not so precocious in evil knowledge. This difference is due largely to the fact that the houses contain three and four families at the most; that the apartment houses in the section are beyond the reach of any but the skilled working man. He holds his own at high rental in the house that shelters but three other families like his own. His neighbors are people of like ambitions as his own, and demand what he demands.

The housekeepers in this section differ essentially in their relation to the tenants from those of the more heterogeneous population of the East Side of the city. One resemblance is recognized—the effect of the character of the housekeeper. Here, as on the East Side, to a very large degree, the comfort, health, peace and goodwill of the tenants in every house depends on the character and the spirit of the woman who controls the property for the landlord.

The law of natural selection holds good. The housekeeper holds the tenants who are satisfied with the conditions she creates. They, especially the children, develop in habits of cleanliness, in care of property, in respect for the rights of others, as the rules of the house enforced by the housekeeper compel. It is in her power to get rid of those who do not accept her dictates, let them be what they may—just or unjust. The housekeeper will make her presence felt. If she violates the law in the disposal of garbage outside of the house, tenants will violate the law she makes for them in the care and disposal of garbage inside the house. If she is compelled to obey the law, she will compel tenants to obey the law. It is this that makes the morale of the Department of Street Cleaning so important. If the part of the house which in renting tenants agree to keep clean is not kept clean, the observer will discover that the housekeeper does not keep her part of the agreement in keeping the entrance clean.

A large factor in the tenement house for character building or destroying is the housekeeper who has charge of it. Where she is well paid she makes the property valuable. She cares for it, for the character of the tenants. Tenants remain in the house because of the advantages her offices control for the poor man and his wife anxious to provide for their children's best welfare. Property under this type of woman resists decay. She holds it in spite of the decay about it. The characterless, slovenly, indifferent housekeeper is a factor in destroying property, because of the destructive character of the tenants who will tolerate her and her methods.

The house that is the property of the man with "a pull" is an obstruction to civilization almost impossible to overcome. By connivance the law is inoperative. If pushed, such an owner can easily rid himself of the tenants who attempt, or have attempted for them, efforts to compel the owners to repair the property. A mill owner on the water front on the lower East Side owned three three-story and basement houses adjoining the mill property. They had been built for one family each. The basements were altered into stores, and the floors above altered at the least cost to accommodate one or two families. This meant two inside bedrooms absolutely without ventilation. The tenants of this property and all in the neighborhood were tormented by the smoke and gas from the chimney of the mill. When the wind blew directly toward the houses, windows were kept closed for hours in the warmest weather. All the tenants dried their clothes on pulley lines. Frequently the soot made the clothes unwearable, and they had to be washed the second time. Ten years of effort have failed to compel the building of the chimney of that mill to the legal height.

The houses the mill owner owned were in a disgraceful condition. The closets in the yards had no flow of water. The engineer of the mill was required to carry a hose from the mill over the fences to the closets to flush them. Sometimes he forgot to turn the water off, and the yards were flooded and made disgusting. Sometimes he forgot for days at a time to flush the closets, when the conditions were even worse. Only people who were helpless or hopeless would endure such conditions. One of the workers of the College Settlement discovered the conditions in these houses. She took immediate steps to compel the necessary improvements. The owner discovered that the wife and children of one of the tenants went to clubs at the Settlement, and he ordered that family to move. Before the mother moved her education had begun, and she imparted to her neighbors the information that the conditions were unlawful and could be changed if they would fight for it. The man exacted his rent on the first of the month; he was hard and unyielding; the tenants continued the warfare until he had evicted every one who spoke English and filled his houses with foreigners. One of the stores is used for storing and sorting rags and paper; next door is a meat shop. The fight was given up. The owner had "a pull," and the law is defied to this day on that property.

All the land on the river front in this neighborhood for blocks is made land, filled in by the city refuse, on which houses were built years ago. This kind of property extends back from the North River for three, and at one point four, blocks. In some of the houses near the river the high tides of spring and fall rise in the cellars. The College Settlement workers who visited families in one of these houses had been distressed by the amount of illness in it. Malaria had attacked every family. Spring and fall wages were lost at times by as many as three wage-earners in one family for two and three days each week. In addition to loss of wages, there was the expense of medicine and doctors. At last came the urgent request that a worker should call on a girl of sixteen who was dying of consumption on the first floor. This consisted of four rooms, two being inside bedrooms, each of which would hold a three-quarter bed and a chair between the bed and the wall. One was absolutely unventilated, except through the doors. It was, in fact, a passage-way between the front and rear rooms. This plan is the usual plan in houses altered from residences for one family to a tenement house.

The door of the other bedroom, which opened into the large room, was closed at night because the large room was used as a bedroom by the male members of the family and one lodger. The girl of sixteen had slept with two others in that room for eight years. The floors of the four rooms were covered with carpets. The odor was sickening. The visitor asked the tenant who brought her to the sick girl what caused the odor perceptible in the hall, with front and rear windows always open, unbearable in the rooms where doors and windows were closed.

"Oh, that! The water has been in the cellar now for two or three weeks. The tides are high now." A visit to the cellar showed the water at the height of the second step of the cellar stairs; also a sewer pipe that had burst. Visits were made to the proper city department once a week for eleven weeks. The clerk, on the last visit, evidently intending to be facetious, said: "Say, what's the matter with those people taking baths in that cellar? They ain't got no bathtubs."

The owner of the property had "pull" enough to escape even an investigation by the department. It was years before the cellar of that house was concreted and the necessary connections of pipes and sewers made. It was done when the property had changed hands and a man comparatively poor and wholly free from political affiliations became the owner.

The people of this whole region are the victims of political corruption. Some of them have more fear of offending a political light, let his glimmer be ever so small, than of offending against even God's law. They could be turned out of house and home, deprived of the means of earning a living, by men who openly defy the law, and who become heroes to the growing boys and girls for no reason but because of their power to use and defy the law.

The moral natures of the men and the women who grow up under this influence are dwarfed and warped until it is impossible for them to have distinct conceptions of right and wrong. The education they receive does not reveal the relations of ethics to life; the struggle for existence dulls the mind: while the depleted physical conditions caused by bad air, malnutrition and ignorance of real values reduce moral resistance almost to zero. Enforce the tenement-house laws, and the moral strength of the people of New York will rise to higher levels of moral resistance. Not poverty, but the burden imposed by political corruption, is the blight of home life in the tenement-house sections of New York.

JOHN J. D. TRENOR
Proposals Affecting Immigration[†]

At the outset of the examination of any proposals affecting immigration there should be a full realization of the magnitude of dependent interests and of the injury that will be wrought by ill-considered and misjudged legislation. No subject of national concern demands more assuredly impartial and thorough consideration—in the colorless light of facts determined and determinable—without any bias of prejudice, of misinformation, or selfish, short-sighted interest.

It is needless to enter into any presentation in detail of the contribution of immigration to the upbuilding of this country. It is conceded that the

† *Annals of the American Academy of Political and Social Science* 24 (1904).

marvellous growth of our nation in every exhibit of industrial progress has been greatly aided by the influx, during the last century, of so many millions of honest, willing and industrious laborers seeking homes and opportunities here for themselves and their children. They have taken part in every memorable achievement and their decisive influence has been cast in the scale to sustain every effort for the maintenance of the life and integrity of the Union.

During the past forty years, there has been a persistent sifting of immigration, with the design of excluding all classes and conditions incapable of assimilation or offensive to our civilization. The Act of 1862 prohibited the importation of "coolie" labor from Oriental countries and subsequent "Chinese Exclusion Acts" have broadly shut out the Chinese as persistently alien and detrimental to the character and homogeneity of our nation. The Act of 1875 excluded convicts, except those guilty of political offenses, and women imported for immoral purposes. By the Act of 1882, lunatics, idiots, and persons unable to care for themselves without becoming public charges, were comprehended in the exclusion. The Act of 1885, by implication, and the Act of 1887 expressly, added "contract laborers." By the Act of 1891, paupers, persons suffering from loathsome or dangerous contagious diseases, polygamists and "assisted" immigrants were specifically excluded. The Act of 1903 added epileptics, persons who have been insane within five years previous, professional beggars and anarchists. By the same Act also, there was a stringent exclusion of persons deported within a year previous, as being "contract laborers." If by any oversight of inspection any of the excluded persons should succeed in obtaining an entrance to this country, their deportation at any time within two years after their entry is secured when their presence is detected.

The comprehensive Act of March 3, 1903, entitled "An Act to regulate the immigration of aliens into the United States," was professedly the crystallization of thirty years of experience, investigation, debate, and legislation in the solution of the so-called "problems of immigration." The testing of the operation of this Act has barely begun; but, without waiting for any exact determination of substantial defects or insufficiency, further proposals of change are hazarded. Of the two deserving special mention, one would effect a radical change in administration through consular inspection and certification at the ports of embarkation; the other urges a sweeping exclusion, not based on moral character or capacity for labor and self-support, but on literary qualification and comprehension of political institutions—the ability to read and presumably to appreciate a text taken from the Constitution of the United States.

Proposal for Consular Inspection

The proposal for a change of administrative method, through consular inspection and certification, is a belated revival of a proposition that has received more careful and expert consideration than any other measure affecting immigration that has been urged upon the attention of Congress. Every material point in the case was raised and determined in the investigation of the "Weber Commission" of 1890–1891. The adverse report of this Commission was formally endorsed by Secretaries Gresham and Carlisle and its conclusion has been enforced by the repeated examination and judgment of successive committees on immigration. In the latest hearings before the Senate Committee on Immigration in 1902, the undesirability of regulation by consular inspection was expressly attested by Mr. Charles Warren, representing the Immigration Restriction League, who stated: "I do not think that there is a prominent man who has taken up the subject, who advocates it;" and the Chairman of the Committee confirmed this conclusion by observing: "I understand that the idea of consular inspection has been practically abandoned."

Proposal for "Educational Tests"

The proposition for the introduction of the so-called "educational test" was judicially considered and rejected in the message accompanying the *veto* of President Cleveland on March 2d, 1897. No statement of the case is more obviously impartial or can carry a greater weight of individual authority.

In this statement he observed: "A radical departure from our national policy relating to immigration is here presented. Heretofore we have welcomed all who came to us from other lands, except those whose moral or physical condition or history threatened danger to our national welfare and safety. Relying upon the jealous watchfulness of our people to prevent injury to our political and social fabric, we have encouraged those coming from foreign countries to cast their lot with us and join in the development of our vast domain, securing in return a share in the blessings of American citizenship.

"A century's stupendous growth, largely due to the assimilation and thrift of millions of sturdy and patriotic adopted citizens, attests the success of this generous and free-handed policy, which, while guarding the people's interests, exacts from our immigrants only physical and moral soundness and a willingness and ability to work.

"A contemplation of the grand results of this policy cannot fail to arouse a sentiment in its defense; for, however it might have been regarded as an original proposition and viewed as an experiment, its accomplishments are such that if it is to be uprooted at this late day, its disadvantages should be plainly apparent and the substitute adopted should be just and adequate, free from uncertainties and guarded against difficult or oppressive administration.

"It is not claimed, I believe, that the time has come for the further restriction of immigration on the ground that an excess of population overcrowds our land.

"It is said, however, that the quality of recent immigration is undesirable. The time is quite within recent memory when the same thing was said of immigrants who with their descendants are now numbered among our best citizens.

"It is said that too many immigrants settle in our cities, thus dangerously increasing their idle and vicious population. This is certainly a disadvantage. It cannot be shown, however, that it affects all our cities, nor that it is permanent; nor does it appear that this condition, where it exists, demands as its remedy the reversal of our present immigration policy.

"The best reason that could be given for this radical restriction of immigration is the necessity of protecting our population against degeneration and saving our national peace and quiet from imported turbulence and disorder.

"I cannot believe that we would be protected against these evils by limiting immigration to those who can read and write in any language twenty-five words of our Constitution. In my opinion it is infinitely more safe to admit a hundred thousand immigrants who, though unable to read and write, seek among us only a home and opportunity to work, than to admit one of those unruly agitators and enemies of governmental control, who can not only read and write, but delight in arousing by inflammatory speech the illiterate and peacefully inclined to discontent and tumult. Violence and disorder do not originate with illiterate laborers. They are rather the victims of the educated agitator. The ability to read and write as required in this bill, in and of itself, affords, in my opinion, a misleading test of contented industry and supplies unsatisfactory evidence of desirable citizenship or a proper apprehension of the benefits of our institutions. If any particular element of our illiterate immigration is to be feared for other causes than illiteracy, these causes should be dealt with directly instead of making illiteracy the pretext for exclusion, to the detriment of other illiterate immigrants against whom the real cause of complaint cannot be alleged."

Hon. Samuel J. Barrows, Secretary of the Prison Association of New York, has characterized this test as a suggestion of literary dilettanteism—not measuring the extent of education in its true meaning as the drawing out of faculty, or the capability for useful and needed service, nor gauging the moral character of any immigrant. In view of this apparent certainty, it may be noted without unfairness that the probable effect of the adoption of this test seems to be of much more concern to the bulk of its advocates than the justice and fitness of its application. It is the simplest and handiest resort for cutting down immigration and it is calculated that it will bear chiefly on the immigration from Southern Europe, which is the most novel and hence least expert in settlement and least supported by widely distributed roots here.

Without discussing further, therefore, the application of this particular device of reduction, it is of prime importance to meet the broader issue—the pressure for the curtailing of immigration. Its advocacy must be based, necessarily, on one of two assumptions—that, in spite of all present safeguards, part of the present influx is unfit to enter this country, or that there is no longer an opening here for the labor seeking admission.

In maintenance of the first proposition, it is alleged broadly that our foreign-born population shows a higher percentage of criminality than the native born; that the immigration from Southern Europe is more burdensome proportionately to our prisons and asylums than the immigration from Northern Europe; and that these immigrants are the makers of the slums of our great cities and are largely thriftless and unprogressive. These are too common impressions through prejudiced and misinformed disparagement, but records of unquestionable authority demonstrate that none of these assertions is correct.

The Immigrant and Crime

In view of the services of the immigrant in upbuilding this country, there might be some just palliation of a percentage of law breaking in excess of that of the native born. The immigrant has not been reared in conformity with our laws and social restrictions and has been negligently housed in the slums. Yet in spite of our slum traps it does not appear that the record of the immigrant needs any special consideration. Hastings H. Hart, General Secretary of the National Conference of Charities and Correction, has contributed a notable demonstration of the comparative criminality of our foreign and native-born population, in a communication to the *American Journal of Sociology* for November, 1896.

Mr. Hart shows from the United States Census returns (*a*) "that as a matter of fact the foreign-born population furnishes only two-thirds as many criminals as the native-born; (*b*) that while it is true that the native-born children of foreign-born parents furnish more criminals proportionately than those whose parents are native born, yet in more than half the States the showing is in favor of the children of the foreign born; (*c*) that the combined ratio of prisoners of foreign birth and those born of foreign-born parents to the same classes in the community at large is only eighty-four per cent. of the ratio of native-born prisoners to the same class in the community at large."

A common error arises, as he notes, "from comparing the criminal population, foreign and native, with the whole of the general population, foreign and native. The young children of the community furnish practically no prisoners, and nearly all of these children are native born, whether the parents are native born or not. The consequence is that Mr. Hawes has not only given the native population credit for its own children, who are not criminals, but has taken the native-born children of foreign parents, adding them to the native-born population and counting them against their own parents."

"Of the prisoners of the United States 98.5 per cent. are above the age of sixteen years; 95 per cent. are above the age of eighteen years; and 84 per cent. are above the age of twenty-one years. The native-born population of the United States in 1890 numbered 53,390,600; the native-born prisoners 65,977; ratio 1235 in a million. The foreign-born population numbered 9,231,381; the foreign-born prisoners 16,352; ratio 1,744 in a million; an apparent excess of foreigners over native of 41 per cent. But the number of native-born males of voting age was 12,591,852; native-born male prisoners 61,637; ratio 4,895 in a million. The number of foreign-born males of voting age was 4,348,459; foreign-born male prisoners 14,287; ratio 3,285; showing an actual excess of natives over foreigners of 50 per cent."

The accuracy of Mr. Hart's conclusions has since been sustained by a number of independent inquiries of less extended range embracing the ascertainable returns of a number of States whose records are most complete and reliable. The basis of his reckoning of parentage is criticized in the statistical report of the United States Industrial Commission on Immigration transmitted to Congress on December 5th, 1901, but his general conclusion is affirmed as follows, viz.: "From this table it will be seen that taking the United States as a whole, the whites of foreign birth are a trifle less criminal than the total number of whites of native birth."

In the report of the Commission there is further noted very significantly the nationality which has contributed far more largely than any other to raise the average of the criminality and pauperism of the foreign born:

"Taking the inmates of all Penal and Charitable Institutions we find that the highest ratio is shown by the Irish, whose proportion is more than double the average for the foreign born, amounting to no less than 16,624 to the million."

There are, unfortunately, too few States that have taken pains to secure and record exact statistics of crime and pauperism for the comparison of nationalities and birth. Among these few is the State of Indiana, and the report of State Statistician Johnson for 1902 significantly shows that a common impression as to the relative criminality of the foreign born is by no means a reliable guide for restrictive legislation. In this report it is noted: "The great majority of Indiana evil-doers who find their way eventually to the State Prison and Reformatory are American born. In the State prison, out of 751 convicts, 531 are white Americans and 122 American negroes, 48 Irish, 27 Germans, 7 English, 4 French, 3 Scotch, 1 Welsh, 1 Russian, 1 Pole, 1 Belgian."

"At the Reformatory at Jeffersonville, with 919 inmates, 696 are white Americans, 191 American negroes, 10 Germans, 2 French, 3 Canadians, 8 English, 1 Scotch, 1 Belgian, 1 Swiss and 2 Irish."

There is a further special contention of the Immigration Restriction League, bearing most severely upon the Italian immigrant, that a "parallelism exists between the criminal tendencies and the illiteracy of the same races." In addressing the Senate Committee on Immigration of the last Congress, Prescott F. Hall, Secretary of this League, cited in support of his contention a tabulated statement from the Twenty-fourth Annual Report of the Massachusetts Prison Commissioners for the year ending September 30th, 1894.

The conclusion which he sought to draw from this report was opposed on the floor of the Senate in December, 1896, by Senators Gibson, Caffery, and others, and the general character of the filtered immigration was attested in particular by an extract from a report of the Commissioner General of Immigration for the year 1895–6 as follows:

"It is gratifying to me to be again able to report to you that I know of no immigrant landed in this country within the last year who is now a burden upon any public or private institution.

"With some exceptions the physical characteristics of the year's immigration were those of a hardy, sound laboring class, accustomed and apparently well able to earn a livelihood wherever capable and industrious labor can secure employment."

There was, however, no direct challenging of the statistical prop of the Immigration Restriction League and its inference until it was picked up and shaken by Samuel J. Barrows, Secretary of the Prison Association of New York, on December 9th, 1902, in a hearing given by the Senate Committee on Immigration. "The Italian people," said Mr. Barrows, "as a whole are a frugal and industrious people. In our statistics we sometimes make discriminations against them that are not correct. We had an illustration of this in Massachusetts. A report was prepared by the Immigration Restriction League which was based upon the criminal record of the Italians in Massachusetts, leaving out all crimes which had been produced through intoxication. That is the way that ingenious plan of statistics was drawn. So they tried to make out a bad case against the Italians.

"Now Massachusetts is the one State in the Union that has made the most thorough examination of the whole question of the relation of intemperance

to crime, and the report on that subject in 1895 by the Bureau of Labor
Statistics there shows that about 87 per cent. of all the crime in Massachusetts grew out of intemperance in some form. When you take then the
Italian population of Boston and of Massachusetts, and ask how many of
those people were imprisoned or arrested or committed crime because of
intemperance, you find that they rise away above all the Northern races—
that is, commit fewer crimes from this cause. The Italian people are a tem-
perate people, and while in Massachusetts three in a hundred of the
Northern races, including the Scotch, the Irish, the English and the Germans, were arrested for intemperance, only three in a thousand of the Italians were arrested. What a remarkable bearing that has upon desirability
and availability."

The evidence of Mr. Barrows is further specifically attested in the
report of the United States Industrial Commission on Immigration, covering the tables compiled by the Prison Commissioners of Massachusetts,
referred to by Mr. Hall. This report states: "It appears from the table that
of prisoners committed to all institutions in proportion to a thousand population of the same nativity those born in Massachusetts numbered 7.5
per thousand, but that, omitting those committed for intoxication, the
number is 2.6 per thousand. Below this proportion stand immigrants
from Portugal, Austria, Germany, Russia and Finland. The leading nationality above this average is that of the Irish, whose commitments per thousand were 27.1, but omitting intoxication was 6. Next in order of
commitments are Welsh, English, Scotch, and Norwegians, all of which
show a large predominance of intoxication. The Italians are a marked
exception, the commitments numbering 12.9 for all causes, and 10 for
causes except intoxication.

The Immigrant and Pauperism

An allied contention of the Immigration Restriction League is the rolling
up of the burden of pauperism through the influx of Southern Latin immigration. As Massachusetts has been picked out by preference on the basis
of its exhibit, invidiously distinguishing the Italian immigrant, Massachusetts authority of unimpeachable character is here cited in flat contradiction of this assumption.

In the Twenty-third Annual Report of the Associated Charities of Boston,
November, 1902, it is stated:

"The variation in the number of Italians applying for assistance is interesting: 54 families came to us in 1891, and only 69 in the last year, though
the Italian population of this city has in the meantime increased from
4,718 to 13,738. This fact seems to corroborate the report of Conference
6 (embracing the North-End District or Italian quarter), which described
the Italian immigrant as usually able to get on by himself except in case of
sickness, when temporary help is needed."

It is obvious that this report marks not only a low rate of pauperism
but a very material decrease in the percentage of applicants for charity
in the face of the much decried influx during the closing years of the last
century.

The report of District 6 Conference, referred to in the above summary,
remarks: "As the Italian families so largely outnumber the others, and as

the Italian element is now predominant in the district, it is worth while to note the chief causes of extreme poverty.

"We observe that intemperance is not found as a chief or as a subsidiary cause in any of this year's list of Italian families. Sickness was the leading chief cause (10) and also the leading subsidiary cause (9); next in order, come the following chief causes: lack of employment due to no fault of employee (4); physical or mental defects (2); roving disposition (3); dishonesty (2); disregard of family ties, lack of training for work, and lack of thrift (1 each).

"If any general inference is fair from so small a number of cases, it is that the Italian families referred to us have not been in the greatest distress. The majority of the Italians are apparently fairly thrifty and those who have trouble are often helped by their countrymen. The little that we have been called upon to do has in some cases set a family at once upon its feet."

The assumption that illiteracy is a prolific source of pauperism is not sustained by the examination of cases known to this Conference, so far, at least, as the Italian immigrant is concerned. "In the matter of illiteracy," the Conference of District 6 states, "we can give positive information about only 45 of the 68 families (applying for aid)—mostly Italians." The record shows 32 Italian families, with 64 parents born in Italy. "Among heads of these families, we find 32 who can read and write; 2 who can read and not write, while 11 can neither read nor write."

As to the burden imposed by recent arrivals the report of Conference 4 is noteworthy: "We found that none of the new arrivals (needing help) were recent immigrants and that almost all of the parents were born in the United States or Great Britain."

Another exact and authoritative record giving an exhibit of pauperism in New York City and its distribution by nationalities is presented in the Thirty-fifth Annual Report of the State Board of Charities of New York, containing the proceedings of the New York State Conference of Charities and Correction at the Second Annual Session held in New York City, November 19th, 20th, 21st, and 22d, 1901. At this Conference an address on "The Problems of the Almshouse" was given by Hon. W. Keller, President of the Department of Public Charities of the City of New York. In the course of his discussion the following table was presented showing the nativity of persons admitted to the Almshouse in 1900:

	MALE.	FEMALE.	TOTAL.
United States	355	199	554
Ireland	808	809	1,617
England and Wales	111	87	198
Scotland	25	14	39
France	19	2	21
Germany	290	84	374
Norway, Sweden and Denmark	22	6	28
Italy	15	4	19
Other countries	50	36	86
Total	1,695	1,241	2,936

"Out of a total of 2,936 only 554 were born in the United States; 2,382 were foreign born, and of this number 1,617 were born in Ireland alone." The determination of the general distribution of pauperism by nationalities has been made in the report of the United States Industrial Commission on Immigration transmitted to the Fifty-seventh Congress. "The proportion of the nationalities among the paupers in our almshouses varies very greatly. The Irish show far and away the largest proportion, no less than 7,550 per million inhabitants, as compared with 3,031 for the average of all the foreign-born. The French come next, while the proportion of paupers among the Germans is somewhat unexpectedly high. The remarkably low degree of pauperism among the Italians is possibly due to the fact that such a large percentage of them are capable of active labor, coming to this country especially for that purpose."

These citations are not made with the design of casting any particular reproach upon the Irish nationality, but simply to correct a prevalent impression discrediting the influx of the Southern Latin races and the alleged relation of illiteracy to pauperism, for it is morally certain that the alleged "educational test" would not be urged, if it bore severely upon the Irish immigrant, whose value to the country is generally conceded.

The Immigrant and the Slum

There has been a strenuous harping on the disastrous effect of immigration in filling the slums of our cities and in the prolific breeding of crime and disease. Fortunately for the credit of the immigrants, there has been of late years a dawning perception that it is the tenement, not the tenant, that makes the slum and that the rational remedy for congestion does not lie in the exclusion of the flow of productive labor, but in its effective regulation and distribution. Our present slums are the natural outgrowth of the reckless laxity of our building laws and sanitary regulations. They are plainly chargeable to our civic blindness and the toleration of greed. It is the native-born rookery, not the foreign-born influx, that must bear the burden of reproach for the slum.

This has been conclusively demonstrated in the partial transformation already effected by the pressure of necessity and the sense of responsibility.

In the pithy conclusion of Jacob Riis: "Wherever the Gospel and the sunlight go hand in hand in the battle with the slum, there it is already won— there is an end of it at once." Sometimes the slum has been conquered by cutting out sections bodily, as was done in the annihilation of the infamous Five Points, in the opening of Paradise Park, a playground for the children. "Mulberry Bend," as Mr. Riis observes, "was the worst pigsty of all." "I do not believe that there was a week in all the twenty years I had to do with the den, as a police reporter, in which I was not called to record there a stabbing or shooting affair, some act of violence. It is now five years since the Bend became a park, and the police reporter has not had business there once during that time; not once has a shot been fired or a knife been drawn."

Reconstruction is not a gift enterprise nor a charitable donation. Street widenings and the opening of squares and little parks are the changing of antiquated, inconvenient and unhealthful conditions for the essential requirements of a modern city. Reconstruction of dwellings to meet proper requirements is not any half-way approach to the erection of almshouses. It has been repeatedly demonstrated that the so-called model tenements will unfailingly pay even higher average returns than the business buildings erected under modern regulations in the best city locations. Even where there is an apparent strain of philanthropy or extraordinary accommodation for the rental charges, as in the erection of the Riverside Tenements in Brooklyn, the return is certified to be never less than six and even seven per cent. on the investment.

Relief of Congestion

The relief of congestion by more effective distribution is undoubtedly desirable. The importance of this provision of relief has been emphasized repeatedly by our Commissioners of Immigration, and it is particulary urged by the present Commissioner General as the only adequate solution of the so-called "problem of immigration." This national concern may rationally and appropriately be a national undertaking, as leading sociologists and practical handlers of immigration have insistently advised.

Wider distribution, so far as it has been effected by local and spasmodic effort and the drift of unassisted settlement, has done away with any complaints of the influx. Recent and searching inquiries among the smaller cities and towns of the country as to the condition and occupation of the immigrants show that they are now fully employed, as a rule, and that their sterling qualities are clearly appreciated.

With scarcely an exception, when they have been drawn into the agricultural districts their settlements have been thriving. Their knowledge of intensive farming enables them to develop exhausted soils and even abandoned farms successfully. The chief obstacle in the way of this drift has been the prejudice against agriculture derived from bitter experience with land monopoly and disproportionate taxation in their native countries, but this prejudice is disappearing with the better information now spreading among them.

There has never been a period in which the Southern States have been so energetic in courting immigration. They see in it the surest and quickest solution of their labor and racial problems. The recent organization of the "Four States League" and the formation, only a few weeks ago, of the "Immigration Association of South Carolina," are significant indications of a rising demand for immigration, notwithstanding the extraordinary flow of recent years to this country. There has been a very considerable attraction of Italians already to the sugar cane plantations, and the influx to the Southern States should grow with the extending familiarity of the immigrants and the rising appreciation of their peculiar adaptation for varied plantation service. Even if the South continues to draw largely from the North and West, as at present, instead of enlisting the newcomers directly, the drain of older settlers must be filled by immigration or the North will suffer.

There is further an expanding demand for the heavy outdoor labor of the recent immigrant in the extension of public works of all kinds, railway building, etc. These elemental undertakings in industrial development are necessarily dependent on the certainty of the supply of willing and sturdy labor, and their progress will inevitably be checked by any shrinkage of this supply. It is apparent that the effect of this employment and the consequent development of the country should be to expand the demand for workers in every line of industry. Hence the entry of immigrants does not operate to exclude American laborers now here from profitable occupation, but surely in the long run to increase the demand for their labor.

JOHN SPARGO

From The Bitter Cry of the Children[†]

The Blighting of the Babies

v

However interesting and sociologically valuable such an analysis might be, the separation of the different features of poverty so as to determine their relative influence upon the sum of mortality and sickness is manifestly impossible. We cannot say that bad housing accounts for so many deaths, poor clothing for so many, and hunger for so many more. These and other evils are regularly associated in cases of poverty, the underfed being almost invariably poorly clad, and housed in the least healthy homes. We cannot regard them as distinct problems; they are only different phases of the same problem of poverty,—a problem which does not lend itself to dissection at the hands of the investigator. Still, notwithstanding that for many years all efforts to reduce the rate of mortality among infants have dealt only with questions of bad housing and of unhygienic conditions in general,—on the assumption that these are the most important factors making for a high rate of infant mortality,—it is now generally admitted that, important as they are in themselves, these are relatively unimportant factors in the infant death-rate. "Sanitary conditions do not make any real difference at all," and "It is food and food alone," was the testimony of Dr. Vincent before the British Interdepartmental Committee, and he was supported by some of the most eminent of his colleagues in that position. That the evils of underfeeding are intensified when there is an unhygienic environment is true, but it is equally true that defect in the diet is the prime and essential cause of an excessive prevalence of infantile diseases and of a high death-rate.

Perhaps no part of the population of our great cities suffers so much upon the whole from overcrowding and bad housing as the poorest class of Jews, yet the mortality of infants among them is much less than among the poor of other nationalities, as, for instance, among the Irish and the Italians. Dr. S. A. Knopf, one of our foremost authorities upon the subject of tuberculosis, places underfeeding and improper feeding first, and bad housing and insanitary conditions in general second as factors in the causation of children's diseases. In Birmingham, England, an elaborate

† New York: Macmillan, 1906.

study of the vital statistics of nineteen years showed that there had been a large decrease in the general death-rate, due, apparently, to no other cause than the extensive sanitary improvements made in that period, but the rate of infantile mortality remained absolutely unchanged. The average general death-rate for the nine years, 1873–1881, was 23.5 per thousand; in the ten years, 1882–1891, it was only 20.6. But the infantile death-rate was not affected, and remained at 169 per thousand during both periods. There had been a reduction of 12 per cent in the general death-rate, while that for infants showed no reduction. Had this been decreased in like degree, the infantile mortality would have fallen from 169 to 148 per thousand.

Extensive inquiries in the various children's hospitals and dispensaries in New York, and among physicians of large practice in the poorer quarters of several cities, point with striking unanimity to the same general conclusion. The Superintendents of six large dispensaries, at which more than 25,000 children are treated annually, were asked what proportion of the cases treated could be ascribed, on a conservative estimate, primarily to inadequate nutrition, and the average of their replies was 45 per cent.

In one case the Registrar in a cursory examination of the register for a single day pointed out eleven cases out of a total of seventeen, due almost beyond question entirely to under-nutrition.

The Superintendent of the New York Babies' Hospital, Miss Marianna Wheeler, kindly copied from the admission book particulars of sixteen consecutive cases. The list shows malnutrition as the most prominent feature of 75 per cent of the cases. Miss Wheeler says: "The large majority of our cases are similar to these given; in fact, if I kept on right down the admission book, would find the same facts in case after case."

VI

As in all human problems, ignorance plays an important role in this great problem of childhood's suffering and misery. The tragedy of the infant's position is its helplessness; not only must it suffer on account of the misfortunes of its parents, but it must suffer from their vices and from their ignorance as well. Nurses, sick visitors, dispensary doctors, and those in charge of babies' hospitals tell pitiful stories of almost incredible ignorance of which babies are the victims. A child was given cabbage by its mother when it was three weeks old; another, seven weeks old, was fed for several days in succession on sausage and bread with pickles! Both died of gastritis, victims of ignorance. In another New York tenement home a baby less than nine weeks old was fed on sardines with vinegar and bread by its mother. Even more pathetic is the case of the baby, barely six weeks old, found by a district nurse in Boston in the family clothes-basket which formed its cradle, sucking a long strip of salt, greasy bacon and with a bottle containing beer by its side. Though rescued from immediate death, this child will probably never recover wholly from the severe intestinal disorder induced by the ignorance of its mother. Yet, after all, it is doubtful whether the beer and bacon were worse for it than many of the patent "infant foods" of the cheaper kinds commonly given in good faith to the children of the poor. If medical opinion goes for anything, many of these "foods" are little better than slow poisons. Tennyson's awful charge is still true, that:—

"The spirit of murder works in the very means of life."

Nor is the work of this spirit of murder confined to the concoction of "patent foods" which are in reality patent poisons. The adulteration of milk with formaldehyde and other base adulterants is responsible for a great deal of infant mortality, and its ravages are chiefly confined to the poor. It is little short of alarming that in New York City, out of 3970 samples of milk taken from dealers for analysis during 1902, no less than 2095, or 52.77 per cent, should have been found to be adulterated. Mr. Nathan Straus, the philanthropist whose Pasteurized milk depots have saved many thousands of baby lives during the past twelve years, has not hesitated to call this adulteration by its proper name, child-murder. He says:—

"If I should hire Madison Square Garden and announce that at eight o'clock on a certain evening I would publicly strangle a child, what excitement there would be!

"If I walked out into the ring to carry out my threat, a thousand men would stop me and kill me—and everybody would applaud them for doing so.

"But every day children are actually murdered by neglect or by poisonous milk. The murders are as real as the murder would be if I should choke a child to death before the eyes of a crowd.

"It is hard to interest the people in what they don't see."

Ignorance is indeed a grave and important phase of the problem, and the most difficult of all to deal with. Education is the remedy, of course, but how shall we accomplish it? It is not easy to educate after the natural days of education are passed. Mrs. Havelock Ellis has advocated "a noviciate for marriage," a period of probation and of preparation and equipment for marriage and maternity. But such a proposal is too far removed from the sphere of practicality to have more than an academic interest at present. Simply worded letters to mothers upon the care and feeding of their infants, supplemented by personal visits from well-trained women visitors, would help, as similar methods have helped, in the campaign against tuberculosis. Many foreign municipalities have adopted this plan, notably Huddersfield, England, and several American cities have followed their example with marked success. There should be no great difficulty about its adoption generally. One great obstacle to be overcome is the resentment of the mothers whom it is most necessary to reach, as many of those engaged in philanthropic work know all too well. One poor woman, whose little child was ailing, became very irate when a lady visitor ventured to offer her some advice concerning the child's clothing and food, and soundly berated her would-be adviser. "You talk to me about how to look after my baby!" she cried. "Why, I guess I know more about it than you do. I've buried nine already!" It is not the naïve humor of the poor woman's wrath that is most significant, but the grim, tragic pathos back of it. Those four words, "I've buried nine already!" tell more eloquently than could a hundred learned essays or polished orations the vastness of civilization's failure. For, surely, we may not regard it as anything but failure so long as women who have borne eleven children into the world, as had this one, can say, "I've buried nine already!"

But circular letters and lady visitors will not solve the problem of maternal ignorance; such methods can only skim the surface of the evil. This ignorance on the part of mothers, of which the babies are victims, is deeply rooted in the soil of those economic conditions which constitute poverty in the broadest sense of the term, though there may be no destitution or absolute want. It is not poverty in the narrow sense of a lack of the material necessities of life, but rather a condition in which these are obtainable only by the concentrated effort of all members of the family able to contribute anything and to the exclusion of all else in life. Young girls who go to work in shops and factories as soon as they are old enough to obtain employment frequently continue working up to within a few days of marriage, and not infrequently return to work for some time after marriage. Especially is this true of girls employed in mills and factories; their male acquaintances are for the most part fellow-workers, and marriages between them are numerous. Where many women are employed men's wages are, as a consequence, almost invariably low, with the result that after marriage it is as necessary that the woman should work as it was before.

When the years which under more favored conditions would have been spent at home in preparation for the duties of wifehood and motherhood are spent behind the counter, at the bench, or amid the whirl of machinery in the factory, it is scarcely to be wondered at that the knowledge of domestic economy is scant among them, and that so many utterly fail as wives and mothers. Deprived of the opportunities of helping their mothers with the housework and cooking and the care of the younger children, marriage finds them ill-equipped; too often they are slaves to the frying-pan, or to the stores where cooked food may be bought in small quantities. Bad cooking, extravagance, and mismanagement are incidental to our modern industrial conditions.

VII

But there is a great deal of improper feeding of infants which, apparently due to ignorance, is in reality due to other causes, and the same is true of what appears to be neglect. In every large city there are hundreds of married women and mothers who must work to keep the family income up to the level of sufficiency for the maintenance of its members. According to the census of 1900 there were 769,477 married women "gainfully employed" in the United States, but there is every reason to believe that the actual number was much greater, for it is a well-known fact that married women, especially in factories, often represent themselves as being single, for the reason, possibly, that it is considered more or less of a disgrace to have to continue working after marriage. Moreover, it is certain that many thousands of women who work irregularly, a day or two a week, or, as in many cases, only at intervals during the sickness or unemployment of their husbands, were omitted. A million would probably be well within the mark as an estimate of the number of married women workers, the census figures notwithstanding. These working mothers may be conveniently divided into two classes, the home workers, such as dressmakers, "finishers" employed in the clothing trades, and many others; and the many thousands who are employed away from their homes in cigar-making, cap-making, the textile industries, laundry work, and a score of other occupations including domestic service.

The proportion of married women having small children is probably larger among those employed in the home industries than in those which are carried on outside of the homes. Out of 748 female home "finishers" in New York, for instance, 658 were married and 557 had from one to seven children each. The percentage could hardly equal that in the outside industries. While there are exceptional cases, as a rule no married woman, especially if she has young children, will go out to work unless forced to do so by sheer necessity. Dr. Annie S. Daniel, in a most interesting study of the conditions in 515 families where the wives worked as finishers, found that no less than 448, or 86.78 per cent of the whole, were obliged to work by reason of poverty arising from low wages, frequent unemployment, or sickness of their husbands. Of the other 67 cases, 45 of the women were widows, 15 had been deserted, and 7 had husbands who were intemperate and shiftless. Of all causes low wages was the most common, the average weekly income of the men being only $3.81. The average of the combined weekly earnings of man and wife was $4.85, and rent, which averaged $8.99 per month, absorbed almost one-half of this. In addition to the earnings of the men and women, there were other smaller sources of income, such as children's wages and money received from lodgers, which brought the average income per family of 4½ persons up to $5.69 per week.

Nothing could be further from the truth than the comfortable delusion under which so many excellent people live, that so long as the work is done at home the children will not be neglected nor suffer. While it is doubtless true that home employment of the mother is somewhat less disadvantageous to the child than if she were employed away from home,—though more injurious from the point of view of the mother herself,—the fact is that such employment is in every way prejudicial to the child. Even if the joint income of both parents raises the family above want, the conditions under which that income is earned must involve serious neglect of the child. The mother is taken away from her household duties and the care of her children; her time is given an economic value which makes it too precious to be spent upon anything but the most important thing of all,— provision for their material needs. She has no time for cooking and little for eating; the children must shift for themselves.

Thus the employment of the mother is responsible for numerous evils of underfeeding, improper feeding, and neglect. She works from early morn till night, pausing only twice or thrice a day to snatch a hasty meal of bread and coffee with the children. Her pay varies with the kind of work she does, from one-and-a-half to ten cents an hour. Ordinarily she will work from twelve to fourteen hours daily, but sometimes, when the work has to be finished and delivered by a fixed time, she may work sixteen, eighteen, or even twenty hours at a stretch. And then there are the "waiting days" when work is slack, and hunger, or the fear of hunger, weighs heavily upon her and crushes her down. Hard is her lot, for when she works there is food, but little time for eating and none for cooking or the care of her children; when there is no work there is time enough, but little food.

In Brooklyn, in a rear tenement in the heart of that huge labyrinth of bricks and mortar near the Great Bridge, such a mother lives and struggles against poverty and the Great White Plague. She is an American, born of American parents, and her husband is also native-born but of Scotch parentage. He is a laborer and when at work earns $1.75 per day, but partly owing to frequently recurring sickness and partly also to the difficulty of obtaining employment, it is doubtful whether his wages average $6 a week the year through. Of six children born only two are living, their ages being seven years and two-and-a-half years respectively. Both are rickety and weak and stunted in appearance. As she sat upon her bed sewing, only pausing to cough when the plague seemed to choke her, she told her story: "It's awful," she said, "but I must work else we shall get nothing to eat and be turned into the street besides. I have no time for anything but work. I must work, work, work, and work. Often we go to our beds as we left them when I haven't time or strength to shake them up, and Joe, my husband, is too tired or sick to do it. Cooking? Oh, I cook nothing, for I haven't time; I must work. I send the little girl out to the store across the way and she gets what she can,—crackers, cake, cheese, anything she can get—and I'm thankful if I can only make some fresh tea." Neither of this woman's two little children has ever known the experience of being decently fed, and their weak, rickety bodies tell the results. From a bare account of their diet it might be inferred that the mother must be ignorant or neglectful, but she is, on the contrary, a most intelligent woman and devoted to her children. Under better conditions she would perhaps have been a model housewife and mother, but it is not within the possibilities of her toil-worn, hunger-wasted body to be these and at the same time a wage-earner. So, without attempting to minimize the part which ignorance plays, it is well to emphasize the fact, so often lost sight of and forgotten, that what appears to be ignorance or neglect is very frequently only poverty in one of its many disguises.

* * *

The School Child

It is common to hear teachers in poor districts say: "When I first came to this school my heart used to ache with pity on account of the poverty-stricken appearance of many of the children and the sad tales they sometimes tell. But now I have grown used to it all." That, in many cases, tells the whole secret—they have grown accustomed to the sight of stunted bodies and wan, pinched faces. There are teachers, earnest men and women devoted to their profession, and consecrating it by an almost religious passion, who study the home life and social environment of the children intrusted to their care; but they are, unhappily, exceptions. The number of teachers having no idea of how a healthy child should look is astonishingly large. The hectic flush of disease is often mistaken by teachers and principals for the bloom of health.

In one large school the principal, in the course of a personally conducted visit to the different classrooms, singled out a little Italian girl, and asked with a note of pride in his voice: "Wouldn't you call this a healthy child? I do. Look at her round, full face." There were a great many signs of ill health in that little girl's appearance which the good principal did not recognize. I pointed out some of the signs of grave nervous disorder, due, as I afterward learned, almost beyond question, to malnutrition. Her cheeks were well rounded, but her pitifully thin arms indicated a very ill-developed body. I pointed out her nervous hand, the baggy fulness under her eyes, and the abrasions at the corners of her twitching mouth, and asked that the teacher might be consulted as to the girl's school record. "She is not a very bright child," said the teacher, "and what to do with her is a problem. She is very nervous, irritable, and excitable. She seems to get exhausted very soon, and it is impossible for her to apply herself properly to her work. I think very likely that she is underfed, for she comes from a very poor home." Subsequent investigation at her home, on Mott Street, showed that her father, who is a consumptive, earns from sixty cents to a dollar a day peddling laces, needles, and other small articles, the rest of the income supporting the family of seven persons being derived from the mother's labor. They occupy one small room, and the only means of cooking they have is a small gas "ring" such as is sold for ten cents in the cheap stores.

Where principals and teachers declined to assist, it was impossible to make inquiries in the schools, and it was useless to make them in schools where the children had already been openly questioned. Wherever it was possible to secure the coöperation of principals or teachers, I got them to question the children privately and sympathetically. In 16 schools, 12,800 children were thus privately examined, and of that number 987, or 7.71 per cent, were reported as having had no breakfast upon the day of the inquiry, and 1963, or 15.32 per cent, as having had altogether too little. Teachers were asked to exclude as far as possible all cases of an obviously accidental nature from the returns, as, for instance, when a child known to be in fairly comfortable circumstances had come to school without breakfast merely because of lack of appetite. They were also requested to regard as having had inadequate breakfasts only children who had had bread only (with or without tea or coffee), or such things as crackers or crullers in place of bread, but without milk, cereals, cake, butter, jam, eggs, fruit, fish, or meat of any kind. That this standard was altogether too low will probably be admitted without question, but there was no way of examining the actual meals of the children, and some sort of arbitrary rule was necessary. The figures given are therefore based on a very low standard, and most certainly do not include all cases either of the unfed or underfed. It is more than probable that some children who had gone without breakfasts refused to admit the fact, and there were several instances in which children known to be desperately poor, and who, the teachers felt, were certainly underfed, gave the most surprising accounts—which must have been drawn from their imaginations—of elaborate breakfasts. Out of 12,800 children, then, 2950, or more than 23 per cent, were found either wholly breakfastless or having had such miserably poor breakfasts as described. And that is certainly an understatement of the evil of underfeeding in those schools.

*   *   *

ANONYMOUS

Neighbors[†]

Friends of Mr. Riis—and who that ever knew the man or his work was not his friend?—will welcome this volume of brief sketches from his pen. They

† New York Times, Dec, 6, 1914.

are mere outlines, some of them, impressions, yet all of them true and vital. Most of the stories are of conditions as they existed ten years or so ago, and to one who knows, they form a cheering milestone that proves that the world does move ahead. In spite of the criticism of the delays of organized charity, for instance, we do not hear today of the "greenhorn" tying his feet together with his prayer shawl and committing suicide to bring relief to his starving family. The Heartsease Home, so sympathetically described, has left its west side slum long ago, and still, though the space and pure air of its new environment are costly, still "the rent is pledged by half a dozen friends, and the rest—comes."

The message of the book is an optimistic one:

I am not learned in such things. Perhaps I am wrong. No doubt dogmas are useful—to wrap things in—but even then I would not tuck in the ends, lost we hide the neighbor so that we cannot see him. After all, it is what is in the package that counts. To me it is the evidence of such as these that God lives in human hearts—that we are molded in His image despite flaws and failures in the casting—that keeps alive the belief that we shall wake with the flowers to a fairer Spring.

LILLIAN D. WALD

From The House on Henry Street[†]

Chapter IV. Children and Play

The visitor who sees our neighborhood for the first time at the hour when school is dismissed reacts with joy or dismay to the sight, not paralleled in any part of the world, of thousands of little ones on a single city block.

Out they pour, the little hyphenated Americans, more conscious of their patriotism than perhaps any other large group of children that could be found in our land; unaware that to some of us they carry on their shoulders our hopes of a finer, more democratic America, when the worthy things they bring to us shall be recognized, and the good in their old-world traditions and culture shall be mingled with the best that lies within our new-world ideals. Only through knowledge is one fortified to resist the onslaught of arguments of the superficial observer who, dismayed by the sight, is conscious only of "hordes" and "danger to America" in these little children.

They are irresistible. They open up wide vistas of the many lands from which they come. The multitude passes: swinging walk, lagging step; smiling, serious—just little children, forever appealing, and these, perhaps, more than others, stir the emotions. "Crime, ignorance, dirt, anarchy!" Not theirs the fault if any of these be true, although sometimes perfectly good children are spoiled, as Jacob Riis, that buoyant lover of them, has said. As a nation we must rise or fall as we serve or fail these future citizens.

Their appeal suggests that social exclusions and prejudices separate far more effectively than distance and differing language. They bring a hope

[†] New York: Henry Holt and Company, 1915.

that a better relationship—even the great brotherhood—is not impossible, and that through love and understanding we shall come to know the shame of prejudice.

Instinctively the sympathetic observer feels the possibilities of the young life that passes before the settlement doors, and sincerity demands that something shall be known of the conditions, economic, political, religious, or, perchance, of the mere spirit of venture that brought them here. How often have the conventionally educated been driven to the library to obtain that historic perspective of the people who are in our midst, without which they cannot be understood! What fascinating excursions have been made into folklore in the effort to comprehend some strange custom unexpectedly encountered!

When the anxious friends of the dying Italian brought a chicken to be killed over him, the tenement-house bed became the sacrificial altar of long ago; and when the old, rabbinical-looking grandfather took hairs from the head of the sick child, a bit of his finger-nail, and a garment that had been close to his body, and cast them into the river while he devoutly prayed that the little life might be spared, he declared his faith in the purification of running water.

It is necessary to spend a summer in our neighborhood to realize fully the conditions under which many thousands of children are reared. One night during my first month on the East Side, sleepless because of the heat, I leaned out of the window and looked down on Rivington Street. Life was in full course there. Some of the push-cart venders still sold their wares. Sitting on the curb directly under my window, with her feet in the gutter, was a woman, drooping from exhaustion, a baby at her breast. The fire-escapes, considered the most desirable sleeping-places, were crowded with the youngest and the oldest; children were asleep on the sidewalks, on the steps of the houses and in the empty push-carts; some of the more venturesome men and women with mattress or pillow staggered toward the riverfront or the parks. I looked at my watch. It was two o'clock in the morning!

Many times since that summer of 1893 have I seen similar sights, and always I have been impressed with the kindness and patience, sometimes the fortitude, of our neighbors, and I have marveled that out of conditions distressing and nerve-destroying as these so many children have emerged into fine manhood and womanhood, and often, because of their early experiences, have become intelligent factors in promoting measures to guard the next generation against conditions which they know to be destructive.

Before I lived in the midst of this dense child population, and while I was still in the hospital, I had been touched by glimpses of the life revealed in the games played in the children's ward. Up to that time my knowledge of little ones had been limited to those to whom the people in fairy tales were real, and whose games and stories reflected the protective care of their elders. My own earliest recollections of play had been of story-telling, of housekeeping with all the things in miniature that grown-ups use, and of awed admiration of the big brother who graciously permitted us to witness hair-raising performances in the barn, to which we paid admittance in pins. The children in the hospital ward who were able to be about, usually on crutches or with arms in slings, played "Ambulance" and the "Gerry Society." The latter game dramatized their conception of the famous Society for the Prevention of Cruelty to Children as an ogre that would catch them. The ambulance game was of a child, or a man at work, injured and carried away to the hospital.

Many years' familiarity with the children's attempts to play in the streets has not made me indifferent to its pathos, which is not the less real because the children themselves are unconscious of it. In the midst of the pushcart market, with its noise, confusion, and jostling, the checker or crokinole board is precariously perched on the top of a hydrant, constantly knocked over by the crowd and patiently replaced by the little children. One tearful small boy described his morning when he said he had done nothing but play, but first the "cop" had snatched his dice, then his "cat" (a piece of wood sharpened at both ends), and nobody wanted him to chalk on the sidewalk, and he had been arrested for throwing a ball.

A man since risen to distinction in educational circles, whose childhood was passed in our neighborhood, told me how he and his companions had once taken a dressmaker's lay figure. They had no money to spend on the theater and no place to play in but a cellar. They had admired the gaudy posters of a melodrama in which the hero rescues the lady and carries her over a chasm. Having no lady in their cast, they borrowed the dressmaker's lay figure—without permission. Fortunately, and accidentally, they escaped detection. It is not difficult to see how the entire course of this boy's career might have been altered if arrest had followed, with its consequent humiliation and degradation. At least, looking back upon it, the young man sees how the incident might have deflected his life.

The instruction in folk-dancing which the children now receive in the public schools and recreation centers has done much to develop a wholesome and delightful form of exercise, and has given picturesqueness to the dancing in the streets. But yesterday I found myself pausing on East Houston Street to watch a group of children assemble at the sound of a familiar dance from a hurdy-gurdy, and looking up I met the sympathetic smile of a teamster who also had stopped. The children, absorbed in their dance, were quite unconscious that congested traffic had halted and that busy people had taken a moment from their engrossing problems to be refreshed by the sight of their youth and grace. For that brief instant even the cry of "War Extra" was unheeded.

Touching as are the little children deprived of opportunity for wholesome play, a deeper compassion stirred our hearts when we began to realize the critically tender age at which many of them share the experiences, anxieties, and tragedies of the adult. I cannot efface from my memory the picture of a little eight-year-old girl whom I once found standing on a chair to reach a washtub, trying with her tiny hands to cleanse some bed-linen which would have been a task for an older person. Every few minutes the child got down from her chair to peer into the next room where her mother and the new-born baby lay, all her little mind intent upon giving relief and comfort. She had been alone with her mother when the baby was born and terror was on her face.

I think the memory never left her, but it may be only that her presence called up, even after the lapse of years, a vision of the anxious little face inevitably contrasted in my mind with the picture of irresponsible childhood.

At about the same time we made the acquaintance of the K——— family, through nursing one of the children. The mother was a large-framed, phlegmatic, seemingly emotionless type, although she did show appreciation of our liking for her children. The father was only occasionally mentioned. We assumed that he was away seeking work, a common explanation then of the absence of the men of the families. One afternoon I stopped at their house to make arrangements for the children's trip to the country. Early the next morning, awakened by a pounding on the door, I opened it to find little Esther beside herself with excitement, repeating over and over, "My mother she die! My mother she die!" Following fast, it was not possible to keep pace with her. When, breathless, I entered their rooms it was to see the mother's body hanging from a doorway. She had been brooding over a summons to testify in court that morning against her husband, who had been arrested for bigamy, and this was her answer to the court and to the other woman.

The frightened little children were scattered among different institutions. From one of these Esther was sent West, to a home that was found for her. Possibly she was so young that the terrible picture faded from her mind. At least there was no mention of it in the first letter which she wrote, announcing that her new home was a farm and that they had "six cows, eighty chickens, eleven pigs, and a *nephew.*" The nephew Esther eventually married.

In the first party of children that we sent to the country were three little girls, daughters of a skilled cobbler. The mother, a complaining, exacting invalid, spent a large proportion of her husband's earnings for patent medicines. Annie, not quite twelve, was the household drudge, and the coming of the settlement nurse lifted only part of her burden. The new friends, determined to get at least two weeks of care-free childhood for the little girls, procured an invitation for them, through a Fresh-Air agency, from a farmer in the western part of the state. It was necessary to secure the mother's admission to a hospital during the time the children would be absent from home—not an easy task, as she was not what is termed a "hospital case." When we met the children at the railroad station on their return, their joyousness and bubbling spirits attracted the attention of the onlookers; but as Annie neared home its responsibilities fell like a heavy cloud upon her, and before we reached the tenement she was silent. Her quick eye discerned the absence of the brick which had kept the front hall door open, and in a second she had darted into the yard and replaced it. Before we left, with sleeves rolled up she was beginning to wash the pile of dishes that had accumulated in her absence. Gone was the gayety. The little drudge had resumed her place. Later, when the child swore falsely to her age, and the notary public, upon whose certificate employment papers could at that time be obtained, affixed his signature to her perjury, the position she secured as cash girl in the basement of a department store was, to her, emancipation from hateful labor and an opportunity for fellowship with children.

Recalling early days, I am constantly reminded of the sympathy and comprehension of those friends who, though not stimulated as my comrade and I were by constant reminders of the children's needs, from the beginning promoted and often anticipated our efforts to provide innocent recreation.

We had not thought of the possibility of giving pleasure to large groups of children in picnics and day parties, when a friend, a few days after our arrival in the neighborhood, asked us to celebrate his sister's birthday by giving "fun" to some of our new acquaintances. I yet remember the thrill I felt when I realized that this gift was not for shoes or practical necessities, but for "just what children anywhere would like."

Two memories of this first party stand out sharply: the songs the children sang,—"She's More to be Pitied than Censured," and "Judge, Forgive Him, 'Tis His First Offense,"—painfully revealing a precocious knowledge, and their ecstasy at the sight of a wonderful dogwood tree. Now, when the settlement children go on day parties, they have another repertory, and the music they learn in the public schools reflects the finer thought for the child.

During the two years that Miss Brewster and I lived in the Jefferson Street house we frequently made up impromptu parties to visit the distant parks, usually on Sunday afternoons when we were likely to be free. After a while it was not difficult to secure comradeship for the children from men and women of our acquaintance, and the parties were multiplied. In the winter, rumors of "a fine hill all covered with snow" on Riverside Drive would be a stimulus to secure a sled or improvise a toboggan, and we found that, given opportunity and encouragement, the city tenement boys threw themselves readily into venturesome sport.

Happily some of the early prejudice against ball-playing on Sunday has vanished. We were perplexed in those days to explain to the lads why, when they saw the ferries and trains convey golfers suitably attired and expensively equipped for a day's sport, their own games should outrage respectable citizens and cause them to be constantly "chased" by the police. The saloons could be entered, as everybody knew, and I remember a father, defending his eight-year-old son from an accusation of theft, instancing as proof of the child's trustworthiness that "all the Christians on Jackson Street sent him for their beer on Sundays."

In our search for a place where the boys might play undisturbed, one of the settlement residents, a never-failing friend of the young people, invoked the Federal Government itself, and secured for them an unused field on Governor's Island.

Now, in summer time, many of the organized activities of the settlement are removed from the neighborhood. Early in the season the "hikers" begin their walks with club leaders. I felt a glow of happiness one Sunday morning when I stood on the steps of our house and watched six different groups of boys set off for the country, with ball and bat and sandwiches, each group led by a young man who had himself been a member of our early parties and had been first introduced to trees and open spaces, and the more active forms of healthful play by his settlement friends.

The woeful lack of imagination displayed in building a city without recognizing the need of its citizens for recreation through play, music, and art, has been borne in upon us many times. New Yorkers need to be reminded that the Metropolitan Museum of Art was effectually closed to a large proportion of the citizens until, on May 31, 1891, it opened its doors on Sundays. It is interesting to recall that of the 80,000 signatures to the petition for this privilege, 50,000 were of residents of the lower East Side and were presented by the "Working People's Petition Committee." The report of the

Museum trustees following the Sunday opening notes that after a little disorder and confusion at the start the experiment proved a success; that the attendance was "respectable, law-abiding, and intelligent," and that "the laboring classes were well represented." They were also obliged to report, however, that the Sunday opening had "offended some of the Museum's best friends and supporters," and that it had "resulted in the loss of a bequest of $50,000."

When we left the tenement house we were fortunate to find for sale, on a street that still bore evidences of its bygone social glory, a house which readily lent itself to the restorer's touch. Tradition says that many of these fine old East Side houses were built by cabinetmakers who came over from England during the War of 1812 and remained here as citizens. The generous purchaser allowed us freedom to repair, restore, and alter, as our taste directed. Attractive as we found the house, we were even more excited over the possibilities of the little back yard. Our first organized effort for the neighborhood was to convert this yard and one belonging to an adjacent school, with, later, the yard of a third house rented by one of our residents, into a miniature but very complete playground. There was so little precedent to guide us that our resourcefulness was stimulated, and we succeeded in achieving what the President of the National Playground Association has called the "Bunker Hill" of playgrounds.

*　*　*

On Saturday afternoons the playground was used almost exclusively by fathers and mothers, but it was a pretty sight at all times, and the value placed upon it by those who used it was far in excess of our own estimate. It was something more than amusement that moved us when a young couple, who had been invited to one of the evening parties, stood at the back door of the settlement house and gazed admiringly at the little pleasure place. Gowned in white, we awaited our guests, and as I rose from the bench under the pergola to cross the yard and give them welcome, the young printer said with enthusiasm, "This must be like the scenes of country life in English novels."

It was a heaven of delight to the children, and ingenuity was displayed by those who sought admittance. The children soon learned that "little mothers" and their charges had precedence, and there was rivalry as to who should hold the family baby. When (as rarely happened) there was none in the family, a baby was borrowed. Six-year-olds, clasping babies of stature almost equal to their own, would stand outside, hoping to attract attention to their special claims. Once, when the playground was filled to capacity, and the sidewalk in front of the house was thronged, the Olympian at the gate endeavored to make it clear that no more could enter. One persistent small girl stood stolidly and when reminded of the condition said, "Yes, teacher, but can't I get in? I ain't got no mother."

There was much illness, unemployment, and consequent suffering the next winter. One day, when I visited a school in the neighborhood, the principal asked the pupils if they knew me. She doubtless anticipated some reference to the material services which the settlement had rendered, but the answer to her question was a glad chorus of, "Yes, ma'am, yes, ma'am, she's our scupping teacher." "Teacher" was a generic term for the residents, and nothing that the settlement had contributed to the life of the neighborhood impressed the children as had the playground. It is worth reminding those who are associated with young people that the power to influence is given to those who play with, rather than to those who only teach, them. Our children on the East Side are not peculiar in this respect. To this day I receive letters from men and women who try to recall themselves to my memory by saying that they once played in our back yard.

An organized propaganda for outdoor gymnasia and playgrounds crystallized in 1898 in the formation of the Outdoor Recreation League, in which the settlement participated. The tireless president of the League eventually succeeded in obtaining the use of a large space in our neighborhood, originally purchased by the city, during a brief reform administration, for a park. Some very undesirable tenement houses had been destroyed, and when a Tammany administration returned to power a hot summer was allowed to pass with nothing done to accomplish the original purpose. Unsightly holes, once cellars, remained to fill with stagnant water, amputated sewer- and gas-pipes were exposed, and among these the children played mimic battles of the Spanish-American War, then in progress.

The accident that the Commissioner of Health, a semi-invalid, felt gratitude to a trained nurse who had cared for him, gave me an opportunity to approach him on the subject. He promised (and he kept his promise) to use his influence to get an appropriation on the score of the menace to the health of the city. The appropriation was sufficient to fill in the space and surround it with a fence, and the Outdoor Recreation League was able to demonstrate the value of playgrounds. In 1902 the Board of Estimate and Apportionment of Mayor Seth Low's reform administration, at its first meeting, appropriated money for the equipment and maintenance of Seward Park, as it was named,—the first municipal playground in New York City. So much interest had been aroused in this phase of city government that two city officials left the board meeting while it was in progress to telephone to the settlement that the appropriation had been passed.

Many friends of the children combined to urge the use of the public schools as recreation centers, and in the summer of 1898 the first schools were opened for that purpose. Those of us who had practical experience helped to start these by acting as volunteer inspectors. The settlement then felt justified in devoting less effort to its own playground, and deflected some of the energies it required to meet other pressing needs.

Contemporary Evaluations of Riis and *How the Other Half Lives*

WARREN P. ADAMS
Boston and "The Other Half"†

The publication of Jacob Riis's "How the Other Half Lives," so fully reviewed in *The Christian Union* at the time, marked an era in the history of the great underworld of human labor. The book has been read in Boston with a great deal of interest, and with a good degree of complacency as well, under the assumption of the non-existence of any similar state of affairs here. But Boston has been shaken from center to circumference recently by a series of sermons, revealing a condition of affairs that was little dreamed of.

The prophet crying in the wilderness to make straight our paths is the Rev. Louis Albert Banks, of St. John's Methodist Episcopal Church, South Boston. He has succeeded in filling his Church—with a capacity of twelve hundred people, situated in one of the remoter and less attractive wards of Boston—Sunday after Sunday, and in commanding the attention of an enormous constituency through the press, which gives generous space to these sermons every Monday. The Boston "Advertiser," an unusually cautious and candid critic, called one of his recent sermons a "gem of eloquence," and the "Transcript," a leading daily of marked literary excellence, besides generous and enthusiastic editorials upon the man and his work, gave a very extended sketch of his life and career up to the present time.

Who is the Rev. Louis Albert Banks, and what is the special work which has created such widespread attention? A sketch of this man would seem to be necessary to a fair comprehension of his work. Born in Oregon in 1855, and licensed to preach at sixteen years of age, Mr. Banks has, while yet a young man, a large experience in the world and in public speaking. Reared among the magnificent scenery of the Northwest, and accustomed to travel afoot among the extensive forests and mountains of that unsurpassed region, the breezes which play through its lofty pines seem but a type of those spiritual forces which have swept through his nature, making it sweet, clear, and stimulating. Nor is it surprising that in the glorious freedom of his surroundings, with an intimate acquaintance with the farming life of the community, and, in the best sense, a son of the soil, he should imbibe a hatred of oppression and a sympathy for those who, in one way or another, are deprived of their liberty. Add to this a familiarity with Indian

† *Christian Union* 44.5 (1891).

life and an intimate knowledge of Indian wrongs, as learned from their own lips, and it will be seen that he enters upon public life more than usually equipped for his work along certain lines.

Mr. Banks has made excellent use of the opportunities of education which have been afforded him. He is not a product of the schools, and while an omnivorous reader and a student, especially along sociological lines, there is a freshness in his utterances which no merely scholarly training would afford. He is, of course, an ardent lover of nature, and like Beecher, Spurgeon, and others, makes free use of his knowledge of farm and outdoor life for illustrations to his discourses.

Mr. Banks is of stalwart build, has a pleasant, ringing voice, and has filled pulpits in Oregon, Idaho, and Washington before coming East. It was in Vancouver, in the latter State, that he was shot down on the street by an infuriated saloonist whom he had angered by his trenchant temperance talks, and preached to crowded houses for some months thereafter with his wounded leg supported by chairs. In the Chinese riot in Seattle he defended these people at the risk of his own life, leaving his pulpit on Sunday to be sworn in as a deputy sheriff, and remaining on duty till the danger was over. His idea is that the topics for sermons are ample if the preacher keeps his eyes open for what is going on about him. His recent efforts have been devoted to calling public attention to the evils of the "sweating shops." Visiting them personally day after day among the slumbs of Boston, he has been able to draw a series of pictures startling in their realism, and stirring to its very depths the community, which has followed the series of sermons with intensest interest. He has been showered with letters of inquiry and sympathy from various sections of the country, so widespread has been the interest in his work. Some of them contain offers of aid for the helpless victims of business rapacity, whose sufferings he has described. To one of the social and intellectual lights of Boston, who, in the coldness of his conservatism, addressed him a letter declaring him to be a dangerous agitator as arraying class against class, and as transcending the office of a Christian minister, he replied from his pulpit: "If to be a 'Christian minister' is to stand as a policeman to hold back the righteous indignation of the robbed and degraded laborer, or preach patience and contentment to empty stomachs, that the sweater may grow rich and fat on the toil of orphans and widows, then I spurn the title as beneath the dignity of my manhood; but if, as I take it, to be a Christian minister is to be like my Master, the brother of all men, rich or poor, standing forever as the unflinching enemy of oppression and injustice, I am proud of the title and thank God for its unspeakable privilege."

Mr. Banks's first sermon was entitled "The White Slaves of the Boston Sweaters." The word "sweater," he explained, "is not in the old dictionaries. It is a foul word born of the greed and infernal lust for gold which pervades the most reckless and wicked financial circles of our times." Some of the cases cited were extremely pathetic. A woman with a child of three years was sewing for a leading dry-goods firm white aprons, a full yard long, hemmed across the bottom and on both sides, making, with the strings, six long seams. For these aprons she is paid fifteen cents a dozen! She receives them in packages of ten dozen, on which she is required to pay fifteen cents expressage each way. By working from seven in the morning until eleven at night she could make four dozen a day, but the care of her child prevents her making but three dozen, and for these she receives, net, forty cents a day! Another is the case of a Portuguese woman with five children, one of them deformed. She is required to make six pairs of pants[1] a day for one of the largest firms in Boston, for which she receives *ten cents* a pair! By working from 6 A.M. to 11 P.M., she can earn sixty cents. Some of these pants were "custom" goods, with the names of the owners attached. She has one bed for herself and the five children, and for two little attic pockets pays $1.50 a week. She can keep up the struggle only by the aid of charity. "And," adds the preacher, "oh, my brothers, this is in sight of the Old North Church and the tower where they hung the lanterns for a signal to Paul Revere when he rode through the darkness to arouse the fathers to fight against oppression. God help us to hang another light for liberty in the midst of this cruel slavery!" One woman makes cheap overcoats at *four cents* apiece; another, knee pants for boys at sixteen cents a dozen pairs. The list of prices, so insignificant as scarcely to add to the cost of the cloth itself, might be extended almost indefinitely. In most cases expressage is deducted from these pitiful sums, and the amount is still further diminished by the cost of needles and thread, many machine needles being broken on the stiffer cloths. "If you want variety we will climb four flights of stairs, with half the plastering knocked off the walls, and talk with an English woman. She is working on fine cloth pants; she gets *thirteen cents* a pair. By working till very late in the evening she can complete four pairs a day, and thinks it would almost be a Paradise if she could make her fifty-two cents every day; but it is one of the characteristics of a sweater to systematically keep all his people hungry for work, and she is seldom able to get more than twelve pairs a week."

Here is a picture of how some of these people live in rich, generous, cultured Boston. Saith the preacher; "Sickness, to be dreaded anywhere, is especially pitiful among these sweaters' slaves in the city. In the country the fresh air, fragrant with the breath of new morn hay or sweetened by ten thousand clover blossoms, is free to the poorest, but to the sick in a tenement-house is something terrible. Yet crowded quarters, poisonous air, and filthy clothing make sickness a common guest in such places. I climbed one day up two flights into a dirty little room, the smell of which was sickening to me in three minutes, and yet there was a man on a little cot that had been given him by the charitable missionary who guided me, who has been lying there for more than three years. For two years and more he had not even a cot, but lay on the floor in his dirt and pain. There are two children. The wife and mother make pants for a rich Washington Street firm, for which she gets twelve cents, and on especially fine custom made pants fifteen cents a pair. Rheumatism has settled in the joints of her fingers and stiffened them till she can turn off nine and ten pairs only a week. Last week she earned $1.15; her rent was $1.25." Mr. Banks found the pants for the new postal uniforms made by Italian women for 9½ cents a pair. One young woman made overalls, in which by actual measurement there were in each pair 32½ feet of sewing, for five cents a pair, less expressage for the

---

1. This objectionable no-word is used in this article throughout, as it is the common trade term, and as such is used by Mr. Banks in his sermons.

lot, to and fro. The poor girl stated that while she was compelled to make a dozen pairs a day, in the House of Correction, where some of the work was done, they had but to finish eight pairs a day and had comfortable lodgings and good food. She had sometimes asked herself whether it would not be better to commit some crime and be incarcerated, where life would be far more endurable than in the close and noisome tenement!

In his second discourse on the "Plague of the Sweat Shop," Mr. Banks makes this terrible indictment: "Putting all other questions aside for a moment, let us remember that these people are setting up a standard of living in our midst, which, if permitted to become established, will dictate its cruel laws to all the laboring people in the community. If this system is allowed to go on, there are people now living in luxury who are now indifferently pooh-poohing this whole question, whose grandchildren will starve to death in a sweat-shop. No investment exacts such fearful ursury as indifference to justice. A wrong uncared for, in a North End tenement-house, will avenge itself sooner or later on Beacon Hill or Commonwealth Avenue."

And so the sickening tale goes on. Out of these wretched dens the articles of clothing go forth laden with the seeds of disease. From a notebook crowded with heart-rending cases Mr. Banks has selected but a few typical ones out of the 150 sweat-shops in Boston. It is a spectacle of intense interest to look over the large audiences and notice the rapt attention with which they listen to the preacher. It is an audience composed largely of laboring men, who seem deeply in earnest, and the various tradesunions have declared that never before has their cause been pleaded so effectively, or reached, through the disseminations of the press, so widespread an audience. Manufacturers, middlemen, "sweaters," and many of the great army of employers of labor, have endeavored to break the force of these disclosures, but the words of the preacher seem to go on and on with ever-accelerating force.

JOSEPH B. GILDER

The Making of Jacob A. Riis†

Nothing could be easier than to write a disparaging notice of this autobiography. In the first place it is egotistical: it fairly bristles with "I's." I did this; I did that; I thought so and so, and was right, and the world has come round to my way of thinking. This will exasperate some readers. Others will stand amazed at the author's utter lack of reserve in telling the story of his courtship, and will revolt at his allusions to "curls and lone eyelashes" in the kitchen. Others, still, will be amused by the awkward English of many a sentence, due, no doubt, to the author's habit of writing as he speaks, and not revising his work with a view to the way it will look when printed. These faults are to be found abundantly in "The Making of an American,"[1] and for some people they will spoil the book. Those whom they may affect that way have our profound sympathy—and commiseration.

† *The Critic* 40.1 (1902).
1. "The Making of an American." By Jacob A. Riis. Illustrated, 2 vols. Macmillan. $2.00 *nett*.

We ourselves have found the egotism too pronounced now and then; have wondered how any man could tell all about his love-affairs (and let his wife retell the story from her point of view); and have laughed at the clumsiness of phraseology here and there. But when all this has been granted— and it is a good deal, we admit—there remains enough, and more than enough, to balance it ten times over. An autobiography that is not egotistical hardly deserves to be called an autobiography at all. If an author is to suppress his personality in telling the story of his life, he should leave the writing of it to other hands. Egotism is to autobiography what nicotine is to tobacco. The personality of Mr. Riis is an exceptionally interesting and attractive one, and the frankness of his self-revelation is the chief merit of his book. The rehearsal of the romance of his life shows merely the defect of an admirable quality: it is due to an overplus of the frankness that is one of his finest traits. "The philosophy of the too much" adequately accounts for it. The slipshod English is a minor matter. That it is due to carelessness, and not to the author's foreign birth, is shown by the excellence of the style in which by far the greater part of the book is written.

The story of Mr. Riis's life would have afforded a congenial theme to his illustrious countryman, Hans Andersen, (of whom, by the way, he relates an anecdote here less well than he tells it orally). It reads like a veritable fairytale. A native of Ribe, Denmark, he disappointed the hope of his father, a school-teacher, that he should become a man-of-letters, by choosing the career of a carpenter; and when, in his youth, he himself was disappointed, as a suitor, he came in the steerage to America. During the first six years of his struggle with poverty, he became only too well acquainted with the slums of New York, and the large share he bore in after years in the abolition of the police lodging-houses and the wiping-out of Mulberry Bend was due in no small degree to his early experiences on the East Side. Having tried day-laboring, carpentry, mining, the doing of "chores," lecturing, muskratting, "travelling in" furniture, flatirons, etc., and what not, he had pretty well settled down to journalism when the way was opened for him to go back to Denmark and take unto himself a wife. From that time, almost to the present, his waking hours have been spent as a reporter in Mulberry Street, New York, opposite Police Headquarters; and his work in behalf of the poor, in connection with tenement-house reform, the improvement of schoolhouses, the creation of parks and playgrounds, etc., has been incidental to the pursuit of his profession as a journalist. As a writer for the magazines and as a lecturer, he has been deservedly successful, and his "How the Other Half Lives," which made a veritable sensation on its first appearance, eleven years ago, is still a popular book.

One might have thought that in this and his later works, "The Children of the Poor," "A Ten Years' War," and "Out of Mulberry Street," he would have exhausted his material. Far from it. "The Making of an American" is a book of absorbing interest, and should hold its own even longer than the picture of slum conditions that made its author famous. That there is much in a name, he himself realized when he copyrighted the title "How the Other Half Lives" long before there was anything but an idea behind it. And in the case of his present work he has shown the same felicity of choice or invention as displayed in former volumes.

The unknown immigrant of thirty years ago, who has done more than any one else to alleviate the condition of the poor of New York by revealing their misery to a sympathetic world,—loved and respected now by many thousands of his fellow-citizens,—widely known and admired as an author,— honored by the King to whom he once owed allegiance, and on terms of intimacy with the President of the republic in which he has made his home,—here, indeed, is an "American" worth the "making," and the story of whose lifework, as related by himself, is of intense psychological and political interest.

MARGARET E. BURTON

From Comrades in Service[†]

A Servant of the City

Into the little tiled-roof house of a schoolmaster of the ancient town of Ribe, on the seacoast of Denmark, there was born one day in 1849 a little boy who was named Jacob. His father wanted him to become a schoolmaster like himself, and one of this little Danish boy's earliest memories was of being led, protesting, through the crooked cobble-stoned streets of Ribe to the schoolhouse. He evidently failed to make a good initial impression on the schoolmistress, for a large portion of that first day in school was spent in an empty hogshead, in whose capacious depths he formed a deep and undying hatred of school and all that pertained thereto.

Ribe was a wonderful place for boys. There was splendid fishing in the river and fine places along the forget-me-not-fringed banks where one could build fires and roast fish and potatoes. Once there had been a great castle in Ribe, and the moat around the green castle hill was now filled with long rippling reeds, growing higher than a boy's head, and making a perfect jungle in which to hunt for tigers and grizzlies, and other wild beasts. * * * The Danish consul [in New York City] registered his request to be sent to Denmark in case of war, but could do no more. The French did not seem to be fitting out any volunteer army, and no one was paying the passage of fighting men back to Europe. Riis pawned his revolver and his top-boots to pay his boarding-house bill, and then, having no money, set out for the country with all that he had left, a linen duster and a pair of socks, in a gripsack over his shoulder.

He walked till about daylight, then curled up in a wagon and went to sleep. It was an unfortunate place to select for a nap, for the wagon proved to be a milk cart, whose irate driver hauled the sleeper out by his feet and dumped him into the gutter before starting on his early morning rounds. About noon, footsore and faint with hunger, for he had had no food since the day before, Riis wandered aimlessly into the open gates of Fordham College. He sat down to rest under a tree, so exhausted and famished that when a kindly monk asked him if he was hungry, he confessed that he was, although he says that he had no intention of making such an admission.

† New York: Missionary Education Movement of the United States and Canada, 1916.

The food gave him strength to go on and at night he found temporary work with a truck farmer.

For several days Riis tramped through the country, doing odd jobs for his meals and sleeping in the fields at night, always trying to reach the sea in the hope of finding some way back to Denmark. Finally, his wanderings brought him back to New York where he pawned his boots for a dollar, fortified himself with a good dinner, and bought a ticket to Perth Amboy, New Jersey, with what was left. From Perth Amboy he walked for two days, sustained by two apples, and at sunset of the second day arrived at New Brunswick. He spent the night curled up on a brownstone slab in the cemetery, and early the next morning was out looking for work. Finding nothing in New Brunswick, he went on to a town called "Little Washington," where he succeeded in securing a job in a brickyard. Here he stayed for six weeks, until one day he heard that a volunteer company was ready to sail for France. That night he started for New York, arriving there just after the company had sailed. Repeated appeals to the French consul were unavailing, and a plea to the captain of a French man-of-war in the harbor was equally so. Finally, however, it seemed as if his persistent efforts were to be rewarded. He succeeded in getting a job as stoker on a steamer which was due to sail for France in an hour. He ran all the way to Battery Place for his valise, and all the way back, arriving breathless just in time to see the steamer swing into the river beyond his reach. This was his last hope and he was again left penniless in New York.

It was now late autumn, too late to get employment on farms or in brickyards. The city was full of idle men and Riis's repeated efforts to find something to do were fruitless. Day after day he walked the streets trying to find work, and to forget the terrible hunger which was his constant companion. Night after night he slept in the shelter of doorways or ash-bins, waked up time and again by the toe of a policeman's boot and told to "move on." But he says: "I was too proud in all my misery to beg. I do not believe I ever did. But I remember well a basement window at the downtown Delmonico's, the silent appearance of my ravenous face at which, at a certain hour in the evening, always evoked a generous supply of meat-bones and rolls from a white-capped cook who spoke French. That was the saving clause. I accepted his rolls as instalments of the debt his country owed me, or ought to owe me, for my unavailing efforts in its behalf."

There was just one bright spot in Jacob Riis's life during these dark days, the devotion of an adoring little black-and-tan, who had shared a doorway with him one cold night and had been the loyal companion of his miseries ever after. One terrible night of storm, Riis, drenched to the skin and unutterably wretched and hungry, with no prospect of shelter or food, was almost overcome by discouragement. Home and Elisabeth seemed hopelessly far away and unattainable and the dark river terribly near. Then the little dog pressed close against him for sympathy and banished the dreadful sense of desolation. Taking him up in his arms, Riis tramped through the torrents of rain to the police station and applied for shelter. The sergeant saw the drenched little dog under the tatters of Riis's ragged coat, and ordered him to put it outside. There was nothing else to do—to stay in the streets through such a night was to perish—and most reluctantly Riis left his little friend curled up in a ball on the steps, waiting for him.

The police station was terribly crowded with the worst type of tramps, but Riis was utterly exhausted and soon fell asleep. He woke up long before morning, put his hand to his throat, and found that some one had cut the string around his neck and stolen the gold locket in which he had kept the little shining curl which he felt to be his last link with home. Heartbroken, he rushed to the sergeant with his story, only to be called a thief, accused of having stolen the locket, and threatened with imprisonment. It was too much, coming after days and nights of suffering, and all the bitterness in his heart poured itself out in angry words. He never remembered what he said, but he remembered that the sergeant ordered the doorman to put him out, and that the little dog, seeing the doorman lay unfriendly hands upon his beloved friend, sprang at him and buried his teeth in his leg. The doorman caught the little beast by its legs and beat out its brains against the stone steps, and Jacob Riis, mad with such rage as he had never before imagined, snatched up paving-stones from the gutter and hurled them at the police station until the frightened sergeant ordered two policemen to disarm him and take him out of the district. They left him at the nearest ferry, and he gave the ferryman his silk handkerchief to take him to Jersey City. For four days he walked along the railroad tracks, living on apples.

* * *

[He] then answered an advertisement for a "city editor" in a Long Island weekly paper. He filled this position for two weeks, and having by that time received conclusive proof that the editor was exceedingly "bad pay," went back to New York no richer than when he had come except for Bob, a Newfoundland puppy which some one had given him.

His next occupation was the peddling of an illustrated edition of *Hard Times*. Long afterward he declared that no amount of good fortune could ever turn his head as long as that book stood on his shelves. He and Bob were a living illustration of "hard times," for they were earning barely enough to keep them alive. Bob fared better than his master, for he was able to coax many a meal from the kitchen doors of the houses they visited, but Riis was almost always hungry. Things went from bad to worse. One day the two had only a crust to eat between them, and the next morning set out faint with hunger, without a cent for food for the day or shelter at night. All day long they went from house to house without making a single sale. Bob's most persuasive tail-waggings and his master's most eloquent praises of Dickens had failed to provide breakfast, dinner, supper, or money for a night's lodging. Without a cent in his pocket Jacob Riis sank down at night on the steps of Cooper Institute utterly exhausted and discouraged. His dismal reflections were suddenly interrupted by the question, "Why, what are you doing here?" and looking up he saw the principal of the business college which he had attended when he first came back to New York. "Books!" snorted this gentleman in response to Riis's answer, "I guess they won't make you rich. Now, how would you like to be a reporter, if you have got nothing better to do? The manager of a news agency downtown asked me to-day to find him a bright young fellow whom he could break in. It isn't much—ten dollars a week to start with. But it is better than peddling books, I know. . . . *Hard Times*. . . . I guess so. What do you say? I think you will do. Better come along and let me give you a note to him now."

To be a reporter had been Riis's dream for many a month, and he could hardly believe that such an opportunity had really come to him. All through the night he and Bob walked up and down Broadway, thinking. "What had happened had stirred me profoundly," he wrote many years later. "For the second time I saw a hand held out to save me from wreck just when it seemed inevitable, and I knew it for his hand to whose will I was at last beginning to bow in humility that had been a stranger to me before. It had ever been my own will, my own way, upon which I insisted. In the shadow of Grace Church I bowed my head against the granite wall of the gray tower, and prayed for strength to do the work which I had so long and arduously sought and which had now come to me; the while Bob sat and looked on, saying clearly enough with his wagging tail that he did not know what was going on, but that he was sure it was all right."

The next morning Jacob Riis presented himself for duty at the New York News Association, and was assigned to report a luncheon in the Astor House. In the midst of such savory food as he had not seen or smelled in many a day, he wrote his report, and won from the editor a brief, "You'll do! Take that desk and report at ten every morning sharp." Then, having had no food for three days, he fell in a swoon on his way up the stairs of a Danish boarding-house, and lay there until some one stumbled against him in the dark and carried him in.

All through the autumn and winter Riis worked with the news agency, beginning his day promptly at ten in the morning and seldom reaching home until one or two in the morning of the next day. In the spring a group of politicians in Brooklyn, who had started a weekly newspaper, asked him to be their reporter, and two weeks after he had joined them made him editor of the paper. When the paper had served its purpose by helping its owners to win in the fall elections, they decided to give it up, but at Riis's earnest entreaty finally consented to sell it to him for the small sum which he could pay down, and his notes for future payments. For the next year Riis was editor, reporter, publisher, and advertising agent of a big four-page weekly, and by an almost incredible amount of work became its sole owner by June. The day on which he made his last payment was Elisabeth's birthday, and that night he sent a letter addressed to her speeding on its way to Denmark.

It was while he was editing the *News* that he became powerfully stirred by the preaching of the Rev. Ichabod Simmons, and definitely consecrated himself to the service of God and his fellows. With characteristic wholeheartedness he decided to give up his editorial work and become a minister, but was restrained by Mr. Simmons, who showed him that the world had need of "consecrated pens" as well as consecrated tongues. "Then and there I consecrated mine," says Mr. Riis. The *News* was promptly dedicated to the cause of reform, regardless of the consequent unpopularity of its owner.

Into the midst of these busy days, there came one early winter afternoon a letter half covered with foreign stamps. Elisabeth did not know how many stamps it took to carry a letter from Denmark to America, and because she was afraid to ask anybody about it, she put on three times as many as were required. When he had taken the letter up to his own little room and finally summoned the courage to read it, the face of the world changed for Jacob Riis. "I knelt down," he says, "and prayed long and fervently that I might strive with all my might to deserve the great happiness that had come to me." The doctor had ordered a rest and change, the newspaper could be sold for five times what had been paid for it, and there was nothing to prevent the prospective bridegroom from going home to claim Elisabeth almost immediately. In a very few weeks in the old Domkirke of Ribe he and the Elisabeth of his dreams were made man and wife.

Soon after Jacob Riis returned to America with his wife he was offered a position as reporter on the *New York Tribune*. For six months he worked hard for a salary so small that he was forced to draw on his little bank account to make both ends meet. Then one night when he had been uptown on a late assignment, and was running at full speed through a blinding snowstorm to get his report in before the paper went to press, he collided with the city editor of the *Tribune* so violently as to throw him off his feet into a snowdrift. The irate remarks which issued from the drift convinced Riis that his days with the *Tribune* were numbered, and he waited in despair for the victim's recognition of his assailant. But the city editor's curiosity as to the cause of Riis's mad haste seemed more pronounced than his wrath. "Do you always run like that when you are out on assignments?" he inquired, after listening to Riis's explanation. "When it is late like this—yes," Riis answered. "How else would I get my copy in?" "Well," was the editor's comment, "just take a reef when you round the corner. Don't run your city editor down again."

The next morning Riis went to the office with a sinking heart. He had not been there long before he was summoned to the city editor's desk, and the first words he heard seemed to confirm his worst forebodings.

"Mr. Riis," the editor began stiffly, "you knocked me down last night without cause."

"Yes, sir! But I——" Riis interrupted.

"Into a snowdrift," the editor continued. "Nice thing for a reporter to do to his commanding officer. Now, sir! this will not do. We must find some way of preventing it in the future. Our man at Police Headquarters has left. I am going to send you up there in his place. You can run there all you want to, and you will want to all you can. It is a place that needs a man who will run to get his copy in and tell the truth and stick to it. You will find plenty of fighting there. But don't go knocking people down—unless you have to."

Riis went out from the editor's office and did two things. He telegraphed his wife, "Got staff appointment. Police Headquarters. $25 a week. Hurrah." And facing what he knew to be the most difficult position on the paper, remembering how hard had been the fight his predecessor had had to wage, he commended his work and himself to the God who gives victory, and took hold! Both actions were characteristic. Prayer in the midst of his tasks was as natural to Riis as breathing, for he regarded his work as a reporter as a God-given opportunity.

"The reporter who is behind the scenes," he once said, "sees the tumult of passions, and not rarely a human heroism that redeems all the rest. It is his task so to portray it that we can see all its meaning, or at all events catch the human drift of it, not merely the foulness and the reek of blood. If he can do that he has performed a signal service, and his murder story may easily come to speak more eloquently to the minds of thousands than the sermon preached to a hundred in the church on Sunday."

With such a conception as this of the opportunity of his work, prayer in the midst of it all was inevitable. "My supplications," he said, "ordinarily take the form of putting the case plainly to him who is the source of all right and justice, and leaving it so."

The first years of work at the Mulberry Street police quarters were years of constant fight for Jacob Riis. "Somebody was always fighting somebody else for some fancied injury or act of bad faith in the gathering of the news," he says, and upon the arrival of the new reporter from the *Tribune* all made common cause against him. The record of his working hours tells of ceaseless strenuous struggle to get for his paper the news which rival reporters and the police were determined he should not get. But the greatest fight of all those fighting years, says Jacob Riis, was with himself. His blood had never ceased to boil at the memory of that night of pouring rain when at the door of the police station his loyal little dog friend had been killed before his eyes. And now that he had a recognized place at the police head-quarters, and the backing of the *Tribune*, nothing would have been easier than to go to the records of the Church Street Police Station, find out the name of the cruel sergeant and demand his punishment. Time after time he went to the station to begin his search in the record books, and again and again he turned away, until one day, as he held in his hand the very book which would have given him the sergeant's name, he thought of a plan of revenge which his heart could approve. He would destroy, not the sergeant, but the system of police lodging-houses of which the sergeant had been only an instrument. With the record book in his hands, he vowed that if God gave him strength he would fight the unutterably filthy police lodging-houses, where hardened tramps and impressionable penniless boys, such as he had been, were herded together in utter wretchedness, until not a lodging-house was left. He set the book down unopened, his fight with himself over, his long fight with those breeders of physical and moral disease begun.

It was a long fight and a slow one, and many a time Jacob Riis kept up his courage only by going out and watching a stone-cutter hammer away at his stone one hundred times without so much as a crack appearing, until finally at the one hundred and first blow the rock would split in two. Riis never lost a chance to strike a blow. He felt sure that if the people of New York understood the evils of the police lodging-houses they would never tolerate them, and he told the truth in no uncertain terms through the columns of newspaper after newspaper, by pictures, by lantern slides, by reports to committees and boards, until finally, more than fourteen years after the fight was started, when Mr. Roosevelt was commissioner of police, the doors of the police lodging-rooms were closed forever, and the murder of the little dog was avenged!

Another fight of the first years as police reporter on the *Tribune* was with Mulberry Bend, a slum district filled with tenements far more congested and dangerous than the Rags Hall which had so displeased the twelve-year-old schoolboy. Mulberry Bend was a center of both disease and crime, and Jacob Riis attacked it single-handed. Article after article he wrote, making apparently little or no impression, but never giving up. Then one day his morning newspaper contained a four-line item telling of the discovery of a method of taking pictures by flashlight. Riis was sure that if he could make people see the Bend at night as he had seen it, he could rouse them to action, and straightway investigated the matter of flashlights. Within two weeks he was invading Mulberry Bend night after night, armed with flashlight cartridges, which in those days were shot from a revolver, and which were more than terrifying to the startled inhabitants of the Bend. Little by little Riis won his fight, and was rewarded for the long hours of voluntary night work, on top of busy days, by seeing the tenement-houses of the Bend condemned by the Sanitary Board, and a park and playground established on the place where they had been.

The fight for the destruction of Mulberry Bend was only the beginning of Jacob Riis' fight with the slum and the tenement-house, which lasted as long as life lasted. Day after day he put the facts before the people of New York City through the columns of his newspaper. Many a night found him in church or lecture hall showing the stereoptican slides which he had had made from his photographs, that both the eyes and ears of the people of that great city might know "how the other half lives." One night an editor of *Scribner's Magazine* heard him lecture and asked him to write an article for the magazine. When the magazine article came out, a firm of publishers asked him to elaborate it into a book, and night after night he came home from his office and wrote *How the Other Half Lives,* while the rest of the family slept. How desperately tired he grew probably no one knows but himself, and even he hardly realized it until one evening in Boston, he went to call on a friend and found, when he tried to give the maid his name, that he had no idea what it was. But he felt repaid for all the hard work when his book came out and thousands of people all over the country were reading *How the Other Half Lives* and learning how to help. This was the first of many books which Jacob Riis wrote to tell the story of the needs of the poor and the way to meet those needs. *Children of the Tenements, The Battle with the Slums, Out of Mulberry Street* are only a few of them.

Always, too, he was helping in other ways. One year he gave all the time and effort he could spare as general agent of the Council of Confederated Good Government Clubs.

"We tore down unfit tenements, forced the opening of parks and playgrounds, the establishment of a truant school system, the demolition of the overcrowded old Tombs and the erection on its site of a decent new prison. We overhauled the civil courts and made them over new in the charter of the Greater New York. We lighted dark halls; closed the 'cruller' bakeries in tenement-house cellars that had caused the loss of no end of lives, for the crullers were boiled in fat in the early morning hours while the tenants slept, and when the fat was spilled in the fire their peril was awful. We fought the cable-car managers at home and the opponents of a truant school at Albany. We backed up Roosevelt in his fight in the Police Board and—well, I shall never get time to tell it all. But it was a great year!" he summarizes. This might be a summary not simply of that one year's work, but of all the later years of his life, for the destruction of the tenements and the establishment of an adequate number of good public schools, truant schools, and playgrounds, were causes to which he gave his strength without reserve.

Jacob Riis was not the kind of man to care greatly for recognition of his work. It was enough for him that the work was done. A great many honors of different kinds came to him, many of them nominations to honorary membership in various societies in America and Europe. Most of them he declined, stuffing the letters which offered them into a pigeonhole labeled tersely with one of Eugene Field's verses, descriptive of "Clow's Noble Yellow Pup":

"Him all that goodly company
Did as deliverer hail;
They tied a ribbon round his neck,
Another round his tail."

There was one honor, however, which he could not refuse, fragrant as it was, with memories of flowers and fields and little children. When the meadows around his house in Richmond Hill were radiant with the gold and white of buttercups and daisies, and sweet with the scent of clover blossoms, his small sons and daughters used to bring him great armfuls of blossoms and beg him to take them to "the poors" in the hot city. But no matter how laden he was when he started from home, he never had a single flower five minutes after he had left the ferry, for wistful little faces sprang up on every side, wild with eagerness for just one of the joy-bringing blossoms. The sight of those for whom there were no posies left, who sat down on the curbstone and dug grimy fists into eyes brimming over with tears, went straight to the heart of Jacob Riis, and one June morning he published an appeal for flowers in the newspapers, offering to dispose of any that were sent to his office.

"Flowers came pouring in from every corner of the compass. They came in boxes, in barrels, and in bunches, from field and garden, from town and country. Express wagons carrying flowers jammed Mulberry Street and the police came out to marvel at the row. The office was fairly smothered in fragrance. A howling mob of children besieged it. The reporters forgot their rivalry and lent a hand with enthusiasm in giving out the flowers. The Superintendent of Police detailed five stout patrolmen to help carry the abundance to points of convenient distribution. Wherever he went, fretful babies stopped crying and smiled as the messengers of love were laid against their wan cheeks. Slovenly women curtsied and made way. . . . The Italians in the Barracks stopped quarreling to help keep order. The worst street became suddenly good and neighborly."

The slum's hungry love for the beautiful was a revelation even to Jacob Riis. Taking flowers there was, he said, "like cutting windows for souls." Although he saw that the ministry of the flowers had assumed proportions far beyond his ability to handle, he knew that somehow, somewhere, the work must be taken care of, for the slums must not starve for want of the fragrance and joyous color which willing hands were ready to pour in so lavishly. Some of the boxes of flowers had the initials I. H. N. on them, and when Jacob Riis learned that they stood for "In His Name," the words which were the motto of the King's Daughters' Society, he thought he knew to whom to entrust the flowers. The members of the society gladly undertook the work, but the needs they saw as they took the flowers from house to house were too great and compelling to allow them to turn away when summer and flowers had gone, and to-day there stands in Henry Street a beautiful settlement house maintained by the King's Daughters' Society. What wonder that when on Jacob Riis's silver wedding day they asked him to let this settlement house bear his name, he could not say them nay.

"I have lived in the best of times," said Jacob Riis, "when you do not have to dream things good, but can make them so." Probably no one has ever known better than he what joy it is to "make them so," nor could say more heartily than he, when working days were nearing their close, "I have been very happy. No man ever had so good a time."

THEODORE ROOSEVELT

From An Autobiography[†]

Chapter VI. *The New York Police*

In the spring of 1895 I was appointed by Mayor Strong Police Commissioner, and I served as President of the Police Commission of New York for the two following years. Mayor Strong had been elected Mayor the preceding fall, when the general anti-Democratic wave of that year coincided with one of the city's occasional insurrections of virtue and consequent turning out of Tammany from municipal control. He had been elected on a non-partisan ticket—usually (although not always) the right kind of ticket in municipal affairs, provided it represents not a bargain among factions but genuine non-partisanship with the genuine purpose to get the right men in control of the city government on a platform which deals with the needs of the average men and women, the men and women who work hard and who too often live hard. I was appointed with the distinct understanding that I was to administer the Police Department with entire disregard of partisan politics, and only from the standpoint of a good citizen interested in promoting the welfare of all good citizens. My task, therefore, was really simple. Mayor Strong had already offered me the Street-Cleaning Department. For this work I did not feel that I had any especial fitness. I resolutely refused to accept the position, and the Mayor ultimately got a far better man for his purpose in Colonel George F. Waring. The work of the Police Department, however, was in my line, and I was glad to undertake it.

The man who was closest to me throughout my two years in the Police Department was Jacob Riis. By this time, as I have said, I was getting our social, industrial, and political needs into pretty fair perspective. I was still ignorant of the extent to which big men of great wealth played a mischievous part in our industrial and social life, but I was well awake to the need of making ours in good faith both an economic and an industrial as well as a political democracy. I already knew Jake Riis, because his book "How the Other Half Lives" had been to me both an enlightenment and an inspiration for which I felt I could never be too grateful. Soon after it was written I had called at his office to tell him how deeply impressed I was by the book, and that I wished to help him in any practical way to try to make things a little better. I have always had a horror of words that are not translated into deeds, of speech that does not result in action—in other words, I believe in realizable ideals and in realizing them, in preaching what can be practiced and then in practicing it. Jacob Riis had drawn an indictment of the things that were wrong, pitifully and dreadfully wrong, with the tenement homes and the tenement lives of our wage-workers. In his book he had pointed out how the city government, and especially those connected with the departments of police and health, could aid in remedying some of the wrongs.

As President of the Police Board I was also a member of the Health Board. In both positions I felt that with Jacob Riis's guidance I would be

---

† New York: Charles Scribner's Sons, 1921.

able to put a goodly number of his principles into actual effect. He and I looked at life and its problems from substantially the same standpoint. Our ideals and principles and purposes, and our beliefs as to the methods necessary to realize them, were alike. After the election in 1894 I had written him a letter which ran in part as follows:

It is very important to the city to have a business man's Mayor, but it is more important to have a workingman's Mayor; and I want Mr. Strong to be that also. . . . It is an excellent thing to have rapid transit, but it is a good deal more important, if you look at matters with a proper perspective, to have ample playgrounds in the poorer quarters of the city, and to take the children off the streets so as to prevent them growing up toughs. In the same way it is an admirable thing to have clean streets; indeed, it is an essential thing to have them; but it would be a better thing to have our schools large enough to give ample accommodation to all who should be pupils and to provide them with proper playgrounds.

And I added, while expressing my regret that I had not been able to accept the street-cleaning commissionership, that "I would have been delighted to smash up the corrupt contractors and put the street-cleaning force absolutely out of the domain of politics."

This was nineteen years ago, but it makes a pretty good platform in municipal politics even to-day—smash corruption, take the municipal service out of the domain of politics, insist upon having a Mayor who shall be a workingman's Mayor even more than a business man's Mayor, and devote all attention possible to the welfare of the children.

Therefore, as I viewed it, there were two sides to the work: first, the actual handling of the Police Department; second, using my position to help in making the city a better place in which to live and work for those to whom the conditions of life and labor were hardest. The two problems were closely connected; for one thing never to be forgotten in striving to better the conditions of the New York police force is the connection between the standard of morals and behavior in that force and the general standard of morals and behavior in the city at large. The form of government of the Police Department at that time was such as to make it a matter of extreme difficulty to get good results. It represented that device of old-school American political thought, the desire to establish checks and balances so elaborate that no man shall have power enough to do anything very bad. In practice this always means that no man has power enough to do anything good, and that what is bad is done anyhow.

In most positions the "division of powers" theory works unmitigated mischief. The only way to get good service is to give somebody power to render it, facing the fact that power which will enable a man to do a job well will also necessarily enable him to do it ill if he is the wrong kind of man. What is normally needed is the concentration in the hands of one man, or of a very small body of men, of ample power to enable him or them to do the work that is necessary; and then the devising of means to hold these men fully responsible for the exercise of that power by the people. This of course means that, if the people are willing to see power misused, it will be misused. But it also means that if, as we hold, the people are fit for self-government—if, in other words, our talk and our institutions are not shams—we will get good government. I do not contend that my theory will automatically bring good government. I do contend that it will enable us to get as good government as we deserve, and that the other way will not.

The then government of the Police Department was so devised as to render it most difficult to accomplish anything good, while the field for intrigue and conspiracy was limitless. There were four Commissioners, two supposed to belong to one party and two to the other, although, as a matter of fact, they never divided on party lines. There was a Chief, appointed by the Commissioners, but whom they could not remove without a regular trial subject to review by the courts of law. This Chief and any one Commissioner had power to hold up most of the acts of the other three Commissioners. It was made easy for the four Commissioners to come to a deadlock among themselves; and if this danger was avoided, it was easy for one Commissioner, by intriguing with the Chief, to bring the other three to a standstill. The Commissioners were appointed by the Mayor, but he could not remove them without the assent of the Governor, who was usually politically opposed to him. In the same way the Commissioners could appoint the patrolmen, but they could not remove them, save after a trial which went up for review to the courts.

* * *

It is difficult for men who have not been brought into contact with that side of political life which deals with the underworld to understand the brazen openness with which this blackmailing of lawbreakers was carried out. A further very dark fact was that many of the men responsible for putting the law on the statute-books in order to please one element of their constituents, also connived at or even profited by the corrupt and partial non-enforcement of the law in order to please another set of their constituents, or to secure profit for themselves. The organ of the liquor-sellers at that time was the *Wine and Spirit Gazette*. The editor of this paper believed in selling liquor on Sunday, and felt that it was an outrage to forbid it. But he also felt that corruption and blackmail made too big a price to pay for the partial non-enforcement of the law. He made in his paper a statement, the correctness of which was never questioned, which offers a startling commentary on New York politics of that period. In this statement he recited the fact that the system of blackmail had been brought to such a state of perfection, and had become so oppressive to the liquor dealers themselves, that they communicated at length on the subject with Governor Hill (the State Democratic boss) and then with Mr. Croker (the city Democratic boss). Finally the matter was formally taken up by a committee of the Central Association of Liquor Dealers in an interview they held with Mr. Martin, my Tammany predecessor as President of the police force. In matter-of-course way the editor's statement continues: "An agreement was made between the leaders of Tammany Hall and the liquor dealers according to which the monthly blackmail paid to the force should be discontinued in return for political support." Not only did the big bosses, State and local, treat this agreement, and the corruption to which it was due, as normal and proper, but they never even took the trouble to deny what had been done when it was made public. Tammany and the police, however, did not fully live up to the agreement; and much discrimination of a very corrupt kind, and of a very exasperating kind to liquor-sellers who wished to be honest, continued in connection with the enforcing of the law.

In short, the agreement was kept only with those who had "pull." These men with "pull" were benefited when their rivals were bullied and blackmailed by the police. The police, meanwhile, who had bought appointment or promotion, and the politicians back of them, extended the blackmailing to include about everything from the pushcart peddler and the big or small merchant who wished to use the sidewalk illegally for his goods, up to the keepers of the brothel, the gambling-house, and the policy-shop. The total blackmail ran into millions of dollars. New York was a wide-open town. The big bosses rolled in wealth, and the corrupt policemen who ran the force lost all sense of decency and justice. Nevertheless, I wish to insist on the fact that the honest men on the patrol posts, "the men with the nightsticks," remained desirous to see honesty obtain, although they were losing courage and hope.

This was the situation that confronted me when I came to Mulberry Street. The saloon was the chief source of mischief. It was with the saloon that I had to deal, and there was only one way to deal with it. That was to enforce the law. The howl that rose was deafening. The professional politicians raved. The yellow press surpassed themselves in clamor and mendacity. A favorite assertion was that I was enforcing a "blue" law, an obsolete law that had never before been enforced. As a matter of fact, I was only enforcing honestly a law that had hitherto been enforced dishonestly. There was very little increase in the number of arrests made for violating the Sunday law. Indeed, there were weeks when the number of arrests went down. The only difference was that there was no protected class. Everybody was arrested alike, and I took especial pains to see that there was no discrimination, and that the big men and the men with political influence were treated like every one else. The immediate effect was wholly good. I had been told that it was not possible to close the saloons on Sunday and that I could not succeed. However, I did succeed. The warden of Bellevue Hospital reported, two or three weeks after we had begun, that for the first time in its existence there had not been a case due to a drunken brawl in the hospital all Monday. The police courts gave the same testimony, while savings banks recorded increased deposits and pawnshops hard times. The most touching of all things was the fact that we received letters, literally by the hundred, from mothers in tenement-houses who had never been allowed to take their children to the country in the wide-open days, and who now found their husbands willing to take them and their families for an outing on Sunday. Jake Riis and I spent one Sunday from morning till night in the tenement districts, seeing for ourselves what had happened.

During the two years that we were in office, things never slipped back to anything like what they had been before. But we did not succeed in keeping them quite as highly keyed as during these first weeks. As regards the Sunday-closing law, this was partly because public sentiment was not really with us. The people who had demanded honesty, but who did not like to pay for it by the loss of illegal pleasure, joined the openly dishonest in attacking us. Moreover, all kinds of ways of evading the law were tried, and some of them were successful. The statute, for instance, permitted any man to take liquor with meals. After two or three months a magistrate was found who decided judicially that seventeen beers and one pretzel made a meal—after which decision joy again became unconfined in at least some of the saloons, and the yellow press gleefully announced that my "tyranny" had been curbed. But my prime object, that of stopping blackmail, was largely attained.

All kinds of incidents occurred in connection with this crusade. One of them introduced me to a friend who remains a friend yet. His name was Edward J. Bourke. He was one of the men who entered the police force through our examinations shortly after I took office. I had summoned twenty or thirty of the successful applicants to let me look over them; and as I walked into the hall, one of them, a well-set-up man, called out sharply to the others, "Gangway," making them move to one side. I found he had served in the United States navy. The incident was sufficient to make me keep him in mind. A month later I was notified by a police reporter, a very good fellow, that Bourke was in difficulties, and that he thought I had better look into the matter myself, as Bourke was being accused by certain very influential men of grave misconduct in an arrest he had made the night before. Accordingly, I took the matter up personally. I found that on the new patrolman's beat the preceding night—a new beat—there was a big saloon run by a man of great influence in political circles known as "King" Calahan. After midnight the saloon was still running in full blast, and Bourke, stepping inside, told Calahan to close up. It was at the time filled with "friends of personal liberty," as Governor Hill used at that time, in moments of pathos, to term everybody who regarded as tyranny any restriction on the sale of liquor. Calahan's saloon had never before in its history been closed, and to have a green cop tell him to close it seemed to him so incredible that he regarded it merely as a bad jest. On his next round Bourke stepped in and repeated the order. Calahan felt that the jest had gone too far, and by way of protest knocked Bourke down. This was an error of judgment on his part, for when Bourke arose he knocked down Calahan. The two then grappled and fell on the floor, while the "friends of personal liberty," danced around the fight and endeavored to stamp on everything they thought wasn't Calahan. However, Bourke, though pretty roughly handled, got his man and shut the saloon. When he appeared against the lawbreaker in court next day, he found the court-room crowded with influential Tammany Hall politicians, backed by one or two Republican leaders of the same type; for Calahan was a baron of the underworld, and both his feudal superiors and his feudal inferiors gathered to the rescue. * * * As with so many other problems, while there must be governmental action, there must also be strengthening of the average individual character in order to achieve the desired end. Even where economic conditions are bad, girls who are both strong and pure will remain unaffected by temptations to which girls of weak character or lax standards readily yield. Any man who knows the wide variation in the proportions of the different races and nationalities engaged in prostitution must come to the conclusion that it is out of the question to treat economic conditions as the sole conditions or even as the chief conditions that determine this question. There are certain races—the Irish are honorably conspicuous among them—which, no matter what the economic pressure, furnish relatively few inmates of houses of ill fame. I do not believe that the differences are due to permanent race characteristics; this is shown by the fact that the best settlement houses find that practically all their "long-term graduates," so to speak, all the girls that come for a long period under their influence, no matter what their race or national origin, remain pure. In every race there are some naturally vicious individuals and some weak individuals who readily succumb under economic pressure. A girl who is lazy and hates hard work, a girl whose mind is rather feeble, who is of "subnormal intelligence," as the phrase now goes, or a girl who craves cheap finery and vapid pleasure, is always in danger. A high ideal of personal purity is essential. Where the same pressure under the same economic conditions has tenfold the effect on one set of people that it has on another, it is evident that the question of moral standards is even more important than the question of economic standards, very important though this question is. It is important for us to remember that the girl ought to have the chance, not only for the necessaries of life, but for innocent pleasure; and that even more than the man she must not be broken by overwork, by excessive toil. Moreover, public opinion and the law should combine to hunt down the "flagrant man swine" who himself hunts down poor or silly or unprotected girls. But we must not, in foolish sentimentality, excuse the girl from her duty to keep herself pure. Our duty to achieve the same moral level for the two sexes must be performed by raising the level for the man, not by lowering it for the woman; and the fact that society must recognize its duty in no shape or way relieves, not even to the smallest degree, the individual from doing his or her duty. Sentimentality which grows maudlin on behalf of the willful prostitute is a curse; to confound her with the entrapped or coerced girl, the real white slave, is both foolish and wicked. There are evil women just as there are evil men, naturally depraved girls just as there are naturally depraved young men; and the right and wise thing, the just thing, to them, and the generous thing to innocent girls and decent men, is to wage stern war against the evil creatures of both sexes.

In company with Jacob Riis, I did much work that was not connected with the actual discipline of the force or indeed with the actual work of the force. There was one thing which he and I abolished—police lodging-houses, which were simply tramp lodging-houses, and a fruitful encouragement to vagrancy. Those who read Mr. Riis's story of his own life will remember the incidents that gave him from actual personal experience his horror of these tramp lodging-houses. As member of the Health Board I was brought into very close relations with the conditions of life in the tenement-house districts. Here again I used to visit the different tenement-house regions, usually in company with Riis, to see for myself what the conditions were. It was largely this personal experience that enabled me while on the Health Board to struggle not only zealously, but with reasonable efficiency and success, to improve conditions. We did our share in making forward strides in the matter of housing the working people of the city with some regard to decency and comfort.

The midnight trips that Riis and I took enabled me to see what the Police Department was doing, and also gave me personal insight into some of the problems of city life. It is one thing to listen in perfunctory fashion to tales of overcrowded tenements, and it is quite another actually to see what that overcrowding means, some hot summer night, by even a single inspection during the hours of darkness. There was a very hot spell one midsummer while I was Police Commissioner, and most of each night I spent walking through the tenement-house districts and visiting police stations to see what was being done. It was a tragic week. We did everything possible to alleviate the suffering. Much of it was heartbreaking, especially the gasping misery of the little children and of the worn-out mothers. Every resource of the Health Department, of the Police Department, and even the Fire Department (which flooded the hot streets) was taxed in the effort to render service. The heat killed such multitudes of horses that the means at our disposal for removing the poor dead beasts proved quite inadequate, although every nerve was strained to the limit. In consequence we received scores of complaints from persons before whose doors dead horses had remained, festering in the heat, for two or three days. One irascible man sent us furious denunciations, until we were at last able to send a big dray to drag away the horse that lay dead before his shop door. The huge dray already contained eleven other dead horses, and when it reached this particular door it broke down, and it was hours before it could be moved. The unfortunate man who had thus been cursed with a granted wish closed his doors in despair and wrote us a final pathetic letter in which he requested us to remove either the horses or his shop, he didn't care which.

I have spoken before of my experience with the tenement-house cigar factory law which the highest court of New York State declared unconstitutional. My experience in the Police Department taught me that not a few of the worst tenement-houses were owned by wealthy individuals, who hired the best and most expensive lawyers to persuade the courts that it was "unconstitutional" to insist on the betterment of conditions. These business men and lawyers were very adroit in using a word with fine and noble associations to cloak their opposition to vitally necessary movements for industrial fair play and decency. They made it evident that they valued the Constitution, not as a help to righteousness, but as a means for thwarting movements against unrighteousness. After my experience with them I became more set than ever in my distrust of those men, whether business men or lawyers, judges, legislators, or executive officers, who seek to make of the Constitution a fetich for the prevention of the work of social reform, for the prevention of work in the interest of those men, women, and children on whose behalf we should be at liberty to employ freely every governmental agency.

Occasionally during the two years we had to put a stop to riotous violence, and now and then on these occasions some of the labor union leaders protested against the actions of the police. By this time I was becoming a strong believer in labor unions, a strong believer in the rights of labor. For that very reason I was all the more bound to see that lawlessness and disorder were put down, and that no rioter was permitted to masquerade under the guise of being a friend of labor or a sympathizer with labor. I was scrupulous to see that the labor men had fair play; that, for instance, they were allowed to picket just so far as under the law picketing could be permitted, so that the strikers had ample opportunity peacefully to persuade other labor men not to take their places. But I made it clearly and definitely understood that under no circumstances would I permit violence or fail to insist upon the keeping of order. If there were wrongs, I would join with a full heart in striving to have them corrected. But where there was violence all other questions had to drop until order was restored. This is a democracy, and the people have the power, if they choose to exercise it, to make conditions as they ought to be made, and to do this strictly within the law; and therefore the first duty of the true democrat, of the man really loyal to the principles of popular government, is to see that law is enforced and order upheld. * * * As I have said, the Senator was an old and feeble man in physique, and it was possible for him to go about very little. Until Friday evening he would be kept at his duties at Washington, while I was in Albany. If I wished to see him it generally had to be at his hotel in New York on Saturday, and usually I would go there to breakfast with him. The one thing I would not permit was anything in the nature of a secret or clandestine meeting. I always insisted on going openly. Solemn reformers of the tom-fool variety, who, according to their custom, paid attention to the name and not the thing, were much exercised over my "breakfasting with Platt." Whenever I breakfasted with him they became sure that the fact carried with it some sinister significance. The worthy creatures never took the trouble to follow the sequence of facts and events for themselves. If they had done so they would have seen that any series of breakfasts with Platt always meant that I was going to do something he did not like, and that I was trying, courteously and frankly, to reconcile him to it. My object was to make it as easy as possible for him to come with me. As long as there was no clash between us there was no object in my seeing him; it was only when the clash came or was imminent that I had to see him. A series of breakfasts was always the prelude to some active warfare.[1] In every instance I substantially carried my point, although in some cases not in exactly the way in which I had originally hoped.

There were various measures to which he gave a grudging and querulous assent without any break being threatened. I secured the reënactment of the Civil Service Law, which under my predecessor had very foolishly been repealed. I secured a mass of labor legislation, including the enactment of laws to increase the number of factory inspectors, to create a Tenement House Commission (whose findings resulted in further and excellent legislation to improve housing conditions), to regulate and improve sweatshop labor, to make the eight-hour and prevailing rate of wages law effective, to secure the genuine enforcement of the act relating to the hours of railway workers, to compel railways to equip freight trains with air-brakes, to regulate the working hours of women and protect both women and children from dangerous machinery, to enforce good scaffolding provisions for workmen on buildings, to provide seats for the use of waitresses in hotels and restaurants, to reduce the hours of labor for drug-store clerks, to provide for the registration of laborers for municipal employment. I tried hard but failed to secure an employers' liability law and the state control of employment offices. There was hard fighting over some of these bills, and, what was much more serious, there was effort to get round the law by trickery and by securing its inefficient enforcement. I was continually helped by men with whom I had gotten in touch while in the Police Department; men such as

---

1. To illustrate my meaning I quote from a letter of mine to Senator Platt of December 13, 1899. He had been trying to get me to promote a certain Judge X over the head of another Judge Y. I wrote: "There is a strong feeling among the judges and the leading members of the bar that Judge Y ought not to have Judge X jumped over his head, and I do not see my way clear to doing it. I am inclined to think that the solution I mentioned to you is the solution I shall have to adopt. Remember the breakfast at Douglas Robinson's at 8:30."

James Bronson Reynolds, through whom I first became interested in settlement work on the East Side. Once or twice I went suddenly down to New
York City without warning any one and traversed the tenement-house quarters, visiting various sweat-shops picked at random. Jake Riis accompanied
me; and as a result of our inspection we got not only an improvement in the
law but a still more marked improvement in its administration.

* * *

LINCOLN STEFFENS

From The Autobiography of Lincoln Steffens[†]

* * *

Jake Riis was a Danish American who "covered" police headquarters, the
Health Department, which was then in the same building, and "the East
Side," which was a short name for the poor and the foreign quarters of the
city. And he not only got the news; he cared about the news. He hated passionately all tyrannies, abuses, miseries, and he fought them. He was a
"terror" to the officials and landlords responsible, as he saw it, for the desperate condition of the tenements where the poor lived. He had "exposed"
them in articles, books, and public speeches, and with results. All the philanthropists in town knew and backed Riis, who was able then, as a
reformer and a reporter, too, to force the appointment of a Tenement
House Commission that he gently led and fiercely drove to an investigation and a report which—followed up by this terrible reporter—resulted
in the wiping out of whole blocks of rookeries, the making of small parks,
and the regulation of the tenements. He had discovered these evils as a
reporter, reporting, say, a suicide, a fire, or a murder. These were the news,
which all the reporters got; only Riis wrote them as stories, with heart,
humor, and understanding. And having "seen" the human side of the crime
or the disaster, he had taken note also of the house or the block or the
street where it happened. He went back and he described that, too; he
called on the officers and landlords who permitted the conditions, and
"blackmailed" them into reforms.

This had been going on for years when I came to police headquarters.
Riis was growing old, but he had found and trained his boy, Max, to see
and to understand as Riis did; and Max could see. It seemed to me that
Max was born and not made. He did the early morning work, which was
the key to the day. The police, stationed all over the city, reported all happenings in their precincts to headquarters—fires, accidents, crimes, and
arrests—which were posted briefly in the basement telegraph office,
where the reporters could see them. The morning newspaper men
watched these bulletins, weighed them, and went out to investigate those
that seemed likely to have a story back of them. They stayed up till their
papers went to press, at two or three o'clock in the morning. When Riis

† New York: Harcourt, Brace, 1931.

first came to police headquarters as a young man, the evening newspaper men appeared at about eight or nine o'clock and began their work by conning the accumulation of bulletins dated from three o'clock on down to eight. These they divided up among themselves, each reporter going out on one. When they returned with their several stories, they exchanged the news, wrote each one all the stories, and then could settle down for the day to a poker game, which only big news could interrupt. Riis did not play poker; he joined in no "combine"; he worked alone, sometimes giving but never asking help. He began to beat the combine, which had to quit poker and work all day, still together, to keep up with and, if possible, beat Riis. They, all veterans, had the advantage of knowing the town and the police, who did not like Riis, but he carried the war into their camp by coming to work at seven o'clock, which gave him time to take two or three of the early morning bulletins, cover and write them all, and since most of the sensational incidents of a city are reported in those late night hours, the *Evening Sun* had such a lead on police news as the *Post* had had on Wall Street. And when the beaten editors drove their police reporters to work at seven o'clock, Riis, the scab, began to come at six, then five, then four. Nobody else started that early: no editor could demand it, and Riis himself could not stand it long. But each reporter had a copy boy, a messenger, to carry his stories downtown. Riis hit upon the idea of a boy who, besides carrying copy, could "cover" the city from three till seven, eight, nine, when Riis turned up to write the news. Max, who began with the facts, soon learned to see and form and deliver to Riis the stories of the night for which the *Evening Sun* was noted. Beautiful stories they were, too, sometimes, for Riis could write.

This, then, was what I was seeing, my first morning at police headquarters: Max furnishing Riis the night's stories, all ready made. I must know Riis. Waiting out in the street till he was through writing—when I saw Max take the copy and set off for his office downtown, I crossed over and called on Riis. In a loud, cheerful, hearty voice, he greeted me.

"Glad you've come," he said. "The *Post* can help a lot up here, and you've begun well."

"Begun well!" I exclaimed. "I haven't begun yet."

Riis roared his great laugh. "Oh, yes, you have. Max says you banged Alec Williams one and disappointed the old man himself."

He meant that I had failed with Superintendent Byrnes! I was about to protest, but Riis was shouting through that open window.

"That's the way to handle them! Knock 'em down, then you can pick them up and be the good Samaritan. It's their own way with us reporters. They put the fear of God into us, then they are kind to us—if we'll let them. Not to me. They are afraid of me, not I of them, and so with you. You have started off on top. Stay there."

He bade me keep out of the combine. "Play alone," he said. "The combine will beat you for a while; so will I, of course. The whole police force will help beat you. Sure. But you'll soon learn the game and hold your own."

He said, still embarrassingly aloud, that he had seen me talking with the other reporter.

"I know what he wanted," he laughed. "He proposed that you share his office, pay him—not his office, him—half the rent costs, be his Max, and—"

"How did you know that?"

"I didn't," Riis shouted, as the reporter we were talking about walked across the street and up the stairs to headquarters. "But ―― tries to get every new reporter to fag for him; and most of them do. No. Don't you do it. I can't show you around much; too busy; but Max will," and he called "M-a-a-x" out of the window; then remembered: "Oh, yes, Max is gone downtown. Come on. I'll show you around."

He broke into all the offices, police and health, walked right in upon everybody he thought I should know, laughed, made them all laugh, and introduced me, not by name, but as the new *Evening Post* man. When we were coming back out of the building, at the front end of the hall, we saw two policemen half forcing, half carrying, a poor, broken, bandaged East Side Jew into the office opposite that of the Superintendent of Police. There were officers and citizens all about us, but Riis grasped my arm, and pointing to the prisoner as he stumbled in through the open door, he shouted—not, I think, for me alone to hear: "There you have a daily scene in Inspector Williams' office! That's a prisoner. Maybe he's done something wrong, that miserable Russian Jew; anyway he's done something the police don't like. But they haven't only arrested him, as you see; they have beaten him up. And look―"

The door opened, showed a row of bandaged Jews sitting against the wall in the inspector's office, and at his desk, Clubber Williams.

"See the others. There's a strike on the East Side, and there are always clubbed strikers here in this office. I'll tell you what to do while you are learning our ways up here; you hang around this office every morning, watch the broken heads brought in, and as the prisoners are discharged, ask them for their stories. No paper will print them, but you yourself might as well see and hear how strikes are broken by the police."

Inspector Williams had heard. He rose from his desk, pointed at the door, shouted something, and the doorman closed the door with a bang. And Jake Riis laughed. But there was no merriment in that loud laugh of Jake Riis; there was bold rage in his face, as he left me, banging out of the building. I stayed, as he suggested, and watched the scene. Many a morning when I had nothing else to do I stood and saw the police bring in and kick out their bandaged, bloody prisoners, not only strikers and foreigners, but thieves, too, and others of the miserable, friendless, troublesome poor.

* * *

VI. Dr. Parkhurst's Vice Crusade

Learning as I was that the newspapers, literature, and public opinion did not picture men and life as they are, it was nevertheless a weekly amazement to me to read in the Monday morning newspapers descriptive reports and caricatures of the Rev. Dr. Charles H. Parkhurst that represented him as a wild man, ridiculous, sensational, unscrupulous, or plain crazy; then to call on him and find a tall, slim, smiling gentleman, quiet, determined, fearless, and humorous; and then, finally, go on down to police headquarters and hear groups of policemen, politicians, and reporters talking in earnest about this fiend. I don't know how he is remembered; Dr. Parkhurst may be not remembered at all. He carried on his vice crusade all through the nineties, charging police and political corruption and forcing the State

Legislature to appoint the Lexow Committee which investigated, proved, and exposed the police and Tammany corruption, caused the election of a reform administration, and led up to the whole period of muckraking and the development of the Progressive party. Such a service is not the kind that is appreciated by public opinion and history, and whenever I speak with old New Yorkers now of Dr. Parkhurst they are puzzled to hear of him as I see him: a man of strength, who was "wise" in the slangy sense and otherwise wise. He never told or preached half of what he knew. His method was simple. He received individuals, sometimes honest victims of police outrage, sometimes disgruntled politicians, policemen, or criminals with axes to grind, and he heard their stories, which multiplied as he went on his steady way of exposure and attack. The facts and hints he collected then had to be investigated by his Society for the Prevention of Crime, with attorneys and detectives who followed up these leads, proved or disproved them, discovered others by the way, and delivered the information with the evidence to the Doctor, who used them—wisely. All he gave in a sermon or a lecture was enough to startle his hearers and to frighten the police world with the suggestion that he knew all. He didn't. As it turned out he did not know "the half of it." But he knew enough, and he understood so well what he knew that by sticking within the provable facts, by selecting those that were the most typical and significant, and using these boldly, he carried his charges every time.

"The police are paid bribe money regularly by the saloons," he would charge. "That is why they do not close them. If they care to show that I am wrong, let them enforce the law and close the saloons. They will not. They cannot. They don't dare."

That is what he would say clearly, even fiercely, of a Sunday. On Monday morning, when I called and asked him how he knew that, he would give me prices, dates, and names, and, smiling, say, "Now you ask Byrnes what he is going to do."

At police headquarters I would call on the Superintendent, who knew, of course, my routine; I soon learned to "spot" detectives watching me. Byrnes was ready for me.

"Well, and what does the reverend gentleman say this morning?"

"He says that you won't close the saloons this week either."

"I'll show you," he shouted in a rage one morning. He pressed a button, and to his Sergeant Mangin, who responded, he commanded: "Summon all the inspectors to report here at eleven o'clock. And"—to me—"you too."

At eleven o'clock all the inspectors in full uniform and all the reporters were in the chief's office. He rose from his desk and said: "Inspectors of police, I have bidden you, again and again, to enforce the law requiring the closing of saloons at certain hours, especially at night and on Sundays. Once more I command you to order your captains to obey and enforce upon others obedience to the laws."

We report the news, describing the scene, and the next morning I call on Dr. Parkhurst, who says, "Good. We'll see," and smiling he adds: "You will see—if you keep your eyes open—you will see the saloon-keepers and district leaders running to police headquarters to ask Byrnes if he means it; if he does, to protest and to threaten him. And as for me, I'll wait till Sunday to say what I see."

I saw the procession of saloon-keepers, politicians, and others, many other people, calling on Byrnes. One day Tim Sullivan, the famous East Side ward boss, came up to me, straight in his direct way, and asked me what th' hell I was trying to do.

"I?" I exclaimed. "I'm not trying to do anything but get the news."

"The hell you ain't," he protested. "You are backing up that damned preacher. Before you came to headquarters the reporters paid no attention to what the blankety-blank said. But now you interview Byrnes, ask him what he's going to do about it, and the other reporters have to report what he says too. You're making it hard for the old man; he says so himself; and you're making it hard for us, too. Why? What's th' game? What do you get out of it all?"

"News," I laughed.

"News!" he echoed. "Say, if that's all you want I'll give you news; we'll all give you news. I can tip Byrnes to put you 'way inside on th' news."

"Go ahead," I answered, jesting, and to my consternation he darted back into Byrnes' office, and coming out, reported, "I've fixed that all right. Now you be good. See?"

This had consequences which I was not "wise" enough to foresee or detect. I did not understand that I was being bribed; nothing happened immediately. Riis joined me in pressing Byrnes to heed Dr. Parkhurst or at least to answer his tirades. The other reporters merely laughed at me and my naïveté, but police officers were polite and obliging. Byrnes offered me a beat on a burglary several days later and looked mystified when I declined it, saying priggishly that the *Post* did not care for that sort of news. What interested me was that the police court cases showed and the reporters reported that the liquor laws were not enforced, as Dr. Parkhurst knew. He said so in his next Sunday sermon; he said it furiously, with scathing sarcasm and jubilant triumph.

"Now," he said amiably Monday morning, "now see what Byrnes does by way of his next bluff."

I think that at that time Dr. Parkhurst was really driving at the closing of the saloons. The appeals of wives and children to him for relief from the week-end drunkenness of their husbands and fathers were worrying the clergyman and making him hope for the enforcement of the early closing laws so as to save some of the workers' wages. My interest was in the glimpses I was catching of the Tammany government, and, by the way, of political morals. The police were protecting from the law and from public opinion the law-breakers they were appointed and paid to protect the public from. That was an apparent fact about the New York government. And by way of morals there was the faithful keeping of the alleged contract of the police with the saloon-keepers. Anyway, I went from Dr. Parkhurst, not to Byrnes, but to Riis. After a talk with him, about the situation as I saw it, he went with me to interview Byrnes.

"What about it, Inspector?" Riis asked for us both.

"What about what?" Byrnes retorted, his Irish showing in his angry eyes and hanging jaw.

"Parkhurst says you were bluffing when you had us in here last Monday to hear you instruct the inspectors to shut up the town. Anyway they didn't do it. What next?"

The chief paced the floor a few times, then halted before Riis and challenged him.

"Is the *Sun* backing Parkhurst? I know the *Post* is, but as I read the *Sun*—"

He was referring to the attacks by the *Sun* upon both Parkhurst and the *Post* for their hypocritical policy of law-enforcement, but Riis, who was not only a reporter, cut him short.

"Never you mind the *Sun*," he said. "Say what you are going to do. That's the news of the day, and the *Sun* prints the news."

"Two o'clock," said Byrnes, pointing us to the door and going to his desk.

"The" inspector, as I have said, had a funny way of affecting the dignity which he thought belonged to his position as the head of the uniformed police force; he would speak English as English as he could, using the broad "a." But under the strain of a sudden temper, he would fall back into his native Irish. This happened that day.

At two o'clock, when the inspectors filed into his office with Riis and me, the Superintendent in full uniform was pretending to write at his desk. He was very busy, too busy to see us till we had stood there silent and waiting and winking at one another for a minute or two. It seemed long before Byrnes looked up, saw us, rose solemnly, and strode slowly around in front of his inspectors, who watched him come. He never looked at Riis and me. He stood glaring at his inspectors.

"Gentlemen," he began, "did not I command you last Monday on this very spot in this same office to enforce to the letter the laws regulating the saloons in this city, and—and to close them one and all at the legally fixed hours for closing?"

No answer of course, only silence and attention, while the chief, crouching low at them and balling his fists, cried, "Well, and what I want to know now is: did youse did it?"

I snorted, couldn't help it; and Byrnes whirled upon me, and his arm lifted at the door, he yelled, "Get out of here!" I ran; Riis stood, but the angry man added, "Both of you." Then Riis came out laughing too.

How Byrnes finished his broken scene, what he said further to his inspectors, we did not learn. The inspectors avoided us, slipping back into their offices with sobered faces and mute lips. But the next Saturday night and Sunday many saloons closed. Not all. There seemed to have been some request sent out from headquarters for a voluntary compliance with the law; the liquor dealers must have decided among them which were to close and which to remain open. Anyway, for the next few weeks different saloons seemed systematically to obey and disobey the law, and there were few raids, though there were some places, the most notorious, which never did close. They had "thrown away their keys" the day they opened up for business, and it was not till Theodore Roosevelt became Commissioner that these powerful men were brought to heel.

Why were these law-breakers so strong? And why was there such an opposition to the simple, superficial reforms of Dr. Parkhurst? I used to wonder at what I was seeing, and the reporters, policemen, politicians, who explained it all to me, wondered at my stupidity. I could understand the bribery and the contributions to political parties; that accounted for the police and Tammany Hall, and that satisfied the minds of my informants. But it did not explain to me the opposition to reform that was most bitter: that of good, prominent citizens who had no apparent connection with the underworld. As Dr. Parkhurst forced such results as the voluntary closing of some saloons, he was hated more and more openly by people whom one might expect to see approving his course: bankers, business men, and even other clergymen. There was something to find out about the organization of society, as it occurred in New York, something the "wise guys" of the underworld did not know or would not tell. I asked my friends in Wall Street to justify their indignation at Parkhurst, but all they would say was that his crusade "hurt business." That was the first time I heard that expression. "How can the closing of saloons hurt business in Wall Street?" I asked James B. Dill, who knew everything. He kicked my shin, hard, and when I exclaimed, he answered my question, "Why does your mouth cry out when only your shin is hurt?" That was the answer, but I could never be satisfied with a fact or a phrase; it was a picture I needed, a diagram of the connection between the saloon business and the banks, just as I had one of the nervous system that linked up my lower and upper extremities.

VII. The Underworld

The inspector, Byrnes, was cultivating my friendship, and he did it by letting me in to a view of his relations with thieves and the underworld generally. It may have been Tim Sullivan's hint that I could be won with "news"; it may have been that, wishing to impress me, he talked, and talking, naturally turned to the field where he was most impressive, his detective work. Before he was promoted to be Superintendent of Police, he had been for years the inspector in charge of the detective bureau. He had enjoyed that work, evidently, and his many miraculous services to prominent people who had been robbed had made him loom in their imagination as the man of mystery and of marvelous effects. They all knew him in Wall Street; big men down there envied me the privilege of knowing personally "the inspector," as they still called him.

"You see him? Every day? And he talked to you, man to man, like that?"

Few of them had seen him. Even those he had helped out of trouble had rarely met him personally. It was his pose to remain in the background, receiving communications through others—detectives or attorneys—and working in the dark, suddenly hand out his results. You saw only the hand and the restored property. Bankers told me tales of how somebody's house had been robbed; the inspector had been told about it, and having listened in silence a moment, had said, "Enough. Your diamonds will be delivered at your house within three days." And on the third day—not on the second or the fourth, but exactly when this amazing man had promised—your diamonds were handed in by two startling men "with the compliments of the inspector." Another banker had had his pocket picked of money and valuable papers; he did not mind the money, but the papers . . . Byrnes had got back the papers, all intact.

One of the most famous of our millionaire families had consulted Byrnes about a foreign nobleman who had won the love of a daughter of the house; what could be done to get rid of the fellow? "I'll see," Byrnes had answered, and a few days later he promised that the family would see no more of the foreigner. "You might let me have enough money for him to pay his passage home and perhaps a little more." Gladly they paid whatever Byrnes thought would "do," and no more was ever seen or heard of that trouble. Byrnes was the man to deal with blackmailers. Wall Street and "Society" had suffered from the possession by unscrupulous scoundrels of personal and more or less scandalous facts against its leaders; true stories. Byrnes could deal with them. You told him "all about it"; perhaps you made one more payment, and—that ended it. Byrnes established Fulton Street as the dead line beyond which no thief could go downtown. It was understood that, in return for these services, Byrnes was tipped on stocks, let in on "good things," and otherwise helped to make money, quite properly; and no doubt the gratitude to Byrnes was an element in the ingratitude to Parkhurst. But that did not explain the connection between the saloon nerves and the big-business brains. There was something else back of all these surface signs. What was it? And how did Byrnes perform his miracles?

While I was pondering these questions he did one for me. Drawing my salary one Saturday afternoon, I went home and took my wife out for dinner. As I was about to pay the waiter, I discovered that my pay envelope with the money was gone. My pocket had been picked. I complained to Byrnes by 'phone; he asked how much was in the envelope, how the envelope was addressed, and what lines of cars I had used to go home and to dinner. When I had answered all his questions, he said, "All right. I'll have it for you Monday morning." And on Monday morning Byrnes handed me the envelope with the money just as I had received it from my paper.

"How did he do it?" I asked the other reporters. They were playing their poker in a basement office and had not much time for me, a greenhorn. I had to repeat my question several times before one of them looked up and answered briefly.

"Huh," he said. "He knew what pickpockets were working the car lines you rode and he told the detectives who were watching them to tell them that they had robbed a friend of the chief's of so much money in such and such an envelope."

"But how—"

"Ah, say, you don't know enough to cover Wall Street, to say nothing of police headquarters. Byrnes passed the word that he wanted that dip back by Monday morning, and so, of course, it came back Monday morning."

What reporters know and don't report is news—not from the newspapers' point of view, but from the sociologists' and the novelists'. It enabled me, when I learned a little of it, to write my *Shame of the Cities*. But it took time and sharp listening to get that little. Though I had nothing to do, professionally, with criminal news, I used to go out with the other reporters on cases that were useless to my paper but interesting to me. Crime, as tragedy and as a part of the police system, fascinated me. I liked to go for lunch to the old Lyons restaurant on the Bowery with Max Fischel or some other of the "wise" reporters. They would point out to me the famous pickpockets, second-story men and sneaks that met and ate there; sometimes with equally famous detectives or police officials and politicians. Crime was a business, and criminals had "position" in the world, a place that was revealing itself to me. I soon knew more about it than Riis did, who had been a police reporter for years; I knew more than Max could tell Riis, who hated and would not believe or even hear some of the "awful things" he was told. Riis was interested not at all in vice and crime, only in the stories of people and the conditions in which they lived. I remember one morning hearing Riis roaring, as he could roar, at Max, who was reporting a police raid on a resort of fairies.

"Fairies!" Riis shouted, suspicious. "What are fairies?" And when Max began to define the word Riis rose up in a rage. "Not so," he cried. "There are no such creatures in this world." He threw down his pencil and rushed out of the office. He would not report that raid, and Max had to telephone enough to his paper to protect his chief.

There were fairies; there were all sorts of perverts; and they had a recognized standing in the demi-world; they had their saloons, where they were "protected" by the police for a price. That raid Riis would not report was due to a failure of some one to come through with the regular bit of blackmail overdue. And so with prostitution, so with beggars, so with thieves, as I gradually learned, first from the reporters, then from police officers I came to know well, then from the crooks themselves who learned to trust me, and all the while from Byrnes. When he discovered that, while and because I did not write criminal news, he could interest and trust me with it, he used to call me in and tell me detective stories of which he was the hero. He was bragging, and he was inventing, too. This I knew because I had found out where he hid the detective story-books he was reading, and borrowing them when he was not looking, I read and recognized in them the source of some of his best narratives. Thus I discovered that instead of detectives' posing for and inspiring the writers of detective fiction, it was the authors who inspired the detectives. For example:

One day a young policeman who had just been appointed a plain-clothes man appeared at headquarters so exultant that I asked him what he had done. He hesitated a moment; detectives are forbidden to tell of their feats; that must be left to the inspector; but he knew that I did not report crimes, and he did want to talk; so he told me that he had "got the dope" on a certain big robbery of a rich man's house up Fifth Avenue.

"You remember the case," he began. "Jewelry and silverware taken on a grand scale, and the owner hollered. That made the old man mad; with the public in on it, he had to make a showing; so we were all instructed to do our damnedest."

The police all over the world caution citizens who are robbed to report to headquarters and never to the press. They explain that detectives can work better if the thieves are not warned by the newspapers that the police are after them. This is absurd, of course. Thieves always know when the police are looking for them after a crime. The true reason of the police for privacy is that they don't like to have the public know how many unsolved crimes are committed, and they do like to deal privately and freely with the criminals. My detective assumed that I understood this; he assumed that I knew everything. His next assumption was that I knew that detectives specialized, as criminals do, in one class of crime, and that the detective's trade consists not in pursuing but in forming friendships with criminals.

"It wasn't any of my business," he said. "My assignment, of course, is to the dips [pickpockets]; I was promoted because I had cultivated them and their girls and was known to be in with 'em. The case was either a burglary or a plain robbery, a good job, too, and the burglars and such that ought to know about it were as mystified as the chief himself. They said that they hadn't any of 'em done it. The old man put some of them through the mill till he was convinced that no crook that is allowed either to operate or to live in New York was in on it in any way. He thought, and I remember I guessed, that it was an inside job: servants. But the servants had all been kept, and the old man couldn't get a word out of them; not to the point. He said that they seemed really as mystified as anybody. A pretty case, eh?

"Well, we heard no more of it for a couple of months. I had about forgotten it and the burglar gang had dropped it, when one night I saw a dip who had been on the bum all dressed up with lots of money. He used to work the Bridge cars [the old Brooklyn Bridge surface lines] but had a row with his pal and got fired. Unable to work, he was down and out. Here he was, all of a sudden, flush and sassy. I naturally asked what t'ell. 'Got a new girl,' they told me in the barroom where the dips hang out. I thought they meant that she was a young, pretty piece that earned him a lot of money, but when she was pointed out to me one night later she turned out to be a homely foreigner; couldn't pick up a dollar a night on the streets. I smelled a rat. 'She must work,' I thinks. 'A servant perhaps. But how, then, did she get the money?' I followed her home, and what do you think? She went to that house on Fifth Avenue. Say, I had something, and I knew it. I got hold of her pickpocket and asked him if he'd like to get back on the cars. He sure would; what would it cost? I said he knew what the price would be, and he said he knew, too. He'd think it over. And the next night he paid the price to the old man himself, me being there.

* * *

CRITICISM

LOUISE WARE

From Jacob A. Riis: Police Reporter, Reformer, Useful Citizen[†]

Chapter IV. Riis and the Reform Movement, 1886–1897

By 1886, Riis was a seasoned reporter. During the preceding ten years he had covered every type of case from crime to death. But in spite of the routine of turning out page after page of copy, year in and year out, he retained the enthusiasm of his cub days. Every story seemed to have its special twist, now weird, now grim, now triumphant in its lesson of human sacrifice. Riis was an odd mixture of the matter-of-fact, the worldly wise, and the romantic. He gave the bare facts of an incident without any attempt to soften or embellish them; but, after recounting them just as they had happened, he would add some compassionate phrase that lifted the reader beyond the world of Mulberry Street to the realm of things of the spirit. He had, in short, become an artist in human-interest appeal.

The years 1886–97 were the period of Riis's greatest activity. In addition to his newspaper work he wrote numerous magazine articles and published three books, one of which, *How the Other Half Lives,* was a pioneer in works of its kind in the United States.[1] He battled against the police-station lodging-houses, urged the razing of Mulberry Bend and the establishment of a park in its place, advocated better schools, pleaded for more adequate working conditions for the laboring man, bespoke further legislation to restrict immigration, and urged wider control of the liquor traffic. In his lectures he showed the astonished public what life in the tenements was like.

To evaluate his work as we encounter it during this period, it is necessary to turn to the general picture of the time.[2] Everybody is familiar with the great growth of industrialism in the country after the Civil War. By 1886, it had become one of the most potent factors in American life. Factory towns had sprung up like mushrooms all over the country and thousands of laborers were flocking into them from the rural districts. The overcrowding in city slums, which had been noticeable as early as the 1860's, had now reached dangerous proportions. European immigration had increased with each decade; there were as yet no restrictions beyond a head tax imposed by the Federal Government and the Contract Labor Law of 1885, which forbade would-be employers to import cheap labor on promises of work. The immigration from Southern and Eastern Europe had begun, and every ship brought its crowd of men, women, and children with their bundles and shawls. Two or three families were often herded into quarters designed for one and the tenants often took in lodgers to eke out their rent. Each slum district came to have its own racial aspect; Italians congregated in one region, Bohemians in another, Russian Jews in another, the Irish in another, and so forth. Unscrupulous manufacturers encouraged

[†] New York: Appleton-Century-Crofts, 1938. Pages 50–59.
1. Charles Loring Brace's *The Dangerous Classes* (1873) carried similar material but was not as comprehensive a work.
2. A. M. Schlesinger, *The Rise of the City* (New York, 1933); H. U. Faulkner, *The Quest for Social Justice* (New York, 1931); V. L. Parrington, *The Beginnings of Critical Realism in America, Main Currents in American Thought* (New York, 1930), Vol. III, pp. 301–334.

sweat-shop labor, indifferent to the sight of fathers and mothers bending over garments in dark, unsanitary rooms. Although some housing legislation had already been effected, the laws in most cities were poorly enforced; only too often corrupt politicians defended the landlords when cases of violation of law were brought into court.

The growth of industrialism, the increase of immigration, and the persistence of overcrowding had brought many problems in their wake. In the late eighties and the nineties the number of poverty-stricken persons in the United States was becoming larger, and the country was faced with the prospect of having a permanent pauper class.[3] Bad environment in the crowded tenements had brought an increase of crime and juvenile delinquency, and the country had not yet made adequate provision for either the adult or the juvenile offender. There was, moreover, a decline in the old spirit of neighborliness which had characterized the simple communities existing before the machine age; bonds of sympathy were harder to form.

Numerous groups in the United States were offering solutions for the serious social problems that had arisen. The doctrine of laissez-faire was rapidly losing the prestige it had enjoyed. Political theorists offered panaceas, among them a changed society in which there should be a wider distribution of wealth and greater benefits for the laboring man. The Socialists presented their plea for public ownership of the means of protection, and a redistribution of wealth. Henry George advanced his economic theory of the single tax. Municipal reform clubs spent time and energy in trying to remove corruption from city government and to bring about social legislation. Not least among the theorists were the Utopians who dreamed of a society where all would work and all would share the benefits of labor. This group had a wide following. One of their number, Edward Bellamy, wrote *Looking Backward from the Year 2000 to 1887* (published in 1888), and William Dean Howells advanced a similar thesis in his *A Traveller from Altruria* (published in 1894).

It was during this period, too, that the American Federation of Labor was founded (1886) with a view to procuring better conditions of labor for the working-man. This organization added its voice to the clamor for legislative reforms.

That the movement for reform should reach into the field of literature was inevitable.[4] Reference has already been made to the Utopian writers, but the movement extended beyond their works. While the romantic school had long tinged American letters with a rosy glow, beginnings of realism were distinctly visible in the works of this period. Magazines carried stories of Bowery life and slum conditions. Books such as *A Hazard of New Fortunes* by William Dean Howells, told of society in the new industrial age. By the middle nineties several realistic works came off the press. Stephen Crane drew a sordid picture of slum life in his *Maggie, A Child of the Streets* (1894); Frank Norris gave his readers the drab *McTeague,* and Hamlin Garland began to publish his harsh sketches of the Mid-West in *Main Travelled*

3. A. J. Warner, S. A. Queen, and E. B. Harper, *American Charities and Social Work* (New York, 1930), pp. 25–141; R. Hunter, *Poverty* (New York, 1904); F. D. Watson, *The Charity Organization Movement in the United States* (New York, 1922); Mrs. C. R. Lowell, "The Economic and Moral Effects of Public Outdoor Relief," *National Conference of Social Work Proceedings,* Vol. XVII (1890), pp. 81–91.
4. V. L. Parrington, *op. cit.,* pp. 301–334.

Roads (1894). Many writers were so depressed by what they saw that their works were filled with gloom. This was not the case with Riis, however, though he was a member of the new realistic school. He retained a cheerful optimism that is hard to understand.

A glance at the social work of the country shows that a great deal of effort was being made to relieve distress among the poor. There were a few national organizations such as the American Red Cross, The National Conference of Charities and Corrections, and the Women's Christian Temperance Union, which aimed at meeting different aspects of the social problems; but, in the main, work tended to be more local than national in scope. There was, as yet, no school of social work where men and women might be trained, and only too often the social workers were merely supplying relief. Yet they often had a friendly spirit which established a bond of sympathy between them and the needy persons under their care, so that much good work resulted. There was a distinct tendency toward group activity in social-work programs and it was during this period that the settlements were first founded in the United States,[5] with their ideal of maintaining neighborhood spirit through joint participation in club work and community activities. The movement for parks and playgrounds gained momentum in this period.[6] Boston led the way with "Sand Gardens" patterned after the German playgrounds, and other cities followed suit. During this decade many churches, realizing the need to extend their work, formed clubs in congested neighborhoods and broadened their activities in behalf of the poor.

No brief account of the New York social work of this period (1886–96) can give an adequate idea of the spirit of the workers, their enthusiasm and earnestness. Life to the ardent New York social workers was a tremendously zestful social experience. They felt that they must somehow meet the material needs of the poor and at the same time "help them to help themselves." By the late eighties and nineties the number of agencies, both public and private, was large. It would take many pages merely to list these organizations. The Association for Improving the Condition of the Poor, the Charity Organization Society, the United Hebrew Charities, the St. Vincent de Paul Society, the State Charities Aid, the Travelers Aid, the Salvation Army, the Children's Aid Society, and the Society for Prevention of Cruelty to Children were among the familiar names. New Agencies, too, were founded.

In the movement to establish settlements in the United States, New York led the way.[7] Stanton Coit, an Amherst graduate, had lived at Toynbee Hall in London, and in August, 1886, he went to live in the New York slums. In the next year he founded Neighborhood Guild (later University Settlement) on the East Side. Charles B. Stover came to help him and was one of the leaders in the movement for playgrounds. In 1889 the College Settlement opened its doors with Miss Jean E. Fine and Dr. Jane E. Robbins as workers, and in 1890 King's Daughters' Settlement was organized. Among the other New York settlements founded in this decade were the Henry Street Nursing Association (founded 1893) with Miss Lillian D. Wald as head, and

5. R. A. Woods and A. J. Kennedy, *The Settlement Horizon* (New York, 1922), pp. 62, 114, 223–242.
6. C. E. Rainwater, *The Play Movement in the United States* (Chicago, 1922), pp. 45–135; J. Lee, *Constructive and Preventive Philanthropy* (New York, 1902); H. S. Curtis, *The Play Movement and Its Significance* (New York, 1917), pp. 15–18.
7. R. A. Woods, A. J. Kennedy (Eds.), *Handbook of Settlements* (New York, 1911), pp. 193–194, 205–207, 228–229.

Hudson Guild (1895) under the leadership of Dr. John L. Elliott. All of these settlements conducted club work and took an active stand in agitating for social reforms, including regulation of sweat-shops and housing conditions.

Two of the well-known organizations with which Mr. Riis had constant contact were the Charity Organization Society[8] and the Children's Aid Society. The Charity Organization Society was founded in 1882 with Mrs. Josephine Shaw Lowell,[9] a woman of Boston ancestry and sister-in-law of George William Curtis of the Civil Service Reform League, as one of the moving spirits. Charles D. Kellogg was the secretary of the society in the eighties and early nineties. There was a staff of visitors, or agents, whose work was allocated to districts, and there were district committees and volunteers. The main steps in the work of the district staff consisted in registration of the case in a central bureau, and investigation of the fitness of the applicant by visits to relatives, employers, and others. The visitors procured jobs for their clients, gave relief, secured loans, and attempted to sustain and develop character.[1] The modern emphasis on individual treatment through the use of psychiatric techniques was yet distant, however. Often the agents stumbled upon a plan by which they could help the troubled client to resolve his difficulties, but the day of mental hygiene and the knowledge of emotional conflicts had not come. The society urged coöperation among the social agencies in order to reduce overlapping of effort. Its executives were active in agitating for housing and other legislative reforms.

The Children's Aid Society was doing a notable work. The Reverend Charles Loring Brace had founded[2] this organization in 1853. Under his genial and kindly leadership the work of the society had expanded until, in the early nineties, it conducted industrial classes, maintained a farm for boys in Westchester County, and placed out and supervised children on farms in the West.

A number of individuals gave their services freely either in individual enterprises or through the work of the social organizations. Dr. Felix Adler of the Ethical Culture Society served on the Drexel Committee to investigate housing. Robert W. DeForest was another of the most prominent figures of the day. He was for years president of the Charity Organization Society and a member of other social organizations. His chief interest lay in housing reform. E. R. L. Gould, a Johns Hopkins lecturer, writer, and later Columbia professor, made a notable contribution to housing improvement by organizing the City and Suburban Homes Company of New York (1896) with the object of providing comfortable homes at moderate prices. The picturesque work of Nathan Straus, the merchant philanthropist, in establishing baby milk stations and in selling coal at a cheap rate to the poor during the panic of 1893, should be mentioned.[3] His efforts to have piers used for recreation were partly successful and a number of such piers were established later in the 1890's. Richard Watson Gilder's work as

8. F. D. Watson, op. cit., Annual Reports of the New York Charity Organization Society: 1889, 1890, 1892–1897; Proceedings of the National Conference of Charities and Correction, 1886–1892.
9. W. R. Stewart, The Philanthropic Work of Josephine Shaw Lowell (New York, 1911).
1. C. D. Kellogg, History of the Charity Organization in the United States (Chicago, 1893); Annual Reports of the New York Charity Organization Society, 1886–1896.
2. E. Brace (Ed.), Life and Letters of Charles Loring Brace (New York, 1894), pp. 426–503.
3. Lina G. Straus (Ed.), Disease in Milk—The Remedy Pasteurization. The Life Work of Nathan Straus (New York, 1917), pp. 119–123, 187–194, 201–206.

philanthropist and reformer merits special notice. He was greatly interested in housing reform and served on the legislative committee appointed in 1894 to investigate housing conditions in New York.

Social-work leaders had frequent contacts with one another and were well acquainted. It was easy to "drop in" at Mrs. Lowell's and discuss various social problems.[4] The doors of the settlements were always open. The pioneer character of the task aroused an enthusiasm which sometimes caused overlapping. But at least it may be seen that there were many agencies and individuals who really cared for the poor and were trying to formulate some program to help.

New York social workers were not unaware of what was going on in social lines abroad. The cable, mails from Europe, travelers returning, kept them in close touch. Europe, they knew, was gripped by the Industrial Revolution and showed urban trends as marked as those in the United States. On every hand socialists were urging redistribution of wealth; and trade unions were clamoring for fewer hours and better pay. Germany,[5] with her program of State Socialism, was striding forward in the hope of a better day. In the last few years of the century, she passed three social insurance laws and lent state aid to employers so that they could improve the homes of their workingmen. France also was waking up to reform of all kinds. She enacted a law for a working-men's council to build better homes for the poor, and the city of Paris opened shelters for homeless women and men. In like manner, England, a leader in reform,[6] had a number of varied activities under way to help the poor. Model-housing associations flourished; settlements, with Toynbee Hall as a shining example, were voicing the need for preserving community life. Birmingham was a leader in housing reform. Various churches and societies were meeting the needs of the poor, and at the same time extending a plan for self-improvement and self-support. Two important works from Salvation Army leaders in England depicted tenement life in all of its squalor. One of these *In Darkest England and the Way Out* had a miraculous sale of about 200,000 copies; while the other, Charles Booth's *Life and Labor of the People,* appalled a large public with its depressing picture.

There is no doubt that numerous organizations and individuals in New York received many of their ideas from Europe. For example, the idea of converting old burial plots into playgrounds for children came from England and was put into use here. So, too, the suggestion of using school buildings as evening recreation centers came from abroad. To find the man or woman who deserved praise for originating the plan would be a well-nigh impossible and perhaps an unnecessary task. Those who went into the work for sheer love of their fellow men would be the last to come forward and demand public acclaim. Many of the reforms for which Jacob Riis agitated so consistently were not his own ideas but were suggested by the reforms of others. He knew this, admitted it, and sent letters to ask for

4. Jacob Riis Papers (*Russell Sage Library*); interviews with Mr. Riis's friends.
5. J. H. Clapham, *The Economic Development of France and Germany—1815–1914* (Cambridge University Press, 1921), pp. 189–190, 271–275, 333–338; W. H. Dawson, *Bismarck and State Socialism* (London, 1890), pp. 87–127.
6. E. P. Cheyney, *Modern English Reform* (Philadelphia, 1931), pp. 151–159, 162–176; E. L. Hutchins and A. Harrison, *A History of Factory Legislation* (London, 1926), pp. 200–222, 280, 283; S. and B. Webb, *The History of Trade Unionism* (Revised edition, New York, 1920), pp. 370–409; R. A. Woods, *English Social Settlements* (New York, 1897), pp. 1–259.

information of what was being done elsewhere. His files fairly bulged with pamphlets.

Thus it is evident that both America and Europe had awakened to the need for social reform. There were thousands of persons interested in trying to do their share to meet needs and to bring about reform legislation. Jacob Riis was in no sense an isolated figure; he was part of the big movement. What then is his contribution? It would seem as though his greatest gift lay in his ability to dramatize his message so that it appealed to a large public who might otherwise have been unmoved by social conditions. Then, too, he had a sincere and lovable personality which inspired men with confidence in him, and drew them to the support of the measures that he advocated. We shall try to follow him to see whether our conclusions are justified as he continues his journey.

CHARLES J. LOTZ

Jacob Riis†

He Emigrates to America

Jacob Riis was one of fourteen children in the home of his Danish schoolmaster father, who hoped devoutly that at least one of his sons should become a man of letters. He was deeply disappointed when Jacob announced that he had decided to learn the carpenter's trade. Reluctantly Father Riis gave in and Jacob journeyed from his native Ribe to Copenhagen, where he spent four years at his apprenticeship.

One of Jacob's principal reasons for becoming a carpenter was to be in the good graces of the daughter of a factory owner. But when she scornfully refused him, he sorrowfully but courageously announced he would journey to America. Some day he would return to claim her as his wife.

He was twenty-one when he went to the Land of Opportunity, and for four years he worked at whatever promised him a living, hoping in the meantime to find his opportunity. Often hungry, terribly hungry, he traveled from city to country and back again to the city. He worked at farming, coal mining, in a clay bank, he sold books, and did a dozen different things. More than once he almost despaired of ever succeeding. It was in one of those moments of despair that a man whom he had previously met told him of an opening on a newspaper as a reporter. He was already in the second day of a torturing fast. He finished his first assignment after going for three days without anything to eat, and, assured that he could now pay for room and board, he went to a boarding house operated by an acquaintance to apply for living quarters and board; but he fell in a faint upon the stairway before he could see the keeper.

He Enters His Life Work

From the first, Riis distinguished himself as a reporter. For only a brief period he owned and edited his own paper; during the rest of twenty-seven

---

† From *Creative Personalities, Volume 1: Vocations and Professions*. Edited by Philip Henry Lotz. New York: Association Press, 1940.

years he was content to unearth news, write his stories of what he saw, and comment upon the events which he reported. He scorned many opportunities to enter other fields both in newspaper work and in politics. He never sought office and never occupied any. He is a remarkable example of unselfish devotion to the social good, which he promoted with determination and success.

In order to succeed, Riis was compelled to compete with seasoned reporters; but he soon demonstrated to them that length of service and experience were not the only qualifications of a good reporter. He irked them by his industry, arriving hours before they did at police headquarters. They had to give up their loafing and gambling in the basement at the station, and found that their pooling of news and the identical stories that they sent to all the newspapers were no longer good enough. Riis was constantly making earlier editions than they were, and his stories far surpassed theirs in reading interest.

But Jacob Riis proved to be more than a reporter: he was a reporter who cared about the events that he chronicled. There was human interest in his stories. People read them because they wanted to help uplift the East Side and Mulberry Bend; and they became increasingly convinced that in Jacob Riis this slum section of the city had found a sympathetic interpreter and a strong advocate.

He Becomes a Reformer

It was in the field of social reform that Jacob Riis most distinguished himself. This is all the more remarkable, since he continued in newspaper work through twenty-seven strenuous years, and never professed to be a reformer. He was like the shoemaker, who said that he cobbled shoes for a living, but his real work was preaching the Gospel of Christ.

But Riis was not an ordinary reporter. He reported with a view to eliminating crime and with a view to uplifting those who were continually finding themselves in the toils of the law. He early saw that life in the slums inclined the people toward violations of the law. He never reported a crime but he also described the surroundings; and always the wretched living quarters of the people involved came in for their just description in his stories. Soon the landlords began to be uncomfortable under the lashings that Riis gave them for compelling the people to live in unspeakable hovels. When he published his first book, *How the Other Half Lives*, in 1890 he awoke to find two camps agitating the problem that was most on his heart, one defiantly attacking him for what they called his unjust portrayal of housing conditions, the other rejoicing that some one had the courage to protest against the tenement situation.

Riis had the satisfaction of being directly or indirectly responsible for the razing of seven blocks of tenements. He worked ceaselessly for better sanitary conditions, safer water supply, decent lodging houses for the wayfarers, and a new jail to supplant one that was a disgrace to the city.

All of these things Riis accomplished by his pen. He won the respect of leading persons throughout the city and the nation. All of these co-operated with him to make his reforms succeed. Among them was Theodore Roosevelt, who treasured him as a true friend. He said of him in an introduction to the 1922 edition of *The Making of an American* (Riis' autobiography):

"Jacob Riis was one of those men who by his writings contributed most to raising the standard of unselfishness, of disinterestedness, of sane and kindly good citizenship, in this country. But in addition to this he was one of the few great writers for clean and decent living and for upright conduct who was also a great doer. . . . Moreover, he was one of those good men whose goodness was free from the least priggishness or self-righteousness. He had a white soul; but he had the keenest sympathy for his brethren who stumbled and fell. He had the most flaming intensity of passion for righteousness, but he also had kindliness and a most humorously human way of looking at life and a sense of companionship with his fellows. He did not come to this country until he was almost a young man; but if I were asked to name a fellowman who came nearest to being the ideal American I should name Jacob Riis."[1]

He Is Honored

At the celebration of his silver wedding he and Mrs. Riis were honored by loving friends at the King's Daughters' Settlement. Of this occasion he writes in his autobiography:

". . . friends . . . gave to the new house my name. . . . It stands, that house, within a stone's throw of many a door in which I sat friendless and forlorn, trying to hide from the policeman who would not let me sleep; within hail of the Bend of the wicked past, atoned for at last; of the Bowery boarding house where I lay senseless on the stairs after my first day's work in the newspaper office, starved well nigh to death. But the memory of the old days has no sting. Its message is one of hope; the house itself is the key-note. It is the pledge of a better day, of the defeat of the slum with its helpless heredity of despair."[2]

Mulberry Bend today is a beautiful park, and the sunlight that Riis so earnestly craved for the stunted, emaciated bodies of the thousands of children of the slums now shines unhindered upon all who walk along the winding paths. This transformation was due almost entirely to the faithful, undiminished efforts through the years of the great Danish writer who wrote with a vision of what might be. Let him tell it in his own words:

"The children who were dancing there in the sunlight were to have a better time, please God! We had given them their lost chance. Looking at them in their delight now, it is not hard to understand what happened: the place that had been redolent of crime and murder became the most orderly in the city. When the last house was torn down in the Bend, I counted seventeen murders in the block, all the details of which I remembered. No doubt I had forgotten several times that number. In the four years after that during which I remained in Mulberry Street I was called only once to record a deed of violence in the neighborhood, and that was when a stranger came in and killed himself. . . . The Bend had become decent and orderly because the sunlight was let in, and shone upon children who had at last the right to play, even if the sign, 'Keep off the grass' was still there. That was what the Mulberry Bend park meant."[3]

1. Riis, Jacob. *The Making of an American*, New York, Macmillan, 1922, pp. xv–xvi.
2. The same, pp. 430–431.
3. *The Making of an American*, pp. 282–283.

After Mr. Riis had moved his family to a delightful plot on Long Island, his children one day gathered armfuls of daisies and asked him to take them to "the poors" in the city. This incident prompted the writing of an article that invited the hundred thousand people who came on the trains into the city every day from country places to bring flowers to the slum children. As a final suggestion he offered to handle flowers brought in by persons who could not distribute them themselves. He was overwhelmed with flowers. Let us read again from his autobiography:

"Flowers came pouring in from every corner of the compass. They came in boxes, in barrels, and in bunches, from field and garden, from town and country. Express wagons carrying flowers jammed Mulberry Street, and the police came out to marvel at the row. The office was fairly smothered in fragrance. A howling mob of children besieged it. The reporters forgot their rivalries and lent a hand with enthusiasm in giving out the flowers. The Superintendent of Police detailed five stout patrolmen to help carry the abundance to points of convenient distribution. Wherever we went fretful babies stopped crying and smiled as the messengers of love were laid against their wan cheeks. Slovenly women curtsied and made way. 'The Good Lord bless you,' I heard as I passed a dark hall, 'but you are a good man. No such has come this way before.' Oh! the heartache of it, and yet the joy! The Italians in the Barracks stopped quarrelling to help keep order. The worst street became suddenly good and neighborly. A year or two after, Father John Tabb, priest and poet, wrote, upon reading my statement that I had seen an armful of daisies keep the peace of a block better than the policeman's club:

'Peacemakers ye, the daisies, from the soil
Upbreathing wordless messages of love,
Soothing of earth-born brethren the toil
And lifting e'en the lowliest above.'"[4]

The King's Daughters took up the work, and it led to a remarkable enterprise among the poor of the East Side. Jacob Riis House was the ultimate outgrowth of the flower mission, which started in such humble way.

His Character

Jacob Riis had many splendid virtues. *The Making of an American,* as he called his autobiography, was likewise the making of a Christian. Numerous statements indicate his deeply religious nature. One of the striking passages from this interesting autobiography is this, in which he tells of the letter that opened the way to his first job as a newspaper man:

"What had happened stirred me profoundly. For the second time I saw a hand held out to save me from wreck just when it seemed inevitable: and I knew it for His hand, to whose will I was at last beginning to bow in humility, that had been a stranger to me before. It had ever been my own way, upon which I insisted. In the shadow of Grace Church I bowed my head against the granite wall of the gray tower and prayed for strength

4. *The Making of an American,* pp. 289–290.

to do the work which I had so long and arduously sought and which had come to me."[5]

He was a frank, impulsive youth with deep convictions. All of these things got him into trouble at first, but as the years of hardship and trouble wore on he became gentle and kind. His story reminds one of the impulsive Peter, the disciple. Their growth in Christian grace was very similar.

But he never lost his convictions. Though he had to learn to see life from new angles and to get the other fellow's point of view, once he was certain of his facts he went at the task that these facts suggested with might and main to correct evils and to accomplish his purposes.

Jacob Riis had a very wholesome outlook upon life. His was a sensitive nature, but he never pitied himself. When the girl of his dreams scorned him, he went to America, partly out of disappointment but more to prove the stuff of which he was made. The first time he returned to his native land he did so for the purpose of bringing that same girl to America as his wife. Though he had letters to acquaintances in America upon whose friendship he might have leaned in those first terrifying years in the new world, he refused to use them. Even when he had to go hungry for days he refused to beg; indeed, more than once when hunger was gnawing at his vitals he refused money that was offered to him, lest he lose his self-respect.

This outlook upon life gave him the courage that it took to achieve his ends despite the almost insurmountable barriers that he encountered. He won the girl he loved passionately though he had to wait long years in a foreign land; he accomplished in the slums what every other reformer had given up as a hopeless undertaking; he won for his friends and admirers those who scorned him and mocked him. He had the satisfaction of being stopped one day by one of his superiors, who years before had snubbed him and who had avoided him for years. This man warmly shook Jacob's hand, and assured him that he considered him a man of the highest type and a superior newspaper man.

Mr. Riis had the good sense to retire from his strenuous professional career before his best years were spent; indeed, he hints in the concluding chapters of his autobiography that he had had a warning of a serious malady. He died at the age of sixty-five. Between his retirement from the newspaper business and his death he lectured far and wide, and was in great demand in every kind of educational, social, and business circle. He was greatly beloved. Thousands who knew him personally, and millions who knew him through his books and by reputation must have felt as Theodore Roosevelt did when he said:

"It is difficult for me to write of Jacob Riis only from the public standpoint. He was one of my truest and closest friends. I have ever prized the fact that once, in speaking of me, he said, 'Since I met him he has been my brother.' I have not only admired and respected him beyond measure, but I have loved him dearly, and I mourn him as if he were one of my own family."[6]

5. The same, p. 121.
6. *The Making of an American,* p. xv.

ROBERT H. BREMNER

From From the Depths: The Discovery of Poverty in the United States[†]

Chapter 5. *The Condition of the Poor; Late Nineteenth-Century Social Investigations*

The helpful result of our study should be to renew the search for the preventive causes of degeneration, and to re-instill a consciousness of the necessity of improving both character and conditions.

Amos G. Warner, American Charities.
A Study in Philanthropy and Economics.

The information on urban social conditions gathered by settlement residents, institutional churchmen, Y.M.C.A. secretaries, and agents of charitable societies was usually obtained as an incident to other activities. Surveys and monographs undertaken by these groups influenced workers in the movements involved and were sometimes consulted by students and teachers of sociology; but as a general rule they were not intended for, or readily accessible to, the general public. Such knowledge as the average citizen possessed on the subject of poverty he acquired (if not by personal experience) from popular journalistic treatments of the problem.

There was no lack of curiosity about the existence of slum dwellers in the latter half of the nineteenth century, much of it excited by the peculiar depravity which was assumed to characterize that life. For a half century after 1842, when Charles Dickens startled the country with his description of the coarse and bloated faces of the inhabitants of the Five Points, a succession of books rolled off the press purporting to expose the mysteries and miseries of metropolitan life. Not infrequently these sensational works, some of them written by authors of dime novels, appealed to prurience behind a mask of outraged respectability, and nearly all of them capitalized on public interest in the details of vice and crime. Yet even the most lurid of these "inside stories" of sin in the big cities recognized that "The deserving poor are a multitude . . ." and acknowledged that "amid all this crime and pestilential influence there are found true hearts beating under breasts of spotless purity. . . ."

On a higher level, newspapers such as the *New York Tribune* and the *Daily Graphic* and periodicals such as *Frank Leslie's* and *Harper's Weekly* devoted considerable space to articles describing life in the slums. *Harper's Weekly* was particularly interested in the tenement-house problem, and during the seventies and eighties it ran several series of papers on Bottle Alley, Gotham Court, Ragpickers Court, and other picturesque but miserable districts in New York City. The article on Bottle Alley told of the enterprising family which occupied one small room in a rear tenement: the family regularly took in from eight to twelve lodgers a night at five cents a head, and also sold sour beer at two cents a pint or three cents a quart. Of Ragpickers Court the *Harper's* correspondent wrote: "The men who live in these wretched hovels pay from five to six dollars a month rent out of earnings that hardly ever exceed fifty cents a day. The agent who lets the property lives in New Jersey. The owner—well, if the name were mentioned it would surprise the people of New York City."

By far the most influential of the popular writers on slum life was Jacob Riis. Through years of experience as a police reporter he had acquired an unrivaled store of anecdotes about the people of the tenements, and he made liberal use of these in his books and articles. In a typical chapter Riis explained the problem of child vagrancy by telling this story: The remains of Harry Quill, aged fifteen, were discovered at the bottom of an air shaft in the tenement where his parents lived; investigation disclosed that two months earlier Harry, while drunk, had attacked another boy on the roof of the building; in the struggle the youth pushed Harry into the air shaft, but felt it best to say nothing about the occurrence; at the time the body was discovered Harry's parents had not yet notified the police that their son was missing.

The best known of Riis's books was *How the Other Half Lives* (1890), a reporter's sketchbook which had the good fortune to be published in the same year as Ward McAllister's picture of the pleasures of the idle rich, *Society as I Found It*, and General Booth's *In Darkest England*, an exploration of the social depths in London. Riis appealed not only to the sympathy but also to the self-interest of his middle-class readers. The strength of his book lay less in the novelty of his material—for by 1890 there had been at least a generation of intermittent discussion of the tenements and slums—than in the journalistic skill that made his description of existing evils seem so authentic and his plea for reform so compelling. He denied that the poor lived in slums simply because they were lazy, immoral, intemperate, and dirty, but, except in the cases of children and virtuous women, he displayed little sympathy for the economic underdog and voiced no protest against the arrangement of society which consigned masses of men to mean lives. His was no cry for social justice, but a call to the propertied classes to bestir themselves lest the crime engendered in the slums and the diseases bred there invade the comfortable quarters where ladies and gentlemen resided.

During the hard times of the nineties serious magazines such as *The Forum* printed numerous essays on philanthropic experiments and on improved methods of dealing with dependency. *The Arena*, edited by B. O. Flower, was especially receptive to articles on social problems. The first issue of the magazine carried a symposium on the causes of the increase in poverty, in which one contributor suggested that not poverty itself but consciousness of it was on the rise. Helen Gardener's "Thrown in with the City's Dead," which appeared in *The Arena* in 1890, was an excellent early example of muckraking. "Suppose you chanced to be very poor and to die in New York," the article began. "We are fond of saying that death levels all distinctions. Let us see." There followed a harrowing report on conditions on tiny Blackwell's Island, to which the city of New York consigned its insane, its "medium term" prisoners, and its pauper dead. Flower himself was the author of *Civilization's Inferno; or Studies in the Social Cellar* (1893), in which he attempted to do for Boston's slums what Riis had done for Manhattan's, and also to plead more vigorously for social justice for the laboring classes.

A series of articles appearing in *Scribner's Magazine* in 1892 and 1893 under the general title "The Poor in Great Cities" was a pioneer effort to examine urban poverty in a broad frame of reference. The introduction referred to the condition of the poor as "the central subject of all social questions" and cited relief of suffering and improvement in the standard of living of the masses as necessary forerunners of all other reforms. "What we need to know," said the editor, "is what is doing, here and elsewhere, in the general and efficient activity that has been the growth of the last few years; and especially, what are the facts with which our own efforts are to deal, and how facts elsewhere compare with them." Articles in the series examined the extent of misery and the preventive and ameliorative activities under way in London, Paris, Naples, New York, Boston, and Chicago. The contributors included Riis, who wrote on the children of the poor, Robert A. Woods, a Boston settlement leader, and William T. Elsing, a city missionary and pastor of a large institutional church in New York City.

The popular books and articles mentioned above were important primarily as indications of a mounting interest in social questions. The best of them admittedly grazed only the surface of the problems examined. Based on personal observation or impressions, they were often intensely, and intentionally, subjective in their approach. As late as 1892 Washington Gladden protested that there was little "definite and reliable" information on poverty in America in print and complained that popular ignorance on the subject was "profound and universal."

One reason why there was such a paucity of systematic knowledge about poverty in America was the widely shared assumption that being poor was a self-inflicted mortification. This attitude had the result of directing toward pauperism and crime most of the sociological research undertaken in the United States prior to the 1890's. Robert L. Dugdale's *The Jukes* (1877), for example, expressed both the contemporary concern regarding the "dangerous classes" and the proclivity to lump dependency in the same category as criminality. The Secretary of the Prison Association of New York introduced Dugdale's book with the observation that "out of the same social soil from which spring the majority of the criminals there also chiefly grow up the vagrants and paupers—the ignorant and vicious and incapable." Even *American Charities* (1894) by Amos Warner, which incorporated the most recent findings of European and American research, treated poverty, no matter what the cause, as synonymous with "degeneration." To the nineteenth-century American few crimes were more reprehensible than inability to make a living.

Preoccupation with the moral and fiscal aspects of pauperism (that is, dependence upon charity for support) long prevented Americans from making serious studies of the causes and results of poverty. The English investigator, Charles Booth, was perhaps more influential than any other intellectual factor in bringing about a shift in the emphasis of social research in the United States. His painstaking study of the *Life and Labour of the People of London,* which began to appear in the late 1880's, was soon well known and highly regarded in this country. To a very considerable extent Booth set the pattern for later American sociological investigations. Like many of his contemporaries he had a tendency to subject persons in lowly economic circumstances to moralistic tests. Nevertheless, the ultimate result of his analysis of London's population was to direct attention away from moral considerations and toward economic factors such as occupations and wages.

Booth had a passion for facts. He was dissatisfied with guesses about the amount of poverty, with theorizing about its probable causes, and with melodramatic descriptions of isolated instances of misery. By means of school-board visitors and other voluntary and official agencies he made a street-by-street canvass of various London districts, obtaining data on the employment, earnings, and housing of a sizable portion of the city's population. On the basis of what he believed to be reliable and pertinent statistics collected in this fashion, Booth estimated that about 30 per cent of the people of London lived in poverty. This conclusion, and also his finding that intemperance was an unimportant cause of poverty as compared to illness and unemployment, awakened great interest in his work. In the long run, however, the lesson of Booth's study was its demonstration that poverty was not an amorphous, intangible, pseudoreligious problem, but a concrete situation capable of economic definition and worthy of scientific scrutiny.

Notable advances were scored in the field of social statistics during the last three decades of the nineteenth century. The Census Bureau, state bureaus of labor statistics, congressional committees, the federal Commissioner of Labor, and the Department of Agriculture compiled and published reports on a multitude of subjects ranging from wages and prices to the incidence of divorce. As a result of the data supplied by these agencies no less a student than Charles B. Spahr asserted in 1896: "In the United States, despite the absence of income-tax returns, we find perhaps the most complete and satisfactory statistics in the world regarding the aggregate of the national income." It is noteworthy, however, that when Spahr estimated the distribution of income among various classes he relied heavily on "common observation" and contended that "upon matters coming within its field the common observation of common people is more trustworthy than the statistical investigations of the most unprejudiced experts."

At the close of the century there were in fact (as there long remained) vast gaps in statistical information on some pressing economic and social issues. For example, in 1891 when Richard T. Ely attempted to ascertain the number of paupers in the United States he discovered that neither the states nor the federal government had accurate records showing the number of persons in public institutions or receiving outdoor relief.

Inadequacies in technique were only partly responsible for the incomplete and unreliable statistical information available at the end of the century. By 1900 only about half the states had established labor bureaus and fewer than half had developed factory-inspection systems. Whether state or federal, legislation creating fact-finding agencies, to say nothing of regulatory bodies, was often so weak that employers were under no compulsion to answer questionnaires or, if they did reply, to submit accurate data. Furthermore, the appropriations granted the bureaus were seldom sufficient to permit them to do a thorough piece of work. Thus in 1892 Congress passed a resolution calling on the Commissioner of Labor to conduct an investigation into the slums of cities with populations of 200,000 or over—and appropriated $20,000 for the task. The number of cities in the category designated was sixteen, but the sum appropriated was barely enough to enable the Commissioner's staff to look into some of the slums in four cities. Another example of congressional parsimony occurred in the mid-nineties when the Commissioner of Labor was "authorized and directed" to make a full-dress survey of the employment of women and children, subject to the provision that the investigation be carried out under the regular appropriation of the office.

Some of the state labor bureaus were weakened by patronage appointments of dubious qualification. At least one was placed under the supervision of a director who had been notoriously hostile to the establishment of the agency. Not infrequently statistical findings were shaped by political pressures. The Michigan labor bureau, by selecting counties in which property ownership was much more concentrated than in the state as a whole, was able to demonstrate that "one two hundredth" of the population owned 60 per cent of the real estate of Michigan. In 1893 the Senate Finance Committee, by garbling the figures submitted to it by employers, managed to show a nearly seventy-per-cent increase in wages between 1860 and 1891. Similarly, as his critics were quick to point out, Carroll D. Wright's summaries of the investigations conducted by his office (Department of Labor) were not always consistent with the observations and statistical data contained in the bodies of the reports. No doubt thirty years of experience as a state and federal officeholder had taught Wright the value of ambiguity in the discussion of controversial issues.

The incomplete and unsatisfactory character of late nineteenth-century statistical inquiries into industrial issues is well illustrated by conflicting estimates of the extent of unemployment. In 1878, when some calculations placed the number of jobless in Massachusetts at as high as 300,000, the director of the state bureau of labor statistics, basing his figures on the returns of police officials and tax assessors, asserted that the actual number was less than 30,000.

Wright devoted his first annual report (1886) as United States Commissioner of Labor to a study of industrial depressions in the United States and Europe in the half century since 1837; and in 1895 a Massachusetts commission prepared a notable report on unemployment relief. In general, however, studies of unemployment long suffered both from inadequate coverage and from a want of scientific spirit. Many seem to have been undertaken less to ascertain the facts than to assure a troubled people that the problem was not really serious at all.

For all their shortcomings, the early reports of the state and federal labor bureaus introduced a greater degree of objectivity into discussions of social and economic questions. In a commentary on studies of unemployment made by various agencies in the eighties and early nineties, the economist Davis R. Dewey listed ten factors which he said were "generally recognized as contributary causes making for nonemployment," not one of which referred to personal defects in the jobless. E. W. Bemis used the statistics on wages and unemployment compiled by the Ohio labor bureau in his inquiry into the standard of living of miners in the Hocking Valley in the mid-eighties. Bemis assigned the major responsibility for the high incidence of unemployment in the region to management's policy of keeping a surplus of labor on hand; and he showed that owing to low wages and frequent layoffs the average yearly expenditure per person in miners' families must have been less than the amount spent by the state of Ohio for the maintenance of an inmate in its asylums or prisons.

Industrial accidents and occupational diseases were among the problems conspicuously avoided by most state labor bureaus. Nevertheless, the Interstate Commerce Commission recorded and published in its annual statistical summary the grisly total of employees killed and injured on the nation's railroads. President Benjamin Harrison, calling attention to this "cruel and largely needless sacrifice," declared in 1889: "It is a reproach to our civilization that any class of American workmen should in the pursuit of a necessary and useful vocation be subjected to a peril of life and limb as great as that of a soldier in time of war." In each of his annual messages to Congress Harrison recommended the passage of legislation, finally adopted in 1893, requiring gradual installation of air brakes and automatic couplers on railway cars employed in interstate transportation. Meanwhile, approximately half of the states had enacted laws of varying effectiveness providing for the use of safety devices and appliances on railways within their jurisdictions.

Much of the credit for arousing public interest in railway safety belongs to a Baptist clergyman, Lorenzo S. Coffin. Beginning in his native Iowa in the 1880's, he gathered such facts as were available regarding work accidents on the railroads and launched a campaign for the adoption of automatic couplers and air brakes. He interviewed railroad executives in an attempt to awaken their consciences, wrote articles, delivered lectures, and preached sermons on the need for protecting brakemen and other railroaders. In one day Coffin is reported to have mailed more than 2,000 letters to prominent citizens in different parts of the country explaining the pressing need for remedial action.

Case workers for charity organizations were among the first persons, aside from the victims and their families, to recognize the part played by industrial accidents in producing poverty. W. F. Willoughby, who made a survey of workingmen's insurance in Europe and America in the 1890's, observed that in no other field of reform was the United States more backward than in legislation regularizing compensation for work accidents. In 1890 only half-a-dozen states required factory accidents to be reported, and only one, Massachusetts, had an employers' liability law of any efficiency. By the middle of the decade one out of seven railroad workers was protected against injury or death at work through insurance schemes voluntarily established by their employers. For the great mass of workers in transportation and industry, however, there was bitter truth in an investigator's statement that in America human life was ordinarily regarded as cheaper than the small cost of protecting it.

The plight of workingwomen was a favorite subject of discussion among mid-century reformers and feminists. A brief review of the problem in 1844 by a Boston clergyman, R. C. Waterston, struck a modern note by examining piece rates paid in garment shops and calculating the impossible number of hours it would be necessary for a hand sewer to work in order to support herself by making shirts at six or seven cents each and pants at twenty-five cents a pair. The author, whose remarks were addressed to the Society for the Prevention of Pauperism, warned that "inadequate wages— both because they are inadequate and because they discourage—have proved to many a source of pauperism." Louisa May Alcott's Work, although not published until 1873, described conditions in a number of different women's occupations in the 1850's. To a modern reader its tone is distressingly sentimental, but, in one passage at least, Miss Alcott spoke with evident sincerity: the best reply to people who advise young girls to go to work as servants or factory hands, she said, was "Try it."

After the Civil War both official agencies and private individuals made rather frequent investigations of female labor. Wright's reports from the Massachusetts Bureau of Labor Statistics were the first trustworthy accounts of the status of women wage earners in American industry, and when he became United States Commissioner of Labor he continued to explore the question. His *Fourth Annual Report* (1889), covering more than 17,000 workingwomen in twenty-two cities, offered valuable data on wages, standards of living, and sanitary provisions in factories. The New York and other state labor bureaus undertook similar studies in the eighties and nineties.

Elizabeth Stuart Phelps obtained the framework for her novel of industrial life, *The Silent Partner* (1871), from the reports of the Massachusetts Bureau of Labor Statistics. Fifteen years later, and in a more realistic spirit, Helen Campbell's *Prisoners of Poverty* (1887) exposed the precarious and ill-rewarded labor of women in New York's needle trades and department stores. Although the style was emotional, Mrs. Campbell's book was marked by a very practical concern with earnings, budgets, and health. She showed how declining piece rates unsettled standards of living, and she presented numerous case records to reveal what it meant, in terms of household economy, to try to exist on three dollars a week. In a later work she described factory employment for women as valuable only as preparation "for the hospital, the workhouse, and the prison," since the workers so often were "inoculated with trade diseases, mutilated by trade appliances, and corrupted by trade associates."

Where Miss Phelps, in *The Silent Partner*, had preached moral reform to manufacturers Mrs. Campbell maintained that the pursuit of "bargains" by well-to-do shoppers forced employers to depress wages below the subsistence level. Her disclosure of the human cost of bargain-counter finery was one of the factors that inspired the formation of consumers' leagues in several cities during the 1890's. These shoppers' organizations investigated wages and working conditions in retail establishments and published white lists recommending patronage of those which met the standards of a fair house. The national organization of the Consumers' League, as will be made clear in a later chapter, was one of the most active forces in working for improved factory legislation to protect women and children and in providing the legal defense when the constitutionality of the statutes was challenged in the courts.

Fairly numerous, but not necessarily effective, legal restrictions on the employment of minors testify that the question of child labor was by no means ignored in the late nineteenth century. Yet on no issue, with the possible exceptions of unemployment and industrial accidents, was factual information more difficult to obtain. Prior to 1870 the federal census did not differentiate between child and adult workers in its statistics on wage earners; thereafter the totals were broken down so as to indicate the number over and under fifteen years of age. These figures did not represent an actual count of working children, since they did not include the large group that was not technically employed but regularly "helped" parents in sweat-shops and mines. For obvious reasons state labor bureaus found it almost impossible to get employers to submit accurate data on the employment of young children in their establishments. Those statistics that were available in 1890, however, indicated that the wage earners under fifteen were increasing at a more rapid rate than the adult workers.

Popular attitudes toward child labor may be gauged by the frequency and enthusiasm with which the heroes of magazine fiction and dime novels assumed the economic burdens of manhood at a tender age. Charles Morris, not so well known as Horatio Alger, but equally devoted to the gospel of youthful endeavor, had one of his model youths, Harry Handy, complain to his employer that he was not worked hard enough. From time to time a novelist wrote of working children with compassion; Elizabeth Oakes Smith described a group of newsboys, some of them dozing, in the pit of the Bowery Theater:

> You look at them, so thin, so like little old men, sharp, eager, self-reliant when awake, and then when sleep comes and muscles relax, and the overtaxed nerve yields to inaction, they grow children again, weary, suffering, hard-wrought children they look, and you gaze at their emaciated forms, the angular shoulders peeping from the ragged shirt, the hollow temple and thin nostril, with an indescribable pang. You feel how pitiful is the childhood of the poor.

For the most part, however, Americans took it for granted that poor children had to work and assumed that, within reason, it was good for them to do so.

The legislation on the subject enacted in about half the states before 1896 was consistent with this view. Ordinarily the laws applied only to manufacturing, excluded only very young children (under ten in some states, twelve or fourteen in others) from employment, and permitted older ones to work ten hours a day. It was common knowledge that statutory restrictions were frequently violated through falsification of age. Compulsory-education laws designed to keep minors out of factories and mines until they had gained at least a common school education were, in most states, so loosely drawn and laxly enforced that, according to one investigator, they were "a farce."

Charles Loring Brace, founder of the Children's Aid Society, devoted one chapter of *The Dangerous Classes of New York* (1872) to "Factory Children." Brace made one of the earliest surveys of child labor when he inquired into the employment of the boys and girls attending the Society's night-school classes. He was far from a doctrinaire opponent of child labor. His society presented a bill to the New York legislature in 1872 which would have authorized factory labor of children over ten years of age for a maximum of sixty hours a week. Nevertheless, Brace was one of the most important figures in the post-Civil War era in the movement for better education for working children. He feared that, unless more attention were paid to their instruction, the child laborers would swell the ranks of the dangerous classes upon reaching maturity.

Critics of child labor became more outspoken during the eighties and the nineties. Clara Potter reported on the working conditions of children in New York City for the *Christian Union,* giving special attention to industrial accidents in which youthful workers were maimed and crippled. Because of the legal fiction that they were employed at their own risk, the children almost never received damages for these injuries. Clare de Graffenried, who investigated the employment of minors in a wide range of retail and manufacturing enterprises in 1889, blamed the large number of cases of tuberculosis among working girls on premature work, unsanitary factory conditions, and poor nourishment. Willoughby, discussing the social aspects of child labor, commented that public opinion would be inflamed if any state subjected the children in its reformatories and poorhouses to the kind of treatment which they received as a matter of course, and without public outcry, in many factories.

Both Miss de Graffenried and Willoughby argued that permitting a young child to work usually meant dooming him to a lifetime of drudgery and helpless incompetence. They believed that boys and girls who went into the factories, mines, stores, and offices when they should have been at school wore out their energies in routine and repetitive tasks without acquiring the skills that would later enable them to earn decent wages. Child laborers consequently entered maturity under such a heavy handicap of ignorance and physical debility that many could never become self-supporting. Several years earlier a writer in a metropolitan newspaper had arrived at a somewhat similar conclusion regarding children employed in the street trades. "It is a popular fallacy that bootblacks and newsboys grow up to be major generals and millionaires," he observed. "The majority of them, on the contrary, become porters and barkeepers."

The best-informed student of child labor in the United States during the 1890's was Florence Kelley, a resident of Hull House and chief factory inspector of the state of Illinois. Mrs. Kelley collaborated with Alzina P. Stevens on a chapter about wage-earning children for *Hull-House Maps and Papers*. Their paper was a fighting document which asserted that "it is not where labor is scarce, but where competition for work is keenest that the per cent of children is largest in the total number of employed" and that "children are found in greatest number where the conditions of labor are most dangerous to life and health."

In 1896 Mrs. Kelley told the National Conference of Charities and Correction that three years of experience as a factory inspector had convinced her that regulation of child labor was impossible; the only way to end the evils connected with it was to prohibit entirely the employment of children under sixteen. Like Helen Campbell, who had urged that it was as necessary to rescue children from the factories as from the slums, Mrs. Kelley denied that child labor was either desirable or necessary. "Why have newsboys?" she asked. "Why not let the unemployed men sell the papers and the newsboys go to school, as our own children do?" She contended that if parents could not provide children with maintenance and education, the state should assume responsibility for their care and instruction. In this paper, read before a meeting of professional philanthropists, Mrs. Kelley recognized that manufacturers' associations, department stores, and the telegraph company (then the largest employer of child labor in the world) would oppose the abolition of child labor; she predicted, however, that the fiercest opponents of such a reform would be the self-righteous, tax-conscious philanthropists. Prophetically, in view of the history of the proposed child-labor amendment in the 1920's, she forecast that the philosophy of self-help, appeals to the stern puritan virtues, and the argument of economy would all be adduced to justify the continuance of child labor.

In the nineteenth century concern with poverty was usually accompanied by hostility to liquor; conversely, concern with intemperance frequently, as in the instance of Robert Hartley, led to interest in poverty. Not always, but in a number of cases (as, for example, Frances Willard), antisaloon sentiment went hand in hand with economic radicalism. To many persons "the liquor interests" represented plutocracy in its most insolent and insidious guise. The temperance crusade also drew adherents from men and women who regarded indulgence in drink as not necessarily a vice but an expensive and dangerous pastime. "What a great amount of time, and strength, and money might multitudes gain for self-improvement by strict sobriety!" exclaimed Channing. "That cheap remedy, pure water, would cure the chief evils in very many families of the ignorant and poor."

Throughout the century the idea was accepted that drink was one of the most important causes, if not the sole cause, of poverty. Those who held to this point of view could point to numerous examples that seemed to prove their point. As the years went by, however, students of poverty—as opposed to the general public—assigned a less prominent role to alcohol as a factor in producing want. In the 1830's Joseph Tuckerman estimated that 75 per cent of American pauperism resulted from drink; in the 1890's, on the other hand, the charity organization societies' records consulted by Amos Warner indicated that intemperance was the cause of distress in only 5 to 22 per cent of the cases investigated by the agencies. By the closing decade of the century, as noted in a previous chapter, there was a growing tendency to think intemperance as much a result as a cause of poverty.

The formation in 1893 of the Committee of Fifty for the Investigation of the Liquor Problem marked the emergence of a more detached and scientific attitude toward this particular social issue than had been apparent in most earlier discussions of it. The Committee was composed of college presidents, prominent clergymen, and well-known social scientists; its announced purpose was "to secure a body of facts which may serve as a basis for intelligent public and private actions." In the ten years after its organization the Committee published five books, one a summary of its work and the others dealing with the physiological, legislative, ethical, and economic aspects of the liquor question.

In gathering data for several of these volumes the Committee utilized the services of charity agents, settlement residents, and teachers and students of economics and sociology. The study of the economic phase of the problem was based on special reports submitted by thirty-three charity organization societies for each "case" handled over periods of from three to twelve months. These reports, as analyzed by the Committee's staff, revealed a higher percentage of want attributable to intemperance (25 per cent) than had been shown in Warner's study of the regular case records. The significance of this finding was undermined, however, by the growing conviction among professional social workers that it was unrealistic to attempt to pick out any single factor as solely responsible for distress.

The inquiry entitled *Substitutes for the Saloon* (1901) contained information furnished the Committee by a variety of correspondents on different grades of drinking establishments in seventeen cities. This report began with a frank recognition that the saloon performed a necessary function in society: "Its hold on the community does not wholly proceed from its satisfying the thirst for drink. It satisfies the thirst for sociability." As the Committee saw it, the problem was to devise other institutions capable of meeting the social needs of working people as effectively as the saloon. Laying prejudice aside, the staff of investigators sought to learn from the saloon by analyzing its nonalcoholic appeal. Altogether it was a unique and enlightening presentation which, if its message had been heeded, might have brought a more realistic spirit into the temperance movement. Present-day students can find in it a wealth of information, not only on turn-of-the-century saloons, but also on the quantity and quality of other recreational institutions then available to the public in representative cities.

In the latter part of the century the tenement problem awakened much interest, partly because of the traditional regard for the home as the bulwark of society, and partly because of the supposed connection between tenements and saloons. "Foul homes" and "intoxicating drink" were the twin causes of poverty, according to Robert Treat Paine, head of the Associated Charities of Boston. He thought that each led to the other and that improvement of the homes of the poor was a necessary preliminary to the elimination of intemperance. E. R. L. Gould, a statistician in the federal labor bureau, expressed similar views in *The Housing of the Working People* (1895). "Bad housing is a terribly expensive thing to any community," he warned, "for its cost is drunkenness, poverty, crime, and other forms of social decline." The reporter and fiction writer, Julian Ralph, who was not entirely sympathetic in his attitude toward tenement dwellers, nevertheless remarked that frequent visits to the saloon must be expected among people who lived in quarters too cramped to encourage use for any purposes save eating and sleeping. Riis pointed out that because of scant water connections it was often easier to get beer than water in the tenements. In his opinion "the scandalous scarcity of water in the hot summer" was the one most important cause of drunkenness among the poor.

State and city boards of health were usually charged with the administration of such tenement laws or ordinances as were adopted prior to 1900. The reports of these agencies provide he most authoritative descriptions of slum and tenement conditions during the last third of the nineteenth century. Their findings, which were rather widely publicized in magazines and newspapers of the period, showed that one of the consequences of being poor was greater than average susceptibility to illness and death. Seventy out of every one hundred deaths in New York City befell residents of the tenement houses; in some notorious rookeries, such as Gotham Court on Cherry Street, the annual death rate was almost 20 per cent—seven times as high as the average in the city as a whole. The mortality rates for the children of the poor were even more shocking than those for adults. A writer in *The Christian Union* cited two New York alleys where the death rates showed that nearly three out of four infants succumbed before reaching five years of age.

Allusions to the depravity of slum dwellers persisted to the end of the century; but, especially in the 1890's, this view was challenged by numerous students. In *The Housing of the Poor* (1893) Marcus T. Reynolds drew together material on the economic condition of tenement dwellers from state labor bureaus, boards of health, tenement commissions, and charity organization societies; the slum investigation conducted by the staff of the United States Commissioner of Labor in 1894 contained almost 250 pages of statistics on earnings, unemployment, and rents paid by residents of slums in four large cities; and Gould's *Housing of the Working People* examined the experience of European and American communities in providing decent low-cost housing for wage earners through public or private initiative. Factual investigations of this sort disclosed that the problem of the slum and the tenement involved the housing of productive elements, not just the dregs, of industrial society.

In itself this was hardly a startling discovery. Fifty years earlier men such as Griscom, Hartley, and Channing had made the point that the tenements were nothing less or more than the homes of the urban working class. Yet the earlier reformers, no matter how sharply they had criticized the bad, expensive, and unhealthful housing of the poor, had usually asserted that the "fault or ignorance of the sufferers" was chiefly responsible for the evils they decried; and they had assumed that the remedy lay in "the elevation of the mind and character of the laborer."

This may have been a valid diagnosis of the situation in the 1840's. A half century later the problem had become much more complex; its solution impinged on all the other issues—wages, working conditions, industrial accidents, health, and unemployment—affecting the standard of living of the urban masses. Relatively little positive action had as yet been taken to rectify the ills and injustices to which tenement dwellers were exposed, but improvement in housing was nevertheless seen to be dependent on economic and legal rather than moral reform.

At the end of the nineteenth century Americans were still ignorant as to the actual extent of poverty in their midst. Only rough estimates based on limited data could be hazarded. Charity organization records, the number of evictions, and pauper burials occurring in a given period were all used as an index of want. Projecting his conclusion from such data, Jacob Riis estimated in 1892 that from 20 to 30 per cent of New York's population lived in penury. Charles B. Spahr's investigation of the distribution of property and income, which indicated a narrower and narrower concentration of wealth, also implied that the number of the poor was disturbingly large.

Although only slight progress had been made in determining the amount of poverty in America, much attention had been given to its causes. The trend of informed opinion was away from the individualistic interpretation of want, and the ground had been prepared for an inductive approach to the problem. There was growing acceptance of the view that no single explanation yet advanced was in itself sufficient to stand the test of facts. Amos G. Warner, a very influential figure in the development of social work in the United States, noted in 1894 that in modern society, "where the individual suffers not only from his own mistakes and defects, but also from the mistakes and defects of a large number of other people," we must expect the causes of destitution to be "indefinitely numerous and complicated."

The opinion that was becoming current among social scientists here and abroad was that poverty could not be studied as a separate phenomenon, isolated from other economic and social maladjustments. Rather, as a Canadian student suggested, poverty must be scrutinized as "a part of the study of the economic life of the people as a whole." This conviction brought with it an eagerness to discover "what life is and how it is now lived by the people." E. B. Andrews criticized both *laissez-faire* and socialist theoreticians for being "in too great haste to generalize." The business of the present, he advised, was "the analysis of social conditions—deep, patient, and undogmatic."

It was not merely disinterested curiosity that led the publicists of the eighties and nineties to tear aside the veil of ignorance and indifference that concealed the suffering of the poor from public view. Men and women such as Riis, Flower, Helen Campbell, and Florence Kelley were propagandists who hoped to alter conditions by rousing the conscience of the nation. Like the muckrakers who followed them they sincerely believed that once the "plain bald statement of facts" had been submitted to the public judgment, nothing could stand in the way of reform.

Perhaps they erred on the side of optimism. Realism in social science was no better received by the polite classes than its counterpart in literature and art. The powerful alignment of groups with a stake in the perpetuation of social wrongs did not disintegrate when its malefactions were exposed. But it was placed on the defensive. In a liberal democracy it is literally true that the first step toward the achievement of reform is the exploration of and diffusion of knowledge about the realities of the prevailing situation. By the latter part of the 1890's a start had been made toward the accumulation of social facts; after the turn of the century the study of mankind was to be carried forward with a vigor and zest that imparted a characteristic tone to the intellectual climate of the Progressive era.

ROY LUBOVE

From The Progressives and the Slums: Tenement House Reform in New York City, 1890–1917[†]

3. Jacob A. Riis: Portrait of a Reformer

I already knew Jake Riis, because his book "How the Other Half Lives" had been to me both an enlightenment and an inspiration for which I felt I could never be too grateful.

THEODORE ROOSEVELT, *Autobiography*

I

Jacob A. Riis, a dozen years after publication of *How the Other Half Lives*, was described as the man "who has done more than any one else to alleviate the condition of the poor of New York by revealing their misery to a sympathetic world." Lincoln Steffens, surveying the former Danish carpenter's achievements up to 1903, observed that "if any rich man could mark a city with as many good works as Jacob A. Riis has thrust upon New York, his name would be called good and himself great." In 1922, eight years after Riis's death, the crusading Episcopal minister, W. S. Rainsford, remembered him as one of the two men most beloved by the poor in his time.[1]

No housing reformer before Riis so successfully captured the public's imagination and affection. One cannot explain Riis's eminence through the novelty of his message—he certainly did not discover the tenement problem. Furthermore, Riis erected no scaffolding of theory to which disciples could turn for inspiration and guidance; he was unsystematic, almost impressionistic, in his thought. Riis never held public office, with its accompanying power and prestige. In part, the architect of Riis's fame was history. It is significant that *How the Other Half Lives* was published in 1890, the first year of a decade of turbulence such as the nation had not experienced since the Civil War.

The social and economic problems which had troubled the postwar generation exploded in the 1890's with accumulated fury. Agricultural prices sank to new lows. Southern and western farmers organized a political party which promulgated such radical doctrines as the free coinage of silver and government ownership of utilities. The Homestead strike of 1892 foreshadowed the labor strife of the lean years of depression beginning in 1893. The Pullman strike in 1894 and Coxey's industrial army, only one strike and one army among many others in that convulsive year, suggested that power, violence, and disciplined organization were fast becoming the arbiters of our industrial life. The Pullman strike, for the time being at least, suggested also that workers would no longer accept the paternal benevolence represented by George M. Pullman as a substitute for their right to organize. The widespread unemployment and pervasive poverty of the depression years seemed to prove, once and for all, that America would not be spared "the discipline of poverty and inherited misery."

It was not only in agriculture and labor-capital relations that the 1890's witnessed a challenge to the old order. The alleged conquest of the West signalized by Frederick Jackson Turner's 1893 essay on the significance of the frontier troubled those who believed that American character and institutions had been shaped by the process of westward settlement. Significantly, the ardent immigration restrictionist, Francis A. Walker, based his argument in part upon "the important fact of the complete exhaustion of the free public land in the United States."[2]

Perhaps more important in the eyes of Riis's contemporaries than the passing of the frontier was the conquest of the town and farm by the big city. Although the growing influence of the city disturbed Americans before 1890, as we have seen, interest in the role of the urban colossus reached a new pitch of intensity after that date. It was not only the city's inexorable expansion in population and wealth that attracted attention, but the fact that many Americans regarded the city as a kind of parasite, draining the hinterlands of their vitality. Youth poured into the city seeking jobs, cultural and social stimulation. The old, the weary, the complacent remained in the

---

1. Joseph B. Gilder, "The Making of Jacob A. Riis," *The Critic*, XL (1902), 64; Lincoln Steffens, "Jacob A. Riis, Reporter, Reformer, American Citizen," *McClure's Magazine*, XXI (1903), 419; William S. Rainsford, *The Story of a Varied Life: An Autobiography* (New York, 1922), 369. The other was Father McGlynn, described by Rainsford as "a saint, a crusader born ahead of his time."
2. Francis A. Walker, "Restriction of Immigration," *Atlantic Monthly*, LXXVII (1896), 826.

country. Unless something were done, America faced the appalling prospect of breeding a "rural American peasantry, illiterate and immoral, possessing the rights of citizenship, but utterly incapable of performing or comprehending its duties."[3] The American was forgetting that his roots lay in the soil: "Not only has he left the pasture and wood, but in the towns his shelter lifts higher and higher, nearer the stars, but surely not nearer heaven."[4]

This "silent tragedy" being enacted in the 1890's—the depopulation and decline of the countryside—represented for many a profound social and economic catastrophe. People forsook the pure air, cheap homes, and equalitarianism of the countryside, heedlessly pouring into cities which deprived them of these advantages. The defenders of country life argued that the city would, in the end, pay dearly unless the balance was restored, for "the degeneration of the rural population means the later degeneration of the urban population also." The city could not survive without the infusion of sturdy, energetic rural stock.[5]

Connected with practically every major social and economic issue of the 1890's was the immigrant. Americans, never so fearful and pessimistic about the future welfare of the Republic since the Civil War, scrutinized the relationship between the immigrant and national life with the deepest misgivings. If the immigrant was not entirely responsible for such developments as urban congestion and crime, industrial warfare and machine politics, he certainly contributed his share.

Two features stand out conspicuously in the immigration controversy of the decade. The first was the pervasive nativism affecting South and West as well as East; the second was the growing sentiment in favor of halting unrestricted immigration. The anti-Italian riots in New Orleans, the anti-Chinese agitation on the West coast, the fear of eastern workers that great immigrant hordes threatened their jobs and standard of living, the rapid growth of the anti-Catholic American Protective Association, the anti-semitism of western and southern agrarians which focused upon the "conspiracy" of Jewish bankers and financiers to exploit the productive classes, the racism circulating in the writings and salons of eastern patrician intellectuals like Henry Cabot Lodge and the Adams brothers, all point to the conclusion that Americans of disparate classes and sections viewed the immigrant as a grave threat.

It seemed as if the immigrant had become a national scapegoat upon whom frustrated Americans could focus their wrath. Hostility to the immigrant provided at least one policy upon which normally antagonistic groups could unite; thus nativism cut across the class and sectional strife of the 1890's. The employer, fearful of imported European anarchy and radicalism, could join with the worker troubled about the threat to his economic security, in common hostility to the immigrant. Conservative patrician intellectuals who parted company with southern and western agrarians on

3. Josiah Strong, *The New Era or The Coming Kingdom* (New York, 1893), 174. See also Henry J. Fletcher, "The Doom of the Small Town," *Forum*, XIX (1895), 223; and A. C. True, "The Solidarity of Town and Farm," *Arena*, XVII (1896–97), 544.
4. Anna R. Weeks, "The Divorce of Man from Nature," *Arena*, IX (1893–94), 230.
5. Henry J. Fletcher, "The Drift of Population to Cities: Remedies," *Forum*, XIX (1895), 738; quotation from Strong, *The New Era*, 177; True, "The Solidarity of Town and Farm," 544. Also Alfred H. Peters, "The Depreciation of Farming Land," *Quarterly Journal of Economics*, IV (1889–90), 32, 33.

economic issues, shared with them a mutual dislike of Jews and other cor-
rupters of American racial purity. In effect, the broad scope and fiery intensity of the nativism of the 1890's cannot be explained by reference only to
the conflict between American and foreigner on concrete economic or political issues. In an era of intense sectional and class disharmony, nativism
was a psychological palliative—a means of affirming national unity in the
face of obvious disunity. The immigrant became the victim of an internally
directed nationalism, just as the Spaniard became the victim of an exter-
nally directed nationalism and jingoism in 1898.[6]

The decade, understandably, gave rise to a vigorous conviction in favor
of closing the gates so indifferently guarded since the nation's founding.
With the frontier at an end and our cities already overcrowded, many feared
that we were losing our capacity to absorb and assimilate the immigrant. It
was "obvious that the time must come when by the advance of population
we shall lose the very advantages that now make this country attractive to
European emigrants." Opponents of free immigration argued that the
recruiting activities of steamship agencies and the extension of rail facilities to interior portions of Europe made immigration too easy. As a result,
it was "now among the least thrifty and prosperous members of any European community that the emigration agent finds his best recruiting-
ground."[7]

Given the temper of the time, restriction would probably have been an
important issue in the 1890's no matter what the source of the immigration. As it happened, the trickle from southern and eastern Europe in the
1870's increased over the next decade and leaped to the crest of the wave
in the 1890's. Italians, Jews, Poles, Russians, and Slavs superseded the
arrivals from the British Isles, Scandinavia, and Germany for the first time.
The "new immigration"—650,000 Italians over the decade compared to
500,000 Germans; 500,000 Russians compared to 250,000 Britons;
600,000 from Austria-Hungary in contrast to 300,000 from Norway and
Sweden—was received by many Americans with fear, contempt, and hostility. Opponents of the new immigration doubted that this flock of uned-
ucated peasantry could be assimilated within the foreseeable future, if at
all. The new immigrants were described as "beaten men from beaten races;
representing the worst failures in the struggle for existence." They had no
inherent aptitude for self-government in contrast to those "descended from
the tribes that met under the oak-trees of old Germany to make laws and
choose chieftains." Their habits were "of the most revolting kind." Contact
with them was "foul and loathsome."[8] Even the moderate and dignified
New York *Times* complained of this invasion of "the physical, moral, and
mental wrecks" of Europe.

---

6. An excellent account of nativism in the 1890's is contained in Chapter Four of John Higham,
   Strangers in the Land: Patterns of American Nativism, 1860–1925 (New Brunswick, N. J., 1955),
   68–105. Also informative is Richard Hofstadter, *The Age of Reform: From Bryan to F.D.R.* (New
   York, 1955), 70–93.
7. New York *Times*, Jan. 30, 1893, 4; Walker, "Restriction of Immigration," 827. On the restriction
   controversy consult, besides Higham, the following: National Conference of Charities and Correction, *Proceedings*, 1890–1900; New York *Times*, Sept. 5, 1892, 4; Peri Ander, "Our Foreign
   Immigration. Its Social Aspects," *Arena*, II (1902), 269–77; Prescott F. Hall, "Immigration and the
   Educational Test," *North American Review*, CLXV (1897), 393–402; Edward G. Hartmann, *The
   Movement to Americanize the Immigrant* (New York, 1948).
8. Walker, "Restriction of Immigration," 828; New York *Times*, Feb. 17, 1890, 4.

The new immigrants poured into our northern industrial cities and towns at a time when Americans already feared that urban pauperism, vice, crime, and political corruption menaced the welfare of the nation. They augmented the unskilled labor force at a time when labor-capital relations were undergoing severe strains. At best the new immigrants—a motley crew of peasants, illiterates, and incompetents in the eyes of extremists— intensified the class and ethnic divisions which were corrupting the ideal of the classless and homogeneous society. At worst it reinforced the numbers of those who actively menaced the law and order of the urban community. New York, for example, sheltered the "hatchet-faced, pimply, sallow-cheeked, rat-eyed young men of the Russian-Jew colony," who drank the "pestiferous milk of Nihilism and dynamite throwing."[9] It bulged also with Italians who imported with them the sinister Mafia and code of personal vengeance. The Italian too often considered himself above the laws and courts of justice.[1] Americans "pretty well agreed," the New York *Times* concluded, that the Russian and Italian immigration was "of a kind which we are better without."[2]

The new immigrants demonstrated an unusually "great resistance to being assimilated and Americanized." This was their greatest fault. Their clannishness negated whatever virtues they may have possessed as individuals or whatever economic utility they may have had. The new immigrants crowded into cities, clustering in ghettos where "the mother tongue is carefully preserved, the English language is ignored, the institutions of the home country are revered, and American habits are despised."[3] In an intensely nationalistic decade, the shadow of the new immigrant seemed to cover the land with the darkness of un-Americanism.

2

The success of Jacob Riis as a housing reformer is incomprehensible apart from the historical context just described. Americans in the 1890's were anxious to learn about those things which he described in his books and lectures. Puzzled and fearful, they needed social critics like Riis to interpret the significance of the big city and immigration, poverty and tenement life; to explain how America could safely make the transition from an agrarian-rural society to an urban-industrial one.

Born in Ribe, Denmark, in 1849, Riis spent his youth in a pre-industrial society. His boyhood town was situated on a wide plain, separated from the nearby river by a marsh. On summer evenings, Riis recalled, he and his companions drifted down the river in a boat "listening to the small talk of

9. New York *Times*, Aug. 23, 1893, 1.
1. "Most of the illiterate immigrants from the southern provinces of Italy, having had no feeling save contempt and hatred for the courts of their native land, do not import with them any disposition to respect the processes of civil tribunals in this country. Taught to seek redress with stiletto or blunderbuss at home, they cannot easily be educated to outgrow that inclination. . . ." New York *Times*, May 16, 1893, 9. Also Robert E. Park and Herbert A. Miller, *Old World Traits Transplanted* (New York, 1921), 238–58; Jacob A. Riis, *How the Other Half Lives: Studies Among the Tenements of New York* (Sagamore Press: New York, 1957), 40–41.
2. New York *Times*, Mar. 6, 1892, 4. Working in favor of the immigrant during these troubled years were such influences as the long tradition of free immigration and the continuing need for cheap labor. It was not until World War I that restrictionists finally triumphed.
3. New York *Times*, Mar. 6, 1892, 4; John T. Buchanan, "How to Assimilate the Foreign Element in Our Population," *Forum*, XXXII (1901–02), 689.

the mother duck with her young, and to the chattering of uncounted thousands of starlings in the reeds." True, a cotton mill had invaded Ribe, but it was "grotesque in its medieval setting, and discredited by public opinion as a kind of flying in the face of tradition and Providence at once. . . ."[4]

Riis grew up in an environment in which primary group ties centering in the family and neighborhood circle of friends and peers exerted a powerful influence over personal behavior. Through the network of primary group relationships the community transmitted its conventions, customs, and traditions, and in this way exercised a social control comparable to that of statutory law in a more stratified, complex society. How different from New York was Ribe where "neighbor knew neighbor and shared his griefs and his joys." There "no one was rich, as wealth is counted nowadays; but then no one was allowed to want for the daily bread." Although the daily salutations, "Good day and God help," were only figures of speech, they were typical of the "good feeling that was over and above all the sign of the Old Town and its people."

Before Riis set down his recollections of his Danish boyhood, many decades had intervened. No doubt his memory was influenced by the nostalgia which afflicts the old when they remember their youth, and by Riis's inveterate romanticism and sentimentality; it was easy for him to believe of faraway Ribe than of Hester Street in New York that "the sun shone always in summer," and that "the autumn days were ever mellow." The important thing, however, was that for Riis the social ideal always remained the warm, friendly life which Ribe personified in his mind.[5]

At the age of sixteen Riis went to Copenhagen to learn carpentry. After four years he returned to Ribe in possession of a certificate from the carpenter's guild. Unfortunately, both the gods of love and trade frowned upon the ambitious young artisan. His childhood sweetheart, Elisabeth, rejected his protestations of love, and work was difficult to find. These setbacks inspired Riis's decision to leave for America in 1870.

For seven years the young Danish immigrant shuffled from job to job. He tried, among others, carpentry, coal mining, and advertising. Having acquired a taste for journalism by helping his father edit the local Ribe paper, Riis gained additional experience working for Brooklyn and Long Island newspapers. An opening on the New York *Tribune* staff in 1877 marked the turning point in his fortunes, for despite the low pay and long hours, it was a triumph to be hired by a metropolitan daily. After only a few months, Riis became the *Tribune's* police reporter. He held the position until 1888, when he joined the *Evening Sun* in the same capacity.

Two years later he published *How the Other Half Lives: Studies Among the Tenements of New York*. In this vivid and impressionistic series of sketches, Riis described the residential environment and ethnic traits of New York immigrant colonies, the weary struggle for subsistence in the tenement sweatshop, the dangers confronting the tenement child and working girl, the lure of the saloon and street gang, the degradation of the stage-beer dive, cheap lodginghouse, and opium den, and the human garbage dumped unceremoniously into the workhouse, almshouse, charity hospital, penitentiary, and Potter's Field. Seven lean years flittering from one unsatisfactory

4. Jacob A. Riis, *The Old Town* (New York, 1909), 6, 7–8.
5. *Ibid.*, 24, 25, 229.

job to another, more than a decade as a police reporter exploring the life of
the outcasts, criminals, and the poor of New York—these were the experiences which Riis distilled into his book. He too, had gone hungry many
days and had slept many nights in the doorways and alleys of the East Side.
When Riis described the case of the "hardworking family of man and wife,
young people from the old country, who took poison together in a Crosby
Street tenement because they were 'tired,'" he could understand the roots
of such a tragedy more than most people. He had contemplated suicide
once when he was unemployed and despondent.[6] Riis understood also
that a man's poverty did not justify an affront to his dignity. Scorched in
his memory was the treatment he had received at the Church Street
police lodginghouse, the dormitory of last resort, filled with tramps and
beggars who could not afford a cot even in one of New York's frowsy
downtown rooming houses. He was ejected by a German police sergeant
who had heard him express sympathy for the French in the Franco-
Prussian war. This was after Riis had complained to the sergeant that his
gold watch had been stolen, only to be called a thief for possessing such a
valuable.

In part, How the Other Half Lives was a plea for understanding and sympathy drawn from Riis's own experiences. He implored his contemporaries
to join in an assault against the degrading influence of poverty and the tenement environment upon the individual. Riis appealed to the conscience of
the middle class, asking it to raise "a bridge founded upon justice and built
of human hearts."[7] He argued that the indifference and greed of the
respectable elements of the community were as responsible for the social
catastrophe he described as any ignorance or vice which might be ascribed
to the poor themselves. One can always detect in Riis's work a plea for
brotherhood and Christian love.

In addition to sympathy for the sufferings of the poor and the indignant
demand for elementary justice, there is another dimension to How the
Other Half Lives, just as there was to Riis's subsequent interpretations of
poverty. One reviewer complained that his first book revealed certain "serious limitations": "a lack of broad and penetrative vision, a singularly
warped sense of justice at times, and a roughness amounting almost to brutality." This criticism is exaggerated, but it contains an important kernel of
truth. Riis sometimes displayed a singular lack of patience with certain
groups. For example, he had nothing but contempt for the beggar, tramp,
pauper, or whoever, in his estimation, preferred to live off charity rather
than earn an honest living. Such outcasts, he said, were the responsibility
of the police and workhouse, not the sociologist or social worker.[8]

Riis's career sheds considerable light upon his attitude toward the tramp
and pauper. His own life personified the promise of America. His was an
American success story in the classical vein. A poor man, handicapped
because he was an immigrant, Riis in time achieved local and national
fame. Like Horatio Alger, he lifted himself out of the mire by force of
brains, ambition, and will power. He took advantage of America's limitless
freedom and opportunities to reward himself and reward America by

6. Riis, How the Other Half Lives, 9; Jacob A. Riis, The Making of an American (New York, 1901), 70.
7. Riis, How the Other Half Lives, 226.
8. The Critic, XVII (1890), 332; Riis, The Making of an American, 75.

becoming a useful and respected citizen. Did he not thus prove his loyalty to his adopted country by justifying the opportunities she lavished upon the individual? By the same token, were not tramps and paupers little better than traitors and parasites? Their laziness and social irresponsibility seemed to mock the ideals and institutions which afforded Riis and other ambitious individuals a chance to advance in life.

For all his social consciousness, Rills was squarely in the American entrepreneurial tradition. His basic economic and social creed was individualism, but tempered by justice, moral responsibility and Christian love—the kind of restraints upon individual assertiveness presumably found in the primary-group. The nation did not need socialism, communism, or any other, form of collectivism to cure its social ills so much as the creation of an environment which insured the individual a chance to realize his potentialities; an environment that did not, like the tenement, stifle his moral sensibilities and choke off his ambitions Riis believed fervently in all the contemporary entrepreneurial, individualistic cliches: "Nothing is more certain, humanly speaking, than this, that what a man wills himself to be, that he will be"; "Luck is lassoed by the masterful man, by the man who knows and who can"; "All the little defeats are just to test . . . grit. It is a question of grit, that is all."[9] Here was the spirit which was to find its most elaborate expression in Wilson's New Freedom.

Individualism and love of nature were two basic components of Riis's moral *Weltanschauung*. They were closely related. "For hating the slum what credit belongs to me?" Riis asked. "When it comes to that, perhaps it was the open, the woods, the freedom of my Danish fields I loved, the contrast that was hateful." Despite a lifetime spent in New York, Riis never reconciled himself to the complexity and impersonality of city life. The city, generally, and the tenement slum in particular, he equated with physical and spiritual decay. The city hindered the individual from growing into a moral and sensitive human being. Too often, it elicited the worst instead of the best in his nature. The child, especially, suffered damnation in the urban wilderness. Any "plan of rescue for the boy in which the appeal to the soil has no place" was false in principle and in practice.[1]

For Riis, the real America most resembled Ribe. It was in the countryside that the values which best exemplified America were born and nourished. Here tightly-knit family life insured the individual's proper moral development; respect for hard work and the dignity of labor was taught; and love of God and nature inculcated respect for human life and all living things. By contrast the city was a babel of moral confusion.

In his nostalgia for the countryside, Riis was not alone. All over western Europe, as in the United States, people were migrating from the farm and village to the city. Many of them found the impersonal and unstable life of the city demoralizing. Those immigrants who settled in New York's tenement quarters were especially shocked by the dehumanizing deficiency of natural life. Thus Gregory Weinstein, a Russian-Jew who emigrated here in the 1880s, remembered that his enthusiasm for New York diminished as soon as he saw the tenements, saloons, and bordellos of the lower East Side.

9. Jacob A. Riis, *Theodore Roosevelt the Citizen* (New York, 1904), 15, 63–64, 125.
1. Riis, *The Making of an American*, 423; Jacob A. Riis, "One Way Out," *Century Magazine*, LI (1895–96), 308.

Depressed in spirit, he felt "terribly homesick for the beautiful green hills and valleys" of his native Vilna. Similarly, the novelist Michael Gold remembered his immigrant mother's joy when the family left its East Side tenement for a day's outing in Bronx Park: "Ach, Gott!" she said, "I'm so happy in a forest! You American children don't know what it means! I am happy!"[2]

We can begin to understand now why Riis's star shone so brightly in the reform firmament of the 1890's. He himself was part of a great drama of human transplantation, and he expressed the deepest sentiments of his less vocal immigrant contemporaries. In a period of doubt and social unrest in this country, he reaffirmed those values which Americans had always believed were the foundation of national greatness. And Riis intensified his affirmations, his tributes to individualism and the countryside, with all the zeal and uncompromising dedication of the convert. In an era of pervasive nativism and troubled questioning of the free immigration policy, the former Danish immigrant stood out as an American among Americans. Riis's nationalism, his loyalty to his adopted country, were as deeply rooted in his character as his rural bias and his individualism. In a sense, Riis's Americanism was the keystone of his entire moral philosophy. Any man who pledged allegiance to God, whose life's work was directed by the code of rural virtues, and who took advantage of his country's freedom and opportunities to realize his maximum potentialities as an individual was simply being a good American.

Proud of his citizenship and grateful to America, Riis was determined that the heritage in which he shared should be transmitted intact to future generations. His hatred for the tenement was strongly conditioned by the belief that it retarded, if it did not preclude, the Americanization of the immigrant. Riis's sharpest criticisms were reserved for an immigrant group like the Chinese, who seemed most clannish and least inclined to adopt American speech, customs, and culture. The real problem of the tenements, in terms of the nation's long-range welfare, was this:

> One may find for the asking an Italian, a German, a French, African, Spanish, Bohemian, Russian, Scandinavian, Jewish, and Chinese colony. Even the Arab, who peddles "holy earth" from the Battery as a direct importation from Jerusalem, has his exclusive preserves at the lower end of Washington Street. The one thing you shall vainly ask for in the chief city of America is a distinctively American community. There is none; certainly not among the tenements.[3]

His "clinching argument" against New York's Jewish ghetto was "it is clannish." Significantly, Riis entitled his autobiography *The Making of an American.* Unlike the native American critic of urban society, Riis could not take his Americanism for granted. He had to prove in deed and thought that he was worthy of his adopted country's hospitality. He had to distinguish himself in American eyes from those immigrants who remained foreigners all their lives—from the East Side Jews, for example, who stood "where the new day that dawned on Calvary left them standing, stubbornly refusing to see the light."[4]

2. Gregory Weinstein, *The Ardent Eighties: Reminiscences of an Interesting Decade* (New York, 1928), 18; Michael Gold, *Jews Without Money* (New York, 1930), 155.
3. Riis, *How the Other Half Lives*, 15.
4. Jacob A. Riis, "The Jews of New York," *Review of Reviews*, XIII (1896), 58; Riis, *How the Other Half Lives*, 83.

3

"It seemed to me," Riis confided, "that a reporter's was the highest and noblest of all callings; no one could sift wrong from right as he, and punish the wrong."[5] It must be remembered that this apostle of Americanism was a reporter by profession, and one of the best. Riis's professional talents are peculiarly important to an understanding of his contemporary appeal and enduring fame.

Riis was a fine journalist whose sensibilities were those of a romantic poet. He remembered the annual fair at Ribe as an "enchanted land" of toys, trumpets, and honeycakes topped with an almond heart in the middle. Perhaps it was there that a wizard who possessed the secret of eternal youth cast his spell, insuring that Riis would never know the weariness and cynicism that comes with age and knowledge of evil. To the day he died at the age of sixty-five, Riis remained the incorruptible idealist, certain that "on the brink of hell itself human nature is not wholly lost."[6] Even in the slum, Riis averred, "the spark of His image" resided in the hearts of men. Riis encountered more evidence of human depravity, suffering, and wreckage in a month than most men would confront in a lifetime. For all that, his faith remained unshaken that justice, truth, and love would eventually govern the affairs of men.

As Lincoln Steffens once said of him, "far deeper than any intellectual faculty lay his sympathy."[7] Riis's perception was that of the poet, not the scholar. Life was always fresh and wondrous for Riis because his powers of imagination and emotional response were inexhaustible. Even the slum, for all its faults, had one thing in its favor—"it was very human." Once Riis watched a group of children playing see-saw:

> The whole Irish contingent rode the plank, all at once, with screams of delight. A ragged little girl from the despised "Dago" colony watched them from the corner with hungry eyes. Big Jane, who was the leader by virtue of her thirteen years and her long reach, saw her and stopped the show.
>
> "Here, Mame," she said, pushing one of the smaller girls from the plank, "you get off an' let her ride. Her mother was stabbed yesterday." And the little Dago rode, and was made happy.[8]

This simple manifestation of human tenderness compensated for much of the meanness and viciousness Riis encountered. It contained the seed and promise of a better world; it was the spirit which would conquer the slum.

Riis's idealism, his poetic sensitivity, his capacity for emotional response, all converged in a passionate, ebullient love of life. And because he loved life, he hated whatever he believed was life-denying, like the slum. Here were no flowers, no trees, no natural growth at all; and very little human growth, either—merely the grim animal struggle for existence. People who toiled in the sweater's shop all their days and all their lives had lost their birthright, the capacity to appreciate the simple beauty and wonder of a child's laughter or of an ocean gently stirring beneath a sun-drenched sky.

5. Riis, *The Making of an American*, 99.
6. *Ibid.*, 261.
7. Steffens, "Jacob A. Riis," 422.
8. Jacob A. Riis, "The Passing of Cat Alley," *Century Magazine*, LVII (1898–99), 176.

Thus Riis justified his work to God and man in terms of every human's right to happiness. "The saddest of all things," he told Richard Watson Gilder, "must be to go to one's grave with the feeling that in nothing one has been able to soothe or help the world's misery."[9]

An incorrigible romantic, Riis tended to view life as a kind of tournament in which the forces of good, like Danish knights of old, galloped forth to joust with the forces of evil. Against one knight, especially, the dragons of the slum, saloon, and political corruption, stood little chance. In his worship of Theodore Roosevelt, Riis displayed openly his sentimental idealism and suspended his faculties of critical judgment. Roosevelt was the personification of all the patriotic, manly, and human virtues which Riis admired:

> A man with red blood in his veins; a healthy patriot, with no claptrap jingoism about him, but a rugged belief in America and its mission; an intense lover of country and flag; a vigorous optimist, a believer in men, who looks for the good in them and finds it. Practical in partisanship; loyal, trusting, and gentle as a friend; unselfish, modest as a woman, clean-handed and clean-hearted, and honest to the core. In the splendid vigor of his young manhood he is the knightliest figure in American politics today, the fittest exponent of his country's idea, and the model for its young sons who are coming to take up the task he set them.[1]

"I loved him from the day I first saw him," Riis unblushingly confided.[2] He found in Roosevelt a kind of superman who could do no wrong, and he needed this superman for reassurance. The romantic temperament is prone to create demi-gods to assure itself that its beatific visions can and do materialize on earth. According to Riis, Roosevelt "nursed no ambitions; he built up no machine of his own. He was there to do his duty as it was given to him to see it. . . ."[3] In this judgment one sees the willful naïvete of a man who wanted to believe that somewhere morality and politics, virtue and power, were not incompatible. Although Tammany employed its power for evil purposes, Riis saw in Roosevelt a man who used power as an instrument of good. With someone like Roosevelt in the ranks, Riis could be certain that the promise of a better world was no idle dream.

Only a man like Riis could have written *How the Other Half Lives* or its sequel, *The Children of the Poor*, a book published in 1893 in which Riis revealed his monumental affection for the tenement young and outlined his program for their redemption through education, clubs, and exposure to nature. These, books did not suggest the ponderous, aloof objectivity of the scholar, the righteous pomposity of the preacher, or the humorless, tiresome certitude of the reformer-pedagogue. Riis did present facts like the scholar, moralize like the preacher, and try to win converts like the reformer, but his infectious love of life and his vivid imagination combined to invigorate his words with a sparkle and vivacity always rare, but especially rare in the prose of reformers and preachers to wayward humanity. Riis brought the tenement slum to life. It became for his readers an immediate and felt

9. Jacob A. Riis to Richard W. Gilder, July 2, 1894, The Century Collection.
1. Jacob A. Riis, "Theodore Roosevelt," *Review of Reviews*, XXII (1900), 186.
2. Riis, *The Making of an American*, 328.
3. Riis, *Theodore Roosevelt the Citizen*, 228.

experience, not simply an abstract and remote evil. No housing reformer, before or after, has equalled Riis's ability to make the slum a reality for those, situated on a different plane of life.

Dramatic and anecdotal, Riis's style reflected his interest in human feelings and emotions. He did not brother much with statistics. Riis realized that one concrete illustration of the demoralizing effects of poverty would arouse the reader's compassion more swiftly and surely than statistics whose magnitude was beyond the power of mind to reduce to human terms. There was, for example, an ocean of human meaning condensed in such a tragedy as had occurred in a seventh-ward tenement. A mother of six children had leaped to her death from a window because, as the neighbors said, she was "discouraged."[4] Although many before and after Riis described every conceivable feature of tenement life, he was the master. With the skill of an artist, he took stale and ordinary material and refashioned it into what seemed new, fresh, and original. When he applied such imagination and sensitivity to the commonplace, it seemed to be a revelation. Through Riis people not only came to hate the slum but, in a sense, discovered it for the first time.

4

Riis's predecessors had emphasized the dual purpose of housing reform. Better housing would, in the first place, contribute to the physical safety of both the poor and the community as a whole. There can be no quarrel with this assumption. The overcrowding, filth, and inferior sanitary facilities in the tenement obviously had an unfavorable effect upon health. Science and common sense confirmed this. But the housing reformer had also considered better housing as an instrument of social control. He observed that tenement neighborhoods, populated often by foreigners and their children, seemed to abound in vice, crime, and pauperism. He assumed, therefore, that the physical environment was at fault. The tenement must cause a deterioration of character, making the individual more susceptible to vice than he would have been in a different environment. Improve his housing, it followed, and you would influence his character for the better.

It is true that a statistical correlation could be drawn between poor housing on the one hand, and a resistance to Americanization or a low individual and neighborhood moral tone, on the other. It did not necessarily follow, however, that improved housing, in and of itself, would have socially desirable effects. The housing reformer never subjected to rigorous analysis his assumption that housing influenced character. He applied a crude environmental determinism to the problem, underestimating the tenacious persistence in the individual of set habits and values.

Riis did not, in any clear and systematic fashion, analyze the relationship between housing and social structure. He accepted without much reflection the assumption that better housing would result in various social blessings. Often, however, Riis broke loose from this simple determinism. Almost unconsciously, he expanded the usual scope of housing reform to include the neighborhood in which the tenement was situated. Like the settlement

4. *Ibid.*, 36.

worker, Riis realized that the tenement neighborhood contained many objectionable features which needed to be eliminated. More than previous housing reformers, he sensed that the tenement, the slum, was a way of life and not simply a problem of sub-standard housing. Thus socially effective housing reform would involve a reconstruction of the whole tenement environment and the customary life-organization of the inhabitants. Indeed, there was much in common between Riis and the settlement movement, striving since the late 1880's to improve neighborhood life through every channel of personal influence and environmental reform available to the middle-class humanitarian. In the Progressive era, the settlement was the profoundest embodiment of the ideal which inspired Riis, the ideal of community and human brotherhood expressed in a common Americanism. It concentrated, like Riis, upon the neighborhood as the unit of social reconstruction. The neighborhood ideal, as Riis observed, was "the heart of the settlement movement." The convictions which led Jane Addams to Halsted Street in Chicago and Lillian Wald to Henry Street in New York were exactly those which inspired Riis to declare war on the tenement and the slum.[5]

Everywhere in the tenement neighborhood, Riis saw the saloon, the poor man's social club. Its brightness and relaxed atmosphere contrasted sharply with the squalor and dinginess of the tenement. But if the saloon satisfied the worker's gregarious instinct, his need for companionship and sociability, it also encouraged him to squander his earnings on liquor while his family went without necessities. The saloon thus contributed to the decline of family life, a process presumably set in motion by the tenement. The saloon also taught a sorry brand of citizenship. Gangs of toughs, useful on election day, congregated there to be regaled by the same Tammany chieftains who sponsored their social clubs and protected them from the law when caught brawling or thieving. The saloon keeper, if not a precinct leader himself, was the friend of politicians. "The rumshop," Riis complained, "turns the political crank in New York." Perhaps worst of all, in Riis's estimation, was the saloon's effect upon the child. It not only solicited his patronage at an early age, initiating him into evil company and habits, but taught him contempt for law and order. Not "one child in a thousand, who brings his growler to be filled at the average New York bar," Riis protested, "is sent away empty-handed, if able to pay for what he wants."[6] What conclusion did the child draw, Riis wondered, as he watched his growler foam with beer in full view of the sign forbidding sale to minors?

As ubiquitous as the saloon in the tenement neighborhood was the street gang, the refuge of children who lacked any sense of identity and turned to their similarly confused peers for protection, security, and a code of values. Every corner had its gang of toughs, hostile to each other but united in their defiance of society.[7] What was the use of improving the tenement child's housing if the street gang waited outside, ready to initiate him into the jungle code of the pack. Riis realized that boys would form into gangs. His object

5. Riis, How the Other Half Lives, 159, 163; Jacob A. Riis, The Peril and Preservation of the Home (Philadelphia, 1903), 187. Riis was highly conscious of the similarity of ideals and purposes between the settlements and himself. See The Making of an American, 316, and his personal tribute to the settlement movement, "What Settlements Stand For," Outlook, LXXXIX (1908), 69–72.
6. Riis, How the Other Half Lives, 159, 163.
7. Ibid., 164.

was to direct this gregarious instinct into socially productive channels. Instead of an instigator of mischief and crime and the promoter of a distorted code of values, the street gang could be revamped into an organized force for good. But reform depended upon the alternatives to the saloon or the street, which were all society offered in the tenement neighborhood, and upon the interest taken in the moral development of the tenement child.

The East Side in the 1890's was in New York's great red light district.[8] Prostitution downtown was unabashedly open. An army of prostitutes, pimps, and madams plied their trade unmolested by the Tammany-ruled police: "On sunshiny days the whores sat on chairs along the sidewalks. They sprawled indolently, their legs taking up half the pavements. People stumbled over a gauntlet of whores' meaty legs," the novelist Michael Gold recalled. "The girls gossiped and chirped like a jungle of parrots. Some knitted shawls and stockings. Others hummed. Others chewed Russian sunflower seeds and monotonously spat out the shells."[9]

Although Riis, a proper Victorian gentleman reluctant to drag sex into the arena of public controversy, wrote little on the subject of tenement prostitution, his less squeamish contemporaries eagerly exposed it as a formidable evil in the lives of the poor. Frederick J. Shackleton, pastor of a Forsyth Street church, complained before the Mazet Committee in 1899 that solicitation was practiced from the stoops and windows of the tenements in his crowded neighborhood.[1] Edward J. Riordan, an investigator for this committee, reported that east of the Bowery he had frequently been "stopped by men and solicited to go into houses to meet girls." He singled out Allen, Chrystie, Rivington, Stanton, and Delancey Streets as especially vice-ridden. Edgar A. Whitney, another investigator, discovered that solicitation on the East Side was as impudent and aggressive as the less harmful kind practiced by the Jewish "pullers-in" of Baxter Street, clothing merchants who dragged reluctant passers-by off the streets and into their shops.[2]

Children in such an environment learned about sex at a tender age; it was cheapened and degraded in their eyes. It took one veteran of the East Side jungle "years to learn that sex can be good as well as evil; more than the thing truck drivers bought for fifty cents on my street." While boys from better neighborhoods played cowboys and Indians at the age of five, Michael Gold and his tenement-spawned companions teased prostitutes: "Fifty cents a night! That's what you charge; fifty cents a night! Yah, yah, yah!"[3] Children were hired by proprietors of bordellos to distribute their cards. Others served as "lighthouses" or "watch-boys," running errands and guarding against possible surprise raids. "It is a fact," Riordan informed the Mazet Committee, that "young people on the east side are brought in daily

---

8. It was unmolested except for the necessary protection money paid to politicians and police officers. Two state investigations in the 1890's, the Lexow Committee in 1894 and the Mazet Committee in 1899, documented the deeply-rooted police corruption in New York City.
9. Gold, *Jews Without Money*, 15.
1. Special Committee of the Assembly Appointed to Investigate the Public Offices and Departments of the City of New York and of the Counties Therein Included. Transmitted to the Legislature January 15, 1900, *Report*, II, 2001. Hereafter cited as Mazet Committee, *Report*.
2. *Ibid.*, 2028, 2029, 2002.
3. Gold, *Jews Without Money*, 26, 17.

and nightly contact with vice, and are obliged to live with it and see it, and are made familiar with it in every way."[4]

None of these things—prostitution, street gangs, saloons—were new to New York's tenement quarters. Reformers before Riis had noticed that squalid housing was usually coupled to a train of associated evils. The AICP, with its strong emphasis upon intemperance as a cause of poverty, always regretted the workers' easy access to saloons. Charles Loring Brace, who organized the Children's Aid Society in the 1850's, listed high among his objectives the removal of the child from the influence of the street and gang. None of the reformers, however, had linked all the disparate elements of tenement life together as the object for a general policy of neighborhood reconstruction. From housing reform they had expected social benefits which were not inherent in the simple act of modifying one defect in the environment of the immigrant and working poor.

Equally important, critics of tenement evils had not always considered alternatives to the vices they struggled to suppress. Riis, however, understood that the saloon and street gang served a functional purpose; they satisfied social needs and desires. The reformer could not abolish them unless he devised wholesome substitutes capable of fulfilling these same needs. In concrete terms, Riis's answer to the street gang was not the policeman's nightstick or the reform school, but rather the playground, boy's club, and public school.

The child was the key to neighborhood reconstruction. According to Riis, "The problem of the children is the problem of the State. As we mould the children of the toiling masses in our cities, so we shape the destiny of the State which they will rule in their turn, taking the reins from our hands." The community, for its own protection, had the solemn duty "to school the children first of all into good Americans, and next into useful citizens." Here was the answer to the troublesome riddle of Americanization and the reunification of the urban community. Since the child was "a creature of environment, of opportunity, as children are everywhere,"[5] it was only necessary to create for him a wholesome environment in which to mature.

Improved housing and the establishment of a neighborhood in which such institutions as the saloon, the house of prostitution, and the street gang were less influential would surely benefit immigrant parents as well as their children. But for all his optimism, for all his faith in the power of environment to shape individual habits and values, Riis realized that the adult was sometimes beyond redemption. Although "we can do almost anything with his boy," Riis pointed out, we could not always "do much for or with the old immigrant who comes to stay with us."[6] The old country, for better or worse, had already determined the main outlines of his personality. The child, by comparison, was putty ready for the hand of the social sculptor.

As Thomas and Znaniecki have explained, the immigrant child in the American city often exhibited a "condition of passive or active wildness in which behavior [was] not controlled by social customs and beliefs but

4. Mazet Committee, *Report,* II, 2029. Further information on the subject of prostitution in New York and the attitude of reformers can be found in *The Committee of Fifteen, The Social Evil, with Special Reference to Conditions Existing in the City of New York* (New York, 1902).
5. Jacob A. Riis, *The Children of the Poor,* (New York, 1893), 1, 8, 4.
6. Jacob A. Riis, "Special Needs of the Poor in New York," *Forum,* XIV (1892–93), 501.

directly conditioned by temperamental tendencies and swayed by momentary moods." Unwilling to organize his life around the scheme of values imported by his parents from abroad, but confused as to his identity and status in the American community, the immigrant child was frequently "a-moral"; the social objective was to expose him to "constructive influences which tend to develop in him a normal life-organization."[7] Although the authors of *The Polish Peasant in Europe and America* theoretically formulated the issue better than Riis ever did, he viewed the problem of the immigrant child in essentially the same light: guide the child's impulses into socially constructive channels, plant in his neighborhood attractive and wholesome counterinfluences to the saloon, street gang, and similar evils, and the tenement would surrender its power to produce moral and social decay.

By transmitting to the tenement child and adult a meaningful life-organization which would facilitate their acceptance of middle-class American values, Riis was striving, in the final analysis, to create a new system of primary group ties in the tenement neighborhood. The confusion of nationalities, religions, and cultural standards in tenement districts had discouraged, he believed, the birth of any sense of community. There was little to nurture social unity and cohesiveness. Apart from individual moral standards and the voluntary submission of the individual to the social norms of his ethnic group, there was no effective instrument of social control except for the law and policeman's club.

New York, of course, was not Ribe, Denmark, where Riis had experienced the powerful control exercised by the primary group over the individual and the security which it offered him in return for his obedience. New York was not the small town which was the only model of primary group control in the experience of native American reformers. The influence of the primary group is most effective in a small, self-contained community characterized by a high incidence of face-to-face relationships and a relative uniformity of ethnic origin and economic status. It depends less for its authority upon rational persuasion, individual choice, and voluntary cooperation than upon an unreflective, spontaneous, and internalized sense of social solidarity. In this respect the attempt to establish a primary group ethos, a feeling of transcendent and universal community, in the heterogeneous and unstable tenement neighborhood was doomed to failure. In a more limited sense, however, the ideal of neighborhood reconstruction was sound. At very least, it implied a comprehensive and pragmatic assault upon the slum. No scheme which promised to improve the physical, moral, or social condition of the poor was foreign to its spirit. As Riis preached, the settlement practiced, reaching beyond the tenement in an effort to influence the total environment and personality of the poor.

The public school, in Riis's estimation, was one critical factor in the reconstruction of the tenement neighborhood. "When the fathers and mothers meet under the school roof as in their neighborhood house, and the children have their games, their clubs, and their dances there," Riis predicted, "there will no longer be a saloon question in politics; and that day the slum is beaten."[8] Thus the public school would serve the same function

7. Thomas and Znaniecki, *The Polish Peasant in Europe and America,* II, 1777, 1778.
8. Jacob A. Riis, *The Battle with the Slum* (New York, 1902), 407.

as the church in the medieval town, peasant village, or American hamlet—the visible symbol of the community's solidarity, the transmitter of its ideals and values. As the neighborhood social center, the school would shed light about American history, government, and customs to the immigrant and his child. A common bond of Americanism would link all those it reached.

Riis promoted a wide variety of educational reforms in this effort to make the school the focus of neighborhood unity. If the school repelled the child for any reason, it could hardly serve its exalted purpose. Thus Riis condemned the disgraceful physical appearance of the average city school. Much as he believed in the importance of education, he sympathized with the hookey-player who preferred to romp outdoors in the sun rather than incarcerate himself in the gloomy vaults of the existing public schools. Herds of rats in the Wooster Street school, Riis complained, shared the premises with the children. Like many others, this institution was poorly lit and ventilated. It was typical of the dirty, cramped, and cheerless quarters in which the immigrant child was expected to learn his American catechism.[9]

Along with an improvement and expansion in physical plant, Riis crusaded for an intensive use of school facilities. The forces of evil, such as the saloon and gambling syndicate, were perpetually in motion, exerting their baneful influence at all times. Why, then, was the school silent except for a few hours a day? This was no way to save the child from the streets. In the summertime, the streets were particularly alluring to tenement youth after a long, cooped-up winter, and Riis endorsed the establishment of summer vacation schools. Since the gang was "nothing but the genius for organization in our boys run wild," Riis asserted, why not put this talent to socially constructive ends by means of the school? Why not, in effect, organize public school children during the summer into a "great military body," ship them out of the city, and "make a real vacation of this for the boys who need it most by drilling them in camp?" And since the street gang was "hardest hit" by the responsible and well-supervised boy's club, the school could make a real contribution to neighborhood welfare by lending its building out of hours to such clubs.[1]

Riis warmly supported two innovations in curriculum to insure the school's all-inclusive influence over the child. One was the kindergarten, a moral as well as an educational experiment. Its function was to "rediscover . . . the natural feelings that the tenement had smothered." If not for its influence, the "love of the beautiful might slumber in those children forever."[2] The kindergarten shepherded the child in the dawn of his consciousness. By teaching him beauty and training his powers of self-expression at so early an age, it assisted in arousing his dissatisfaction with the ugly barbarism of the slums. He was then more likely to turn to the school, church, social settlement, and similar agencies devoted to his moral welfare to satisfy the yearnings aroused by the kindergarten.

9. Jacob A. Riis, "Playgrounds for City Schools," *Century Magazine*, XLVIII (1894), 657. In connection with his work in educational reform, Riis strongly urged the establishment of special truant schools. He objected to the commitment of truants in reformatories, where they mixed with hardened juvenile criminals. He also advocated the creation of special juvenile courts. In each case, he wanted to insure that the erring, but potentially decent, child was not pushed by society into a life of crime.
1. Jacob A. Riis, "The Making of Thieves in New York," *Century Magazine*, XLIX (1894–95), 115; Riis, *The Children of the Poor*, 238.
2. *Ibid.*, 180.

In manual or vocational training Riis discovered a second curriculum innovation with manifold possibilities for influencing the child's future. The industrial school which taught boys a useful trade helped transform the tough street urchin into a respectable citizen. In the opinion of Joseph Lee, the prominent Massachusetts humanitarian for whose book on philanthropy Riis wrote an introduction, the industrial school made a civilized being out of a barbarian.[3] Vocational training, presumably, would allure the boy who saw no useful purpose in learning history, geography, and other academic subjects which had no relevance to his immediate experience. But this same boy, who perhaps had to lug heavy sacks of garments each day between his parents' tenement workshop and the manufacturer, could appreciate a school which promised to teach him a trade and equip him for a better life than that of his parents. And a boy with a respectable trade, in Riis's eyes, was a better candidate for good citizenship than an untrained boy.

Riis thought that training in home economics contained the answer for the needs of the tenement girl. It would perform wonders in keeping the tenement family together. "I am well persuaded," Riis declared with characteristic hyperbole, "that half of the drunkenness that makes so many homes miserable is at least encouraged, if not directly caused, by the mismanagement and bad cooking at home."[4]

As part of his crusade to rescue all children, Riis struggled to bring opportunities for wholesome play and recreation to the tenement districts. The park and playground, as well as the public school, were fundamental to the reconstruction of the tenement neighborhood.[5] In his emphasis upon the need for neighborhood recreation facilities, Riis participated in a more general movement in the 1890's to direct, consciously and rationally, leisure activities. This movement grew out of the belief of middle-class reformers that the urban poor was being weaned on an unsavory diet. Gambling, low-grade melodrama, vaudeville, burlesque with its appetizing promise of "50—Pairs of Rounded Limbs, Ruby Lips, Tantalizing Torsos—50," beer-gardens, dance halls, and concert saloons, these were the staples of recreation. They satisfied, however, an important need in the life of the urban working class. The quest for pleasure was a natural response to sordid surroundings and long hours of dreary, unremunerative work.[6]

Recreation, play, and the constructive use of leisure time were not problems in the primary group environment of the peasant village in Europe or the American small town. In the peasant village, especially, play was an expression of community solidarity. It was closely integrated into religious, social, and economic life. Religious festivals, local ceremonies and pageants of one sort or another, celebrations of birth and marriage—in all these the family participated as a unit. Leisure was less a matter of individual taste and preference than an affirmation of family and communal solidarity. How different things were in the American industrial city where

3. Joseph Lee, *Constructive and Preventive Philanthropy* (New York, 1902), 203.
4. Riis, *The Children of the Poor*, 197.
5. On the history and significance of the play movement in the 1890's and after consult the following: Henry S. Curtis, *The Play Movement and Its Significance* (New York, 1917); Clarence E. Rainwater, *The Play Movement in the United States: A Study of Community Recreation* (Chicago, 1922); Charles M. Robinson, "Improvement in City Life: Philanthropic Progress," *Atlantic Monthly*, LXXXIII (1899), 533–36.
6. The quote from a temporary burlesque advertisement is found in Foster Rhea Dulles, *America Learns to Play: A History of Popular Recreation, 1607–1940* (New York, 1940), 217, 212.

leisure activity was both individualized and commercialized. Far from being an expression of solidarity, play was, on the contrary, an expression of disintegration:

> The East Side, for children, was a world plunged in eternal war. It was suicide to walk into the next block. Each block was a separate nation, and when a strange boy appeared, the patriots swarmed. "What streeter?" was demanded, furiously.
> "Chrystie Street," was the trembling reply. Bang! This was the signal for a mass assault on the unlucky foreigner, with sticks, stones, fists and feet.[7]

There was no guarantee, of course, that slum children or their parents would take advantage of parks, playgrounds, clubhouses, and other facilities provided for their use. They might be used in the wrong way. As we realize today, a park can be as perfect a setting for juvenile gang warfare or mugging as for wholesome play. "To suggest," furthermore, "that a boy will not be delinquent because he plays ball is no more valid than to say that he will not play ball because he is delinquent. He may do either, neither, or both."[8] This does not imply, however, that putting parks or playgrounds where none had existed would do harm, or fail to do good. The tenement inhabitant sought diversion from the monotony of his work and the depressing squalor of his home. He was not likely to travel outside of his neighborhood to satisfy his yearning. At the very least, Riis believed, he should be given the opportunity for wholesome diversion and not have to resort to the saloon or dance hall.

The movement to reconstruct the tenement neighborhood by directing the leisure of the poor sparkled with ideas and suggestions. Some of Riis's contemporaries concentrated on the adult. The Committee of Fifty for the Investigation of the Liquor Problem, a leader in the struggle for adult recreation in tenement districts, recommended that the city build "large plain buildings" in different parts of the city to serve as club-houses[9] in which the immigrant worker could satisfy his social needs without resort to the liquor and unsavory company of the saloon. Such organizations as The People's University Extension Society of New York, and the Educational Alliance, hoped to elevate the moral and aesthetic standards of the poor by stimulating their intellects and instinct for beauty. They might then turn more often to the city's libraries, museums, and art galleries, and less frequently to the concert saloon and vaudeville show.

Although Riis heartily endorsed any and all such proposals to guide the adult's leisure time into socially constructive channels, his interest in recreation was predominantly a reflection of his ceaseless effort to capture the mind and emotions of the child. "In the matter of healthy play," Riis complained, "the school-boy in New York does not have a chance. Any village boy is better off than he." Play was the child's safety valve. Unfortunately, "with the landlord in the yard and the policeman on the street sitting on his safety valve and holding it down," the child was "bound to explode." The community which made no provision for allowing the child to release his

---

7. Gold, *Jews Without Money*, 42–43.
8. Henry D. McKay, "The Neighborhood and Child Conduct," in Paul K. Hatt and Albert J. Reiss, Jr., eds., *Cities and Society: The Revised Reader in Urban Sociology* (Glencoe, Ill., 1957), 822.
9. Raymond Calkins, *Substitutes for the Saloon* (New York, 1901), 72–73.

excess energies through harmless play was criminally negligent. It encouraged the mischief and delinquency of the street gang, and the commercial exploitation of the young. The community was obligated to provide alternatives to those agencies which pandered to the lowest sensual instincts of the child. "Under the rough burr" of the tenement child lay "undeveloped qualities of good and of usefulness." The right kind of play would help draw them out. The wrong kind would simply smooth the path to the reformatory and prison. As a disciple of Froebel, whom he described as "the great kindergartner who gave us the best legacy of the nineteenth century to its successor," Riis agreed that play was the true occupation of the child, through which he first perceived moral relations.[1]

Riis, as we have seen, hated the tenement partly because he loved the green purity of nature. It was not surprising, therefore, that he combined his passion for the outdoors with his belief in the redeeming potentialities of wholesome play. Thus he enthusiastically advertised and promoted the *Tribune* Fresh Air Fund, the summer excursions sponsored by churches, settlements or charities, and every other such attempt to bring the slum child into contact with nature. A splendid vision came to Riis, which he set forth in almost apocalyptic terms:

> And then if you were to ask me to point to the goal we are striving after, where we shall be quite safe, where the slum cannot come, I should lay before you a map of the city and put my finger upon the islands that lie in the East River, stretching their green length five miles or more from Fiftieth street or below clear up into Hell Gate to the mouth of the Sound. And I should tell you that on the day when we shall have grown civic sense and spirit robust enough to set them apart as the people's playground forever, on that day we shall be beyond the reach of the slum and of slum politics for good and all.[2]

Riis worked as hard to bring nature to the tenement world of brick, asphalt, and concrete as he did to bring the tenement child to nature. He wanted to see small parks built where antiquated tenements took their toll in human life and suffering.[3] These would be lungs for the poor, oases of fresh air, flowers, trees, and grass for mothers with babies, and children whose only playground had been the congested streets. Riis expected miracles from these parks, from the contact between nature and the tenement child: "Down in the worst little ruffian's soul there is, after all, a tender spot not yet pre-empted by the slum. And Mother Nature touches it at once. They are chums on the minute."[4] The school and the park, joining forces to touch the head and the heart of the tenement child, were surely the means to bring light into dark places.

1. Riis, "Playgrounds for City Schools," 659; Jacob A. Riis, *A Ten Years' War: An Account of the Battle with the Slum in New York* (New York, 1900), 147; Riis, *The Children of the Poor*, 64; Jacob A. Riis, *The Peril and Preservation of the Home*, 166, 167; Riis, *The Children of the Poor*, Ch. X.
2. Jacob A. Riis, "The Island Playgrounds of the Future," *Charities*, XI (1903), 205.
3. For Riis's story of the long struggle to raze Mulberry Bend and build a park in its place see his article "The Clearing of Mulberry Bend: The Story of the Rise and Fall of a Typical New York Slum," *Review of Reviews*, XII (1895), 172–78. The Bend, located in the Italian quarter of the lower East Side, was detested by Riis as the symbol of all the degradation of slum life.
4. Riis, *The Children of the Poor*, 173. Similarly: "I have seen an armful of daisies keep the peace of a block better than a policeman and his club, seen instincts awaken under their gentle appeal, whose very existence the soil in which they grew made seem a mockery." *How the Other Half Lives*, 136.

Riis had another vision. Why not attach a park-playground to every school? If we did this in New York, then children would undoubtedly "be attracted to a school that was identified with their playground. Truancy would cease."[5] Here was a real community center which would put the street gang out of business. It would constitute a kind of neighborhood commons, a visible symbol of unity transcending ethnic and religious differences. If the school became, as Riis hoped, a social and intellectual beacon for adults as well as children, it would help restore the family cohesiveness which the tenement had wrecked. The school, park, playground— these were the tools which would civilize the child, Americanize the immigrant, reconstruct the tenement neighborhood, and reduce the importance of the policeman's night stick as an instrument of social control. In Riis's eyes, no greater challenge confronted the housing or social reformer than the creation of new primary group relationships based on the neighborhood in geography and a common Americanism in spirit.

ALEXANDER ALLAND SR.

From Jacob A. Riis: Photographer and Citizen†

Preface

To my list of intense experiences in photography, including a preview of some Strand negatives in Taos, the Portraits and Shells of Weston, the Equivalents of Stieglitz and the magnificent human affirmation of Dorothea Lange, I must add the Riis-Alland prints displayed at the Museum of the City of New York.

For me these are magnificent achievements in the field of humanistic, photography . . . I know of no contemporary work of this general character which gives such an impression of competence, integrity and intensity.

I find it difficult to explain my convictions. I am not thinking of Riis's achievement in terms of comparative equipment and materials (that is a line worn thin by now). Obviously, Alland's beautiful prints, by exalting the physical qualities of Riis's work, intensify their expressive content. The factual and dated content of subject has definite historic importance, but the larger content lies in Riis's expression of people in misery, want and squalor. These people live again for you in the print—as intensely as when their images were captured on the old dry plates of ninety years ago. Their comrades in poverty and suppression live here today, in this city—in all the cities of the world. I have thought much about this intense, *living* quality in Riis's work; I think I have an explanation of its compelling power. It is because in viewing those prints I find myself identified with the people photographed. I am walking in their alleys, standing in their rooms and sheds and workshops, looking in and out of their windows. And they in turn seem to be aware of me.

In so much photography of people in our time I feel that the photographer is cloaked in invisibility; he captures a fragment of the world without

5. Riis, "Playgrounds for City Schools," 665.
† Pages 6–7, 11–48. Reprinted by permission of Alexander Alland Jr.

identifying himself with his immediate environment. Perhaps he thinks he achieves identification—but only the spectator of his photograph can be sure. He seems to avoid detection; no one in his pictures seems to recognize him or acknowledge his presence. It is a peephole—or keyhole—view point: the sly capturing of the private moment, the time-slice of turmoil, the "observation" of the little man who wasn't there!

I remember a photographic educator who violently condemned any picture in which the subject "mugged" the camera. His concept of a picture was suspiciously reminiscent of an aquarium thronged with weary, uninterested fish, or a stage of posturing puppets. I fortified myself by recalling Strand's wonderful Mexican photographs; in many of these the subjects are looking at you—you are there with them, you may almost speak to them. Because of this intimacy, reality is magically intensified, another dimension of response is added to the dimensions of statement. Do I hear the word "empathy"?

Many of the people shown in Riis's work looked at the camera and the photographer at the moment of exposure. They did not realize that they were looking at you and me and all humanity for ages of time. Their postures and groupings are not contrived; the moment of exposure was selected more for the intention of truth than for the intention of effect.

It would be difficult to imagine these photographs as single images apart from the great matrix of Riis's project. Riis's photographs, books, articles and lectures exist as a *unit statement*, a consuming lifework. This is what photography should be—an integrated creative and constructive statement, not a series of disconnected and unorganized images of more or less superficial appeal. The photographer when "expressing himself" or reflecting an ideological or purely aesthetic line is, in effect, shadowboxing with reality. The larger aspects of reality—humanity, nature in implied or direct relation to humanity—cannot be compressed into stylized, intellectual patterns. Statements which are built upon and express truthful intention will seldom be ineffective. The mechanics of communication partake of truth when truth is the objective. The techniques of the pictorialist and the esoteric abstractionist often reflect the weakness of their concept and expression. In Riis's work I am never conscious of technique, methods or means—only of appropriate and efficient mechanical necessities. As revealed in the Alland prints, the quality of his flash illumination is extraordinary; the plastic shadow-edges, modulations and textures of flesh, the balance of interior flash and exterior daylight—what contemporary work really exceeds it in competence and integrity?

Ansel Adams

Chapter 1. *"The Mightiest Lever"*

Two unique attributes of photography attracted Jacob Riis and enabled him to become—nearing forty and a reporter by trade—America's first true journalist-photographer. First, the camera is unsurpassed for recording what is there; words describe, the camera shows. Second, formal training is not a necessity; even with the primitive equipment of Riis's day, a neophyte could become a proficient photographer in a relatively short time. What mattered, then as now, was the use one made of the camera. To some early photographers it was a toy for passing the time, to others an instrument for expressing artistic sensibility. To a humanist like Riis it was a weapon, to be taken up as he had taken up the pen, to battle for social justice. "The power of fact is the mightiest lever of this or of any day," he wrote in his autobiography *The Making of an American*. He saw in the photograph a supreme weapon of fact, a mighty lever for exposing, persuading, convicting. A half-century before Henry Luce made publishing history with a magazine devoted to pictures, Riis knew the truth of Luce's assertion: "The photograph is not the newest, but is the most important instrument of journalism which has developed since the printing press."

Riis's extraordinary photographic legacy was accomplished in a short duration. In 1887 he enlisted two amateur photographers and then two professionals to illustrate his stories with pictures made instantaneously by means of a new technique—flash powder. A few months later Riis himself bought a camera outfit and went to Potter's Field to make his first photographs. Only one plate turned out: a dramatically overexposed view of a common grave. Some ten years later, he put away the camera and apparently never again took it up. He had made enough photographs to document his writings and lectures. The collection that survived him is testimony to the extreme practicality with which he approached photography. It embraces 412 glass-plate negatives consisting of original pictures taken by Riis and by four other men, a large number of copy negatives of pictures and drawings Riis obtained from the files of the Society for the Prevention of Cruelty to Children, Rogues Gallery, Board of Health, and the Children's Aid Society, and a few subjects copied from commercially sold stereographs. The negatives by Riis himself probably do not exceed 250, though those he made for his newspaper stories undoubtedly disappeared into the files of the newspaper and were lost. He photographed only what he needed. Moreover, the new flash-powder technique filled the room with such dense smoke that taking more than one exposure often was out of the question. "I came to take up photographing . . . not exactly as a pastime," Riis wrote. "It was never that with me. I had use for it, and beyond that I never went. I'm downright sorry to confess here that I'm no good at all as a photographer."

The marked contrast between Riis's work and that of his better-known contemporary Alfred Stieglitz encapsulates two divergent streams of twentieth-century photography. Stieglitz, who almost single-handedly elevated the status of photography to that of a fine art, used the camera to create; Riis used it to record. One believed that the camera should portray the beauty that nature wrought, the other used it to record the ugliness wrought by man. The work of Stieglitz is photography at its creative best— living facsimiles of nature's images, expanded vistas caught in a mirror. Riis's photographs are not pretty pictures. Sordid documents, they aroused the public indignation that led to many vital reforms. Both men were visionaries, whose photographs today are treasured, studied and often exhibited side by side. Between the two extremes lies the spectrum of human experience and the range of individual preference.

Stieglitz, returning to New York in 1890 after several years abroad, found himself assaulted "almost physically" by the naked squalor of the city's streets. Walking down Broadway one evening, he happened upon the performance of a then unknown actress Eleonora Duse; only the prospect of occasionally seeing something with the quality and beauty of her performance made it possible for him to stay on in America. In that same year Riis published *How the Other Half Lives*, his compassionate account of the people-strewn streets that seemed so stifling to Stieglitz. "The belief that every man's experience ought to be worth something to the community from which he drew it . . . made me begin this book," Riis wrote in his introduction. "The story is dark enough, drawn from the plain public records, to send a chill to any heart. If it shall appear that the sufferings and the sins of the 'other half' and the evil they breed, are but a just punishment upon the community that gave it no other choice, it will be because that is the truth."

Lewis Mumford has written of Stieglitz: "One of the most moving and impressive pictures Stieglitz ever made was that of a little tree in Madison Square Park, young and vernal in the rain, with a street sweeper in the foreground, and the dim shape of a building in the background: the promise of life, its perpetual re-awakening and renewal are in that print. Wherever Stieglitz turns his head in the city he looks for the touch of life."

To me, Riis's most moving picture is that of a little child with waxen skin lost in the emptiness of a dank stair landing. The child has the saddest eyes I have ever seen. In stark drama this photograph matches the paintings of Francisco Goya who, before Riis, had used his pictures to show man's gross immorality and cruelty. Riis described how he took the child's picture: "I went up the dark stairs in one of the tenements and there I trod upon a baby. It is the regular means of introduction to a tenement house baby . . . but I never have been able to get used to it. I went off and got my camera and photographed that baby standing with its back against the public sink in a pool of filth that overflowed on the floor."

Before Riis's day, photography was pretty much the province of a small group of professionals. They took portraits on commission or produced for sale remarkably beautiful, sharp and clear views of faraway places. I remember how, as a boy in my hometown of Sebastopol in the Crimea, I marveled at the pictures taken under fire by the Englishman Roger Fenton in the Valley of the Shadow of Death. He traveled to Crimea during the war in 1855 to become the first combat photographer in history. A few years after him the scenes most in demand were the pyramids of Egypt and the wonders of other little-known lands. In America, of course, Mathew Brady's celebrated photographs of the Civil War were widely collected. Later, grandiose views of the West came into fashion, especially those taken with a stereoscopic camera. Called stereographs, these pictures created lifelike, three-dimensional images when seen through a viewer.

The invention of dry plates and albumin printing paper in the late 1880's simplified photography. By Riis's day it no longer was necessary to transport huge cameras, chemicals and portable darkrooms to the scene. Photography clubs sprang up all over the country and began squabbling about whether photography was a fine art, a science or a craft. Many photographers, striving to be artists, resorted to all kinds of tricks to make their prints look like paintings—throwing the image out of focus, interposing it with screens, using multiple printing and chemical manipulations. The final product, greatly admired then, is still highly prized, costly and scarce.

About the turn of the century, Alfred Stieglitz and a small group of followers repudiated their dependence on such manipulation and began to practice straight photography. They had learned to correlate the visible and hidden factors that control the qualities of a photograph. Stieglitz's vehicle for propounding his new views was the New York Society of Amateur Photographers, which in the 1890's had been so intrigued by the advent of the bicycling era that it considered transforming itself into a bicycle club. Stieglitz saved the society from the beckoning asphalt of Broadway by promising to rebuild the club, organize exhibitions and publish the new *Camera Notes*. His work raised the standards of photography to the point where it ceased to be considered an imitative medium. Actually, Stieglitz and his friends did not invent anything new but went back full-circle to the original intent of Daguerre and Niépce, the inventors of photography, who sixty years before had found a mechanical means for recording images that approximated those seen by the human eye.

After photography was recognized as a fine art, that recognition embraced only pictures for pictures' sake. In the credo of one group, the Pictorial Photographers of America, this meant: "Pictures of beauty, originality and of artistic self expression as distinguished from mere record photography." (This credo was at least a model of clarity. Other aesthetes fed photo-club members hogwash such as: "The esthetic, selfless, sympathetic touch of man upon his fellows, masculine or feminine, subhuman and inanimate as well as human which it organizes and the sense of life itself, and the intense respect for it in all its forms, and the feeling of its wonders communicated by it, provide a basis for relationships and a commonwealth of responsible, self-regulatory individuals, and democracy. . . .") It was many years before museums overcame their aversion to documentary photography. The simple yet magnetic appeal of Jacob Riis's pictures helped break down the resistance. In 1970 twelve of his prints were included in a group show at the Metropolitan Museum of Art—an event that would have caused a riot forty years earlier.

Even today, some critics question Riis's credentials as a photographer. They are disturbed by the relatively brief duration of his photography and his technical shortcomings. Millions of citizens take pictures today, but are they photographers? My son, an anthropologist, constantly uses still and motion-picture cameras in his work. Countless others make snapshots for pleasure. Riis qualifies as a photographer by at least two definitions: Webster's "one who is engaged in the business of taking pictures" and the more exalted standard laid down almost a century ago by the celebrated spokesman for naturalistic photography, Dr. P. H. Emerson, who said pictures should be judged by "the truth of sentiment and high intellectual standards." The allegation of poor technique is more difficult to rebut. And yet every time I doubt Riis's photography because of its unquestioned technical shortcomings, I recall a story that puts technique in proper perspective. In 1939 that photographer of impeccable technique, Edward Weston, toured the Hollywood storage lots of Metro-Goldwyn-Mayer. "Edward was in seventh heaven," his wife wrote, "he couldn't take a step in any direction without seeing something he had to photograph. When he found a whole street full of stairways leading to nowhere he nearly went mad with delight."

Ultimately, not technique but point of view determines whether the photograph will have lasting value. The photographer chooses what image his camera is to record. The power of the choices Riis made is borne out by the tremendous and enduring appeal of his pictures to large and erudite groups of viewers. Given such choices, technique tends to take care of itself. Riis's photographs are like children's drawings—spontaneous, uninhibited, honest. Like things in nature, the people who are his subjects fall into place by themselves and create a visual harmony that at once makes us aware of their reality and of the truth they project.

Riis's passionate social viewpoint sets him apart from photographers who have achieved much greater renown. I remember vividly the first time I ever heard a talk by Edward Steichen, some thirty-five years ago when he was the most sought-after photographer in the advertising field. He told of a conversation with the great dancer Isadora Duncan, who had come to New York from Russia to give a concert. She asked him: "Edward, why are you wasting your time here? Come back with me to Moscow. They will give you there a studio and everything you may ask for, and you'll be free to create meaningful art for the people." Steichen looked at the audience and asked, "Do you know what I told her? I said, No, Isadora, no. My place is here in America. There is plenty of hell to be raised right here!" As far as I know, Steichen was not in the habit of making public comments on any of our social, political or economic problems. In two world wars and in Korea, Steichen was in charge of combat photography. He had seen and had access to millions of photographic records of the devastation, brutality and suffering brought on by war. Compiled in his famous book *Family of Man*, these records would have spelled DEATH in any language and would have warned humanity against another global holocaust. While his book shows that the world has become man's single environment, it reeks of the same familiar sentimentality and blind faith in the continuity of the "status quo."

Jacob Riis's photographs are inseparable from his activities as a journalist, his journalism from his own incomparable standards of citizenship. He was one of the first of the great investigative reporters—the muckrakers—and he brought all his considerable skills as a reporter, author, photographer and lecturer to exposing corrupt politics, inhuman housing and the plight of neglected children. For much of his life, his arena was New York City. Others like Lincoln Steffens and Upton Sinclair attacked corruption and social injustice on a national scale. Muckraking, Steffens once suggested, is as old as the prophets of the Old Testament. About the time Riis came to America, reporters from *The New York Times* exposed the machinations of the infamous Boss Tweed. His chief assistant in the infamous ring of "Forty Thieves" was Richard Connelly, known as "Slippery Dick"! About the time I came to America the press was pouring out the details of the Teapot Dome Scandal. Today, the heirs of the muckrakers have brought to light Watergate and other colossal abuses of governmental power. Columnist Jack Anderson was asked recently on a television show if he minded being called a muckraker. "Not at all," said Anderson. "Unfortunately, there are too few muckrakers for too many muckmakers."

Riis's immediate heirs in photography were a score of idealistic men and women, many of whom worked on documentary assignments for civic organizations that Riis had founded or supported. But the great boom in documentary photography came when social and economic conditions were again at their visible worst, during the 1930's Depression. Nearly everyone who owned a camera fancied himself a documentary photographer.

Young artists and photographers transformed lofts and basements into clubs and galleries where they could show their work and debate endlessly whether it was of social value. Some of their photographs helped the cause of social justice. Like Riis, such photographers found a way—in the words of Roy Stryker, who headed the Farm Security Administration documentary team—to "speak, as eloquently as possible, of the things to be said in the language of pictures [and knew] enough about the subject-matter to find its significance in itself and in relation to its surroundings, its time, and its function." Other pictures were not worth the paper they were printed on. There were more photographs taken of ashcans and garbage heaps, of slums and drunken bums, of broken windows and street urchins, than in the entire previous history of American photography. "There was very little truly constructive imagery," wrote Ansel Adams, "photographs that expressed hope or a positive possibility of solutions to the sad Depression situation. It was this blind devotion to an *approach* which disturbed. 'Social significance' to me had at that time the same semantic integrity as 'law and order' does today."

I remember one instance where overzealousness defeated the best of intentions. An exhibit of photographs on housing, "Roofs for 40 Million," was to be held at Rockefeller Center. The directives to photographers read: "The theme is housing but don't limit yourself to slum horrors. The subject is very broad and can be treated satirically, realistically, imaginatively, optimistically, pessimistically, etc., in terms of causes, results, Utopian dreams. The implications of bad housing can be told in tragic human terms: crime, juvenile delinquency, fire hazards, prostitution, disease, crowded schools, sordid interiors. . . ."

The spirit of social concern fostered by the Depression carried over into the formation of the American Artists Congress, some eight hundred nationally recognized artists, sculptors and photographers who came together to oppose Hitler's theories and to strengthen the ideas of democracy at home. Its credo stated: "Art is one of the forms of social development and consciousness, which is in constant interaction with the other social forms. The character of art at any given time stands in definite relation to the social environment . . . including its political, social, economic and cultural aspects, and is a matter of direct concern to all artists who wish to develop as rational human beings." Riis believed that the ills that beset the other half could be remedied only by the will of society once it knew the truth. I learned the value of exposure when in 1939 I was on a photographic assignment to promote tourism in the Virgin Islands. The housing conditions of the inhabitants were so bad that I decided on my own to document them. The photographs appeared in the New York newspaper *PM* and resulted in a Congressional appropriation for housing in the Virgin Islands. The newspaper's "News of Photography" editor, Ralph Steiner, said of the photographs: "Pictures must have roots which are planted below the superficial level to make people feel and act. Certainly no photographic salon will hang these pictures. But they have been used in Congress to promote good housing in the Islands."

Out of the documentary explosion of the 1930's emerged the new form of photography known as photojournalism. Newspapers gave vastly more space to photographs; new magazines devoted to journalistic pictures came into being. In the last two decades television, with its immediacy and simultaneous transmission of words, pictures and sound, has become the newest form of photojournalism. But there remain the documentary still photographers who, in newspapers and books, carry on the tradition of Jacob Riis.

Ever since 1947, when Riis's photographs were exhibited for the first time, I heard only one adverse criticism of him and his work. His critic perused a *single* Riis volume and saw pictures which were facsimiles of prints made from copy negatives which in turn were made from poor prints. While conceding Riis's effectiveness as a reformer, the critic said: "There is no denying Riis's humanitarianism and energy, and there is no question that he is one of the most effective reformers this country has ever seen, and that he has a place too, in the history of photography. But frankly I see no way, nor reason to obscure the fact that he's crippled as well as ennobled by his intentions, that his awesome single-mindedness, the source of much that is admirable and honorable in him, has as its flipside a simple-mindedness that lands him as often on his head as his feet. . . ."

Perhaps without realizing it, the critic had pinpointed Riis's greatest strength. Riis was a simple man, though hardly simple-minded. His biographer, Dr. Louise Ware, noted that he cared little for music or the theater and "the niceties of literary taste were beyond him." He was not an artist, not a literary stylist. But his very simplicity as a man permitted a single-minded pursuit of social justice rarely matched in journalism. Humanitarian zeal led him to take up in turn the weapons with which he excelled—pen, camera, his own voice on the lecture platform.

Far more complex is the task of finding the sources of Riis's zeal. Saints are not ordained and social reformers not born: they come to their calling through a chain of experiences, influences, even coincidences. Certainly Riis's early immigrant days in the slums of New York provided him with both firsthand knowledge and powerful motives for his later crusades. Among the many other attempts at accounting for the evangelistic eloquence of his pen and camera, none is more dramatic nor plausible than a story told by Riis himself: "In a Methodist revival . . . I had fallen under the spell of the preacher's fiery eloquence. Brother Simmons was one of the old circuit rider's stock . . . the spirit burned within him; he brought me to the altar quickly, though in my case conversion refused to work the prescribed amount of agony. With the heat of the convert, I decided on the spot to take to preaching, but Brother Simmons would not hear of it. 'No, no, Jacob,' he said, 'not that, we have preachers enough. What the world needs is consecrated pens.'"

When Riis came to realize that his pen was not enough, he took up the camera and consecrated it in his crusade. His writing, he said, "did not make much of an impression—these things rarely do, put in mere words—until my negatives, still dripping from the dark-room, came to reinforce them. From them there was no appeal."

Chapter 2. *The Young Immigrant*

One day in mid-May 1870, Jacob Augustus Riis boarded a small ship in his native Denmark and left for Glasgow, Scotland. There he changed to the steamer *Iowa* and sailed for America. The voyage took sixteen days on stormy seas. Riis, twenty-one and virtually penniless, rode it out in steerage, the notorious stinkhole deep in the hull where immigrants were packed like cattle. He wrote nothing of the voyage except a description of one incident, which reveals a trace of the diplomacy that later tempered his zeal as a reformer. "The meat served to us became so bad as to offend not only our palates, but also our senses of smell. We got up a demonstration, marching to see the captain in a body. . . . As the spokesman, I presented the case briefly and respectfully, and all would have gone well had not the hot blood of Adler risen at the wrong moment. . . . With a sudden upward jerk he caused that official's nose to disappear in the dish."

I too came to America in steerage, fifty years after Riis, and the same kind of salted beef, black and reeking with saltpeter, was served. I would have starved if not for a good Samaritan traveling in first class. She was a call girl, young and pretty, who had come to my photography studio in Constantinople for a portrait sitting whenever she bought a new hat. She spotted me on the deck below her and every night lowered a little bag of leftovers to me. When we docked in New York, steerage passengers had to wait a day to go ashore because the immigration inspectors were on holiday. First-class passengers did not have to wait; they strolled down the gangplank soon after arrival and were taken ashore by launch, my friend among them.

Riis's ship arrived in New York at daybreak on June 4 and, after a twenty-four-hour delay because of fog, cast her anchor before the U.S. Immigration Station, Castle Garden. "It was a beautiful spring morning," Riis wrote, "and as I looked over the rail at the miles of straight streets . . . my hopes rose high that somewhere in this teeming hive there would be a place for me. . . . The love of change belongs to youth, and I meant to take a hand in things as they came along."

Jacob Riis was born May 3, 1849, in the ancient town of Ribe in southwest Denmark. He was the third in a family of fourteen children and one foster daughter. His father, Niels Edward Riis, taught at a centuries-old preparatory academy. The elder Riis, in addition to being a master of Latin and Greek, was well-versed in history and current affairs. To supplement his modest salary he did occasional part-time editorial work for the town newspaper and served as an interpreter when foreign vessels foundered on the nearby coast. Jacob's mother, Caroline, was a cheerful woman with a gift for recounting stories. By the word of relatives, it was an orderly and most affectionate family.

Young Jake received in his father's school a solid foundation in classical subjects and, like all Scandinavian children, was compelled to acquire a good knowledge of English. He preferred playing outdoors, where he invented games based on his favorite stories of the American frontier by James Fenimore Cooper. His independent streak is foreshadowed in the class journal for 1861, when young Jacob was eleven: "J. Riis showed such unseemly behavior that I found it advisable to dismiss him from the classroom; Riis without pencil; Riis without a pen; Riis has forgotten his book; Riis has neglected a written assignment; Riis inattentive [the last three entries were by his father]; Riis has failed to write his Danish compositions; Riis disobedient. . . ." His foster sister once remarked: "Jake was a good boy—his heart was always warm—but he could be as fire to a powder." When Riis was sixty, he recalled his schooldays in *The Old Town*, a proud history of Ribe where kings once lived interspersed with childhood vignettes. "There were 15 of us in the Latin School. The 13 took the straight and narrow road. They were good and they prospered. Hans and I were the black sheep who perennially disputed the dunce seat. . . . Now, after a lifetime, what was my surprise to find out that of the whole fifteen whom the king had singled out for decorations were Hans and myself!"

Jacob's father wanted him to prepare for a literary career, but young Jake wasn't interested. He wanted to be a carpenter. In fact, there appears to be little in his boyhood to account for his later career, other than occasional help lent in his father's part-time newspaper job. Many years later a magazine article about Riis found a foreshadowing of the reformer: he had found a rat-infested tenement built over a sewer and waged war against the vermin. Actually, the house in question was Jacob's own home and his battles with the rats earned him the nickname "Jacob the Delver."

After a year's apprenticeship with a local craftsman, Riis moved on to Copenhagen to study with a well-known master builder. His son, Roger William, would later theorize that Riis's passion for reform stemmed from the contrast between sylvan Denmark and the tenement-strewn streets of New York. But the Copenhagen where Riis spent four years had its share of poverty and overcrowding. "Curiously enough," wrote Dr. Louise Ware in her biography, "young Jacob appears not to have been aware of these social conditions, which were almost identical with those that shocked him into action a few years later in New York." Much of the four years in Copenhagen he had his mind on a girl from back home. He had met young Elizabeth—he was fifteen and she not yet thirteen—when he was helping build her foster father's new factory. Her presence had so overwhelmed him that in quick succession he sliced his shinbone with an adz, chopped off a forefinger with an ax and fell off a roof. Now a full-fledged member of Denmark's Carpenters' Guild, he returned home from Copenhagen to find a job and claim his love. He failed at both. Denmark was in the grip of serious unemployment. Elizabeth's foster father rejected him as a suitor. Jacob had heard there was plenty of work in America, a chance perhaps to get rich quick and become a more desirable suitor for Elizabeth. Years later Riis— who was not above poetic license—embellished their parting: "I kissed her hand and went away, my eyes brimming over with tears, feeling that there was nothing in the world for me anymore and that the further I went from her the better. . . . So I went out in the world to seek my fortune."

The America Riis came to was in the midst of enormous change. It was booming with industry and corruption as the nation evolved from an agricultural economy and suffered growing pains. Congressmen connived with lobbyists; votes for huge appropriations were bought with cigars, costly dinners and outright bribes. The industrial revolution required infusions of cheap manpower, which was recruited in foreign lands. People were on the move along Europe's paths and roads, on foot and by horse and wagon. First by the hundreds then by the thousands they stole across the borders in the dark of night to fulfill their dream, "On to America!" The new immigrants flocked to New York and other big cities where, along with thousands of ex-slaves up from the South, many found themselves unemployed and living in wretched tenements. (Eventually, the new immigrants would fare better than the ex-slaves. Many years later a young black girl spoke for blacks in a white-dominated society when, in answer to the question of what should be done with Hitler after World War II, she wrote, "Put him in a black skin and let him live the rest of his life in America.")

As soon as Riis stepped off the boat, he began preparing himself for the rigors, real and imagined, of life in the new land. In Denmark his friends had given him a going-away gift of $40 and he had thanked them, saying, "I have not forgotten my religion or the 11th commandment: 'Do not let yourself be overtaken by surprise.'" Riis stopped at the first general store he saw in New York and used half the $40 to purchase a huge Navy revolver. He strapped the revolver to his waist and marched up Broadway ready for the worst. Later he wrote that he was "cut . . . to the heart to find the streets actually paved, with no buffaloes in sight, and not a Red man or a beaver hat." A friendly policeman spotted the revolver and suggested Riis put it away.

After a few days of fruitless job-hunting, Riis hired on as a carpenter for an ironworks in Brady's Bend on the Allegheny River in upstate New York. Soon homesickness and the monotony of building huts for the miners overtook him. He tried his hand as a miner. He made more money, but the long back-breaking hours in the black pit proved too strenuous and he went back to carpentry. Unexpected news stirred him out of his melancholy: France had declared war on Germany. He thought that surely Denmark would join France to punish Prussia for stealing the Danish province of Schleswig in the War of 1864. "All the hot blood of youth was surging through me, I remembered the defeat, the humiliation of the flag I loved. . . ." He may also have seen the war as a way of getting home to see Elizabeth. He quickly sold some tools and clothes to buy a train ticket as far as Buffalo, where he pawned his trunk and watch to get to New York—with one cent in his pocket. In New York he walked straight to the French consulate to join the ranks, only to learn there were no plans to outfit a volunteer army in America nor funds for his transportation to France. At the Danish consulate the clerks could do no more than register him for military service in the event Denmark entered the war.

Dispirited and broke, Riis was again out on the streets. In order to square a previous account with a New York landlady, he pawned his revolver and a pair of top boots. All he had now, was a linen duster, an extra pair of socks and the prospect of sleeping on the street. At daybreak he set out for open country where a farmer might welcome a strong and willing hand. He walked all day and, exhausted and hungry, collapsed into an empty wagon to sleep. Before dawn the milkman who ran the wagon jerked him out of his slumber. He took a bath in a river and walked on, reaching Fordham College, where he wandered through the gates in a daze. A teacher, an old cleric in a cowl, invited him to breakfast—his first solid meal in days and the first time he had ever sat at ease with a Catholic priest.

Soon Riis was back in the city. For a while he had hoed cucumbers in exchange for meals and a haystack bed, but could find no job at decent pay. At least he wasn't broke; he had a silver quarter, the goodwill token of a young man who had come upon him sleeping in a wagon shed by the roadside. Now, glancing at the headlines in the New York Sun, Riis saw that the paper was helping recruit a regiment of volunteers to fight for France. He rushed to the Sun office, where he sought out the editor. The man shrugged his shoulders and said, "Editors sometimes do not know everything that is in their papers." Then, realizing that Riis looked hungry, he pulled out a dollar. "Go and get your breakfast; and better give up the war." Riis spurned the offer. "I came here to enlist, not to beg money for breakfast." He strode out of the office, proud and still hungry. The editor was the famous Charles Dana, and years later Riis would return as one of Dana's star reporters. After three unsuccessful attempts to fight for the French, Riis gave up the idea. Years later he rejoiced that fate had prevented him from joining the army that used a scapegoat for its own troubles when they charged a Jewish army captain named Dreyfus with spying for Germany. Dreyfus was subsequently exonerated and made a member of the Legion of Honor.

Riis carried with him letters of introduction to the Danish consul and to a businessman who was indebted to the Riis family for saving his life in a shipwreck near Ribe. Earlier, Riis had called on both men but they were in Europe at the time. Now, when he needed help the most, he was too proud to try using the letters again and he destroyed them. He was also too proud to correspond with his family. He didn't want them—or Elizabeth—to know he was having such a hard time in America. "The city was full of idle men," he wrote later. "My last hope, a promise of employment in a human-hair factory failed, and homeless and pennyless I joined the great army of tramps, wandering about the streets in the daytime with one aim of somehow stilling the hunger that gnawed at my vitals, and fighting at night with vagrant curs or outcasts as miserable as myself for the protection of some sheltering ash-bin or doorway. I remember well a basement window at the downtown Delmonico's, the silent appearance of my ravenous face at which, at a certain hour of the evening, always evoked a generous supply of meat-bones and rolls from a white-capped cook who spoke French."

One morning, after a few excursions out of New York had convinced him he could do better elsewhere, Riis left the city vowing never to return. He followed the railroad tracks into western New York, where he found a more congenial atmosphere among the Scandinavians clustered in small towns there. He held jobs longer and his pay got better, enabling him to buy his first suit in America. On one job he contracted to plane and finish doors at 15 cents a door. In the first week Riis earned $15. When his employer realized that this was $5 more than Riis's predecessor had earned, he cut the price to 12 cents a door. The next week Riis worked extra hard and made $16. "The boss examined my work very carefully, said it was good, paid my wages, and cut the price to 10 cents. He did not want his men to earn more than $10 a week, saying it was not good for them." (Such exploitation was still prevalent fifty years later when I came to America. In 1923 I found a job in a large pencil factory. The company hired mostly immigrants—they would work for less pay and the fact that few spoke English made it difficult for them to organize into unions. One of the engineers, a countryman of mine, helped me become an overseer in the lead-cutting department. I showed the workers how to increase their production and earn higher wages under the piecework system. By the next week they had almost doubled their pay. Management then lowered the rate of pay—like Riis's employer—and thus became the sole beneficiary of my good intentions.)

Over the next two years Riis tried his hand at numerous occupations. He was carpenter, farm hand, common laborer, lumberjack, hunter and trapper, cabinetmaker, railroad hand, salesman. To break the boredom he felt in the small rural communities, he made his first tentative attempts as a lecturer and writer. In Jamestown, New York, he lectured to the local Scandinavians about astronomy and geology but got so bogged down in longitude and latitude that an old sea captain stood up to object and the entire audience walked out. "Other ambitions than to milk cows . . . were stirring in me," Riis wrote. "I had begun to write essays for the magazines, choosing for my topic the maltreatment of Denmark by Prussia, which ranked fresh in my memory, and the duty of all Scandinavians to rise up and avenge. The Scandinavians would not listen when I wrote in Danish, and my English outpourings never reached the publishers. I discovered that I lacked words—they didn't pour."

Nowhere in his diaries or books does Riis mention amorous encounters in the new land. Though he was a remarkable raconteur, there isn't a single tale about girls he might have liked. Perhaps his love for Elizabeth had sealed his heart against other girls. But he also kept before him a constant vision of his mother, who was the last to see him off on his journey to America. He had bidden her goodbye at the door of the wife of the miller, who comforted his mother by saying, "Jacob will come back President of the United States." Riis enjoyed the comradeship of men, but he worshiped women, whom he put on a higher plane than men. Many years later, when his oldest daughter became engaged to be married, Riis was overcome by hopelessness at the prospect of losing her.

Of his many jobs during this period, Riis was most successful as a salesman. After several good months of peddling flat and fluting irons, he was made factory representative for the State of Illinois. He hired subagents to help him cover the huge territory. The enterprise looked good—orders were mounting—but in Chicago Riis ran afoul of local sharpies. Among them were some of his childhood chums, who had immigrated from Denmark. "In six weeks they had cleaned me out bodily, had run away with my irons and with money they borrowed of me to start them in business. I returned to Pittsburgh as poor as ever, to find that the agents I had left behind in my Pennsylvania territory had dealt with me after the same fashion. The firm for which I worked had contrived at the frauds. My friends had left me."

Down and out once more, Riis wandered up the Allegheny River where he fell ill with fever. Bedridden in a riverside tavern, he received the worst blow of all. A letter from home that had been forwarded to him announced that Elizabeth was engaged to be married to a cavalry officer. "In all my misadventures that was the one thing I had never dreamed of," he wrote. "That she should be another's bride seemed so utterly impossible. . . . At the thought I turned my face to the wall and hoped that I might die."

In this lonely tavern, toward the end of his third year in America, Riis nursed himself back in health and heart. Then, on foot, he started his slow trek back East, peddling flatirons to pay his way. Later he would remark that at twenty-four one does not die of a broken heart.

Chapter 3. "Noblest of All the Callings"

When he reached New York after spending the entire summer on the trip East, Riis's wanderlust was ebbing. He decided to seek a permanent job and invested all his money in a training course for telegraphers. Before completing the course, however, he turned again to an ambition he apparently had harbored for some time—perhaps since his boyhood days when he helped his father with newspaper work. "It seemed to me that a reporter was the highest and noblest of all the callings," he wrote later, "no one could sift wrong from right as he, and punish the wrong . . ." Once before, while knocking around the state, he had dropped into a newspaper office in Buffalo to apply for a job. "What are you?" asked the editor. "A carpenter," replied Riis. The editor laughed in his face and pushed him out of the office. "You laugh," shouted Riis, shaking his fist, "but wait . . ." Riis wrote, "In that hour it was settled that I was to be a reporter."

Now, seeing a classified ad placed by a small Long Island weekly, Riis skipped telegraphy class and rushed to the newspaper. He got the job, city editor. Afterward he learned that the job was usually open because the editor in chief was dishonest, a scandalmonger and heavily in debt. After two weeks Riis quit, forfeiting his pay. Broke, but having endured a brief baptism in journalism, he returned to his old haunts in the Five Points section of downtown New York. The area had long been notorious at home and abroad as a place of misery, degradation and lawlessness. Thirty years earlier, Charles Dickens had vividly described Five Points:

> This is the place; these narrow ways, diverging to the right and to the left, and reeking everywhere with dirt and filth. . . . The coarse and bloated faces at the doors have counterparts at home. . . . Debauchery has made the very houses prematurely old. See how the rotten beams are tumbling down and how the patched and broken windows seem to scowl dimly, like eyes that have been hurt in drunken frays. Many of the pigs live here. Do they ever wonder why their masters walk upright in lieu of going on all-fours? Where dogs would howl to lie, women and men and boys slink off to sleep, forcing the dislodged rats to move away in quest of better lodgings. Here too . . . are . . . hideous tenements which take their name from robbery and murder; all that is loathsome, drooping and decayed is here.

By Riis's time little had changed. A contemporary author noted the appalling statistics: "Forty thousand vagrant and destitute children . . . too dirty, too ragged . . . to be admitted to the public schools. Over a thousand young girls, between the ages of twelve and eighteen, can be found in the Water Street drinking saloons . . . children can be seen who come up daily from the brothels and dens of infamy which they call their homes." Many of the lodging houses were underground, without ventilation; lodgers slept on canvas bags filled with rotten straw, which they rented for five or ten cents a night. Riis himself spent many nights in the police lodging cellars, which were free. The misery of his existence in Five Points cannot be discounted, and yet he was drawn to it again and again. For him Five Points proved to be a kind of hard-knocks school of journalism.

One day he was sitting disconsolately on the steps of the Cooper Institute. He was back where he had begun three years before, broke, hungry and now, "bankrupt in hope and purpose." In his hand was a copy of the new Dickens book *Hard Times*, which he had been futilely attempting to peddle door to door. The principal of his telegraphy school happened by and saw him. He glanced at the title of the book and snorted: "Books . . . I guess they won't make you rich. Now how would you like to be a reporter if you have nothing better to do? News Agency's manager asked me today to find him a bright young fellow whom he could break in. It isn't much—$10 a week to start with. But it is better than peddling books, I know."

Riis spent another night on the streets, rose early, washed up at a horse-watering trough and rushed to the New York News Association where the editor looked up incredulously at the rumpled young man. But he was impressed by Riis's willingness to begin work so early and told him to wait. At 10 A.M. he was sent on the first assignment of the day, covering a luncheon at the Astor House. Three days without food must have sharpened his perception: despite the distraction of the savory meal being served, he submitted a good report and got the job. "That night, when I was dismissed from the office, I went up the Bowery . . . where a Danish family kept a boardinghouse up under the roof. I had work and wages now, and could pay. On the stairs I fell in a swoon and lay there till someone stumbled over me in the dark and carried me in. My strength had at last given out. So began my life as a newspaper man."

This first job of collecting general news wherever it happened gave Riis the chance to get acquainted with parts of the city beyond his familiar tenement district. New York, already America's chief financial and cultural center, had 11,000 factories devoted to clothing, cigars, furniture and printing. Millionaires from all over the country came there to live in the magnificent edifices along Fifth and Madison avenues. Its seaport drew 30,000 ships annually and was the gateway for the immigrants—German, Swedish, Norwegian and Danish, Irish, Italian, Jewish, French—with whom Riis felt at home. The immigrants tended to settle among their own kind where they could find cheap lodgings and home-operated, sweatshops. They struggled to make a better life for their children, many of whom grew up to become, like Riis, celebrated citizens of the new land.

Riis wrote about pushcart vendors who lost their profits to police graft, about sweatshop slaves, about homeless boys. Writing came easy to him, even though English was not his native tongue. No literary stylist, he had the storytelling gift of a homespun narrator. He worked sixteen hours a day. Any time now, he expected to hear from home that Elizabeth was married and a "furious kind of energy took possession of me at the mere idea."

He earned a reputation as a good reporter and soon accepted the title of editor and a higher salary on a small local weekly. It turned out that the *News* was a front for a group of politicians and heavily in debt. Just as the debt-ridden paper was going out of business—it was Christmas Eve—a letter arrived from Riis's father. Never since Riis had left home had a letter from his family reached him in time for Christmas, his favorite holiday. This one bore extraordinary news. His two older brothers and a favorite aunt had died. Riis wept. But the most important tidings were saved for the postscript: Elizabeth's fiancé, too, had died. In the next few days new hope of having Elizabeth surged unashamedly through him. He wrote her a long letter pouring out his feelings. Then, with his savings, $75, and some promissory notes, he purchased the assets of the *News*.

"The *News* was a big four-page sheet," he recalled. "Literally every word in it I wrote myself. I was my own editor, reporter, publisher and advertising agent. In the early morning hours I shouldered the edition and carried it down to the ferry. . . . When I got home, I slept on the counter with the edition for my pillow, in order to be up with the first gleam of daylight to skirmish for newsboys."

In five months he saved enough to pay off his debts on the paper. No longer financially obligated to the politicians, he became their scourge.

Finally, the politicians bought him off with a sinecure as a court interpreter. He continued to publish his paper but toned down his attacks. He had Elizabeth on his mind and didn't want to jeopardize their future together. For the rest of his life, Riis regretted his weakness in giving in to the politicial bosses. Though he was asked many times to be a public official, he never again accepted.

It was agonizing months before he received Elizabeth's reply: she was willing to go with him to America if he would come for her. He answered immediately that he would be back in Denmark within a year. Then came another stroke of luck. The politicians wanted to buy back the *News*. They gave him five times the price he had paid for it, and Riis took the next steamer for home. He had left Denmark with $40; he was coming back a hundred times richer. When he arrived in Ribe, Elizabeth's palatial home at last opened its doors to the one-time carpenter boy. Three months later Elizabeth and Jacob were married. "I hear people saying . . . there is no such thing as luck," Riis often said. "They are wrong. There is; I know it. It runs in streaks, like accidents and fires. The thing is to get in the way of it and keep there till it comes along, then hitch on, and away you go."

When Riis arrived in New York with his bride, America was in the grip of another depression. With his savings to fall back on, he and Elizabeth busied themselves with the pleasant task of setting up housekeeping in a small Danish neighborhood in Brooklyn. At length, he hired himself out to edit the newspaper of a south Brooklyn political machine but couldn't stomach it for long. Then, looking around for another means of livelihood, he hit upon an idea that was to impress upon him, perhaps for the first time, the immense power of the visual image. Some time before, he had bought at a rummage sale a magic lantern, an early version of today's slide projector. The device could project enlarged images of slides—either photographic transparencies or pictures painted on glass in transparent watercolors— and Riis thought it might provide entertainment for his future children. It first came into use at the end of the seventeenth century—for amusement, anatomical lectures and even to dupe the superstitious.

Riis brought out his magic lantern from basement storage and launched a highly innovative advertising scheme. He started modestly, projecting ads for neighborhood merchants on a sheet stretched between two trees. When cold weather came, he moved into an empty store and flashed his pictures onto a screen in the window. His shows attracted large crowds of fascinated viewers. He shrewdly interspersed the ads with beautiful scenic views. "I advertised nothing I would not have sold the people myself, and I gave it to them in the way that was distinctly pleasing and good for them; for my pictures were real works of art, not the cheap trash you see nowadays on street screens."

Successful in Brooklyn, Riis and a friend decided to take their advertising business to small towns. In upstate New York and western Pennsylvania they moved from town to town with nightly displays. After several months of thriving, the operation ended when Riis and his partner got caught unwittingly in the violence between the law and a group of striking railroad workers. "I heard a word of brief command, the rattle of a score of guns . . . and a volley was fired into the crowd point blank. A man beside me weltered in his blood. There was an instant's dead silence, then the rushing of a thousand feet and the cries of terror as the mob broke and fled. We ran with it. In all my life I never ran so fast."

Jobless again, and now with a baby to support, Riis ran into one of those happy coincidences he liked to remark upon. One of his neighbors happened to be the city editor of the New York *Tribune*. Through his recommendation Riis got a job as a probationary reporter. All that winter he covered news, mostly on foot, for long hours at little pay. Just as he was about to look for a better job, his boss offered him an assignment as police reporter. The editor told him: "It is a place that needs a man who will run to get his copy in, tell the truth and stick to it. You will find plenty of fighting there. But don't go knocking people down, unless you have to." Riis ran to the telegraph office to send Elizabeth the news: GOT STAFF APPOINTMENT. POLICE HEADQUARTERS. TWENTY-FIVE DOLLARS A WEEK. HURRAH!

At first the press office, across the street from police headquarters on Mulberry Street, gave Riis a cold reception. The other reporters thought him overly ambitious; they went at their work leisurely, taking turns gathering the news and then sharing it with all. After Riis achieved several scoops, they accepted him and soon nicknamed him "the boss reporter." Riis wrote: "Of the advantages that smoothed the way to newsgetting, I had none. I was a stranger, and I was never distinguished for detective ability. But good hard work goes a long way toward making up for lack of genius."

Mulberry Street, around which Riis was to spend a quarter of a century, was nicknamed "Death's Thoroughfare." It was here, where the street crooks its elbow at the Five Points, that the streets and numerous alleys radiated in all directions, forming the foul core of the New York slums. Until about 1767 Mulberry Street was a path lined with mulberry trees over which cows with tinkling bells came home from pasture. The old people still remembered scavenger pigs roaming the neighborhood; now the tinkling bells proclaimed the homecoming of ragpickers. There is a negative in the Riis Collection of a yard behind an ancient homestead. It is inscribed: "The Last Mulberry. It isn't. It is probably an old Ailanthus."

Riis doubted his ability to last on the police beat. The hours were late, and Elizabeth waited up for him, homesick for Denmark and singing to keep up her courage. After a year he asked for a transfer. The editor refused, saying that Riis was irreplaceable. "Go back and stay," he said. "Unless I'm much mistaken you are finding something there that needs you."

For the next ten years Riis kept at it, investigating, absorbing, writing, hammering away at indifference and graft. Walter Lippmann once remarked: "The rewards in journalism go to specialty work . . . to men with a knack and flavor of their own. If he sees a building with a dangerous list, he does not have to wait until it falls into the street." Riis was just that kind of journalist: he didn't wait for the building to fall before he probed its rotting foundation. The range of his reportorial interests is revealed in this sampling of headlines from his scrapbook for the years 1883–87: VIRUS FARM, REMOVING THE DEAD, EPIDEMIC DANGERS, CUTE TRICKS OF THIEVES, MEN WITH PISTOLS, RED TAPE EXTRAVAGANCE, WHAT IT COSTS TO KEEP RATS, A CHURCH WITH A NEW IDEA.

He was accused of being one-sided, of prejudice, of overemphasizing certain facts. In the end he was virtually always vindicated. He didn't despise the rich, nor even criticize them. He only criticized poverty. Years later, when a Russian theoretical anarchist, Prince Peter Kropotkin, complimented him for his relentless exposure of social conditions in America and called him a revolutionary, Riis retorted: "I don't like the Reds." At every opportunity he stepped out of the slum to solicit support from people of influence and financial standing. John Haynes Holmes observed: "What moved Riis most was the spectacle of helpless human beings robbed of their sheer joy of living which was his own richest treasure."

Others were exposing the seamy side of New York life, but their writings exploited the slums for profit. Books filled with advice to visitors on where to go for slumming and adventure bore such titles as *Sunshine and Shadow*, *Darkness and Daylight* and *Light and Darkness*. The text in such books was enhanced with artists' drawings that made the narration more vivid. Riis also felt the need for pictorial documentation of his stories. He tried his own hand at drawing the scenes he reported, but had to admit he was a poor artist. Besides, he knew that the line drawings of even the most skilled artist could not convey the impact of what he saw and wished to document. Aware that words were not enough, he was "frustrated, dissatisfied and anxious. . . . In anger I looked around for something to strike off . . . fetters with. But there was nothing." Then, when he least expected it, the tool he desperately needed presented itself.

Chapter 4. *Light for the Darkest Corner*

Jacob Riis had never even thought of buying a camera, much less using one to record the misery his own eyes saw with such righteous anger. It was a slow, cumbersome instrument, built for the brightness of day; what Riis wanted to expose cowered in dark tenements. Then, early in the spring of 1887 four lines of newspaper type brought Riis his flash of light. "One morning scanning my newspaper at the breakfast table, I put it down with an outcry that startled my wife sitting opposite. There it was, the thing I had been looking for all these years. A four-line dispatch from somewhere in Germany, if I remember right, had it all. A way had been discovered, it ran, to take pictures by flashlight. The darkest corner might be photographed that way."

The new method was a forerunner of the modern flash gun, a pistol lamp that fired magnesium cartridges to provide light for instantaneous unposed photographs. Riis immediately saw its potential for his own crusades and told his friend Dr. John Nagle, an enthusiastic amateur photographer who was chief of the Bureau of Vital Statistics in the City Health Department. Nagle enlisted a couple of other amateur photographers. With Riis in the lead, they began a series of nighttime forays into the slums—armed with cameras and the new pistol lamp. The drama of these bizarre expeditions was vividly described by Riis some months later in an unsigned article that appeared in the New York *Sun* on February 12, 1888. It was the first published account of the use of the new technique in America.

Flashes from the Slums
Pictures taken in dark places by the
Lighting Process
Some of the Results of a Journey Through the City
with an Instantaneous Camera—
The Poor, the Idle and the Vicious.

With their way illuminated by spasmodic flashes, as bright and sharp and brief as those of the lightning itself, a mysterious party has lately been startling the town o'nights. Somnolent policemen on the street, denizens of the dives in their dens, tramps and bummers in their so-called lodgings, and all the people of the wild and wonderful variety of New York night life have in their turn marvelled at and been frightened by the phenomenon. What they saw was three or four figures in the gloom, a ghostly tripod, some weird and uncanny movements, the blinding flash, and then they heard the patter of retreating footsteps, and the mysterious visitors were gone before they could collect their scattered thoughts and try to find out what it was all about. Of course, all this fuss speedily became known to the Sun reporters, and equally as a matter of course they speedily found out the meaning of the seeming mystery. But at the request of the parties interested the publication of the facts was delayed until the purpose of the expedition was accomplished. That has now been done, and its history may now be written.

The party consisted of members of the Society of Amateur Photographers of New York experimenting with the process of taking instantaneous pictures by an artificial flashlight and their guide and conductor, an energetic gentleman, who combines in his person, though not in practise, the two dignities of deacon in a Long Island church and a police reporter in New York. His object in the matter, besides the interest in the taking of the pictures, was the collection of a series of views for magic lantern slides, showing, as no mere description could, the misery and vice that he had noticed in his ten years of experience. Aside from its strong human interest, he thought that this treatment of the topic would call attention to the needs of the situation, and suggest the direction in which much good might be done. The nature of this feature of the deacon-reporter's idea is indicated by the way he has succeeded on Long Island in the work of helping the destitute children of the metropolis. The ground about the little church edifice is turned into a garden, in which the Sunday school children work at spading, hoeing, planting, and weeding, and the potatoes and other vegetables thus raised are contributed to a children's home in the city. In furtherance of such aims the deacon-reporter threw himself with tireless energy into the pursuit of pictures of Gotham's crime and misery by night and day to make a foundation for a lecture called "The Other Half: How it Lives and Dies in New York." to give at church and Sunday school exhibitions, and the like.

The entire composition of the night rousing party was: Dr. Henry G. Piffard and Richard Hoe Lawrence, two accomplished and progressive Amateur Photographers; Dr. John T. Nagle of the Health Board, who is strongly interested in the same direction, and Jacob A. Riis, the deacon-reporter. . . . Mr. Riis kindly furnished a number of his photographs to the Sun artist and they are given here.

The article was accompanied by twelve line drawings based on photographs taken by Riis's companions—then the newspaper's accepted way of reproducing pictures. His amateur photographers were fascinated by the flashlight process but soon tired of the late-night hours. Riis next tried hiring professionals. One, an *Evening Sun* employee named Collins, was too slow to suit Riis. The other photographer was in all probability A. D. Fisk, who had a studio at 18 Ann Street. Riis wrote of the second photographer: "He was even less willing to get up at 2 a.m. than my friends, who had a good excuse. He had none, for I paid him well. He repaid me by trying to sell my photographs behind my back." Riis went to court and established that he owned the negatives—probably a precedent in winning for an employer the rights to pictures taken for him. It cost Riis a lawyer's fee of $15, no small amount then. Riis later wrote this footnote to his exasperating experiences with the photographer: "He was a pious man, I take it, for when I tried to have him photograph the waifs in the baby nursery at the Five Points House of Industry, as they were saying their 'Now I lay me down to sleep,' and the plate came out blank the second time, he owned up that it was his doing: it went against his principles to take a picture of anyone at prayers. The spectacle of a man prevented by religious scruples from photographing children at prayers, while plotting at the same time to rob his employer, has been a kind of chart to me that has piloted me through more than one quagmire of queer human nature. Nothing could stump me after that."

Riis again sought help from his friend Dr. Nagle, who suggested the obvious. So, in January 1888, Riis bought a camera, loaded the plateholders and went to Potter's Field on Hart Island to experiment. On that cold morning there were no burials and no one in sight to distract him. He trained his camera on an open trench and made two exposures. Then he made his first error as a photographer: he put the two exposed plates back among the other ten plates he had brought and thus had to develop all twelve to get one picture. His photograph of the snow-covered common grave was much overexposed, but dramatically right to accentuate the feeling of desolation in a paupers' cemetery.

The entire photographic outfit cost him $25. It consisted of a 4×5 wooden box camera, the plateholders, a tripod, a safety lantern, developing trays and a printing frame. By this time a safer and less startling flashlight technique had replaced the pistol lamps brandished by Riis's earlier raiding parties. ("Our party carried terror wherever it went," Riis observed. "The spectacle of strange men invading a house in the mid-night hours armed with pistols which they shot off recklessly was hardly reassuring . . . and it was not to be wondered at if the tenants bolted through the windows and down fire-escapes.") The pistol lamp cartridges contained highly explosive chemicals, which had seriously burned several photographers. The newer method, developed by Armstrong of London late in 1887, used magnesium powder blown through an alcohol flame. Riis ignited the powder on a frying pan. "It seemed more homelike," he explained. Even so, Riis once blew the light into his own eyes and only his glasses saved him from being blinded for life.

The circumstances of Riis's photography make the resulting pictures all the more remarkable. Unlike modern flash systems, his home-rigged frying pan device was not synchronized with the camera. He had to remove the cap from his lens, quickly ignite the flash powder, then replace the cap. Some of his pictures show a slight blur—movement of his subjects just before the firing of the powder. Once, Riis set fire to a tenement room and, because the tenants were blind, had to smother the blaze by himself. He also faced obstacles more familiar to documentary photographers today. He and his camera were driven off by a band of angry women who pelted him with stones. A tramp accepted 10 cents to pose for a picture, then demanded a quarter when Riis asked him to put his clay pipe back in his mouth. Other subjects insisted on posing when Riis wanted a candid picture. A group of young ruffians who called themselves "the Montgomery Guards" set up an elaborate tableau to show how they picked pockets: one of them slouched against a shed to simulate the sleeping victim while two others ransacked his pockets. Riis's lament about subject-staged pictures would be echoed by future legions of documentary photographers: "Their determination to be 'took' the moment the camera hove into sight, in the most striking pose that they could hastily devise, was always the most formidable bar to success I met."

Riis time and again expressed wonderment at the process by which an image emerged from apparent nothing. "To watch the picture come out upon the plate that was blank before, and that saw with me for perhaps the merest fraction of a second, maybe a month before, the thing it has never forgotten, is a new miracle every time. If I were a clergyman . . . I would preach about it." Most of all, Riis marveled at the practical impact of his pictures. Truth had previously boiled down to the reporter's word against someone else's; in the courts the only pictorial evidence was in the form of artists' sketches, which often were ruled out because such drawings relied on faulty memory and the bias of the human imagination. Now Riis had the most tangible proof to back his allegations. Few listened when he reported that tenement lodgers slept fifteen to a room; his pictures proved it. When typhus broke out in the city, he warned that the police lodging rooms were ripe for it; he photographed the effects of typhus in these crowded dens and took his pictures directly to the Academy of Medicine to alert the doctors. From his pictures, "there was no appeal."

When Riis had enough pictures to illustrate several articles, he began making the rounds of magazine publishers. At Harper's he ran into one of those unhappy ironies of the trade: the editor liked the pictures and offered to buy them, but he wanted someone else "who could write" to do the article.

Riis was so disheartened that he stopped his extracurricular writing attempts and sought another forum—speaking at church meetings. As soon as the churches learned he was a Mulberry Street police reporter, they turned him down. Some churches thought his tales of slum life would be offensive to parishioners; others derived considerable income from their ownership of tumble-down tenements. It was true even of the most fashionable Trinity Corporation, which managed the endowment properties. "[They] held delapidated rookeries, so they were called, vile tenement blocks, for rental to the poor. These were dark close-built 'old law' cold-water housings, in the 'long blocks'. . . . Many children went heavenward from the dark damp hovels." Riis's own church on Long Island prevented him from delivering an address there and he angrily resigned from the diaconate. Then he met two prominent churchmen, Dr. Adolph Schauffler, superintendent of the City Mission Society, and Dr. Josiah Strong, whose book *Our Country* was a pioneer work in sociology. The two men were impressed by his photographs and plans and agreed to sponsor his lecture at the Broadway Tabernacle, a progressive church long famous for its anti-slavery meetings.

Riis had only a few weeks to have lantern slides prepared from his negatives for the lecture, and he had practically no money. The upkeep on his family was growing—he and Elizabeth now had four children—and he had recently gone in debt to build their new house in Richmond Hill on Long Island. To purchase the land alone, he had been forced to take part-time work revising Danish insurance policies. The manager of the Press Bureau for which Riis worked put up the money for the construction of the house and took a mortgage on the entire cost. Behind the house Riis built a charming writer's study that looked like a dollhouse. Though the children were instructed that "Papa is not to be disturbed," the children found reasons to invade his privacy. Without admitting it, he delighted in their visits. Riis wanted a house and lawn for every child in New York. He wrote that his secret wish was "to go around and pay off mortgages on the little homes, so that the owners when they had got the interest together by pinching and scraping should find it all gone and paid up without knowing how." To help finance his new lecture enterprise, he took a partner. He was Riis's friend W. L. Craig, a Health Department clerk who paid all the bills for several months.

The lecture at the Broadway Tabernacle was a huge success—except in the pocketbook of the new partnership. Riis and Craig received nothing. The Mission Society netted $143.50. "I had my say and felt better," Riis wrote. But the $143.50 in proceeds provoked a flash of grim humor—"The fifty cents would have come in handy for lunch that day." The expense accounts kept by Riis and his partner indicate how little they profited from the early lectures: "Jamaica Town Hall, March 7—32.50; Plymouth Church, April 12—46; Lexington Avenue Baptist Church, April 26—25." On June 28, 1888, Riis summed up the accounts: "Expenses of entire business 219.69, deduct amount paid 116.50. Leaves to pay Craig 103.19. Understanding fixed that $1/2$ of all net income goes to Craig until full outlay is paid. Thenceforth he receives a one fourth and owns a one fourth interest in the concern and all that comes from it in any way."

The lectures proved immensely profitable in other ways. They gave him large new audiences for his message and the occasion to meet and form lasting friendships with such celebrated reformers as Dr. Charles Parkhurst, the crusading clergyman who later helped beat Tammany Hall. Riis's lantern slides electrified his audiences. He already knew the selling power of visual images—from his magic lantern advertising venture and from his early days as a traveling salesman when he took along an album of pictures to clinch his sales of furniture. Now pictures and the spoken word were selling his deepest convictions about human misery. "Almost before I knew it, my tongue was enlisted in the fight as well as my pen and the pictures. . . . I lay no claims to eloquence. So it must have been the facts."

Among the listeners and viewers at a Riis illustrated lecture was an editor of the influential *Scribner's* magazine. He was so moved by the story of "bitter poverty, of landlord's greed, of sweatshop slavery, of darkness and squalor and misery" that he asked Riis to submit an article with pictures. The story, titled "How the Other Half Lives," appeared in *Scribner's* at Christmas 1889. The layout covered eighteen pages and carried no less than nineteen of Riis's photographs converted into line drawings. It was the first time his photographs appeared in a national publication. The extraordinary number of pictures used by the magazine—high engraving costs ordinarily limited illustrations to a handful—was a tribute to their unique power.

The article was a breakthrough. A few days later Riis came home to find a letter from a magazine writer suggesting he expand the article into a book—she knew a publisher who might be interested. Riis was jubilant, but his wife looked troubled. Riis wrote: "I saw a tear in her eye as she bent over the baby's cradle. 'Shall we lose you now?' she whispered and hid her head on my shoulder. I don't know what jealous thoughts of authors being wedded to their work had come into her mind. . . . I registered a vow which I have kept. It was the last tear she shed for me."

Actually the idea for the book came to Riis at a meeting of ministers of every sect who were concerned about the losing fight the church was waging among the masses when a man cried out, "How are these men and women to understand the love of God you speak of when they see only the greed of men?" Riis wrote, "I wanted to jump up in my seat at that time and shout Amen! But I remembered that I was a reporter and kept still. It was that same winter, however, that I wrote the title of my book . . . and copyrighted it. The book itself did not come out until two years after, but it was as good as written then. I had my text."

Riis began his first book within weeks after the Scribner's article. Sensing that the popularity of the article might be partly attributable to its catchy title, he chose the same title for the book. It was an abbreviation of the one he copyrighted as: "The Other Half, how it lives and dies in New York, with 100 illustrations, photographs from real life, of the haunts of poverty and vice in a great city." The writing put a tremendous strain on him. His duties as a reporter—he had switched from the Tribune to the Sun in November 1890—took up the days; his lectures took up many of the evenings. He wrote late at night, a regimen that left him so exhausted that one evening at a friend's house, when the maid asked him who he was, he could not remember his own name. Thereafter he never left home without a calling card in his pocket.

The book was published in late 1890, ten months after he began writing. The text was tough, biting, aimed at the conscience of America. Photographically, How the Other Half Lives was a landmark—the first account of social conditions to be documented with action pictures. It was also apparently the first book to use a large number of pictures reproduced by the new halftone process. The book used seventeen halftones, in addition to the eighteen line drawings reproduced earlier in the Scribner's article. (Strangely, this fact went unnoticed in Robert Taft's account of the first use of halftones in Photography and the American Scene, which mentions books published in 1890 and 1891 that carried only a few halftones. In fact, the first large-scale use of halftones occurred in a picture magazine, Sun and Shade, which began publication in July 1888 and had to abandon the practice a year later because of the high costs.)

Riis's first book went into several editions and was widely quoted from the pulpit. Magazine critics praised it, some with reservations. "His aim is to let us know the worst," said the liberal weekly The Nation, "and it is not surprising that special emphasis should be laid upon whatever intensifies the darkness, but he allows us at least to see that there is another side." The Critic, whose staff member had originally suggested the book to Riis, was less enthusiastic: "His book is literally a photograph and as such has its value and a lesson, but also serious limitations. There is a lack of broad and penetrating vision, a singularly warped sense of justice at times, and a roughness amounting almost to brutality." Some reformers, such as Ellen Collins, a prominent worker in the better housing movement, objected that

Riis had painted an overly dark portrait. Riis agreed, but like another great muckraker, Lincoln Steffens, he believed that readers would often accept an ironical statement of facts they might otherwise reject. Wrote Riis: "There is a standing quarrel between the official sanitarian and the unsalaried agitator for sanitary reform over the question of overcrowded tenements. The one puts the number a little vaguely at four or five hundred, while the other asserts that there are thirty-two thousand. . . . It depends on the angle from which one sees it. . . ."

Riis believed that the popular success of his book was due in part to interest in reform aroused by a recent exposé of London's slums, *In Darkest England and the Way Out* by Charles Booth. He also felt that another, quite different book helped draw attention to his own work: Samuel Ward McAllister's *Society As I Have Found It*, a flippant saga of the other "other half"—New York's very wealthy.

Other publishers attempted to capitalize on the popularity of the new documentary approach. One such book published in 1892, *Darkness and Daylight; or Lights and Shadows of New York Life*, carried at least eleven photographs from the present Riis Collection. These included Murderers' Row in the Tombs Prison, opium dens in Chinatown and other scenes that were out of bounds to those who, unlike Riis, did not have the privileged access of a police reporter. Though the book's preface hailed the new technique of flashlight photography—paraphrasing Riis's old *Sun* article—it failed even to mention Riis's role in establishing the method in America. Most of the pictures in the book were obviously taken in daylight; the preface asserted many were taken by flashlight. A further irony was the sermon-like introduction written by Rev. Lymen Abbott, who was both pastor of the Plymouth Church, where Riis had given one of his first illustrated lectures, and editor of the magazine *Outlook,* which later published some thirty-five articles by Riis. The book's text turned out to be just another attempt to titillate a thrill-seeking audience. One of its authors was the superintendent of the New York police detective bureau, a Mulberry Street colleague about whom Riis had decidedly mixed feelings. "Byrnes stood for the old days that were bad," Riis wrote. "He was unscrupulous, he was for Byrnes—he was a policeman, in short, with all the failings of the trade."

Riis's first book proved there was an audience that was genuinely concerned about social conditions. Publishers clamored for more and Riis responded with a sequel. *The Children of the Poor* was published in 1892 and dedicated to his own children: "May the love that shines in their eager eyes never grow cold within them; then they shall yet grow up to give a helping hand in working out this problem which so plagues the world today." The book related individual case histories from Riis's firsthand knowledge and contained a comprehensive list of charitable institutions helping to care for children. Thanks in part to photography, Riis now had a promising new career as an author. He also had a new alliance with a fast-rising young political star, one that would help thrust Riis into the forefront of reform across the nation.

Chapter 5. *"The Most Useful Citizen"*

Shortly after the publication of his first book, *How the Other Half Lives*, Riis found on his office desk a card bearing the name Theodore Roosevelt. On the back of the card, hastily scribbled, was a one-line message saying that Roosevelt had read the book and had come to help. Years later Riis wrote, "The message was short, but it told the whole story of a man. I loved him from the day I first saw him; not ever in all the years that have passed has he failed of the promise made then. No one ever helped as he did."

Roosevelt was then just coming into political prominence. He and Riis began a friendship that followed Roosevelt's rise: president of New York City's police board, governor of New York, vice-president, president of the United States. The two men shared many of the same characteristics: personal honesty, uncompromising stubbornness, a decisiveness in seeing things through. They also were both Republicans, though Riis seldom participated in partisan politics. Originally a Democrat, he switched parties because of the corruption of Tammany Hall.

In May 1895 Roosevelt was appointed president of the city police board and began making good on his promise to Riis. He immediately asked Riis to guide him on a midnight inspection tour of police posts. On their first round they found nine out of ten patrolmen missing from their posts. Riis whipped up a story about it for the next day's paper. As a result, the entire police force woke up and stayed awake for the next two years, the duration of Roosevelt's term. During one of their middle-of-the-night tours, Riis took Roosevelt to the lodging rooms at the Church Street police station. There he told his friend the story of the most traumatic experience of his life, which had occurred at this station some twenty-five years before. The story he told already had been recounted several years before in a full-page article in the *Tribune*, "Vice Which Is Unchecked." Riis was both the author of the piece and the "poor boy" who is the victim in this story within a story. The article first describes a recent visit of two distinguished English women to the lodging rooms of the Church Street station. After painting the horrors of the lodging rooms in fulsome detail, Riis gets to the point of his story:

> The ladies turned away with loathing, after a brief look. "Is it possible," said Lady Summerset to her conductor, "for a man to sleep there a night and come out a decent, self-respecting being?" "Once, yes!" said he drily, and as they went upstairs he told them this story: "One rainy October night in the year 1870, a poor boy sat on the bulwark down by the river, hungry, footsore and drenched to the skin. He sat thinking of friends and home thousands of miles away over the sea, whom he had left six months before to go alone among strangers. He had been alone ever since, but never more so than that night. His money gone, no work to be found, he had slept in the streets for nights, too proud to appeal in his wretchedness to those who could and would help him for the sake of those over there. That day he had eaten nothing; he would die rather than beg. And one of the two he must do soon. There was the dark river, rushing at his feet; the swirl of the unseen waters whispered to him of rest and peace—it was so cold—and who was there to care, he thought bitterly. No one who would ever know. He moved a little nearer the edge, and listened more intently. Just then a little whine fell on his ear, and a cold wet face was pressed against him; a little black and tan dog that had been crouching beside him, settled in his lap. It was his only friend. He had picked it up in the street, as forlorn as himself, and it had stuck to him. Its touch recalled him to himself. He got up hastily and taking the dog in his arms went

to this same police station and asked for shelter. It was the first time he had accepted even such charity, and as he lay down on his hard plank in that room downstairs he hugged a little gold locket he wore around his neck, the last link with better days, and thought with a hard dry sob of home.

When he awoke the next morning, the locket was gone. One of the tramps who slept with him had stolen it. He went up and complained to the sergeant at the desk and the sergeant ordered him to be kicked out in the street as a liar, if not a thief. How should a tramp boy have come honestly by a gold locket? The doorman put him out as he was bidden, and when the little dog showed his teeth a policeman seized it and clubbed it to death there on the step.

"And the boy?" said one of the ladies when the story was told. "He went out to battle with the world and to conquer," was the reply. "He lived to become a useful man. That one night in the police station cured him of dreaming."

Now, as Riis related the long tale to Roosevelt, his friend turned red with anger. "Did they do that to you?" Roosevelt asked. Then he brought his clenched fists together. "I will smash them tomorrow." Roosevelt closed the police lodging rooms in February 1896, and in a single stroke ended Riis's years of battling these infamous holes. "Among all the things which I have been credited with," wrote Riis, "it is one of the few in which I really bore a strong hand. And yet it was not mine which finally wrought that great work, but a stronger and better than mine, Theodore Roosevelt's . . . we together drove in the last nail in the coffin of the bad old days."

The only time Riis may have had second thoughts about his relationship with Roosevelt came later, during the days preceding the outbreak of the Spanish-American War. When rumors began to fly that the United States planned to stop Spain's mistreatment of the Cubans, some liberal groups approached Riis to investigate the situation. They believed that the real instigators of the coming conflict were the U.S. Naval authorities looking for a pretext to seize a strategic island lying near the Caribbean ports on the path to the projected Panama Canal. Riis wrote to his sister: "I had a very good offer . . . and it would have brought me about $150 a week. . . . A large part of our population, especially in New England, do not think the war against Spain is just. The Universities, especially disapprove. It would have been my work to find out the truth and write about it." He declined to accept any position offered him, saying of he did not wish to become involved in politics. He was glad when his two sons, for physical reasons, were prevented from entering the war. The Cuban campaign wrecked Riis's career as a foreign correspondent when the Danish papers took opposite views to the American attitude. Riis was accused of being overpatriotic in his youthful enthusiasm. He retorted, "The bottom fact was the distrust of the United States that was based upon a curiously stubborn ignorance, entirely without excuse in a people of high intelligence like Danes." At the start of the war Theodore Roosevelt began outfitting a company of volunteers, the "Rough Riders," and asked Riis to help him. Riis performed routine tasks, but declined to be an official.

Later, when Roosevelt succeeded to the presidency after the assassination of William McKinley in 1901, Riis became a frequent visitor to the

White House. He was known as a personal friend of the president, a reputation that opened many doors otherwise barred to an investigative
reporter. Roosevelt wrote a stirring tribute to his friend, saying in part:

> Recently a man, well qualified to pass judgment, alluded to Mr. Jacob
> A. Riis as "the most useful citizen of New York. . . ." The countless
> evils which lurk in the dark corners of our civic institutions, which
> stalk abroad in the slums, and have their permanent abode in the
> crowded tenement houses, have met in Mr. Riis the most formidable
> opponent . . . to Mr. Riis was given, in addition to earnestness and
> zeal, the great gift of expression, the great gift of making others see
> what he saw and feel what he felt. . . .

For his part, Riis stumped ardently for Roosevelt and wrote a laudatory
campaign biography. ("It is strenuous," said a critic. "It is loud, it is fer-
vent. . . . It is hoarsely enthusiastic, and it is all pitched in one high monotonous key of laudation.") Riis never publicly differed with his friend, except
in the most roundabout way. On one occasion he told an audience:
". . . permit me to say it, that your great and splendid city has been . . .
pauperized in its citizenship by great wealth and perilous prosperity. . . .
However, this is politics, which I shall not discuss. The President of the
United States says that my opinion in that quarter is no good at all, and you
are free to adopt his view. I will endorse his views—most of the time—
anywhere."

Though Riis was most often associated with the battle against the slums,
he helped bring about reform in many areas—child labor laws, playgrounds
for schools, establishment of small neighborhood parks. One of his most
important pieces of investigative reporting may have saved thousands of
New York residents from the scourge of cholera—an exposé of the city's
contaminated water supply. The story appeared in the *Evening Sun* August
21, 1891, under the headline SOME THINGS WE DRINK. With the story were
six of his photographs, which apparently later vanished into the files of the
newspaper. "I took my camera and went up in the watershed photographing my evidence wherever I found it. Populous towns sewered directly into
our drinking water. I went to the doctors and asked how many days a vigorous cholera bacillus may live and multiply in running water. About
seven, said they. My case was made." His words and pictures led to the purchase of the extensive Croton Watershed.

Many of Riis's stories were controversial, even among progressives sympathetic to his crusades. Himself an immigrant, he occasionally spoke out
against unrestricted immigration. He knew that the tenements to which the
newcomers flocked already were dangerously overcrowded and that every
new boatload of cheap labor further depressed wage scales in the city's
sweatshops. (In sharp contrast to Riis's practical viewpoint was the brazen
bigotry of the man known as "the father of American photography," Samuel
F. B. Morse, the portrait painter and inventor of the telegraph. Morse
wanted to deny U.S. citizenship to all new immigrants, whom he labeled
"priest-ridden slaves of Ireland and Germany" and "outcast tenants of the
poor houses and prisons of Europe.")

Riis justifiably could be chided for his occasional exaggerated characterization of some groups in the polyglot population of New York. Some of his

remarks have disturbed those of us who have lent their voices in protest against the use of racial and ethnic stereotypes by public figures. My own faith in racial brotherhood was set forth in a book that I co-authored in 1945, *The Springfield Plan*. It was based on the biblical injunction "Thou shalt love thy neighbor as thyself and that, if America is to endure as a free and united country, the many races and faiths that make America must live together in mutual respect. The racist senator from Mississippi, Theodore Bilbo, so detested the book that soon after its publication he said its supporters "should be totally ostracized from decent, right-thinking and right-living white people in every community in America." In Jacob Riis's case, I am sure he wrote without malice. He had to develop a folksy style using the jargon of the lower depths where he worked. Because of his down-to-earth approach, he was read and listened to in greater degree than any of his more sophisticated colleagues. "I had no stomach for abstract discussions," he said. "I wanted to right those of them that I could reach."

Throughout the 1890's Riis continued his newspaper and magazine broadsides. His pen was the incisive edge of a growing reform movement that had been augmented by young enthusiasts who flocked to the settlement houses and other progressive new groups and institutions. Riis's stubbornly enduring single-mindedness served them as an example. Before Riis took up the cudgel, most New York reform efforts tended to ebb and flow. In the 1870's, Frank Leslie's *Illustrated Newspaper* described a lecture meeting about poverty: "The lecture was delivered to a room full of people, who listened, sympathized and went away—doing nothing." To those who got discouraged at the length of the battle, Riis would counsel patience and remind them of "the Israelites that marched seven times around Jericho and blew their horns before the walls fell."

His battle to raze the dreadful slums around the Five Points area to replace them with a park took fourteen years. His exposés helped spark the Drexel Committee Investigation of ramshackle firetrap tenements, which existed in defiance of laws relating to light, air and sanitary requirements. Riis himself sat in on the investigation and learned many of the techniques that enabled him to dig out facts for his reporting. The investigation resulted in the Small Park Act of 1887, but it took nine more years of boat-rocking by Riis and others before the infamous Mulberry Bend was replaced by a park.

The formal opening of the park was held on June 15, 1897. Riis wasn't even invited to the ceremonies, though he was formally entitled to an invitation as secretary of the Small Parks Committee, a citizens' group. He went anyway, accompanied by his fellow muckraker Lincoln Steffens. They were pleased to find thousands of boys and girls eagerly waiting for the ceremonies to start. A band played. There were speeches by the mayor and lesser dignitaries—some of whom had for years opposed the efforts of the Small Parks Committee. The final speaker was the street-cleaning commissioner, who placed credit for the park where it belonged and called for three cheers for Jacob Riis. The crowd roared, "Hooray, Jacob Riis!" Other such parks were created and Riis came to be known as "the father of the small parks movement."

New reform agencies sprang up—among them the Citizens Union and the Social Reform Club. Riis's tenacious reporting and superhuman optimism set their model of good citizenship. "Have we not all seen it? Have we not seen the boss dethroned, graft and iniquity exposed, the muckrake plied until the stench of it was sickening? Yet let us be comforted. The muck has to be raked up before it can be carted away, and the devil is not cast out without a prodigious noise. He is wedged in the doorway now, but he is going out, and that soon. It is good to live in this strenuous day that took him by the throat."

Chapter 6. Evangelist for Reform

One of the happiest and most fulfilling years in Jacob Riis's life was 1901. He and Elizabeth celebrated their silver wedding anniversary; their good friend Theodore Roosevelt became President; Tammany Hall's hold on New York City was broken by the forces of reform; his highly successful autobiography was published; and finally he felt secure enough as a writer and lecturer to give up his daily job as a newspaper reporter.

Even as his income from lectures and books grew, Riis still had to struggle to make ends meet. The family now numbered five children—Edward, Clara, John, Kate and Roger William, plus his first grandchild—and only after fifteen years of arduous effort had he managed to pay off the mortgage on their Long Island home. When friend Lincoln Steffens told him he didn't charge enough for his lectures, Riis only shrugged and turned away. As the following entry from one of his account books shows, he tended to count his blessings as well as the money. "Took in $3450.60 in 1895. Gosh what a lot of money. Where did it all go to? I am . . . earning as much as I ever will, with nothing going in the bank for a rainy day. . . . Let us see what I have against it: a good wife, the best that ever lived, good children, none of whom will ever be rich, but all of whom I hope and believe, will be always good, standing up for the right and fight for it if need be. A place of usefulness for myself, friends, good and true—what more can a man want?"

Riis's autobiography *The Making of an American* sold out two editions in three weeks. It was the ideal saga of an immigrant boy who had made good. What's more, it told in detail the story of the rich girl he had lost and then regained, including a chapter by Elizabeth herself on their long courtship. One critic attacked Riis's "little regard for dignity or domestic privacy," but readers loved the romance of the book and Elizabeth became a kind of national figure in her own right. By August 1902 Riis had yet another book out, *The Battle with the Slum*, which was dedicated to Theodore Roosevelt as a record of the battles they waged together. The book contained much material that Riis already had published in magazines—slum life, the inadequacies of schools and playgrounds, exploitation of little children who worked at home, the slave labor system in the sweatshops. The book also carried his reminiscenses of the wretched alleyways, the notorious landmarks of human degradation now long gone—Battle Alley, Kerosene Row, Poverty Gap, Bandit's Roost, Thieves' Alley, Hell's Kitchen, Cat Alley. "It thrills you as much as the most exciting romance," said one critic, "and for far better purpose. Its brief, crackling sentences tell of the noblest most high minded, most desperate fight ever waged—that for decency, cleanliness, and a chance to breathe and live like a man."

There were now seven books by Riis, some in several editions. They were on the lists of recommended reading in schools and libraries, and their homespun philosophy was often quoted by sociologists and reformers.

Riis's observations may seem commonplace today, but they were radical in his time. Some examples:

> The tenement is a destroyer of home and character, of the individuality that makes character tell. A homeless city—a city without civic pride, without citizen virtue is a despoiler of children, a destroyer of the tomorrow.

> You cannot make a good citizen out of the lad whom you denied a chance to kick a ball across lots when that was his ambition and his right; it takes a whole boy to make a whole man.

> A man cannot be expected to live like a pig and vote like a man.

> The very enforcement of law has sometimes seemed a travesty: the boy who steals fifty cents is sent to the House of Correction; the man who steals a railroad goes free.

> The bad environment becomes the heredity of the next generation, given the crowd, you have the slum ready-made.

> There is needed only the strong and informed public opinion that sees clearly the peril, to set a barrier against the inroads of the slum. Without that we fight in vain.

> Our country has grown great—our cities wealthy—but in their slums lurk poverty and bitterness—bitterness because the promise has not been kept that every man should have an even chance to start with.

> The poor we shall have always with us, but the slum we need not have. These two do not rightfully belong together. Their present partnership is at once poverty's worst hardship and our worst blunder.

> Every baby is entitled to one pair of mother's arms.

By the early 1900's the writings of Riis, Steffens and the other muckrakers had popularized the subject of social reform. New national organizations sprang forth to serve as clearinghouses for reform projects of every kind. At a gathering of the National Conference of Charities and Corrections, representatives from all over the country came to give testimony about the many movements under way. Civic leaders everywhere regarded Riis as an expert who could give them encouragement and point the way to enactment of practical reforms in their cities and towns. So Riis left his familiar slum battleground in New York and became a nationwide evangelist for reform. He had learned on one of his early ventures out of the city that his crusade was needed everywhere. "Standing . . . on a mountainside in New Hampshire with a matchless view stretched out before me, I said to my friend, the good rector . . . Here everybody must surely be good. How can they help it? He looked at me sadly and said, pointing to the scattered farms lying so peacefully in the landscape: 'If you could go with me into those homes and see the things I see in many of them you would quit your Mulberry Bend and transfer your battle with the slum to our hillside!'"

Each of Riis's two main activities were of twenty-five years' duration. He became a full-fledged reporter in 1876 and gave it up in 1901. He started to lecture in 1888 and continued through 1913. "Now my winters are spent on the lecture platform altogether," he wrote after leaving newspaper work. "I always liked the work. It tires less than the office routine and you feel the touch with fellows more than when you sit and write your message." At the height of his popularity Riis kept three lecture bureaus busy. His engagements sometimes brought him as much as $150 per lecture, though part of the proceeds went for transportation and lodging. All would have been well but for his failing health. For some time he had experienced painful attacks, which he attributed to indigestion brought on by hastily swallowed meals. He finally consulted a doctor who found a serious heart condition, angina pectoris. In an epilogue for a new edition of *The Making of an American*, Riis's grandson, Dr. J. Riis Owre, described the intensity of his grandfather's lecture schedule: "The first of his long lecture tours began in January 1902. It took him from East to the Middle West and back again to New England. According to his pocket diary for 1902, some seventy lectures were scheduled in the period from Jan. 2 to April 11—a rigorous schedule for one who had had a major heart attack only two years earlier."

Despite his poor health and advancing years—he was now in his fifties—Riis liked the lecture circuit. The warmth of his audiences made him optimistic about the future of reform. In an article entitled "Experiences of Popular Lecturer," he related some causes for optimism:

> I was to lecture at Cedar Falls and was laid up at a Junction, waiting for my train. At the lunchtable were three typical Iowa farmers, all bound for the lecture. They are great people. I have known them to travel forty miles across the frozen prairie to hear a lecturer in whom they were interested. In that same winter I spoke in a little town a dozen miles beyond the bluffs of the Mississippi River, where the population, men, women, and children, numbered three hundred. To my amazed inquiry of where the audience was to come from, the manager of the lecture said simply, "You wait." And when at night I found the hall jammed with a crowd that numbered at least six hundred, he took me to the window and pointed to a great host of teams and wagons below. Some of them had come from the next county. I have sometimes wondered how they got home. When I started at four in the morning a sleet-storm was raging, with the snow lying foot-deep. . . . I go across the country in the course of the winter sometimes twice. And I record without hesitation my conviction that we are very much awake. The evidence is, on every hand, that the people are thinking. . . . Every day it is brought home to us that we "belong," that as people we have to solve our problems together since apart we never can. . . . Compare that, now, with the day that was, when we in my city stood by unprotesting while a church that had grown wealthy moved uptown from Mulberry Street, trading off its House of God to the devil in human shape of conscienceless builders who cut it up into rooms and filled it with tenants who in their cubbyholes knew neither light nor air and died like flies. . . . I have struggled with the Mulberry Bend and seen it go down . . . all about me I see the dawn breaking. Are we gaining? Here, yesterday, came a letter asking me to come to Scranton, where they are getting ready to give the children playgrounds. They wanted me to help. . . . Do you wonder that I think we are gaining?

Riis did not have to vary his lectures greatly since his audiences were widely scattered around the country. He banged away at the same basic stories, as he did in his writing, building on true stories from his personal experience. One of his favorite subjects was the "Battle with the Slum" of the 1880's and 90's, the struggle that resulted in the passage of many reforms. He would preface the show of his lantern slides with these prophetic words: "Think not that any of them are irrelevant because of things that were. Those things are but shadows of what may come again, if we lose our grip and once more let our conscience fall asleep, believing that we have done so much that all is well." Another lecture was "Tony," the story of a boy of the streets who needed help if he was to grow up as a useful member of society. His words described the suffering of the poor; his photographs, blown up large on the projection screen, brought home the reality of it.

In January 1905 Riis took time out from his lectures to attend the second inauguration of his friend Teddy Roosevelt. Elizabeth and the children were already in Washington waiting for him, and it was a big day for all of them. Riis felt a sense of personal triumph—he had campaigned for Roosevelt and his biography of the President had sold widely and contributed to his friend's victory. In March he left home again for a two-month lecture tour. This time he went on the road reluctantly; Elizabeth had been ill for several weeks and he was worried. He was nearing the end of the tour when the urgent telegram reached him. He hurried home to find the entire family assembled: Kate and young Roger William who lived at home, Clara from her nearby home, Edward from California, John from Colorado. Riis's diary tells the story: "May 5—Dr. Jewett came. Said lungs involved. May 6—Dr. . . . said Bronchial-Pneumonia. May 18—Lammeth died. God help us all." "Lammeth" means little lamb in Danish; it was the nickname he had given to Elizabeth on their first Christmas together when, to cheer up his homesick wife, he had brought her a picture of the Good Shepherd protecting his flock. The tenderness of the scene had made him think of her, and from that day on he had called her by no other name. Elizabeth was buried at Maple Grove Cemetery, in sight of their home.

Newspapers across the country carried long obituaries and from the White House came a telegram: BELOVED FRIEND: IN THE TERRIBLE ELEMENTAL GRIEF NO ONE, NO MATTER HOW CLOSE, CAN GIVE ANY REAL COMFORT. . . . YOU KNOW HOW MY WIFE AND I LOVED THE DEAR, DEAR ONE WHO HAS GONE BEFORE YOU; YOU KNOW HOW WE LOVE YOU, HOW WE THINK OF YOU, HOW WE FEEL FOR YOU IN YOUR CRUSHING CALAMITY. THE LIFE OF YOU TWO WAS AN IDEAL LIFE. . . .

Riis was overcome by grief. "I can hardly weep any more," he wrote to a friend. "But in the still of night-watches the loneliness of it all comes upon me and it is dreadful. Still I shall try to take up a man's work and do it, and so it may be that the road shall not seem so long or so hard anymore. . . ." Two months after her death, Riis took up his work. He wrote a magazine article, spoke at memorial services for a friend and resumed a heavy lecture schedule. Nothing could break him, but the next two years were an ordeal of constant travel and deep loneliness. Other things went wrong. His older children were not doing well and depended on him for support. The two youngest were boarded out and needed care and planned education. Expenses mounted and, because of his failing health, he worried more than ever about money. The house in Richmond Hill was rented: the family scattered.

Chapter 7. The Last Years

In the spring of 1907 Riis broke the news of his plans to remarry. To his son John he wrote: ". . . the nest is empty, and I am a lonely homeless man. . . . Miss Phillips is thirty, and she is a woman who has seen much of life. Like myself, she longs for a home. . . . Sometime in late summer we will quietly marry." And to his younger daughter: ". . . I too have to begin over again, and it is well so, for a man may not lay down his work and still live. . . . I shall do my best, and be glad for the old home and for a voice at the gate to hail my coming."

Mary Phillips was twenty-eight years younger than Riis, a St. Louis society girl who had heard one of his lectures and been greatly impressed by his sincerity and dedication. She became his secretary and, during his time of grief, an energetic and cheerful companion. A native of Memphis, she grew up in St. Louis where her father was president of the cotton exchange. She finished her education in England and France and had a short stint as an actress in New York. Riis considered himself fortunate to have merited a woman so much younger than he. There is a letter that he wrote to her five months after Elizabeth's death addressed "Dearest girl" and signed with an informality unusual for Riis: "So long, sweet—your old Jake."

Dr. Owre speaks warmly of his step-grandmother: ". . . she had a rare and beautiful zest for living; there were few things that did not arouse her curiosity. . . ." She and Riis had waited a year and a half before deciding to marry, and Dr. Owre indicates she must have had reservations even then. She told Dr. Owre in 1964: "I really did not love your grandfather, when I married him. I admired him enormously. I was fascinated by him. He was the most exciting man I had ever met, but I did not love him. It was not until several months later, when I went to meet him on one of his lecture tours, that I realized I really loved him." Dr. Owre notes that Riis's second marriage was thus not unlike his first: "Devotion and admiration and respect and loneliness . . . were to turn into mutual love—adoration even—and what followed was to be an idyll." (Many years later Mary Riis made refreshingly clear that her husband was no saint: "I've heard a little swearing, of course, but nothing to compare with Jake, the first time I heard his anger aroused. His swearing simply swept me off my feet.")

After a brief honeymoon late in the summer, Riis brought his bride to Richmond Hill and the old home was opened again. Under Mary, the home's Danish atmosphere gradually became distinctly American, but its friendliness and courtesy did not change. Once again it was a house open to Riis's friends and a refuge where he could write and relax. His youngest son Roger William—known as "Vivi"—had a home to come to from boarding school. Mary took to the boy immediately, an affection that developed into a lifelong friendship. Riis himself went at his work with renewed zeal. He planned another book and a trip to Europe, wrote magazine articles and resumed his lectures. Thanks to his wide-ranging lecture tours, he now wrote knowledgeably about the entire country. In 1908 his articles included "Heading off the Slums in the West," "How Helena Became a City," "Playgrounds in Washington and Elsewhere" and "The Plight of St. Louis."

The contrasting roles played by Riis's two wives are revealed in a letter he wrote to his sister. Of Elizabeth he wrote: "She made me all that I am. It isn't much, but it is her work. . . . There was always something sacred about her to me. . . ." Of Mary: ". . . of an entirely different sphere than myself—but I saw the genuine true soul in her, and I was not mistaken." He made special note of her acute business sense: "I have always written my stories and let them pay what they thought them worth. Mary told me they did not pay enough. That never occurred to me. At her request I notified them all to pay me hereafter 5 cents a word. They yelled yes! and just begged me to write. But heretofore everybody paid me 1½ or 2 cents a word."

In the summer of 1908 Jacob and Mary went to Germany, taking young Roger William with them. Riis's heart had been giving him trouble, and they hoped that the famous baths at Nauheim would help him. From Germany they went to his hometown Ribe, where Mary met his relatives and friends. While in Ribe, Riis gathered research for a book about the town and his own youth. Back home, rested and feeling better, he finished the book by late fall and it was published the following year as *The Old Town*. The illustrations in the book were freely drawn, unlike several previous Riis books, which carried line drawings or halftones from his photographs. The drawings were by Vladyslaw T. Benda, a well-known American artist. The antiquarian at the Museum of Ribe, Mogens Bencard, noted that the drawings were a "mixture of free version of old photographs and Riis' and Benda's combined imagination."

Mary Riis, pleased that the trip abroad had reinvigorated her husband, encouraged him to write more about his native land. He decided to undertake a volume of short biographies of some Danish heroes. The project, quite different from his previous writing based on personal experience, required researching old records that could be found only in Copenhagen. In the summer of 1910 they sailed for Denmark. They again visited Ribe, where the entire town gave them a very warm reception, and the baths at Nauheim. The trip home was leisurely and took them through Switzerland and Italy, with short stopovers in Greece, Algiers and Spain.

Riis felt better, but he continued to fret about finances. When he remarried, Mary had insisted he put his savings in trust for his children. She did not want to be the beneficiary of his years of hard work and self-denial. Now, wrote Dr. Owre, "he knew his earning years were limited and every cent thus expended diminished the provision he wanted to make for his wife. It was a problem that was to be with him to the end of his days—one of those unhappy mixtures of economics and personality for which there was no solution."

The family's decision to move to the country added to the financial worries. Richmond Hill was no longer the open, quiet country that they wanted. In Barre, Massachusetts, they found and bought Pine Brook Acres, a hundred-year-old house and two hundred acres, and set about restoring both house and land. "The next May," Dr. Owre wrote, "Mary and Jake established themselves there, in a tent while the house was being renovated and for the summer only, since there was no furnace. It was an adventure, a new experience, for both. Mary was the farmer. She pored over textbooks, planted twenty acres of potatoes, planted apple trees, picked potato bugs, bossed farm hands, began to recondition the soil by raising clover and rye and vetch and plowing them under."

Restoration of the farm was expensive and Riis would not slacken his lecture pace. In the late summer of 1912 he interrupted his lecture tour to stump for Teddy Roosevelt, who hoped his party would nominate him for a second full term in the White House. Riis's diary shows that, from September 16 to October 24, he spoke in fifteen cities for Roosevelt—often three and four times a day. Now past sixty, he found the lecture trips more and more tiring. He was dissatisfied with the bookings provided by his agents: they were too few and too many miles apart. In the early fall, in a letter to his daughter, Riis appeared resigned to slowing down: "My heart is very much enlarged and has only a small margin to run on. . . . I expect henceforth to limit my activities and, as far as possible, to let my lecturing go. It is too bad—a couple of years more would have put our farm on a paying basis so that we might live off, and on it. . . ."

Riis fulfilled his current lecture engagement, then returned to the sanitarium in Battle Creek, Michigan, where he had previously gone for a rest. In November he went on a short speaking tour, a trip eased by the companionship of his wife. Toward Christmas they returned to New York and rented an apartment. He felt well enough in early December to cover for three New York newspapers the proceedings of the National House Conference in Philadelphia. He also wrote an article for *The Century* under the old familiar title "The Battle with the Slum." The article acknowledged the gains made in the past twenty-five years but appealed for an intensified fight against sweatshops and the elimination of bad housing conditions, which were conducive to the spread of tuberculosis. Riis was particularly concerned about that dread disease; it had claimed the lives of six of his brothers. Christmas in New York was an unusually cheerful one. He loved the holiday season, wrote many stories about it and originated several new American Christmas traditions, including the idea of Christmas seals for the benefit of tuberculosis research. This holiday season he and Mary attended a Riis-inspired New York ritual—the huge New Year's celebration in Madison Square where 100,000 gathered to sing songs that were projected onto enormous screens with stereopticons.

The following spring Riis completed another lecture tour, then spent the summer at Pine Brook Farm. Mary's mother had come to live with them. Roger William was home from college. Riis's other children made frequent visits. In December he wrote to his sister: "Yes, I am well again and I have been out lecturing. But you are right. I cannot do it the way I could before and the risk is really too great. On the last journey I caught a terrible cold. Had that turned into pneumonia it would have been over with my heart. But it is, of course, my livelihood." He went again to the sanitarium in Battle Creek, then took up his lecture tour to Chicago, and south through Texas and Louisiana. In New Orleans he collapsed and hurried back to Battle Creek, where he came down with bronchitis. Mary's last letter to her husband begged him to discontinue the tour and come home: "Billy and I have had a long talk about money, and we both feel that you must give up this lecturing entirely. We will slowly build up a good farm business and a preserve business and in a few years we will be really well off. Don't ever think that you are a burden to me, heart of my heart, you are my reason for living, my joy of life."

Early in May, she received urgent word from her husband in the sanitarium. Though spent with his illness, he wanted to come home. She and Roger William rushed to Battle Creek to bring him back. "The railroad journey was almost more than his strength could endure," wrote Dr. Owre. "Then came the automobile trip, over a rough road. Just before they came in sight of the farm, Riis collapsed again. He rallied briefly, and then began to lose strength each day. Friends gathered and messages of sympathy poured in. Riis fell into a coma; occasionally he was able to recognize those around him. On May 26, 1914, he died . . . he was . . . buried, as he had specified, under an unmarked granite boulder in the cemetery situated down the hill from the farm."

Chapter 8. An Epilogue

Long before his death, Jacob Riis had ended his career as photographer. There is no evidence that he made pictures for his own use after 1898. He had prepared a sufficient number of lantern slides for his lectures; by his pragmatic standards, he had no further need for the new craft he had taught himself. On his visits to Ribe he purchased pictures of whatever Danish scenes he required for lectures and books. In his ledger there are entries for two such purchases. He apparently did not make family snapshots. I asked Dr. Owre about his grandfather's photographic activities and received the following reply: "I don't remember my mother or my aunts and uncles talking of their father as a photographer. . . . In his letters—I have read most of them—he never mentions a camera. He bought post cards of scenes he liked. I remember when he visited us in Minneapolis in 1912, and I am sure I should have remembered him taking pictures if he had done so."

While his photography was quickly forgotten, Riis's voluminous writings and other papers took their place in major libraries and archives, including the Library of Congress. In addition to his letters and diaries, there were fifteen books, more than one hundred magazine articles and at least two hundred major newspaper feature stories—plus the countless newspaper reports that were unsigned and difficult to attribute to him. As the years went by, even the reputation of Riis the writer and reformer became obscured by the worldwide tumult of events. By modern times his name was scarcely known, except for a park and a settlement house in New York and a boulder with a plaque in Riis Park in Chicago bearing the name Jacob Riis.

I first became interested in Riis in 1941 when a book critic compared my own work to that of the great muckraker. I knew that there were certain similarities in our lives—both of us were immigrants, both of us were involved in social reform. In a secondhand bookstore I found Riis's autobiography and discovered that we had something else in common. I came to the page where Riis described how he learned about taking pictures by flashlight and became a photographer. The next morning I rushed to the bookstores along the Bowery, where Riis had spent many of his newspaper days. Among the half-dozen Riis books I found—all of them long out of print—was How the Other Half Lives. The title page bore the confirmation I sought: "With illustrations chiefly from photographs taken by the author."

Though a documentary photographer for many years and a teacher of the subject, I had not heretofore learned of Riis's photography. Nor had I seen old photographs that could compare with the simple, powerful immediacy of those in his books. Seeking Riis photographs, I went to the Museum of the City of New York, the New-York Historical Society, the New York Public Library, city and social agencies and finally the Jacob A. Riis Neighborhood Settlement House. I could not find a single Riis photograph; I could not find anyone who knew anything about his photography. My search widened. I inquired of the Library of Congress, the Smithsonian, the George Eastman Museum of Photography. I contacted photo agencies, newspaper morgues, manufacturers of lantern slides. I checked books and magazines devoted to photography during the years from 1880 to 1900. Not one mentioned Riis.

Finally, in January 1942, I located Jacob Riis's second wife Mary and sent her a letter. To identify myself, I noted that I was the photo editor of *Common Ground*, the publication of the Common Council for American Unity, of which she was a member of the board of directors. I told her that I was most eager to bring to light her husband's photography and asked if she had his negatives. When no reply came, I telephoned Mrs. Riis at her office in a Wall Street brokerage firm. She said she was too busy to talk then. After months of unsuccessful attempts to discuss the matter with her by phone, I was referred by Mrs. Riis to her stepson Roger William Riis. I had a long talk with Roger William at his Fifth Avenue public relations office. He agreed that his father's pictures ought to be found and put to some use, but said he had no idea where they were and doubted they could be found. I sensed that he wondered why I was so interested. At any rate, he promised to see what he could find. Later I learned that the Riis family had been rather careless with memorabilia: among the first editions that I picked up in secondhand bookshops was a copy of *The Old Town* inscribed to the eldest son, "Edward Riis, affectionately, from his father, Jacob A. Riis."

Over the next few years I kept up my search for the Riis negatives. I rummaged without success through antique and junk shops, finding in the process a number of other old glass-plate negatives that enriched my own collection of early photographs. The war was on and I went off on frequent assignments to take photographs for military training manuals. I also completed my book *American Counterpoint*, a photographic study of American ethnic groups, and began discussions for an exhibition of the original prints at the Museum of the City of New York.

I stayed in touch with Roger William Riis, but there was no new information. He was always very gracious and kept my hopes up. In 1945 I went to see him again. Together we reconstructed Jacob Riis's whereabouts shortly before his death and concluded that the negatives and lantern slides must have been left on the farm in Massachusetts. I suggested Roger William should visit Pine Brook Farm to search the attic where some of his father's personal effects were stored after the funeral.

At this point, my frustration was mounting. The many years of procrastination by the Riis family led me to resort to a slightly devious strategy. I suggested to Miss Grace Mayer, a curator at the Museum of the City of New York, that she write Riis saying that the museum was trying to locate his father's pictures. A month later Riis brought to the museum a box containing 163 lantern slides which had been found at the farm. I was delighted to see the old pictures in any form and began work in the darkroom. Lantern slides are positive images; they must be converted into negatives from which prints can be reproduced. Many of the slides were cracked, faded or discolored. These had to be enlarged into paper negatives and turned into positives through contact printing so that the damage could be retouched. Only then could they be photographed as negatives and the final prints made. After several months of tedious work I had a portfolio of satisfactory prints. I rushed them to the office of *U.S. Camera*, certain that the editors would want to break the news of my discovery in their 1947 Annual. Two months later I received an apologetic note saying, "Although the story is good, the decision is, unfortunately, in the negative."

I was perplexed but decided to prepare a brief monograph that would include Riis's photographs, a condensed biography and the story of discovering his work. I asked my secretary to type the manuscript without making copies. Alas, the young lady was more disposed to helping a friend than being loyal to her employer. It soon came to my attention that a popular photographic magazine had accepted a feature on Jacob Riis and scheduled it for publication. The author had thinly disguised what I had written and added a number of paragraphs from Riis's own writings. As it turned out, publication of his piece was delayed and was not the first account of Riis's photography to appear.

Then occurred the event that made worthwhile my nearly five years of searching, prodding and hoping. Some time before, I had suggested to Roger William Riis that he look for the negatives in the old family house in Richmond Hill on Long Island. He promised to alert the occupants. A few months later the house was sold and about to be torn down. The owners, rummaging around the attic, found stored between the rafters the priceless photographs of Jacob Riis—412 glass negatives, 161 lantern slides and 193 prints. They took the collection to Roger William's home in Manhattan and, finding no one there, left it outside the door.

On November 15, 1946, R. W. Riis presented the collection to the Museum of the City of New York. Now the road was open for presenting his father's photography to the world. Miss Mayer, curator of prints, and I decided an exhibit of his prints should open the following May, the month of Riis's birth. I selected fifty negatives I considered to be most representative of his work and began preparing prints. At first I was dismayed when I saw the original negatives. In his haste to bring before the public the evidence contained in his negatives, Riis had neglected to fix and wash them properly and some had deteriorated. The negatives presented an even more serious problem, which required a carefully controlled method of printing. In Riis's day, photographic emulsion was not as sensitive to all colors as it is in modern film. It did not reproduce tonal values correctly and, as a result, parts of the negatives were either overexposed or underexposed, thus creating unnatural contrast. If an old glass negative is held up to the light, the image is seen in full detail because our eyes concentrate on the darker areas while skimming over the lighter ones. In printing from such negatives, however, an even exposure does not render the gradation of tones from black to white in the same relationship as they appear to the eye. Riis could not possibly have visualized precisely the entire gamut of values that would appear in the final prints. He was totally unaware of the "interrelation of the three principal variables—subject brightness, exposure and development"—and I don't think he was much concerned about technical perfection in his photographs. In making lantern slides, Alfred Stieglitz worked out ingenious chemical techniques for controlling contrast and tone and a means of expanding the range of values by the use of a mask. In printing Riis's negatives, I similarly controlled the exposure by masking out various parts.

Meanwhile, my search for additional historical material to enhance the show led me to a trunk filled with Riis manuscripts and letters at the New York Public Library. I first heard about the trunk from Mitchell Kennerley, a pioneer in publishing and exhibiting photographs. He told me the first of three dramatically different versions of how the trunk had come to the library. His story had it that agents of the library had snatched the manuscripts and letters from the Massachusetts farm while Riis's family were still at his funeral. Another version came from Riis's grandson Dr. Owre, who heard it from the former chief of the library's research section. This man told him that many years ago, hearing that tenants of the farm were using Riis's papers to light fires, he had sent agents to rescue the papers. The third version was related to me by Paul R. Rugen, the library's keeper of manuscripts. According to Rugen, the library had learned of the papers in 1936 from Jacob Riis Praeger, president of the Jacob A. Riis Youth Foundation in Boston. "The farm at Barre was owned (not rented)," said Rugen, "and the story of 'using the Riis papers to light fires' would appear to be apocryphal."

The show was announced as "Special Exhibition, 'The Battle With the Slum,' 1887–1897. Fifty Prints by Alexander Alland from the original negatives by Jacob A. Riis, presented to the Museum by Roger William Riis. May 20 through September 14, 1947." In her introduction for the show Miss Mayer wrote:

> About 5 years ago Alexander Alland—himself engaged in the battle for which Jacob A. Riis gave his life—made a discovery that eventual led to the present exhibition. Searching for early pictorial records of the lives of newcomers to America's shore, he came upon a group of illustrations by Jacob A. Riis that antedated all others. Searching further, he established the fact that Jacob A. Riis was the first journalist photographer to make use of the flashlight to document the social scene. Through Alexander Alland's efforts the monumental Riis Collection was rediscovered and generously given to the Museum by Roger William Riis. As a labor of love, Alexander Alland has made the fifty exhibition prints from the fading 4 × 5 glass negatives, brilliantly surmounting the most difficult technical problems to bring back these epic documents of the eighties and nineties to fight again "The Battle With the Slum."

Much credit for the show must go to Miss Mayer, whose labors far exceeded her normal duties as a curator. She did painstaking research for the preparation of captions, the introduction and publicity for the show. For text that appeared with each picture, she extracted lengthy passages from Riis's copious writing. This approach made each photograph an independent unit, which then reinforced the other photographs so as to create an intensely fascinating narrative.

From the start the show was one of the most popular ever held at the museum. It was not dismantled until January 1948, long beyond the scheduled closing date. Beaumont Newhall said in his *History of Photography:* "The photographs are direct and penetrating, as raw as the sordid scenes which they so often represent. Riis chose unerringly the camera stand which would most effectively tell the story." Newhall commented to me when he first saw the prints: "I was bowled over by the Riis prints . . . Miss Mayer showed me some of the original negatives, and I could quickly see that you have done wonders with them." The 1948 *U.S. Camera Annual,* which devoted ten pages to the Riis pictures, called them "one of the greatest sets of documentary pictures in American photographic history."

I wanted the whole world to know about the pictures. Years of research had convinced me that most of the material in museums is relegated to oblivion and seen by few. I did not want this to happen to Riis. I knew that he would have wanted his pictures used by reform forces in furtherance of his lifelong crusade. I outlined my intentions to Roger William Riis— traveling shows, magazine articles, lectures, a book—and he acknowledged approval. At the outset of our association he had written to me: ". . . anything you wish to do with my father's pictures and slides, is entirely agreeable to me. . . ."

To expedite wide distribution of Riis's photographs here and abroad, I engaged a reputable photo agency. Within a few months, features on Riis were accepted by publications in Holland, Sweden and America. Then came an unexpected snag. The editors of *Harper's Bazaar* questioned my agent's right to sell Riis's photos in view of the fact that the same pictures were being released by the museum free of charge. The museum had assured me that Riis's negatives would be given out only to me, and I had taken it for granted that all requests for his photographs would be referred to me. I conveyed to Roger William Riis my fears that indiscriminate release of the photographs by the museum might jeopardize their meaningful use. He responded immediately with a request to the museum: ". . . as to the use of my father's negatives or photos . . . I think there should be one condition, in justice to Mr. Alland, and the marked service he has performed on his own initiative and at his own expense: I believe that when the Museum receives a request for use of those negatives or photos from a profitmaking concern, such as a magazine or newspaper, the request should go through Mr. Alland . . . he ought to have a chance to recoup a little, at least, in exchange for his great services to history and to the city."

My attempts to preserve the Riis photographic heritage in other museums ran into difficulties at first. New York's Metropolitan Museum of Art and the Museum of Modern Art both offered thanks and regrets. I was more successful at the New-York Historical Society, which now has some 150 Riis prints I made from the original negatives, along with several hundred prints made from my own collection of historical glass plates by other early photographers. The lack of foresight shown by some museums was not greatly surprising to me. Too often such institutions as the Library of Congress ask that photographers and artists bequeath them important documents and artifacts. This practice is unfair and undignified and does not ensure a flow of valuable materials into our national museums and archives. What is needed is a U.S. Department of Antiquity; until that day, Congress should earmark annual monies for acquiring historical material. As it stands now, many treasures are in danger of being lost. Once, I was present in the office of a museum when someone telephoned to offer for sale a photographic collection found in the attic of an old Dutch colonial house. The caller was advised that the museum did not have funds for such purchases but did accept gifts. I spoke to the caller and acquired, for a token payment, the work of a very skilled photographer, the one-time secretary of Stieglitz's New York Camera Club.

Even the Museum of the City of New York, home of the Riis Collection, failed to give full and proper acknowledgment of the manner in which the photographs were saved. In the fall of 1973 I wrote to the director, Joseph Veach Noble: "I am proud that I have made a noteworthy contribution to the preservation of our Nation's and the City of New York's historical heritage, and I think that the users of Riis' pictures should also be aware of it. . . ." He responded by awarding me the museum's commemorative medal and acknowledging "a debt to you which the Museum can never adequately repay." Writing of the museum's "expanding years" 1932–1959, Albert K. Baragwanath, senior curator, noted that among the great treasures of New York history that came to the museum during these years were Eugene O'Neill's manuscripts, a complete room with Duncan Phyfe furniture, a man's suit worn to Washington's Inaugural Ball, and the negatives taken by Jacob Riis. (The question of the museum's right to the Riis Collection was raised by Riis's wife long before her death at the age of ninety. Nothing came of her letter to the museum, though the man who was then director was prepared to battle it out in the courts if she brought suit. Mrs. Riis received no remuneration for the use of her husband's pictures.)

The rediscovery of Riis's photographs sparked a long resurgence of interest in the great reformer. The Riis Collection, one of the most popular in America, has averaged nearly five hundred print requests a year for the past twenty years—for books, exhibitions, films and classrooms. They are used here and abroad to promote the cause of human decency. In Denmark an exhibition of his pictures—including the showing of a film in which Dr. Owre and I participated—toured some thirty-five cities. Riis's old Richmond Hill home was designated a National Historic Landmark in 1971 by the U.S. Department of Interior—through the efforts of Felix J. Cuervo, president of the Native New Yorkers Historical Association. A commemorative plaque was purchased with contributions from schoolchildren, but when the owner of the house refused to cooperate Mr. Cuervo had to nail the plaque to a tree. The plaque was lost when municipal workers trimmed the tree. Two years after being declared a landmark, the house was razed to make way for new homes. Not long after, Riis's dollhouse-like study, with its teakwood walls and handsome fireplace, also fell to the bulldozer.

But many years before, in 1949, occurred two events that fittingly memorialized the two essential aspects of Jacob Riis which have concerned me—photographer and citizen. One was a huge show at the Museum of Modern Art called "The Exact Instant," for which Edward Steichen assembled more than 300 photographs covering camera reporting for the past century. The list of 180 photographers included many celebrities. Most of them were represented by one or two prints; Jacob Riis had six. The publicity release for the show mentioned only four names and said of Riis's work, "a camera crusade never surpassed." Never before had there been space for Riis in a group photographic show; indeed, the museum previously had refused to buy his original prints. Now here he was holding his own among the five-star generals of photography. I watched large groups of people absorbed in his pictures. I was thrilled—for he was my "protégé." Later when I asked Roger William Riis if he had seen the show, he replied, "Yes, you bet, I got the notice of the Modern Arters and realized that all this springs out of the Alland pioneering."

The second event that year went beyond the parochial concerns of photography as an art and honored Riis the citizen. New York's Mayor William O'Dwyer proclaimed Jacob A. Riis Week in honor of the man who "gave to New York and to all America a newer and wider sense of civic conscience and responsibility." A dinner commemorating Riis's one hundredth birthday was held at the Waldorf Astoria. Inviting me to serve on the sponsoring committee Roger William Riis wrote: ". . . there will be many glittering stuffed shirts on the Committee, that is why we want an occasional unstuffed shirt." Speakers representing every segment of New York's peoples praised the citizenship of Jacob Riis, which had brought the city better housing, parks and playgrounds. I too felt honored, for Riis's photography was mentioned from the rostrum. Many years have passed since that night when I sat and listened to the speakers ring out the words of Jacob Riis. Today his words and his pictures speak to us with a power undiminished by the passing years. They speak, as Riis himself put it, with the power of fact—"the mightiest lever of this or of any day."

JAMES B. LANE

From Jacob A. Riis and the American City[†]

4. How the Other Half Lives

It was not unnatural, considering his personal ordeals in America, his newspaper career, and his interest in urban reform movements, that Jacob Riis became the preeminent publicist for bridging the chasm between the rich and the poor. For over a decade he had perfected his attention-getting style of writing in the rough-and-tumble world of his Mulberry Street beat. He experimented with photography as a journalistic tool to capture the essence of slum life. An immigrant who suffered many of the indignities of poverty himself, he nevertheless shared most of the values of his middle and upper class audience. All these experiences went into his first book, *How the Other Half Lives*. Merging his vocation with his reform work, Riis became one of the first crusaders for a moral and political awakening to the virulent consequences of urbanization.

THE OTHER HALF: LECTURES, PHOTOGRAPHS AND ARTICLES

In 1888 Riis became interested in presenting illustrated lectures on life in New York's slums. The idea came to him during a tour which he took with sanitation inspectors. Riis later wrote that the sights he saw "gripped my heart until I felt that I must tell of them, or burst, or turn anarchist, or something." Remembering the stereopticon displays that he had given a decade earlier in Brooklyn, he decided that photographs would best attract attention to the horrid conditions. His first attempt to speak misfired. After failing to interest his own church in listening to him, he angrily resigned his post as deacon. On 25 January 1888 he made his first address to a club of amateur photographers to which he belonged on the topic of "The Other Half, How It Lives and Dies in New York." The New York *Tribune* reported that Riis was so ingenious in his descriptions and "brought to his task such a vein of humor that after two hours every one wished that there was more of the exhibition, sad as much of it was."

---

† Kennikat Press, 1964. Pages 46–68. Reprinted by permission of the author.

Just as Riis was putting together his lecture, he learned about a German invention of a new flash lighting process that enabled the camera to capture dark indoor scenes that heretofore had been inaccessible to its eye. In February 1888 Riis and three friends tested the idea in the interior of tenements and lodging houses. The experiment's success meant that for the first time he could present indisputable evidence of the squalor in which some people lived. While explaining his discovery to members of the press, Riis excitedly told about a picture that he took inside a cheap lodging house. It reminded him of a slave ship, the New York *Sun* reported him as saying on 12 February. Here a hundred snoring and groaning tramps lay in stacks of rickety beds, polluting the air with their putrid breath.

When Dr. A. F. Schauffler, the director of the City Mission Society, heard about Riis's slides, he asked him to speak at Broadway Tabernacle. Riis's performance on 28 February impressed Schauffler and others in attendance, including the zealous moralist the Reverend Charles H. Parkhurst, and Josiah Strong, author of the influential indictment of urban ills *Our Country*. The audience afterwards donated $143.50 to the Tabernacle. Of even more consequence, Schauffler. Strong, and Parkhurst helped arrange other speaking engagements for Riis. In a letter of recommendation, Schauffler called the lecture an object lesson. He added that Riis used no material "that could shock the taste of any in the audience."

During the next nine months, Riis traveled throughout the state repeating his address. He accepted fees of from twenty-five to fifty dollars for traveling expenses and remuneration for time lost from his normal job. The pathetic revelations of misery fascinated his audiences. Sensing in this response the possibilities of marketing his material in book form, he secured a copyright to the title "The Other Half, How It Lives and Dies in New York, with One Hundred Illustrations, Photographs from Real Life, of the Haunts of Poverty and Vice in a Great City."

Yet Riis's first lectures were not a total success. Many people questioned whether the conclusions of a mere reporter were worthy of serious attention. One critic who called him a German immigrant wrote that Riis had a "peculiar, rasping voice" that distracted from the presentation. Furthermore, a considerable number of churches still closed their doors to him, saying that his topic was irrelevant to their purpose. In December when one congregation turned down his offer to speak, Riis angrily declared that churches such as this were no more sanctified than newspaper offices.

In 1889 Riis wrote several articles on the theme of the two Americas which he had enunciated in his lectures. Warning the public about the evils that the slums bred, he characterized the more than a million New York tenement dwellers as "that other half, uneasy, suffering, threatening anarchy and revolt, the despair of our statesmen and the joyful opportunity of the politician." The slums were an evil cancer born of public neglect and nurtured by private greed, Riis declared, and they "touch the family life with deadly moral contagion." In graphic and passionate phrases, he guided his readers on a tour of the tenements. "Do not stumble over the children pitching pennies in the hall," Riis wrote; "not that it would hurt them. Kicks and cuffs are their daily diet." He told of one small child whose job it was to transport beer from a saloon to workers in a nearby factory. One day the lad drank too much beer himself, fell asleep in a cellar, and was gnawed to death by rats.

In these articles Riis recommended tighter health laws, better public schools, and the prohibition of child labor as viable government programs for ameliorating the suffering of the poor. Finally he urged individuals to support the activities of private organizations such as the Children's Aid Society.

Also in 1889 Riis received $150 from *Scribner's* magazine for an article entitled "How the Other Half Lives." The phrase, originally uttered by the Frenchman Francois Rabelais, had been used by several New York writers, including John H. Griscom in his bellwether work, *The Sanitary Condition of the Laboring Population of New York* (1845). Just as his camera had helped to launch his career as a lecturer, so had his photographs caught the eye of editors more than his prose. When the article appeared in December, *Scribner's* offered to publish an expanded version of it as a book. Riis later recounted how he and Elisabeth reacted to the news that he would become an author: "I should have thought I would have shouted and carried on. I didn't. We sat looking into the fire together, she and I. Neither of us spoke. Then we went up to the children." Elisabeth began to weep and asked Jacob if this meant that she and the family would lose him. Riis embraced her and made a silent vow not to become heady with conceit.

Revising "How the Other Half Lives" into a book was hard work, but for Riis it was a labor of love and the culmination of his newspaper work. He personalized his experiences of two decades into impressionistic vignettes and crystallized the insights he had formed as a reporter. In fact, for many chapters Riis merely expanded upon material which he had used in previous articles and columns. To accentuate the importance of his personal anecdotes, he drew upon statistics which he got from the health and police departments. His tour-guide descriptions were reminiscent of the writings of Charles Dickens, one of Riis's favorite authors. From the English master, who combined the skills of a novelist, a historian, a social critic, and a reformer, Riis learned how to blend humor, indignation, and pathos. Both writers were expert craftsmen in developing a mood of penetrating realism by the use of picturesque and recurring portraits of the commonplace. Having been virtually weaned on Dickens as a child, having sold *Hard Times* on the streets of New York two decades previously, and having read Dickens's account of his visit to the slums of the Empire City in the 1840s—called *American Notes and Pictures from Italy* (1857)—Riis was emulating his mentor in his first book.

Riis began the manuscript in January 1890, and the book appeared in print ten months later. Since he continued working as a police reporter during the day, he did most of his writing at night, after his family had gone to bed. His habit, he later recalled in *The Making of an American*, was "to light the lamps in all the rooms of the lower story and roam through them with my pipe, for I do most of my writing on my feet" (p. 303). In his study he had a desk with fifty pigeonholes, each with a heading such as "The Bend" or "Slum Tenements." On weekends when the work went slowly, Riis often transplanted flowers or pulled up weeds in his garden. He believed that putting his hands in the earth and on nature's harvest helped to put things in their proper perspective. Riis's proofreader rejected his handwritten drafts and urged him to make several drastic revisions in tone and style. He hired a typist but refused to bow to his editor's blue pencil. During 1889 he continued to give lectures but became so burdened with his manuscript that he suffered lapses of memory. He claimed that once while in Boston he became so weighted down with the project that he temporarily forgot his own name. Whether true or not, this incident became one of his favorite stories.

During the 1880s several men had written tracts concerning the malaise of large cities. Among the most popular books were Charles Loring Brace's *The Dangerous Classes of New York and Twenty Years' Work among Them* (1880), Josiah Strong's *Our Country: Its Possible Future and Its Present Crisis* (1885), and Samuel L. Loomis's *Modern Cities and Their Religious Problems* (1887). Each noted the enormous growth of urban industrial centers and regretted the trend away from the the values of a rural society. They viewed the rising tide of immigration with concern and emphasized the sinful and devious aspects of urban life. Brace had spent his adult life relocating orphans away from New York. Strong warned that cities menaced civilization, whereas Loomis found them a natural habitat for crime, drunkenness, and sexual immorality since their impersonality was incompatible with the traditional ties of family, church, and community and fraught with temptations for the weak. Similarly in 1887 J. O. S. Huntington wrote in the *Forum* that in the tenements "The bad almost inevitably drag down the good; and the good have not the chance to lift up the bad." While large segments of the populace shared these fears, almost all Americans were anxious to learn about the cities. The popularity of books with this theme augured well for Riis.

Prior to 1890 most social critics had contrasted the pure country with the depraved city, whereas Riis's concept of two Americas centered on the disjunction between the rich and the poor. "The half that was on top cared little for the struggles, and less for the fate of those who were underneath," Riis wrote in *How the Other Half Lives*, "so long as it was able to hold them there and keep its own seat." He had many of the antiurban biases that were so common at the time. He extolled the virtues of rural Denmark, even though he had fled from its boring ways twenty years before. An admirer of the work of Josiah Strong and Charles Loring Brace, Riis nevertheless counseled his readers to accept, not abandon, the city and "make the best of a bad bargain" (pp. 1–2).

Brace and Strong criticized the urban milieu rather than the economic system which spawned the slum. Henry George's *Progress and Poverty* (1879) and Edward Bellamy's *Looking Backward* (1888). two widely read radical critiques of American society, usually scared rather than converted their affluent audiences. Going further than Brace's philanthropic solutions but stopping short of Bellamy's advocacy of socialism, Riis demonstrated the urgency of a workable middle path that utilized all resources. Everyone had a stake in combating the slums, Riis stated in *How the Other Half Lives*, because they bred crime, epidemics, paupers, moral decay, and corrupt government. To remove this blight would require a moral crusade and a multifaceted assault combining charity work, individual regeneration, governmental action, and shrewd business enterprise. Once people answered all problems with "law and order," he proclaimed, but "with our enormously swelling population held in this galling bondage, will that answer always be given?" (pp. 2–4).

THE IMMIGRANT QUARTERS

Riis subtitled his book *Studies among the Tenements of New York*. His focus was on the effect that bad housing had on immigrant families, especially the so-called children of the tenements. "All life eventually accommodates itself to its environment, and human life is no exception," he wrote. He warned that without sufficient space to move, fresh air to breathe, or esthetic pleasures to enjoy, people would lose their capacity for any "gentle thought and aspiration above the mere wants of the body. . . ." By the standards of the slum a respectable neighborhood was one that had a trace of greenery and no more than four saloons to each block. Yet in the midst of these degrading circumstances Riis wondered at the countless personal struggles of heroism "against fearful odds" to overcome the oppressive milieu (pp. 120–22).

Riis traced the genesis of the tenement to the spacious homes of New York's former knickerbocker aristocracy, who sold out to real estate dealers early in the nineteenth century. Reacting to the new conditions of industrialization and immigration, the owners subdivided the floors, partitioned the rooms, and constructed rear tenements "in the old garden[s] where the stolid Dutch burgher grew his tulips or early cabbages . . ." (pp. 6–7). By the 1840s the tenement districts in east Manhattan were already squalid and overcrowded. After viewing the scene, Charles Dickens castigated the buildings as leprous and unspeakable, worse than in London. During the 1880s, 290,000 people lived on 1 square mile of land, often 20 in a room, paying more for their dilapidated quarters than others paid elsewhere.

Using his favorite device of acting as a tour-guide, Riis recreated Mulberry Bend, which lurked in the shadows of his newspaper office and was to the reporter the apotheosis of evil and neglect. During the 1860s governmental officials had declared that almost all of the Bend's 609 tenements were a menace to public health. But in 1889 they still stood. Riis wrote that "the whole district is a maze of narrow, often unsuspected passageways— necessarily, for there is scarce a lot that has not two, three, or four tenements upon it, swarming with unwholesome crowds" (p. 43). Sections of the Bend had appropriate sobriquets such as Kerosene Row, Bone Alley, Bottle Alley, Thieves' Alley, and Bandits' Roost. Murder and abuse were common in this locale, with absentee landlords conspicuous among the criminals.

In graphic detail Riis took his readers into a back alley which was "just about one step wide, with a five-story house on one side that gets its light and air—God help us for pitiful mockery!—from this slit between brick walls." One wall had no windows; a fire escape straddled the two sides, touching each. He stated that the sun "never shone into the alley from the day the devil planned and man built it." In a typical dwelling were a darkened hallway and the odors of poisoned sewage, a saloon was adjacent. "Here is a door. Listen! That short hacking cough, that tiny, helpless wail— what do they mean?" Riis asked. Another child dying. "With half a chance it might have lived but it had none. That dark bedroom killed it," he concluded (pp. 31–34).

Summer in the tenements was the worst time of the year. The heat made indoor life almost insufferable, and the crowded quarters caused epidemics. Riis told of a woman who attempted to kill her own child after she could obtain no food with which to nourish the infant. On another occasion Riis and a doctor visited a three-room flat that housed six adults and five children who slept on straw-filled boxes. Near the stove a baby lay dying from malnutrition and a lack of fresh air. From the physician's thermometer Riis learned that the temperature of the room was 115 degrees. The pains of life and the shortage of good water drove people to the plentiful taverns, often the only cheerful and "humanly decent" place on the block. Yet Riis believed that the saloons undermined decency by breaking up families, corrupting youngsters, and further pauperizing the downtrodden. He concluded that it "saps the very vitals of society, undermines its strongest defenses, and delivers them over to the enemy" (pp. 48–49, 124–29, 159–63).

In the fourth ward there lived a colony of blind beggars in an area which residents named Blind Man's Alley. Daniel Murphy, their landlord, made a half-million-dollar profit from his occupants, and then in his old age he lost his sight also. When the Board of Health forced him to repair his property, Murphy protested that his tenants were "not fit to live in a nice house." Once every June the city distributed twenty thousand dollars to the blind. On that evening the sightless beggars sang and drank and played their fiddles in celebration. Riis recounted that on this occasion, "Even the blind landlord rejoices, for much of the money goes into his coffers" (pp. 24–26).

Riis's descriptions of living conditions shocked most of his readers but commanded their attention, and his personal sketches of slum residents gained their affection. With vivid strokes he described the multitude of cultures and personalities among New York's polyglot population which he called "this queer conglomerate mass." Concerning the mixed crowd of Italians, Irish, Germans, eastern Europeans, Poles, Chinese, Bohemians, and other national groups, Riis declared with considerable exaggeration that "the one thing you shall vainly ask for in the chief city of America is a distinctively American community. There is none; certainly not among the tenements" (pp. 15–16).

Measuring immigrant societies against his own cultural traditions, which had more in common with the upper class than with the "other half," Riis's yardstick of approval corresponded in part to how well an ethnic group adopted American habits and values. Although he showed much compassion for the plight of immigrants, the Danish-American author was somewhat cavalier in describing their manner of living and used simplistic clichés in characterizing groups. To Riis the Italians seemed clannish, the Bohemians easygoing, and too often the Jews worshiped at the altar of greed. He desired the Americanization of the immigrant, and so he was insensitive at times to habits that were barriers to this goal. Yet he did not so much denigrate ethnic customs as social patterns that were exaggerated or even created by conditions in the American ghetto. The dislocations of the slum caused many foreign-born residents to cling tenaciously to old-world customs. Often their offspring mocked them and abandoned respect for all primary-group ties. Both of these extremes Riis thought to be dangerous.

Riis devoted a chapter of his book to the Italian immigrants. He pilloried the padrone system whereby financiers lured peasants to the United States with false promises of opportunity and then exploited their ignorance by locating them in vile tenements and hiring them out to employers for a pittance. Many Italians became scavengers and ragpickers for contractors who paid officials for the privilege of inspecting the refuse at the city dump. The Italians made less trouble than the Irish, he said, and were usually "gay, light-hearted and . . . inoffensive as a child" (p. 41). They seldom protested against their wretched housing but were clannish and preferred to avenge feuds privately than to call upon the police. Italian society had a closeknit, hierarchical structure with well-defined obligations and rights. Riis understood the need for this tight organization for maintaining order, stability, and status in the face of a hostile and atavistic environment. Nevertheless, while admiring certain Italian customs, he felt it necessary to pry apart others to make the Italians better Americans. For instance, he praised the colorful religious festivals which symbolized hope and unified the community, but he condemned the rowdy Sunday card playing and the frequent vengeance murders which occurred in the Italian districts.

Riis's pen captured the colorful and picturesque culture of the Italian communities, the swarms of laughing children, the earnest hucksters and peddlers with their fish and sausages and fruit and vegetables, the lively gossip of the women, and the fragile dignity of the old patriarchs. He admired the warm ingenuity and zestful nature of the people, even though he thought their habits were somewhat sloppy. He wrote that "When the sun shines the entire population seeks the street, carrying on its household work, its bargaining, its love-making on street or sidewalk, or idling there when it has nothing better to do, with the reverse of the impulse that makes the Polish Jew coop himself up in his den with the thermometer at stewing heat" (p. 43).

Riis's portrayal of New York's Jews was paradoxical because he admired the premises of their ethical code but believed that Jews were, on the whole, too materialistic. Revealing his religious prejudices, Riis wrote that despite the exhortations of Christian preachers, the Jews were "stubbornly refusing to see the light." In the Jewish neighborhood, he stated, thrift was "at once its strength and its fatal weakness, its cardinal virtue and its foul disgrace" (pp. 77–78). Children labored almost from birth, and families packed in lodgers in the hope that they could turn from the exploited to the exploiters. Riis praised the work of Jewish philanthropic organizations such as the Baron de Hirsch Fund and the United Hebrew Charities, but he added that the ignorance of the immigrants often frustrated such admirable programs as farm colonies and vocational schools.

Many Jewish immigrants from Russia, Poland, and other eastern European countries worked in tenement sweatshops. Riis described how the typical sweater in the clothing industry took advantage of the plentiful labor supply and the financial distress and isolation of his employees to circumvent factory and child labor laws. With "merciless severity" the sweater smothered "every symptom of awakening intelligence in his slaves" (p. 90). During a visit to a two-room apartment, the author came upon a family of five who worked from daybreak until nine at night, sewing, finishing, and ironing trousers. They sold them to a manufacturer at a profit of 5 cents a dozen. Supplementing this income by taking in boarders, the family earned $25 a week and paid $20 a month rent for the two rooms. Riis concluded: "At the least calculation, probably, this sweater's family hoards up thirty dollars a month, and in a few years will own a tenement somewhere and profit by the example set by their landlord in rent-collecting" (p. 94).

Rivaling the clothing sweatshops in abasement were the tenement cigar factories. Legions of workers, primarily Bohemians, made cigars by stripping tobacco leaves, breaking bits into filler, and then wrapping it up into a finished product. Landlords held this class of tenants "in virtual serfdom" by binding their rent to the terms of their employment. The exploitation of the Bohemians, according to Riis, constituted "a slavery as real as any that ever disgraced the South" (p. 101). Entire families labored from seventy-five to one hundred hours a week each. Riis reported that a typical household received only $11 for the three thousand cigars they made each week, and then they had to pay $12.25 a month rent to the manufacturer. Such outrageous and barbarian treatment, Riis predicted, would make it not unnatural for the Bohemians, a gregarious and passionate people, to rebel against the system which perpetrated the injustices upon them.

Of all the ethnic groups which Riis analyzed, he had least sympathy for the Chinese, perhaps because he saw little hope of assimilating them into American life. "Between the tabernacles of Jewry and the shrines of the Bend," he wrote, "Joss has cheekily planted his pagan worship of idols, chief among which are the celestial worshiper's own gain and lusts." Riis was unable to understand the mysterious Chinese; he needlessly concluded that "In their very exclusiveness and reserve they are a constant and terrible menace to society. . . ." Even their cleanliness he compared to a cat which lived by cruel cunning. Riis ridiculed their pigtails and fan tan games and decried the way the Chinese trapped white girls into their lairs with opium. He urged the police to use the "harshest repressive measures" against this vice. On the other hand, he suggested that the government allow Chinese women to come to America in order to transfer the Chinamen's lusts for white girls. Undesirable and useless as they were, he concluded, "they are here, and . . . having let them in, we must make the best of it" (pp. 67–76).

Riis's commentary on New York's black residents mixed compassion with condescension. This dichotomy sprang from his partial acceptance of racist stereotypes and concurrently his deeper commitment to the premise that environment was the controlling factor in personality development. In the past Riis had sometimes portrayed black men as strong but dimwitted. In 1885, writing of a man who got up unhurt after he fell head-first from a third-story window, he foolishly stated, "No one but a Negro could possibly have performed that feat."

In *How the Other Half Lives* Riis presented an image of the black man as cheerfully working at menial jobs for which "his past traditions and natural love of ease" perhaps fit him best. He wrote, however, that "his ludicrous incongruities, his sensuality and his lack of moral accountability, his superstition and other faults . . . are the effect of temperament and of centuries of slavery. . . ." What happened, he concluded, was that the black people emulated the worst characteristics of their former masters, as evidenced by their love of expensive luxuries. He looked with horror on the mixing of black men and white women at lewd dance halls that were "the worst of the desperately bad." Than the mingling of "the utterly depraved of both sexes, white and black, on such ground, there can be no greater abomination," Riis concluded (pp. 111–17).

Despite the misgivings which Riis harbored as a result of his inaccurate and simplistic understanding of black culture, in *How the Other Half Lives* he expressed admiration for the Negro's religious faith, his love of citizenship and his desire for education. And he came out squarely against the closed system of housing which black people faced when they immigrated to New York. Landlords, in their lust for profits, deliberately and brutally drew color lines and heightened racial tensions, Riis wrote, in order to make "the prejudice in which he traffics pay him well" (p. 110). He rejected the myth that Negroes were inherently dirty, pointing out that black tenements on 99th Street were cleaner than the Italian ghettos. If vile surroundings debased men, Riis believed, then good housing could uplift them.

One group whom Riis despised fitted no exclusive ethnic or social category: the tramp. Borrowing the rhetoric and using the statistics of the Charity Organization Society, Riis fulminated against paupers who eschewed work for panhandling. Such men contributed nothing to society and consumed all of their energy in inventing ways to deceive the public. Some of them even mutilated children whom they used to gain alms, he claimed. On seventeen separate occasions one lady requested money to give her deceased husband a proper burial. In *How the Other Half Lives* he declared that "There is enough of real suffering in the homes of the poor to make one wish that there were some effective way of enforcing Paul's plan of starving the drones into the paths of self-support: no work, nothing to eat" (p. 191). Riis recommended the outlawry of begging, except for the blind. He believed that labor bureaus, workhouses, asylums, and private philanthropy could take care of the needy.

THE WRECKS AND THE WASTE

All immigrant groups in the tenements shared common problems, and the weak perished. Riis cogently told of the toll in wasted lives. In 1889, 140,000 people were jammed into the city's jails, workhouses, almshouses, foundling homes, insane asylum, or charity hospital. In addition, 14,000 men each night slept in unsanitary lodging houses. One of ten New Yorkers ended up in Potter's Field, the burial ground of paupers. Riis wrote: "The Potter's Field stands ever for utter, hopeless surrender. The last the poor will let go, however miserable their lot in life, is the hope of a decent burial" (p. 185).

Children were the most helpless against the slum. Life denied most of them the joys of childhood or the benefits of formal education. Many worked almost from infancy to help their family keep from starving. Young girls often labored eighty hours a week to earn a paltry two dollars and had to pay fines for tardiness and other mistakes. Orphans who escaped the founding asylum often became "street Arabs" or runaway vagabonds, who lived or died in the streets by their cunning. Gangs of young toughs were common on every corner. They offered the sons of immigrants a source of identity, companionship and pride, but Riis lamented that their objectives were usually crime and bravado.

With intolerable conditions in existence and with the gap ever widening between rich and poor, Riis held up the specter of revolution if reform was not forthcoming. "The sea of a mighty population, held in galling fetters, heaves uneasily in the tenements," he warned, and the time for counseling patience or preaching a hollow Christianity had passed (p. 226). Churches had to cease being slum landlords and accessories to an inadequate system. They needed to take up the social gospel in order to keep the faith and save themselves. The only possible paths were justice or violence. Riis warned the wealthy of the consequences of inactivity in an oft-quoted parable:

A man stood at the corner of Fifth Avenue and Fourteenth Street the other day, looking gloomily at the carriages that rolled by, carrying the wealth and fashion of the avenues to and from the big stores down town. He was poor, and hungry, and ragged. This thought was in his mind: "They behind their well-fed teams have no thought for the morrow; they know hunger only by name, and ride down to spend in an hour's shopping what would keep me and my little ones from want a whole year." There rose up before him the picture of those little ones crying for bread around the cold and cheerless hearth—then he sprang into the throng and slashed around him with a knife, blindly seeking to kill, to revenge (pp. 199–200).

In contrast to Riis's optimistic temperament, a foreboding tone pervaded the book. In part Riis did this for shock value rather than as a prediction of doom. Hoping for a moral awakening, he nevertheless knew well the failures of a half-century. The foes of change were ignorance and apathy. The floodtide of immigration rendered useless today the palliatives of the past, he wrote. Often do-gooders faced the resistance of the poor themselves, whose short-term necessities conflicted with their long-range interests. Merely to survive, many families had to take in boarders, send their children to work, act as strikebreakers, or even steal. Slum dwellers, he wrote, were often "shiftless, destructive, and stupid, in a word they are what the tenements made them." He cited an example of a benevolent owner who installed new plumbing, faucets, and wooden closets in his tenement. The occupants used the wood for fires, pawned the faucets, and flooded the building when they pulled up the pipes. After that debacle, the owner became "a firm believer in the total depravity of tenement-house people." The tragedy, Riis said, was that the landlord could have turned his model tenement into a profitable enterprise if he had been a better teacher and manager (pp. 207–8).

In *How the Other Half Lives* Riis called for an end to the economic policy of laissez-faire, which he branded as a smokescreen for selfishness. Private rights had to bend to public interests. Should not laborers have the right to decent housing, even if it infringes on the property rights of others, Riis asked. He pointed out that some absentee landlords even resided in Europe. "It is easy enough to convince a man that he ought not to harbor the thief who steals people's property," he stated; "but to make him see that he has no right to slowly kill his neighbors, or his tenants, by making a death-trap of his house, seems to be the hardest of all tasks" (p. 205).

The final chapter of *How the Other Half Lives* examined "How the Case Stands." Riis concluded that the health and security of all Americans depended upon decent housing. He wrote that if there was a revolution of the poor, "no human power may avail to check it." Cognizant that tenements would not disappear since suburban housing was too costly and impractical for most workers, he called for governmental regulation to make it "unprofitable to own a bad tenement." The state had the duty to tear down the worst buildings and force owners to remodel others. And private enterprise, spurred by moral purpose and self-interest—"philanthropy and five per cent"—should build model tenements. In order to underscore his theme that reform was more than a matter for the idealists, Riis concluded his book with this admonitory poem by James Russell Lowell: "Think ye that building shall endure/Which shelters the noble and crushes the poor?" Thus, slum conditions constituted a clear and present danger to the established institutions, whose military arsenals were scant insurance against a bitter harvest (pp. 215–22, 226).

IMPACT OF HOW THE OTHER HALF LIVES

How the Other Half Lives received favorable critical acclaim and quickly gained great popularity, thereby establishing Riis as an expert on urban life. James Russell Lowell told the author that "I had but a vague idea of these horrors before you brought them home to me." Through his dramatic and anecdotal style, Riis had brought the slum to life, made it comprehensible and therefore not quite so fearful. How the Other Half Lives was extremely timely in unraveling the mysteries of the big city in a manner that reenforced the traditional values of love, justice, and moral responsibility that were rooted in small communities. Riis defined the slums as the symbol and gauge of society. Their inhabitants were neither immoral dolts who deserved their fate nor happy and noble people. Rather, they were what environment made them, potentially dangerous but, more hopefully capable of becoming good citizens. Riis wanted to wipe out poverty before the culture of the slum affected younger generations and hardened into permanent patterns for individuals, families, communities, and ultimately, the nation. He called on Americans not to construct a new system but to modernize their methods to realize the goals of the past.

How the Other Half Lives reached the public during the same year as did a book about the manners of New York's upper class, Samuel Ward McAllister's Society As I Have Found It. McAllister's portrayal of opulence and ostentatious display reenforced Riis's central theme of poverty in the midst of plenty. Reviewers contrasted the two books and repeated Riis's warning of an impending storm. The True Nationalist wrote: "The bullet-proof shutters, the stacks of hand-grenades and gatling guns of the sub-treasury" show that society foolishly chose to arm itself rather than reform "our cursed, unclean and disgraceful tenement-house system. . . ."

Reviewers also compared How the Other Half Lives with two other contemporary books, John Peter Altgeld's Live Questions and William Booth's In Darkest England. Altgeld's book, a reprint of his speeches and articles, focused on the problems of workingmen in Chicago. Although it concentrated more on labor-management relations than did How the Other Half Lives, the tone of Live Questions was similar to that of Riis's book. In Darkest England, which William T. Stead ghost-wrote for the leader of the Salvation Army, was a comprehensive study of the slums of London and an indictment of public apathy toward the victims of industrial progress. Riis believed that it sparked sales of his own book. Most reviewers agreed with Lyman Abbott of the Christian Union that Riis's work was the more graphic and effective, largely because of the realistic photographs of the Bend, the lodging houses, the sweatshops, back alleys, and, most of all, the chilling expressions of the poor. Booth himself admired How the Other Half Lives, and his magazine War Cry reprinted some of its more poignant passages. A reviewer for the Critic, however, called Booth's treatment of London's poor more sympathetic and noted Riis's "lack of broad and penetrative vision, a singularly warped sense of justice at times, and a roughness amounting almost to brutality."

Riis's portrayal of the Chinese and, to a lesser degree, other ethnic groups warranted criticism. While not unsympathetic toward immigrants, *How the Other Half Lives* contained racial slurs which others could use to support nativistic shibboleths and restrictionist legislation. Ironically, the racial stereotypes, which detracted from the book's veracity, probably widened its appeal with middle class readers. Riis's goal of Americanizing the immigrant perhaps blinded him into too great a desire for cultural homogeneity. Other humanitarian reformers, faced with the magnitude of their problems and the frustrations in improving the quality of urban life, made similar charges. The gentle Jane Addams mentioned the "pathetic stupidity" of so many tenement house residents in her autobiographical *Twenty Years at Hull-House* (1910). In *Civilization's Inferno* (1893) Benjamin O. Flower, the muckraking editor of *Arena*, referred to Boston slums as "reservoirs of physical and moral death. . . . But while Booth and Flower emphasized sin as the root of human misery and degradation, Riis held the cause to be largely environmental and thus amenable to public treatment.

Within Riis's mind warred two contradictory impulses regarding ghetto residents, one benign and the other backward-looking. On the one hand, he rejected explanations of poverty based upon inherent biological differences among races. Since all people were basically alike in potential, Riis argued, tenement ghettos were unnatural aberrations. Their residents were decent human beings whose aspirations were the same as native Americans but whose poverty sprang from inequality of opportunity. On the other hand, he believed in the cultural superiority of Anglo-American institutions and in an upright code of conduct. Describing habits of ghetto residents which he found loathsome, such as sloth, vice, clannishness, intemperance, and superstition, he explained that they were vestiges of Old World ways or spurious by-products of the slums. But at times his indictments of ethnic customs revealed a class and race snobbery. This trace of condescension toward "this queer conglomerate mass" became less pronounced later in life, but Riis never totally suppressed it.

More important than the shortcomings of *How the Other Half Lives* were its beneficial consequences. Ushering a generation of examination into all aspects of American life, the book educated great numbers of middle and upper class Americans about the seamier side of the American scene but also the human side of that scene. It evoked the compassionate lump in the throat, the tears of sorrow or perhaps guilt, in the place of vague uneasiness. In the words of Sam Bass Warner, Jr., he "painted a colorful landscape of the lower East Side, so that poverty became an interesting subject for social tourism. . . ." Patrician organizations such as the People's Municipal League of New York, which prior to 1890 had been interested primarily in honest government, began compiling remedies for slum conditions. *How the Other Half Lives* stirred the conscience of a generation of young activists, many of whom worked to blot out the ills which Riis described. Louis H. Pink, a settlement house worker and housing expert, John Jay Chapman, an innovator in neighborhood redevelopment, and Ernest Poole, an author, social worker, and socialist reformer—all three men and many more attested to the book's effect in jolting them out of their complacency. Riis also set conditions for a new emphasis on realism in fiction. After *How the Other Half Lives*, the public searched out books such as Stephen Crane's *Maggie: A Girl of the Streets* (1893) and William T. Stead's *If Christ*

Came to Chicago (1895). Establishing Riis as an expert on urban problems, the book opened up new opportunities for his espousal of the gospel of reform. And hereafter his utterances had a new authority.

Thus, fame came to Riis because he was able to make life in the slums knowable to affluent Americans. Almost a half-century after the publication of *How the Other Hall Lives,* James Ford concluded that "Jacob A. Riis probably had greater influence than any other publicist [during the 1890s] in calling attention in a graphic manner to the evils of slum dwelling. . . ." Riis believed that if people knew the facts about the tenement house ghettos, they would act to eradicate the evils. Otherwise, their ignorance, apathy, and shortsightedness threatened the health, morals, prosperity, and political system of the nation. *How the Other Half Lives* was a book "whose time had come in 1890," to quote historians Charles N. Glaab and A. Theodore Brown, but it also has a timeless relevance. Despite the author's limitations as a social scientist, Sam Bass Warner, Jr., concluded, Riis conveyed the message that every city dweller deserved "a decent house, a decent job, a decent school, fresh air, clean water, and safety against fire, epidemic, and crime. He never lost sight of these basic urban rights of being human."

PARK DIXON GOIST

From From Main Street to State Street: Town, City, and Community in America[†]

7. *Social Workers, Reformers, and the City: Jane Addams and Jacob Riis*

The emphasis of the urban novels written by Hamlin Garland, Theodore Dreiser, and Henry Blake Fuller was essentially on the consequences of city living for individuals. In Garland there is some notice taken of a limited social network in which Rose Dutcher attempts to find her place. In Fuller's novel the Marshall family, though badly weakened by events, still plays some role. But the real concern of these novelists is with the individual. This is even more noticeable, of course, in Dreiser's work. Here the focal point is entirely on the unattached individual; no sustained social group ties or family bonds are enjoyed by the lonely characters in *Sister Carrie*. The perspective of the early urban novelists focused, then, on the impact upon the indivudal of the urban milieu.

Contemporaneous with this emphasis on the individual was a growing consciousness among middle class reformers of the important role played in cities by groups. Theodore Brower's proposed justice center for the poor, the settlement work of Isabel Herrick's university friends, even Jane Marshall's lunchroom for working girls and Mrs. Granger Bates's camp for needy children, were fictional counterparts of efforts actually being made by social workers to understand and cope with changing urban conditions in terms of group needs. In Chicago the work of Jane Addams (1860–1935)

† Kennikat Press, 1977. Pages 89–95. Reprinted by permission of the author.

at Hull-House is the best-known of such endeavors. In her work one notices a shift from individual to group concerns in dealing with the industrial city. Also, her life provides an opportunity to trace the relationship between a particular kind of nonurban upbringing and the social work approach to urban society. A similar perspective, which also offers some interesting contrasts to Addams, can be seen in the work of the famous New York newspaperman and reformer Jacob Riis (1849–1914). An immigrant himself, Riis personally experienced the awful poverty and lonely isolation which was the fate of many in late nineteenth-century American cities. But he was fortunate enough to survive and eventually achieve success as a police reporter in New York. These experiences shaped his view of the city which he tried so hard to change. Addams and Riis were two of the outstanding reform figures of their day, and they provide an insight into an important middle class response to the rapidly changing turn-of-the-century American city.

Jane Addams was born in the northern Illinois village of Cedarville. This settlement (founded in the 1830s) is just south of the Wisconsin border, and a few miles north of the small city of Freeport. Addams's parents had settled here on the Cedar River in 1844. By the time of Jane's birth her father, John, who had previously been a miller in Pennsylvania, was the most prominent man in the area. He owned a flour mill and a sawmill, was president of an insurance company and of a Freeport bank, which he had helped organize, and had invested money in railroads and land. A self-made man, he was also a community builder. He helped organize the first school, the first church, and the first library in Cedarville, and was instrumental in bringing a railroad into the Cedar River region. John Addams was also an Illinois state senator for sixteen years (1854–70) and one of the organizers of the Republican Party, to which he remained loyal throughout his life. He died in 1881 at the age of fifty-nine, leaving an estate worth a quarter of a million dollars.[1]

Jane was two years old when her mother died at the age of forty-nine. Sarah Addams had given birth to nine children, five of whom lived. Jane was the youngest; she had three sisters and a brother. She was eight when her father married Anna Haldeman, the attractive widow of a prominent Freeport man. Anna brought a son with her to live in the Addams household, and he became a close companion and playmate of his stepsister Jane. The second Mrs. Addams had intellectual and cultural aspirations, and was a talented musician. She provided her new home not only with a piano but also with an insistence upon the daily use of linen table cloths, good china, and silver. The emphasis upon culture and taste meant for young Jane drawing and music lessons in Freeport, stylish clothes, and, following college, a grand tour of Europe. It also meant the lectures, concerts, and fashionable parties of Baltimore, where Mrs. Addams moved after her second husband's death.

Jane Addams's recent biographer Allen Davis points out that, despite her rather complex family structure and early illnesses (the most serious of which left her with a slight curvature of the spine), she had a happy childhood.

---

1. Except where indicated, biographical material on Addams is based on Allen Freeman Davis, *American Heroine: The Life and Legend of Jane Addams* (New York: Oxford University Press, 1973).

Davis also maintains that in spite of her father's prominent position and the cultural aspirations her second mother had for Jane, she attended the one-room village school and played with the children of millhands. These were not the sons and daughters of immigrants, however, and nearly all were Protestants. Davis finds further evidence of the "natural equality" of the small town in the fact that the Addamses' "hired girls" were not treated as servants. They agreed to work for a year or two in order to learn to cook and sew, and were included in the Addams family circle. Davis's point here is that the rather aristocratic tendencies of her stepmother conflicted with the easy equality of village life, thus producing some of the ambivalence and contradictions in Addams's character.

At seventeen Jane entered Rockford Female Seminary, where she was an undergraduate from 1877 to 1881. Although nearby Rockford did not yet have official college ranking, those attending were self-conscious of being college women. They were in fact among the first generation of full-fledged college educated women. The purpose of this "Mount Holyoke of the West" was to combine domestic training with religious and cultural instruction. Addams was somewhat formal and aloof as a student, but entered fully into the life of the school. She was president of the literary society and an editor of the school magazine, she read widely and debated, struggled with religious questions, became interested in science, did well in class work, and developed the habits of a writer. In her essays she broke with Rockford tradition and argued for the special role of women in world affairs. Upon graduation she planned to go on to Smith College for a Bachelor of Arts.

But for the next eight years, until the opening of Hull-House, Addams was buffeted by family tragedy and responsibility, physical disability, and severe mental depression. For convenience, this time in her life can be divided into four periods. During the two years following graduation from Rockford, Addams was generally ill and despondent. She gave up hopes of going to Smith for a B. A., was forced to leave the Women's Medical College in Philadelphia because of her health, spent a good deal of time as an invalid, and had major surgery on her back. She also faced family tragedy, including the sudden death of her adored father and the mental breakdown of her brother. With other members of the family scattered, Jane took on the burden of managing family business affairs. Between August, 1883, and June, 1885, she and her stepmother and a small party of friends lived and traveled in Europe. Returning to the United States in the summer of 1885, for the next two and a half years she spent the winters with her stepmother in Baltimore, the rest of the time in Cedarville. It was during the winter months of 1885 and 1886 in Baltimore when, according to her recollections some twenty-five years later, "I seemed to have reached the nadir of my nervous depression and sense of maladjustment."[2] In December, 1887, she departed again for Europe, in a party which included her close friend Ellen Starr. During this trip the scheme which resulted in the founding of Hull-House apparently took shape. Addams and Starr returned to America in October, 1888, moved to a Chicago boarding house in January

2. Jane Addams, *Twenty Years at Hull-House, With Autobiographical Notes* (New York: New American Library, 1981) p. 67. All page references are to the New American Library edition.

of the next year, raised money for their scheme, and took up residence in the old Charles Hull mansion the following September.

The question remains: Why did Jane Addams turn to social work and become a leader of the social settlement movement at the turn of the century? The two most interesting recent efforts to answer this question have been put forward by Christopher Lasch in 1965, and Allen Davis in 1973.

Lasch discusses Jane Addams and the founding of Hull-House within the framework of his analysis of *The New Radicalism in America (1889–1963): The Intellectual as a Social Type* (1965). Indeed, the key date in locating this phenomenon is the very year Addams and Starr moved to the house on Halsted Street. According to Lasch, the growth of a new radicalism coincides with the emergence of intellectuals as a "status group" alienated from the general life of society. This, in turn, is an aspect of a more general cultural fragmentation, characteristic of industrial and postindustrial societies.

> The decline of a sense of community, the tendency of the mass society to break down into its component parts, each having its own autonomous culture and maintaining only the most tenuous connections with the general life of the society—which as a consequence has almost ceased to exist. . . . (Introduction, p. x)

The new radicals, in rebelling against culture, conventional family standards, and values of the middle class, acquired a "radical reversal of perspective." They identified with what Jacob Riis called the "other half" of humanity, thus seeing society from the bottom up.

Within this context Addams's involvement in the settlement is seen as a resolution of certain debilitating personal tensions caused by the effect of those general cultural and domestic crises. In the first place, the social settlement was an outlet for the combined moral piety and intellectual energies which she could not satisfy by religious missionary work or by a purely secular career like medicine. According to Lasch, tension was created by the persistence of the old moral urge in face of the failure of religious theology to provide an adequate medium for intellectual speculation. Jane Addams needed an outlet for both urges. Social work was a successful resolution because "it combined good works with the analysis not only of the conditions underlying urban poverty but also of one's own relation to the poor" (p. 12). The settlement combined good works and intellectual excitement.

Equally important for Lasch's understanding of Addams is the tension caused by her resistance to and final rejection of "the life her [step] mother was trying to get her to lead" (p. 35). She came to realize that the educational and cultural advantages of the first generation of college women often acted as a barrier to understanding and responding to the "real," changing world around them. In comparing her generation to that of her grandmother's, she wondered during the first European trip if the younger women "had taken their learning too quickly" and "departed too suddenly from the active emotional life led by their grandmothers and great-grandmothers." Education for her generation had been all taking and no giving, merely "acquiring knowledge" and "receiving impressions." Thus, she remarked in *Twenty Years at Hull-House* (1910), ". . . somewhere in the process of 'being educated,' they had lost that simple and almost automatic response to the human appeal, that old healthful reaction resulting in activity from the mere presence of suffering or of helplessness . . ." (p. 64). Addams and many of her intellectual and cultivated friends, ironically like plodding and inarticulate Hugh McVey, had great difficulty "making real connection with the life about them." The smothering advantages enforced "the assumption that the sheltered, educated girl has nothing to do with the bitter poverty and the social maladjustment which is all about her" (p. 65).

But reality can break through the cultural barrier. In Addams's case that breakthrough was symbolized in her own mind by an experience at a Madrid bullfight during the second European trip in April, 1888. She was initially fascinated by the spectacle, "rendered in the most magnificent Spanish style," during which five bulls and a number of horses were killed. Seeing the scene through historic Christian imagery, where the ring became an amphitheater, the riders knights, and the matador a gladiator, she outlasted the rest of her party as an enthralled witness of the bullfight. That evening revulsion at her endurance set in, and she generalized the scene to include "the entire moral situation which it revealed." Prior to this event Addams claims she had begun to think about the plan which eventually led to the establishment of Hull-House.

> It may have been even before I went to Europe for the second time, but I generally became convinced that it would be a good thing to rent a house in a part of the city where many primitive and actual needs are found, in which young women who had been given over too exclusively to study might restore a balance of activity along traditional lines and learn of life from life itself. . . . (P. 72)

Then, with the bullfight scene freshly in mind, she realized that her "dreamer's scheme" was a mere paper reform which "had become a defense for continued idleness" and a rationale for indefinitely continued study and travel. The moral reaction to the bullfight experience revealed that she had become "the dupe of a deferred purpose," that she was caught in "the snare of preparation." But no longer: she soon revealed her plan to Ellen Starr, visited Toynbee Hall (a university settlement in East London) in June, and six months later moved to Chicago to carry out her plan.

Lasch accepts the importance which Addams attached to the bullfight. But he interprets it within the context of his discussion of the new radicalism:

> The bullfight was more than a reminder of her self-deception, her end-lessly deferred plans and projects. It was the embodiment of the aesthetic principle toward which she was appalled to find herself so strongly drawn. Nothing could have made more clear to her what was wrong with a life devoted to beauty alone, the kind of life represented by her stepmother; for here was beauty intertwined with and depending upon the most outrageous cruelty—beauty bought with blood. . . . Henceforth not only the pursuit of beauty for its own sake but all those intellectual pursuits which had so long confused and misled her, those tangled theological speculations which she could neither resolve nor put aside, were to give way before her conviction that the only god she could worship was a god of love—a god, that is, of doing rather than of knowing. (Pp. 27–29)

In his recent study *American Heroine: The Life and Legend of Jane Addams* (1973), Allen Davis rejects Lasch's interpretation. Davis dismisses the importance of the bullfight scene and places less emphasis than Lasch on Addams's rebellion against an upper class Victorian family. Instead, he argues for a more multifaceted explanation of motivation. Davis stresses the influence of various reform movements which Addams came across in London, and the warm support of Ellen Starr. Davis asserts that in letters written at the time of the event there is no indication that the bullfight experience caused any change in Addams's plans or thinking. But she did respond to the reform spirit and new awareness of the poor which was widespread in London during the late 1880s. She found Toynbee Hall "so free from 'professional doing good,' so unaffectedly sincere and so productive of good results in its classes and libraries . . . that it seems perfectly ideal."[3] During those June weeks in London Addams visited the People's Palace, a philanthropic institute for workers. She also read the settlement-oriented novels of Walter Besant. "The mission side of London is the most interesting side it has," she wrote to her sister. From such evidence Davis concludes it was probably during these two weeks in London that she decided to move to a working class neighborhood in Chicago.

> Her decision to establish a settlement in a poor section of Chicago was essentially a religious commitment, but the kind of Christianity she witnessed at Toynbee Hall and the People's Palace was a religion of social action, a version of religion that solved her doctrinal difficulties and doubts, which demanded also a desire to serve. (P. 51)

Ellen Starr's enthusiasm and her eager willingness to aid in every way possible are seen by Davis as the needed incentive for Addams's pursuit of the project.

When one turns to Jane Addams's own reflections on the motives behind social settlements, the combination of elements emphasized by both Lasch and Davis is striking. Less than three years after moving into Hull-House, she gave a lecture entitled "The Subjective Necessity for Social Settlements," at a summer school sponsored by the Ethical Cultural Societies. Reflecting in *Twenty Years at Hull-House* on the group of settlement workers who attended that summer session, she remarked that they seemed convinced that in the settlement "they had found a clue by which the conditions in crowded cities might be understood and the agencies for social betterment developed" (p. 91). She noted further that those who were most enthusiastic about the movement in the early 1890s had continued active for some twenty years because they had found "the Settlement was too valuable as a method, as a way of approach to the social question to be abandoned . . ." (p. 91). Thus, as a method for understanding cities the settlement satisfied her intellectual needs, and as an agency for social betterment it answered her desire for action.

In her 1892 speech Addams posited three trends which she felt had led to the founding of Hull-House. She defined them as (1) an urge to socialize democracy, (2) the progressive thrust to better the conditions of mankind, and (3) a regenerated Christian humanitarian impulse to share the

---

3. Letter cited by Davis, p. 40.

lives of the poor. Taken together, these felt needs constituted the subjective necessity behind the settlement movement. In light of her own experience, it follows that she found a growing desire on the part of educated young people to overcome the burden of their cultural backgrounds which had shut them "off from the common labor by which they live." Such young people, she argued, sought to socialize democracy and develop a fuller civic life by making universal the cultural advantages they enjoyed. Addams was sure that more and more people like herself had a strong desire to make contact with those who were engaged in "the starvation struggle." The settlement was a means of achieving this contact. It provided communication where alienation had existed previously, the kind of alienation which she described in the following passage:

> You may remember the forlorn feeling which occasionally seizes you when you arrive early in the morning a stranger in a great city: the stream of laboring people goes past you as you gaze through the plate-glass window of your hotel; you see hard workingmen lifting great burdens; you hear the driving and jostling of huge carts and your heart sinks with a sudden sense of futility. The door opens behind you and you turn to the man who brings you in your breakfast with a quick sense of human fellowship. . . . You turn helplessly to the waiter and feel that it would be grotesque to claim from him the sympathy you crave because civilization has placed you apart, but you resent your position with a sudden sense of snobbery. (P. 93)

In this striking passage Addams has connected her own class sense of guilt to the feeling of an entire generation of educated upper and upper middle class men and women.

The settlement, continued Addams, provides these young people an opportunity to break away from "elaborate preparation" and to satisfy their need for action and involvement in life. Now the young girl returning from college who wants to fulfill her feeling of social obligation to the "submerged tenth" need not let the family claim be so strenuously asserted. No longer need educated and informed young people suffer, as Addams herself had, from a "sense of uselessness" and inaction, for the settlement offers them something definite to do. "Our young people feel nervously the need of putting theory into action, and respond quickly to the Settlement form of activity" (p. 95). Addams felt the settlement was also related to a "renaissance of the early Christian humanitarianism" which saw Christ's ideas best expressed in the social life of the community. Thus, the settlement aims "to develop whatever of social life its neighborhood may afford, to focus and give form to that life, to bring to bear upon it the results of cultivation and training . . ." (p. 97). The function of the settlement, then, was to focus on the neighborhood as a basis for urban community, and as a basis for bridging the gap between social classes in the city.

Addams concluded her essay by asserting that the settlement sought to relieve destitution at one end of society and the sense of uselessness at the other. "The Settlement, then, is an experimental effort to aid in the solution of the social industrial problems which are engendered by the modern conditions of life in a great city" (p. 98). The key figure in this effort was the settlement resident. She/he must be flexible, tolerant, hospitable, patient, committed to the idea of the solidarity of the human race, humble, and respectful of the differences of neighborhood residents. The settlement resident must be ready to arouse and interpret neighborhood opinion, to understand the needs of neighbors, and to furnish data for needed legislation. "In short [settlement] residents are pledged to devote themselves to the duties of good citizenship and to the arousing of the social energies which too largely lie dormant in every neighborhood given over to industrialization" (p. 100).

The work of Jane Addams was aimed at creating an atmosphere conducive to community in the urban environment. In the first place, she hoped the settlement would be a place, where the growing disparity between classes could be checked, and where greater harmony between upper class natives and lower class immigrants could be achieved. In other words, she sought to encourage and maintain social interaction among immigrants and native Americans. Second, she envisioned the settlement house as a bridge between European peasant patterns and the urban industrial environment of America. It was a difficult task, but she sought to encourage pride in certain ethnic practices while also instilling respect for American values and institutions. Among the various groups she worked with at Hull-House, Addams tried to foster a sense of sharing both in ethnic accomplishments and in the advantages of local life in Chicago. The locale in which she sought to facilitate interaction and sharing was the city neighborhood. To a large extent, then, the social settlement efforts of Jane Addams were aimed at creating and sustaining community in the same sense that recent sociologists have defined that phenomenon.

Jacob Riis, journalist and reformer, was among those many people from nonurban backgrounds who sought to come to terms with the late nineteenth- and early twentieth-century American city. Unlike any of the other figures looked at so far in this study, Riis was an immigrant who had also to adjust to a new culture. Born in the small Danish town of Ribe (population 3,000), he migrated to this country at the age of twenty-one in 1870. After years of struggle and privation he became a nationally known newspaper reporter and writer, active campaigner for numerous reform movements, and close personal advisor to President Theodore Roosevelt.

Hamlin Garland started his literary career as a spokesman for the downtrodden middle western farmer but lived the majority of his life in cities. Jacob Riis became a publicist for the city tenement dweller, but like Garland always felt deep ambiguity toward the city. He lived in New York City until about a year before his death. Of his move to a farm in Massachusetts, Riis's biographer has remarked, "Riis's personal move to Pine Brook Farm and his continuing interest in urban reform represented in microcosm his ambivalence about the city." Indeed, one of the main themes in James Lane's biography of Jacob Riis is the interesting dynamic between Riis's rural background and inclinations on the one hand, and his involvement in city life and reform on the other.[4]

4. James B. Lane, *Jacob A. Riis and the American City* (Port Washington, NY: Kennikat Press, 1974), p. 216. Except where indicated, the biographical material on Riis is based on Lane.

Riis experienced hard times and near-starvation upon his arrival in the United States. He knocked about the country from one job to another until he landed a position with the *New York Tribune* in 1877. But he was from a well-placed and educated, though not wealthy, family (his father was a schoolmaster). Thus, even when reduced to accepting handouts from understanding cooks and bakers he "did not consider himself of the lower class." On the contrary, he "considered himself a young man of culture rather than a common laborer."[5] His background and his experience in America thus confirmed Riis in a belief that coincided perfectly with one of his adopted land's major credos, individualism. He firmly believed that "nothing is more certain, humanly speaking, than this, that what a man wills himself to be, that he will be." While some immigrants and native radicals were socialists critical of capitalism, Riis was an avid advocate of individualism and privatism. When he wrote his autobiography, he portrayed himself as a prime example of the fulfillment of the American dream of success—an individual who by hard work and will power had risen from humble origins to the position of counselor to presidents.[6]

Riis established his reputation as a police reporter, first for the *Tribune* and then with the *Evening Sun*. He wrote articles about people in the slum areas of New York's East Side. Here he set up shop on Mulberry Street, across from police headquarters. He gathered much of his information by accompanying inspectors from the city's health department on their nightly rounds in the area of Mulberry Bend. As a result of this work, his social consciousness was raised. Using a new flash lighting technique which allowed cameras to photograph dark interiors, he started to record in graphic pictures the slum living conditions in the Bend area. In 1888 he began presenting illustrated lectures on conditions in the tenements and writing magazine articles about what he saw. Two years later, encouraged, by the fascinated response of audiences to his vivid portrayal of urban misery, he turned his work into a book.

How the Other Half Lives (1890) is a classic of American reform journalism. It was an exposé of urban conditions largely unfamiliar to the middle class reading public. In this sense it was in the same genre as such earlier books as Charles Loring Brace's *The Dangerous Classes of New York and Twenty Years among Them* (1872) and Benjamin O. Flower's contemporaneous *Civilization's Inferno, or, Studies in the Social Cellar* (1893). Brace argued for the need of greater organization among charitable institutions devoted to the poor, supplemented by state aid, in order to prevent "an explosion from this class which might leave this city in ashes and blood" (p. 29). Flower, who found "deplorable conditions existing at our very door which are a crying reproach to the Republic" (p. 99), was both fascinated and shocked by what he discovered. Causes and cures, however, escaped him.

Riis's perspective was somewhat different from that of Brace or Flower. To some extent Riis was attempting to make sense of his own experiences, first as a threadbare drifter and then as a police reporter. In this important sense, he "had been there," the others hadn't. It should be emphasized that such experiences do not automatically guarantee greater understanding,

---

5. Ibid., p. 20.
6. Jacob A. Riis, *The Making of an American* (New York: The Macmillan Company, 1901).

but in Riis's case they did provide an alternative perspective for viewing "the other half" in the city. What Riis concluded about the other half is that they were largely a product of the conditions under which they lived, and those conditions were summed up in one word, "tenements." Thus, beyond providing vivid descriptions of slum life, the focal point of his inquiry was the impact that living in New York's 37,316 tenements had on their estimated 1,230,000 occupants in 1890. The impact was potentially explosive, and Riis concluded *How the Other Half Lives* by expressing a fear similar to that of his friend Charles Brace: "The sea of a mighty population, held in galling fetters, heaves uneasily in the tenements. . . . If it rise . . . no human power may avail to check it" (p. 226). But he was generally optimistic that the challenge could be met, and met within the boundaries of the American system of free enterprise.

Riis's suggestions for improving the condition of the tenement districts included providing more open space by replacing the worst tenements with parks and playgrounds; encouraging neighborhood clubs, settlement houses, and better schools; establishing clean municipal lodging houses; building model tenements under the aegis of limited-dividend companies; enacting and enforcing tenement house laws (including state-enforced ceilings on rents); and the remodeling of certain tenements. While Riis had progressed beyond the emphasis on the organized charity and Christian voluntarism of a Josiah Strong (in *The Challenge of the City*, 1907) to solve the problem of urban poverty, he remained committed to the principles of private enterprise as the best way of providing improved housing for the city's poor immigrants.

Riis argued that while it is easy to convince a man that he should not harbor a thief, it is more difficult to make the same man understand that he has no right to kill tenants by allowing his property to become a death trap. It is, he continued, a matter of education, and there were "men and women who have mended and built with an eye to the real welfare of their tenants as well as to their own pockets" (p. 205). He was insistent that these two, the general welfare and individual profit, were inseparable. Workingmen had a just claim to a decent home—"at a reasonable price." "The business of housing the poor, if it is to amount to anything, must be business, as it was business with our fathers to put them where they are" (p. 205). In listing the three effective ways of dealing with the tenements in New York—housing laws, remodeling older tenements, and building model tenements—Riis was sure that "private enterprise—conscience, to put it in the category of duties where it belongs—must do the lion's share under the last two heads" (p. 216).

In writing of Riis such students of urban history as Sam Bass Warner, Jr., James Lane, and Roy Lubove have noted the close connection between his reform proposals and his commitment to nature, family, the local neighborhood, and individualism.[7] Lubove maintains of Riis that "he could not literally recreate New York in the image of Ribe, but he wanted an environment compatible with stable family life, neighborhood cohesiveness,

---

7. Sam Bass Warner, Jr., introduction, Jacob A., Riis, *How the Other Half Lives: Studies Among the Tenements of New York* (Cambridge: Belknap Press of Harvard University Press, 1970). Roy Lubove, *The Progressives and the Slums: Tenement House Reform in New York City, 1890–1917* (Pittsburgh: University of Pittsburgh Press, 1963).

and not least, the rejuvenating contact with nature he had known as a youth."[8] According to Lane, Riis "sought to apply to his urban surroundings the values which he had acquired in a traditional rural environment" (p. 4). Thus, the values of individual effort and hard work, love of nature, and a concept of community based on family, local place, and religion were translated under urban conditions into an advocacy of improved housing, neighborhood social centers, settlement houses, and better schools, parks, and playgrounds. Riis did not advocate a radical alteration of the economic system, but rather a gradual change in the environment to be brought about by educating the public to the needs of the other half.

What the slum and tenement were doing, Riis told his largely middle class audience, was destroying individual initiative and undermining the traditional family and primary group foundations of community. Housing and neighborhoods must be improved because they make up the environment in which community either flourishes or decays. "Where home goes, go family, manhood, citizenship, patriotism."[9] Essentially the slum was a ruinous environment because it destroyed family life and the home.

The neighborhood was of equal importance with the family. Lane quotes Riis as saying his main purpose in urban reconstruction was "to arouse neighborhood interest and neighborhood pride, to link the neighbors to one spot that will hold them long enough to take root and stop them from moving" (p. 91). For Riis, then, an important element in community was the rooted continuity over time which he had known as a child in the Danish village of his birth. In a book entitled The Old Town (1909), written three years before his death, Riis paid tribute to the continuity and community which Ribe and villages like it always symbolized for him. In his ambivalence toward American culture, Hamlin Garland had sought stability and continuity in Europe; in his devotion to American values Riis sought social stability and control in improved housing and neighborhood conditions.

Riis's response to the city is interesting because in it we are provided an example of a certain kind of ambiguity. He sought to meet the challenge of changing urban conditions primarily on the basis of values frequently equated with nonurban areas. His passionate conviction regarding individual worth and responsibility led him to condemn the tramp (whose rootlessness undermined the stability of society). It also led him to speak out against those landlords whose greed was seen as the cause of the slum tenement. If individual landlord greed and immigrant ignorance produced dangerous tenements, then the education of the individual toward fair play and giving the other guy an even break was essential. But the hand of the law would also have to be asserted on occasion. Thus, the need for certain restrictive, minimum-standard housing legislation. More frequently, however, he looked to limited-dividend model tenements, and the "fairplay between tenant and landlord" exhibited by a handful of paternalistic managers and owners.

Both Jane Addams and Jacob Riis were moderate, middle class reformers. They were committed to the idea of the importance of the localized

---

8. Roy Lubove, introduction, Jacob Riis, The Making of an American, pp. xi–xii.
9. Cited by Lane, p. 205.

community as a basis for individual worth. In their emphasis upon the urban neighborhood, both assumed that a specific geographic place was essential as an arena for the social interaction and sharing of common ties which are today taken to be basic characteristics of community life. In this sense, they were the early twentieth-century antecedents of those in the 1960s and 1970s who are advocates of the "resurgent neighborhood," and participants in neighborhood improvement organizations.[1] On this issue they were thus closer to recent neighborhood organizers than to such of their own contemporaries as Theodore Dreiser and Henry Blake Fuller, who held out little or no hope for community in the city.

The significant point of difference between a Dreiser and an Addams on the issue of the possibilities of community in the urban setting was that Addams assumed that there had to be a group basis for the, realization of individual significance. Groups that fulfilled that function in the city included families, ethnic clusters, and settlement houses. Such groups operated within a given locale, the neighborhood. Dreiser, on the other hand, saw the city individual as bereft of any meaningful family or group ties, alone and adrift amidst forces over which he/she had no control. The impact of the city upon the individual was, then, to impose its own kind of lonely isolation. The isolation that Addams perceived was an isolation of groups. Her efforts were aimed at using ethnic group solidarity first as a means of encouraging individual worth, and then at employing the settlement as a cultural bridge between ethnic group isolation and the larger system of the city. Her assumption and that of Riis was, in contrast to Dreiser and Fuller, that community based on locale, interaction, and sharing was as natural in the city as in the small town.

RICHARD TUERK

Jacob Riis and the Jews†

During the Great Migration of European immigrants to America (roughly from 1875 to 1924), as more and more people entered the country, anti-immigrant sentiment grew, finally culminating in the series of discriminatory laws passed during the 1920s. As anti-immigrant sentiment grew, anti-Semitism grew, for the Jew was often seen as a newly arrived foreigner bringing Eastern European customs and manners to America.[1] Many individuals and groups, however, refused to follow these trends. Jacob A. Riis, for example, came to the attention of a large segment of the American public through his first book, *How the Other Half Lives*, published in 1890, before anti-Semitism had risen to a peak. Yet in its treatment of Russian Jews living in New York City, this book is blatantly anti-Semitic. As the American public became increasingly antagonistic toward the immigrants

---

1. For example, James V. Cunningham, *The Resurgent Neighborhood* (Notre Dame, Ind.: Fides Publishers, 1965), and Marshall Kaplan, *Urban Planning in the 1960s: A Design for Irrelevancy* (New York: Praeger, 1973).
† *The New-York Historical Society Quarterly* 63.3 (1979). Reprinted by permission of the author.
1. See Maldwyn Allen Jones, *American Immigration* (Chicago, 1960), 247–77.

and concomitantly more anti-Semitic, however, Riis became more compassionate and even militant in his defense of immigrants in general and Jews in particular.

Riis is, of course, particularly worthy of study by one who desires to understand America—and especially New York City—at the turn of the century. He was one of the most influential men of the Progressive Era. In addition to pioneering photojournalism, he was probably the single most important person in the tenement-house reform movement in New York from 1890 to 1910. Riis's friend President Theodore Roosevelt called him "one of those men who by his writings contributed most to raising the standard of unselfishness, of disinterestedness, of sane and kindly good citizenship, in this country."[2] Modern historians of the Progressive Era also single out Riis for special attention as one of the most influential men in the area of urban development.[3] Moreover, he is worth studying by one interested in properly assessing American attitudes toward Jewish immigrants if only because several recent studies have chosen to attack him. Finally, one of the most influential men of his day, Riis was able to sway large segments of public opinion. Thus, his changing attitudes toward Jews are significant in terms of the treatment of Jews and Jewish immigrants, for during a period of widespread anti-Semitism, Riis was one of the leaders of the vigorous minority that argued for and eventually won fair treatment for the Jews in America.

In his foreword to the 1970 reprint of *The Poor in Great Cities*, Sol Cohen writes that many historians point to the rural bias and anti-immigrant sentiment in the writings of Progressive Era reformers; one of these reformers, Cohen states, is Riis.[4] His being included here is, of course, ironic, for Riis was born in Denmark in 1849 and arrived in New York almost penniless in 1870. For about seven years he tried unsuccessfully to live in rural America; he finally had to return to New York City, where he began a successful career as a journalist. Curiously, he never entirely lost his rural bias, but he did lose most of his anti-immigrant sentiments, including those directed against Eastern European Jews.

Two recent studies of Eastern European Jewish immigrants in America that treat Riis rely exclusively on his first book to make their points about him; other studies also base their final judgments on statements Riis makes in his first book. All consequently paint a picture of him as being interested in alleviating the plight of the Jews in New York City but extremely prejudiced against them. The uses to which these authors put Riis's book become clear in the following quotation from one of them, Irving Howe:

> Riis wrote *How the Other Half Lives*, the most influential of the early
> muckraking books, out of a reformer's zeal but with only a limited
> capacity for seeing the people he proposed to help. What he described
> of "Jewtown" was accurate and—in behalf of tenement reforms yet to
> come—very useful. But Riis was a cold writer, deficient in that play of

---

2. "Introduction" in Jacob A. Riis, *The Making of an American* (New York 1929), x, reprinted from *Outlook*, June 6, 1914.
3. For a modern study of Riis's position in the history of tenement-house reform, see Roy Lubove, *The Progressives and the Slums: Tenement House Reform in New York City, 1890–1917* (Pittsburgh, 1962), 49–80. Lubove's praise of Riis is at times excessive.
4. Sol Cohen, "Foreword," in Robert A. Woods et al., *The Poor in Great Cities: Their Problems and What Is Doing* [sic] *to Solve Them* (1895; reprint, New York, 1970), vii.

humane sympathies which lights up the work of [Lincoln] Steffens and Hutchins Hapgood. "Money," Riis could say about the immigrants, "is their God. Life itself is of little value compared with even the leanest bank account." This not only restated an ancient stereotype but was also painfully obtuse, for never in his book did Riis ask himself why the immigrants were so eager to save a few dollars or to what uses they might put their savings. His eye was sharp, but it was the eye of an outsider content to remain one, and eager as he was to remedy the conditions of the immigrant poor, he was equally clear in his mind as to the distance he meant to keep from them.[5]

Unlike Steffens and Hapgood, Riis always remained an outsider looking in. During his newspaper years, he often relied on Max Fischel, his assistant, to provide him with inside information about the immigrant quarters.[6] Nonetheless, in relying only on Riis's more blatantly anti-Semitic statements in *How the Other Half Lives*, Howe and similar writers distort, for Riis did not write only one influential book. Yet no studies in print of Eastern European Jews—and indeed no studies in print of Riis—trace his shifting views concerning the Jew in America, even though he wrote numerous books and articles and gave countless lectures, many of which directly influenced the lives of the immigrants about whom he spoke and wrote. And these works show a growth on Riis's part toward an understanding of and even admiration for the Eastern European Jews he so severely attacked in *How the Other Half Lives*.

To assess Riis's growth away from prejudice one must first gauge the extent of that prejudice. Howe's quotation from *How the Other Half Lives* only begins to show some of the stereotypes Riis used. This book contains numerous additional anti-Semitic statements, especially in the chapters on "Jewtown" and "The Sweaters of Jewtown." As one might guess, the Jews' supposedly inordinate desire for money supplies a nexus for many of these statements. In saying that Jews worship money, Riis was, of course, repeating a common stereotype of his day.[7] Nonetheless, for one who claimed to have firsthand knowledge of life on the Lower East Side, he here displayed an inexcusable callousness.

In *How the Other Half Lives* he wrote that the Jews' "constitutional greed" drives them to starve "themselves to the point of physical exhaustion, while working night and day at a tremendous pressure to save a little money." But, "an avenging Nemesis pursues this headlong hunt for wealth; there is no worse paid class anywhere." He attributed the Jews' being underpaid to the Jews themselves: the Jew's "price is not what he can get," Riis wrote, "but the lowest he can live for and underbid his neighbor." In

5. Irving Howe, *World of Our Fathers* (New York, 1976), 396–97. See also Ronald Sanders, *The Downtown Jews: Portraits of an Immigrant Generation* (New York, 1976), 180–81. For similar statements see Thomas Kessner, *The Golden Door: Italian and Jewish Immigrant Mobility in New York City 1880–1915* (New York, 1977), 62–63, 76. Additional similar treatments are cited below. The most puzzling treatment of Riis in connection with Jews occurs in Joseph Brandes, *Immigrants to Freedom: Jewish Communities in Rural New Jersey Since 1882* (Philadelphia, 1971), 175, in which Riis's statement from the 1890 book that "Money is their [the Jews'] God" is quoted in a discussion of American attitudes toward the Jews on the eve of World War I. Howe's criticisms are similar to those found in a contemporary review in the *Critic*, XXVII (December 1890). For excerpts from contemporary reviews, see Louise Ware, *Jacob A. Riis: Police Reporter, Reformer, Useful Citizen* (New York, 1938), 73–75. The review from the *Critic* is excerpted on pp. 74–75.
6. See Lincoln Steffens, *The Autobiography of Lincoln Steffens* (New York, 1931), 203–07.
7. See for example E. Lyell Earle, "Character Studies in New York's Foreign Quarters," *Catholic World*, LXVIII (March 1899), 782–93.

an earlier discussion of both Jews and Italians he even wrote that "they carry their slums with them wherever they go, if allowed to do it," implying that they lived in slums because they liked to.[8]

Riis's picture of the Jew in his first book is extremely unpleasant. "Oppression, persecution, have not shorn the Jew of his native combativeness one whit," he wrote. The Jew "is as ready to fight for his rights, or what he considers his rights, in a business transaction—synonymous generally with his advantage—as if he had not been robbed of them for eighteen hundred years." This passage is about as sympathetic to the Jews as Riis ever gets in this book.

Riis's most ludicrous criticism involves "decorum" in the sweatshops. In the hot summer months the workers in these usually unventilated, sweltering rooms naturally removed as much of their clothing as possible, working, Riis wrote, "half-naked." To this fact Riis added: "Proprieties do not count on the East Side; nothing counts that cannot be converted into hard cash." Even the poverty in the Jewish quarters, Riis insisted, is largely sham. "The direst apparent poverty in Jewtown" he wrote, "unless dependent upon absolute lack of work, would, were the truth known, in nine cases out of ten have a silver lining in the shape of a margin in the bank."[9] Riis's portrait of the Jews obviously fanned the fires of anti-Semitism in the New World.

The early Riis could not forgive the Jews for their refusal to accept Christianity. Both Eastern European and second-generation German Jews did not accept Christianity, but Riis found the Eastern European Jews alone offensive in this regard because they would not put on even the outward appearance of Christians. In an unpublished note to the manuscript version of *How the Other Half Lives*, Riis explained: "There is a broad line of distinction to be drawn between our home Hebrews [German Jews] and the Polish [Eastern European Jews] immigrants. It is with the latter only we have here to do."[1] They spoke an unfamiliar and to Riis, an unpleasant sounding language; they adhered to strange customs; and they worshiped in ways that hardly resembled Protestant practice. Furthermore, many of them refused to abandon these ways even after many years in America. Riis attributed this refusal to sheer stubbornness. "So, in all matters pertaining to their religious life that tinges all their customs," he wrote, "they stand, these East Side Jews, where the new day that dawned on Calvary left them standing, stubbornly refusing to see the light."[2] That the residents of Jewtown could hold honest religious convictions differing from those of Riis or of the Reformed German Jews did not occur to him. He seems to have reasoned that if his friend Felix Adler could form the Ethical Culture Society, the Jews of Jewtown could at least act a little like Protestants.

The idea of unity in multiplicity or of strength in diversity seems alien to Riis's thinking. In fact, his criterion for determining whether an immigrant group was to be admired seems to have been Americanization, a word he defined in terms of assimilation. He admired the groups he felt were likely

---

8. Jacob A. Riis, *How the Other Half Lives: Studies Among the Tenements of New York* (New York, 1890), 26, 107–22.
9. *Ibid.*, 107–10, 124–33.
1. Jacob A. Riis, "How the Other Half Lives," MSS, 137, Jacob A. Riis Papers, New York Public Library, Astor, Lenox and Tilden Foundations. The author wishes to express his gratitude to Dr. J. Riis Owre for permission to quote from Jacob Riis's unpublished writing.
2. *How the Other Half Lives*, 112.

to become good citizens and scorned those he felt were unlikely to do so. Thus, he especially scorned Chinese immigrants, for he felt that they deliberately kept themselves from becoming good citizens by leaving their families in China and by having their bones returned to China.[3] Similarly, in 1890 he scorned the Eastern European Jews for their refusal to imitate their Protestant neighbors. What happened to Riis after 1890 to change his mind about the Jews' ability to become "good" citizens is a matter of speculation. All that is certain is that he did change his mind.

Perhaps his work in connection with the Brodsky family contributed to this change. Riis repeatedly wrote of the child Jette Brodsky, who at the age of three wandered from her parents' home on the Lower East Side and disappeared. Her parents' strength and faith as they searched for their lost daughter inspired Riis. Especially appealing was one visit he paid the family. Forgetting that their Sabbath began on Friday evening, he went to their home and found them gathered around the Sabbath table, with a highchair ready and a place set in case their lost daughter should appear. All efforts to find the child failed, but the family still hoped. Finally, two years after Jette disappeared, she was found in a children's home not twelve blocks from her own home. As far as Riis could tell, she had wandered the streets until a policeman took her to police headquarters. Unable to discover who she was, the authorities sent her to the children's home, where she was given a new name. In 1900 Riis was to write of this episode as "my first meeting with the Russian Jew."[4] Although this individual contact probably helped him overcome some of his anti-Semitism, one must recall that Riis told the story of Jette in *The Children of the Poor* (1892), the companion volume to *How the Other Half Lives*. In the former volume he was only a little less blatantly anti-Semitic, at least toward the immigrants themselves, even though he felt confident that their American-born children would become good citizens.[5]

Nonetheless, personal contact probably helped change Riis's mind. His attitude toward the assimilation of the Jews also underwent a change. No one has yet fully explored Riis's ideas about the possibilities of assimilation of various ethnic groups; to do so would require a lengthy study of his writings about such diverse groups as the Italians, the Syrians, the Bohemians, the American Indians, the blacks, the Chinese, and, of course, the Jews. Yet there is good reason to believe that Riis tended to judge ethnic groups and their members in terms of what he felt to be their ability to become assimilated. His autobiography, *The Making of an American*, is a hymn in praise of assimilation in which he uses his own life as an example for other immigrants to follow. Riis's message is the Franklinesque one that if he, a poor Danish immigrant, could become wholly Americanized, so could any other person. Thus he could not completely forgive the Russian Jews for their refusal to become assimilated.

As noted earlier, the culture of the German Jews in New York did not antagonize Riis, for they spoke English, they dressed like other Americans,

---

3. See, for example, *How the Other Half Lives*, 29; and Jacob A. Riis, *The Children of the Poor* (New York, 1892), 8–9.
4. Riis told the story at length in fictitious form, using the name Yette Lubinsky for the girl, in the story entitled "Lost Children" in Jacob A. Riis, *Children of the Tenements* (1903; reprint. Freeport, N.Y., 1970), 54–58. He also told it in *Children of the Poor*, 43–44; and in "The Heart of New York," *Independent*, LXXVI (December 4, 1913), 450.
5. See *Children of the Poor*, 8, 14, 52.

and they worshiped for the most part in temples that resembled in structure, ritual, and decorum the Protestant churches to which Riis was accustomed. But the Eastern European Jews, who often refused to give up their Orthodoxy and consequently their practice of seemingly strange religious customs, and who spoke Yiddish instead of English, presented problems. Riis's dislike of Yiddish persisted throughout his life. He never recognized it as a distinct language: in his early works it was "the queer lingo that passes for Hebrew on the East Side" and "the gutterals of the Russian Jew"; in later works it was "the jargon of the East Side" in which he thought the Russian Jew prayed as well as spoke. He never lost the notion that he expressed in *The Children of the Poor* that Yiddish is "the strange jargon that passes for Hebrew on the East Side, but is really a mixture of a dozen known dialects and tongues and of some that were never known or heard anywhere else. In the census it is down as just what it is—jargon and nothing else."[6] Consequently, Riis was blind to the rich Yiddish culture evolving in America at the turn of this century. It is not surprising that Riis harbored such sentiments, however, for even a writer as sympathetic as Hutchins Hapgood called Yiddish a language "which, on account of its poor dialectic character, is an inadequate vehicle of thought," and contemptuously labeled it "the 'jargon,' the Yiddish of the people."[7]

In January 1896, Riis's essay entitled "The Jews of New York" was published. In terms of thoroughness, this essay nicely complements the treatment of the Jews in *How the Other Half Lives*. Yet in tone it is markedly different. It is essentially a defense of Eastern European Jews. Its major premise is that just as German Jews had been Americanized, so their Eastern European brethren are being Americanized and are already making positive contributions to American life.

Riis began his essay by writing about "the great Hebrew Fair in Madison Square Garden," designed to raise money for "Hebrew" charities. He then contrasted the fair with "the strike among the garment workers on the East Side."

> On the one side the mayor of America's chief city opening the great fair with words of grateful appreciation of the civic virtues of a prosperous and happy people, wealth and fashion thronging to its doors and the whole community joining in the glad welcome. On the other, this suffering multitude in its teeming tenements, fettered in ignorance and bitter poverty, struggling undismayed to cast off its fetters and its reproach, and winning in the fight against tremendous odds by the exercise of the same stern qualities that won for their brothers prosperity and praise.

Riis had indeed come a long way in less than six years from his descriptions in *How the Other Half Lives* of money-grubbing Jews. He commented on the struggle of the Eastern European Jew: "Truly this is a spectacle well calculated to challenge every feeling of human and manly interest; alas! and of human prejudice as well."[8]

6. *How the Other Half Lives*, 56, 60; Jacob A. Riis, "The Snow Babies' Christmas," in *Neighbors: Life Stories of the Other Half* (New York, 1914), 194; *Children of the Poor*, 45.
7. Hutchins Hapgood, *The Spirit of the Ghetto* (1902; reprint. Cambridge, Mass., 1967), 25, 44. For a discussion of Yiddish as "jargon," see Sanders, *Downtown Jews*, 13–16.
8. Jacob A. Riis, "The Jews of New York," *Review of Reviews*, XIII (January 1896), 58.

In 1895 Riis estimated that of the 250,000 Jews in New York City, Orthodox Jews outnumbered Reformed Jews by nearly two and one half to one. The Orthodox "are of the tenements"; the Reformed, "of the Avenue. Those of the strike, this one of the fair. Those the newcomers, struggling hand to hand with the dim realities of poverty which these, having won home and welcome, are attacking in the rear, faithful none the less, as their problem." Riis then discussed the lives of the Orthodox Jews. About "the tenement hordes" he wrote: "They perplex at times the most sanguine optimist. The poverty they have brought us is black and bitter; they crowd as do no other living beings to save space, which is rent, and where they go they make slums." Although this passage sounds like the old Riis, he then added: "They slave and starve to make money, for the tyranny of a thousand years from which freedom was bought only with gold has taught them the full value of it. It taught them, too, to stick together in good and evil report since all the world was against them, and this is the clinching argument against New York's ghetto: it is clannish." Here Riis at least attempted to do what Howe rightly says he did not do in his first book, namely, to understand "why the immigrants were so eager to save a few dollars." Riis in part explained their clannishness too by their feeling that they could rely only on themselves.[9]

Instead of being negative, as it may seem at first, the essay is positive, live, presenting first the accusations against the Eastern European Jews and then defending them. "As to the poverty," Riis wrote, "they brought us boundless energy and industry to overcome it. Their slums are offensive, but unlike those of other less energetic races, they are not hopeless unless walled in and made so on the old world plan. They do not rot in their slum, but rising pull it up after them. Nothing stagnates where the Jews are."[1] Retaining this idea for the rest of his life, Riis wrote about the Jew in *The Battle With the Slum* (1902): "He is the yeast of the slum, if given time. If it will not let him go, it must rise with him." This picture contrasts markedly with the one painted in an earlier essay, "Special Needs of the Poor in New York" (1892). There, he wrote that every "new attack of Jew-baiting in Russia or Germany, every threatened famine . . . every fresh political persecution sends its hordes of destitute emigrants over the sea to swell the army of the unemployed and needy." After they arrive in New York, the "able bodied" and "ambitious" move on, leaving "the sediment that settles in the slums, too helpless to strike out for itself, all its energies exhausted in that generation in the uprooting from the old soil." Curiously, a modern historian, Moses Rischin, echoes this idea: "The East Europeans landing in New York between 1870 and 1914 arrived with energies spent, nerves frayed, and purses emptied." Nerves frayed and purses emptied? Yes. But "energies spent"? Rischin's own pages describing the tremendous energy in the ghetto belie this overgeneralization, as do the writings of such contemporary critics as Steffens, Hapgood, and Riis himself.[2]

In "The Jews of New York" Riis was the champion of the Eastern European Jew, stronger in his defense than many modern historians and sociologists. For example, he wrote that the Jews' "slums on the East Side are

9. *Ibid.*; Howe, *World of Our Fathers*, 397.
1. "Jews of New York," 58.
2. Jacob A. Riis, *The Battle With the Slum* (1902; reprint. Montclair, N.J., 1969), 193; Jacob A. Riis, "Special Needs of the Poor in New York," *Forum*, XVI (December 1892), 492; Moses Rischin, *The Promised City: New York's Jews, 1870–1914* (Cambridge, Mass., 1962), 53, 55–61.

dark mainly because of the constant influx of a new population ever beginning the old struggle over. The second generation is the last found in those
tenements, if indeed it is not already on its way uptown to the Avenue."
Here, of course, Riis also overgeneralized. Yet he clearly disavowed his earlier idea that the Jew carries the slum with him wherever he goes.[3]

Riis then countered another charge. The Jew's "clannishness, at all
events, does not obstruct his citizenship," he wrote. "There is no more
patriotic people than these Jews, and with reason. They have no old allegiance to forget. They saw to that over yonder." In *The Battle With the Slum*
he repeated the idea in even stronger terms: "If ever there was material for
citizenship, this Jew is such material. Alone of all our immigrants he comes
to us without a past. He has no country to renounce, no ties to forget.
Within him there burns a passionate longing for a home to call his, a country which will own him, that waits only for the spark of such another love
to spring into flame which nothing can quench."[4] One modern author criticizes Riis for calling the Jews in this passage a people "without a past," yet
Riis clearly wrote here of a recent past of willful allegiance to a regular government, something the Eastern European Jews surely did not have.[5]

No longer seeing Jews as always willing to underbid their neighbors, Riis
no longer thought them happy to live and work in terrible circumstances. Nor
did he think they loved life in the sweatshop, either as workers or as bosses.

> Trade organization conquers the sweat shop, and the school drills the
> child, thenceforth not to be enslaved. The very strike of today is an
> instance. It is waged over a broken contract, extorted from the
> sweaters, which guaranteed to tailors a ten-hour working day and a
> fixed wage. Under this compact in a few brief months the tenement
> sweat shop was practically swept from the trade. And it will not be
> restored. I verily believe these men would starve to death rather than
> bend their backs again under the yoke.[6]

"Clannishness" here is replaced by patriotism and a willingness to work
together for the common good, and "constitutional greed' is replaced by a
feeling for the dignity of the individual and the power of cooperation.

Riis defended the Jews against the negative charge of clannishness in yet
another way: "Their poor are not, and never were, a burden upon the community. The Jewish inmates of the workhouse and the almshouse can be
counted on the fingers of one hand any day. They are not paupers. Of the
thousands who received help through the dreadful winter of two years ago
[1893–94], scarce half a dozen remained to be aided when work was again
to be had for wages." In particular, he praised the Jewish charities that the
Hebrew Fair supported, the managerial skills of the people who ran the
charities, the schools they established to teach English, and the technical
schools they supported. He also praised the work of the Baron de Hirsch
Fund in connection with its support of agricultural colonies like the one in
Woodbine, New Jersey, about which he wrote extensively in a later essay.
He praised the Jews' industriousness which led them to become teachers,
doctors, and lawyers. Moreover, "Their temples and synagogues are centres

3. "Jews of New York," 58; for a more balanced discussion of the same topic, see Howe, *World of Our
Fathers,* 159–68.
4. "Jews of New York," 59; *Battle With the Slum,* 192–93.
5. Ande Manners, *Poor Cousins* (New York, 1972), 202–03.
6. "Jews of New York," 59.

of a social energy," he wrote, "that struggles manfully with half the perplexing problems of the day." In a later essay (1913) he added to this praise when he described "The Gemilath Chasodim [sic], an orthodox Jewish charity [that] lends money to Christian, Jew and pagan, asking neither pledge nor interest; it is enough that he is a neighbor and in need." Riis, of course, had no idea what the name of this society meant or what kinds of charitable and benevolent activities it implied. He was simply impressed by the forerunner of the Hebrew Free Loan Society he found behind a door inscribed with the name. Here, however, the Jews' "clannishness" became a virtue extending far beyond the "clan."[7]

In "The Jews of New York" Riis even tackled the perplexing problem of crime in the ghetto. "Jewish liberalism takes a different course in New York on the Avenue and in the tenement," he wrote. "With still its strong backing of old faith morality, it runs uptown to philanthropy, to humanitarianism. . . . 'Religion and humanity' is the watchword of the advanced Jew, sufficiently indicating his spirit. In the slum the loosening of the old ties lets in unbelief with the surrounding gloom and leads directly to immorality and crime. The danger besets especially the young." To Riis's way of thinking, when the Eastern European Jew arrived in America, he was always Orthodox in beliefs and practices; in this essay Riis seemed unaware of the socialists and anarchists among the Jewish arrivals who disavowed affiliation with Judaism as a religion and in many cases even with the peoplehood of the Jews.[8] He also showed a naive unawareness of the complex causes of crime. He admitted, however, that elements other than the weakening of religious convictions might be at work: "Whether it be the tenement that corrupts, the new freedom, or the contrast between the Talmud schools, to which the children are sent when young, and the public school, the fact appears to be that crime is cropping out to a dangerous degree among the Jewish children on the East Side." He explained that the Talmud schools, usually held "in dark and repulsive tenement rooms, become identified in the child's mind from babyhood with his faith. By contrast the public school appears so much more bright and beautiful."[9]

Riis concluded his essay on a slightly ambiguous note.

> The Jew in New York has his faults, no doubt, and sometimes he has to be considered in his historic aspect in order that the proper allowance may be made for him. It is a good deal better perspective, too, than the religious one to view him in, as a neighbor and fellow citizen. I am a Christian and hold that in his belief the Jew is sadly in error. So that he may learn to respect mine, I insist on fair play for him all around. That he has received in New York, and no one has cause to regret it except those he left behind [that is, his persecutors in Europe]. I am very sure that our city has to-day no better and more loyal citizen than the Jew, be he poor or rich—and none she has less need to be ashamed of.[1]

7. Ibid., 59–60; "Heart of New York," 449–50. For the relationship between the *Gemillat Hasodim* Society, as Rischin terms it, and the Hebrew Free Loan Society, see *Promised City*, 106.
8. "Jews of New York," 62. Ronald Sanders' tracing of the career of Abraham Cahan is especially instructive along these lines. See his book *Downtown Jews*, 119–22, 344–62. For a summary of information concerning crime in the New York ghetto in the beginning of this century, see Howe, *World of Our Fathers*, 263–64.
9. "Jews of New York," 60.
1. *Ibid.*, 62.

Even here he retained a slightly patronizing attitude and tone. At least, however, he no longer condemned the Jew for not being a Christian, and he did not attribute the Jew's refusal to convert to sheer stubbornness. But he did think Christianity "superior" to Judaism. It is interesting to note that in his assertion that the Jews have received "fair play" in New York, Riis displayed a lack of knowledge of his own earlier contribution to anti-Semitism. He seems to have remained unaware of his own lack of "fair play" in his first book. Riis's defense of the Jews here, however, is remarkable on at least two counts. First, it contrasts greatly with his earlier anti-Semitic stance, especially in *How the Other Half Lives*. Second, it contrasts markedly with the anti-Semitism that was becoming fashionable around the turn of the century.

Although Riis had consistently argued for limits on immigration, he changed his tone markedly here too. In "Special Needs of the Poor in New York," for example, he had written in "protest against having our city made the dumping ground for half the poverty and ignorance and vice of the Old World." Yet as anti-immigration feelings rose, Riis became a defender of certain kinds of unlimited immigration. Whereas he always advocated the exclusion of criminals, he wanted to "hold the door wide open for the man who comes here for conscience sake, the victim of unjust political persecution," he wrote in 1911. In an address in 1912 he declared: "I for one am not afraid of the immigrant who comes here, or is driven here by persecution at home and comes to be one of us." And he added: "We welcome to our shores the people of Europe, who will come to make common cause with us." Thus, he would keep the door open for Jews escaping pogroms and persecution in Eastern Europe, no matter how poor or ignorant they might be.[2]

In a short story that appeared in *Out of Mulberry Street*, published two years after "The Jews of New York," Riis gave a remarkably sympathetic glimpse of the lives and motives of Eastern European Jews in America. The story, entitled "Merry Christmas in the Tenements," consists of a series of vignettes, including one about a Jewish wedding in Liberty Hall. "Liberty!" Riis exclaimed:

> Strange how the word echoes through these sweaters' tenements, where starvation is at home half the time. It is as an all-consuming passion with these people, whose spirits a thousand years of bondage have not availed to daunt. It breaks out in strikes, when to strike is to hunger and die. Not until I stood by a striking cloak-maker whose last cent was gone, with not a crust in the house to feed seven hungry mouths, yet who had voted vehemently in the meeting that day to keep up the strike to the bitter end—bitter indeed, nor far distant—and heard him at sunset recite the prayer of his fathers: "Blessed art, thou, O Lord our God, King of the world, that thou hast redeemed us as thou didst redeem our fathers, hast delivered us from bondage to liberty, and from servile dependence to redemption!"—not until then did I know what of sacrifice the word might mean, and how utterly we of another day have forgotten.[3]

2. "Special Needs of the Poor in New York," 501; Jacob A. Riis, "The Man Who is an Immigrant, a letter," *Survey*, CXXV (February 18, 1911), 869: Jacob A. Riis, "Citizenship and What It Means," in *Exercises in Commemoration of the Birthday of Washington, Twenty-second February, Nineteen Hundred Twelve* (Chicago, 1912), 37–38.

3. Jacob A. Riis, "Merry Christmas in the Tenements," in *Out of Mullberry Street: Stories of Tenement Life in New York City* (New York, 1898), 34.

From the ideas that money is the Jews' only God and that Jews always work for the least money available, Riis has here moved to an understanding that money is only a part of the lives of the Eastern European Jews in America, a part often sacrificed to some higher goal. For all of its compassion however, the passage still subtly illustrates Riis's lack of complete understanding of Judaism's place in the modern world; as the last clause illustrates, he felt that even though Christians can learn valuable lessons from Jews, Judaism is a religion only of the past, a notion which strangely refuses to die, as shown by Maurice Samuel's need to write *The Professor and the Fossil* (1956) in reply to Arnold Toynbee's similar accusation in this century.

As noted earlier, Riis was greatly interested in the work of the Baron de Hirsch Fund with the Russian-Jewish farming colonies in the Vineland area of New Jersey. His most sympathetic extended treatment of Jews appears in his essay "Making a Way Out of the Slum" (1900), in which the "way out" was through agricultural colonies like those in Woodbine, New Jersey. Perhaps his enthusiasm was so great because these colonies seemed to fulfill his own desire to see an agrarian, agricultural answer to the problems of the slums.

The first of these colonies was established under the auspices of the Hebrew Emigrant Aid Society in 1882 at Alliance, New Jersey. A number of other colonies were formed in South Jersey, including Rosenhayn and Carmel, both established later in 1882. Other, later colonies included Norma, Brotmansville, Garton Road, Six Points, Estellville, Hebron, Mizpah, and Zion. The most successful and the largest of the colonies was Woodbine, founded in 1891 under the auspices of the Baron de Hirsch Fund. Woodbine was to be a model agricultural colony, but during its first year of operation manufacturing was also introduced. In 1894, the Baron de Hirsch Agricultural School was established at the Woodbine colony, the purpose of which was to teach the immigrants and their children modern farming methods. Because the colonies drew their settlers mostly from the tenements of New York City, they naturally attracted Riis's attention.

On visits to the New Jersey colonies Riis saw many reasons for hope. He once went to the farming colonies to deliver an address to the students of the agricultural school there. He told them that "as far back as I can remember I have cherished in my heart a picture of the Jew as husbandman, happily content in his toil, all his troubles over," even though he admitted that the only two Jewish families he knew in his youth in Denmark were not farmers. He then told of his encounter with Jews in New York City, where he saw their "traditional virtues conquer even the physical perils" of life in the slum. After recounting the story of Jette Brodsky and telling of the joy of his first visit to the colonies, he declared: "*Here* you are lifting the Jew out of the slough of centuries, to live a free man upon the land."[4]

More significant, however, is the essay "Making a Way Out of the Slum," which he wrote as a result of his experiences at Woodbine.[5] As one might guess, he began by retelling the story of Jette Brodsky, saying that that was

4. Jacob A. Riis, "On Jews," unpublished typescript with holograph corrections, Jacob A. Riis Papers, Library of Congress.
5. Jacob A. Riis, "Making a Way Out of the Slum'," *American Monthly Review of Reviews*, XXII (December 1900), 692–93, 696–97.

his first meeting with Russian Jews. He then said he met Russian Jews again in New Jersey. On the whole, Riis's evaluation of the colonies and of the lives the Jews led there seems accurate. "Theirs is not Paradise," he wrote. "It is a little world full of hard work, but a world in which the work has ceased to be a curse." He also did not see the colonies as having particularly visionary goals. The "scheme" at Woodbine is, he wrote, "intensely practical. It is to make, if possible, a Jewish yeomanry fit to take their place with the native tillers of the soil, as good citizens as they. With that end in view, everything is 'for present purposes, with an eye on the future.'"

In addition to describing his trip through the Jewish colonies at Woodbine, Carmel, Rosenhayn, Alliance, and Brotmansville, Riis discussed similar experiments in New England. There, the colonists "are mostly dairy-farmers, poultrymen, sheep-breeders." The Russian-Jewish farmer, he wrote, "works hard and faithfully. The Yankee, as a rule, welcomes him. He has the sagacity to see that his coming will improve economic conditions, now none too good. As shrewd traders, the two are well-matched." No longer seeing Eastern European Jews as greedy money-grubbers ready to take unfair advantage of employees, employers, and competitors, Riis here praises them for their shrewdness in business. As he traveled through New Jersey, he joyfully noticed that "everywhere there were signs of reawakened thrift." Ten years earlier he had attacked the Jews for this same thrift.

As though to answer his own earlier criticism, he wrote concerning the Jewish farming colonies in New England: "If the showing that the Jewish population of New England has increased in 17 years from 9,000 to 74,000 gives anybody pause, it is not at least without its compensation. The very need of the immigrant to which objection is made, plus the energy that will not let him sit still and starve, make a way for him that opens it at the same time for others. In New York he *made* the needle industry, which he monopolized. He brought its product up from $30,000,000 to $300,000,000 a year, that he might live, and founded many a great fortune by his midnight toil. In New England, while peopling its abandoned farms, in self-defense he takes up on occasion abandoned manufacturing plants to make the work he wants." The very people who, because of their greed, could never make a worthwhile contribution to anything now have become, in Riis's opinion, good for the economy.

In the final analysis, Riis realized that the agricultural colonies were at best only partial answers to the problems of the teeming tenements. Although the colonies "have given hundreds the chance of life," he wrote, "it cannot be said for them that they have demonstrated yet the Jews' ability to stand alone upon the land, backed as they are by the Hirsch-Fund millions. In fact, I have heard no such claim advanced. But it can at least be said that for these they have solved the problem of life and of the slum. And that is something!" The forming of the agricultural colonies, Riis wrote, "had two objects: to relieve the man and to drain the Ghetto. In this last it failed. In 18 years 1,200 families have been moved out. In the five months from October to March last [1899–1900], 12,000 came to stay in New York City. The number of immigrant Jews during those months was 15,233, of whom only 3,881 went farther. The population of the Ghetto reaches already 250,000. It was like trying to bail out the ocean." Riis nonetheless concluded his article: "When, say, 10 per cent of those now in the Ghetto have been removed, argue the enthusiasts, a rut will have been made for so much of the immigration to follow to the new places, and to that extent it will have been diverted from the cities. To that extent, then, a real 'way out' of the slum will have been found."[6]

Riis retained his hope that movements like the one behind the New Jersey colonies, especially Woodbine, might alleviate the plight of Jews (and other ethnic groups) in the slums of New York. In *The Battle With the Slum*, for example, while admitting their limitations, he again praised the Jewish farming colonies.[7] And he chose to reprint his essay "Making a Way Out of the Slum" in *Children of the Tenements*.[8]

Although Jews still live and work in the area of the Woodbine colony and although many children of the colonists became leading agricultural scientists, including soil chemists, plant pathologists, and agronomists, the experiment ultimately did not relieve the crowding of the ghetto, nor did it produce the sturdy Jewish yeomanry it (and Riis) sought.[9] Even the support of a person of Riis's stature and influence could not make this dream come true to any large extent in turn-of-the-century America.

Riis's understanding of the Russian Jew was, of course, far from complete. In "Making a Way Out of the Slum" he himself told an anecdote that humorously shows his failure to comprehend the reasons why many Jews fled Russia. At supper the night he stayed in the colonies, he recalled, "I caught the burning eyes of a young nihilist fixed upon me with a look I have not yet got over. I had been telling of my affection for the Princess Dagmar, whom I knew at Copenhagen in my youth. I meant it as something we had in common; she became Empress of Russia in after years. I forgot that it was by vitrue of marrying Alexander III. I heard afterward that he protested vehemently that I could not possibly be a good man." Then Riis added: "Well for me I did not tell him my opinion of the Czar himself! It was gleaned from Copenhagen, where they thought him the prince of good fellows."[1] In later years Riis retained his affection for Dagmar but felt less affection for the tsar, as is shown by an account of a meeting he had with Alexander's son, Nicholas II, in 1909. Riis encountered the tsar at Bad Neuheim, Germany. "I took off my hat to him for his mother's sake," Riis wrote, "but I itched to tell him that it was not because of what he is doing to poor Finland, or to his Jewish subjects, I saluted him. I wonder what he would have thought of an indignant American citizen's opinion of it all. I shall never find out now; he went his way unenlightened, too."[2]

Less than a month after Riis's death, in 1914, Stephen S. Wise, then rabbi of the Free Synagogue of New York City, recalled that soon after Wise returned to New York in 1906, Riis came to him and said, "You know I have no wish to proselytize among your people. I want them to be Jews; I want them to be good Jews; I want them to be the best of Jews; and I want you to come down to the Riis settlement and tell them so." Riis's choice of

6. *Ibid.*, 689, 692–93, 696–97.
7. *Battle With the Slum*, 212–16.
8. *Children of the Tenements*, 365–87.
9. For an informal account of the Woodbine experiment, see Manners, *Poor Cousins*, 137–72; for a more extended treatment, see Brandes' book-length history, *Immigrants to Freedom*.
1. "Making a Way Out of the Slum," 693–94.
2. Jacob A. Riis, "A Kindly Journey," *Outlook*, XCVI (December 31, 1910), 1022.

Rabbi Wise is significant. The two men were both involved in the tenement-house reform movement. By 1906 Wise and Riis had been friends for several years. Wise, the leader of a Reformed congregation, was born in Budapest in 1874. Thus he could serve as a bridge between Riis and the Eastern European Jews living near the Riis settlement. Riis asked Wise to talk to the Jewish children at the settlement about "the heroic story of the Maccabees." Riis "could not have spoken with deeper admiration," Wise added, "if he had been thinking and telling of his own Danish forebears."[3] Riis's choice of the Maccabees is also significant. Earlier he was pleased to report that a Jew was among the Rough Riders, and he predicted that if called upon, Jews would serve well in the armed forces.[4] Wise wrote that "we had that Maccabean celebration," and he concluded that "this was Riis's way of answering those who protested against what they conceived to be his attempt to wean children from Judaism and win them to his own faith."[5]

Riis obviously still felt uncomfortable with an Orthodox rabbi, preferring to deal with what he considered to be Americanized Jews. Nonetheless, his sincere desire that Jewish children remain Jews is clear here. Also, his choice of Rabbi Wise, an Eastern-European-born American Jew, later to become one of the foremost spokesmen for American and indeed world Jewry, indicates his sympathetic understanding of the concern of the Jewish parents whose children frequented the Jacob A. Riis Settlement. By 1906, the harsh anti-Semitism of *How the Other Half Lives* was obviously gone. Riis's idea that Jews remain Jews out of sheer stubbornness was nowhere to be seen. Instead, he honestly desired that the Jews remain Jews, but that they be good, sincere Jews, as he desired that Christians be good, sincere Christians.

The time between *How the Other Half Lives* and "Making a Way Out of the Slum" is only ten years. The distance between New York City and the Woodbine colonies is only 130 miles. Yet the psychic time and distance Riis traveled between these two works is immense. In his introduction to Hutchins Hapgood's book, *The Spirit of the Ghetto*, Rischen asserts that it "clearly was an effort to redress, in part at least, Riis's one-dimensional portrait of 'the other half.'"[6] Yet by the time Hapgood published his book (1902) Riis's portrait was by no means one dimensional. He himself had added a great deal of the depth and breadth his earlier portrait lacked, and he had corrected many of the earlier portrait's errors. By the time of his conversations with Rabbi Wise, Riis may even have been able to accept the idea that people could remain different from one another and still live in harmony and contribute to the common good. After 1898 he consistently saw Eastern European Jews and especially their children as good citizens. He defended them when others were attacking them and when it would have been far easier for him to have remained silent. The virulence of his

3. Rabbi Stephen S. Wise to the Reverend Newell Dwight Hillis, June 12, 1914, Jacob A. Riis Papers, New York Public Library, Astor, Lenox and Tilden Foundations. The author wishes to express his gratitude to the Honorable Justine Wise Polier and James Waterman Wise for permission to use this letter.
4. Jacob A. Riis, *Theodore Roosevelt, the Citizen* (1904; reprint. St. Clair Shores, Mich., 1970), 188; *Battle With the Slum*, 193—here Riis actually invokes the Maccabees in predicting the Jews will make excellent soldiers.
5. Rabbi Wise to the Reverend Hillis, June 12, 1914.
6. Moses Rischin, "Introduction," in Hapgood, *Spirit of the Ghetto*, XXIII.

early anti-Semitism makes his later defense of Jews extraordinary. To dismiss him facilely as an anti-Semitic reformer who tried to help the people he despised is, of course, to do Riis a disservice. More important, it is to distort one of the phases of American ethnic history in which Riis played an extremely important role.

PETER BACON HALES

From Silver Cities: Photographing American Urbanization, 1839–1939[†]

Chapter 5. *The Hidden Hand: Jacob Riis and the Birth of Reform Photography*

One of the signal mutations in American urban photography occurred between 1885 and 1895. Until that decade, the genre seemed immutably bonded by technology and tradition to a celebratory, monumental style, whereby the outer surface of the city served as a metaphor for its inner strength and civilized grandeur. But those years brought about a revolution in photographic technology, exploding the neat tautology of the urban grand-style taxonomy and introducing a new vision of the city. Acceptance of supersensitive dry-plate technology, the introduction of flexible film into the professional and amateur marketplace, the development of a new artificial light technology for photography, the advent of cheap, simple cameras that made use of these innovations—all served to break down the old strictures of professionalism and the outdated conceptions of urban style.

But there was more to this revolution than a response to technological innovations. Long before snapshots became everyday affairs, long before flash-lit scenes became *de rigeur* for the ambitious photographer, pioneers in the medium had made photographs that presaged the wave of new forms that would wash over urban photography. In the surrounding fields of lithography and wood engraving, imagery that ranged far afield from the lightstruck business corridors into the darkened dens of poverty and desperation were readily to be seen. Yet urban photographers shied from expanding into these areas.

Larger social and cultural trends swept urban photography back into the forefront of the American vision of the city as reality and as possibility: trends in public health, in epidemiology, in social reform, in religion and philosophy under-girded the photographic revolution.

From this revolutionary decade, one name stands out clearly—that of Jacob Riis. Probably more than any other single individual in the history of the genre, Riis brought together the technological, philosophical, and stylistic strands of his time and his culture. An outsider to the photographic establishment, he created a body of work that altered the terms of debate within the medium of photography and had a nearly equal effect on the way Americans saw the city as environment and as metaphor.

The photographs Riis made (or, more accurately, presided over, as we shall see) enlarged the vista of urban photography, but they also cemented

† Copyright © 2005, University of New Mexico Press. Reprinted by permission of the Publisher.

the link between photography and social reform, making it not just the visual medium of an American intellectual and social movement but the preeminent mode of proof in the rhetoric of social and urban reform for the next ninety years.

The photographs Riis produced operated by a rhetoric of realism, of verisimilitude: one believed them to be true to life, visual records of a moment in a larger experiential continuum. Riis's photographs promised access to worlds alien, dangerous, and seductively fascinating. This fascination might range from the obsessive—horrified looking at gruesome photographs—to the voyeuristic—staring at the lives of others far removed from one's own—and end at the extreme of catch-in-the-throat sentimentality, as emotionally charged stereotypes from recognizable sources surfaced in novel, exotic surroundings.

Riis's photographs didn't depend, particularly, on the rigorous aesthetic discipline of later so-called documentarians whose aspirations were very different—artists appropriating the documentary mode, "concerned" photographers exploiting its moral uplift to personal ends, propaganda producers, mass-market advertisers, museum curators. There wasn't meant to be art in documentary, even if the pictures were supremely artful. To call attention to the skill of the maker was a distraction, not a goal. But Riis's photographs *did* depend upon a strongly directive moral presence, an authorial voice that might speak with the authority of experiences not held by his audience.

Indeed, in social documentary photography, as Riis's photographs exemplified and anticipated the form, authority replaced authorship as the critical catalyst for what might broadly be called the *picture event*. In documentary, simply looking at or, more fully, understanding a photograph is not the end—the completion point or the goal. Instead, documentary linked the event of the picture's making backward to a hidden world that predated the picture and would live on after the image was made; documentary also linked the act of looking and parsing out the picture *forward*, to some changed circumstance in the consciousness of the viewer that impelled further action to influence those events, social circumstances, and tragedies that the picture revealed and that now continued and would continue unless the viewer *acted*.

Finally, though, Riis's work made the photograph a part of a larger directorial, even dictatorial, process on the part of the authority standing behind the picture. Looking at a documentary photograph, as Riis catalyzed the form, meant subjecting oneself to moral imperatives—the judgments, even commandments, of the man or woman who had entered that world, had risked something to witness the scene and bring it back, had understood its tragedy and now stood before the viewer demanding something in return. The picture compelled action; the documentary authority pointed out what action was required.

Just how that moral direction might be successfully administered was one of the problems of documentary to which Riis proposed lasting solutions. Riis's photographs could in many cases stand alone because they contained a clear visual language—borrowed from other experiences common to their viewers or, more ambitiously, built from the event of looking sequentially at a larger body of pictures so that themes, ideas, images, and symbols developed a common set of meanings that carried over from picture to picture. They could stand, in other words, as single pictures if they borrowed a clear iconography (as his famous "Home of an Italian Rag-picker," which drew so blatantly from popular Christian images that it soon became known as the "Slum Madonna"), or they could form a visual narrative, as the authority behind them ordered them into a directive sequence. Or documentary photographs could come to their meanings by their imbeddedness in other forms—in books, in lectures, in sermons, in performances more generally—where words, tones of voice, even the associations with the publication or the venue (a theater, perhaps, or the rectory of a church, even the sanctuary) might serve to dike the flood of possible meanings and direct the stream of comprehension into a wider estuary of response.

All of these qualities of documentary photography had predated Riis's excursions into the New York underclasses. But Riis was the first to unite them, to hone them, to develop a near-completed strategy of visual rhetoric that was simultaneously dependent upon photography for its power even as it invested in photography powers drawn from other traditions and other media.

Previous to Riis, reform photography had existed only in the scattered experiments of a few photographers. In England during the 1840s, daguerreotypist Richard Beard had produced a body of "character studies" for Henry Mayhew's model urban reform study, *London Labour and the London Poor* (finally published in 1851). In America, U.S. Geological Survey photographer John K. "Jack" Hillers had made a revolutionary collection of photographs depicting the destruction of American Indian tribal cultures and the horrendous conditions of Indian life. Both photographers had empirically discovered the powerful link between their medium and the social concerns of reform, but the technical difficulties of Beard's single-image daguerreotypes and the limited audience for Hillers's Indian studies prevented any real growth of reform photography within the genetic pool of photographic traditions and strategies.

Riis, however, provided the model from which a reform tradition in photography could be developed. Because of Riis, social reformers from 1890 to the present would look to photographs as the logical source of publicity for their efforts, as an imperative part of every report, call for funds, discovery of inequity, or angry polemic aimed at the public or even at their own ranks. Because of Riis, photographers of the city would come to see themselves not simply as passive describers of the surface of things but as active investigators delving beneath the deceptive surface of the city to its hidden realities, its darker truths. Lecturing before civic improvement associations, upper-class social clubs, church congregations, reform groups, academic meetings and conventions, and reform organizations, Riis used his lantern-slide views of urban poverty to give authority and credence to his insistence that the city and its residents had been too long denied a true vision of their environment and its effects. His articles and books—beginning with *How the Other Half Lives* in 1890 and continuing through *Children of the Poor*, *The Making of an American*, and others—introduced a generation of readers in America and Europe to the rhetoric of reform and the crucial place of photography within that rhetoric.

So great an effect did Riis and his photographs have that within twenty years his photographic and reform models would hold absolute sway in urban social study, and in forty-five years the terms he had defined would pervade rural reform and its rhetoric as well. It is one of the great ironies that, as a direct effect of his own influence, Riis himself would be nearly forgotten for most of a century. The intellectual tide that he set in motion engulfed him; his photographs, too, disappeared in the flood of reform photography his example engendered, only to be returned to prominence and controversy at the end of another century.

Since I initially wrote about Riis in the first edition of this book, the photographer-reformer has become the linchpin of an engrossing debate concerning the nature of reform photography and, by extension, the underpinnings of reform ideology more generally. For some, Riis has served as the object of a poststructuralist critique of the dominant liberal reform paradigm; examining his work has revealed—in what was emphasized and what suppressed—the ways dominant and dominating individuals, social groups, and institutions fought to maintain their domination in a cultural landscape increasingly polyglot and polymorphous. In caricatures, Riis has become a straw man for polemicists; in the hands of sophisticated and deft analysts (Keith Gandal, Maren Stange, Douglas Tallack, and Sally Stein most notably), the complexities of Riis's place in American culture have been brilliantly redefined.

Knowledge of Jacob Riis remains crucial to an understanding of the intellectual and social movements of the American city and equally crucial to a history of urban photography in America. The fascinating interplay of cultural revolutionary and cultural conservative that Riis embodied is more than just a revelation of his personality or even his moment: to trace the strands that converged on him; to look at the resulting photographs and their variants (prints, lantern slides, halftone reproductions, forgeries, appropriations, and variations), teasing out the meanings within them; and to explore the results over the decades that followed, is to find the opportunity to weave together some of the seeming disparities of nineteenth- and twentieth-century American urban culture.

*   *   *

This was the world that Jacob Riis entered on February 12, 1888, with the publication of "Flashes from the Slums," a telegraphic article in the *New York Sun* illustrated with a set of crude wood engravings from photographs. The article was the culmination of fifteen years of experience with the underworld of American urban life, most of it garnered as a night-beat police reporter. It was also the first suggestion that a major new urban photography was in the process of being born.

Police reporting was Riis's métier. He began his beat at a time when both urban and rural residents hungered for information about the slums, for confirmation of their fears about the growing chaos of urban life, and for the vicarious excitement and sensational rhetoric that police-beat reporting offered them. Ostracized by his fellow reporters for his habit of actually investigating his turf rather than rewriting police reports, Riis immersed himself in the life of the streets. Every morning after work, Riis would walk "the whole length of Mulberry Street, through the Bend, and across the Five Points down to Fulton Ferry." In short, he traversed one of the worst slums in history. "There were cars on the Bowery," he recalled in his autobiography, "but I liked to walk, for I saw the slum when off its guard."

This obsession with the gritty life of the city made Riis one of the most popular police reporters of his age. But it also revealed what, to him, seemed a compelling logic to the slums. Crime, he began to argue, was not the result simply of moral and genetic failures. Rather, it was the effect of an environment that suppressed all positive impulses and influences and substituted—even demanded—greed, desperation, and moral laxity. "Survival of the Fittest," Herbert Spencer's most famous slogan, engendered not moral progress but moral regress.

Riis wasn't alone in this discovery, and the influence of others, more scientifically sophisticated and more firmly connected to the strands of New York's privileged classes, profoundly altered Riis's attitude. By 1881, Riis had begun to cultivate friendships among the scientists and statisticians in the city's health department: the men who investigated conditions, compiled reports, and lobbied for action. These men, notably Dr. Roger S. Tracy and amateur photographer Dr. John T. Nagle, provided Riis with "pretty much all the understanding I have ever had of the problems I have battled with."

Like him, they were pragmatists with experience. Unlike him, they had less of sensationalism and more of dispassion in their method. What they offered Riis was a pseudoscientific causal system that, while simplistic, was to form the core of the social environmentalism of the Social Gospel and Progressive movements. In a culture still intellectually dominated by laissez-faire social theories, and within a social and economic class more concerned with protecting itself than helping others, the environmentalism of Riis and his health department compatriots put them in the social avant-garde of the era. While a noted economist was reporting in a speech to the American Social Science Association that few Americans were "so poor nowadays as not to be able to afford some sort of carpet for their parlor," Riis and his friends were touring the tenements just a few blocks away, seeing for themselves the conditions of urban poverty.

Out of this, Riis came to understand, better than most reformers of his era, the fundamental logic that saw crime, ignorance, vice, and poverty as effects rather than causes. By 1883, Riis had begun to write the earliest of his attacks on slum conditions, arguing that petty moralisms could not eradicate the logic that linked environment to sickness, crime, and social disorder. By 1885, he had cemented relations with Lowell of the COS and Felix Adler, founder of one of New York's earliest social work institutions, the Ethical Culture Society.

Yet Riis was not the morally unambiguous paragon that he might seem. His vision was set within a very specific cultural frame: he did not see the relationship between himself and his "subjects" to be one of brotherhood or kinship. Often they were "a race apart," as he once wrote, capable, perhaps, of "rising" from "the depths" to the elevated regions occupied by the middle-class citizens who were truly American, but until then still the objects of pity rather than empathy, of observation, judgment, paternalism, not of kinship. Just as today conservative ideologues use the phrase "underclass" to define a world beneath the floor of social identity, in his time Riis coined and exploited "the other half" as a means of separating his audience from his subjects and identifying himself firmly with the former. Similarly (as Douglas Tallack has pointed out) Riis's subjects served not as examples but as "specimens," in Riis's parlance: the chilling quality of this word today may not have rung so clearly then, but the underlying sense of the "other half" as a race separate, subject to scrutiny rather than sympathy, was one part of the complex admixture that comprised Riis's ideology.

But it was not the only side: these "specimens" were also meant to be understood—by him and, before him, by the health department specialists who taught him—as victims of a mysterious disease that was striking at the American body politic—a disease that threatened not just the poor but all

Americans. Riis's contradictions might thus be resolved in this way: the souls he described were already lost—dead, they could serve as specimens for a postmortem. But their deaths came not at their own hands. Their fate required detectives, journalists, judges, juries to bring to justice those who had so injured, crippled, or killed them. One didn't have to be of them, or even move within their world, to participate in the process that might redeem them and damn their oppressors. In the chain of justice, every faction of urban society might find a proper role.

This explains why, for Riis as for so many of his generation of reformers, children were so important to his ideology: they proved his argument that all souls were innocent but vulnerable, open to corruption, open to *influences*—evil or good. In this, then, Riis *did* see the American population as united into one great mass, fluid—dangerously fluid—sharing the streets, the air, the urban space most broadly. It was, finally, Riis's contribution to propose the impossibility of successfully isolating one class from another, and thereby the necessity of *creating* a united social landscape.

*   *   *

Riis was a thinker whose attention was always simultaneously drawn to the narrowly specific and to the broadest thematic sweeps. A single child stood for all children, to him; a single child mistreated, harmed, starved, driven to crime was an indictment of all humanity by every child: in this he was the preacher first and last. In his double role as detective and prosecutor, the smallest details of the crime scene were redolent, and he sought constantly to assemble these richly persuasive facts. In his memoranda books, he scribbled hasty notes about the places he visited with his health department friends and the sanitary police—here is one evening's notes, scribbled as he paced out the sizes of rooms and interviewed the residents of one floor of one tenement:

> Dimensions: front 14'–11'
> middle 7×11
> rear 7×8–½
> 9.7 fl. To ceiling
> for all 2784 cubic feet
>
> 3 rooms—Finelli [?]
> 3 families
> front room 3 children
> man and wife
> . . .
> 2 men—2 in middle
> 3/man sleep in 3 [?]
> " "1 bed
> cigarmaker [?], works
> part in hall
> rent for all $12-½
>
> 2 floors
> rent 12 dollars
> 6 [rooms?]
> Rent_____

3 fl.
Rear 11 per[sons].
2 women sew
  one with baby in lap
3 . . . children
lamp with . . . paper shade
one girl disappeared
. . .
7 cent per parl [? Pan? Panel? Parcel?]
4 pan a day.

"It was upon my midnight trips with the sanitary police that the wish kept cropping up in me that there were some way of putting before the people what I saw there," he recalled later. "A drawing might have done it, but it would not have been evidence of the kind I wanted."

Riis's statement is a telling one, for it reminds us just how closely allied was his thinking, and his work, to the world of visual journalism that had come increasingly to dominate the newsstands and subscription services in America after the Civil War. Riis's writing was, after all, directed toward making his readers believe in him, in his vision and in his response; he had become a master of word pictures, increasingly aware of the limits of credibility in that mode of rhetoric. He sought a practice outside words but closely allied to them. "Evidence of the kind I wanted" meant evidence in which the passion and prejudice of the detective might be rendered invisible or confirmed from another source.

* * *

MAREN STANGE

From Symbols of Ideal Life: Social Documentary Photography in America, 1890–1950†

Chapter 1. From Sensation to Science: Documentary Photography at the Turn of the Century

* * *

How the Other Half Lives, written on behalf of tenement reform in New York, addressed its message directly to the propertied middle class. Dismissing "tardy enactment of law" and "political expedient," Riis placed the solution to the tenement problem squarely in the hands of private capital: "neither legislation nor charity can cover the ground," he said, and "the greed of capital that wrought the evil must itself undo it." Model tenements, with profits held at five percent and much personal involvement by the Christian landlord, were the solution he proposed. His conclusion reiterated that the "lion's share" of dealing with the tenement problem must fall to "private enterprise" or "conscience, to put it in the category of duties, where it belongs." And, Riis's final paragraphs insisted, this is a duty that the middle class owed first and foremost to itself: the law and philanthropy, when powerfully aided by "conscience," would preserve it from the effects of disastrous social upheaval. "The sea of a mighty population, held in galling fetters, heaves uneasily in the tenements," Riis warned. "If it rise once more, no human power may avail to check it." There was, however, a bridge to "carry us over safe," and it was "built of human hearts," he avowed, ending the book with a monitory couplet from James Russell Lowell: "Think ye that building shall endure/Which shelters the noble and crushes the poor?"

Already a consummate publicist, Riis was proposing in essence that conscientious personal philanthropy might function both as good public relations and as self-improvement, reaffirming the benignity of middle-class values, and of wealth itself, even as the respectable classes girded themselves anew against the threat breeding in the slums. That such a "solution" in no way challenged capitalist social and economic relations, Riis himself tacitly admitted when he compared "the extra trouble of looking after . . . tenement property" to a penance or "penalty" exacted for "the sins of the fathers." Far from radical, Riis's solution affirmed the centrality and social worth of traditional individualist and entrepreneurial values even as it specified a new class duty, and the enthusiasm of his wide readership affirmed that his proposal had struck a responsive chord.

There was, as well, an ethnic dimension to Riis's plan. At the time he wrote, a system for building tenement houses as speculation was well entrenched in New York. The existence of middlemen made tenement ownership possible for a relatively small investment of $5,000 to $15,000, which was within the reach of many small tradesmen among the Irish, Italians, and Jews. However, the speculative nature of both building and ownership involved the assumption of various loans and mortgages, so that tenements were shoddily built and landlords did all they could to maximize their profits. "Years ago we all had American landlords, who went once a month to every room and collected rents, and looked to see if the rooms were clean and how the people were," a witness for the Tenement House Committee testified in 1900. "Now the landlord cares only for the rent."

Thus, rather than addressing the majority of actual landlords, Riis's texts proposed to the wealthy that they take up tenement ownership as a form of philanthropy. Such an initiative would introduce a new group, "wealthy owners with time to spare to look after their tenants," into an arena increasingly occupied by "foreign" speculators. Although the book never spells out the point, Riis's audience might easily have understood his plan as proposing a method to restore control over tenement housing to "Americans."

Riis was settled in Brooklyn and had been a police reporter for ten years when, encouraged by the recent invention of magnesium flash powder, he assembled and delivered for the first time in 1888 his exhibition on "The Other Half, How It Lives and Dies in New York." Generally using over a hundred slides, Riis presented material which, contemporary accounts would have it, provoked "many a shudder" in "the more sensitive of his hearers," especially outside New York. Yet, as a Buffalo reporter perceived, "running through" Riis's "racy description of the infected district there was a vein of earnestness that lifted the lecture quite above the level of a mere passing away of the time." A part of the lecture concerned "what we [are] going to do to protect ourselves," noted the Washington *Post*.

As such reports suggest, Riis carefully pitched his presentation to middle-class fears and concerns, and he often tailored his material to particular audiences. Though his first lecture, to the New York Society of Amateur Photographers, was reported (perhaps by Riis himself) to be an "ingenious" set of "Pictures of Police life" enlivened by "a vein of humor," he quickly revised his approach. Adopting the more reformist perspective observed in Buffalo, he succeeded in interesting religious reformers in his material. He went on to give the majority of his early lectures as benefits for evangelical Christian churches, so that his efforts were associated with their programs to promote missions among the city's "unsaved masses."

In the famous "Flashes from the Slums," an illustrated article that appeared in the New York *Sun* on Sunday, February 12, 1888, two weeks after Riis's initial lecture, Riis described his role as "guide and conductor" for a party of amateur photographers "experimenting with the process of taking instantaneous pictures by artificial flashlight"; the resulting slides of "Gotham's crime and misery by night and day" would illustrate talks he planned to give at churches and Sunday schools. The men whose interest in photography had prompted them to join Riis's party in the late fall of 1887 were Dr. John T. Nagle of the health department, Dr. Henry G. Piffard, consulting surgeon to the New York City Hospital, and Richard Hoe Lawrence, a gentleman banker and clubman, later president of the Iconophile Society. Both Piffard and Lawrence were active in the Society of Amateur Photographers of New York; Lawrence was chairman of the society's lantern slide committee, and Piffard, chiefly interested in learning to manipulate the newly developed magnesium flash powder, gave a lecture and demonstration on the subject to the society on October 11. Lawrence seems to have retained the greatest interest in photography, and he is apparently the only one besides Riis who has left behind a body of work, now held by the New-York Historical Society. The society's Richard Hoe Lawrence Collection consists of copy prints made from Lawrence's lantern slides, which were donated to the society by his widow in 1950; captions on the backs of the prints were copied from the slide mounts.

※   ※   ※

Some images in Riis's collection, such as those of model tenements, are obviously from other sources, and as we have seen, Riis's writing implicitly credits other photographers. On the evidence of his autobiography, it was not until January 1888 that he bought and learned to use his own camera. "The slum and the awkward hours [soon] palled upon the amateurs," he explained, and "I found myself alone just when I needed help the most." Though virtually the opposite seems true—the amateurs evidently participated generously, offering critical manpower, photographs, and a lecture opportunity—Riis's lectures and books never, as far as I can determine, credited other photographers outright for images he showed; and he told stories of his photographic exploits that describe the making of photographs in the Lawrence collection as if they were his own. This situation prevailed despite the fact that from the beginning some of his audience, particularly those in the Society of Amateur Photographers, were apparently aware that Riis was not the sole author of many of the photographs he showed. Whether, as it seems, Lawrence (and Piffard) willingly let Riis take sole credit for photographs evidently made by themselves, and if so, why, remains, for the moment, a mystery.

Relying on a variety of representational and narrative strategies to get their message across, the lectures serve as a testing ground upon which Riis worked out both his techniques and his ideology. They turned out, when assembled, to hold only a small number of images—perhaps one-fourth to one-third—hailed as the pioneering flash photographs. Many images were posed—such as Lawrence's *Bandit's Roost,* his portrait of the tramp, or his tableau showing young boys picking the pockets of a drunk, which imitates a similar image in woodcut that appeared in the *Police Gazette* in the 1840s. Lawrence's *22 Baxter Street,* a tenement court, took its iconography from scenes such as well-known illustrator William A. Rogers's *Ragpickers' Court,* done in 1879; ragpicker subject matter was familiar at least from the 1860s and probably earlier. Even the flashlit "night pictures," though "realistic" in their unposed immediacy, must have seemed to their audiences, in some respects at least, much more conventional and less startling than we might think, because many of them rehearsed imagery familiar to any reader of illustrated periodicals. For example, a *Harper's* artist had drawn police station house lodgers in 1869, and Winslow Homer had gone to station houses and to opium dens for the magazine in 1874. In 1880, *Harper's* artist C. A. Keetels sketched a "Bottle Alley" saloon; his composition resembles Lawrence's well-known *A Downtown Morgue* and again suggests photographers' reliance on pictorial conventions governing the representation of such scenes. Riis's photographs of the newsboys' lodging house, which included washroom and night school, re-presented scenes that appeared in *Harper's* in 1867 [see page 119]. Like the illustrations they were modeled on, a number of the slides are in decorative circular vignettes rather than square frames, and some are handcolored.

As I have suggested, however, the interest and impact of individual slides was not dependent solely on visual appeal, for in the course of a lecture the slides never appeared unmediated. Various dramatic devices and Riis's accompanying narrative identified and named, or captioned, individual images, directing viewers to assign them specific meanings consonant with Riis's larger text—the representation of "Gotham's crime and misery." In Brooklyn, Riis used music, reported the Brooklyn *Times,* and the pathos evoked by a slide of boys asleep in the street, "a touching scene," was "greatly heightened by a cornet duo played in the wings of the stage— "Where Is My Wandering Boy Tonight?" A typical anecdote, repeated and elaborated in his book, purported to describe the origin of Lawrence's tramp, who poses, of course, with a clay pipe. The lecture narrative called him a "tramp and thief" because, offered ten cents to pose for Riis's camera, the old man removed his picturesque pipe and "struck," Riis claimed, demanding another five cents (an amount increased to a quarter in the book) before agreeing to replace it for the picture [See page 49].

As the lectures proceeded, slides were related to each other in pairs or groups for which Riis's remarks served as "relay," moving audiences along through story-telling sequences of images like those encountered in comic strips or films. He "had a fancy" for contrasting the opposites of New York life, wrote one reporter, so that "the most dismal alley or filthiest dive was often followed by a brown-stone mansion on Fifth Avenue." He put photographs of "saved" children, such as those shown at prayer in the Five Points House of Industry, to good use as a foil for other images of less well-tended children, and he showed "portraits of children side by side, of how they looked when taken from their hovels, and cruel and wretched parents, and after they were cleaned and cared for by Mr. E. Gerry's 'Society for the Prevention of Cruelty to Children,'" reported the *Photographic Times*. In Washington, where his lecture was preceded by scripture reading, prayer, and gospel music, Riis organized his slides of children to portray the life of the homeless "street Arab" from "his birth in a dive to his burial in an unknown grave on Hart's Island," a technique borrowed from the reformer Charles Loring Brace, whose *The Dangerous Classes of New York and Twenty Years' Work Among Them*, published in 1872, was illustrated by a similar series in woodcut.

These narrative and rhetorical strategies functioned in several ways. Humorous or adventuresome anecdotes imposed a reassuring order on content whose "crime and misery" might otherwise overwhelm. They also confirmed the privileged position of the viewer by implying that he or she had a right to be entertained by an encounter with such material even while absorbing Riis's moral strictures. Riis's actual physical presence as mediator between the audience and the photographs virtually embodied the overseeing "master" narrator familiar to readers of realist literature. Not only were the pleasures of reading recalled, but also the ostensibly incontrovertible authority of such a "point of view" was evoked on Riis's behalf, dismissing any possibility that the photograph itself might offer an alternative, or even oppositional, meaning to his. In the same way, Riis's blunt title, framing his content as "the other half," simultaneously designated his audience as "this half," thus assigning to them a relation to the proceedings that offered an attractively secure and collective point of view from which to survey the show.

As Riis's project developed, he spoke of it in language that affirmed his regard for the supposed universal benignity of middle-class interests and social perspectives, and he specifically associated the powers and pleasures of photography with them. As Riis explained to an interviewer early in 1888:

> The beauty of looking into these places without actually being present there is that the excursionist is spared the vulgar sounds and odious scents and repulsive exhibitions attendant upon such a personal examination.

A revealing rhetoric, which Riis elaborated in *How the Other Half Lives*, this language of tourism seems to owe more to literature than to the ideas of earlier reformers. The literary convention of an urban landscape so fragmented as to make quarters of the city "another country" was of course well established in the press and popular literature of the 1880s. "The other half" was not least among a battery of well-worn tropes evoking "nether" regions that presented an "excursionist" with scenes so alien, forbidding, or disgusting that they required the mediation of journalists or artists. William Dean Howells remarks of a "wretched quarter," for example, that "in a picture it would be most pleasingly effective, for then you could be in it and yet have the distance on it which it needs"; but actually to be there was to experience

> the stenches of the neglected street and . . . that yet fouler and dreadfuler poverty-smell which breeds from the open doorways . . . [and] to see the children quarreling in their games and beating each other in

the face and rolling each other in the gutter like the little savage outlaws they are.

Riis's comment implied just such a distinction. But more than this, he
rephrased the claims of countless earlier exhibitors who offered urban
"excursionists" vicarious travel to exotic, unknown, and distant territory.
Forbears among such purveyors may have been the entrepreneurs who
emerged during the craze for moving panoramas of the rural South and the
unsettled West that swept the country in the 1850s. Such exhibitions were
often intended to simulate for audiences a steamboat trip down the Mississippi. Imbued with patriotism and imperialist sentiment, their purveyors
sought ultimately not to mystify but to domesticate the western territories.
Panoramas showed the wilderness "giving way to commerce and settlement," and in addition to entertaining and exhorting, they functioned as a
form of surveillance, offering potential settlers a reliable "visual inventory
of objects in the [western] landscape." Helping to bolster urbanites'
courage and desire to settle the distant places, they implied that their "aesthetic appropriation prepare[d] the way for physical colonization" of the
West, according to art historian Angela Miller.

Like slide shows, these edifying spectacles featured music and were narrated by authoritative "professors" or "directors" who vouched for the
verisimilitude of the painters' renditions. Audiences were solicited to enjoy
the pleasures of vicarious westward travel in language much like Riis's:
"Whilst storing the mind with information never to be effaced, the viewer
congratulates himself at not being actually exposed to the dangers and
inconveniences of so extended a pilgrimage," promoters enthused, noting
"how much more convenient and pleasant it is to sit comfortably amid the
beauty, fashion and intelligence of our great metropolis for two or three
hours and view this mighty river as it flows past, than it is in reality to
boat . . . up and down it."

As an "exhibitor," Riis stood closer to the panoramists who would
domesticate than to the journalists who would mystify, and his evocation
of spectacle and tourism in regard to New York's slums used the rhetoric
and its associations for purposes akin to those of the western imperialists,
Riis's representation of the touristic point of view offered a "respectable"
perspective on the photographs he showed; in addition, it helped him further flatter his audience, implicitly assuring them that they were the "half"
designated by history and progress to colonize and dominate. Just as the
panorama promoters' fulsome congratulation of their audience affected to
assume not only their curiosity, but also their privileged position as those
who would soon colonize the uncivilized landscape, so Riis's phrases convey his understanding that his "excursionist" is at once tenderly refined
and sternly reform minded. He or she deserves both the information
needed to transform or control the slums, and the security and privilege
of distance that obviates the "vulgar, odious and repulsive" experiences
that the actual slums would inevitably present. By conflating the language
and perspective of geographical inventory and settlement with that of
social surveillance and control, Riis was able to imply as well that his audience's mobile and "colonial" position in relation to the slums it "visited"
was a natural one.

※   ※   ※

It is not my intention especially to discredit or unmask Riis—tempting as that may be, after so many years of hagiography. Rather, in attempting to reconstruct the historical context and meaning of his work and to recover the authorship of photographs he showed, I have hoped to represent Riis's actual photographic practice and to place it at the beginning of the complex process by which social documentary gradually emerged as a photographic discourse distinct from other forms of urban visual culture and other photographic practices. Clearly, these origins were complicated, and less benign and straightforward than we may have thought; and for reasons that may now be evident, Riis is not an altogether reliable guide to them.

In this connection, it is interesting to note that Riis claims in his autobiography never to have understood the enormous popularity of *How the Other Half Lives*. Ever the skillful publicist, he did not justify his annexation of documentary photography to middle-class interests by asserting photography's unique claim to verisimilitude. Rather, he insisted on linking his appreciation of the medium, and of his subject, to current notions of refinement and estheticism. Riis does take pains to distinguish his interest in the slums from "the delight of the artist"; nevertheless, he subtitled his book "studies among the tenements," and he uses the metaphors of art to embellish his text. "Why complete the sketch?" he concludes a typical vignette. More than this, Riis specifically associates photography with the traditionally sanctioned "magical" powers of art and poetry rather than with innovation and social insight:

> I do not want [photography] explained to me in terms of . . . formulas, learned, but so hopelessly unsatisfying. I do not want my butterfly stuck on a pin and put in a glass case. I want to see the sunlight on its wings as it flits from flower to flower, and I don't care a rap what its Latin name may be. Anyway, it is not its name. The sun and flower and the butterfly know that. The man who sticks a pin in it does not, and never will, for he knows not its language. Only the poet does among men.

Even Riis's somewhat disingenuous assertion of bumbling incompetence with the camera serves to dissociate his use of the medium from official record keeping or social control, as well as from other uses of photography. "I am no good at all as a photographer, [but] I would like to be," he wrote in his autobiography, and the remark seems to identify him as a connoisseur and appreciator of photography rather than as a producer. Just as Riis firmly rejects the status and ambitions of a professional, he also disengages himself from the practice of a leisured amateur such as the patrician Richard Hoe Lawrence. His studied admission may even be construed as a belated and backhanded acknowledgment or apology to Lawrence and others whose images Riis had appropriated into his enterprise—obliquely crediting them, and not himself, for any visual impact to be found in the materials. At the same time, as a consumer rather than a producer, Riis could draw closer to the mainstream of his middle-class audience, who were not photographers or patricians either, and use himself as a model to enact for them, once again, a role of properly distanced spectatorship in relation to the alarming possibilities presented not only by the images, but also by the society, that confronted them.

* * *

KATRINA IRVING

From Immigrant Mothers: Narratives of Race
and Maternity, 1890–1925[†]

4. Sentimental Ambitions: Americanization and the "Isolated and Alien" Mother

> But surely there is another scene of colonial discourse in which the native or Negro meets the demand of colonial discourse. . . . The colonial fantasy. . . . proposes a teleology—under certain conditions of colonial domination and control the native is progressively reformable.
>
> —Homi K. Bhabha

> Can we permit thousands of foreign mothers to hold their old country ideals unchanged and expect their homes to be truly American? . . . We must bring the mother out of her home. . . . When we can do that we shall save families from disruption, for the mother determines the home; we shall save America, for the home determines America.
>
> —Bessie Olga Pehotsky

Despite nativist assertions to the contrary, a number of writers and reformers proclaimed the immigrants' potential for rehabilitation and directed their energies toward achieving that task. The momentum of this project, known as the Americanization movement, peaked during and in the years immediately following America's participation in World War I. Its inception can be traced to the early 1890s and located specifically in the work of the social settlements, in the various programs launched by the Daughters of the American Revolution to educate immigrants in American customs, and in the work of individual activists such as Jacob Riis (Higham, *Strangers* 236–37)[1]

Buttressed by the accounts of scientists such as Franz Boas (whose report for the Dillingham Commission asserted that modification of immigrants' living conditions and nutritional habits led to a definitive change in the racial constitution of their descendants), Americanizers proclaimed that the aliens could jettison their Old World cultures.[2] They perceived the immigrant to be eminently malleable. Their difference no longer sprang from a genetic and inalienable source but was susceptible to modification. Key tactics in this collective effort at racial renovation included forays into

---

1. In a sense, I will be using the term *Americanization* somewhat anachronistically, because the term did not achieve widespread currency until World War I. I follow Higham, however, in seeing the early work of Riis and others as linked to the later, full-blown Americanization movement. What ties the two forms of activism together is a belief in the social and cultural origin of racial difference, the idea that the alien was assimilable, and an urge to intervene in the lives of immigrants in order to facilitate that process.

2. In that report, *Changes in Bodily Form of Descendants of Immigrants*, Boas presented findings, based on a comparative study of the skull measurements of first- and second-generation immigrants, that identified culture and sociology rather than biology as paramount in the formation of racial differences: "In most of the European types that have been investigated the head form, which has always been considered one of the most stable and permanent characteristics of human races, undergoes far-reaching changes due to the transfer of the people from European to American soil. . . . We are compelled to conclude that when these features of the body change, the whole bodily and mental makeup of the immigrant may change. . . . Permanence of types in new surroundings appears rather as the exception than as the rule" (5).

tenements to gather information (the photographic missions of Jacob Riis), attempts to recolonize the "wilderness" (the settlement movement), and direct visitation of immigrant homes in order to teach American ways by example.[3]

The immigrant mother was a particular target of these reformers' correctional zeal.[4] In 1920 Kate Waller Barrett, a special agent for the U.S. Immigration Service, summarized the prodigious effort required of native Americans if the ever-burgeoning immigrant population were to be successfully assimilated. She pinpointed the immigrant family home as the critical site for the native's assimilationist endeavors and reiterated an imperative at least three decades old: "The importance of reaching the alien woman is paramount if we are going to Americanize our foreign population" (224). Continuing, she asserted that the immigrant mother was "the crux of the whole subject" (224). Frances Kellor, chief of New York State's Bureau of Industries and Immigration, agreed, arguing that "the foreign-born woman and her home are . . . the most vulnerable spots in our . . . democracy" ("Neighborhood Americanization" 9).[5] Peter Speek, a contributor to the Carnegie Series on Americanization Studies, articulated the opinion of the bulk of these reformers when he argued, "Whether immigrant women vote or not, they are an inevitable influence in the political life of the country. . . . The first question is how to reach them" (227).

Part of the reason the immigrant mother and home were particular targets of concern is that they were seen to fall outside the network of institutions (public schools, factories, and prisons) in which the inculcation of American ideals might otherwise occur. Kellor explained, "The foreign born child is Americanized by the public school. . . . Men become Americanized at work," but the mother still wears "a shawl over her head" ("Neighborhood Americanization" 9, 10). Americanizers (in the face of abundant evidence to the contrary) conceived the immigrant woman to be isolated within the tenement and stressed the need to penetrate into that region in order to bring her within the ambit of Americanization.[6] More important, it was these activists' conception of the role of the mother in the reproduction of racial difference that positioned her at the forefront of their

---

3. Americanizers' methods of justifying intervention into tenements cannot be read apart from the larger backdrop of the growth of social sciences and the professions (particularly social work) that occurred in turn-of-the-century America. These developments were, as John Tagg has pointed out, intimately connected to the restructuring of the state during the same period. The new social sciences and professions "redefin[ed] the social as the object of their technical interventions," interventions that during the 1930s became important in "securing social regulation and consent within a social democratic framework" (5, 10). Thus Kellor and Breckinridge's depiction of the immigrant as unable to carry out her maternal duties effectively in the New World also provides a powerful argument legitimizing, even demanding, state intervention. Gwendolyn Mink has illustrated how that intervention was made on the basis of culturalist and racist assumptions about normative gender roles.
4. George Sanchez discusses a similar focus among Americanizers on the West Coast who attempted to force the assimilation of Mexican families. "Motherhood," he argues, "in fact, became the juncture at which the Mexican immigrant woman's potential role in Americanization was most highly valued" (289).
5. Frances Kellor undertook graduate work in sociology at the University of Chicago although she left without taking a degree (Fitzpatrick 58). Her involvement in Progressive causes eventually led to her career as chief of New York State's Bureau of Industries and Immigration and later to her role as "close advisor to Theodore Roosevelt . . . member of the Progressive party's National Committee and head of the Bull Moose's innovative Progressive service" (Fitzpatrick 131). Higham discusses her participation in immigration issues in *Strangers*, 239 passim.
6. See the discussion of Katherine Anthony, *Mothers Who Must Earn*, in this chapter.

campaign.[7] This conception, in turn, owed to the convergence of cultural racist presuppositions and sentimental ideology within the activists' racial schema.

Cultural racists typically see the home as the critical space for the transmission of racial difference: "The family. . . . is portrayed as the crucial site for the reproduction of those correct social mores, attitudes and behaviours that are thought to be essential to maintaining a 'civilized' society" (Lawrence, "Just Plain Common Sense" 50).[8] Accordingly, Americanizers pinpointed the immigrant home as a key location for implementing their normative coercion and positioned it, in their cultural-racist terms, as the place in which a retrogressive culture would issue in a dysfunctional family. The logic informing this project was thoroughly sentimental. The immense popularity that sentimental novels had enjoyed during the middle decades of the nineteenth century had largely waned by the early 1900s.[9] As Laura Wexler has demonstrated, however, that fictional genre's political agenda came to inform several reform movements during the Progressive Era.[1] Sentimental novels typically stage the desire of marginalized characters such as slaves or working-class children to replicate white, middle-class codes of conduct. By remaking themselves in the image of the dominant culture, such individuals prove their eligibility for normative citizenship.[2] In other words, sentimental fiction contains an assimilationist vision at its core.

Wexler maintains that Progressive programs designed to Americanize immigrants (along with educational efforts aimed at native American and African-American populations) coupled the imperial agenda of sentimental fiction with "the social control of marginal domestic populations" (18). The Americanization movement implemented the reform agenda of sentimental fiction within a variety of institutional settings, both in its conviction of the other's mutability and in the modes by which it proposed to effect that transformation (namely, through the media of instruction and affective connection). The political program underpinning Jacob Riis's documentary chronicle of immigrant life in the slums or Sophinisba Breckinridge's sociological analysis of the immigrant woman's assimilatory potential in *New Homes for Old* was, therefore, directly linked to the fiction of such mid-

---

7. In both *Wages of Motherhood* and "The Lady and the Tramp," Gwendolyn Mink analyzes the convergence of racial and gender ideologies in middle-class women's reformist politics She argues cogently that "[reformers] made the imitation of a middle-class, Anglo American maternal ideal the price of woman's citizenship" (*Wages* 73). My argument is parallel to hers in that I, too, argue that different conceptions of the origin of racial difference marked off the nativist conceptualization of the immigrant problem from that of Americanizers. Similarly, she discusses the reformers' connection of "the problem of racial order to the material and cultural quality of motherhood. . . . the only way mothers from new races could produce ideal American democrats would be through reform and reward of maternal practice" ("Lady" 93). Mink's chief concern in the essay, however, is with the emergence of the American welfare state at the site of this complex of race and gendered assumptions. This chapter, by contrast, concerns itself with the debate over immigration itself being waged through and around the figure of the immigrant mother.
8. See Errol Lawrence, "Just Plain Common-Sense," for a discussion of how cultural racist discourse operated in Britain during 1970s and 1980s.
9. The exception here is the turn-of-the-century explosion of sentimental fiction written by and for African American women. See Claudia Tate, *Domestic Allegories of Political Desire,* for an account and analysis of this phenomenon.
1. Wexler's "Tender Violence" is an important and incisive account of sentimentalism's cultural work at the end of the nineteenth century with respect to these "marginal domestic populations" (18).
2. Philip Fisher (chapter 2, esp. 91 passim) sees this aspect of sentimentalism as constituting an expansive, democratic agenda.

century writers as Maria Cummins, Harriet Beecher Stowe, and Susan Warner.[3]

The Americanizers' focus on the immigrant mother and their forms of representing her are equally indebted to sentimental ideology. The power afforded therein to the woman within the home, the idea that "the mother is the greatest educator of the nation" (Speek 227), rendered the alien woman critical to the success of their movement. Her formative influence on the next generation made her racial reconstruction imperative if immigrants were to be reshaped into American citizens. The success of the assimilationist efforts of those home nurses, settlement house workers, and social workers who ventured into tenements to teach the necessity for, and pragmatics of, accomplishing rapid and thorough Americanization largely depended upon the immigrant mother's acquiescence to these regulatory interventions. Margaret Sangster, drawing from the sentimental credo, warned, "The tenement mother, whatever her creed, or race, or country, impresses herself upon her family with an ineffaceable stamp" (242). "Reaching the immigrant woman" became the critical component of the reformers' campaign. Their task was to impart those practices and skills that would enable the immigrant woman to carry out her sentimental maternal role.

Of course, this was more than a little ironic because such a position was not an option for the vast majority of immigrant women. Evelyn Nakao Glenn has pointed out that the "idealized division of labor" upon which the ideology of sentimental motherhood depended "was largely illusory for . . . immigrant and racial-ethnic families" (4).[4] To the degree that the immigrant woman engaged in activities calculated to aid her family in negotiating the economic conditions of the new world (home-work, taking in boarders, and putting her children to work as early as possible), she violated the precepts of normative maternity. To the extent that she herself engaged in waged labor, she moved outside of the intensely privatized world of the home to which the True Mother was confined and upon which depended her claim to normative citizenship. Americanizers elided these economic exigencies, however. Instead, they presented inadequate training combined with retrograde cultural practices as the factors militating against the alien woman's achievement of the ideal. Successful Americanization depended largely on an innate capacity and willingness to absorb those New World mothering practices modeled by social workers.

The Americanizers' immersion in sentimental "ways of seeing" produced a thorough ambivalence in their representations of the immigrant mother.[5] Whereas nativists had posited an antithetical relationship between the

---

3. As Wexler puts it, in Riis's slide-lantern shows the "consciousness of the social and historical reciprocity of those who see and those who are seen is effaced precisely along the lines of deflection that sentimentality had entrenched" (37).
4. Similarly, Bonnie Thornton Dill indicates that "being a racial-ethnic woman in nineteenth-century American society meant having. . . . a contradictory relationship to the norms and values about women that were being generated in the dominant white culture" (429). Glenn, however, drawing on the work of Phyllis Palmer, points out that the cult of domesticity created incompatible demands on white middle-class women, too. For example, the demand for cleanliness faced off against the ideal of purity and refinement. The contradiction was resolved by hiring racial ethnic women to perform such tasks, thereby "saving" middle-class white women for true womanhood ("From Servitude to Service Work" 8 passim).
5. The phrase "ways of seeing" is John Berger's.

immigrant woman and sentimental maternity, Americanizers stressed her aspirations toward that ideal and read those aspirations as testament to her desire to assimilate. Her circumstantial inability to approximate that ideal (given that her culture and education left her inadequate to its demands) rendered the alien mother a figure of particular pathos for these activists. Their texts frequently depicted her as a suffering Madonna in order to convey that pathos. The premier journal of social work, *The Survey*, typically construed the immigrant mother in this way. The cover of the April 5, 1913, issue carried an illustration of a sculpture of "The Immigrant Mother" by Antoinette B. Hollister. Hollister's image was also reproduced inside the December 6, 1913, issue, this time accompanied by verses on the same theme by Madelaine Sweeny Miller and Gordon Thayer. In the October 11, 1913, issue, a sketch of "A Bohemian Immigrant Mother" by E. Benedict of Hull House appeared, and the December 11, 1915, issue contained a reproduction of a postcard produced for the National Child Labor Committee and entitled "The Immigrant Madonna," with verses on the same topic by Helen C. Dwight. Even after the cessation of the war and the curtailing of foreign immigration, the December 1, 1922, issue carried an illustration of "The Immigrant Madonna" from a monotype by Joseph Stella. As Stephanie Smith explains, "Sanctified maternity [had] become . . . a central image for the nineteenth-century white, middle-class Cult of True Womanhood" (75).[6] Americanizers drew repeatedly upon that familiar icon in the first two decades of the twentieth century. The suffering alien woman whose maternal effectivity could be restored by native intervention proved a powerful sign of the necessity as well as the tenability of their project.

Notwithstanding their investment in conveying the immigrant woman's sentimental ambitions, Americanizers' narratives were invariably shadowed by accounts of her refractoriness with respect to their pedagogical efforts. For example, "Old Country Mothers and American Daughters," Christina Merriman's review of Louise Montgomery's *The American Girl in the Stockyards*, was accompanied in *The Survey* by a photograph of immigrant women clad in head scarves and shawls. The photograph appears taken from a considerable distance, and the women seem to be hurrying out of the camera's field of vision. "Immigrant Mothers, Immune to American Influences" runs the rather ominous caption. The women's distance from and apparent ignorance of the camera bespeak that immunity, as does their stubbornly traditional garb. The image taps into what by 1913 was a familiar narrative about the immigrant mother's particular imperviousness to instruction. In fact, the narrative was so commonplace that the writer felt no need to explain or expound upon it and left the photograph and caption to speak for themselves. Neither in the accompanying review nor across the range of Americanizers' texts, however, is the immigrant woman's recalcitrance presented as a consequence of her active resistance to Americanization. Rather, her perceived inability to retrofit herself is also a product of her construal within the terms of sentimental discourse. Ultimately, these reformers' construction of the immigrant woman as a sentimental mother immobilized her with respect to the process of assimilation. The

6. In particular, see Stephanie Smith's discussion (*Conceived by Liberty*, chapter 2) of the construction of an American Madonna in *Women in the Nineteenth Century* by Margaret Fuller.

discourse of Americanization ultimately joined with that of nativism in reifying the immigrant mother as constitutionally unassimilable.[7]

Jacob Riis's texts provide an early and comprehensive treatment of the "immigrant problem" from an Americanizer's perspective. A police reporter turned agitator for tenement-house reform, Riis was concerned to speed assimilation through the improvement of the immigrants' environment, and he conducted several fact-gathering expeditions into New York's tenements in order to record and report the conditions that obtained there. His books detailing the need for reform within the tenements—*How the Other Half Lives* (1890), *The Battle with the Slum* (1901), and *The Peril and the Preservation of the Home* (1903), among many others—were the first on this topic to reach a large audience. They largely consist of photographs embedded within a written narrative, a novel format that was especially effective in the case of *How the Other Half Lives*, which went through eleven editions in five years (Szasz and Bogardus 422).

The use of photography augmented the "authenticity" of Riis's representations (Szasz and Bogardus 429). Sally Stein has demonstrated, however, that despite the use of new photographic and reproductive technologies his work was firmly located in the "literary tradition of the urban picturesque" that characteristically mixed sketches and narrative exposés of the seamy underworld of city life (10). Despite the fact that the photographs' effectiveness depended on the willingness of his contemporaries to extend to the photographic apparatus the capacity to reproduce the "truth," Maren Stange has shown that his images were far from being unmediated reproductions of a spontaneous reality. Rather, Riis composed the tableaux in his snapshots, sometimes paying subjects to pose in certain attitudes and often cropping both his own prints and those he borrowed from other photographers in order to achieve a more satisfactory effect (Stange 7).[8] In the case of "Bandit's Roost," a photograph taken by Richard Hoe Lawrence but included in the Riis Collection at the Museum of the City of New York, Stange has shown how Riis cropped the photograph horizontally in order to excise two women from the tableau. The image, which reveals a tenement alley crowded with men, some of whom wield sticks, is thereby rendered considerably more threatening (Stange 7–9). Such techniques, although undeniably detracting from the images' documentary status, are congruent with Riis's conception of the nature of his photographic practice. As Stange argues, Riis conceived his work to be closer to art than to objective journalism. He "uses the metaphors of art to embellish his text" and "specifically associates photography with the traditionally sanctioned 'magical' powers of art and poetry rather than with innovation and social insight" (25–26).

7. In *The Wages of Motherhood,* Mink argues (72 passim) that these reformers, whom she dubs "maternalists," liberalized race discourse while inscribing gender inequality in the newly emergent welfare state. My argument is that the articulation of cultural racism with a biologically rooted conception of gender difference, within the thinking of the Americanizers, helped reify racial difference no less solidly (although along a different axis) than the nativists' arguments.
8. See Stange's extended discussion of Riis's photographic practices in *Symbols of Ideal Life* (1–26). Stange also points out that Riis himself did not take many of the photographs that were used in his lectures and later cataloged as part of the Riis Collection. Of the 412 glass-plate negatives that constitute that collection, only about 250 are assumed to be taken by Riis. The others were collected from various sources, including newspaperwoman Jessie Tarbox Beals and amateur photographer Richard Hoe Lawrence.

Riis's reworking of the nativist image of the immigrant mother was fundamental to the rhetorical power of his lectures and texts. That reworking was extremely influential. In *Battle with the Slum* he maintained that "there is nothing better in all the world" than "the mother heart" (251) and defined his task as reformer to be the institution of a normative family life among the immigrants, a task vital to the well-being of the state: "Unsafest of all is any thing or deed that strikes at the home, for from the people's home proceeds citizen virtue, and nowhere else does it live" (7).

For Riis, the home was always metonymically connected with the mother. His reform efforts, directed toward the immediate goal of eliminating overcrowded tenement conditions (in other words, rectifying a situation in which homes were without mothers and mothers without homes), were largely an attempt to institute the conditions in which a normative motherhood could operate. According to the dictates of sentimentality, however, Riis's immigrant mother had to emerge as sorely inadequate, because it was the perceived breakdown of the maternal bond in the tenement that legitimated his intervention. The lack of fit between the idealized mother and immigrant reality was a gap into which Riis, and by extension his native readers, would have to step.

The rhetorical appeal of the photograph entitled "In the Home of an Italian Ragpicker, Jersey Street" is largely a result of its depiction of the foreign woman as an aspirant sentimental mother.[9] As with many of Riis's photographs involving immigrant women, the intimacy of context (the viewer penetrates into the inner recesses of immigrant family life) is striking. Riis's use of the novel technology of flash photography allowed him to photograph domestic spaces that middle-class readers had hitherto only imagined.[1] The passivity of the maternal figure, however, here delivering herself up to the controlling gaze of Riis's lens, allays anxieties potentially attendant upon this unprecedented proximity. The effectiveness of the image turns on what John Tagg has called "a social division between the power and privilege of *producing* and *possessing* meaning and the burden of *being* meaning" (6, emphasis in the original).[2] The utter acquiescence of the woman to Riis's disciplinary surveillance is key to Riis's argument about her assimilatory potential. The willingness with which she yields herself to the camera bespeaks her susceptibility to being remolded in the American context, would Americans only intervene to facilitate it.

Riis's mother and child are posed in a conventional Madonna and child tableau, the mother centered, seated, and holding her young baby in her arms. Yet it is the depiction's deviations from, as much as correspondences to, the familiar representation that compel attention. The Italian mother's gaze is not cast at her baby; she does not return the baby's look but instead directs her gaze above the camera level. Although the traditional iconography of the Madonna often depicts her with eyes cast upward as a sign of submission, within this context the interplay of looks not only conveys the

---

9. A sketch by Kenyon Cox modeled on the photograph, rather than the photograph itself, was used in early editions of *How the Other Half Lives*.
1. For more on Riis's use of flash photography, see Maren Stange's discussion of his work (*Symbols of Ideal Life,* chapter 1).
2. He sees the division as instantiated both in documentary photography and across a range of different institutional contexts in this period, always invested in producing new forms of knowledge about the social body and new ways of exercising power over it.

notion of supplication but also, combined with the mother's physical posture, reinforces the separation of the mother and child. Rather than bending protectively over it, she seems split from the baby, defying the usual monadic image that the tableau of Madonna and child offers. Nancy Theriot has pointed out that a critical part of the nineteenth-century "motherscript" assumed a total commitment on the part of mothers toward their children, a commitment that "involved physical and attitudinal expectations that bound mothers spatially, behaviorally, and emotionally to their children's welfare" (27).[3] Thus, the physical separation between Riis's mother and child stresses their emotional separation. The mother's body is not surrendered to the baby (Theriot 27). Instead, in direct contrast to the devotion that Riis had elsewhere declared as vital—"every baby is entitled to one pair of mother's arms around its neck; that is its God-given right" (*Peril* 23)—the mother mechanically clasps the child as if it were a bundle to be held rather than something to be nurtured. Once again, its rigid form emphasizes its spatial and emotional separation from the mother. The rolled-up mattresses stacked on barrels and the grimy buckets that surround the Italian woman attest to the circumstantial conditions that contribute to her maternal inadequacies.

Then, too, the fact that the baby is swaddled points to the existence of archaic and outmoded mothering practices that demand modernization and the intercession of the reformer. Breckinridge argued that because immigrant parents came from "countries . . . which . . . are not republics," they tended to insist, in un-American fashion, on "the absolute obedience of child to parent" (152).[4] That relationship was antithetical to democratic participation because only "early placing of the responsibility for his acts on the child himself would "train citizens for . . . democracy" (151). The child's swaddling is part of the narrative's argument about this immigrant mother's ignorance of American child-rearing practices and her consequent inability to fulfill her nationally significant maternal role.

Lillian Wald's *The House on Henry Street* (1915) also employed a rhetoric of deficient maternity that simultaneously underscored the conflict between the woman's desire to fulfill the ideal of sentimental motherhood and her inability to do so.[5] It details an encounter between Wald and an Italian mother: "Once in searching for a patient in a large tenement near the Bowery I knocked at each door in turn. An Italian woman hesitatingly opened one, no wider than to give me a glimpse of a slight creature obviously stricken with fear. Her face brought instantly to my mind the famous picture of the sorrowing mother. 'Dolorosa!' I said. The tone and the word sufficed, and she opened the door. . . . In a corner of the room lay two children with marks of starvation upon them" (286–87).

---

3. Besides child-centeredness, the other two parts of the mother-script were "a new realm of feminine power" accrued through the mother-child relation and "a promise of fulfillment" pursuant to the association of womanhood and maternity (Theriot 26).
4. Sophonisba Breckinridge received a Ph.D. in political science from the University of Chicago and later earned a doctor of jurisprudence degree (Fitzpatrick 80 passim). She subsequently founded the School of Social Service Administration and became full professor there. I have drawn upon biographical accounts of Breckinridge, Kellor, and Edith Abbot in Fitzpatrick, *Endless Crusade*. The Breckinridge quotations are drawn from *New Homes for Old,* volume 6 in the series on Americanization sponsored by the Carnegie Corporation.
5. Lillian Wald was trained as nurse and founded the Henry Street social settlement. *The House on Henry Street* is her account of her experiences therein.

Wald's relation to the immigrant is shown to be an aestheticized one
before her textualization of the event: "Her face brought instantly to my
mind *the famous picture of* the sorrowing mother" (emphasis added). Inherent maternal sentiment provides a shared language that is assumed to tran-
scend cultural and ethnic barriers ("Dolorosa! I said . . . she opened the
door"). Equally important, the immigrant woman's failure to approximate
the maternal ideal calls for Wald's intervention. She subsequently fetched
food for the children and obtained the release of the woman's husband,
who had been wrongfully imprisoned.[6] The passage is a striking example of
how the rhetoric of sentimental motherhood can be mobilized both to legitimate native intervention into immigrants' lives and mount an argument for
their potential recuperability for the American way of life.

As the new century unfolded, the definition of deficient maternity shifted
as mothering became reformulated on a scientific basis and the acquisition
of specific knowledge and skills became necessary. Correspondingly, the
imperative to intervene into the immigrant mother's life became all the
more urgent. Breckinridge now insisted that it was not merely an unwholesome environment that prevented immigrant women from carrying out
their maternal duties, because "looking after the physical well-being of the
children is. . . . a peculiarly difficult problem for the foreign-born mothers.
Modern knowledge of child-feeding and modern ideas with regard to daily
bathing are of recent origin" (150–51). Kellor likewise urged the appointment of home teachers who would visit immigrant homes, and she repeatedly underscored the necessity to impart to immigrant mothers information
concerning the "use and preparation of American foods, care of children
and homes" ("Neighborhood Americanization" 11).[7] The narratives of these
later Americanizers are striking because activists, rather than replace the
old rhetoric of sentiment with the new ideas of science, generally articulated that rhetoric with the emergent, scientific conception of maternity.

The photograph by Jessie Tarbox Beals that accompanied Dan Feeks's
"Putting Mother in Her Right Place" in *World Outlook* (1918) encapsu-
lated the shift to the scientific ideal of motherhood while rearticulating elements from both the discourse of sentiment and the traditional iconography
of the Madonna. A product of native intervention (Feeks recommended
home education of immigrant mothers by social workers), the immigrant
mother is dressed in spotless medical white. The baby's unencumbered
body, free of swaddling, attests to freedom from archaic and handicapping
mothering practices. The infant is alert, sitting up and gazing at something
out of the photograph's frame, testament to a nascent individualism pre-
saging the emergence of a fit democratic subject. At the same time, the circular form of the photograph, which contains nothing besides the pair,
emphasizes their unity and invokes the familiar tableau of Madonna and
child. The emotional bond between the two is evoked by the immigrant

---

6. This presentation of the white female as liberator of the benighted immigrant mother accords with
a similar tradition in abolitionist literature. Jean Fagan Yellin has pointed out that many abolitionist texts present the "relationship between the passive female slave and the empowered white
female liberator" (Nudelman 943 passim). See also Stephanie Smith's discussion of Stowe, who
not only thematized the idea of suffering maternity in *Uncle Tom's Cabin* but also presented "her
authorial destiny . . . as a sanctified mother" (94).
7. See Levenstein, *Revolution at the Table*, especially chapter 8, for a discussion of native attempts
to influence immigrant foodways.

mother's gaze, which is directed at her baby, as well as by her attitude of protective support. Here, science, imparted by the social worker, enables the procession of the sentimental ideal, which in turn retrofits the immigrant as a normative subject-citizen.

Riis's texts, predating this shift to science, largely content themselves with gesturing to the break-down of the requisite emotional bonds in the tenement. The photograph "Organized Charity: A Home Nurse" continues to deploy the traditional iconography of mother and child but reverses it. The young boy rather than the mother is the nurturer. While the "mother script," in which Riis's readers were well schooled, called for a "commitment of body and soul to the service of the offspring. . . . [in which the] mother was to be constantly available, constantly selfless," in this photograph the impossibility of such commitments in the tenement is heavily underscored (Theriot 27). Once again, the mother does not return the gaze of her child. Represented as an inert, defeminized lump, she stares out past him at something out of the picture's frame. The angle from which the photograph is taken, as well as the cropping that cuts off the top of the pictures hanging on the wall, reduces the apparent size of the room. The futility of the attempt to institute a domesticity modeled on middle-class patterns, evidenced in markers such as the china cup, framed prints, intricately carved wooden door behind the mother's bed, and elaborately patterned quilt, is ironically underscored by the little boy's grime, loose shirt, and bare feet and, of course, by the prone mother. Yet those very markers, absent in Stephen Crane's depiction of Mrs. Johnson's domicile, witness the assimilatory potential of this malfunctioning family and urge the need for American intervention to facilitate it.

Reformers invariably hedged descriptions of immigrant women with doubts concerning her capacity to attain the ideal to which she aspired. In some cases she appeared stubbornly resistant to their instructional projects. Dan Feeks's shrill insistence that the "immigrant Mother. . . . must get . . . out of herself, out of a rut, out of her too-foreign habits" (9) insinuated a woman disturbingly unresponsive to reformers' agendas. What remained implicit in Feeks became explicit in the texts of many others. Again and again, reformers' texts described scenes of conflict between the immigrant mother and the native reformer, often enacted over the site of children. Joseph Mayper, writing of the resistance social workers encountered from immigrant women, explained that "great difficulty was experienced in this healthwork in overcoming the superstitions of ignorant mothers" (57). Consequently, "A decidedly threatening attitude had to be assumed by the nurse in several cases to convince the mothers of their folly" (57). The immigrant mother's dogged clinging to Old World ways was seen to lessen her control over children and husband, forcing a rupture in the family that led to the much-discussed criminal tendencies of the second generation of immigrant youth. In the face of the alien woman's "prefer[ence for] her own foods and ways" ("Neighborhood Americanization" 12) and tendency to become "suspicious and resentful and sullen" (17) in the face of Americanization efforts, Frances Kellor exhorted listeners at the Colony Club to "show them [immigrants] the advantages of the American standards and *insist* on their prevalence" (12, emphasis added).

In Elsa Herzfeld's 1905 account of her social work among immigrant women, a discussion of the foreign woman's ignorance of normative childcare practices slides, almost imperceptibly, into condemnation of her refusal to implement them. Herzfeld at first attributed the immigrant mother's inability to provide appropriate care for her children to ignorance: "The cultural status of many a tenement-house dweller is not far removed from that of primitive man. His world is a world of ghosts and spirits, of the reality of dreams and the efficacy of the amulet" (983). In the face of such "primitivism," it was essential for natives to school immigrants in the new technical expertise of domesticity. Herzfeld also acknowledged poverty as a factor influencing the procession of child care in tenements: "Children are not warmly wrapped. They have little underclothing. . . . The poor physical condition of the older children I attribute to the lack of suitable dietary" (986). Although poor mothering practices here derive from poverty ("little underclothing") and ignorance ("lack of a suitable dietary"), a subtle modulation in the paragraph shifts the blame onto the foreign mother's turpitude: "Sometimes the young child goes to school without breakfast because the mother is not up on time" (986). Again, although Herzfeld pointed out the need to educate the women—"most families are entirely ignorant of the precautions necessary to preserve the purity of milk" (986)—she went on to stress the foreign woman's resistance to advice: "[Although] they were glad to be taught how to pasteurize or sterilize the milk for baby . . . it 'took up too much time to do it regularly'" (986).[8]

For most of these writers, however, the immigrant mother's resistance was depicted as the result of apathy or incapacitation rather than as an active refusal to change. Isabelle Horton, superintendent of social and educational work in Chicago's Halsted Street Institutional Church, summarized the reformers' general perspective when she wondered, "How can these indifferent, these ignorant, these discouraged mothers be stimulated, taught, inspired?" (100). That imputed incapacitation is a critical part of the texts' rhetorical appeal. Riis's "In the Home of an Italian Ragpicker" clearly constructs the immigrant mother in this way, and the mothers literal prostration in "Organized Charity: A Home Nurse" surely gestures to a more generalized paralysis on her part in the face of New World demands. In *How the Other Half Lives*, Riis carefully recorded the contents of a note found with a baby abandoned in front of the Foundling Asylum and thereby staged the immigrant mother's admission of ineptitude. "'Take Care of Johnny, for God's Sake. I cannot,'" the note; penned "in a woman's trembling hand," read (145).

Later Americanizers, including Wald, Kellor, and Breckinridge, similarly defined the immigrant mother in terms of a generalized and intractable debility. Wald wrote that immigrant mothers are "not indifferent, but rather helpless, in the face of the modern city's demands upon motherhood" (198). Kellor particularly harped on that theme, arguing that the first step in the Americanization process was showing the immigrant woman "friendliness," because only that would enable her to "do her own thinking and changing . . . we [need to] . . . help create in her the *desire* for it" ("Neighborhood Americanization" 17). One typical description in Katherine Anthony's volume of case histories of working immigrant mothers concerns

---

8. See Levenstein for an account of the attempt to develop methods for sterilizing milk in the face of massive child death rates in tenement areas. At the time Herzfeld was writing, the sterilization methods advocated by reformers proved so cumbersome that only upper- and middle-class families able to hire servants to carry out the process were able to implement them.

a Mrs. Furhmann, in whom "patience rather than enterprise is the chief trait" (179). The opening to Anthony's text asserts that "the mother of the family . . . least often sees beyond the neighborhood limits. . . . [is] even less adventurous in seeking recreation" (6–7). Acknowledging that these people "once had the enterprise to journey from the old world to the new" (11), she then proves that, as far as women are concerned, "Somehow they have lost it on the West Side" (11).

Breckinridge's *New Homes for Old* also cataloged the many difficulties facing the immigrant wife and mother in her new context. Subject to the tyrannical dictates of her husband, in conflict with her children whose rapid Americanization pries them free of her control, and unschooled in the "art of spending," she becomes "uncertain of herself" (175). For Breckinridge, the prototypical immigrant woman was "a Ukrainian mother, who admits being afraid to go beyond her own neighborhood" (123–24). The text represents the immigrant woman as an isolated and alien unit whose cultural stasis estranges her children. Breckinridge cited daughters who "said [they] were ashamed to go out with their mother who remained unprogressive. . . . [who] would do nothing but sit at home and cry" (184).

No doubt many immigrant women did find it difficult to adjust to new conditions. Yet the uniformity of this characterization of a hapless and refractory immigrant mother, as well as the narrative energy invested in the depiction, owes more to the reformers' immersion in a sentimental regime of intelligibility, combined with their need to legitimate their own activities, than to any anterior reality.[9] Depictions of immigrant mothers unable to fulfill their maternal functions constructed a domain for the authoritive expertise of the newly developed profession of social work. Ellen Fitzpatrick and many other critics have shown how closely the individual careers of professional women such as Breckenridge, Kellor, and Wald were linked to the figure of the immigrant woman. Wald became nationally known as a settlement-house worker; Breckinridge's reputation was secured, despite her academic position at the University of Chicago, as a social worker among immigrants (Fitzpatrick 190); and Kellor's various government positions

9. This depiction of the backward immigrant mother is one that many contemporary texts by immigrant daughters seem at pains to combat. See, for example, Anzia Yezierska's contrast between her savvy mother (a Russian Pole) and her naive immigrant father in the semiautobiographical *Bread Givers*.

Historians discussing the immigration of various ethnic groups have, by and large, reproduced this narrative of the assimilatory resistance of the "innately conservative" immigrant woman. In *Immigrant Women in the Land of Dollars* Elizabeth Ewen ponders the accuracy of reformers' description of the immigrant mother's backwardness, finally seeming to concur with it: "If immigrant mothers were consumed by the realities of home life, some of their daughters were quick to notice the new world. . . . While the mothers attempted to reassemble the terms of a known life, their daughters . . . step[ped] into the present" (67).

Some work stressing the central role the immigrant woman played in acculturating her family has begun to emerge, however. For example, in *Adapting to Abundance*, Andrew Heinze stresses consumption as a critical avenue to assimilation for Jewish immigrants at the turn of the century. A Jewish woman, as principal consumer for her family, was a key agent in forging the family's American identity. "Through her command over the household's consumers, the *baleboste* [housewife] initiated newcomers in the adoption of American ways. . . . and incorporated the demands of children for an American lifestyle" (114). Similarly, Ardis Cameron analyzes how immigrant women's twin tasks of child-rearing and wage labor coupled with the need to forge "strategies of survival translate[d] into 'street smart' concepts of life and labor" (57). She argues that in Lawrence, Massachusetts, "Women utilized the proximity of neighbors, friends, and kin to mutual advantage, socializing a variety of domestic tasks and customizing Old World principles of mutuality and collectivity. . . . Female collaborative activities, forged out of necessity, fostered networks that took root and strengthened. . . . Mutual dependence and cooperative assistance bound women together in a lattice-work of reciprocity" (60, 61).

were a function of her expertise on the issues of immigration and Americanization. The recurrence of the incapable immigrant mother within their
texts can be traced, in part, to their own need to forge an acceptable professional role for themselves, as women, in a society still committed to the
ideology of dual spheres. Positioning themselves as the necessary adjunct
to the dysfunctional immigrant family, these women assumed the role of
public mothers (Smith-Rosenberg 264). Their professional competence was
secured against the backdrop of the inefficient immigrant mother.[1] And
Sally Stein and Maren Stange have shown that Jacob Riis, in exposing to
the middle-class public the neediness and threat of the immigrants and presenting himself as capable of mitigating that neediness, forged a prominent
social and public position for himself.[2]

It is important to note, however, that this conception of alien women as
almost imbecilic in their inability to adapt to a changed milieu is also
a function of the reformers' immersion in sentimental "ways of seeing."
Although demonstrating her assimilatory ambitions, the alien mother's
proto-sentimental construction immobilized her with respect to the process
of Americanization. A brief look at the gendered assumptions underlying
sentimentalism demonstrates why. Sentimental discourse assigned women
to the domestic sphere, where they were "charged with preserving old values and a safe and stable haven against change" (Evans 69). The literal and
symbolic function of preserving the nation's traditions and cultural mores
was a natural adjunct to her innate (biologically based) conservatism.
Nineteenth- and early-twentieth-century biology assumed that "woman
was in evolutionary terms 'the conservative element' to the man's 'progressive'" (Stepans 40). As Nearing and Nearing rehearsed this biological wisdom, "Since women are less specialized they are more conservative. That
is, they have more of a tendency to adhere to the past, and less inclination
to branch out in new directions" (16). Thus, the female "conserv[es] the
qualities which have been developed and handed down from the past" (17).
For reformers, the female sex's biologically mandated conservatism made
the immigrant woman a particular point of concern because, unlike her
male counterpart, it rendered her innately resistant to their instructional
project. In order to assimilate, she would have to throw off her sex-
determined conservatism and renege on her biological function of reposi-
tory and transmitter of her own culture's mores.

Thus, the urgency impelling Kellor's assertion that "immigrant women
are very generally years behind the men in Americanization" ("Straight
America" 24) was largely an outcome of the projection of the sentimental
ideal onto the immigrant female. Although her sentimentalized construal
demonstrated a desire for cultural citizenship, it simultaneously implied
assumptions about her innate aversion to change.[3] In other words, the
sentimentalized immigrant woman was constitutionally at odds with the

---

1. In "The New Woman as Androgyne," Smith-Rosenberg maintains that new women such as Wald
and Addams used "old arguments" concerning women's innate nurturing capacity to "justify public roles that, in their eyes, merely carried their 'mother's' ideas to a logical conclusion" (171).
2. In "Making Connections with the Camera," Stein argues that Riis's role as reformer of the aliens'
physical context enabled him to move from the position of penniless immigrant, to that of
respected citizen, and eventually to confidante of Theodore Roosevelt.
3. William Ripley, too, had argued that "woman always is the conservative element in society" and
pointed to "many thousand cases of destitution among foreign-born women . . . [whose] husband
has outdistanced her in adaptation" ("Races" 750).

Americanizer's project; within the logic of sentimentality, the phrase "Americanized immigrant mother" is oxymoronic. Consequently, reformers' texts oscillated between reclaiming the immigrant woman for national belonging by depicting those factors that mitigated against the procession of her maternal duties and evincing a more or less muted animus against the alien female, who was, given the reformers' immersion within the gendered assumptions of sentimentality, biologically resistant to reformation.

Nowhere is evidence of the Americanizers' investment in biologically based explanations of gender difference more abundant than in the texts of those writers and activists who continued to stress the immigrant woman's dependence and conservatism even though clearly confronted with activities on her part that demonstrated enterprise and flexibility. Anthony's *Mothers Who Must Earn*, a fascinating and highly readable account of the experiences of laboring immigrant mothers on New York's West Side, is one such narrative. It combines descriptions of the work engaged in by the women, statistics pertaining to rates of pay and hours of work, and interviews with working immigrant mothers. Most pertinent to my argument is Anthony's dogged cleavage to the script of immigrant mothers as anachronistic, tradition-bound, and dependent despite being confronted time and again with evidence confirming their adaptability and survival skills. She insisted that immigrant mothers who worked did so out of maternal considerations only: "They had become wage-earners in obedience to the most primitive of maternal instincts. Their children would have suffered seriously had they failed or refused to earn" (199). Anthony reclaimed the laboring immigrant mother for sentimental motherhood by defining her as doubly dependent. Contrasting the father's and children's job-seeking with that of the mother, she wrote: "Looking for work. . . . has for the boy or girl the spice of adventure. . . . But the mother who must earn finds it no adventure" (84). She continued, "A more helpless figure than the middle-aged mother of a family starting out to look for work would be hard to imagine" (85). A scant few pages later, however, she pointed out that "the women feel a strong mutual responsibility to help one another to find employment. . . . they roughly co-operate to help each other in work. . . . news of a vacant job is quickly passed around" (88–89). This clear conveyance of communal cooperation in the matter of employment opportunities surely bears witness to the women's enterprise. Anthony acknowledged the cooperation only to quickly subordinate it to the overriding agenda of the text: the reproduction of the immigrant woman as a sentimental mother and hence as hapless and inflexible.

Again, discussing the large number of immigrant mothers who become janitresses, a much-coveted job, Anthony observed, "Occasionally, a janitress will develop very fair business capacity for her work. A large real estate dealer in the district says that he depends on the character of his janitresses to keep his apartments rented" (75). Yet Anthony continued to maintain that the women experienced a "complete stultification of spirit" from their "life of monotonous toil" (100). At one point, however, she edged very close to acknowledging that work, rather than being solely waged labor and an arena of travail, for many immigrant mothers provided a forum in which a welcome sociality could occur: "None of the women expressed a direct preference for outside work over housework. . . . some expressed a preference for cleaning jobs because of their social character. 'The work is hard,' said one, 'but we all pull together'" (158). Despite such evidence of resourcefulness and affirmation of paid labor, Anthony maintained that the immigrant mother's innate passivity and conservatism rendered her doubly disadvantaged. The tension between adaptive reality and sentimental template indicate that the Americanizers' sentimentalized understanding of the immigrant mother precluded recognition of her competence in the New World and in turn rendered her a well-nigh intractable problem in terms of their rehabilitatory project.

The convergence of nativist and Americanization arguments with respect to the immigrant woman's racial intransigence helps explain the periodic eruption into reformers' texts of maternal images at odds in every respect with the image of sanctified immigrant motherhood. Any account of Riis's texts is incomplete without consideration of those moments when an immigrant mother surfaces whose monstrosity clearly echoes nativist arguments and images. In *How the Other Half Lives*, Riis described two police record entries that were "far from uncommon" and pertained to "mothers in West Side tenements, who in their drunken sleep lay upon and killed their infants" (131). Similarly, his photograph "Girl and Baby on Doorstep" depicts a baby in the arms of a young girl (presumably his sister), underscoring the physical absence of the maternal figure and raising the specter of generational reproduction of inefficacious mothering. He commented that the House of Industry [an orphanage] contained "a score of babies, rescued from homes of brutality and desolation. . . . their white nightgowns hide tortured little bodies and limbs cruelly bruised by inhuman hands" (151). At such moments Riis's arguments about the deleterious effects of environment and maternal ignorance slid into an argument that constructed the heinous rather than the incapacitated immigrant mother as the cause of family breakdown. The congruence of nativist and Americanizers' representation of her at such points must be traced to their mutual investment, although differentially located, in notions of the immigrant woman's racial intractability.

If Riis's photographs convey the immigrant mother's amenability to the reformer's regulatory interventions by the docility with which she yielded herself to the lens, then the opposite effect is achieved in images such as "The Dive", which was included in both *The Battle with the Slum* and *Peril and Preservation of the Home*. Distracted by something to the left and out of the frame, the women do not readily accede to Riis's fact-gathering mission. He typically characterized such resistant women in terms that clearly echoed nativist thought. They were "utterly depraved" and frequented "the borderland where the white and black races meet in common debauch" (*How the Other Half Lives* 156).

A similar dichotomy occurred in Breckinridge's *New Homes for Old*. Embedded within a narrative largely invested in construing the foreign woman as "Dolorosa" are immigrant women who "find themselves unequal to the task of readjusting their lives" (52) and a particular wife who "drank and was immoral. Instead of caring for the home and the two-year-old child, she spent her time . . . in her brother's saloon [leaving her child]. . . . alone in the house while she went to the 'movies'" (52–53). And in Ruth True's *The Neglected Girl*, the ineptness of the immigrant mother in her new context slides quickly and repeatedly into an account of her immorality: "The worry and strain of insecurity become too great for many a woman. She grows apathetic, careless, and stolid, or she becomes querulous and neurotic. Perhaps she takes to drink" (27). The immigrant mother "is spent, dragged, and worn, in pitiful need of the younger, more vigorous life at her side" (53). In this text, the proximity of mother to daughter is a danger to the latter because "the daughter of fourteen in the tenements must share the experience of the mother of fifty, who, even with the best intentions, cannot shield her girl from her own fifty-year-old materialistic morals" (78).

This facet of the Americanizers' discourse helps explain the increasing hysteria of the Americanization movement during and immediately following the war years. John Higham has argued that the period witnessed the victory of the coercive, nationalist approach of groups such as the Daughters of the American Revolution and the 100 percent Americanism movement over the more meliorative, liberal approach of those settlement workers and social reformers who stressed an educative and humanitarian approach to Americanization. My argument has suggested that the movement may not have been, in its aims, essentially bifurcated. It was the logic of the Americanizers' particular form of racialism rather than the victory of one impulse over another that led to the extreme coercion and xenophobia of their later activities.[4] The hysteria that accompanied Americanizers' activities during the war years resulted from the reformers' assumptions about the obdurate traditionalism of the immigrant woman. Such feminine intractability issued, at best, in an un-Americanized second generation and at worst in a generational schism liable to produce criminal sons and wayward daughters.

JOEL SCHWARTZ

From Fighting Poverty with Virtue:
Moral Reform and America's Urban Poor, 1825–2000[†]

* * *

In his classic account of late-nineteenth-century urban poverty, *How the Other Half Lives,* Jacob Riis voiced the ambivalence (at best) of moral reformers about the immigrant thrift that was made possible by a below-normal standard of living:

> Thrift is the watchword of [New York's] Jewtown, as of its people the world over. It is at once its strength and its fatal weakness, its cardinal virtue and its foul disgrace. Become an overmastering passion with these people who come here in droves from Eastern Europe to escape persecution, from which freedom could be bought only with gold, it has enslaved them in bondage worse than that from which they fled. Money is their God. Life itself is of little value compared with even the leanest bank account. . . . Over and over again I have met with instances of these Polish or Russian Jews deliberately starving themselves to the point of physical exhaustion, while working night and day at a tremendous pressure to save a little money.

---

4. This is Higham's interpretation in *Strangers.*
† Copyright © 2000 by Joel Schwartz. Reprinted by permission of Indiana University Press.

If we can ignore the anti-Semitic overtones of this passage, how should we evaluate its substance? Since Riis elsewhere lauded the development of "habits of thrift and ambitious industry" (around the "sound core of self-help"), it is tempting to attack the hypocrisy of moral reformers who advocated thrift but then criticized the immigrant practitioners of the very virtue that had been preached to them.

On the other hand, a more sympathetic assessment of the reformers is possible. It is to the reformers' credit—not their shame—that they understood thrift as a situational virtue, more valid in some circumstances than others. To have done otherwise, to have suggested that additional belt-tightening was always appropriate for the poor, would surely have been still more unfair to them. Although Riis might (and should) have shown more sympathy for the plight of the self-denying residents of "Jewtown," he was not wrong to warn against underconsumption as a genuine danger. Nor was [Mary] Brown[1] wrong to see child labor as a strategy that had costs for the poor as well as the obvious benefit—increased income—that made greater savings possible.

In effect, Riis's critique constitutes an acknowledgment that material poverty itself frustrated many of the moral strategies that were meant to reduce it (e.g., migrating westward in search of employment or renting larger and cleaner apartments). For that reason, the "morals" strategy of the reformers was not and could not be altogether effective on its own, but instead needed to be supplemented by an "income" strategy. Greater virtue was surely desirable in the poor (as it would have been in the nonpoor as well). Ultimately, though, the poor needed to earn more money as well as to improve their morals. In some ways, earning more would actually facilitate moral improvement, for example by making it possible to migrate in quest of jobs or to occupy housing that was less demoralizing and also conducive to better health.

Riis himself explained that material privation and not moral failure was at issue only two paragraphs after his critique of Jewish miserliness. There he approvingly quoted this statement from doctors who ministered to charity cases on the Lower East Side: "The diseases these people suffer from are not due to intemperance or immorality, but to ignorance, want of suitable food, and the foul air in which they live and work." Clearly Riis understood that the poor could benefit from using their income wisely (by spending it wisely as well as saving it wisely), but he also realized that simply increasing their income (so that they could eat more and work less) would also benefit them greatly.

Riis (like Brown) recognized that thrift was desirable in some circumstances but not all, that it could solve some problems but not all. His discussion of thrift amounted to an implicit critique of those who saw working-class thrift as a panacea. Significantly, the qualified defense of thrift that Riis and Brown espoused is supported by Thernstrom's assessment of the historical evidence. Thernstrom criticizes those who regarded savings banks as a remedy for all the ills of the poor: their position could be sustained only by adopting the untenable "premise that the problem of working class poverty was not essentially a deficiency of total income, but only a failure to use income rationally."

*   *   *

1. A Baltimore charity worker [editor].

ROBERT M. DOWLING

From Slumming: Morality and Space in New York City—from "City Mysteries" to the Harlem Renaissance[†]

* * *

With the waning influence of Victorianism on contemporary images of nineteenth-century New York, we are discovering that the city is shown in the popular urban fiction of the mid-nineteenth century as the ultimate proving ground for the success or attrition of the United States. Those elements of New York that required direct discourse and definition: the growing reliance on a perceived need for a moral center, the rapid increase of poverty, and the seeming loss of the original American ideal, were all uniquely engaged by this fiction. City mysteries writers took the first deliberate textual soundings of urban morality. They were born into a generation which powerlessly stood by as New York's population sprang from 100,000 to 500,000. Cities across the country grew in kind, and the publishing world responded to their audience's apprehensions. From the 1840s through the 1860s, over 400 urban novels were published, three times as many as were set in the West (Siegal 6). Authors and publishing houses were scrambling to meet their audience's exigent demands for guidance. Men like George Thompson, George Foster, George Lippard, and John Vose, four vanguards of the popular urban form in American literature, did their best to help supply meet demand.

After the Civil War, textual representations of New York slum life began to reflect the growing popularity of the social sciences to address the issue of New York's increasingly identifiable and morally problematic "lower" districts. The corollary in literary history is the transition from sentimentalism to realism, from a preoccupation with plot-driven pathos to social concerns and unheroic character play. Sentimental and sensational modes of representing New York slum life spliced with the social sciences during America's Gilded Age into a new mode that might be called "moral realism," a fusion of the romantic and the pragmatic practiced by such reform writers as Charles Loring Brace, Helen Campbell and Jacob Riis—a group whose explicit aim was nothing less than to change the face of urban America.

Campbell and Riis in particular argued their cases by intermingling Protestant gospel with sociology, stark melodrama with appalling statistics, romantic characterization with interviews, and caricatured settings with very specific sites of inquiry which readers were encouraged to explore for themselves. Poverty then became a provable, tangible lifestyle that had deeply-rooted and seemingly irreversible social effects. Like the sentimental or sensational text, characters in the new mode were rewarded for choosing the right moral path after experiencing a series of temptations, but the stories were "real" and the characters could be literally sought out at a neighborhood mission or downtown saloon. Moral realists condemned "low class" neighborhood cultures in favor of acculturation. And rather than being passive observers, they immersed themselves in the society of each site by exercising an inductive process of gathering material. Rather

† Reprinted by permission of the author.

than rely on commonly held universal principles of social progress that promoted conclusions based on hearsay and preconceptions, they met the poor on their own ground.

But though texts like Campbell's *The Problem of the Poor* (1882) and Riis's *How the Other Half Lives* (1890) reflect an altruistic middle-class concern for the inhabitants of the slums, New York society and its slum reporters still retained their "moral interpretations of poverty." (Ward 43). A process of polarization was at work, regarded as both necessary and repugnant by uptown New Yorkers. This was precipitated by increasingly isolated job sites, inadequate housing, and neighborhood displacement. Reform movements were organized to manage the crisis. The slums both emerged and were transformed during this period, and by the 1870s, the distinctive qualities of many neighborhoods that had been singled-out by moral suasion efforts were effectively incapacitated. If Paula Rabinowitz defines "slumming" in the 1930s as "more likely the regulation of working people's desires than the expression of middle-class pleasures" which is manifested in "ritual encounters between those whose lives were privileged to observe, regulate, and detail the behaviors of others" (188), the 1870s and '80s were, in fact, the heyday of slumming as social regulation. By 1895, for example, the notorious Five Points area had been, as urban reformer Helen Campbell recalls, "long ago reduced to order and decency by farces working for good" (Campbell *Darkness* 51).

In the 1880s and '90s, more and more writers began to investigate these affected neighborhoods in uniquely introspective and realistic modes. Walt Whitman, Stephen Crane and Henry James, for example, have all descriptively revealed to what extent the middle-class had coerced the immigrant and laboring classes into the Victorian "cult of respectability." All of them slumming on the Bowery—Whitman in the late 1880s, Crane in the early 1890s, and James as late as 1907—found there a milieu that was being stripped of its cultural identity; the idiosyncratic Bowery lifestyle of the 1830s and '40s existed only residually. The moral reform efforts of the 1860s, '70s, and '80s, had given way to a culture of consumption. Entertainment venues in particular were guided by the principles of middle-class Victorian conduct Consumer culture, such as might be found in New York's theaters, dance halls, and museums, proved far more effective for bringing urban "low life" into the "respectable" fold.

Needless to say, moral suasion had its limits. Moral regions continued to crop up throughout the city, becoming increasingly self-contained and foreign. As commercial regionalism—as seen on the Bowery and the waterfront—gave way to ethnic isolationism—the Tenderloin's "black Bohemia," the Jewish Lower East Side, Harlem—it became transparently clear that the urban slums often had more power on the regulators of decency than those reformers had on them. With the immigration of the Chinese, the Italians, and the Eastern European Jews at the turn of the century, and blacks from the West Indies and the American South in the 1920s and '30s, the "slum" had become the "ghetto" in the popular usage of the term: "the residential segregation of ethnically defined migrants in the inner-city slums" (Ward 2).

Literary naturalists slumming in the modern city, as June Howard relates, began to recognize the "crucial difference between omniscience and omnipotence" (x). It was one thing to investigate slum life, and even to write about it, but if there was to be any change in moral perspective, it would be the privileged spectators even more than the objectified Other that would now do the changing. Howard continues,

> The author and reader and the characters who represent them inhabit a privileged location [in literary naturalism], assuming a kind of control over forces and events through their power to comprehend them. Yet the privilege of the spectator, constructed by contrast, is necessarily vulnerable; fear and desire—sexual passion and violence, the fatal spell of the commodity, the fascination of the Other—constantly disrupt the design of safety. To venture any dealings with the powers that inhabit causality proves hazardous; characters who go slumming in the realm of determinism risk their freedom and expose themselves to the dangers of paralysis and proletarianization. (x)

Realist and naturalist writers like William Dean Howells and Paul Laurence Dunbar consciously rendered the impact of New York's neighborhoods on "outsider" sensibilities. Dunbar sardonically warns in 1902 that after a short time in New York, outsiders unaccustomed to the city will become intoxicated by "the subtle, insidious wine of New York." Singling out the Bowery, Broadway, and Central Park, Dunbar entreats the wise traveler to avoid such temptations—they might "even go over to Jersey" (71). In contrast, Howells welcomes the new aestheticism offered by working-class street life, such as that which his character Basil March perceived while transversing the "shapeless, graceless, reckless picturesqueness of the Bowery" (159).

Indeed, as Amy Kaplan argues in *The Social Construction of Realism*, realism was as often as not "a strategy for imagining and managing the threats of social change—not just to assert a dominant power but often to assuage fears of powerlessness" (8). There exists in many realist texts an "if you can't beat 'em, join 'em" sensibility; slumming becomes a means of unifying, for better or for worse, an otherwise fragmented urban environment. Commenting on Frederic Jameson's "strategy of containment"—the means by which to isolate a working-class culture in order to destroy it, a strategy Helen Campbell and Jacob Riis most certainly employed—Kaplan further asserts that "by containing the threats of social change, realistic narratives also register those desires which undermine the closure of that containment" (10).

✳ ✳ ✳

JOSEPH ENTIN

From "Unhuman Humanity": Bodies of the Urban Poor and the Collapse of Realist Legibility†

1. Realism, Legibility, and the Turn-of-the-Century City

Recently, several scholars of late nineteenth-century urban fiction, photography, and social science discourse have stressed the complicity of these

† From *Novel: A Forum on Fiction* 34.3 (2001). Copyright © 2001 NOVEL Corp. Reprinted with permission.

cultural forms with emerging modes of social discipline. In particular, critics have argued that the desire to represent the lives of socially subordinate populations—tenement dwellers, immigrants, vagrants—in novels, photographs, and scientific studies converged with governmental and private-sector reform and social service programs to establish an extensive, tightly-woven web of surveillance through which the poor and disenfranchised were analyzed, regulated, and policed.

Literary historian June Howard contends, for example, that naturalist writing reinforced Progressive-era structures of social dominance in which the poor become objects of professional-managerial class scrutiny. Howard argues that naturalism is characterized by an organizing dichotomy between a privileged, autonomous narrator, with whom the reader is aligned, and a "brute," a degraded inhabitant of a deterministic world. Rather than an a self-governing individual, the "brute" is the central subject in a spectacle of determinism that confirms the power of the narrator's gaze and the moral authority and freedom of the readers. "[T]he menacing and vulnerable Other"—the "brute"—"is incapable of acting as a self-conscious, purposeful agent[;] he can only be observed and analyzed by such an agent" (104). However, although the spectator describes and explains the brute, he (rarely she) retains his autonomy from the deterministic environment the brute inhabits; while "we explore determinism, we are never submerged in it and ourselves become the brute" (104). Ultimately, Howard argues, the narrator/brute split anticipates the Progressive movement, which placed reform in the hands of a small cadre of ostensibly enlightened, nonpartisan experts. "It is a very short step," Howard contends, "from naturalism's gesture of control to progressivism's, from the sympathy and good intentions of the naturalist spectator to the altruistic and ultimately authoritarian benevolence of the progressive reformer" (131).

Along similar lines, Mark Seltzer has recently argued that realism's drive to render the social world legible operates as a form of cultural surveillance. Seltzer contends that realism's and naturalism's diverse "registers" "are coordinated within a single technology of regulation" ("Statistical" 84), "a flexible and totalizing machine of power" (Bodies 44). "[T]he realist vision of the urban underworld," Seltzer contends, "involves a disciplinary relation between seeing (seeing and being seen) and the exercising of power": "the realist project of making-visible is perfectly in line with the techniques of a certain social discipline—the opening of the everyday ordinariness of every body to, and the fabrication of individuals under, the perfect eye of something like the police" ("Statistical" 85, 84). Realism and social discipline overlap seamlessly, Seltzer suggests, forming a "single," "totalizing" mechanism of power. In his account, vision is inherently, invariably regulative, a perfect policing eye, always enforcing social control.

This essay examines a counter-current embedded within this matrix of regulating and order-producing technologies. The scenes of tramping and of urban looking examined below frequently destabilize the relation between seeing and social power that underwrites many dominant realist and naturalist narratives. The stories, articles, and sketches explored here suggest that the dynamics of late nineteenth-century literary spectatorship cannot invariably and completely be subsumed under the umbrella of "surveillance" or placed neatly within a rubric of social control. On the contrary, the array of works I analyze—by William Dean Howells, Jacob Riis,

Stephen Crane, and Walter Wyckoff—suggest that professional efforts to survey the bodies of the urban lumpenproletariat often result in various forms of cognitive dissonance that undermine realism's will-to-legibility. In contrast to Howard's claims, these writings—especially those by Wyckoff and Crane—suggest that the dichotomy between omniscient narrators and "brute" characters is unstable and insecure; in contrast to Seltzer's contentions, these writings indicate that the links between realist writings about the bodies of the poor and "techniques of a certain social discipline" are far from seamless.

The writings explored below represent efforts to fashion post-sentimental modes of narrating the poor—to circumvent what many realists and naturalists perceived as sentimental literature's overly emotional identification with the underprivileged and over-wrought stylistic tendencies. Writings by Riis and Howells mitigate potentially threatening scenes of urban unruliness and potential class conflict by lending their readers a disembodied position of distance from urban blight and "alien" bodies. Disembodiment is a form of privilege—in contrast to embodied subjects who are anchored to the material world, bound by physicality, disembodied readers and viewers are free to see and move beyond the confines of their bodies, to survey the embodied classes without placing their own bodies at risk.[1] For Crane and Wyckoff, both of whom enter the urban underworld disguised as tramps, encounters with the bodies of the dispossessed prove much more unsettling; the lodging house "stiffs" they describe disorient them, engendering narratives in which realism's desire for legibility is disrupted and naturalism bleeds into an early form of modernism. Their efforts to delineate the experience and bodies of the poor produce forms of sensory disorientation and cognitive confusion that undermine the narrative clarity that Howard and Seltzer contend gives realism and naturalism their "disciplinary" capacity.

The ambiguities of cross-class viewing that I examine echo the larger ambiguities that characterized turn-of-the-century urban visual experience. At the end of the nineteenth century, the growth of department stores and spread of advertising, the rise of mass circulation magazines, the proliferation of city daily newspapers, and the development of new technologies of lithographic and photographic reproduction all contributed to the explosion of new visual forms and new modes of seeing which were especially prevalent in the nation's cities.[2] However, if the late nineteenth- and early twentieth-century city was increasingly a site of visual stimulation and activity, urban spectators faced a social space that was much more fractured and opaque than the city of previous generations had been. Scholars such as Lawrence Levine and David Harvey have argued that American culture was undergoing a process of fragmentation and segregation during the late nineteenth century, a process that was especially acute in urban areas. Social, economic, and material changes to the shape of urban space altered the ways the city was conceived, imagined, and narrated. As the urban social landscape grew more complexly

1. On the privileges of disembodiment, see Scarry 243–77.
2. Reviewing the transformation of urban culture at the end of the nineteenth century, Trachtenberg has argued, "Viewing and looking at representations, words and images, city people found themselves addressed more often as passive spectators than as active participants, consumers of images and sensations produced by others" (*Incorporation* 122).

stratified and densely compacted during the process of economic and cultural incorporation, the ways in which individuals perceived and understood this new social space fractured. Describing the period, Fredric Jameson argues that "an objective fragmentation of the so-called outside world is matched and accompanied by a fragmentation of the psyche which reinforces its effects" (229). This psychic fragmentation led to the emergence of a variety of new aesthetic styles—early modernist styles—such as the Jamesian point-of-view and Impressionism, in which the exercise of perception and the perceptual recombination of sense data become the focus of artistic endeavor.

According to Jonathan Crary, the process described by Jameson, in which individual perception becomes increasingly autonomous and subjective, began to occur in American visual culture as early as the first third of the nineteenth century, with the emergence of industrial capitalism. Beginning in the 1830s, Crary contends, the site of visuality is relocated from the stable, incorporeal relations of the camera obscura to the more subjective position within the human body. Vision acquires a previously unknown flexibility and autonomy: "what occurs is a new valuation of visual experience: it is given an unprecedented mobility and exchangeability, abstracted from any founding site or referent" (14). Echoing Crary's emphasis on the increasingly subjective quality of visual experience, Martin Jay points out that although many of the new technologies of visual production (especially photography) were employed to reinforce positivist and rationalist ways of thinking and regulating the social world (for example, Frederick Taylor's industrial management plans and Bertillon's system of criminal classification), these new modes of visuality also created the possibility of challenges to Cartesian perspectivalism and the longstanding Enlightenment ideology of dispassionate cognition.

Late nineteenth-century urban spectators, then, were placed in an unsettling and uncertain position. On the one hand, the rise of consumer culture and new technologies of reproduction inaugurated a proliferation of viewing activities. Inducements and opportunities to look expanded; spectating became an activity in and of itself. On the other hand, the city was becoming an increasingly opaque and impenetrable space—densely packed yet segregated and stratified. Crary assigns to this moment an "atomization of sight" in which spectating becomes an increasingly subjective act, unloosed from fixed or transcendental coordinates. If, as many critics contend, looking was increasingly an instrument of social control—if urban viewers were increasingly active, vigilant, discriminating—then a counter tendency was also present: urban space was increasingly opaque, vision was increasingly subjective.

One cultural genre that emerged to confront this new urban space and to explore new modes of looking was the journalistic "sketch." Like a snapshot, a sketch offered a quick and partial glimpse of city life. Written to capture the newspaper reader's scanning, scrambling gaze, sketches are studies in narrative perspective, exercises in point of view that suggest the city can best be described in bits and slices, fragments of a totality. One of the primary functions that sketches performed was to bring images and views of the foreign or unfamiliar elements of the increasingly segmented city—the poor and immigrants, the "other half"—home to readers, generally in terms that made the city's alien people and places seem more familiar, less threatening. Typically, turn-of-the-century sketches on the urban poor fell into one of three veins: pieces warning readers of the dangers and vices that permeate the city; pieces describing the picturesque nature of poor immigrants; pieces participating in a sentimental crusade to aid and reform the poor and their environment.[3] However, within this popular genre, several authors produced articles that, in a variety of ways, challenged as well as reaffirmed their readers' sense of social security and specular privilege, underscoring not only the contingency of spectatorial view points, but the potential reciprocity, even mutuality, that active and aggressive cross-class looking makes possible.

✻ ✻ ✻

3. Danger and Containment in How the Other Half Lives

✻ ✻ ✻

Jacob Riis's *How The Other Half Lives* (1890) performs a similar double movement—introducing potentially disturbing scenes, but, through a variety of rhetorical framing techniques, protecting the reader's position of specular distance and security. A passage that opens one of the text's final chapters, entitled "The Man with the Knife," illustrates the semiotic double-take Riis frequently enacts:

> A man stood at the corner of Fifth Avenue and Fourteenth Street the other day, looking gloomily at the carriages that rolled by, carrying the wealth and fashion of the avenues to and from the big stores down town. He was poor, and hungry, and ragged. This thought was in his mind: "They behind their well-fed teams have no thought for the morrow; they . . . would keep me and my little ones from want a whole year." There rose up before him the picture of those little ones crying for bread around the cold and cheerless hearth—then he sprang into the throng and slashed about him with a knife, blindly seeking to kill, to revenge. (207)

On the one hand, this might have been a very unsettling passage for Riis's readers: it begins by challenging the indifference of middle-class consumers to the indigent by shifting the narrative perspective from the carriage (the position from which Riis's readers—like Howells's friend perusing the bread line in "The Midnight Platoon"—were accustomed to viewing the poor) to the sidewalk. In addition, the passage endows the hapless man with the foundations of a sentimental subjectivity (he has a family and a hearth), demanding that the reader (who, in other circumstances, is the carriage occupant) consider the personal predicament of a "ragged" man on the street. The most potent incentive to take the man seriously, however, is undoubtedly the threat of violence that the scene portrays—it is the very indifference of the carriage riders that sparks the man's terrifying attack (terrifying because it is unpredictable from inside the carriage and yet directed at carriage riders and shoppers). On a certain reading, then, this

---

3. These categories are based largely on my own survey of turn-of-the-century periodicals. For further detail about the varieties of urban journalism that sought to decipher and delineate the contours of the city's mysteries, see Gandal.

passage insists that the apathy of the wealthy bears responsibility for lower-class insurrection.

On the other hand, however, the menace that the passage presents is mitigated by the readers' privileged narrative position. Although the violence is potentially disturbing, from our vantage point it is comprehensible, even predictable—the ragged man's mind is transparent to us, his motives and actions immanently legible. The readers are neither in the carriage nor on the sidewalk but in a floating position that affords both security and insight. We are disembodied, in a position of omniscience and immunity. Read in this manner, the passage describes a threat for the purposes of affirming the readers' safety and perceptiveness—the man's attack inspires a sense of urgency about reform but does so in a way that confirms our social privilege.

Recently, Peter Stallybrass has argued that it was the very horrible, virtually undescribable quality of the urban poor that consolidated the gaze of middle-class viewers. Stallybrass contends that in mid-nineteenth-century Britain, an array of painters, journalists, and novelists set out to describe the lives and living places of the urban lumpenproletariat. In this "hysteria of naming," the urban underclasses were presented as a "spectacle of multiplicity" against which the homogeneity of the bourgeois subject was produced (72). The grotesque, exotic, even unrepresentable quality of the underclasses confirmed, through contrast, the "homogenizing gaze of the bourgeois spectator" (79). The dynamic that Stallybrass describes approximates the effect of Riis's survey of New York's tenements, back alleys, and flophouses: the disarray, decay, and destitution depicted confirms the social power as well as, Riis hoped, the social obligations of the wealthier classes. Riis prevents potentially unsettling sights from threatening his readers by enforcing a sense of social and aesthetic distance between his readers and the slums. The poor constitute a spectacle that Riis's viewers observe, inspect, and scrutinize from a distance; he allows readers access to the deepest recesses of the tenements through a rhetoric that paradoxically confirms social separation. The "other half" remains thoroughly "Other"; the possibility of an exchange of points of view is avoided.[4]

The vicarious insight Howells and Riis offer to their readers differs dramatically from the account of urban disorientation published by sociologist Walter Wyckoff and the shadowy, opaque world of urban interactions depicted by journalist Stephen Crane. For Wyckoff and Crane, the protections of narrative privilege prove much less secure.

* * *

Works Cited

Crane, Stephen. *The New York City Sketches of Stephen Crane and Related Pieces.* Ed. R. W. Stallman and E. R. Hagemann. New York: New York UP, 1966.
Crary, Jonathan. *Techniques of the Observer: On Vision and Modernity in the Nineteenth Century.* Cambridge: MIT P, 1990.

4. The debate on the politics of Riis's work and methods is a hotly contested one. Stange contends that Riis's images provided a fundamentally "safe" viewing experience for the urban middle-class, "assigning to them a relation to the proceedings that offered an attractively secure and collective point of view from which to survey the show" (291). In contrast. Hales argues that Riis's images

Gandal, Keith. *The Virtues of the Vicious: Jacob Riis, Stephen Crane, and the Spectacle of the Slum.* New York: Oxford UP, 1997.

Hales, Peter B. *Silver Cities: The Photography of American Urbanization, 1839–1915.* Philadelphia: Temple UP, 1984.

Howard, June. *Form and History in American Literary Naturalism.* Chapel Hill: U of North Carolina P, 1985.

Howells, William Dean. "An East-Side Ramble." *Impression and Experiences.* New York: Harper & Bros., 1896. 127–49.

———. "The Midnight Platoon," *Literature and Life: Studies.* New York: Harper & Bros., 1902. 154–60.

Jameson, Fredric. *The Political Unconscious: Narrative as a Socially Symbolic Act.* Ithaca: Cornell UP, 1981.

Jay, Martin. *Downcast Eyes: The Denigration of Vision in Twentieth-Century French Thought.* Berkeley: U of California P, 1993.

Levine, Lawrence W. *Highbrow/Lowbrow: The Emergence of Cultural Hierarchy in America.* Cambridge: Harvard UP, 1988.

Ohmann, Richard M. *Selling Culture: Magazines, Markets, and Class at the Turn of the Century.* New York: Verso, 1996.

Riis, Jacob. *How the Other Half Lives: Studies Among the Tenements of New York.* 1890. New York: Dover Publications, 1971.

Robertson, Michael. *Stephen Crane, Journalism, and the Making of Modern American Literature.* New York: Columbia UP, 1997.

Scarry, Elaine. *The Body in Pain: The Making and Unmaking of the World.* New York: Oxford UP, 1985.

Seltzer, Mark. *Bodies and Machines.* New York: Routledge, 1992.

———. "Statistical Persons." *Diacritics* 17 (1987): 82–98.

Stallybrass, Peter. "Marx and Heterogeneity: Thinking the Lumpenproletariat." *Representations* 31 (1990): 69–95.

Stange, Maren. "Jacob Riis and Urban Visual Culture: The Lantern Slide Exhibition as Entertainment and Ideology." *Journal of Urban History* 15 (1989): 274–303.

Trachtenberg, Alan. "Experiments in Another Country: Stephen Crane's City Sketches." *Southern Review* 10 (1974): 265–85.

———. "Image and Ideology: New York in the Photographer's Eye." *Journal of Urban History* 10 (1984): 453–64.

———. *The Incorporation of America: Culture and Society in the Gilded Age.* New York: Hill & Wang, 1982.

Wyckoff, Walter A. "The Workers—The West." *Scribner's Magazine* 23 (1898): 259–75, 429–47, 582–604, 730–47; 24 (1898): 91–111, 321–32, 422–37, 561–72.

"make [the viewers] uncomfortable, threaten their worldview" (193). While Stange contends that Riis offered both ideology and entertainment, Hales asserts that "Riis's lantern slides and his books were not meant to entertain; they were meant to demand of his middle-class Victorian audience a complete and active commitment to the cause of social justice and economic reform" (193). For the most part, I find Stange's argument—that what Riis offered his viewers tended to confirm rather than challenge their sense of security and privilege—more persuasive. Hales's claim that Riis's images "demand" a "complete and active commitment to the cause of social justice" exaggerates, I feel, the progressive quality of Riis's enterprise. However, it is the case that Riis employs threatening scenes and imagery to encourage reform and that his efforts to recontain the dangers he presents are, while largely successful, never entirely complete. My reading of Riis—and the other figures in this essay—is indebted to Trachtenberg, who argues that the moral stance adopted by most slum reformers "supplied the necessary screen of protection from an exchange of subjectivities" ("Experiments" 273).

VINCENT DiGIROLAMO

Newsboy Funerals: Tales of Sorrow and Solidarity in Urban America[†]

In a small write-up about the death of a newsboy, the *Boston Globe* observed in 1890 that there was "nothing more pathetic in all the 'short and simple annals of the poor' than some of the scenes connected with the burial of one of their number." The reporter noted that "the surviving members of the fraternity gladly forego their meals for an entire day, if necessary, for the sake of bringing flowers to lay upon the cheap coffin." The writer then described the exchange between a "deputation" of newsboys and a prominent florist over the order of a ten-dollar wreath:

> "And, Mister, we want his name fixed in it somehow," said the spokesman.
>
> "Certainly," said the obliging clerk, "what is his name?"
>
> "We allus called him 'Skinney,' cos he was a lean little rat."
>
> The clerk demurred against embalming in flowers this somewhat striking cognomen, on the ground that the feelings of the family might be hurt.
>
> "He ain't got no family," stoutly maintained his comrades. "He b'longs to us fellers as much 's anybody, and we won't have nothin' but Skinney—that or nothin'. We pays for it, and we've got a right to boss it. Who'd know who 't was by any other name?"

The article ended with a direct appeal to *Globe* readers: "Do something besides drop a sympathizing tear. The tear is all right if it materializes into dollars and cents." Signed, "THE NEWSBOYS' FRIEND."[1]

While many Bostonians no doubt skimmed over this little item unmoved by its blatant sentimentalism, such a callous response can only blind modern readers to its deeper meanings. The story's value no longer rests in its capacity to elicit tears or tips, but to reveal the historical significance of one of the more obscure rituals of childhood—newsboy funerals.

Newsboy funerals were pitifully elaborate rituals of pomp and poverty. Most children of the poor were buried as members of a family, church, or ethnic group, not a trade. But between the 1850s and the 1910s dozens of orphaned or homeless newsboys in Boston, New York, Brooklyn, Philadelphia, Louisville, St. Louis, Chicago, and other cities were publicly laid to rest by their peers and the institutions that ministered to them. In addition to flowers, newsboys took up collections for coffins, plots, and gravestones. They hired hearses, undertakers, and ministers. They drafted letters of sympathy, passed resolutions of condolence, and marched in funeral trains through the same streets in which they sold their papers.

If we take the view that newsboy funerals were stories that young people told about themselves, then what exactly were they saying, to whom were they speaking, and for what purpose? One way to answer these questions is

---

† From *Journal of Social History* 36.1 (2002). Reprinted by permission.
1. *Newsboys' Reading Rooms of Boston* (Boston, 1890), 5.

via an ethnographic reading of several such funerals. Most historical studies of child mortality and mourning practices have focused on the home, but
newsboy funerals compel us to expand our understanding of children and
death beyond the domestic and into the public sphere.[2] Indeed, they enable
us to see children's grief not simply as products of familial loss, religious
faith, or even journalistic convention, but as expressions of class feeling.
  Take the story about Skinney. While the haggling between the florist
and the newsboys reads more like fiction than reportage, it demonstrates
that the boys regarded themselves—and were regarded by others—as a
"fraternity," as members of an organized body that had a right to mourn
a fellow trader. When the florist objected to their request because it might
offend the feelings of relatives, the boys asserted the primacy of their own
feelings, the value of their own relationship with the deceased, and the
power of their own money to "boss" the job. Their streety dialect served
to contrast the lowness of their station with the nobility of their gesture.
The fact that Skinney's friends knew him by a nickname speaks not to the
superficiality of their association, but to its totality. "Who'd know who 't was
by any other name?" they asked. Who indeed? To this day we know the boy
only by his nickname and through the tribute of his friends, among whom
the journalist counted himself. The writer's closing appeal for charity further shows how a newsboy's death occasioned concern not just for the
deceased, but for all members of the trade.
  Given their association with the press it is not surprising that stories of
newsboys' short lives, tragic deaths, and humbly ostentatious funerals occasionally found their way into the papers. Yet they were also the subject of
tracts, sermons, poems, memoirs, illustrations, and not a few Tin Pan Alley
tearjerkers. These sources are all part of the vast consolation literature that
nourished what Karen Halttunen refers to as "the sentimental cult of
mourning."[3] So lachrymose are works of this genre that Ann Douglas has
called them "exercises in necrophilia."[4] Such phrases unfortunately imply
that middle-class Americans were deluded, if not perverted, in their most
cherished beliefs. Sentimentalism, argues Douglas, was the way the bourgeoisie, particularly women and ministers, feigned concern yet evaded
responsibility for the evils of a capitalist industrial order they were helping
to usher in. It was an unconscious strategy, says Halttunen, for middle-class
Americans to distinguish themselves as a class while still denying the class
structure of their society. Working folks who adopted these forms and rituals, she says, were simply trying to establish a public claim to bourgeois gen-
tility. Newsboys were both exemplars and casualties of capitalism, and thus

2. See Richard A. Kalish, "The Effects of Death Upon the Family," in L. Pearson, ed., *Death and Dying*
   (Cleveland, 1969), 79–107; David E. Stannard, "Death and the Puritan Child," *American Quar-
   terly* Vol. 26, No. 5 (1974), 456–76; and Peter G. Slater, "'From Cradle to the Coffin': Parental
   Bereavement and the Shadow of Infant Damnation in Puritan Society" and Peter Uhlenberg,
   "Death and the Family," in N. Ray Hiner and Joseph M. Hawes, eds., *Growing Up in America: Children in Historical Perspective* (Urbana, 1985), 27–43 and 243–52. On the significance of public
   mourning rites among the poor in England during the early industrial age see Thomas Laqueur,
   "Bodies, Death and Pauper Funerals," *Representations* Vol. 1, No. 1 (Feb. 1983), 109–31. See also
   the essays in Gillian Avery and Kimberley Reynolds, eds., *Representations of Childhood Death* (New
   York, 2000).
3. Karen Halttunen, *Confidence Men and Painted Women: A Study of Middle-Class Culture in America, 1830–1870* (New Haven, 1982), 130, 195.
4. Ann Douglas, *The Feminization of American Culture* (New York, 1977), 200, 12. See also Douglas'
   "Heaven Our Home: Consolation Literature in the Northern United States, 1830–1850," in David
   E. Stannard, ed., *Death in America* (Philadelphia, 1975), 49–68.

could hardly avoid being sentimentalized in song and story. Yet even these sources suggest a more complex pattern of cultural influence. Moreover, if we read between the lines of these tracts and songs and human interest stories, we can glimpse the social and emotional lives of working-class kids.

Historians have only recently begun to write an emotional history of the United States, to trace how people's feelings of love, anger, jealousy, and grief are not so much natural, immutable impulses as reflections of changing social structures and movements, passing fads and fancies, new ideas and technologies.[5] Capturing such reflections is difficult, especially when dealing with poor youths who did not often commit their feelings to paper. Newsboys usually were literate; some did write letters and even memoirs. But most expressed their sorrow ritualistically, and so it is to these rituals we must look if we wish to discover who they were and how they really felt about matters of life and death.

Newsboys were legion in nineteenth-century America and they came from the lowest ranks of society. They were the sons—and occasionally the daughters—of day laborers, piece workers, and petty traders. Many were immigrants or the children of immigrants. In the 1850s and 1860s New York and Philadelphia claimed between five hundred and six hundred newsboys, most of whom came from poor Irish or German families. This juvenile labor force swelled in the 1880s and 1890s as the number of daily and Sunday newspapers quadrupled, circulations doubled, and eleven million new immigrants (mainly Jews and Italians) poured into the country.[6] By the turn of the twentieth century there were more than five thousand newsboys in big cities like New York, Boston, and Chicago, and two thousand in smaller cities like Detroit, St. Louis, and Cincinnati.[7] Most newsboys were between six and fifteen years old, the age working-class children typically entered the adult labor force. But adults also sold papers if they had lucrative routes or corners or needed to get through hard times.

Unlike Skinney, relatively few newsboys were orphans. Most lived in cramped apartments with one or both parents, but any number of events— the arrival of a new baby, the loss of a job, money disputes, and domestic violence—could send parents and children reeling in opposite directions. Thousands of children wound up living or working on the streets of New York in the 1850s. They were feared and reviled as street rats and guttersnipes, vagrants and beggars. Yet they were also admired and ministered to. In 1854, the Rev. Charles Loring Brace opened the first Newsboys' Lodging House, a kind of cheap hotel for working boys, and dozens of similar institutions sprang up across the country.

5. See Peter N. Stearns and Jan Lewis, eds., *An Emotional History of the United States* (New York, 1998).
6. The number of U.S. dailies rose from 574 in 1870 to a high of 2,600 in 1909; two-newspaper towns became four-newspaper towns, and their average circulation more than doubled from 4,532 to 9,312. Six cities set the pace; New York, Chicago, Philadelphia, Cleveland, Boston, and San Francisco boasted 277 daily and Sunday newspapers in 1909 with a combined circulation of over 16 million. See Alfred McClung Lee, *The Daily Newspaper in America: The Evolution of a Social Instrument* (New York, 1937), 65, 718–19, 728, 732. For immigration figures see Alan M. Kraut, *The Huddled Masses: The Immigrant in American Society, 1880–1921* (Arian Heights, Ill., 1982).
7. "The News-Boys," *The Child's Paper* Vol. 3, No. 10 (Oct. 1854), 37; Ninth U.S. Census (1870), Table LXV. Occupations, 604–15; John F. Fitzgerald, "Street Life in Boston in the '70s," *The Hustler* Vol. 1 (March 1911), 3. See also David Nasaw, *Children of the City: At Work and At Play* (New York, 1985) and Vincent DiGirolamo, "Crying the News: Children, Street Work, and the American Press, 1830s–1920s," unpublished Ph.D. dissertation, Princeton University, 1997, 3–4, 305–06.

Whether they lived with or apart from their families, young people of all classes were familiar with death. In the 1870s nine out of ten Americans over fifteen had lost a parent or a sibling.[8] Child mortality rates were high, though declining, throughout the second half of the century. In Massachusetts, for example, infants died at a rate of 205 per thousand in 1865 and 190 per thousand in 1900. The odds of survival improved as one got older, but the average life expectancy in the United States then stood at forty-seven years. Death rates were higher for the working class than for the general population due to their more dangerous jobs and less adequate medical care, sanitation, and diet.[9] Skinney, if his name is any indication, may well have died from the effects of malnutrition. Nationwide, the biggest killers of children were infectious diseases such as diphtheria, tuberculosis, pneumonia, typhoid, and measles. Accidents accounted for about 10 percent of deaths of children. Statistically, children of working, renting, unemployed, illiterate, foreign-born, African American, or city-dwelling parents died at a much higher rate than did other children. In short, poverty killed, and urban poverty killed the most.[1]

Some commentators thought such familiarity with death inured poor children to the ravages of grief. This was the message of a sketch in *Frank Leslie's Illustrated Newspaper* that depicted a tenement funeral in New York's notorious Five Points slum district in 1865. Neighbors watch impassively from stoops, sidewalks, and upper-story windows as four men load a small wooden coffin into a horse-drawn hearse. Oblivious to the solemnity of the moment, three boys drag a dog through the mud by its hind leg.[2] A generation later the crusading police reporter Jacob Riis took perverse consolation in the heartlessness of the slum child. "If the delights of life are few, its sorrows do not sit heavily upon him either," he wrote. "He is in too close and constant touch with misery, with death itself, to mind it much. To find a family of children living, sleeping, and eating in the room where father or mother lies dead, without seeming to be in any special distress about it, is no unusual experience."[3]

Riis mistook distress shown for distress felt. He also failed to recognize that sitting with the dead at home was part of Irish, Jewish and other ethnic mourning customs.[4] Yet he accurately observed that these customs differed according to the age of the deceased and the resources of the survivors. Infants were often buried in anonymous paupers' graves, or, in cases of extreme poverty, abandoned. "Seventy-two dead babies were picked up in the streets last year," wrote Riis of New York in 1890. "Some of them were doubtless put out by very poor parents to save funeral

8. Daniel E. Sutherland, *The Expansion of Everyday Life; 1860–1876* (New York, 1989), 127.
9. *Historical Statistics of the United States, Colonial Times to 1970*, pt. 1, Series B, 193–200, 201–213, 63.
1. Samuel H. Preston and Michael R. Haines, *Fatal Years: Child Mortality in Late-Nineteenth-Century America* (Princeton, 1991), xviii–xix, 4–5, 86, 99, 117, 119, 125–26.
2. "End of the Poor," *Frank Leslie's Illustrated Newspaper* (July 1,1865). Peter J. Eckel Collection. Department of Rare Books and Special Collections. Princeton University Library.
3. Jacob Riis, *The Children of the Poor* (1892), in Francesco Cordasco, ed., *Jacob Riis Revisited: Poverty and the Slum in Another Era* (Garden City, NY, 1968), 163–64.
4. See Richard E. Meyer, ed., *Ethnicity and the American Cemetery* (Bowling Green, 1993); Richard A. Kalish, *Death and Ethnicity: A Psychocultural Study* (Los Angeles, 1976); and two interesting case studies, Joan Moore, "The Death Culture of Mexico and Mexican Americans" and Maurice Jackson, "The Black Experience with Death: A Brief Analysis through Black Writing," in Kalish, *Death and Dying: Views from Many Cultures* (Farmingdale, NY, 1980), 72–91, 92–98.

expenses."[5] Older children, whose individuality was more manifest, usually merited a humble service and their own grave. Working men received the biggest funerals, for they died at a more rapid clip than women and school-age children, and the economic repercussions of their death were more devastating to their families.[6]

Children also encountered the mysteries of death outside the family. They listened to fire-and-brimstone sermons in church and read stories about fallen heroes in school. Some boys and girls incorporated these teachings into their play, reciting morbid nursery rhymes and staging funerals for their pets or dolls.[7] Newsboys supplemented these lessons with those learned on the job and in the cheap theaters they patronized almost religiously. Newsboys virtually trafficked in death, shouting headlines of " 'orrible murders," "bloody battles," and "tragic accidents." On slow news days children such as Henry Dockter in New York would invent shocking or humorous cries to attract customers: "Extra! Extra! Big shipwreck in the subway! Two dead men found alive!"[8] Death to them was a commodity, a source of profit. Yet the reported death of a beloved president or a famous general could also be a deeply felt vicarious experience similar to that engendered by a novel or a play.

Newsboys loved the theater and therein formed their most basic ideas about death, damnation, and resurrection. Those who frequented the gallery of the Bowery Theatre were called "aficionados of death" because they so enjoyed a bloody finale.[9] They would recite the last words of the expiring hero or villain right along with the actors, never failing to point out a missed line. The boys were generous with their applause, yet they would hiss and boo if a character expired too quickly or without sufficient agony or pathos. The most talented boys would later reenact their favorite death scenes on the street or in declamation contests at the Newsboys' Lodging House.[1]

The play that made the biggest impact on the spiritual thinking of newsboys in the antebellum era was Uncle Tom's Cabin. The New York stage adaptation of Harriet Beecher Stowe's sensational 1852 novel led to the formation

5. Jacob Riis, How the Other Half Lives: Studies Among the Tenements of New York (Orig. pub. 1890) (New York, 1989), 142. On this phenomenon in an earlier period, see Paul A. Gilje, "Infant 'Abandonment in Early Nineteenth-Century New York: Three Cases," in Hiner and Hawes, Growing Up in America, 109–117.

6. In Pittsburgh between 1870 and 1900, for example, male workers between 15 and 24 died at a rate of 12 per 1,000, or about twice the rate of females in the same age group. Nearly a third died as a result of industrial accidents. The mortality rate of younger boys, between 5 and 14 years old, was 8 per 1,000. See S. J. Kleinberg, "Death and the Working Class," Journal of Popular Culture Vol. 11, No. 1 (Summer 1977), 194/56–196/58.

7. New York newsboy Johnny Morrow recalled that when his cat died back in his native England, "I made a little grave for it, and put a tombstone at its head with this inscription, which I had persuaded some one to write upon it:-'Here lies poor puss, who died in the year A.D. 1847; may she rest in peace!'" Johnny Morrow, A Voice From the Newsboys (New York, 1860), 21. On doll funerals see Miriam Formanek Brunell, Made to Play House: Dolls and the Commercialization of American Girlhood, 1830–1930 (Baltimore, 1998), 20–23.

8. Gayle Goodman, interview with Henry Dockter, 1989, in author's possession. On death as news, see Robert V. Wells, Facing the "King of Terrors": Death and Society in an American Community, 1750–1990 (New York, 2000), 245–53.

9. Madeline Leslie, Never Give Up; or, The News-Boys (1863) (Chicago, 1881), 46. Cornelius Mathews also observed that newsboys had a "profound passion for the Theatre," and would carve their names into the benches of the Chatham or the Bowery, securing a right to the spot no less sacred than that guaranteed by the pew rents at Grace Cathedral or St. Patrick's. Newsboys preferred dramas with "thunder and lightning long-swords, casques, and black-whiskered villains," he said, and were devoted to actors who demonstrated a "convulsive, awful manner of yielding up the ghost on the stage." See Mathews, A Pen-and-Ink Panorama of New-York City (New York, 1853), 187–88.

1. Sol Eytinge, "The Streets of New York—A Tragic Story," Harper's Weekly (Oct. 11, 1879), 801.

of the "O-de-Ram Society," a club open to all newsboys who vowed to be good enough to become angels in heaven like Little Eva. It took its name from the boys' mispronunciation of the hymn Uncle Tom sang to Eva on her deathbed, "O, de Lamb, de bressed Lamb." According to one journalist:

> The tender-hearted little fellows used to cry, as all the rest of us did, over Eva's dying advice and farewell to Uncle Tom; and they also resolved, with Uncle Tom, to meet the dear child in Heaven. That vision of inno-cence and beauty was the absolute incarnation of angelhood; and the scene amid which she nightly took her mimic departure for the Land of the Blessed was to them an actual foretaste of eternal life.[2]

Not only did *Uncle Tom's Cabin* stir the moral imagination of newsboys, it taught them to grieve together in public, which they did whenever one of their own died.

Some accounts of newsboy funerals come to us via evangelical reform-ers like Brace. The deaths and burials they recorded in most detail were usually of children who died as a result of their years on the street or from some selfless act. For example, "Mickety," the first boy to sign the ledger of the Newsboys' Lodging House and the first to expire there, died of con-sumption, "perhaps brought on by exposure in early days," said Brace, "when he slept in boxes or on the damp ground." In one of his many short sermons to newsboys Brace told how Mickety grew so weak one afternoon that he had to lie down on the counter of a newspaper shop. His friends wanted to call a carriage, but he would not let them, "feeling too modest to ride in a carriage in the day." According to Brace, "The boys clubbed together and bought a handsome mahogany coffin, and buried him in Greenwood, paying the whole expenses themselves."[3]

Greenwood was one of the lush new suburban cemeteries or "memorial gardens" that had begun to replace overcrowded churchyards. Fancy hard-wood caskets were another new phenomenon in the 1850s. Protestants in the antebellum era regarded ostentatious funerals as vain and sinful. Rich and poor alike buried their dead in simple fashion, with friends and neighbors—usually the womenfolk—taking responsibility for laying out the body and arranging the service. The Civil War, which claimed nearly 620,000 men and left tens of thousands of widows and orphans, profoundly changed Americans' attitudes toward death and mourning. Death declined as a theme in popular literature, and, when taken up, was treated much more euphemistically. Funerals became more elaborate, especially in cities. Fam-ilies started hiring undertakers to prepare the deceased for burial. A "decent" funeral came to include a lacquered hearse, ornate casket, floral wreaths, and rented banners, crape, gloves, and sashes.[4] It was this commercialized

---

2. Oliver Dyer, "The New York Sun; Its Rise, Progress, Character, and Condition," *American Agri-culturalist* (Dec. 1869), 463–67. Eckel Collection.
3. Charles Loring Brace, *Short Sermons to Newsboys* (New York, 1866), 234–36.
4. On the evolution of the funeral and the dimunition of the religious aura surrounding death, see James J. Farrell, *Inventing the American Way of Death, 1830–1920* (Philadelphia, 1980); Charles O. Jackson, "American Attitudes to Death," *Journal of American Studies* Vol. 11 (Dec. 1977), 297–312; Lewis O. Saum, "Death in the Popular Mind of Pre-Civil War America," in Charles O. Jackson, ed., *Passing: The Vision of Death in America* (Westport, Conn., 1977), 65–90; Lewis O. Saum, *The Popular Mood of America, 1860–1890* (Lincoln, 1990), 104–33; and Maris A. Vinovskis, "Death," in Mary Kupiec Cayton, Elliott J. Gorn, and Peter W. Williams, eds., *Encyclo-pedia of American Social History*, Vol. III., (New York, 1993), 2063–70.

funeral that the newsboys—symbols of commerce themselves—saw as the ideal.

Another newsboy who realized this emerging ideal was John Ellard in Philadelphia. Nicknamed Didley Dumps, Ellard was a small hump-backed boy who slept in newspaper bags in printing offices before churchmen founded a Newsboys' Home in 1858. Ellard lived at the home for a year and a half; he attended Wednesday classes and Sunday services, saved and loaned money to his colleagues and eventually became proprietor of a little newsstand next to the county building. Never of strong constitution, Ellard had to be carried back and forth to work on the shoulders of the other boys. In November 1859 he caught a severe cold from which he never recovered. A biography written by a director of the home, F. Ratchford Starr, and published by the American Sunday School Union describes his last days in great detail. Starr refused to withhold the doctor's grim prognosis from Ellard:

> I felt it my duty to acquaint him with it at once. The poor lad revolted at the thought of death, and irritably denounced the physician and declared he would go out the next day. But this was not to be. The hand that now held him was the relentless hand of the angel of death. I felt most sensibly that much was to be done for his soul, and that there was but a brief and uncertain period in which to do it.[5]

Ellard died a "happy death" in the manner of Little Eva. During his last days he prayed with his friends and guardians, forgave two outstanding loans, and made up with a boy with whom he had quarreled. Three newsboys were praying at his bedside when he died on December 15, 1859 at the age of sixteen. He was given a "grand" funeral that included a cortege of fifty-six newsboys, six of whom carried his body from the home on Pear Street to St. Joseph's Church. At Sixth and Chestnut they passed Ellard's newsstand, which had been draped in black crape and tied with white ribbon, "indicating that the adornment was for one of tender years."[6]

Processions, according to the *Atlantic Monthly*, were "a source of great gratification to the street boy," and funeral parades were no exception.[7] Most memorable were the corteges of prominent soldiers or statesmen. Newsboy funerals were self-conscious imitations of these lugubrious ceremonies. In 1861, Brace explicitly compared newsboy Johnny Morrow's funeral procession with that of Col. Elmer Ellsworth, the twenty-four year-old commander of New York's Eleventh Regiment and the first Union combat fatality of the Civil War. While Ellsworth's "grand funeral procession, with slow and mournful step, and wailing music was following down Broadway," said Brace, "another coffin was being followed, with many tears, by little children and poor boys, in the city of Brooklyn."[8]

Morrow was seventeen when he died. His family had emigrated from England when he was about ten. They were poor; his father was a hard-

5. F. Ratchford Starr, *Didley Dumps or John Ellard The Newsboy* (Philadelphia, 1884), 148.
6. Ibid., 160.
7. Charles Dawson Shanly, "The Small Arabs of New York," *Atlantic Monthly* Vol. 23, No. 137 (March 1869), 281.
8. Charles Loring Brace, "Reminiscences" and "The Little Newsboy's Funeral," *N. Y. Evangelist & S.S. Times* (June 1861), in Morrow, *A Voice From the Newsboys*, 137–39. Both articles appear in later editions of Morrow's memoir, which still bear the 1860 publication date. For other versions see "A Newsboy's Funeral," *New York Independent* (June 6, 1861); *Ninth Annual Report of the Children's Aid Society* (Feb. 1862), 34–37; and *Short Sermons to Newsboys* (New York, 1866), 238–44.

drinking, frequently out-of-work carpenter. Morrow, who limped due to a childhood accident, helped support the family by peddling newspapers and matches, scavenging for coal and wood, and selling little stools that his father made. Nevertheless, his father beat him regularly for his low earnings and growing appetite. Morrow and his brother eventually ran away from home. They ended up at the Newsboys' Lodging House, where Morrow befriended theological students, attended classes, and dreamed of becoming a clergyman himself. At age sixteen he published his life story, *A Voice from the Newsboys*, to earn money for college. Unfortunately, he died the next year after undergoing surgery on his bad leg. He bled to death when he tried to change the dressing himself rather than trouble his doctor to do it.

Morrow's funeral procession started from the State Street Congregational Church, which had been filled to capacity with students from three Sabbath schools and the Newsboy's school in New York. After eulogies by Brace, two ministers, and Morrow's attending physician, the mourners marched to Evergreen Cemetery. His gravestone identified him by occupation: "Johnny Morrow, the Newsboy, died May 23, 1861, aged 17."[9]

Newsboys had two things in common with the more celebrated recipients of public funerals. One was their sex: the funeral cortege appears to have been an exclusively male privilege. The other was their hero status. During the post-war years New Yorkers of every age and rank witnessed impressive memorial parades for President Lincoln (1865), Admiral Farragut (1870), Horace Greeley (1872), and Ulysses S. Grant (1885).[1] Their effect on children's inchoate notions of mortality and propriety cannot be overestimated. Although news selling was an unreliable form of subsistence labor, it had been idealized in art and literature since the 1840s as a patriotic, character-building occupation in the tradition of Benjamin Franklin. As the market for children's literature burgeoned in the 1860s and 1870s stories featuring newsboy heroes proliferated in books and magazines.[2] Real boys like Mickety, Ellard, and Morrow were easily cast as heroic figures. In eulogizing Morrow, the Rev. W.A. Bartlett of the New York Theological Seminary unabashedly asserted that he "was no less a hero than any who ever fell on the field of battle." Morrow himself evoked a military allusion in his autobiography when he wrote "the newsboy's cause is a warfare on the battle-field of life, where he who fights the *hardest* comes off triumphant from strife."[3]

9. Peter J. Eckel located and photographed Morrow's grave in 1977.
1. Brooks McNamara, *Day of Jubilee: The Great Age of Public Celebrations in New York, 1788–1909* (New Brunswick, 1997), 110–117, 130–36. On the gender politics of public ceremonies see Mary P. Ryan, *Women in Public: Between Banners and Ballots, 1825–1880* (Baltimore, 1990).
2. See, for example, Horatio Alger, *Rough and Ready; or, Life Among the New York Newsboys* (Boston, 1869); James Otis, *Left Behind, or Ten Days a Newsboy* (New York, 1884); and Oliver Optic [William Taylor Adams], *Watch and Wait; or, The young fugitives* (Boston, 1866). Among the leading juvenile publications that featured newsboy stories were *Harper's Young People, St. Nicholas for Young Folks,* and *Oliver Optic's Magazine*. Cheap serials such as Ornum's & Co.'s Fifteen Cent Romances, Beadle's Half Dime Library, and Fame and Fortune Weekly also made newsboy protagonists a stock in trade.
3. Morrow, *A Voice from the Newsboys*, 144, 128. One casualty of this battlefield was newsboy Giuseppe Margalto, who died Feb. 14, 1891, when a fire broke out while he was sleeping in the ventilation chute of a New York post office. Jacob Riis poignantly recalled this was the same night that General William Tecumseh Sherman died. Riis, *The Children of the Poor,* in *Jacob Riis Revisited,* 29.

Another advocate of newsboys was Col. Alexander Hogeland, a military man himself. Hogeland was one of the many emulators of Brace's pragmatic form of child saving. He founded the Newsboys' and Bootblacks' Association and Night Schools in Louisville, Kentucky, and, like Brace, was a well-traveled lecturer and author. He, too, published an account of his years among the newsboys and compiled a book of inspirational readings for young people. His most dismal duty was burying indigent members of the Association. He said he was often the only adult present besides the undertaker or a widowed parent. Among those he buried in 1881 were Fred Fisher, who had asked that his life savings of thirty-three dollars be spent on his funeral; Jimmy Hart, who died after his foot was crushed in an accident; and twelve year-old Robert Maxie, who for some reason was buried outside the fence of the local Cave Hill Cemetery. Hogeland tried to persuade the newsboys that it didn't matter how or where they were buried:

> No, boys, our heavenly Father cares as much for the soul of little Robert as for the richest in the land, and will cause the moon and stars to shine there as brightly as if it rested under a monument of marble on the Cave Hill side of the fence.[4]

It is doubtful that many of the boys were convinced. Ellard, Morrow, and Fisher all revealed their fear of being buried in a potter's field. Such fears were widely shared by working-class youth, as is evident in this little street rhyme from Milwaukee in the 1880s: "Rattle his bones over the stones. He's only a pauper nobody owns."[5] It was all too common, Riis observed, for the "little army of waifs" to be reunited "in the trench in the Potter's Field where, if no medical student is in need of a subject, they are laid in squads of a dozen."[6]

In contrast to these stark burials was the princely funeral of fifteen year-old Sammy Stout in Louisville in 1883. Hogeland described it as "one of unusual solemnity."[7] The service was held at the Association's headquarters on West Jefferson Street. "Sympathizing friends sent quite a supply of blooming flowers," said Hogeland, "while eight of the newsboys' late companions acted as pallbearers." An illustration of the burial shows the eight boys carrying Stout's flower-laden ebony casket from a horse-drawn hearse toward an open grave.[8] Each boy is wearing a dark suit and clutching a cap in his free hand as he trudges over the snowy ground. Above them looms the Association banner, properly draped in mourning, followed by the boy's aunt, also heavily veiled, and still more boys. Their lame dog Jack watches the procession while the gravedigger, shovel in hand, stares into the glass walls of the hearse. Hogeland and the officiating minister stand over the grave ready to lead the final prayers. There is no telling if the picture captures the ceremony with any degree of accuracy. What it does depict is a vision of the

4. Alexander Hogeland, *Boys and Girls of 100 Cities* (Louisville, 1886), 117–18.
5. Cited by David Overstreet in "Children of Poverty: The County Paupers' Cemetery and Milwaukee Children," a panel at the Children in Urban America Conference, Marquette University, Milwaukee, Wisconsin, May 6, 2000.
6. Riis, *How the Other Half Lives*, 142. New York had several potter's fields until 1869, when the city acquired Hart Island, a forty-five-acre site in Long Island Sound. About a million indigents have been interred there in graves numbered but otherwise unmarked. See, Edward F. Bergman, "Potter's Field," in Kenneth T. Jackson, ed., *The Encyclopedia of New York City* (New Haven, 1998), 931.
7. Hogeland, *Boys and Girls of 100 Cities*, 60, and *Ten Years Among the Newsboys* (Louisville, 1884), 31–32.
8. C.F. Reilly, "Burial of a Newsboy," in Hogeland, *Boys and Girls of 100 Cities*, 60.

ideal funeral. Hogeland's express purpose in dwelling on these matters was to encourage righteous behavior by helping youths to appreciate "the uncertainty and shortness of life."[9]

Songs about dying newsboys conveyed a similar message to a different audience. They typically sought to instill a sense of *noblesse oblige* among the middle-class—those who could afford pianos and parlors. One of these songs, "Found Dead in the Street," written in 1882 by the music instructor of the Louisville House of Refuge, was dedicated to Hogeland. Its climactic verse goes:

> Once more hear him cry, "My papers, who'll buy?
> Oh! Is there not some one that cares though I die?"
> A shivering chill, and then all is still,
> While softly the snow-flakes come down from the sky.[1]

Other songs were tributes to real boys. The 1893 song "The Little Newsboy's Death," for example, documented in verse the *esprit de corps* of those who worked with newsboy Johnny Vantanno. According to the song's dedication, shortly after Vantanno was struck down by a street car his friends "took his bundle of evening papers and sold them, turning the money over to his mother, one of the boys remarking, 'She needs de stuff, see?' "[1]

Pathetic deaths and pitiful rhymes also characterized much of the poetry written about newsboys during this period. Poems such as Miss H.R. Hudson's "The Newsboy's Debt" (1873), Mrs. Emily Thornton's "The Dying Newsboy" (1886), Madeline S. Bridges' "The Newsboy" (1900), and Irene Abbott's "Only a Little Newsboy" (1903) appeared in *Harper's*, *Leslie's*, and other popular magazines. Written primarily by women, these works sought not to expose and ameliorate deadly social conditions, but to remind readers of their sacred duty to aid the least of God's children. Thus these poets and songwriters shared much in common with evangelical philanthropists like Brace, Starr, and Hogeland: they all saw newsboys' deaths as opportunities for moral instruction.

The 1880s and 1890s witnessed dramatic changes in philanthropy, trade unionism, and the funeral industry, all of which affected newsboys' mourning rituals. A new generation of professional charity workers appeared; many of them were college trained women who practiced "scientific philanthropy" in settlement houses, orphan asylums, juvenile courts and reformatories. They saw child street trading as part of the problem, not the solution, to urban poverty, delinquency, and homelessness. They accused newsboy homes and associations of perpetuating that which should be abolished.[4] Meanwhile, the labor movement, hobbled during the depression

9. Hogeland, *Ten Years Among the Newsboys*, 118.
1. Thomas P. Westendorf, "Found Dead in the Street" (Nashville, 1882). Eckel Collection; Hogeland, *Boys and Girls of 100 Cities*, 39–40.
2. Benjamin C. and Gus B. Brigham, "The Little Newsboy's Death," (Chicago, 1893). Eckel Collection.
3. Miss H.R. Hudson, "The Newsboy's Debt," *Harper's New Monthly Magazine* Vol. XLVI., No. CCLXXVI. (May 1873), 876–77. Thanks to Christine Stansell. Mrs. Emily Thornton, "The Dying Newsboy," Eckel Collection; Madeline S. Bridges' "The Newsboy," *Leslie's Popular Monthly*, reprinted in *The Book and News-Dealer* Vol. 11, No. 136 (Dec. 1900), 31; and Irene Abbott, "Only a Little Newsboy," *The Ministry of Love* (Topeka, 1903), 103–04.
4. See Walter Trattner, *From Poor Law to Welfare State: A History of Social Welfare in America*, 5th ed., (New York, 1994), esp. chs. 5 and 6; and Trattner, *Crusade for the Children: A History of the National Child Labor Committee and Child Labor Reform in America* (Chicago, 1970).

of the 1870s, bounced back. The Knights of Labor increased its membership seven-fold among skilled and unskilled workers in the mid-1880s. It
led colorful marches for the eight-hour day, advocated producer coopera-
tives, and ran candidates for political office. Newsboys also formed unions
and mounted strikes during this period. Their unions were usually short-
lived and their strikes unsuccessful, but their identification with organized
labor was strong.[5]

Undertakers also professionalized at this time. They formed the National
Funeral Directors' Association in 1882, and promoted embalming and other
changes in funeral services. Most morticians were small businessmen who
earned $4,000 to $5,000 a year, but some had grown into large companies.
One establishment in New York occupied an entire building on Eighth
Avenue. It had salesrooms on the ground floor, vaults in the basement, and
an auditorium, "larger than a village church," on the second floor. Fitted with
pews and an organ, it was the site of four to five services a day, some of which
were officiated by the president of the company, an ordained minister. The
upper stories housed a floral shop and a casket factory. The firm had only one
hearse, but it was considered "the most remarkable one outside of India."
Long as the longest electric streetcar, it carried mourners on the inside, bore
the casket atop the roof, and required a team of eight horses to pull it.[6] At the
other end of the spectrum were "circular" hearses, smaller, lightly built vehi-
cles named for their rounded corners and elliptical windows. Those painted
white were used exclusively for the funerals of children.[7]

The floral arts also evolved and sometimes featured innovative occupational designs. In 1886, William Henry Ortel, better known in St. Louis as
"Dutch Hiney, King of the Newsboys," received an arrangement that
included copies of the *Post-Dispatch, Globe-Democrat, Republican,* and
other local papers, all bordered by half opened buds of white roses. Placed
diagonally across the arrangement were the words 'Latest Edition' in purple immortelles, surrounded by white carnations. Created by Tony Faust,
the city's leading florist, it measured 16 by 14 inches and rested on a small
stand. It is not clear who paid for the offering, but it may well have come
from Oriel's fellow workers. According to the *Post-Dispatch,* "A large number of newsboys of all age and descriptions attended the funeral service and
followed the body to its last resting place."[8]

There were six thousand funerals a day in the United States at the turn
of the twentieth century, and they cost Americans a hundred million dollars a year.[9] In 1897, the *New York World* estimated that one poor family on
the Lower East Side spent over $140 on a funeral, which included sixty dol-
lars for the casket, thirty dollars for five coaches, and $10.50 for the
hearse.[1] Middle-class reformers decried the fact that poor families paid
between seventy-five and three hundred dollars for a "proper burial." Many

5. DiGirolamo, "Crying the News," 393.
6. Gilson Willets, *Workers of the Nation,* Vol. 2 (New York, 1903), 1043. See also Robert Wesley
   Habenstein, *The History of American Funeral Directing* (Milwaukee, 1955), and Habenstein and
   William M. Lamers, "The Pattern of Late Nineteenth Century Funerals," in Jackson, *Passing,*
   91–102.
7. One such vehicle may be found at the Farmers' Museum in Cooperstown, New York.
8. "'Dutch Hiney's' Funeral," *St. Louis Post-Dispatch* (May 3, 1886), 7. Thanks to Bert Hansen.
9. Willets, *Workers of the Nation,* Vol. 2, 1043.
1. *New York Evening World* (May 6, 1897), cited in Irving Howe, *World of Our Fathers: The Journey
   of the East European Jews to America and the Life They Found and Made* (New York, 1976), 221.

of these critics advocated cremation as a cheaper alternative. But cremation was never popular with the working class: Many regarded it as a repulsive form of scientific management, the aim of which, according to one
Pittsburgh labor paper, was to reduce "the body to a shovelfull of ashes" and
thereby bury people in smaller packages.[2]

To meet the rising cost of burying their dead many working-class families took out burial insurance or joined burial clubs, which, for a few cents
a week, offered similar protection. Between 1882 and 1902 more than
three million children were insured for burial, earning insurance companies a hundred million dollars a year in premiums.[3] Jacob Riis and Benjamin Waugh, president of the English Society for the Prevention of
Cruelty to Children, were two of the many reformers who wanted to ban
children's insurance on the grounds that it gave parents incentive to let
their children die, or, in Waugh's words, to finance the "little funeral" and
the "big drink."[4] Child insurance plans continued nonetheless. In 1892, a
group of prominent citizens established the News Boys Association of
Detroit to promote the boys' "moral, social, personal and intellectual and
religious welfare," and to provide for the "relief of the sick" and "the burial
of the dead."[5] Participating newsboys paid weekly dues, and thus became
accustomed to saving for their death and that of their comrades.

The custom of buying family plots was also popular at this time. When
Chicago newsboy Ole Jacobson, better known as Young Waffles, died of
exposure on a government pier in 1894 at the age of twenty-five, he was
found with only one possession: a water-soaked deed to a grave in a family
plot in Graceland Cemetery. Except for his spot, it was fully occupied by
his parents and four siblings. As historian John Gillis has noted, such plots
made modern cemeteries into domestic spaces devoted to the symbolic
reconstruction of the family. This shift matched middle-class perceptions
of heaven itself as a domesticated haven.[6]

Nevertheless, it was Waffles' comrades, not his family, who laid him to
rest. A "soliciting committee" of three boys secured the coffin at cost and
raised money for other expenses. The *Chicago Tribune* reported that less
than half the city's usual number of newsboys was on the streets the day of
his funeral. Waffles had been a fixture downtown for fifteen years, and one
hundred of the older news vendors gathered at the morgue for a final look.
Also in attendance were several ex-newsboys who had become regular
employees of the newspaper. "They were the forerunners of the entire
craft," reported the *Tribune,* "and for two hours a steady steam of individuals from the old man who sells papers at the entrance to the La Salle
Street tunnel to the 4-year old beginner, filed by the coffin, and many a one
came out with two white streaks down an otherwise dirty face."

2. Kleinberg, "Death and the Working Class," 203/65; Rev. Quincy L. Dowd, "Burial Costs Among
   the Poor," *Proceedings of the National Conference of Charities and Corrections* (June 12–19, 1912),
   121. I am also indebted to Eric Love's unpublished paper, "Fire or the Worm: Cremation and Burial in Fin de Siecle America," presented at the Princeton University Graduate History Conference,
   Oct. 7, 1995.
3. Viviana A. Zelizer, *Pricing the Priceless Child: The Changing Social Value of Children* (New York,
   1985), 116.
4. Benjamin Waugh, "Child Life Insurance," *Contemporary Review* Vol. 58 (July 1890), 41, cited in
   Zelizer, *Pricing the Priceless Child,* 124.
5. Articles of Association of the News Boys Association of Detroit, Feb. 20, 1892.
6. John R. Gillis, *A World of Their Own Making: Myth, Ritual, and the Quest for Family Values* (New
   York, 1996), 203; Douglas, *The Feminization of American Culture,* 220–26

Viewings were rarely held at city morgues, but apparently an exception was made in this case. Waffles' funeral is also noteworthy in that his fellow newsboys did not deem it necessary to invite a minister to conduct the service. Despite the massive turnout, and a funeral that included a hearse, casket, and all the trimmings, no clergyman was in attendance. The boys said they were afraid to ask a minister for fear of being refused. They conducted the ceremony themselves; as the casket was lowered into the grave one of the pall bearers picked up a handful of earth, threw it on the coffin, and said, "Dust to dust." The others followed his example, said the *Tribune*, "and the obsequies of 'Waffles' were over."[7]

Although working-class and middle-class males generally regarded excessive grieving as effeminate, there is little to suggest that newsboys held back tears or felt embarrassed at expressing their sorrow. According to Brace, sobbing and singing went hand in hand at Johnny Morrow's funeral: "sobs sounded in the stillness as the news boys, with voices hoarse with feeling, sang—'There's a rest for the weary—A rest for thee'."[8] On learning of Ellard's death, a former colleague wrote from Memphis, Tennessee, to say that "it made the tears come out, and I could not stop for half an hour."[9] Likewise, a letter from the mother of New York newsboy Willie Crawford acknowledging the receipt of his life savings of $40.50 had a similar effect when read aloud at the lodging house. "Many of them were moved to tears, for they all had a rough affection for Willie," said one news account. Another reported that the boys "sobbed and cried as if they had lost their only friend on earth, and in their simple, rude way expressed their regret for their lost companion."[1]

If newsboys ignored masculine prescriptions against mourning too hard, they generally conformed to those against mourning too long. On the walk home from Morrow's funeral, for example, rival gangs from Brooklyn and New York clashed in a rock-throwing "war" that left one boy with a bloody head and sent another to jail for twenty days.[2] Such were the limits of their unifying inconsolability.

Like members of any respectable labor fraternity, newsboys sometimes passed resolutions of sympathy when a prominent person or one of their own passed away. They sent them to newspapers for publication and saw that they were forwarded to relatives of the deceased. When Ulysses Grant died, for example, Chicago newsboys expressed their sorrow both publicly and collectively. On July 30, 1885, several hundred of them marched to city hall seeking an audience with the mayor. Since he was out of town they met with the chief of police. The boys presented him with a unanimous resolution stating, in part, "whereas, we, the newsboys of Chicago, though comprising the most humble of the callings, trades, or professions, feel that it is our privilege to give expressions of regret and sympathy so universal." They ordered a copy to be sent to Grant's family, bowed their heads for a

7. "'Waffles is Buried," *Chicago Tribune* (May 26, 1894), reprinted in *Newsboy* (HAS) Vol. 24, Nos. 9 and 10 (March–April 1986), 3. The soliciting committee included Robert McMara, William Swaufield, and Severs Johnson, who, along with Bennie Ross, George Campbell, and Epper Kenna, served as pall bearers.
8. *New York Independent* (June 6, 1861).
9. Starr, *Didley Dumps*, 163–64.
1. "Newsboys Wept For Lost Chum," New York *Journal* (Feb. 7, 1898). Heig Scrapbook. Eckel Collection.
2. "War Among the News Boys," *Brooklyn Daily Eagle* (May 27, 1861).

final prayer, and left. Their action was taken seriously. Within weeks Grant's son, Col. Fred Grant, acknowledged receipt of the resolution and thanked the newsboys on behalf of his mother and family.[3]

New York newsboys passed a similar resolution after the death of fifteen year-old Willie Crawford in 1898. They wrote:

> Whereas, Willie Crawford was a good fellow, and
> Whereas, He was always square and honest, and
> Whereas, He should have lived longer, we, his partners and friends when he was alive, hereby
> Resolve, That it is no more than right to let his mother know what a good fellow he was when he was with us, and
> Resolve, That we feel just as bad about his going so far away as we can, and
> Resolve, That we sympathize with his mother.

Conversely, some resolutions reveal newsboys' shame over the failure of fellowship. Such was the case with Little Joe Every, who was routinely robbed of his papers and otherwise "misused" by the bigger boys. The night he died in 1895 one hundred boys met in front of city hall and passed a resolution declaring that "Everybody is sorry he has died." Afterwards, the boys took up a collection and chose four delegates to accompany Joe's small, plain coffin as it was transported in a donated hearse from the county hospital to Holy Cross Cemetery at Flatbush. There was no funeral service, but each delegate placed a flower on the coffin, which bore a metal plate purchased by the boys. It read, "Little Joe, Aged 14. The Best Newsboy in New York. We All Liked Him."[4]

Cleveland, Ohio newsboy Alfred Williams also received a plaque from his comrades after he killed himself. The eleven year-old drank poison and died on October 11, 1900. His friends buried him nine days later under a memorial that sought to put his last act in perspective. It read, "This boy committed suicide because of the hardships of life."[5]

One death and burial that demonstrated interracial working-class solidarity was that of nineteen year-old Aaron "the slave" Charity, a black newsboy from Wilmington, North Carolina. Charity lived in the Newsboys' Lodging House and worked on the New York side of the Brooklyn Bridge. He was engaged to be married to "a pretty mulatto girl" when he took sick in the winter of 1899. As he lay on his deathbed Charity expressed his fear of potter's field. The *New York World* and Steve Brodie, a famous ex-newsboy, spared him that fate by treating him to a "first class funeral." Charity's body was laid in state at the lodging house, where scores of his former colleagues filed past to pay their last respects. A minister gave a funeral oration on "The Value of Manliness" and a chorus of newsboys sang "Nearer My God to Thee." Two hired carriages carried a delegation of newsies to Mount Olivet Cemetery on Long Island, where Charity's body was interred in a private plot.[6]

3. *Chicago Evening News* (July 31, 1885), in Hogeland, *Boys and Girls of 100 Cities*, 17, 19.
4. Carter J. Beard, "The Newsboys of New York. A Study from Life," *Demorest's Family Magazine*, Vol. 31 (May 1895), 381–82. Eckel Collection.
5. Eckel Collection.
6. "Brodie Will Bury Aaron 'The Slave,'" *New York Evening Journal* (Feb. 6, 1899). "Evening World Buries a Boy," *New York Evening World* (Feb. 8, 1899). Heig Scrapbook. Eckel Collection. (The *World* identified the deceased as Aaron Clarity.)

Newspapers were frequently called upon to help bury newsboys. In 1880, George W. Peck, publisher of the *Milwaukee Sun,* furnished an omnibus so newsboys could accompany the remains of their friend, "little" Dan Palmer, to the grave. This philanthropic act was reported not by the *Sun* but by its competitor, the *Sentinel.* Similarly, in 1893 Lucius Nieman of the *Journal* granted the request of a delegation of newsboys who showed up in his office, "hands washed and hair combed," to borrow money to save fourteen year-old Freddy Munk, one of twenty-five *Journal* newsboys, from burial in a potter's field. "And if I lend you the money, how will you pay it back?" Nieman reportedly asked. "We're willing to donate our pay for the next two months, sir," one of them said. "That ought to be enough to do it." Nieman feigned that it was a sound business proposition and agreed to go along with it if he could make a small donation. His contribution paid for the entire funeral.[7]

Running obituaries was another way newspapers paid tribute to newsboys. Most big city dailies published death notices only of their more prominent citizens, but newsboys were the exception. Ellard's demise was reported by two newspapers in Philadelphia and one in Baltimore; Morrow's exit was written up by the *New York World, Sun,* and *Tribune,* as well as the Brooklyn *Daily Eagle.* And Crawford's losing battle with consumption was the subject of no fewer than four articles in New York City papers. They told of his origins in Goldsboro, North Carolina, and the fact that he was a champion speller at the Newsboy's Lodging House.[8]

Some newsboys took the initiative of writing the obituaries themselves and submitting them to the periodicals they sold. In July of 1900 the editors of *Success* magazine ran one such notice saying, "This morning, one of our faithful newsboys handed us the following, which we publish in all its originality:—

> Joseph Rathburn, beter known as "Whistlin' Jo," dide last nite, he was a delicate litle feller and was sick only a week. Us fellers wanted him to go to the hospital or to hav a doctor, but he dident bleve in them he said. His folks was dead but he was workin hard to get a educaitn and be a big musician like he said his father was, but he couldent make it go, an' we are all aful sory he dide cause we had great hopes for him."[9]

Crawford the spelling champ could surely have helped polish up this draft, but what's noticeably absent from this obituary besides proper spelling and grammar is the religious rhetoric of their middle-class protectors. In the resolutions, too, the boys' language is secular not sacred. There is no mention of the deceased going to their heavenly reward, enjoying eternal rest, meeting their Maker, joining the angels, or even reuniting with relatives. The boys simply praise their companions' qualities and unsentimentally lament their death, which in their cosmology was mainly just a big gyp. "He should have lived longer," declared Crawford's friends.

---

7. Milwaukee *Sentinel* (Jan. 28, 1880), 4; Robert W. Wells, *The Milwaukee Journal: An Informal Chronicle of its First 100 Years, 1882–1982* (Milwaukee, 1981), 43–44.
8. Heig Scrapbook. Eckel Collection.
9. Rosebud Folsom, "Whistlin' Joe, 'the Best feller 'T Ever Live," *Success* (Jan. 1900), 15. Eckel Collection.

In whatever literary form they have survived, such utterances ought to be taken seriously as vernacular expressions of genuine sentiment. The same principle applies to newsboy funerals, for even sentimental accounts of them can provide a way into the heads and hearts of working-class youth. Their words and rituals are just the surface ripples of a vast inner ocean of emotion which historians have long found inaccessible. To be sure, many newsboy funerals reflect the influence of the middle-class adults who helped the boys to bury each other, but newsboys did not simply ape bourgeois standards of propriety and spirituality. Rather, they drew on a host of cultural influences, both bourgeois and plebeian, to develop their own codes of affection and rituals of mourning. Just as in their strikes and boycotts, newsboys demonstrated a kind of craft and class consciousness when they laid a fellow hawker to rest. This is most apparent if we define class consciousness broadly, along with Raymond Williams, as "a structure of feeling."[1] Newsboy funerals clearly show how poor children *felt* in class ways.

These rituals also compel us to reconsider just how injurious or ennobling life was on the streets. Most Americans have learned to distrust Horatio Alger's formulaic novels in which plucky street boys pull themselves up by their bootstraps, progressing from rags to respectability in each and every volume. The death and burial of real newsboys described by writers, reformers, and the children themselves remind us that a certain "downward mobility," measurable in six-foot increments, was the fate of more than a few of them. Moreover, their funerals force us to redefine respectability not as some vague middle-class virtue, but in concrete working-class terms as the boys defined it themselves. Respectability, to them, was taking care of their own, which somehow became more important in death than in life.

This caring is best symbolized by their efforts to save each other from the potter's field. Johnny Morrow was most articulate about what such an ignominious ending represented. In comparing his parents' graves, he wrote:

> I thought of my own precious mother, whose remains had slumbered for years in a quiet and beautiful spot, marked with a clean and tasteful slab of marble; and then of my dear father, who was buried in a very different way almost uncared for, in the Potter's Field. Some very sad thoughts came up in my mind.[2]

Morrow was an atypical newsboy for having attended seminary and written a book, but he was able to half express what many of them felt—that there was a correlation between the quality of one's grave and the condition of one's soul. They felt that to be buried in a potter's field was to be denied eternal rest. A pauper's funeral was not just the last indignity; it was an everlasting one. Newsboys wanted better for their families and for each other, and expressed such feelings in their words and actions.

A hero's funeral, however humble, allowed newsboys to assert their collective and individual identities. It was their way of saying that they were not just street rats and guttersnipes, but human beings; not just vagrants and beggars, but members of a trade, and not just anonymous hawkers, but

---

1. See Raymond Williams, *The Long Revolution* (London, 1960) and *Marxism and Literature* (Oxford, 1977), 128–35.
2. Morrow, *A Voice from the Newsboys*, 109.

individuals who had names. That's why Skinney's friends were so intent on honoring him by the name they knew him by, even if inscribed in such an ephemeral form as flowers. The fact that we can still remember obscure boys like Skinney, Mickety, John Ellard, Johnny Morrow, Fred Fisher, Jimmy Hart, Robert Maxie, Johnny Vantanno, Dutch Hiney, Young Waffles, Willie Crawford, little Joe Every, Alfred Williams, Aaron "the slave" Charity, Dan Palmer, Freddy Munk, and Whistlin' Jo Rathburn suggests that the efforts of those who buried them were not in vain. Only through ritual could the death of one enhance the status of all.

TIMOTHY J. GILFOYLE

Street-Rats and Gutter-Snipes: Child Pickpockets and Street Culture in New York City, 1850–1900[†]

For over half a century, the street child was an inescapable fixture of the nineteenth-century industrial city. Lacking formal education, adult supervision, and sometimes even a home, such youths were derided as "rats," "gamins," "Arabs," "urchins" and "gutter-snipes." "Street-rats," concluded one Children's Aid Society (CAS) report, "gnawed away at the foundations of society undisturbed." In a country which identified geographic mobility and physical movement as freedom, the street kid represented the logical nightmare—the replacement of community, familial and even spiritual bonds with the rootless individualism of the nomad. "[T]hose who have once adopted the semi-savage and wandering mode of life in early youth seldom abandon it," wrote *Harper's Weekly* in 1868. Rather, they "continue to the end of their existence Arabs by second nature."[1]

Even those who rejected such pejorative imagery and moralistic judgements recognized this new urban reality. In 1851, the wealthy attorney and diarist George Templeton Strong complained about "the hordes of . . . children who live in the streets and by them." Many labored at casual, unskilled "street-jobs"—blackening boots, sweeping side-walks, hauling bags and other goods, scavenging, or selling newspapers. They lived, slept and ate in streets, alleyways and hallways. "The bad times," admitted detective John Warren referring to the depression of the 1870s, "has driven a small army [of children] into our streets." By 1893, the reformer Helen Campbell concluded that the second half of the nineteenth century witnessed little change in the conditions of Gotham's street children.[2]

The first historical studies of urban children and street life in the U.S. focused on interventionist programs of reformers, "the invention of juvenile delinquency," and the emergence of new systems of penology.[3] Only

---

† From *Journal of Social History* 37.4 (2004). Reprinted by permission. The notes have been edited.
1. *Harper's Weekly*, 19 Sept. 1868 (hereafter *HW*); Children's Aid Society (hereafter CAS), *Sixteenth Annual Report* (New York, 1869), 6. "Annual Report" is abbreviated as "AR" hereafter. ❋ ❋ ❋
2. Allan Nevins and Milton Halsey Thomas, eds. *The Diary of George Templeton Strong* (New York, 1952), 11:57; John H. Warren, Jr., *Thirty Years' Battle with Crime* (Poughkeepsie, N.Y., 1875), 227; Campbell, *Darkness and Daylight*, 117–18. ❋ ❋ ❋
3. The literature on "child saving" and reform is vast. The most useful in this study have been: Thomas Bender, *Toward an Urban Vision: Ideas and Institutions in Nineteenth Century America*

recently have historians recognized the distinctiveness and complexity of urban youth subcultures. Historians like Christine Stansell have documented antebellum New York's public reaction to street children and their changing uses of public thoroughfares. Between 1846 and 1860 the urban bourgeoisie transformed the "urchin" into an image of fearful pathology, a danger to public health, a threat to domestic, family life. By contrast, David Nasaw has argued that city streets in the first decades of the twentieth century offered a separate world for children with its own distinct milieu. The street proved more formative than either educational or municipal institutions, ultimately compelling youths to place their primary loyalty and identity with their peers.[4]

Most historians of American childhood, however, have largely ignored the "criminal" aspects of this subculture, specifically the fluid movement between the licit and illicit street trades. As a child, for example, George Appo admitted that he and fellow newsboy George Dolan pickpocketed with impunity and without interruption for two years before his first apprehension. Similarly, pickpocket Larry Caulfield bragged that from ages 13 to 15, "I made a great deal of money at picking pockets, without getting into difficulties with the police." Sophie Lyons testified that when her father went to fight in the Civil War, her stepmother taught her how to steal. "All during my early childhood I did little but steal, and was never sent to school." Her frequent arrests mattered little, "as my stepmother knew how to bring influence to bear in my favor." Lyons claimed that she pickpocketed on a daily basis, frequently returning home with sums of money in excess of $100. "I did not know it was wrong to steal; nobody ever taught me that."[5]

The world of the street child and juvenile pickpocket was organized, in part, around an unwritten, oral culture. Such youths left few, if any, printed

(Lexington, Ky., 1975), 1–70, 129–193; Paul Boyer, *Urban Masses and Moral Order in America* (Cambridge, Mass., 1978), 94–107; Edward K. Spann, *The New Metropolis: New York, 1840–1857* (New York, 1981), 256–77; Robert S. Pickett, *House of Refuge: Origins of Juvenile Reform in New York State, 1815–1857* (Syracuse, 1969); Anthony Platt, *The Child Savers: The Invention of Delinquency* (Chicago, 1969); Joseph M. Hawes, *Children in Urban Society: Juvenile Delinquency in Nineteenth-Century America* (New York, 1971); LeRoy Ashby, *Saving the Waifs: Reformers and Dependent Children* (Philadelphia, 1984); Marilyn Irvin Holt, *The Orphan Trains: Placing Out in America* (Lincoln, Neb., 1992); Catherine J. Ross, "Society's Children: The Care of Indigent Youngsters in New York City, 1875–1903" (Ph.D. dissertation, Yale Univ., 1977); Bruce Bellingham, "The 'Unspeakable Blessing': Street Children, Reform Rhetoric, and Misery in Early Industrial Capitalism," *Politics and Society*, 12 (1983), 303–30; idem, "Waifs and Strays: Child Abandonment, Foster Care, and Families in Mid-Nineteenth-Century New York" in Peter Mandler, ed. *The Uses of Charity: The Poor on Relief in the Nineteenth Century Metropolis* (Philadelphia, 1990), 123–60; idem, " 'Little Wanderers': A Socio-Historical Study of the Nineteenth Century Origins of Child Fostering and Adoption Reform, Based on Early Records of the New York Children's Aid Society" (Ph.D. dissertation, Univ. of Pennsylvania, 1984); Michael B. Katz, *In the Shadow of the Poorhouse: A Social History of Welfare in America* (New York, 1986), 117–50; Peter C. Holloran, *Boston's Wayward Children: Social Services for Homeless Children, 1830–1930* (Boston, 1989). On the creation of "youth crime panics" in the nineteenth century which exaggerated levels of juvenile crime, see Robert Wegs, "Youth Delinquency and 'Crime': the Perception and the Reality," *Journal of Social History*, 32 (1999), 603–21.
4. David Nasaw, *Children of the City: At Work and at Play* (Garden City, 1985), 26–27, 91–100; Christine Stansell, *City of Women: Sex and Class in New York, 1790–1860* (New York, 1986), 193–216. Also see John E. Zucchi, *The Little Slaves of the Harp: Italian Child Street Musicians in Nineteenth-Century Paris, London, and New York* (Montreal, 1992); Vincent DiGirolamo, "Newsboy Funerals: Tales of Sorrow and Solidarity in Urban America," *Journal of Social History*, 36 (2002), 5–30.
5. The Autobiography of George Appo (typewritten manuscript), p. 3, Box 32, Society for the Prevention of Crime Papers, Rare Book and Manuscript Library, Columbia University, New York, N.Y. (hereafter Appo); Hutchins Hapgood, ed., *The Autobiography of a Thief* (New York, 1903), 34; Sophie Lyons, *Why Crime Does Not Pay* (New York, 1913), 11–14. Appo claimed he made as much as $600 per day pickpocketing. See Appo, 29.

documents. Inconsistent arrest records, exaggerated eyewitness accounts, and little participant testimony thus present difficult interpretive problems for historians interested in discerning the complexities of child street life. Furthermore, juvenile pickpocketing was, in certain respects, an invisible crime. Few pedestrians ever witnessed such activities; young pickpockets claimed working for years at a time before any apprehension. The CAS and others concurred, believing that child pickpockets were so "quick and cunning" that they usually avoided detection, much less arrest. In 1875, the *Times* declared newsboy "pocket-pickers" so adroit "that the real offender is scarcely ever captured, and the accomplice, if arrested is generally acquitted for lack of proof."[6]

Consequently, most historians have paid only cursory attention to child pickpockets and their informal subcultures. Some conclude that by the 1840s pickpockets and shoplifters alike tended to be adults and professional thieves. Juvenile crime focused primarily on merchants or less organized forms of thievery in semipublic areas such as dumps, junkyards, and railroad yards. Even Christine Stansell, in her otherwise exemplary study of this underworld milieu, equivocates.

"While robbing people—pickpocketing and 'baggage smashing'—seems to have been limited to professional child thieves (properly trained by adult sponsors), appropriating random objects was another matter."[7]

More importantly, the youthful pickpocket activity of Appo, Caulfield, Lyons and undoubtedly others raises difficult and complicated questions about the impact and importance of this youth subculture. Were children involved in illicit street activity trained by adults? Or was such activity the outgrowth of a youth culture organized on city streets by other youths? How did this form of theft, in both its actual and symbolic effects, reflect new social divisions emerging within the industrial metropolis? In what ways, if any, did child pickpockets represent an alternative or oppositional subculture?[8]

6. CAS, *Sixteenth AR*, 6 (quick and cunning); *Times*, 6 April 1875; Hapgood, *Autobiography*, 32–35; Appo, 2–3. Some believed that police officials undercounted the number of such crimes in order to stem fears and criticism.

7. Stansell, *City of Women*, 204; Eric H. Monkkonen, *The Dangerous Class: Crime and Poverty in Columbus, Ohio, 1860–1885* (Cambridge, Mass., 1975), 60–61; David R. Johnson, *Policing the Urban Underworld: The Impact of Crime on the Development of the American Police, 1800–1887* (Philadelphia, 1979), 44, 54; idem, "Crime Patterns in Philadelphia, 1840–70" in Allen F. Davis and Mark H. Haller, eds., *The Peoples of Philadelphia: A History of Ethnic Groups and Lower-Class Life, 1790–1940* (Philadelphia, 1973), 89–110, esp. note 8. For an insightful account of female shoplifting, see Elaine S. Abelson, *When Ladies Go A-Thieving: Middle-Class Shoplifters in the Victorian Department Store* (New York, 1989). Only in 1881 did the state begin prohibiting children from "begging, gathering or picking or sorting rags, from collecting cigar stumps, or bones or refuse from markets." See *HW*, 30 July 1881. "Baggage smashing" was also applied to baggage handlers at railroad and transport stations. See CAS, *Sixteenth AR*, 6. I am indebted to the anonymous reviewer for pointing out this nuance.

8. On certain forms of criminal behavior as a form of political resistance, see Robin D.G. Kelley, " 'We Are Not What We Seem': Rethinking Black Working-Class Opposition in the Jim Crow South," *Journal of American History*, 80 (1993), 75–112, especially 82; idem, "The Black Poor and the Politics of Opposition in a New South City, 1929–1970" in Katz, *"Underclass" Debate*, 293–333; Alex Lichtenstein, " 'That Disposition To Theft, With Which They Have Been Branded': Moral Economy, Slave Management, and the Law," *Journal of Social History*, 21 (1988), 413–40; James Scott, *Domination and the Arts of Resistance: Hidden Transcripts* (New Haven, 1990); idem, "Everyday Forms of Peasant Resistance," *Journal of Peasant Studies*, 13 (1986), 5–35; idem, *Weapons of the Weak: Everyday Forms of Peasant Resistance* (New Haven, 1985); Terry Williams, *The Cocaine Kids: The Inside Story of a Teenage Drug Ring* (Reading, Mass., 1989), 97–105. On the differences between alternative and oppositional subcultures and their relationship to a dominant culture, see Raymond Williams, *Problems in Materialism and Culture: Selected Essays* (London, 1980), 40–42.

The precise number of New York's street children was always subject to debate, but few doubted it was substantial. By the 1850s, Police Chief George Matsell and the Rev. Samuel Halliday separately estimated that 5,000 to 10,000 boys lived in New York's streets. Another minister, while criticizing exaggerated figures of 50,000, nonetheless admitted the number was large, between 10,000 and 30,000. In 1870, the CAS treated over 24,000 different children, including nearly 6,000 orphans and 15,000 homeless youths. In 1876 alone, city police "recovered" 5,593 "stray" children found wandering the streets (roughly 15 per day), 97 percent of whom were returned to their parents. One report in 1886 claimed 12,000 homeless youths could be found nightly "wandering in the street."[9]

The Connecticut Yankee, Protestant minister and social reformer Charles Loring Brace epitomized the contradictory views on street children. On one hand, Brace admired their autonomy, describing them as "sharp, ready, light-hearted, quick to understand and quick to act, generous and impulsive, and with an air of being well used 'to steer their own canoe' through whatever rapids and whirlpools." Elsewhere, he invoked horrors of high crime. Street children were the "dangerous class," the element most threatening the property, morals and political life of civil society.[1] In effect, Brace articulated the paradoxical stereotypes of the street child: a cute, fastidious urchin with nascent entrepreneurial values and pragmatic wits, and a corrupted, irredeemable devil full of evil motives and selfish desires, the dangerous class writ small.

Observers noted that certain street children—notably newsboys—had a distinct subculture. Newsboys, wrote one, "have their rules." Every day, young males showed up outside the offices of specific newspapers. Passersby recounted how they heard them "bargain and swap and giggle and sell." One observer claimed that newsboys were informally divided into two classes—"speculators" and "working bees." The former were older, entrepreneurial youths, who took large quantities of papers from editors and then hired younger boys. Working bees were "the children of poor parents, forced into their occupation by privation and suffering." Once they received their newspapers, they scattered throughout lower Manhattan, many going to the ferry wharves and entrances to the principal hotels. Some specific

9. Halliday, *Little Street Sweeper*, 142–43; CAS, *First AR* (New York, 1854), 3–4; idem, *Sixteenth AR*, 6, 51; idem, *Seventeenth AR* (New York, 1869), 47–48; Brace, *Dangerous Classes*, 31 (20,000–30,000), 132–33; Warren, *Thirty Years'*, 218 (6,000); Campbell, *Darkness and Daylight*, 112, 153, 213 (15,000 homeless children); David Dudley Field, "The Child and the State" *Forum*, April 1886, reprinted in Titus Munson Coan, ed. *Speeches, Arguments, and Miscellaneous Papers of David Dudley Field* (New York, 1884), III:343 (12,000); *Tribune*, 17 Jan. 1877 (5,593 stray children); Nasaw, *Children of the City*, 67–68. On bootblacking and newspaper-selling being the most popular callings, see Browne, *Great Metropolis*, 426. The exact figures in 1870 were 5,886 orphans and 14,822 homeless children. See CAS, *Nineteenth AR* (New York, 1871), 6. By the 1870s, the Newsboy's Lodging House provided assistance to 8,000 different boys annually. See Brace, *Dangerous Classes*, 344. Between 1860 and 1880, New York City officially had between 230,000 and 305,000 children, ages five to nineteen, more than a quarter of the city's total population. See New York Secretary of State, *Census for 1855* (Albany, N.Y., 1857), 8, 38–39; idem, *Census for 1865* (Albany, N.Y., 1867), 39–45; United States Department of the Interior, Census Bureau, *Population of the United States in 1860; Compiled from the Original Returns of the Eighth Census* (Washington, D.C., 1864), 322—23; idem, *The Statistics of the Population of the United States . . . From the Original Returns of the Ninth Census* (Washington, D.C., 1872), 1:633; United States Department of the Interior, Census Office, *Statistics of the Population of the United States at the Tenth Census* (Washington, D.C. 1883), 1:422, 660; idem, *Statistics of the Population of the United States at the Tenth Census: Report on the Social Statistics of Cities* (Washington, D.C., 1886).
1. Brace, *Dangerous Classes*, ii, 26–27, 344; CAS, *Nineteenth AR*, 5. For a deeper analysis of Brace's motives and ideology, see Bellingham, "Unspeakable Blessing," 303–30.

spots—even particular boats in the case of ferries—were "considered the private property of particular boys." Any intrusion by a competitor was fiercely resented. "Let a strange boy make his appearance on any of these consecrated grounds," noted one observer, "and he fares worse than a wounded porpoise in the midst of a school."[2]

These street children reflected one grim reality of the new industrial metropolis, or as the popular writer George Foster put it, "[t]he Newsboy is a result of the modern civilization." After 1840, apprentices virtually disappeared from artisan workshops. Factories and sweatshops rapidly replaced craft households and artisanal workplaces. At the very moment that the close supervision of adult craftsmen declined, New York experienced an unprecedented flood of European immigrants into the city. Between 1840 and 1855, 68 percent of all United States immigrants passed through Gotham. By 1860, half the city was foreign-born. Increasingly, certain parts of the working class, especially those trapped in the casual labor market, were pushed into street trades and the informal, underground economy. Newspaper editor Horace Greeley estimated that two-thirds of antebellum New Yorkers lived on one dollar per week. New York was, in the words of historian Edward Spann, "a sparkling gem set in a pile of garbage."[3]

One boy's predicament epitomized the impact of this economic transformation. Writing to Mayor William Wickham in 1875, Henry Barton begged: "I am seventeen years of age, have neither farther [sic], mother, sisters, brothers, home, or friends. I have been working at printing, but my work has give out [sic] and I have been all over looking for work but in vain and I ask your honor to please get me work at anything that will pay my board as I am in debt for it now. I pray your honor do not throw this aside without a thought but send an answer to a poor boy's letter."[4] The combination of declining apprenticeships, the increasing proletarianization of industrial occupations, and poorly enforced school attendance provided fertile conditions for street children to engage in theft. The more astute and adventurous became pickpockets. Larry Caulfield, for example, not only believed that most of his pilfering colleagues were young teenage males, but that such youths enjoyed distinct advantages over older males. "[A] boy can get next to a woman in a car or on the street [for the purpose of pocketpicking] more easily than a man can," he reminisced. "He is not so apt to arouse her suspicions." Appearances were important, insisted Caulfield.

2. *The Flash*, 14 Aug. 1842, vol. 1, no. 9, American Antiquarian Society, Worcester, Mass.; HW, 19 Sept. 1868 (early age). On newsboys working as bootblacks, see HW, 3 Sept. 1881. On the hard work associated with newsboys and the newspaper business, see James Parton, *The Life of Horace Greeley* (Boston, 1872), 357–60.
3. George Foster, *New York in Slices; By an Experienced Carver* (New York, 1849), 103; Spann, *New Metropolis*, 23–44, 71 (Greeley), 137 (garbage). On the bootblack as a "modern innovation," see HW, 19 Sept. 1868. On the decline of artisanal trade and rise of factory-based production, see Sean Wilentz, *Chants Democratic: New York City and the Rise of the American Working Class, 1789–1850* (New York, 1982), especially 107–44, 299–361; Stansell, *City of Women*, 203–09; Elizabeth Blackmar, *Manhattan for Rent, 1785–1850* (New York, 1989).
4. Harry Barton, 525 Pearl Street, to Mayor William Wickham, 12 Feb. 1875, Folder 208, Box 1259, Mayors' Papers, New York City Municipal Archives and Records Center (hereafter MP). For another example of street trades encouraging children to resort to criminal activity, see Eddie Guerin, *I Was a Bandit* (New York, 1929), 5. On the crisis in U.S. economy from 1870 to 1900, see David M. Gordon, Richard Edwards, and Michael Reich, *Segmented Work, Divided Workers: The Historical Transformation of Labor in the United States* (New York, 1982); Alexander Keyssar, *Out of Work: The First Century of Unemployment in Massachusetts* (New York, 1986), 1–4, 340–44.

"[I]f he is a handsome, innocent-looking boy, and clever, he can go far in this line of graft."[5]

Others charged that certain kinds of street work evolved into pickpocketing. "From these [child vagabonds] come the pickpockets, petty thieves, small burglars, 'cotton-baggers,' copper-stealers, young prostitutes, peddlers, street-sweepers, and boot-blacks that swarm in various parts of the city," claimed the CAS in 1869. Two decades later, Helen Campbell concurred: the newsboys' "views of life have come from association with 'flashmen' of every order, with pugilists, pickpockets, cockfighters, and all the *habitués* of pot-houses or bucket-shops."[6]

Indeed, the period from 1866 to 1887 might be described as the "age of larceny." During those two decades, larceny comprised between one-third and one-half of all crimes in New York State. In the words of one pickpocket, the decades following the Civil War were "the halcyon days for us."[7]

The "newspaper dodge" epitomized how selling newspapers and picking pockets often overlapped. Newsboy pickpockets routinely waved a newspaper in the face of a potential customer while reaching into the victim's pocket. Larry Caulfield described how he boarded streetcars, approached male passengers, and shoved a newspaper in their face, yelling "News, boss?" The diversion gave him enough time to pick their watch and chain. Caulfield bragged: "If you will stand for a newspaper under your chin I can get even your socks.[8]

The rise of child pickpocketing was rooted in the changing social ecology of the city. For most children, the street was a workplace, a social center, a place of amusement. At a time when parks (excepting small squares) were nonexistent and playgrounds almost half a century away, streets served multiple functions in a child's life. By the 1860s, parts of Park Row and the Bowery—not to mention numerous post offices, hotels, elevated railroad stations, and ferries—were filled with youthful panhandlers. In the vicinity of the Western Union Building, child pickpockets ranging from 10 to 16 in age preyed on messengers, customers, and even company executives. The most congested pathways of metropolitan commerce became the

5. CAS, *First AR*, 3 (80 percent); idem, *Eighteenth AR* (New York, 1870), 51 ("boy's crime"); idem, *Nineteenth AR*, 8 ("boy's crime"); idem, *Sixteenth AR*, 6; *Times*, 6 April 1875; Hapgood, *Autobiography*, 32–35; Appo, 2–3. For a later examination reaching similar conclusions, see Josiah Flynt, *The World of Graft* (New York, 1901), 26.

6. Hapgood, *Autobiography*, 35; *Tribune*, 12 Aug. 1876; CAS, *Seventeenth AR*, 48; Campbell, *Darkness*, 117. Police and other law enforcement officials rarely broke down pickpocket arrests from other forms of petty larceny. * * *

7. Hapgood, *Autobiography*, 35 (halcyon days). Nearly half (48 percent) of all crime in 1866–1867 was some type of larceny, and never dropped below 36 percent until after 1887. In 1927, robbery (24 percent) surpassed larceny (24 percent) for the first time. See NYSS, *Proceedings Before the Special Committee of the New York State Senate* (Albany, 1876), 1192a (statistics before 1876); and table no. 1 in New York State Crime Commission, *Report to the Commission of the Sub-Commission on Penal Institutions–1928* (Albany, 1928), 33. On the pervasiveness of pickpocketing and the prominent position of pickpockets among "professional" criminals at this time, see Allan Pinkerton, *Thirty Years a Detective* (Chicago, 1884), 36; Josiah Flynt, *Notes of an Itinerant Policeman* (Boston, 1900), 67–68; idem, *World of Graft*, 24–30. Arrest records on pickpocketing were inconsistently kept and remain a poor measure of the amount of the crime. Police reports, however, claimed the crime decreased nearly 50 percent from 1861 to 1870, before nearly tripling by 1875.* * *

8. The term "newspaper dodge" is found in People v. Joseph Brady, 20 Oct. 1874, New York City District Attorney Papers, Court of General Sessions, New York City Municipal Archives and Records Center (hereafter DAP). Helen Campbell also believed bootblacks were often "practised [sic] pickpockets." See *Darkness*, 152. For similar views on the transformation of newsboys into pickpockets, see *Times*, 29 July 1877; *National Police Gazette*, 27 May 1882. On Lower Broadway and Fulton, Nassau, and Wall streets as havens for pickpockets, see Hapgood, *Autobiography*, 51. On the distinctive newsboy subculture and the many newsboys on Nassau Street and its adjoining streets, see Foster, *New York in Slices*, 98, 104–06. * * *

workplaces of child pickpockets. Appropriately, lower Broadway was soon identified as "pickpockets' paradise."[9]

Arrest records confirmed popular charges that petty larceny was "a boy's crime." One grand jury reported in 1854 that 80 percent of felony indictments and 50 percent of petty offenses in New York were committed by minors under 21 years of age. Between 1859 and 1876, the number of pickpockets brought to trial by the district attorney nearly quintupled, increasing from 52 to 242. Although indictments are an imperfect measure of the amount of pickpocketing—most were simply never arrested—they provide one of the few windows into this hidden, secretive activity. In a sampling of seven selected years between 1859 and 1876, the New York district attorney indicted at least 166 juveniles (17 years-old or younger) for pickpocketing. The overwhelming majority were between the ages of 14 and 17 (84 percent), native-born (82 percent), and male (95 percent). In fact, over half of all males arrested in the seven sampled years (56 percent) were 15 to 24 years of age.[1] Most of these larcenies occurred in the street (79 percent), and only a small percentage (19 percent) were physically aggressive assaults where the perpetrator violently snatched an object and ran away.[2]

These arrested youths diverged from popular stereotypes in important ways. Unlike Larry Caulfield, a self-described "moll buzzer" who pickpocketed women, child pickpockets did not prey on the most vulnerable pedestrians; only one out of five victims, for example, was female. The most common purloined object—in two-thirds of all cases—was money. The median value of stolen goods was $10.30. While this seems like very little money, regular working men averaged only $5 to $10 per week. Newsboys were lucky to make a dollar.[3]

The term "child pickpocket," in some respects, was an oxymoron, as such arrested youths rarely considered themselves children. Although they ranged in age from 10 to 17, the vast majority of these young pickpockets identified themselves as adult wage earners, not children. A mere six percent of those indicted affirmed they were students, only one of whom exceeded 14 years of age. In fact, a greater number (7 percent) claimed to be "unemployed" rather than in school.

9. CAS, Seventeenth AR, 48 (City Hall Park); Howe and Hummell, In Danger, 20; unmarked clipping, 2 Feb. 1884 ("paradise"), New York City District Attorney Scrapbooks, New York City Municipal Archives and Records Center (hereafter DAS).
1. I examined grand and petty larceny cases which involved removing personal property from a person, the charge under which most pickpockets were prosecuted by the New York district attorney in the Court of General Sessions. The database totaled 1,176 individuals in the years 1859, 1864, 1869, 1871, 1872, 1874 and 1876. See DAP. I eliminated any case which was not described as a pickpocket. The indictments numbered 1,010 adults (male and female) and 166 children (age 17 or less). Incomplete descriptions of specific events forced me to define pickpocketing broadly. In cases when a pickpocketing attempt went array, the foiled perpetrator sometimes grabbed or "snatched" the object of desire and ran. The victim was then blocked or tripped when they tried to pursue the larcenist. Descriptions of such cases were frequently incomplete, making it impossible to distinguish if the incident was a botched pickpocketing attempt, a "knockdown pickpocketing" attempt, or a simple purse snatching. Consequently, I included cases involving 146 individuals charged with such larcenies. I also included larcenies which occurred in "panel houses" and brothels. In such establishments, when male clients removed their clothes, accomplices hidden behind a wall panel or door picked the client's pockets as their clothing lay on a chair or table. * * *
2. The gender distribution of child pickpockets was: 158 males (95%) and 8 females (5%), four of the latter robbing their victims in brothels or panel houses. * * *
3. Hapgood, Autobiography, 34 (moll buzzer). Items stolen included: pocketbook and/or money–115 (69%); watch and/or chain–46 (28%); handkerchief–3; jewelry–2. Newsboys received 100 papers for sixty cents from newspaper offices and then sold them for a penny each, earning a profit of 40 cents. See CAS, Sixteenth AR, 51.

Their vocational opportunities, however, were neither stable nor lucrative. Most occupied positions of part-time employment or worked in downwardly-mobile crafts. Newsboys and bootblacks accounted for 27 percent of all arrested. Those in service jobs such as clerks, errand boys, messengers and telegraph operators represented another eight percent. A mere four percent labored in factories. The remainder were scattered among a variety of occupations. Particularly striking was the breakdown of the craft system: only two boys (a cooper and a tailor) claimed they were apprentices.[4]

Most of these youths had experienced a swift and sometimes brutal introduction into the market. "Strictly speaking, they have neither childhood nor boyhood," lamented Junius Browne. "They pass from neglected infancy, almost by a bound, to an immature and unnatural manhood, compelled by a sense of self-protection to a rugged and semi-savage independence." Formal education had even less impact because most never darkened the door of a school. Indeed, throughout the nineteenth century, fewer than half of New York's children regularly attended school. Some, like pickpocket George Appo, never spent a single day in a classroom. In 1860, the average daily attendance was only 58,000 (out of 153,000 registered school-age children in public and private schools). In 1870, the figure rose to 103,679 out of 270,000. On average, males left school at age 14. Passage of the Compulsory Education Act of 1875 did little to change the situation; in 1894, Jacob Riis complained, "our compulsory-education law remains a dead letter."[5]

Contrary to popular belief, most child pickpockets were not homeless. Rather, 85 percent of those brought to trial gave specific street names and house numbers when asked where they resided.[6] This is not to say they came from economically or emotionally secure families. While observers continually commented in hyperbolic language on the "broken homes" of such youths, domestic life for many was indeed fraught with difficulty. In one informal survey of 400 street children in 1871, the CAS found that 34 percent

4. The occupational breakdown was: newsboys 32 (19%); unemployed 14 (8%); bootblacks 13 (8%); errand boy/messenger/ hallboy/clerk 11; printer/bookbinder 11; student 10; laborer/teamster 8; unknown 8; factory worker 7; peddler 5; tinsmith/iron moulder 4; servant 3; telegraph operator 3; tailor/shirtmaker 3 (includes one apprentice); machinist 2; plumber 2; bartender 2; brushmaker 2; cigarmaker 2; shoemaker 2; cooper 2 (includes one apprentice); boilermaker 2; 1 each of: baker, birdcage maker, brass worker, coffinmaker, corkcutter, dyer, butcher, fanmaker, goldpen maker, iceman, lamplighter, "married," paper hanger, plasterer, soda water maker, umbrella maker, waiter, "works for uncle."
5. Browne, *Great Metropolis*, 425; George Appo's statement on 6 Oct. 1896, pp. 18, 22 (never went to school), People v. George Appo, 24 July 1896, New York District Attorney Records, Cases #9126, Box B-2, Location 12817, Supreme Court Cases, New York City Municipal Archives and Records Center; New York State Legislature, *AR of the Board of Commissioners of the Metropolitan Police* (Albany, 1864), 9; *National Police Gazette*, 18 Feb. 1880; Jacob Riis, *The Battle with the Slum* (New York, 1902), 231 (dead law); idem, "The Making of Thieves in New York," 49 (1894), 114 (dead letter). Elsewhere, Riis's figures actually showed school attendance improved at the end of the century. See Riis, *The Children of the Poor* (New York, 1892), 118–28. The Compulsory Education Act did not go into effect until 1 Jan. 1875, and even thereafter mandatory attendance was rarely enforced. See *Second AR of the Board of Police Justices of the City of New York for 1875* (New York, 1876), 20. On the failure of the 1853 law, see idem, *AR of the Board of Commissioners of the Metropolitan Police* (Albany, 1865), 8–10. On males leaving by age 14, see Carl F. Kaestle, *The Evolution of an Urban School System: New York City, 1750–1850* (Cambridge, Mass., 1973), 96. On school attendance, see Diane Ravitch, *The Great School Wars: New York City, 1805–1973* (New York, 1974), 405–06. For specific figures on truancy, see New York State Legislature, *AR of the Board of Commissioners of the Metropolitan Police* (New York, 1864), 78–79; ibid., (New York, 1865), 8–10; ibid., (New York, 1867), 49–50; ibid., (New York, 1868), 66–67; ibid., (New York, 1869), 57–58; ibid., (New York, 1870), 62–63; New York City, *First AR of the Police Department* (New York, 1871), 49.
6. See sampled years in DAP.

were orphans or without known parents, while another 23 percent were victims of abandonment, abuse, or desertion. Some lodging houses even claimed that over half their child patrons were without parents. Traditional or secure family structures for such youths were at best weak, at worst non-existent.[7]

In certain ways, pickpocketing emerged as an underground alternative to the traditional but vanishing forms of apprenticeship in the new urban market economy. Most often, older teenage pickpockets taught the secrets of the trade to young "apprentices." One detective claimed pickpockets literally went through "a course of instruction." Older pickpockets, "incapacitated for work on their own hook," instructed the younger charges, reducing the subject "to a science." Others insisted that in saloons and pool rooms, street youths were "instructed by New York Fagins in the arts of petty pilfering, of pocket-picking, sneak-thieving, circulating counterfeit coin," and other kinds of crime. Police chief George Matsell believed that as early as 1854 that "crime among boys and girls has become organized, as it never was previously."[8] While informal and fluid, such instruction was part of the clandestine activity of child street culture.

These complaints were not simply middle-class paranoia. Fourteen year-old Edward Logenstein, after being arrested for pickpocketing, admitted that he was part of a "thieves' school" run by an older man on Ludlow Street. Every afternoon, boys were sent to different parts of the city accompanied by older teenagers who instructed and watched them work. Whenever they stole a purse, claimed Logenstein, "a bigger boy would come up and take the things." After his first successful theft, Larry Caulfield was approached by an adult counterpart. "He had heard of our achievement and kindly 'staked' us, and gave us a few private lessons in picking pockets," remembered Caulfield. "We were proud enough, to be taken notice of by this great man. We felt we were rising in the world of graft, and began to wear collars and neckties." According to Caulfield, the picture of Fagin in Dickens's *Oliver Twist* was "true to life."[9]

A certain fraternity among teenage pickpockets thus emerged. Larceny had its own division of labor, an informal apprenticeship system and a com-

---

7. In 1868, the 11th Ward Lodging-House treated 553 different boys, 359 of whom were orphans (65 percent), 130 "half-orphans" (24 percent); only 64 (12 percent) came from households with both parents living. See CAS, 16 *th AR*, 32–33, 65. In the 1871 survey, only three indicted children even claimed to be homeless. The specific residential information given by the indicted children was: specific house number and street name—141 (85%); street name only—12 (7%); city name only—7; homeless—3; no answer—3. * * * mature youth, lived in domestic groups (usually parents), and mostly returned home after brief periods of foster care. See Bellingham, "Waifs and Strays," 123–60, esp. 131–33; "'Little Wanderers,'" 63. The data in these studies, however, is derived from Record Book #1 of CAS, which only covers the period from April, 1853 to September, 1854.
8. CAS, *First AR*, 3–4 (Matsell); New York State, Metropolitan Police, *AR* (New York, 1865), 9–10 (armies); *HW*, 30 July 1881 (Fagins); J.H. Madan to Judge Bedford, 26 Dec. 1872, in *New York Star*, 8 Oct. 1883, in DAS (course of instruction); Hapgood, *Autobiography*, 33.
9. New York *Sun*, quoted in Minneapolis *Evening Journal*, 18 March 1881 (thieves school); People v. James Scott and James O'Neill, 18 April 1876; J.H. Madan to Judge Bedford, 26 Dec. 1872, in People v. John Hanley, 23 Oct. 1872, all in DAP; Hapgood, *Autobiography*, 33 ("staked"), 149–50 ("true"). Stories of street boys being trained by "professional criminals" or "Fagins" were commonplace in the second half of the nineteenth century. See *HW*, 27 Feb. 1869; *Tribune*, 12 Aug. 1876, 7 April 1895; *National Police Gazette*, 27 May 1882 (pickpocket school); Howe and Hummell, *In Danger*, 28; Brace, *Dangerous Classes*, 340; unmarked clippings, 22 June 1895, vol. 142, DAS. On Abe Solomon's "pickpocket school" on Suffolk Street, see *Tribune* and other clippings, 15 May 1894, vol. 127; unmarked clipping, 10 Sept. 1894, vol. 132, both in DAS. Also see reports on Lawrence "Young Irish" Lutterer in *New York Recorder*, *Times*, and other clippings, 1, 22 Aug. 1896, vol. 157; on Harry Gablinsky (or Jablinsky), 7, 9 Oct. 1896, vol. 159, all in DAS. On Sophie Lyons being taught to steal by her stepmothers, see Lyons, *Why Crime Does Not Pay*, 11–14.

munity of colleagues with patterns of support and exclusion of outsiders. Youth crime was typically the work of small, intimate groups of youths who collaborated together, often for long stretches of time as Appo described working with George Dolan. Picking pockets, like other forms of street life, produced a subculture with arcane, intricate and complex forms of communication which described all the salient roles and procedures of the craft. "Those who have been to the business [of thievery] use this *argot* to such an extent," pronounced one reporter, "that a stranger finds it as impossible to understand them as he would if they were speaking in a foreign tongue." Pickpockets referred to their accomplices, usually numbering two to four, as "mobs." The streets, parks, or trolleys where they worked were "beats." The actual larceny was a "touch" which was performed by a "wire," a "pick," a "bugger" or a "tool" while "stalls" distracted or jostled the victim. Pocketbooks were "leathers" and money was a "roll." The novelist Herman Melville described the underworld vocabulary as "the foulest of all human lingoes, that dialect of sin and death, known as the Cant language, or the Flash."[1]

The special argot bespoke a fraternity with shared affinities extending beyond child larcenists. After having his pocket picked, for example, the adult Julius Rocholl entered one William Street establishment in search of the perpetrator. He found a group of youths crowded around a bench. "I shoved the boys aside and found under the bench this little boy with his coat off" who Rocholl believed had purloined his property. Without warning, the pickpocket's peers raced to his defense. "I had to let go my hold of the boy as there was a crowd of boys all around who immediately rushed between this boy and myself," many of whom "were jeering and laughing at me," claimed the victimized Rocholl. In response, he simply relinquished his captive.[2]

Similarly, George Appo described an uncertain community support to his pickpocketing. As a teenager, he once pilfered a money-filled wallet from a man walking along Wall Street. Upon hearing the cry "Stop thief," a police officer chased Appo in hot pursuit. He managed to escape, but not before the officer shot him in the stomach. Quickly, Appo retreated into the Pearl Street residence of the Maher family, "with whom I was acquainted," he recounted. Rather than report him to authorities, "the good woman, Mrs. Maher, hid me between the mattress of the bed where I remained until her

1. Hapgood, *Autobiography*, 34; Allan Pinkerton, *Thirty Years a Detective* (Chicago, 1884), 37; *Sun*, 4 March 1861 (stage buzzers); Herman Melville, *Pierre, or The Ambiguities* (New York, 1984), 281; Johnson, *Policing*, 54; James D. McCabe, Jr. [Edward Winslow Martin], *The Secrets of the Great City* (Philadelphia, 1868), 358 ("foreign tongue"), 359 ("bugger"), 369 ("beats"); Jonathan Slick, *Snares of New York; or, Tricks and Traps of the Great Metropolis* (New York, 1879), 37–38; A.E. Costello, *Our Police Protectors: History of the New York Police* (New York, 1885), 417; *Tribune*, 2 July 1883, 25 Dec. 1887. On pickpockets usually working in couples, see *Times*, 6 April 1875. On the argot of newsboys, street children and pickpockets, see Campbell, et al., *Darkness*, 123–25, 706–09; *Tribune*, 11 April 1897. The best source for nineteenth-century underworld vocabulary is George W. Matsell, *Vocabulum; or, The Rogue's Lexicon* (New York, 1859). For other lists of underworld slang, see McCabe, *Secrets*, 358–59; idem, *New York by Sunlight and Gaslight* (New York, 1881), 509–10; Pember, *Mysteries*, 26–27; "Our Hot-Beds of Crime," *World*, 19 March 1888, in vol. 46, DAS. One linguist defines "argot" as a "specialized language used by organized, professional groups operating outside the law; these groups normally constitute criminal subcultures, and the language is usually secret or semisecret." See David W. Maurer, *Whiz Mob: A Correlation of the Technical Argot of Pickpockets with Their Behavior Pattern* (University, Ala., 1955), 4. Recent ethnographic examinations of urban youth culture that place considerable importance on street talk include Williams, *Cocaine Kids*, esp. 87; Irving Lewis Allen, *The City in Slang: New York Life and Popular Speech* (New York, 1993).
2. People v. Edward Kilbain, 18 March 1874, DAP.

son went out, looked around and returned, saying everything was all right."[3]

For street children and their sympathizers, the distinctions separating legal and illegal activities proved to be overlapping and fluid. Unbeknownst to adults, youths regularly met, socialized, played, and even reproduced their subculture over time. By the 1860s, street kids were regular *habitués* of Bowery theaters, museums, and similar entertainments. The Bowery Theater, in particular, was described as "a common ground for the gamins." Arthur Pember remarked in 1874 that Saturday evenings at the Bowery Theater were "a night on which all the *elite* of the bootblacks and newsboy world make a point of going to the play." As more upscale establishments moved uptown, the Bowery became a popular outpost for street kids. In its "old-fashioned pit," noted one, "the juveniles of the Bowery region are packed like sheep." The writer George Foster described how newsboys, while occupying the middle benches in the pit of the Chatham and Olympic theaters, inscribed their names with knives, thereby "securing them against invasion, and occupying them by as good a right, and with more regularity nightly, than the rich frequenters of Grace Church and St. Patrick's, their pews."[4]

The Bowery, in particular, served as a surrogate home for street children. Into the 1880s, reformers complained that young boys "infest[ed] the Bowery at all hours of the day and night." The pull of the Bowery was allegedly so great that juveniles often remained away from their real homes for days and even weeks. Their daily regimen included selling papers, begging, stealing from stores, and "going through" drunken men to pilfer money, much of which was then spent at the theater. "Thus they live till arrested or picked up," concluded one Society for the Prevention of Cruelty to Children report. Investigator George McDermott, after visiting Volk's Theater in 1882, was "most astonished" by the many unchaperoned children. Out of an audience consisting mostly of minors, he counted at least 200 children between 7 and 10 years of age, 500 under 14. "For the purpose of corrupting the minds of children," concluded McDermott, "this place affords better advantage than any other resort I know."[5]

Streetboys even had their own theater. In 1871, newsboys, bootblacks and other street children founded the Grand Duke's Opera House. Located in a Baxter Street cellar, the establishment's managers, stage hands, musicians, actors and audience were composed entirely of young boys, many of whom were bootblacks and newsboys. For years, the Grand Duke's Opera House was the only theater which successfully defied municipal efforts to collect the license fee.[6]

3. Appo, 93–94.
4. McCabe, *Secrets*, 262, 265, 442 ("sheep"); Brown, Great *Metropolis*, 430 ("gamins"); Pember, *Mysteries*, 184 ("elite"); Foster, *New York in Slices*, 105–06 (pews). Also see Hapgood, *Autobiography*, 18; Smith, *The Newsboy*, 25–33, 99; Herbert Asbury, *The Gangs of New York* (New York, 1927), 25–26. Howe and Hummell, *In Danger*, 25, claimed youths could be found in both Bowery and Broadway leisure establishments. For other reports of children in concert saloons and theaters, see Application Hearing for New York Museum, 210 Bowery, 30 Nov. 1883, Box 85-EF-12, MP. On the popularity of the theater among street children, see Campbell, et al., *Darkness*, 116. On saloons promoting delinquent juvenile subcultures, see *HW*, 19 Sept. 1868, 30 July 1881. For more on the subculture of newsboys, see DiGirolamo, "Newsboy Funerals," 5–30.
5. Society for the Prevention of Cruelty to Children, *AR* (New York, 1884), 23; George McDermott to Mayor William R. Grace, 2 May 1882, Box 84-GWR-14, MP. Volk's was located at 199 Bowery.
6. The Grand Duke's Opera House or Theatre (or "newsboy's theatre" as it was sometimes called) was originally located in a cellar at 17 or 19 Baxter Street. See *Frank Leslie's Illustrated Newspaper*, 17

The world of the child pickpocket was heavily, but not entirely, masculine. Newsgirls were to be found, but young females generally enjoyed fewer opportunities within the rough-and-tumble street culture milieu. "Girls can only sell papers, flowers or themselves," acknowledged criminal attorneys William Howe and Abraham Hummell, "but boys can black boots, sell papers, run errands, carry bundles, sweep out saloons, steal what is left around loose everywhere, and gradually perfect themselves for a more advanced stage and higher grade of crimes." Like their male counterparts, young girls were found City Hall Park, the Battery, Union Square and Madison Square, playing, sitting on the benches, and accosting passing pedestrians. Sophie Lyons worked mostly as a pickpocket, but she also used sharp, little knives "to slit open the bags so that I could get my fingers in. One pickpocket remembered a teenage female friend so talented at pickpocketing "that older guns of both sexes were eager to take her under their tuition and finish her education."[7]

In most cases, child pickpockets and street children were bound together because of their shared poverty and social marginalization. Their experiences on city streets, for example, broke down common forms of collective identity. "As a rule," concluded Helen Campbell in 1893, street boys "are known by nicknames and nothing else, and in speaking of one another they generally do so by these names." Rather than identifying each other according to categories based on race, ethnicity or religion, Campbell noted that, "these names indicate some personal peculiarity or characteristic." Commentators and criminals alike rarely a discussed the ethnic or immigrant origins of New York's street children, much less any notice of self-described national identity. More often, contemporaries described such youths by their street occupation or activity: newsboys, copper pickers, wood-stealers, ragpickers, swill-gatherers, bootblacks. The one social condition that they all shared was poverty. Perhaps the native-born origins of the majority of Gotham's child pickpockets muted any shared ethnic, racial or religious bond, for undoubtedly a large percentage of these children had immigrant parents. Street life, however, seemed to level those forms of identity.[8]

Pickpocket memoirs reflected this. Although few, if any, child pickpockets directly addressed questions of ethnic or national identity, adult pickpockets reminisced on their childhood. George Appo, for example, remembered

Jan. 1874 (17 Baxter), 30 June 1877; *Herald*, 20 Feb. 1874 (19 Baxter). It later moved to 21 Baxter Street. See Howe and Hummell, *In Danger*, 26; James L. Ford, *Forty-Odd Years in the Literary Shop* (New York, 1921), 104, 197; Digirolamo, "Newsboy Funerals," 9. Critiques of children in the theater appear in: Alger, *Mark, the Match Boy*, 254–56; idem, *Julius the Street Boy* (New York, 1904); Brace, *Dangerous Classes*, 345; Smith, *The Newsboy*, 102–03. Lodging houses, hoping to divorce theater attendance from child street life, deliberately served dinner at the hours of theatrical performances. See Monkkonen, "Nineteenth-Century Institutions: Dealing with the Urban 'Underclass'," in Michael B. Katz, ed., *The "Underclass" Debate: Views From History* (Princeton, N.J., 1993), 358–59.

7. Hapgood, *Autobiography*, 55; Howe and Hummell, *In Danger*, 20–22; Lyons, *Crime*, 12–14. For reports on other child female pickpockets, see *Mercury, Morning Journal*, and other clippings, 3, 5 May 1895, Vol. 140, DAS. Others reported that female pickpockets traveled with male companions, usually preyed on other women, and were rarely caught. See *New York Star*, 8 Oct. 1883, in DAS. Some sources indicate male youngsters were expected to "take advantage" of their female counterparts. See Hapgood, *Autobiography*, 40–41.

8. Campbell, *Darkness*, 124 (quote), 151–54. In the sample of prosecuted child pickpockets in DAP, 82 percent were native-born. Among the 2,095 youths served by three Newsboys' Lodging Houses in 1868, 85 percent were native-born. See CAS, *Sixteenth AR*, 6 (unconscious), 27–33, 65–66. Similarly, of the 6,950 teenagers sent to the Workhouse on Blackwell's Island or the Tomb's Prison in 1878, 6,369 (or 92 percent) were born in the United States. See *World*, 13 Jan. 1879.

pickpocketing as a teenager with another youth with the Irish surname of Dolan. But neither then nor later did Appo ever identify himself as Irish, Chinese or even Roman Catholic, although he was all of these by birth. Like the polyglot world of Five Points where he grew up, Appo never labeled himself by a single, ethnic category. Significantly, as an adult he conspired with Chinese criminal entrepreneurs like Tom Lee, Irish-Americans Barney Maguire and Jimmy McNally, and German-Americans Ike Vail and Bill Vosburgh. Appo's individual experience confirmed observations by some like the CAS that ethnic identity was incidental among their charges; instead street children were part of "an unconscious society for vagrancy and idleness."[9]

Street children in their attitudes toward work, family, life and property presented a competing value system to pious, middle-class ways. What horrified adults—the absence of parental authority, the rejection of formal schooling and legitimate employment, the disregard for law and order—was functional for children. Critics failed to acknowledge how child thieves imitated the middle-class values of consumption and accumulation.[1] As a youth, George Appo admitted that he admired his pickpocketing peers because they "always were well dressed and had plenty of money." Similarly, one burglar and safe robber who grew up in New York admitted that he became a river thief because he believed he made ten times the income of a machine shop apprentice. "I wanted a lot o' dough, an' the only way 't I know how to get it was to steal it." On another occasion, Charles Loring Brace asked a group of street urchins: "My boys, what is the great end of man? When is he happiest? How would you feel happiest?" Their blunt retort: "When we'd plenty of hard cash, sir!"[2]

The secret pilferings of child pickpockets also challenged the vague boundaries of urban consumption. Pickpocket crimes were, in part, the result of an expanding market economy with fashionable and expensive consumer goods. The symbolic and concrete evidence of these new patterns of consumption were the diamond-studded stickpins, gold pocketwatches, and hard cash pedestrians conspicuously paraded while traversing the streets. "Everybody seems to have the idea that unless they are more or less furnished with ornaments they are not properly presentable," commented one fashion journal. Worn for purposes of display and spectacle, these advertisements of personal prosperity invited their secret removal.[3]

Such conspicuous displays of wealth and prosperity alongside homelessness and poverty not only generated resentment by many a child turned

9. Appo; CAS, *Sixteenth AR*, 6 (unconscious), 27–33, 65–66. Other examinations of criminal life which never discuss ethnicity or immigration as factor in criminal or "underworld" identity include Flynt, *Graft*; Hapgood, *Autobiography*.
1. For typical examples of outrage at the behaviors of street children, see New York State Legislature, *AR of the Board of Commissioners of the Metropolitan Police* (New York, 1865), 9–10; idem, *AR of the Board of Commissioners of the Metropolitan Police* (Albany, 1864), 9; *National Police Gazette*, 18 Feb. 1880; Browne, *Great Metropolis*, 425, 432–33; Brace, *Dangerous Classes*, 342; CAS, *Sixteenth AR* (New York, 1869), 6. For sympathetic or tolerant views of child pickpockets, see Benjamin P. Eldridge and William B. Watts, *Our Rival, the Rascal* (Boston, 1897), 22; Howe and Hummell, *In Danger*, 28.
2. Brace, *Dangerous Classes*, 81; Howe and Hummell, *In Danger*, 27; Appo, 3; Flynt, *Graft*, 91–93 (dough); Pember, *Mysteries*, 191 (grin and bear it); Rocco Corresca, "The Biography of a Bootblack" in David M. Katzman and William M. Tuttle, Jr. *Plain Folk: The Life Stories of Undistinguished Americans* (Urbana, Ill., 1982), 3–13 (entrepreneurial).
3. *Elite Dressmaker and Milliner*, 3 (Dec. 1878), 6 (ornaments); Charles Stelzle, *A Son of the Bowery: The Life Story of an East Side American* (New York, 1926), 17.

pickpocket. Some articulated an alternative morality. Asked if he knew the difference between right and wrong during one later court interrogation, George Appo replied, "I know that I ain't doing wrong in picking pockets." When queried further if he thought he enjoyed a right to steal, he acknowledged, "To a certain extent, yes, I do."[4]

On the other hand, even if youthful pickpocketing like Appo's was an ongoing, daily strategy, the overwhelming majority of thefts presented no overt or even symbolic protest to authority or to property arrangements. What was an act of personal maintenance or economic sustenance for impoverished youths was playful rebellion for others. Pickpocketing was integrated into the daily street life of many children, at times irrespective of class. Even well-off youths at times engaged in petty theft. Such boys treated the pilferings not as a crime, but rather a contest, a form of mischief, a product of peer pressure. For example, 16 year-old Joseph DeBoe admitted that he stole Elizabeth O'Rourke's pocketbook at the behest of two acquaintances who wanted to rent a boat and go sailing. At his trial, victim and district attorney alike concurred that the DeBoe was "of good character." The charges were dropped.[5]

In general, the social institutions created and developed by street children functioned as networks of resistance, propagating sentiments of exasperation, disaffection and indignation. With their own ideas about public space, respect for personal property, and standards of family domesticity, street kids represented an alternative subculture. Their institutions allowed for indulgence in adult, male activity, socialization with likeminded friends, while catering to those with a penchant for risk-taking and danger. Coffeehouses, saloons, theaters, museums, even prisons, were an extension of this street milieu. Here youths shared common experiences with their friends, defended themselves against adult outsiders like the police, truant officers, school authorities, even parents and their surrogates. This alternative community of child pickpockets embodied a new struggle, played out on the streets of America's exploding urban centers, between adults with money, consumer goods and power and unsupervised children with little of each.

As this internal, underground, informal child economy grew more pronounced, the dominant society became less tolerant. New Yorkers initially resorted to private forms of social control. Rather than utilizing direct, coercive forms of state power, voluntary groups tried to intervene and change the behavior of street children. Organizations like the CAS resisted methods of repression or coercion associated with municipal police and state prosecutors. They employed persuasion, rhetoric, symbolism, and tangible rewards to solve child criminality. In 1872, Elbridge Gerry founded the Society for the Prevention of Cruelty to Children (SPCC), which enjoyed certain forms of policing power and acted as a conduit between municipal courts,

---

4. George Appo statement to the Commissioners of Public Charities and Corrections, 6 Oct. 1896, pp. 17–18, in People v. George Appo, 24 July 1896, New York City District Attorney Records, New York Supreme Court, New York City Municipal Archives and Records Center, New York, N.Y.
5. People v. Joseph DeBoe, 15 Feb. 1876, DAP. John Hollahan and Henry Flavin, 14 and 12 years-old, respectively, stole a watch at the behest of another teenager who got them intoxicated on gin. See People v. Henry Flavin and John Hollahan, 12 Jan. 1874, DAP. For cases where the "respectability" of parents was reason for forgiveness and the dropping of charges, see People v. Conklin Pearsall, 10 Sept. 1872; People v. Thomas Walsh, 9 July 1872; People v. John Hanley, 23 Oct. 1872, all in DAP.

private institutions, and poor children. Judges routinely followed the SPCC's recommendations, which exercised unparalleled influence on child care in New York.[6] Unable to police families and children, local government resorted to private agencies to fight juvenile delinquency.

Even private ameliorative institutions like the Newsboy's Lodging Houses administered by the CAS were of questionable influence. Undoubtedly, numerous street children passed through their doors: between 1854 and 1885, over 150,000 different boys entered the multiple CAS lodging houses. By 1872, nearly 12,000 individual youths (roughly 400 per night) annually sought refuge in at least five such establishments.[7] Yet, some argued that the autonomy lodging house juveniles enjoyed did little to discourage most forms of street life culture. The average stay lasted only one week, hardly enough time to counteract criminal and other delinquent behaviors. Not surprisingly, a newspaper reporter observed, "the lodging houses and other places where boys assemble are training schools for vice." One former lodging house resident admitted his fellow lodgers included youths who became "respectable citizens" and others, "the swellest of crooks."[8]

Municipal institutions of law enforcement—specifically jail and the police—proved equally inadequate to control pickpockets. Larry Caulfield described how older youths taught him how to "bang a super" (pickpocketing a watch by breaking it off the chain) as a 15-year-old Tombs inmate. Other pickpockets repeated similar experiences while incarcerated. Jails like the Tombs were little more, concluded another, than "seminaries of crime."[9]

Outside, Gotham's police were undermanned. For most years between 1855 and 1900, New York had one police officer for every 400 residents; some years the figure exceeded 500 residents. By contrast, in 1975, the city employed one officer for every 177 residents. As historian Eric Monkkonen has argued, nineteenth-century U.S. municipalities suffered from an inadequate number of police, poor funding, the state-control of punishment systems, and the inability of local courts to mete out justice. Such conditions

6. Ross, "Society's Children," 23–28; Katz, *In the Shadow of the Poorhouse*, 117–50; Timothy J. Gilfoyle, "The Moral Origins of Political Surveillance: The Preventive Society in New York City, 1867–1918," *American Quarterly*, 38 (1986), 637–52. By 1869, the CAS promoted children's courts, compulsory education, and licensing child street-sellers. See CAS, *Seventeenth AR*, 9, 49; Brace, *Dangerous Classes*, 347. Despite these efforts, over 25 percent of the more than 900 cases in the SPCC first ten annual reports involved families and children occupied in some form of street life. See Ross, "Society's Children," 30.

7. From 1854 to 1896, the CAS also sent over 93,000 youths to western states. See CAS, *Sixteenth AR*, 19–22, 63–64, 68 (emigration statistics); idem, *Twentieth AR* (New York, 1872), 5; idem, *Thirty-third AR* (New York, 1885), 5 (300,000 boys and girls) idem, *Forty-fifth AR* (New York, 1897), 13 (93,000); Brace, *Dangerous Classes*, 97–113.

8. Hapgood, *Autobiography*, 89 (swellest crooks); *National Police Gazette*, 27 May 1882 (training schools); CAS, *Sixteenth AR*, 20–21; Hawes, *Children*, 96–98. Despite their names, only a small percentage of the youths in these establishments were newsboys. See CAS, *Sixteenth AR*, 20, 27–33, 65–67.

9. HW, 29 March 1873 (seminaries of crime); Hapgood, *Autobiography*, 45–46; Brace, *Dangerous Classes*, 399; John Josiah Munro, *New York Tombs: Inside and Out!* (Brooklyn, 1909), 12–13, 120–25 ("Schools of Crime"), 241. Other examples that jail and prison contributed to the growth of this subculture can be found in Myer Stern to Mayor William Havemeyer and Board of Public Charities and Correction, 12 Aug. 1873, Folder 7, Box 1220, MP; *World*, 13, 27 Jan. 1879; Warren, *Thirty Years'*, 226; Inspectors of the State Penitentiary for the Eastern District of Pennsylvania, *56 th AR for the Year 1885* (Philadelphia, 1886), 100. For other reports of teenage male incarceration, see *Times*, 9 Jan. 1882; *Herald*, 13 Jan. 1882, both in DAS; *World*, 13, 27 Jan. 1879. From 1857 to 1871, the number of 15 to 20 year-old males in city jails rose from 2,592 to 2,936. Throughout the 1860s, more than 1,800 males under 15 years passed through Gotham's local carceral institutions. See CAS, *Eighteenth AR*, 51–52; idem, *Nineteenth AR*, 8.

did little to discourage teenage boys from pickpocketing or engaging in other forms of street crime.[1] By 1875, police justices admitted that pickpocketing was a growing problem in New York; some even expressed fears that it was overwhelming the city's law enforcement apparatus. Public officials consequently resorted to new measures to stem the problem. In the same year, the state legislature passed the "Children's Law" decreeing the removal of all healthy children ages 3 to 16 from the state's poorhouses in order to remove them from "pauper influences." In 1876, another state statute prohibited theatrical, concert, and musical performances by children under 16 without the written consent of the mayor.[2]

Following legislators' lead, the criminal justice system responded with even more coercive solutions. Between 1869 and 1876, for example, district attorney prosecutions of pickpockets more than tripled, increasing annually from 91 to 302, while juries proved increasingly willing to convict child pickpockets. By 1876, 79 percent of all such cases resulted in conviction. And judges meted out even harsher sentences. Before 1873, only a handful of teenagers were ever sent to prison, and never more than six in a single year. But in both 1874 and 1876, judges sentenced 25 such youthful offenders to Sing Sing.[3]

Most striking was the draconian severity of some punishments. For stealing one dollar, for example, the fourteen-year-old, Irish immigrant Henry Ducketts was sent to the House of Refuge for a year. When teenagers John

1. On municipal police officers and the low level of expenditures, see the following table:

YEAR	NO. OF POLICE	BUDGET (MIL.)	POPULATION	RATIO	$ PER CAPITA
1855	1,116		@665,000	596	
1860	1,473	$1.395	813,669	552	$1.71
1865	2,474		@878,000	355	
1870	2,325	$2.901	942,292	405	$3.08
1875	2,544	(1869)	@1,053,482	414	
1878		$3.316			
1880	2,159	$3.227	1,164,673	539	$2.77
1885	2,898		@1,303,000	450	
1890	3,525	$4.588	1,441,216	423	$3.18
1895	3,825		@1,645,654	430	
1900	7,426	$11.993	3,437,202	463	$3.49
1926				446	
1950	19,789	$101.965	7,891,957	399	$12.92
1975	42,165		@7,483,000	177	
	(highest)				
1990	26,911	$1,627.488	7,322,564	272	$222.26

Sources: Edward T. O'Donnell, "Number of Police Officers in New York City;" and O'Donnell and James Bradley, "The Growth of the Budget of New York City, 1830–1990," both in Kenneth T. Jackson, ed., *The Encyclopedia of New York City* (New Haven, Conn, 1995), 166, 911; *Herald*, 9 March 1855. On the low level of criminal prosecution in nineteenth-century New York, see NYSS, *Proceedings Before the Special Committee of the New York State Senate, Appointed to Investigate in Respect to the Departments of the Government of New York City* (Albany, 1876), table of convictions; Eric H. Monkkonen, *Murder in New York City* (Berkeley, Ca., 2001), 167; idem, "Racial Factors in New York City Homicides, 1800–1874," in Darnell F. Hawkins, ed., *Ethnicity, Race, and Crime: Perspectives Across Time and Space* (Albany, N.Y., 1995), 113; idem, "The American State from the Bottom Up: Of Homicides and Courts," *Law and Society Review*, 24 (1990), 521–31.
2. *World*, 13 Jan. 1879 (Children's Law, pauper); "An Act to Prevent and Punish Wrongs to Children," *Laws of 1876*, chap. 122, copies in Folder 271, Box 1265; and Folder 181, Box 1256, MP. Between 1874 and 1875, the number of arraigned pickpockets rose from 581 to 728. See Board of Police Justices of the City of New York, *Second AR* (New York, 1876), 9. From 1860 to 1895, the number of orphanages in New York City grew 300 percent. See Ross, "Society's Children," 23; Katz, *In the Shadow of the Poorhouse*, 123.
3. See sampled years in DAP. ☆ ☆ ☆ For recent theories of criminal law, see Michael Moore, *Placing Blame: A General Theory of Criminal Law* (Oxford, Eng., 1997).

Golden and Alfred Johnson, in separate cases, were convicted of pickpocketing 50 cents, they each received three year sentences. Similarly, 19-
year-old Lawrence Dixon was sent to Sing Sing for five years for stealing 80
cents; John Kelly was given four years for absconding with five cents.[4]
    This was part of a larger trend. In the final quarter of the nineteenth cen-
tury, law enforcement authorities "got tough" on juvenile offenders. After
1875, municipal courts annually convicted over 1,500 (sometimes more than
2,000) children age 14 years or younger. In 1876 alone, New York's police
justices convicted more than 9,500 teenagers; over 2,600 of them were
under 14, a figure which exceeded the number of convicted African-
American adults.[5] By the time a male pickpocket reached age 15 he was just
as likely to end up in the penitentiary as the House of Refuge, the Juvenile
Asylum, or the Catholic Protectory. For 16 and 17 year-old males, the odds
were worse: 85 percent ended up in Sing Sing.[6] To judges, teenage pickpockets were adults.
    Street children worked and lived outside the paradigm of middle-class
domesticity, enjoying few, if any, traditional familial influences. Their collective identity was shaped primarily by a peer group of immediate friends
and associates, not the "civilizing" social structures of a bourgeois Victorian
household. Absent such influences, street children almost by necessity
developed a confrontational and oppositional subculture relative to adult
authority. Yet, while alienated in certain respects from the dominant culture, street children simultaneously adopted certain entrepreneurial
behaviors as a survival strategy. And why not? They labored as independent
contractors at a pace, place and time they chose. Free to set their own
schedule, they enjoyed more autonomy than in the school, factory, or
home. Such individualistic, entrepreneurial values mirrored elements of
the dominant society, thereby discouraging a broader collective, communal
outlook in most cases. Absent was any long-lasting system of reciprocal
obligation fundamental to group cohesion and solidarity.[7] Based on personal experience, the identity of child pickpockets never embodied a larger

---

4. People v. Henry Ducketts (14 years old), 24 June 1879; People v. John Kelly (19 years old), 16
   March 1871; People v. John Golden (17 years old), 14 Jan. 1874; People v. Alfred Johnson (19 years
   old), 3 June 1874; People v. Lawrence Dixon (19 years old), 6 Feb. 1874, all in DAP. For an earlier charge against Ducketts when he was nine years of age, see People v. Henry Ducketts, 21 April
   1874, DAP.
5. Conviction figures were:

	under 14		15–19 yrs		
	M	F	M	F	African-Americans
1874					590
1875	1,536	336	4,327	1,418	1,121
1876	2,076	565	5,069	1,525	1,536
1877	1,930	796	5,890	1,891	1,222
1888	1,836	1,224	5,312	1,116	
1890	2,031	1,159	4,382	832	

   See Board of the Police Justices of the City of New York, Third AR for the Year 1876 (New York,
   1877), 21–22.; idem, Fourth AR for the Year 1877 (New York, 1878), 14–15; idem, Fifteenth AR
   for the Year 1888 (New York, 1889), 23; idem, Seventeenth AR for the Year 1890 (New York, 1891),
   24. The police courts did not publish annual reports before 1875.
6. Whereas no one thirteen years or younger was ever sent to prison, at least three fourteen year-olds
   were, including one Irish-born newsboy who was sentenced to Sing Sing for three and one-half
   years. See People v. Joseph Dodge, 20 Dec. 1859, DAP (Irish newsboy). * * *
7. On the importance of the family in developing class consciousness, see Scott, "Everyday Weapons."
   On the importance of shared obligation to group cohesion, see William F. Whyte, Street Corner Society: The Social Structure of an Italian Slum (Chicago, 1943), 255–65; Williams, Cocaine Kids.

conception of mutuality and shared suffering. Political revolution or economic redistribution were not their end; individual gain and personal accumulation were. Theirs was a different avenue of upward mobility. The goal was not to turn the world upside down, but rather inside out.

Street kid ideology—broadly defined as those values originating in their ordinary experiences and validated in their social life—was personal and immediate, delineated by their daily struggles to survive in an urban market economy, and grounded in the experience of city streets.[8] These were children who literally slept with rats, who lacked the knee of a supportive adult on which to sit, or a shoulder on which to cry. Absent was any family to love them. Struggling to negotiate a terrain between personal autonomy and adult authority, between self-sufficiency and economic dependence, the personal ideologies of child pickpockets were framed in the context of everyday street life. Child pickpockets thus cultivated their own conception of freedom and independence. But in trying to carve out a place for themselves, they found a world where few adults cared to understand, and many wished they would go away. By avoiding the factory, the school, the church, child pickpockets spoke with their feet, and frequently their hands.

---

8. On the importance of social conditions shaping ideology, see Barbara Jeanne Fields, "Slavery, Race and Ideology in the United States of America," *New Left Review*, 181 (1990), 111–112; and Winthrop Jordan, *Tumult and Silence at Second Creek: An Inquiry into a Civil War Slave Conspiracy* (Baton Rouge, La., 1993), 181–211, esp. 200.

Jacob Riis: A Chronology

1849	Carolina and Neils Riis's third child, Jacob, is born (May 3, Ribe, Denmark).
1865	Jacob Riis becomes apprenticed to a carpenter (Ribe, Denmark).
1870	Sailing aboard the *Iowa*, Riis arrives in New York, landing at Castle Garden (June 5).
1870–73	Takes a variety of odd jobs, traveling around the northeastern United States.
1873	Gets his first exposure to journalism as city editor of a Long Island weekly newspaper, *The Review* (fall). He stays with the job for two weeks.
1874	The *South Brooklyn News* hires him as a reporter (May). Puts down a deposit of $75 to buy the paper, which is being sold for $650 (December).
1875	Pays off his debt to the *South Brooklyn News*, which he then sells for five times what he paid. Makes a return journey to Denmark (December).
1876	Marries Elisabeth Gortz, whom he had fallen in love with at age sixteen (March 5). Jacob and Elisabeth return to the United States, and he resumes his position as editor of the *South Brooklyn News*.
1877	Leaves the newspaper and decides to enter the advertising business, in which he uses a stereopticon. Abandons the advertising business and accepts a job as a reporter for the *New York Tribune*.
1885	Becomes a U.S. citizen.
1886–87	The Riis family moves from Brooklyn to Richmond Hill, a suburb on Long Island. Riis learns to use flashlight powder.
1888	Teaches himself photography. Offers his lecture "The Other Half: How It Lives and Dies in New York" to the New York Society of Amateur Phographers (January 25). Publishes "Flashes from the Slums: Pictures Taken in Dark Places by the Lightning Process," in the *New York Sun* (February 12). Gains copyright of the title "The Other Half: How It Lives and Dies in New York. With One Hundred Illustrations, Photographs From Real Life, of the Haunts of Poverty and Vice in the Great City" (March 19).
1889	*Scribner's Magazine* publishes "How the Other Half Lives" (December).
1890	*How the Other Half Lives* published by Charles Scribner's Sons (November 15).

1895   Escorts Theodore Roosevelt, then serving on the New York City
          Board of Police Commissioners, on a tour of the eastside slums
          (June 6).
1898   Campaigns for Roosevelt in his run for the governorship of
          New York State (October).
1900   Publishes *A Ten Years' War*, describing efforts, his own
          included, to clean up the slums.
1901   Quits the *Evening Sun* and takes up a full-time career as a free-
          lance writer, lecturer, and housing reform advocate. Publishes
          his autobiography, *The Making of an American*.
1903–04   Campaigns for Theodore Roosevelt's bid for the presidency.
1905   Elisabeth Riis dies.
1907   Marries a second time, Mary Phillips, his secretary.
1912   Campaigns for Theodore Roosevelt and the Progressive ("Bull
          Moose"). Party.
1913   Moves to Barre, Massachusetts.
1914   Dies of heart disease at age sixty-five (May 26).

Selected Bibliography

Jacob Riis's Major Writings

How the Other Half Lives. New York: Charles Scribner's Sons, 1890.
The Children of the Poor. New York: Charles Scribner's Sons, 1892.
Nisby's Christmas. New York: Charles Scribner's Sons, 1893.
Out of Mulberry Street. New York: Century, 1898.
Ten Years' War. New York: Houghton, Mifflin, 1900.
The Making of an American. New York: Macmillan, 1900.
The Battle with the Slum. New York: Macmillan, 1902.
Children of the Tenements. New York: Macmillan, 1903.
The Peril and Preservation of the Home. Philadelphia: G. W. Jacobs, 1903.
Theodore Roosevelt, the Citizen. New York; Outlook, 1904.
Old Town. New York: Macmillan, 1909.
Hero Tales of the Far North. New York: Macmillan, 1910.
Neighbors. New York: Macmillan, 1914.
Christmas Stories. New York: Macmillan, 1915.

About Jacob Riis and How the Other Half Lives

• indicates a work included or excerpted in this Norton Critical Edition

• Adams, Warren P. "Boston and 'The Other Half.'" *Christian Union* 44. 5 (1891): 222.
• Alland, Alexander. *Jacob A. Riis: Photographer and Citizen.* New York: Aperture Foundation, 1993.
• Betts, Lillian W. *The Leaven in a Great City.* New York: Dodd, Mead, 1903.
• Brace, Charles Loring. *The Dangerous Classes of New York, and Twenty Years' Work among Them.* New York: Wynkoop & Hallenbeck, 1880.
• Bremner, Robert H. *From the Depths: The Discovery of Poverty in the United States.* New York: New York University Press, 1954.
• Burton, Margaret E. *Comrades in Service.* New York: Missionary Education Movement of the United States and Canada, 1916.
• Byrnes, Thomas. "Nurseries of Crime." *The North American Review* 149 (1889): 355–62.
• Cope, Francis R. Jr. "Tenement House Reform: Its Practical Results in the 'Battle Row' District, New York." *The American Journal of Sociology* 7.3 (1901): 331–58.
• DiGirolamo, Vincent. "Newsboy Funerals: Tales of Sorrow and Solidarity in Urban America." *Journal of Social History* 36.1 (2002): 5–30.
• Dowling, Robert M. *Slumming: Morality and Space in New York City from "City Mysteries" to the Harlem Renaissance.* Ann Arbor, Mich.: Bell & Howell Information and Learning Company, 2001.
• Elsing, William T. *The Poor in Great Cities.* New York: Charles Scribner's Sons, 1895.
• Entin, Joseph. "'Unhuman Humanity': Bodies of the Urban Poor and the Collapse of Realist Legibility." *Novel: A Forum on Fiction* 34.3 (2001): 313–37.
• *First Report of the Tenement House Department of the City of New York, 1902–3.* New York: Tenement House Department, Jan. 1, 1902–July 1, 1903.
• Fried, Lewis. *Makers of the City.* Amherst: University of Massachusetts Press, 1996.
Fried, Lewis, and John Fierst. *Jacob A. Riis: A Reference Guide.* Boston: Hall, 1977.
• Gandal, Keith. *The Virtues of the Vicious: Jacob Riis, Stephen Crane, and the Spectacle of the Slum.* New York: Oxford University Press, 1997.
• Gilder, Joseph B. "The Making of Jacob A. Riis." *The Critic* 40.1 (1902): 63–64.

- Gilfoyle, Timothy J. "Street-Rats and Gutter-Snipes: Child Pickpockets and Street Culture in New York City, 1850–1900." *Journal of Social History* 37.4 (2004): 853–62.
- Goist, Park Dixon. *From Main Street to State Street: Town, City, and Community in America.* Port Washington, N.Y.: Kennikat Press, 1977.
- Hales, Peter B. *Silver Cities: The Photography of American Urbanization, 1839–1915.* Philadelphia: Temple University Press, 1984.
- Huntington, J. O. S. "Tenement-House Morality." *Forum* 3.5 (1887): 513–23.
- Irving, Katrina. *Immigrant Mothers: Narratives of Race and Maternity, 1890–1925.* Urbana: University of Illinois Press, 2000.
- Lane, James B. *Jacob A. Riis and the American City.* Port Washington, N.Y.: Kennikat Press, 1974.
- Lotz, Charles J. "Jacob Riis." In *Vocations and Professions,* ed. Philip Henry Lotz, New York: Association Press, 1940, 33–41.
- Lubove, Roy. *The Progressives and the Slums: Tenement House Reform in New York City, 1890–1917.* Pittsburgh: University of Pittsburgh Press, 1962.
- "Matters We Ought to Know: How the Other Half Lives, Studies Among the Tenements of New York City" by Jacob A. Riis. *New York Times,* January 4, 1891, p. 19.
- "Neighbors." *New York Times,* December 6, 1914, p. BR552.
- Newhall, Beaumont. *The History of Photography from 1839 to the Present Day.* New York: Museum of Modern Art, 1949.
  Prager, Ya'akov Segal. *"The Lone Crusader": Denmark's Contribution to America.* Boston: Barnard Press, 1935.
- Reynolds, Marcus T. *Housing of the Poor in American Cities. Publications of the American Economic Association,* 8, 2, and 3. Ithaca, N.Y. 1893.
- Roosevelt, Theodore. *An Autobiography.* New York: Charles Scribner's Sons, 1921.
- Schwartz, Joel. *Fighting Poverty with Virtue: Moral Reform and America's Urban Poor, 1825–2000.* Bloomington: Indiana University Press, 2000.
- Spargo, John. *The Bitter Cry of the Children.* New York: Macmillan, 1906.
- Stange, Maren. *Symbols of Ideal Life: Social Documentary Photography in America, 1890–1950.* Cambridge: Cambridge University Press, 1989.
- Steffens, Lincoln. *The Autobiography of Lincoln Steffens.* New York: Harcourt, Brace, 1931.
- Townsend, Edward W. *A Daughter of the Tenements.* New York: Lovell, Coryell, 1895.
- Trenor, John J. D. "Proposals Affecting Immigration." *Annals of the American Academy of Political and Social Science* 21 (July 1904): 223–36.
- Tuerk, Richard. "Jacob Riis and the Jews." *The New York Historical Society Quarterly* 63.3 (1979): 179–201.
- Wald, Lillian D. *The House on Henry Street.* New York: Henry Holt, 1915.
- Ware, Louise. *Jacob A. Riis: Police Reporter, Reformer, Useful Citizen.* New York and London: D. Appleton-Century, 1939.